THE OXFORD HISTORY OF
The Twentieth Century

Sir Michael Howard is former Regius Professor of Modern
History at the University of Oxford; **Wm. Roger Louis** is Kerr
Professor of English History and Culture at the University of
Texas at Austin and Fellow of St Antony's College, Oxford.

THE
OXFORD
HISTORY
OF

The

CONTENTS

LIST OF FIGURES AND TABLE

FIGURES

TABLE

LIST OF CONTRIBUTORS

Hugh Brogan was born in 1936 and graduated from Cambridge in 1959. He was a journalist on *The Economist*, 1959–63, and a Fellow at St John's College, Cambridge, 1963–74. Since 1974 he has taught in the Department of History at the University of Essex, where he is R. A. Butler Professor of History. His works include *History of the United States* (1984), *Correspondence et conversations d'Alexis de Tocqueville et Nassau Senior* (1991), *Kennedy* (1996), and *Penguin History of the United States of America* (2001).

Archie Brown, FBA, was born in 1938 and graduated from the London School of Economics in 1962. He was Lecturer in Politics at Glasgow University, 1964–71, Lecturer in Soviet Institutions at Oxford, 1971–89, and has been Professor of Politics at Oxford since 1989. He is a Fellow of St Antony's College, Oxford. His works on Communist and post-Communist politics include *The Gorbachev Factor* (1996), (as co-editor and co-author) *The Cambridge Encyclopaedia of Russia and the Former Soviet Union* (1994), *Contemporary Russian Politics* (2001), and *Gorbachev, Yeltsin & Putin* (2001).

Judith M. Brown was born in India in 1944, educated in England, and graduated from Cambridge in 1965. She was a Fellow of Girton College, Cambridge, 1968–71, and subsequently Senior Lecturer at Manchester University, 1971–90. Since 1990 she has been Beit Professor of Commonwealth History at Oxford University, where she is a Fellow of Balliol College. Her publications include two monographs on Gandhi's civil disobedience movements, *Modern India: The Origins of an Asian Democracy* (1985), and a biographical study, *Gandhi: Prisoner of Hope* (1989). She has also co-edited collections on Asian migration and Hong Kong.

Lord Dahrendorf, KBE, FBA, was born in Hamburg in 1929, and has held chairs in Sociology at Hamburg, Tübingen, and Konstanz. He was a member of the European Commission, 1970–4, Director of the London School of Economics, 1974–84, and Warden of St Antony's College, Oxford, 1987–97. His works include *Class and Class Conflict* (1959), *Society and Democracy in Germany* (1966), *Essays in the Theory of Society* (1968), and *The Modern Social Conflict* (1988). In his own view, his most significant book is *LSE: A History of the London School of Economics 1895–1995*.

Anne Deighton is a Lecturer at Oxford University, and former Fellow of St Antony's College. She is now a Fellow of Wolfson College. She has written on the Cold War, the development of post-war European integration, and European security. Her publications include *The Impossible Peace: Britain, the Division of Germany and the Origins of the Cold War* (1990). She has edited *Britain and the First Cold War*

(1990), *Building Postwar Europe* (1995), and *Western European Union, 1954–1997: Defence, Security, Integration* (1997).

Lawrence Freedman, CBE, FBA, was born in 1948. He was educated at the Universities of Manchester, York, and Oxford, and held research positions at Nuffield College, Oxford, and the International Institute for Strategic Studies before becoming head of Policy Studies at the Royal Institute of International Affairs, 1978–82. He has been Professor of War Studies at King's College, London, since 1982. His works include *The Evolution of Nuclear Strategy* (1981), *Britain and the Falklands War* (1988), (with Efraim Karsh) *The Gulf Conflict, 1990–91* (1993), *Kennedy's Wars* (2001), and *The Cold War* (2001).

W. Travis Hanes III received his Ph.D. from the University of Texas in 1990. He is the author of *Imperial Diplomacy in the Era of Decolonization: The Sudan and Anglo-Egyptian Relations, 1945–1956* (1995), *World History: Continuity and Change* (1996), and *Imperialism or 'Expatriate Nationalism'? The Sudan Political Service and Decolonization in the Sudan 1899–1956* (forthcoming). A scholar of world history, he has written textbooks as well as articles on both Western and non-Western history.

Sir Michael Howard, CBE, FBA, was born in 1922. After war service he graduated from Oxford in 1946, and taught at King's College, London, 1947–63, becoming Professor of War Studies, 1963–8. From 1968 to 1977 he was Fellow in Higher Defence Studies, All Souls College, Oxford. Subsequently he became Professor of History of War (1977–80) and Regius Professor of Modern History (1980–9) at Oxford, and Professor of Military and Naval History at Yale (1989–93). His works include *The Franco-Prussian War* (1961), *The Continental Commitment* (1972), *War in European History* (1976), and *The First World War* (2002). With Peter Paret he edited and translated Clausewitz, *On War* (1992).

Akira Iriye was born in Tokyo in 1934. Educated at Haverford College, he taught at the University of Chicago before becoming Charles Warren Professor of History at Harvard University in 1991. He is a past President of the American Historical Association. His books include *After Imperialism* (1965), *Across the Pacific: An Inner History of American–East Relations* (1976), *Power and Culture: The Japanese-American War, 1941–1945*, (1981), *Cultural Internationalism and World Order* (1995), and *Japan and the Wider World* (1997).

Alan Knight, FBA, received his D.Phil. from Oxford University. As an undergraduate at Balliol he studied under the late Jack Gallagher. He taught at the University of Texas before becoming Professor of the History of Latin America, Oxford University, and Fellow of St Antony's College. His publications include *The Mexican Revolution* (2 vols.), *US–Mexican Relations, 1910–1940*, and *Mexico* (2002).

Michael Leifer is Professor of International Relations and Director of the Asia Research Centre at the London School of Economics. His speciality is the history and politics of South-East Asia. He has held teaching posts at the Australian National University, the University of the Philippines, Cornell University, and the National University of Singapore. His most recent publications include *ASEAN and the Security of South-East Asia* (1990), *Dictionary of the Modern Politics of South-East Asia* (1996) and *The ASEAN Regional Forum* (1996).

Wm. Roger Louis, FBA, is Director of British Studies and Kerr Professor of English History and Culture at the University of Texas, Austin, and Fellow of St Antony's College, Oxford. As a Marshall Scholar at Oxford, 1960–2, he studied under A. J. P. Taylor. He is the Editor-in-Chief of the *Oxford History of the British Empire*. His books include *Imperialism at Bay* (1976) and the *British Empire in the Middle East* (1984). His study *Leo Amery and the British Empire* is based on the Chichele Lectures, All Souls College, Oxford, in 1990. With Robert Blake he has edited *Churchill* (1993).

Norbert Lynton was born in 1927. He studied at the Courtauld Institute and taught at Leeds and Chelsea Schools of Art while acting as London correspondent for *Art International* and art critic for the *Guardian*. He was Director of Exhibitions, Arts Council of Great Britain, 1970–5, Professor of Art History (1975–89) and Dean of the European School (1985–8), now Professor Emeritus, at the University of Sussex. His books include *The Story of Modern Art* (1980), *Victor Pasmore* (1992), *Ben Nicholson* (1993), and *Painting the Century* (2001).

Peter Lyon has been Academic Secretary and Reader in International Relations at the Institute of Commonwealth Studies, University of London, since 1969. He has been Editor of *The Round Table: The Commonwealth Journal of International Affairs* since 1983. He is a life Vice-President of the Royal Commonwealth Society and was a member of the Commonwealth Monitoring Team for South Africa's first post-apartheid general elections in 1994. He is completing a biography of the Commonwealth statesman Malcolm MacDonald.

William H. McNeill was born in Canada in 1917 but moved to the United States as a boy and attended the University of Chicago, 1934–9. After starting work on a Ph.D. at Cornell University, he served with the army for five years and thereafter taught at the University of Chicago, 1947–87. He is a past President of the American Historical Association. His books include *The Rise of the West: A History of the Human Community* (1963), *Plagues and Peoples* (1976), and *The Pursuit of Power: Technology Armed Force and Society since 1000 AD* (1982).

Sir John Maddox was born in 1925 and graduated from Oxford in 1947. After research at King's College, London, he taught Theoretical Physics at Manchester University, 1949–55, became Science Editor of the *Guardian*, 1955–64, and Editor of *Nature*, 1966–95. He was Director of the Nuffield Foundation, 1975–80. His works include *Revolution in Biology* (1963), *The Doomsday Syndrome* (1972), and *Beyond the Energy Crisis* (1974).

Roger Owen was a Fellow of St Antony's College and Lecturer in the Recent Economic History of the Middle East at Oxford before becoming A. J. Meyer Professor of Middle East History and Director of the Center for Middle Eastern Studies at Harvard University. His works include *Cotton and the Egyptian Economy 1820–1914* (1969), *The Middle East in the World Economy, 1800–1914* (1981), *State, Power and Politics in the Making of the Middle East* (1992), and *A Revolutionary Year* (2001).

James Patterson took his Ph.D. at Harvard in 1964 and taught at Indiana University, 1964–72, and has been Professor of History at Brown University since 1972. His books include *Congressional Conservatism and the New Deal* (1967), *Mr Republican: A Biography of Robert A. Taft* (1972), *America in the Twentieth Century: A History* (1976), *The Dread Disease: Cancer and Modern American Culture* (1987), and *America's Struggle against Poverty, 1900–1994* (1995), *Grand Expectations: The United States, 1945–1974* (1996), which won the Bancroft Prize in 1997.

Terence Ranger, FBA, was born in 1929 and took his D.Phil. at Oxford in 1960. He taught at the College of Rhodesia and Nyasaland, 1957–63, the University of Dar-es-Salaam, 1963–9, the University of California, Los Angeles, 1969–74, and the University of Manchester 1974–87, before becoming Rhodes Professor of Race Relations and a Fellow of St Antony's College, Oxford, in 1987. His works include *Revolt in Southern Rhodesia 1896–97* (1967), *The African Voice in Southern Rhodesia, 1889–1930* (1970), *Dance and Society in Eastern Africa* (1975), and *Peasant Society and Guerilla War in Zimbabwe* (1985).

Adam Roberts, FBA, was born in 1940, graduated from Oxford in 1962, and taught at the London School of Economics, 1968–81. He was elected Alastair Buchan Reader in International Relations at Oxford in 1981 and Montague Burton Professor of International Relations in 1986. His books include *Nation in Arms: The Theory and Practice of Territorial Defence* (1986), (ed. with Richard Guelff) *Documents on the Laws of War* (1989), and (ed. with Benedict Kingsbury) *United Nations, Divided World: The UN's Role in International Relations* (1993).

Alan Ryan, FBA, was born in 1940 and taught at the Universities of Keele and Essex before being elected a Fellow of New College, Oxford, and Lecturer in Politics, 1969–87. He was Professor of Politics at Princeton University, 1987–96, and was elected Warden of New College, Oxford, in 1996. His works include *The Philosophy of John Stuart Mill* (1970), *Bertrand Russell: A Political Life* (1988), and *Dewey* (1995).

Lord Skidelsky, FBA, was born in 1939, took his D.Phil. at Oxford, and taught at Johns Hopkins University and the Polytechnic of North London before becoming

Professor of International Studies at Warwick University in 1978 and Professor of Political Economy in 1990. His works include *Politicians and the Slump* (1967), *Oswald Mosley* (1975) and *John Maynard Keynes*, i. *1883–1920* (1983), and ii. *1921–37* (1992).

Jonathan Spence, FBA, was born in 1936, and studied at Winchester College and Clare College, Cambridge. In 1959 he travelled to Yale University, and switched to Chinese studies, receiving his Ph.D. in 1965. He joined the faculty at Yale the following year, and has taught there ever since, being currently Sterling Professor of History. His books include *The Death of Woman Wang* (1978), *The Memory Palace of Matteo Ricci* (1984), *The Question of Hu* (1900), *The Search for Modern China* (1990), *God's Chinese Son* (1996), and *Treason by the Book* (2001).

Richard Stites took his Ph.D. at Harvard in 1968 and taught at Brown University and Ohio State University before becoming Professor of History at Georgetown University in 1977. His works include *The Women's Liberation Movement in Russia: Feminism, Nihilism and Bolshevism, 1860–1930* (1978), *Revolutionary Dreams: Utopian Vision and Social Experiment in the Russian Revolution* (1989), and *Russian Popular Culture: Entertainment and Society since 1900* (1992).

Steven Weinberg was educated at Cornell, Copenhagen, and Princeton, and held professorships at Berkeley, MIT, and Harvard before coming to the University of Texas at Austin in 1982. For his contributions to the theory of elementary particles and cosmology he has been awarded the Nobel Prize for Physics in 1979 and the US National Medal of Science in 1991. His works include *Gravitation and Cosmology* (1972), *The First Three Minutes* (1977), *The Discovery of Subatomic Particles* (1982), *Dreams of a Final Theory* (1993), and *The Quantum Theory of Fields I* (1995), *II* (1996), and *III* (2000).

Adolf Wood has been an editor with *The Times Literary Supplement* since 1975. Born in South Africa, he emigrated to Britain, where he worked in book publishing before joining the *TLS*. In 1992 he was a Guest Scholar at the Woodrow Wilson Center in Washington, DC. He has lectured widely in the US on the history of the *TLS*.

ABBREVIATIONS

Aids	acquired immune deficiency syndrome
AIOC	Anglo-Iranian Oil Company
ANC	African National Congress
APEC	Asia-Pacific Economic Cooperation
APRA	Alianza Popular Revolucionaria Americana
ARF	ASEAN Regional Forum
ASA	Association of South-East Asia
ASEAN	Association of South-East Asian Nations
BSPP	Burma Socialist Programme Party
CFTC	Commonwealth Fund for Technical Cooperation
CIS	Commonwealth of Independent States
CHOGM	Commonwealth Heads of Government Meetings
CROM	Confederación Regional Obrera Mexicana
CSCE	Conference on Security and Cooperation in Europe
DNA	deoxyribonucleic acid
EC	European Community
ECLA	Economic Commission on Latin America
EEC	European Economic Community
EFTA	European Free Trade Association
EU	European Union
FIS	Front Islamique de Salut
FLN	Front de Libération Nationale
FRG	Federal Republic of Germany
GATT	General Agreement on Tariffs and Trade
GDP	gross domestic product
HIV	human immunodeficiency virus
ICS	Indian Civil Service
ILO	International Labour Organization
IMF	International Monetary Fund
ISI	import substitution industrialization
LAFTA	Latin American Free Trade Association
LDP	Liberal Democratic Party (in Japan)
MNR	Movimiento Nacionalista Revolucionario
NAFTA	North Atlantic Free Trade Agreement
NATO	North Atlantic Treaty Organization
NEP	New Economic Policy
NIES	newly industrialized economies
NLF	National Liberation Front (of South Vietnam)
OAS	Organization of American States
OECD	Organization for Economic Coordination and Development
OEEC	Organization for European Economic Coordination
PKK	Turkish Workers' Party
PLO	Palestine Liberation Organization
PRC	People's Republic of China
RNA	ribonucleic acid
SDS	Students for a Democratic Society

ABBREVIATIONS

SEAC	South-East Asia Command
SEATO	South-East Asia Treaty Organization
SLORC	State Law and Order Restoration Council
UDI	Unilateral Declaration of Independence
UMNO	United Malays National Organization
UN	United Nations
UNDP	United Nations Development Programme
UNEF	United Nations Emergency Force
UNTAC	United Nations Transitional Authority in Cambodia
WHO	World Health Organization
WTO	World Trade Organization
ZOPFAN	Zone of Peace, Freedom, and Neutrality

FOREWORD

The twentieth century opened with a paradoxical combination of hope and fear. The hope rested on the expectation that the world was entering a new Golden Age and that such scientific discoveries and technological developments as electricity, the internal combustion engine, aeronautics, and advances in medical science would free humanity from all the sufferings—poverty, disease, famine, war—that had afflicted it since the beginning of recorded history. The fear arose from the apparent disintegration of traditional values and social structures, both secular and religious, that had bound society together in the face of all those evils, and from the prospect that the world was therefore confronting a future in which only the strongest and most ruthless would survive.

Today the century is closing with a similar paradox but with one profound difference. One hundred years ago those hopes and fears were largely confined to the industrialized societies of the West. Today they are global. Scientific knowledge has advanced even further than could have been conceived at the beginning of the century, opening yet vaster opportunities and horizons. Medical science has increased life-expectancy, and with it the size of the world's population. Agriculture has been revolutionized to provide abundant crops and has gradually transformed the lives of those who live on the land—still about half the world's inhabitants. What was once seen as a living standard available only to the rich in the West has become a feasible aspiration for many throughout the world. But these beneficent transformations do not come cost-free. Their global extension is today arousing on a far wider scale many of the same fears that they did in Europe a century ago. The gloomy forebodings that rapid changes might destroy the certainties of life now reflect deeper anxieties. To give but one example, the uncontrolled consumption of natural resources is now beginning to press against the finite resources of the planet.

The first part of the volume deals with the underlying causes and symptoms of this process of change throughout the world from the opening years of the century. The change was reflected in demography and urbanization, in the growth of scientific knowledge, in art and culture, and in the development of a global economy. The second part is concerned with events up to the end of the Second World War, when, to those in the West at least, Europe still seemed to control the destinies of the world. Part III deals with the years between 1945 and 1990 when the course of world affairs was powerfully affected, though by no means entirely determined, by the 'super power' confrontation of the 'Cold War'. Part IV attempts to correct any Eurocentric vision of history by examining the changing structures of societies and the sweep of events in Asia, the Middle East, Africa, and Latin America. Since most of the chapters in Parts III and IV draw to a close in the early part of the 1990s, Part V includes a survey of the last decade of the twentieth century together with a final reflection on the legacy of the present century to its successor.

One major theme that emerges from this volume is the continuing significance of nationalism. The beginning of the twentieth century, as is stated in Chapter 1, saw the apotheosis of the nation-state. National loyalties alleviated the impact of rapid change, binding together social groups looking back to the past with nostalgia with those looking forward to a future which their nation and its values would dominate. Such sentiments lay at the root of two terrible world wars. Today, at least in western societies, there is a widespread belief that such extreme national-ism may be a spent force. Many indeed believe that the nation-state itself is obso-lete, but the passions aroused by football matches and the Olympic Games provide a useful corrective to this view. (In an Oxford History, it is perhaps appro-priate to recall the resurgence of British jingoism during the Falklands/Malvinas War of 1982.) Elsewhere the principle of self-determination on which nationalism is based, so far from creating greater social cohesion, has led to fragmentation as previously suppressed aspirations for autonomy find expression in bitter regional confrontations. Nationalism in one form or another is thus likely to survive, if in new forms and unexpected places, and to provide new sources of conflict. The attempts made during the past century to pre-empt, limit, and resolve such con-flicts, only partially successful at best, are surveyed in a chapter on the United Nations and international law, which traces the continuity of international organ-izations from the turn of the century.

Today tensions within societies are at least as great, if not indeed greater, than those between them. Even the most stable of societies have deep systemic cleav-ages. Advances in agriculture and preventive medicine, together with job oppor-tunities created by new industries, may have solved the problem of mass-poverty as it was known at the beginning of the century, but urban and even rural over-crowding has produced political as well as social instability, especially in Asia, Africa, and Latin America. In Europe social and economic tensions are often ex-acerbated by the increasing immigration from less fortunate societies that mass transportation now makes possible. The existence of a single global market makes it perhaps even more difficult to bridge the gap between urban and rural commu-nities and between immigrants and those in 'host' countries. Further, it means that all states, rich or poor, now find it harder to protect their own economies, and that the intractable problems of the past are made even more severe. When an economy fails, it is still the state that ultimately has to deal with the social and political consequences. For poor states those consequences may be dire.

We thus enter the twenty-first century as we entered the twentieth, with the open question: will the technological advances achieved during the last hundred years enable us to solve the problems that those advances have themselves very largely created?

We face in this volume the problem of historical periodization. Historians have begun to speak of a 'short twentieth century' stretching from 1914 to 1989. Certainly such a period has more coherence than an arbitrary division at 1900 and 2000. The era that saw much of the world dominated by the great powers of Europe, many of them still ruled by an *ancien régime* of land-owning aristocracy, did effectively come to an end with the First World War. The pattern that emerged from the Second World War, of a world in which the United States and the Soviet Union struggled for hegemony, did disintegrate even more suddenly in 1989. The years thereafter are probably best viewed as a prelude to the twenty-first century in which not only nations but international organizations, especially the United Nations, have attempted to define a post-Cold War era.

In fact such sharp historiographical breaks are never entirely satisfactory. The *ancien régime* did not come to an abrupt end with the First World War. Although the emergence of Japan as a modern nation challenged western hegemony, the international order in the first four decades of the century was still dominated by the European powers. Within Europe itself the balance of power, both domestic and international, had certainly shifted drastically, but the course of world affairs was still determined by the outcome of European wars, as it had been since the eighteenth century. The United States was emerging as the world's strongest economic power, but the isolation imposed by the US Senate after the First World War limited in many ways its direct influence to the Western hemisphere and the Pacific. This isolation was effectively ended only when the Japanese attacked the American fleet at Pearl Harbor in December 1941. The European war that had broken out in 1939 suddenly became global. Only then did European dominance finally collapse and the old world order come to an end, almost overnight.

The Second World War was thus the pivotal event of the century, and this volume treats it as such. The nations of Europe no longer had the power, even if they had the will, to sustain their empires, and such legitimacy as they retained was destroyed by the nationalist movements which the war had encouraged. The collapse of the colonial empires left two ideologically hostile and militarily victorious 'super powers' to compete for world dominance. On the one hand the economic strength and the global reach of the United States made it appear—especially to Americans—that the twentieth would be the 'American century'. On the other hand the collapse of the historic centre of capitalism in Europe as well as the striking military successes of Soviet armed forces in the Second World War made it seem plausible that the ideology of Marxist-Leninism might prevail, and that the disintegration of European-based capitalism would lead to the triumph of 'the world proletariat'. For the emerging elites in the former European colonies, the Soviet Union and the vision it embodied often seemed more appealing than the United States, which, although it could provide all the tools and expertise needed for economic advancement, seemed to share many of the attitudes and characteristics of the old colonial powers. In consequence the United States found that the peaceful and benign hegemony that it had hoped to create throughout the world, in which its values would be underpinned by its economic and if necessary its military power, came under increasing challenge from a rival system. Soviet ability to exploit local nationalism and to keep abreast in the development of nuclear weapons made it a formidable adversary. The world seemed to lie in a precarious balance. Probably only the existence of nuclear weapons on both sides prevented the confrontation from erupting into military violence.

The third section of the book deals with the era of the Cold War which provided the framework for world politics for forty years. The framework, however, was very loose. During the last half of the century the peoples of different regions of the world developed their own distinctive political aspirations, however much they might have been affected, for better or worse, by the continuing impact of the West. Then in the late 1980s the failure of the Soviet Union to solve its own internal economic problems not only destroyed it as a superpower but discredited Communist ideology as a model for the rest of the world. That failure was largely economic, but it was also affected by technological developments. The growth of communications technology, which provided instant information, visual as well as verbal, throughout the world, did much to erode the authoritarian control on which the Soviet regime rested. With the collapse of the Soviet Union, the Cold War came to an end with almost cataclysmic suddenness.

In the fourth section of the book we balance the western view of the world by focusing on non-western regions over the span of the century. (The exception is the chapter on Canada, Australia, New Zealand, and South Africa, which is included in this section as part of the world beyond Europe.) Each of these regions or countries have histories in their own right. To take the most obvious example, in China the century began with the Boxer Uprising against foreign intrusion. It continued with the collapse of the traditional regime and thereafter led to war-lords, civil war, invasion, and famine. The disastrous experiment in collective agriculture and the terrifying Cultural Revolution contributed to the death of hundreds of thousands, perhaps millions of Chinese. Yet China's population in the 1980s rose beyond the one billion mark, and today the Chinese economy enjoys one of the fastest economic growth rates in the world. It remains an open question as we approach the next century whether the Chinese can continue to develop economically in a new age of communications technology and corporate internationalism without liberalization or democratization. Similar comments could be made in different ways about all the regions dealt with in this part of the book. Our theme throughout is global yet varied transformation. Each region has its own history distinct from that of the West.

In the last section, the chapter on the close of the century discusses the Four Horsemen of the Apocalypse as an image as appropriate for the 1990s as it has been throughout history. It considers what events in the final decade of the century will be remembered as having tipped the balance for or against those agents of destruction. Has it, on the whole, been a good century or will it be remembered as one of the most murderous in human history? The same questions are taken up in the final chapter, with its look at possibilities for the future.

Michael Howard   Wm. Roger Louis

The Framework of
the Century

1 The Dawn of the Century

MICHAEL HOWARD

The peoples of Western Europe and North America seemed to have every reason to greet the twentieth century as the dawn of a new and happier age in the history of mankind. Science and technology were already improving their standard of living almost beyond recognition, and they dominated the world with their trade, their finance, and their military power. Most of the Western hemisphere, the continent of Africa, the Indian subcontinent and much of Asia outside China had been either directly colonized by Europeans or deeply penetrated by European culture; and it seemed self-evident that such societies as still maintained their independence would be able to do so in future only if, like the Japanese, they successfully imitated the European model.

That model has since become known as 'liberal capitalism'. Those who benefited from its material advantages were conscious primarily of its political framework: freedom of speech, freedom of commercial interchange, freedom of scientific enquiry, mobility of labour, and democratic self-government on an ever-extending franchise. But underlying this liberal ideology was an economic process that Karl Marx had correctly identified fifty years earlier as the most revolutionary that the world had ever seen. Basic to this process was the accumulation of financial resources and their investment in industry and communications. This investment had made possible the development of mechanization, initially by the application of steam power but now increasingly by that of electricity, on a scale that had already transformed Western European society, and was in the course of the coming century to do the same for the rest of the world.

This transformation consisted in the transition from agrarian-based, hierarchically governed, and largely self-sufficient communities whose social structure had been legitimized by a millennium of tradition and reinforced by ecclesiastical authorities claiming supra-natural sanction, to highly mobile, globally interlinked urban or urbanized societies in which political authority was legitimized by at least the appearance of popular consent and public life was increasingly secularized.

Meanwhile religious beliefs which had hitherto been socially mandatory were marginalized (where they survived at all) as largely private matters. This process, generally known as 'modernization', appeared for better or worse ineluctable; but it was to create frequent and often ferocious backlashes throughout the world, both religious and secular, as the century wore on.

By 1900 the forces of science, reason, and progress associated with the Enlightenment of the eighteenth century appeared to have won the battle in Europe itself. The advent of railways and steamships had destroyed the self-sufficiency of the old agrarian communities. By linking them with a continent-wide economy, they had not only compelled farmers to modernize traditional means of production, but made possible a mobility of population that resulted in the huge expansion of cities and, as trans-oceanic transport improved, of mass overseas emigration—a movement that reached its peak in the early years of the twentieth century. The extension of transcontinental rail links in the Americas and, to a lesser extent, in Euro-Asia, made this economy global.

The latter development, the completion of the trans-Siberian railway in 1901, led to gloomy forecasts by West European geopoliticians about the forthcoming dominance over the world by an ill-defined 'Heartland' of Central Asia—warnings that were to surface again during the Cold War but which, even a century later, appear at best premature. The former, however, by opening up the prairies of North and the pampas of South America, made available to Europe grain and meat in quantities, and at a price, that both fed the growing cities and tested the capacity of European cereal producers to compete, often to destruction.

The prospects for European agrarian producers at the beginning of the century thus appeared bleak. They agitated for the imposition of high tariffs, which everywhere created friction with the interests of city-dwellers who needed cheap food. In any case, the standard of living of the new urban populations in Europe and North America was rapidly being improved. Medical advances and good sanitation were bringing disease under control and improving life expectancy. With the growth of representative government and the extension of the suffrage, which by 1900 was on the way to becoming universal, the urban masses were increasingly seen, even by elements within the traditional ruling classes, not so much as a revolutionary menace to be feared but as votes to be won. The advent of electricity in the 1880s had perhaps done more than anything else to improve the standard of life in cities, although decades would pass before its benefits were extended to the countryside. In general there seemed every reason to suppose, as the new century dawned, that these improvements would indefinitely increase.

The most revolutionary scientific discoveries were the slowest to take effect. The discovery of the electron by J. J. Thomson in 1897 and of radium by the Curies a year later, the development by Max Planck of the quantum theory in 1900 and by Albert Einstein of the theory of relativity five years later were to transform man's understanding and control of the universe, but it was to be a further half-century before the application of that understanding, through electronics and nuclear physics, was to have a serious impact on society as a whole. Of more immediate relevance to 'the man in the street' (a phrase in itself indicative of the urbanization of society) were developments in communication. The cinema had already shown its potential for mass entertainment before the new century opened, as had the gramophone for private enjoyment. Further, Guglielmo Marconi had transmitted wireless messages across the Channel in 1899, and these were to cross the Atlantic two years later. In the field of transport, the internal combustion engine was already providing automobiles for the rich. Within a decade Henry Ford was to make them far more generally available; while the bicycle had already extended the range of mobility of all save the very poor.

Even more significant, the internal combustion engine made it possible for the Wright brothers to carry out the first powered flight at Kitty Hawk, North Carolina, in 1903, and for Louis Blériot to cross the Channel in 1909. The central role which the horse had played for a millennium as mankind's principal means of transport and traction was fast disappearing, and an entire social universe vanished with it. Everywhere stables were being replaced by garages. In consequence a further dimension was added to the expanding world economy; the dependence of industrial societies upon oil supplies that few of them were able to produce in the increasing quantities in which they would be needed.

These changes were reflected in the development of European high culture. The term 'modern' had previously been used to distinguish the post-Enlightenment period from that which had looked back to the classics for its authorities. Now it came to signify a yet more total break with the past—the rejection of a cultural tradition reaching back to the Renaissance and beyond. In music the work of Webern, Schoenberg, and Stravinsky; in painting, that of Mondrian and Picasso; in architecture and decoration, the pioneering work of the Bauhaus in Europe and of Frank Lloyd Wright in the United States; in literature, the experiments with new forms conducted by Ezra Pound and James Joyce; in general culture, the deliberate shock administered by Marinetti and the Futurists in Italy, followed elsewhere by vorticism, Dadaism, and surrealism; all indicated a contemptuous rejection of the past and a search for modes of expression appropriate to an age of science and secularism. For some this meant hope and liberation. For others it was anathema. In most lay observers it evoked a degree of bewilderment and incomprehension that was long to outlive the artists who created it.

It was these advances in science and technology that had made possible European world-dominance, and created, on both sides of the Atlantic, an almost unquestioned belief in the cultural and indeed racial superiority of the 'white' races over the rest of mankind. This belief was usually combined with a sense of obligation to bring the blessings of 'civilization' to 'backward' peoples; an obligation combined with one very much older, to spread the Christian gospel among the heathen. The impact of that civilization on the non-European world, for better or worse, is discussed elsewhere in this volume. In 1900 it would have been almost impossible to find a voice in Europe or the United States to suggest that it was anything other than beneficial. The only difference lay between those who believed that the more 'backward' races could in due course be raised up to the level of the 'advanced', and those who were convinced that this 'backwardness' was genetically ineradicable, leaving the white races with the responsibility of governing their inferiors in perpetuity.

The impact of these attitudes on non-Western peoples varied. In China the century opened with the Boxer Uprising, an ethnic upheaval against Western cultural penetration that evoked one of the few cooperative efforts of the Western world to crush it. Elsewhere indigenous élites sought security by cooperating with their conquerors, as they did in India; or by grafting Western technology on to their own culture, which the Japanese did with such success that, after their victory in the Russo-Japanese War of 1904–5, doubts were expressed as to whether the coming century would be that of the white man at all. But even where Western imperialism seemed most triumphant, indigenous cultures remained largely intact, making no more concessions to the conqueror than was strictly necessary until, as the twentieth century progressed, the penetration of Western communications, trade, and technology undermined their traditional life-styles as irresistibly as it had that of the Europeans themselves.

Yet in Europe at the turn of the century this belief in the peaceful inevitability of progress was already rather dated. The inevitability was still widely taken for granted, but the peacefulness was not. Instead there was a growing belief that progress would take the form of conflict—a belief rooted in the thought of those two mid-nineteenth-century giants, Karl Marx and Charles Darwin.

For Marx and his followers the conflict was one between social classes that would result in a revolution of the industrial proletariat to overthrow the entire capitalist system and usher in a classless society in which all contradictions had been eliminated and mankind would find total fulfilment. It was a creed that appealed not only to the leaders of an industrial working class whose wages had been kept at near subsistence level by the competition of their employers, but also to intellectuals who could no longer look for explanations of the world to traditional religion, and who welcomed the prospect of an earthly paradise promised, not by divine revelation, but by the rigorous scientific analysis of social dynamics.

By the end of the nineteenth century, as we have seen, such expectations of violent revolution had markedly ebbed as the physical conditions of the working classes improved, suffrage became more widespread, and the leaders of working-class movements were assimilated into the parliamentary system. But the class struggle was no less intense for being waged by votes, propaganda, and, above all, strikes. In Russia, the most backward of the 'capitalist' economies, such agitation resulted only in more ferocious repression. There revolution—or the threat of it—remained firmly on the agenda of a hard core of Marxist leaders, especially those living in exile in the West. The spectre of communism may not have haunted Europe as Marx had claimed before 1848, but it had not yet been exorcised.

The work of Charles Darwin was if anything even more influential than that of Marx. Darwin's view, that species survive by adapting themselves to the changes in their environment and only those survive that prove themselves fittest to do so, had led by the end of the century to a widespread belief, on both sides of the Atlantic, that this applied as much to social organisms as it did to the natural world. This Social Darwinism was a creed that suited the increasingly competitive economic atmosphere, as Germany and the United States surpassed Britain with their more up-to-date technology. It suited an age of imperial rivalries. It lent an edge to the dialectical struggle of the class war; and it reinforced some of the deepest fears held about the long-term implications of urbanization by those whose ideas were still rooted in values derived from agrarian societies.

The basic fear was that of decadence. If cities were no longer seen as hotbeds of revolution, they were feared yet more as seedbeds of degeneracy and anomie, where not only would the social framework that provided meaning and purpose for individual lives be lost, but where peoples who no longer had to face the challenges and hardships that had moulded their ancestors in the countryside would deteriorate both physically and morally. The fear of overpopulation, bringing with it the dominance of the physically and morally 'unfit', was becoming a nightmare for some political leaders especially in the most urbanized European societies, Britain and Germany. For the British, a solution seemed ready to hand in the colonies of settlement, and emigration was encouraged to Canada, South Africa, and the Antipodes. From Germany, as indeed Italy, there was a constant haemorrhage to the United States. But the Italians had their own dreams of an empire of settlement beyond the Mediterranean, which would also give them the status of a Great Power. As for the Germans, the vision of a Greater Germany colonizing the half-empty lands of western Russia, which was to crystallize so horribly during the middle years of the coming century, were already being formulated within the minds of a few fanatics.

Behind these fears and reinforcing them there lay a yet deeper social cleavage: that between those who welcomed the dawn of a new age, even if it brought with it new problems and conflicts, and those who dreaded the destruction of a society and of values rooted in centuries of tradition. Those who had flourished best in the old soil, the great landowners (and, even more, the not-so-great landowners) and their dependents, were naturally those who dreaded it most, and they remained socially and politically powerful everywhere east of the Rhine. The resistance of these old ruling classes was everywhere reinforced by the enormous power of the Roman Catholic Church; and, though that Church under Pope Leo XIII was slowly and reluctantly coming to terms with the new age, it would be decades before that adjustment penetrated into the rural parishes of Italy, France, and Spain. In those countries a cultural civil war had long been waged between the forces of progress and those of tradition; a conflict that was brought to a head at the turn of the century by the efforts of their governments to control and laicize national education. It was a struggle that was already tearing France apart over the Dreyfus Affair. In Italy the refusal of the Vatican to recognize the legitimacy of the secular Kingdom of Italy was to make much of that country virtually ungovernable from Rome until

MICHAEL HOWARD

the advent of Mussolini in the 1920s; while in Spain the conflict was to erupt four decades later into bloody civil war.

Nor was it only the reactionary survivors of the old order who looked on the developments of the new age with deep apprehension. They were joined, especially in Central Europe, by many who had hitherto benefited from the economic developments of the previous century—a whole mass of petty bourgeoisie employed in the service industries and government administration, as well as small shopkeepers who were finding themselves squeezed between the forces of international capitalism on the one hand, and the growing power of the organized working classes on the other.

These groups, fearful of losing the status and the benefits they had acquired during the happier years of economic expansion, were especially prone to anti-Semitism, as indeed were the landowners, great and small, in the countryside. For the poorer elements, both in town and country, the Jews represented the money-lenders to whom they were becoming indebted. For the possessing classes, they embodied the forces of international capital that seemed to be accumulating more and more power. For all, they were an alien and easily identifiable element that could be cast as a scapegoat for all manner of social ills. It was a tendency that the Catholic Church did little to discourage. Throughout Europe, from St Petersburg to Paris, demagogues found the Jews an easy target. It was in this atmosphere that Theodore Herzl, the creator of Zionism, came to the conclusion that Judaism could survive only if the Jews could found a nation of their own.

By far the most powerful force binding together the disrupted societies of Europe as they moved into the new century was that of nationalism. In 1900 the nation state had reached its apogee. For a century past the power and reach of state authorities had become increasingly intrusive as improved communications enabled them to increase their control over the administration, welfare, and education of their citizens, and to conscript them to serve in their armies. That control would hardly have been feasible unless the old personal loyalties and sense of obligation to a ruling dynasty that had held European societies together since the sixteenth century had not been powerfully reinforced by a broader sense of belonging to a 'nation'—a country, a *Vaterland*, a *patrie*. As the power of the state increased, so did this sense of nationhood. It found expression throughout Europe in military parades and ceremonies, in monumental neo-Baroque architecture, in anthems and flags and patriotic symbols. Historians created patriotic myths and lexicographers nurtured distinctive languages. The person of the hereditary ruler was converted into a quasi-religious icon. Pride in country created a sense of common dignity and purpose. Its appeal reconciled all but the bitterest reactionaries and the most dogmatic socialists. Nationalism, in short, was one of the most powerful instruments of social mobilization that the world had yet seen.

But, like modernization itself, nationalism was subversive of older orders of society. It may have been a force for cohesion and stability in Western Europe, but in the less advanced societies further east, still ruled by traditional dynastic empires, its impact was deeply disruptive. The management of nascent nationalism within the multinational empire of the Habsburgs and the European possessions of the Ottoman Empire—'the Eastern Question'—had occupied European statesmen for the past quarter-century, and was still to trouble them a hundred years later. As for Europe's overseas empires, the British for one had already found in Ireland, and were beginning to discover in India, that it was difficult to proclaim the ideal of national self-government at home while denying it to those they ruled overseas.

Moreover the unity created by national sentiment within the states of Western Europe was bought at the cost of embittering relations between them. Great national ceremonies were explicitly celebrations of past military triumphs and implicitly preparations for new ones. The prospect of another war, fought with all the destructive weapons that technology now made possible, was indeed terrible—so terrible, indeed, that the leaders of Europe had met in conference at The Hague in 1899 to see what could be done to mitigate, if not prevent, it. But the result had not been encouraging. It did little to erode the widespread belief that, even if war was terrible, it still remained the ultimate test of the fitness of nations to survive.

If the peoples of Europe had been told in 1900 that fourteen years later they would enter on the greatest war in the history of mankind, few would have been surprised. Some would not have been ill-pleased. But only a tiny minority foresaw that it would destroy for ever the hopes and the self-confidence with which the century began.

2 Demography and Urbanization

WILLIAM H. McNEILL

An intelligent visitor from outer space, observing the earth as a whole in 1900 and again a hundred years later, would surely find the increase in human numbers and urbanization, together with associated alterations in the planet's array of other life forms, the most remarkable change of the century. Humankind more than tripled in number, from something like 1.63 billion in 1900 to a projected 6 billion plus in 2000. Such growth is without historical parallel. Perhaps in the prehistoric era, when our ancestors began to shift from hunting and gathering to food production some 10,000 years ago, comparable rates of population growth may have set in locally for a while. But effects were limited. Human hunters, like lions and other predators, were comparatively rare in the balance of nature. Food production allowed much greater numbers, but new population ceilings soon asserted themselves as the limits of subsistence agriculture were reached in one locality after another.

Presumably limits to the modern demographic surge will also assert themselves. Indeed, demographers expect that increments to human numbers, now cresting at about 79 millions a year, will decline with the onset of the next century. If so, the year 2000 will symbolize for future generations the apex of an unparalleled transformation of human society and global ecology—a transformation whose repercussions profoundly affect all living beings, human and non-human alike.

Most obvious is the fact that an expanding human presence has inflicted drastic perturbations on other life forms. Everywhere, wild species have shrunk back, while crops, domesticated animals, and all the weeds and pests attuned to coexistence with humankind have multiplied. In addition, deforestation, ploughing, and other human actions have accelerated erosion in many parts of earth, while wholesale use of fossil fuels and other artificially initiated chemical processes have diffused new sorts of molecules throughout earth's air and water on a scale that may alter climate. Accordingly, the earth's ecosystem finds itself evolving much faster than usual, thanks to strains and tears in older balances created by human activity.

Human beings are, and always have been, part of that ecosystem, but exactly how older natural balances were upset, opening a path for the modern multiplication of human numbers, is a matter of dispute. The gross outline of what happened is clear enough. Experts agree that systematic population growth gathered headway about 1750 in Europe and China, spread to nearly all of the globe by 1850, and assumed a new velocity after 1950, when the World Health Organization (WHO) succeeded in checking the ravages of the principal lethal infections that had formerly decimated humankind. Relatively simple public-health measures, such as vaccination, water purification, and spraying against mosquitoes, drastically reduced the incidence of common diseases such as measles, dysentery, malaria, and many others. In addition, newly discovered antibiotics cured once lethal infections like bubonic plague, and a systematic worldwide campaign succeeded in eradicating smallpox entirely. Death rates declined accordingly, especially among children; and, as larger numbers lived to maturity and produced children of their own, the accelerated population surge of the second half of our century got under way.

The extraordinary demographic history of the twentieth century therefore seems primarily due to death control through widespread application of preventive medicine. Before 1950, effective public-health measures were largely confined to wealthy countries, and, for the most part, dated back only to the 1880s, when disease germs and their routes of infection were unambiguously identified for the first time. Then, in the second half of the century, the WHO launched a campaign against infections that extended to poor countries as well. Meeting with general support and cooperation around the globe, a relatively small number of public-health officials and doctors quickly demonstrated an unparalleled capacity to alter the conditions of human life for the better.

Obviously this triumph of science and skill was only possible in tandem with other factors. In particular, the world's governments had to cooperate with medical experts, and other social institutions had to tolerate, even if they did not actively support, what public-health officials were up to. Violence, too, had to be restrained. Surprisingly it was. Despite the losses of two world wars and all the other lethal confrontations that figure so largely in the news, violent deaths entirely failed to inhibit population growth.

In addition, more food was needed to keep growing populations from starvation. In some parts of the earth, clearing new land and working harder in the fields was the principal response; but use of new, higher-yielding seeds, and the application of larger amounts of artificial fertilizer—the so-called Green Revolution—were more important in allowing food supplies to keep up with (and even outstrip) population growth. How to distribute food equably remains problematic; and sporadic famine, especially in parts of Africa, required emergency efforts to distribute food to starving people, despite their inability to pay. The elementary fact that global food supplies still suffice (and more than suffice) to feed the world's population made this sort of public international response to human suffering possible.

Compared with earlier human efforts to evade the ravages of disease and hunger, the twentieth-century triumphs of medical and agronomic science in reducing infection and increasing food production are indeed remarkable. None the less, modern science does not allow humans to escape the trammels of our place in earth's ecosystem entirely. Factors that have not been brought under deliberate public management are still at work, and are sure to affect human life, wealth, and comfort in times to come in ways that are largely unforeseen and, in detail, will probably remain permanently unmanageable.

Paradoxical though it may seem, one such factor is birth control. The recent invention of cheap and effective methods of preventing births allows private persons to decide how many children they will have; and a growing number of people in more and more parts of the earth are, in fact, acting accordingly. But the statistical, long-term effects of such decisions are far from clear. Demographers commonly speak of a 'demographic transition', and often assume that birth control following in the footsteps of death control will eventually stabilize human numbers at some heightened level. But stability seems improbable. Zero population growth cannot be discovered in the imperfect records of times past. Presumably it figured as an evanescent transition between growth and decay rather than as a steady state, since population history—for humans and for all other forms of life—is one of irregular ups and downs.

Moreover, different segments of humanity behave differently, affected by religious and other cultural ideals and by diverse economic and social environments. In the twentieth century, for instance, populations as diverse as civilized Frenchmen and hunters and gatherers of the Amazon jungle have declined in numbers, while overall global population has continued to mount. Public efforts to persuade prospective parents to increase or decrease the number of their offspring have not led to stable populations. In China, for instance, where in recent years the prohibition of more than one child per couple has been energetically enforced, at least in some parts of the country, not stability but an extreme disbalance between the sexes and among age cohorts promises to be the result.

Similarly, when private decisions are not invaded by public law, the introduction of birth control seems likely to produce sharp demographic fluctuations, similar to the one which affected French Canada after the Second World War. French birth rates had long been higher than those of other Canadians, but when wartime urban employment broke up the *habitant* style of rural life, a sudden resort to birth control among young French Canadians reduced their birth rate so sharply that it sank below that of other Canadians and beneath replacement levels as well. At least in the short run, resort to birth control may therefore produce declining populations. It has already done so among the Germans and Hungarians; and, if present trends continue, other rich, urbanized nations will soon begin to experience declining numbers as well.

Generational shifts in behaviour also alter demography in unforeseen ways. For example, the baby boom during and after the Second World War departed from pre-war projections in a way no one anticipated; while the marked decay of births that set in during the 1960s in rich and urbanized countries of the world coincided with the peak of population growth rates among African, Asian, and Latin American populations. So far at least, instability seems to inhere in a situation where private, personal wishes have begun to exercise hitherto unparalleled power over human births.

Shifting gender roles and, in particular, the redefinition of women's status that working for wages permits are other factors that have affected demography in many parts of the world. In general, in proportion as women gained greater economic independence and left home to work for wages, they had less time and energy for the nurture of infants and small children. Postponement of marriage and fewer children often resulted. But it is not clear that responses were everywhere the same. Diverse cultural heritages and different local circumstances affected gender and family relations, whether or not women worked for wages outside the home, and are sure to continue to do so. Cultural diversity therefore constitutes yet another variable affecting population growth and decay.

Still another source of demographic instability arises from the fact that other organisms—disease germs in particular—have begun to adapt to the new conditions created by prophylactic medicine. Powerful antibiotics in effect presented disease germs and other micro-organisms that live inside human bodies with a crisis of survival. Some few, like smallpox, were extinguished; but others evolved resistant strains. As a result, ever since the use of penicillin was introduced in 1940, human ingenuity in discovering new antibiotics entered into a race against the evolution of resistant strains of disease organisms. Human inventiveness retains the initiative, but, with the exception of smallpox, germs have not been destroyed. Complete elimination of age-old infections that seemed within reach at mid-century turned out to be impossible. Instead, some formidable diseases, most notably malaria and tuberculosis, have begun to come back, despite the doctors' best efforts.

In addition, new infections, most famous of which is the virus that causes Aids, have also taken advantage of changes in human behaviour to spread themselves widely around the world. The exact path whereby the HIV virus escaped the older limits on its habitat before being propagated along truck routes in Africa and then around the world by aeroplane is not known, but its global propagation in less than two decades is not in doubt. Air travel (interlinked with bird migrations, which also help to generate and propagate new forms of the influenza virus) also allows variant forms of flu to spread annually over much of the globe; and other diseases obviously have access to the same mode of dispersal. Indeed, the possibility of worldwide lethal epidemic is inherent in the juxtaposition of rapid global transport with the weeks, months, or years required to discover, produce, and distribute immunization doses capable of checking a completely new infection.

In general, twentieth-century advances in medicine have speeded up organic

13

evolution enormously by drastically altering life conditions for infectious organisms. As a result, the initial triumphs over disease that attained spectacular success in the decades of the 1950s and 1960s are wearing thin. Nothing like a stable balance between medical skill and infection is yet in sight as the demographic impact of infectious diseases starts to increase once again.

An additional factor facilitating the return of infections is the difficulty of administering public-health measures—even simple ones like inoculations—in poor countries, beset by political unrest and disturbed by massive migrations. Rapidly growing cities of the Third World commonly lack adequate water sanitation and sewage disposal systems. Rats and other pests multiply incontinently in such circumstances. Recent epidemics of cholera in South America and of bubonic plague in India illustrate how deficient public-health administration can allow old diseases to reclaim a lethal role once more—at least briefly and sporadically.

If one adds to this catalogue of instabilities currently affecting human population the possibility of global climate change and other unintended by-products of atmospheric and oceanic pollution, it seems clear that the surge of human numbers that started about 1750 and rose to a climax during the second half of the twentieth century has begun to generate powerful counter forces that make its indefinite prolongation entirely improbable. If so, the biological expansion of our species that has taken place between 1900 and 2000 will remain unique and truly exceptional in human history.

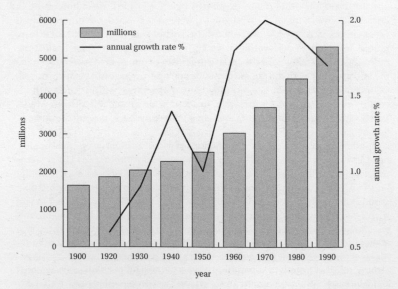

Figure 1. Estimated world population totals, 1900–1990
Source: Massimo Livo-Bacci, *A Concise History of World Population* (Oxford, 1992), 147.

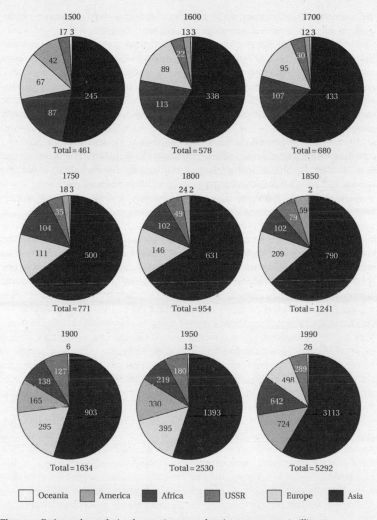

Figure 2. Estimated population by continents and regions, 1500–1990 (millions)

Source: Massimo Livo-Bacci, *A Concise History of World Population* (Oxford, 1992), 31, based on J. N. Biraben, 'Essai sur l'évolution des nombres des hommes', *Population*, 34 (1979), 16.

Clearly, population growth constituted a basic context for twentieth-century history. The extraordinary character of the prevailing demographic regime affected public and private life pervasively, though often indirectly and always in combination with other circumstances and initiatives. None the less, public discourse among urban dwellers commonly takes population growth so completely for granted as to overlook its role in shaping the course of events.

This was not true for a majority of humankind, who in 1900 lived in villages and depended on surrounding fields to produce most of what they consumed. In such communities the effect of population growth was always obvious. Every time more than two children came of age within a family, it became impossible for the young simply to succeed their parents on the land and carry on daily routines as before. If uncultivated soil was accessible, established patterns of life needed only minimal adjustment. Creating new fields was arduous and harvests were commonly inferior; but by working harder life could continue almost as before.

When empty land was unavailable, however, rising numbers confronted rural families with hard, inescapable choices. Partitioning family holdings among a plurality of children was feasible only when new methods of cultivation could increase yields sufficiently to support larger numbers at an acceptable level of comfort. More often, emigration offered the only practicable escape from immiseration.

Where to seek one's fortune then became a capital question for all those who could not stay at home. Young people compelled to roam in search of new modes of livelihood often lost touch with those they left behind; but sooner or later a few achieved a more or less satisfactory lodgement in a city (or more rarely discovered a place where land was available) and notified relatives back home. Others then followed, often assisted by those already established in the new locality. Chain migration of this sort sometimes created odd and unpredictable links between very distant places and, when conditions of life in the new environment were favourable, could persuade almost everybody to leave. For example, I happen to be acquainted with a remote mountain village in Greece that established daughter communities in Toronto, Canada, and in Sydney, Australia, in the 1920s, each of which, by 1976, comprised a far larger number of persons than the handful remaining behind in Greece.

Removal to towns and cities close at hand was, of course, easier and more common, since it did not (usually) require the migrants to learn a new language and accommodate themselves to a radically alien society. On the other hand, the advantages were less, and, correspondingly, depopulation of the sending community seldom or never occurred because conditions of life were almost equally harsh in easily accessible city slums and surrounding overcrowded villages.

Systematic migration from village to city was nothing new. Indeed, from their inception cities had needed migrants from the surrounding countryside to maintain their numbers against the intensified ravages of disease that urban crowding produced. But in the twentieth century this age-old pattern altered. Public-health measures checked urban deaths from infections, so that cities no longer needed immigrants to fill existing jobs. But this narrowing of opportunity was counteracted by an amazing proliferation of urban occupations incident to the intensification of world-girdling commerce, the growth of industrial production, and an enormous expansion of bureaucratic administration, both private and public.

These dimensions of modern urban growth depended in turn on cheaper and more capacious transport which made it possible for more and more people to gather in cities, eating food produced at a distance and delivered to urban consumers as part of an ever more complex exchange of goods and services that extended around the globe.

Until the twentieth century, the vast majority of human beings lived on the land and worked at producing food. Most of them used hand tools that had not changed much for hundreds of years. In 1900, Great Britain was the only important country in the world where less than half of the population was employed in agriculture. But, as the decades proceeded, more and more people abandoned agriculture and learned to live in cities, so that, as the year 2000 approaches, it is probably true that more than half of the world's population has become urbanized, with all the radical changes in daily experience this implies.

Certainty is impossible because statistics are inexact and definition of how large a settlement must be (and where its boundaries lie) before it counts as a city remains arbitrary. But how we classify the places people live in is less important than the changes brought about by the rapid incorporation of rural populations in urban-managed economic and information networks. These changes did not depend on migration into town, for, in proportion as buying and selling penetrated rural communities, urban-style occupations and outlooks seeped into the countryside, narrowing the age-old gap between food producers and food consumers. Subsistence agriculture, which had defined our ancestors' way of life since neolithic times, decayed. In its place, specialized production transformed agriculture throughout most of the earth. Food production was also largely (though not completely) mechanized. Starting in 1901, when the first commercially successful tractor was introduced in Iowa, mechanically powered tractors began to drag new forms of farm machinery across fields formerly tilled by animal and human muscles. Human labour in rice paddies continued to prevail in the densely inhabited parts of Asia, but even there new seeds, fertilizers, and small gasoline-powered cultivaters transformed traditional methods of cultivation.

Only by selling part or all of the harvest could rural food producers acquire the machinery, fertilizer, and seed they needed for such farming. And only because they sold an increased proportion of larger and larger harvests was enough food available to feed the growing urban population of the earth. Parts of Africa and Latin America lagged noticeably behind in the commercialization and technical transformation of agriculture. None the less, this extraordinary change in rural routines means that, by the close of the twentieth century, the vast majority of the world's population has begun to participate, willy nilly, in global interactive networks. Old-fashioned rural isolation has diminished when it has not disappeared entirely. Village and all other forms of local autonomy, both economic and cultural, have been correspondingly curtailed.

This constitutes a fundamental transformation in the texture of everyday experience for humankind. Our ancestors lived in small communities where everyone knew one another, and where customary definitions of what to do prevailed in all ordinary situations. By comparison, anonymity and uncertainty pervade global networks—both economic and informational—and become especially acute in the sprawling cities that constitute their nodes. Rules of behaviour deriving from face-to-face rural experience do not apply easily or automatically among strangers, especially when culturally and physically diverse groups find themselves in competition for advantageous roles and positions. Stability is, therefore, hard to achieve. Anything else would be surprising inasmuch as adaptation to the modern scale of urban living has barely begun. Moreover, the possibility of catastrophe inheres in the radical vulnerability of exchange networks to any prolonged interruption of the long-distance flows of goods and services that, so far, have sustained increasing human numbers so successfully.

The attraction of the new style of living was and remains very powerful. What may be called 'emergent global urbanity' extended its reach abruptly with the new forms of communication that arose in the course of the twentieth century. In particular, broadcasting via radio (beginning in the 1920s) and television (beginning in the 1940s) quickly blanketed nearly all of the globe, thereby bringing local cultural autonomy to an end. Timing differed from one country to another; but in most of the earth the traditional isolation of village communities from contact with urban bustle and excitement broke down soon after the Second World War. Sometimes governments set up radio receivers in village squares to spread official propaganda from the capital. Often it was only when tavern keepers or individual families acquired radios, then television sets, that the outer world began to impinge regularly and unceasingly on village consciousness.

In either case, the effect was extraordinary. Entertainment programmes produced in sophisticated circles of Hollywood, Cairo, Bombay, and other film centres carried devastatingly delightful messages about the comfort and convenience of urban existence. The hardship and laboriousness of rural routines seemed horridly unattractive by comparison, even when villagers knew that life in the slums as actually experienced by those who had left home was very different from what announcers' radio voices or the behaviour of television actors suggested. Yet dissatisfaction with everything around them because they felt excluded from the superior charms of urbanity made many young persons unwilling to stay at home, even when they could expect to live as well as (or modestly better than) their parents had done.

The effect was profoundly unsettling. The new intimacy established by radio and television between rural folk and urban spokespersons did not imply harmony or even a comfortable coexistence. Instead, long-standing inequalities and injustices came to the fore, as rural folk became more acutely aware of how their lives differed from those of wealthy and privileged urban dwellers. From a rural point of view, the market often rewarded ruthless wheelers and dealers extravagantly, despite the fact that such people often evaded honest muscular work entirely. And since those who did work in the fields were selling more and more of their harvest to intermediaries who sold it again at marked-up prices, they commonly felt systematically cheated. Why was the same thing worth more at a distance? Why did they not get what others eventually paid for the crops they had sold?

Communist regimes, both in Russia and China, acquired much of their initial support by appealing to these rural grievances. In the name of social justice, both revolutionary governments sought to suppress private traders who lived by marking up prices. But, once in office, Communist officials proceeded to exploit the countryside ruthlessly, forcibly collecting quotas of food for distribution to city dwellers. In practice, Russians and Chinese both allowed small-scale private marketing of food, even when the rigours of revolutionary ideology were most in vogue, and the Chinese have recently removed almost all restrictions on buying and selling. But policies favouring city dwellers remain in force both in China and in post-Communist Russia. Correspondingly, rural discontent probably simmers somewhere beneath the surface in both countries, but—so far at least—without attaining explicit or significant public expression.

Not surprisingly, migrants from the countryside who found themselves living precariously in city slums all round the world were also dissatisfied with their changed circumstances. Earning a living was hard when so many newcomers competed with one another for whatever jobs were on offer. Success as an independent entrepreneur required skills and moral attitudes that most newcomers lacked. Urban anonymity and specialized activity tended to undermine the moral rules and constraints inherited from the rural past without providing clear or easily accessible substitutes. Ruthless amoralism, on the one hand, and desperate loneliness, on the other, were poor substitutes for the tight-knit village communities of older times.

Various new groups began to form—religious sects first and foremost; but also street gangs, political movements, social clubs, and more informal neighbourhood gatherings at taverns and water taps. In time, one may perhaps expect that human inventiveness will form new primary groups and define more satisfactory codes of conduct to fit human beings into global networks more firmly and comfortably than has yet been done. But the initial transition is difficult and painful; and resulting resentment makes for political instability, especially in Asia, Africa, and Latin America, where rural overcrowding, migration into cities, and incorporation into global exchange networks are most recent, massive, and abrupt.

Old urban residents did not find floods of newcomers easy to accept. This was especially evident in European and North American cities in the second half of the century, when immigrants of alien culture and distinct physical appearance began to arrive in unprecedented numbers. Public policy towards them varied markedly. In particular, Germany and Japan took different paths from the other rich countries.

Germany's peculiar policy started as a response to the erection of the Berlin Wall in 1961. This interrupted the flow of Germans from the east that had helped to sustain the remarkable expansion of the West German economy, so the FRG decided to invite 'guest workers' from the Balkans and southern Europe to fill the gap. To obviate exploitation, and prevent undercutting German wage levels, pay scales and other conditions of employment were carefully negotiated with the governments from whose countries such workers came. As a result, hundreds of thousands of guest workers eagerly signed contracts for work in Germany at wages that far exceeded local pay scales. Initially, all concerned assumed that the migrants would return home after their work contracts expired. Some did so, but many preferred to stay, since their pay far exceeded anything they could earn at home. This presented the German government with an awkward problem of how to cope with immigrants who were expected to retain their national identities and were therefore excluded from German citizenship. No satisfactory resolution has been reached, even though many of the guest workers are unlikely to return voluntarily, and their children, growing up in segregated guest-worker housing, constitute a substantial and growing population that belongs neither to German society nor to the country of origin.

When, a decade or two later, the Japanese began to experience serious labour shortages, they refrained from following the German example of inviting foreigners to work in their country. Instead they began to export capital, building factories abroad where local persons were employed to produce a great variety of goods, usually under Japanese supervisors. Whether the Japanese will sustain this policy when, as demographers predict, the labour pool at home starts to shrink, so that less attractive existing jobs will not be filled, remains to be seen. But so far, in spite of a small population of Koreans and some other illegal immigrants, the Japanese have escaped ethnic frictions in their home islands and remain unique among the rich countries of the world in this respect.

In the United States, France, Britain and most other rich, industrialized countries, immigrants were allowed and expected to become citizens after satisfying relatively simple legal requirements. Throughout the first half of the century, an unspoken condition of this policy was the expectation of assimilation to the host nation. But after the Second World War the ideal of assimilation lost most of its credibility. The long-standing failure of the United States fully to assimilate the descendants of African slaves was not cured by earnest efforts at legal reform in the 1960s. Instead, the limited success of the American civil-rights movement showed how hard it was to achieve genuine freedom and equality when outward bodily appearance assigned a group identity to individuals that was far more powerful than judgements based on personal behaviour, preference, or capability. The fact that more and more of the new immigrants to Western Europe and the United States had darker skins than the receiving nations made imperceptible merger into the host community far more difficult than had been the case earlier, when most newcomers were physically indistinguishable from the majority of existing inhabitants.

All concerned also became aware of the cost immigrants had formerly paid by being asked to surrender religious and other treasured dimensions of their inherited culture. Consequently, multiculturalism with equal political rights for all concerned tended to displace assimilation as an ideal. But intensified friction inhered in the claim of equal rights for culturally diverse groups. The trouble was that some groups did far better than others, relying upon inherited cultural patterns of behaviour to take advantage of educational and other ladders for advancement. Those lagging behind resented their marginality, and, not infrequently, a culture of defiance took root among disadvantaged youths that had the effect of confirming their continued exclusion from free and equal participation in civil society.

Resulting dilemmas are acute in all the wealthy countries of the world. Freedom and equality are easy to invoke, hard to achieve, and less and less apparent in a world where information about how the rich and privileged disport themselves is available to more and more of the world's poorest and most disadvantaged inhabitants. What seems to be at stake is whether or not the gap between rural and urban patterns of life and the plurality of existing cultures in all the different parts of the world can be closed successfully by incorporating everyone into what is fast becoming a global exchange economy. Rewards are enormous. Only specialized production and exchange can sustain existing levels of human population. But adjustment of inherited attitudes and behaviour to safeguard global exchanges from disruption by organized political violence has a long way to go. Public policy is a blunt instrument for making such adjustments. None the less, local initiatives and inventions that satisfy human wants better than before are sure to spread whenever they appear; and in the course of the next two or three centuries one can imagine that human beings may succeed in learning to live under the drastically new conditions created by the runaway population growth and intensified transport and communications that marked the twentieth century off from all earlier ages.

The prehistoric shift from hunting and gathering to food production required comparably pervasive adjustment of personal habits and group behaviour. None the less, our ancestors learnt how to survive by working in the fields, and sustaining all the historic variety of political and cultural institutions. Perhaps it is not unreasonable to suppose that our successors may also learn to live under new and very different conditions of global urbanity thanks to the inventiveness that marks us off from other forms of life.

3 The Great Reduction: Physics in the Twentieth Century

STEVEN WEINBERG

By the end of the nineteenth century scientists had achieved a fair understanding of the world of everyday experience. Sciences such as mechanics, thermodynamics, chemistry, optics, cell biology, and even electrodynamics had become part of the armamentarium of industry and agriculture. In return, industry had provided science with the apparatus, the vacuum pumps and spectroscopes and so on, that would be needed for further advances. Science had also been the beneficiary of the growing intellectual technology of mathematics. Differential and integral calculus, complex analysis, differential geometry and group theory had become well-enough developed by 1900 to satisfy the needs of science for decades to come.

One great thing was missing from science at the nineteenth century's end: a sense of how it all fitted together. In 1900 scientists generally supposed that physics, chemistry, and biology each operated under its own autonomous laws. The empire of science was believed to consist of many separate commonwealths, at peace with each other, but separately ruled. A few scientists held on to Newton's dream of a grand synthesis of all the sciences, but without any clear idea of the terms on which this synthesis could be reached.

We catch echoes of this confusion in complacent statements of late-nineteenth-century physicists, asserting the near completion of physics. Those who made such remarks could not have thought that physics had completed its task of explaining the rules of chemistry, or that physics and chemistry had succeeded in explaining the mechanisms of heredity and embryology. Rather, they did not suppose that it was part of the task of physics to explain chemistry, or of physical science to explain life. The complacency of late-nineteenth-century physicists is a measure of the limitations of their ambitions for physics.

Matters are very different now, at the end of the twentieth century. We understand in principle and often in practice how the laws of chemistry arise from the laws of physics. Biology, of course, involves historical accidents in a way that physics and chemistry do not, but hardly anyone would seriously consider the possibility that there are autonomous universal laws of biology, independent of those of physical science.

This has been reduction in the grand sense—the explanation of a wide range of scientific principles in terms of simpler, more universal ones. It has also largely been reduction in the petty sense—the explanation of natural phenomena at one scale in terms of the principles governing matter at much smaller scales. Just as the rules of chemistry have been explained in terms of the dynamics of electrons in atoms, the mechanism of heredity which drives biological evolution is now understood in molecular terms.

This chapter will not deal with all of twentieth-century science, or even all of twentieth-century physics, but only with that part of physics research that has followed the reductionist tradition of seeking the deepest principles underlying all of nature.

If only for physicists, the twentieth century began in 1895, with Wilhelm Röntgen's accidental discovery of X-rays. Röntgen found that the electric current driven by a powerful electric battery through an evacuated glass 'Crookes' tube (the first particle accelerator) produced mysterious rays on striking the glass wall of the tube, rays that could not be refracted by lenses or deflected by matter or by electric or magnetic fields. In itself, this discovery marked no great revolution. We know now that these X-rays are just light waves of short wavelength, but Röntgen's discovery was a dramatic sign that, outside the range of natural phenomena that had been illuminated by nineteenth-century physics, there were plenty of mysteries waiting to be discovered.

Almost immediately, the discovery of X-rays spurred other, more important, discoveries. Early in 1896 Henri Becquerel, searching for new kinds of rays, found by accident that uranium emits rays that can expose photographic plates. Pierre and Marie Curie soon discovered that thorium, polonium, and radium produce similar effects, and gave the phenomenon its modern name, *radioactivity*. After a good deal of confusion Ernest Rutherford and Frederick Soddy identified radioactivity as being due to transmutation of elements, in which energy is released and carried off by particles of various sorts. Beyond its importance for the understanding of matter, the discovery of radioactivity soon suggested solutions to the fundamental problems of the source of the heat of the sun and the earth, and thereby resolved the discrepancy between the short age of the earth previously inferred from its present heat and the much longer age that had been deduced from the fossil record.

Only two years after the discovery of X-rays, both J. J. Thomson in Cambridge and Walter Kaufmann in Berlin measured the ratio of mass to electric charge of the currents flowing in a modified Crookes tube. This mass/charge ratio turned out to be thousands of times smaller than for the ions that carry electric currents in electrolysis. On this basis, Thomson proposed that the current in a Crookes tube is carried by particles that he called *electrons*, thousands of times lighter than whole atoms, that are universally present in all matter.

The idea that matter consists of atoms had proved useful to chemists and physicists of the nineteenth century, but there was still no direct evidence of their existence. This was provided in the first decade of the twentieth century by a variety of measurements of the masses of atoms, generally giving consistent results. Most of these new measurements had been made possible by the discoveries of 1895–7.

Until 1911 there was no idea how masses and electric charges are arranged within atoms. Then Rutherford used the results of experiments in his Manchester laboratory, on the scattering of particles from a radioactive source by gold atoms, to show that the mass of an atom is almost entirely concentrated in a tiny positively charged nucleus. He pictured the electrons that are responsible for chemical, electrical, and optical phenomena as revolving around the nucleus like planets revolving around the sun. The age-old question of the nature of ordinary matter had thus been answered, with only the composition of the atomic nucleus still entirely mysterious.

In the great work of 1895–1911 described so far, experimenters played the leading role. Where physical theory was used to analyse the experimental results, it was the familiar classical theory of the nineteenth century. But the picture of the atom that emerged from this work raised disturbing questions that could not be answered within the classical framework.

According to the principles of electrodynamics, atomic electrons revolving in their orbits should emit light, losing energy and quickly spiralling into the nucleus. Yet every ordinary non-radioactive atom has a state of lowest energy that seems perfectly stable. Furthermore, although an atom that has absorbed energy from light or from collisions with other atoms will lose it again by emitting light, this emitted light does not have a continuous spectrum of wavelengths, as would be expected for electrons spiralling inwards to a state of lowest energy; rather, it is emitted only at certain sharp wavelengths that are characteristic of the type of atom. Such atomic spectra were discovered early in the nineteenth century, and had become a tool for chemical analysis, including even the analysis of the elements in the sun and other stars, but no one could explain the spectrum of wavelengths at which various atoms emit light.

The solution lay not in a new theory of electromagnetism or atomic structure, but in a radically new framework for all physical theory, known as quantum mechanics. Here are the highlights of this revolution:

1900   Max Planck explains the spectrum of black-body radiation (the intensity of light emitted at various wavelengths by a heated opaque body) by assuming that, when atoms emit light of a given wavelength, they do not lose energy continuously, but rather in multiples of a 'quantum' of energy, inversely proportional to the light wavelength.

1905   Albert Einstein interprets Planck's conjecture (over Planck's objections) as showing that light itself consists of individual particles, later called photons. Photons have no mass but have energy and momentum, inversely proportional to the light wavelength. Experimental evidence for Einstein's photon is found in the photoelectric effect, and later in the scattering of X-rays by electrons.

1913   Niels Bohr offers a tentative interpretation of atomic spectra. Atoms can exist only in certain states of definite energy. When an atom drops from a state of higher to one of lower energy, it emits a photon with an energy equal to the difference of the energies of the final and initial atomic states, and hence, according to Einstein, with a definite wavelength, inversely proportional to this energy difference. Bohr uses the Rutherford picture of atomic electrons revolving around a nucleus to give an *ad hoc* though successful prescription for calculating the energies of the states of simple atoms like hydrogen with just a single electron. But it is not clear how to apply this prescription to more complicated atoms and molecules, or why it should work for any atoms.

1923   Louis de Broglie offers an explanation of Bohr's prescription. Electrons are associated with waves, with a wavelength inversely proportional to the electron momentum, just as for photons. The Bohr prescription for the energy of an atomic state is interpreted as the requirement that a whole number of these wavelengths should just fit around the electron orbit. But, again, this approach works only for the simplest atoms.

1925   Werner Heisenberg makes a fresh start at interpreting atomic spectra. The dynamics of atoms is expressed, not in terms of the trajectories of electrons revolving around the nucleus, but in tables (matrices) of numerical quantities whose squares give the rates at which atoms make transitions from one atomic state to another. Soon after, in a mathematical *tour de force*, Heisenberg's former classmate Wolfgang Pauli uses Heisenberg's formalism to calculate the spectrum of hydrogen, recovering Bohr's 1913 results. But it still seems hopeless to use these methods in more complicated problems.

1925–6 Erwin Schrödinger returns to de Broglie's electron waves, and proposes a differential equation that governs the amplitude of the wave (the so-called wave function) in general electric fields. He shows how Heisenberg's matrices and the algebraic conditions they satisfy can be derived from his wave equation. For the first time, there is a method that can be used to calculate the energies of states, not just in hydrogen, but in atoms and molecules of arbitrary complexity. But the physical significance of the electron wave function remains obscure.

1926   Max Born explains that the waves of de Broglie and Schrödinger are 'probability amplitudes'; the probability that an electron will be found in a small volume around a given point equals the square of the wave function at that point, times the volume.

After 1926 quantum mechanics was rapidly and successfully applied to the calculation of the properties not only of atoms in isolation, but also of atoms joined in chemical molecules and even in macroscopic solids. It became clear that the rules of chemistry are not autonomous scientific principles, but mathematical consequences of quantum mechanics as applied to electrons and atomic nuclei. This was arguably the single greatest triumph of science in the reductionist mode. Paul Dirac expressed the exuberance of the times when, in 1929, he proclaimed that

The underlying physical laws necessary for the mathematical theory of a larger part of physics and the whole of chemistry are thus completely known, and the difficulty is only that the application of these laws leads to equations much too complicated to be soluble.

A price had to be paid for this success. There is an irreducible strangeness to quantum mechanics. A particle does not have a definite position or momentum until one or the other is measured; what it does have is a wave function. The wave function evolves deterministically—knowing the wave function at one moment, one can use the Schrödinger equation to calculate the wave function at any later time. But, knowing the wave function, one cannot predict the precise result of a measurement of position or momentum—only the probabilities of the various possible results. How do these probabilities arise, if observers and their measuring apparatus are themselves described by a complicated but deterministic Schrödinger equation?

The strangeness of quantum mechanics raised a barrier to communication not only between physicists and non-physicists, but also between the young physicists of the 1920s and their older colleagues. Einstein and Planck never accepted the consensus version of quantum mechanics, and its meaning continued to be debated throughout the century. Yet quantum mechanics proved remarkably resilient. The triumphs of atomic, condensed matter, nuclear, and elementary particle physics from the 1920s to the present have been based on the quantum-mechanical framework that was already in place by 1926.

The other great revolution of twentieth-century physics was the development of the theory of relativity. Although not as radical a break with the past as quantum mechanics, relativity was in one way more remarkable. Quantum mechanics was developed over a quarter-century by successive contributions of many physicists, while relativity was almost entirely due to the work of a single physicist, Albert Einstein, from 1905 to 1915.

From an early age, Einstein had worried about the effect of an observer's motion on observations of light. By the end of the nineteenth century this problem had become acute, with experimenters' efforts continually failing to detect changes in the speed of light caused by the earth's motion around the sun. Several theorists addressed this problem dynamically, through hypotheses about the effect of motion through the ether (the medium that was believed to carry light waves) on the measuring apparatus used to measure the speed of light. Then in 1905 Einstein put the ether aside, and asserted as a fundamental law of physics the special principle of relativity—that no uniform motion of an observer could have any effect on the speed of light or anything else.

Relativity was not new. A principle of relativity had been an important ingredient of Newton's mechanics; the Newtonian equations of motion of masses moving under the influence of their mutual gravitational attraction appear the same to all unaccelerated observers, whatever their velocity. But the 'Galilean' transformation that relates the coordinates used by a moving observer to those of an observer at rest, and which leaves the Newtonian equations of motion unchanged, would not leave the speed of light unchanged. To implement his new principle of relativity, Einstein needed to replace the Galilean coordinate transformation with a new sort of transformation, known as a Lorentz transformation, in which the motion of the observer affects not only the spatial coordinates of events but also their time coordinates. But, if the equations of mechanics as well as the speed of light were to be invariant under such Lorentz transformations, then these equations too would now have to be changed. One of the most dramatic consequences of the new mechanics, pointed out by Einstein in 1907, is that a system that loses energy will experience a proportionate decrease in mass, given by the energy loss divided by the square of the speed of light. The energy available in a radioactive transmutation of one atomic nucleus into another could thus be determined by simply weighing the initial and final nuclei.

After 1905 only the theory of gravitation appeared inconsistent with Einstein's version of the principle of relativity. Einstein worked on this problem for the next decade, and finally found the answer in an extension of the principle of relativity. According to what he now called the general principle of relativity, the laws of nature appear the same not only to all uniformly moving observers, but (in a sense) to *all* observers: the familiar inertial forces felt by accelerated observers are nothing but a species of gravitation. Since gravitational forces of any sort are just a function of the coordinate system, they can be described geometrically, in terms of the curvature of spacetime, a curvature produced, according to Einstein's field equations, by the presence of energy and momentum.

Special and general relativity, like quantum mechanics, contradicts our everyday intuitive notions of physical reality. But the public reception of relativity and quantum mechanics was very different. Quantum mechanics was immediately confirmed by a wealth of pre-existing data on atomic spectra, so there was no need for a dramatic critical experiment to prove it right. This, together with its greater conceptual difficulty, reduced its immediate impact on general culture. In contrast, there was little evidence at first for relativity, and particularly for general relativity. Then, after the First World War, a British expedition set out to measure an effect predicted by general relativity, a tiny deflection of light from a distant star by the gravitational field of the sun. The news in 1919 that observations of this effect agreed with Einstein's prediction made headlines around the world, and raised Einstein to a unique public status among the scientists of the twentieth century.

Even though relativity had been much on the minds of de Broglie and
Schrödinger, the successful initial applications of quantum mechanics in 1925–6
were based on the older mechanics of Newton. The electrons in the outer orbits of
atoms travel at only a few per cent of the speed of light, so the effects of relativity
on atomic spectra are difficult to detect. But it was apparent that relativistic
mechanics (like everything else) would have to be recast in a quantum framework.

This was not easy. In special relativity the observed flow of time is affected by
the speed of the observer, so that even the order of events in time may vary from
one observer to another. Nevertheless classical special relativity respects the condition that all observers should see effects following their causes, because the
order of events can depend on the speed of the observer only when the events are
so close in time that light would not have time to travel from one event to the other,
and Einstein assumed (for this reason) that no physical influence can travel faster
than the speed of light. The problem of causality is more troublesome in quantum
mechanics, because the positions and velocities in quantum states cannot both
be specified with sufficient precision to rule out the propagation of physical
effects at speeds faster than light.

The near incompatibility of special relativity with quantum mechanics was to
have a profound effect on the style of theoretical physics. Both pre-quantum relativity and non-relativistic quantum mechanics had provided general frameworks
for physical theories, but one always had to rely on experiment for information
about particles and forces in fashioning any specific theory. Relativistic quantum
mechanics, in contrast, is so nearly internally inconsistent that one can go far in
describing nature by demanding mathematical consistency, with little input from
observation.

Theory in this new style began with the work of Dirac in 1928. His approach was
to revise the Schrödinger equation for a single particle moving in a given electromagnetic field to make it consistent with the special principle of relativity. On this
basis Dirac was able to calculate the strength of the electron's magnetic field and
fine details of the hydrogen spectrum. More dramatically, several years later he
predicted the existence of antimatter, a prediction unexpectedly confirmed with
the 1932 discovery of the antielectron in cosmic rays by Carl Anderson and P. M. S.
Blackett.

Dirac's approach gained great prestige from these successes, but it proved
inadequate to deal with radioactive processes in which particles change their
identity. The need to reconcile quantum mechanics and relativity soon gave rise to
a more general formalism, that of the quantum theory of fields.

Quantum field theory began in 1926 with the application (by Born, Heisenberg,
and Pascual Jordan) of quantum mechanics to the familiar fields of electromagnetism. But electrons were still pictured as point particles, not as fields. Then in
1929–30 Heisenberg and Wolfgang Pauli proposed a more unified view of nature.
Just as there is an electromagnetic field, whose energy and momentum come in
tiny bundles called photons, so there is also an electron field, whose energy and
momentum and electric charge are found in the bundles we call electrons, and

likewise for every species of elementary particle. The basic ingredients of nature are fields; particles are derivative phenomena.

Quantum field theory reproduced the successes of Dirac's theory, and had some new successes of its own, but the synthesis of quantum mechanics with relativity soon ran into a new difficulty. In 1930 both J. Robert Oppenheimer and Ivar Waller discovered that processes in which electrons emit and reabsorb photons would apparently shift the energy of the electron state by an infinite amount. Infinities soon turned up in other calculations, and produced a mood of pessimism about the validity of quantum field theory that persisted for decades.

The forefront of physics shifted in the 1930s from atoms to atomic nuclei, and to new phenomena revealed by the study of cosmic rays. Here are some highlights.

1932   James Chadwick discovers the neutron, an electrically neutral particle with a mass close to the proton's. Heisenberg proposes that the neutron is not a bound state of an electron and a proton, as was thought at first, but a new elementary particle, a constituent along with protons of atomic nuclei. Because they are electrically neutral, neutrons can penetrate atomic nuclei without being repelled by the strong electric fields near the nucleus, so they become a valuable tool for exploring the nucleus, especially in the hands of Enrico Fermi.

1933   Fermi develops a successful quantum field theory of beta decay (the radioactive process discovered by Becquerel). It describes how neutrons spontaneously change into protons and emit electrons and neutrinos (light neutral particles that had been proposed in 1930 by Pauli).

1935   Hideki Yukawa offers a quantum field theory intended to account for both beta decay and for the strong nuclear forces that hold protons and neutrons together inside the nucleus. This theory requires the existence of a new particle, a 'meson', with a mass of about 200 electron masses.

1937   S. H. Neddermeyer and Anderson, and C. E. Stevenson and J. C. Street, independently discover a new particle in cosmic rays. It has a mass close to that predicted by Yukawa, and is at first confused with his meson.

1939   Hans Bethe lays out the primary nuclear reactions by which stars gain their energy.

Basic research was in abeyance during the years of the Second World War, while the discoveries of science were applied to war work. Applied research is outside the scope of this chapter, but it is hardly possible to ignore entirely the most spectacular application of twentieth-century physics, the development of nuclear weapons. In 1938 Otto Hahn and Fritz Strassmann discovered that isotopes of the medium-weight element barium were produced when the heavy nuclei of uranium were irradiated with neutrons. A few months later in Sweden Otto Frisch and Lise Meitner calculated that the capture of a neutron could cause a heavy nucleus like uranium to break into medium-sized pieces, like barium nuclei, releasing some 200 million electron volts of energy. In itself, this would be just another nuclear reaction, not really so different from hundreds of previously studied reactions. The thing that made neutron-induced fission so important was the prospect that, along with the barium and other nuclei, several neutrons would be released in each fission, each of which might trigger another fission, leading to an explosive chain reaction. It would be like a forest fire, in which the heat from each burning tree helps to ignite more trees, but vastly more destructive.*

As war came closer, most of the great powers began to study the possibility of using uranium fission as a weapon or a source of power. Britain took an early lead in this work, which was then transferred to the United States. In December 1942 a group under Enrico Fermi at the University of Chicago succeeded in producing a chain reaction in a uranium pile. The fission took place not in the common isotope U^{238}, but in a rare isotope U^{235} that makes up only 0.723 per cent of the natural uranium used by Fermi, but that, unlike U^{238}, can be made to fission even by very slow neutrons. Another nuclide, the isotope Pu^{239} of plutonium, has the same property of easy fissionability, and, though it is absent in nature, it would be produced in uranium piles.

The problem then was either to isolate enough U^{235} or to produce enough Pu^{239} to make a bomb, and to develop a method of setting it off. These problems were successfully attacked by a team of scientists and engineers headed by Oppenheimer. In August 1945 Hiroshima and Nagasaki were largely destroyed by U^{235} and Pu^{239} bombs, respectively, leading soon after to the surrender of Japan and the end of the war.

It would take us too far from our subject to comment on the effect of nuclear weapons on world affairs, but it may be appropriate to say a word about the effect of nuclear weapons on physics itself. The achievement of the bomb project in helping to end the war gave many of its physicists a natural feeling of pride, often tempered with a sense of responsibility for the damage done in Hiroshima and Nagasaki, and for the danger that nuclear weapons now posed to humanity. Some physicists devoted themselves from then on to working for arms control and nuclear disarmament. Politicians and other non-scientists now tended to look at physics as a source of military and economic power, and for decades gave unprecedented support to basic as well as applied physical research. At the same time, the image of the Hiroshima mushroom cloud had a powerful effect on the attitude of many cultural leaders and other citizens towards science; in many

---

* This is a good place to dispel the common misapprehension, that nuclear weapons are somehow an outgrowth of Einstein's special theory of relativity. As originally derived in 1907, Einstein's famous equation $E = mc^2$ says that the liberation of an energy E by any system will cause it to lose a mass m equal to E divided by c^2, the square of the speed of light. This is just as true of a burning tree as of a nuclear bomb, except that the energy released in ordinary burning is too small to allow a measurement of the decrease in mass of the products of combustion. If one insists on saying that mass is converted to energy in nuclear reactions, then one must say the same of ordinary burning. The true source of the energy released when a tree burns is the sunlight absorbed during the tree's life, and the true source of the energy that is released in a uranium fission is the energy stored in the nucleus when it was formed in a supernova explosion long before the earth condensed from the interstellar medium.

cases their former indifference changed to outright hostility. Time has moderated all these effects, though at the century's end they are not entirely gone.

By 1947 physicists were ready to return to fundamental problems. The use of improved photographic emulsions soon revealed a menagerie of new particles in cosmic rays. One of them, the pi meson, could be identified with the particle predicted by Yukawa.

To discuss these and other new developments, a meeting was convened at Shelter Island, off the coast of Long Island, in June 1947. The high point of the meeting was a report by Willis Lamb. He presented convincing experimental evidence of a small difference in energy between two states of the hydrogen atom—states that, according to Dirac's version of relativistic quantum mechanics, should have precisely the same energy. Evidence was also presented from I. I. Rabi's group at Columbia, showing that the electron's magnetic field is about a tenth of a per cent stronger than had been calculated by Dirac. Effects of this sort would be produced by so-called radiative corrections, due to the emission and reabsorption of photons by electrons in atoms. In fact, the Lamb energy shift was a special case of the effect that Oppenheimer had been trying to calculate in 1930 when he first encountered the troublesome infinities.

The theorists at Shelter Island engaged in intensive discussions of how to carry out these calculations, and, in particular, how to make sure that the answers would come out finite. One idea had already been widely discussed in the 1930s. Perhaps the masses and electric charges appearing in the field equations for the electron and other particle fields are themselves infinite, and the infinities encountered in calculations of radiative corrections just go to correct or 'renormalize' these masses and charges, giving them their observed (and of course finite) values. Soon after Shelter Island the renormalization idea was used in successful calculations of the Lamb energy shift by Bethe, J. Bruce French and Victor Weisskopf, and Norman Kroll and Lamb, and of the electron magnetic field by Julian Schwinger. It was not known at the time in the West, but similar calculations were being carried out at the same time by a group in Japan headed by Sin-itiro Tomonaga.

These successes led to a renewed confidence in quantum field theory. Various radical ideas that had been put forward as solutions of the problem of infinities in the 1930s by Dirac, Heisenberg, and others were now put aside. But the method of calculation remained obscure and difficult, and it was hard to see whether renormalization would continue to resolve the problem of infinities in future calculations.

In the next few years after Shelter Island powerful methods of calculation were developed by Schwinger and Richard Feynman. The essence of these methods was the treatment of processes involving antiparticles in parallel with the corresponding processes involving particles, in such a way as to maintain explicit consistency with special relativity. Finally in 1949 the work of Feynman, Schwinger, and Tomonaga was synthesized by Freeman Dyson, putting quantum field theory in its modern form.

After 1950 the forefront of physics moved again, away from nuclear physics and radiative corrections, and towards the physics of a growing list of (supposedly) elementary particles. The tools of this research also changed; powerful accelerators supplanted cosmic rays, and particle detectors of increasing size and sophistication replaced the Geiger counters and photographic emulsions of the 1930s and 1940s. These technical improvements were accompanied by institutional changes, which, though probably inevitable, were not all improvements. Experimental research steadily moved from the basements of university physics buildings to national or international laboratories, and physics articles appeared with increasing numbers of authors, some of them by the end of the century with a thousand authors from scores of institutions. The demarcation between theorists and experimenters became rigid; after the 1950s, no one again would do both experimental and theoretical work of high calibre in elementary particle physics.

The great task after 1950 was to bring all the known elementary particles and all the forces that act on them into the same quantum field–theoretic framework that had been used before 1950 to understand electrons and electromagnetic fields. The immediate obstacles were, first, that calculations in Fermi's theory of the weak nuclear forces responsible for beta decay revealed infinities that would not be removed by renormalization, and, secondly, that the forces in Yukawa's theory of the strong nuclear forces are too strong to allow the kind of calculation by successive approximations that had worked so well in electrodynamics. Beyond these problems lay a deeper difficulty: there was no rationale for any of these theories.

By the mid-1970s these problems had been overcome, with the completion of a quantum field theory known as the standard model of elementary particles.

The standard model was the product of a century-long preoccupation with principles of symmetry in theoretical physics. In general, a symmetry principle is a statement that the equations of physics appear the same from certain different points of view. Symmetry principles had always been important in physics because they allow us to draw inferences about complicated systems without detailed knowledge of the system, but they attained a new importance in the twentieth century as aspects of nature's deepest laws.

Already in 1905 Einstein had elevated a principle of symmetry—invariance under Lorentz transformations of spacetime—to a status as a fundamental law of physics. Measurements of nuclear forces in the 1930s suggested a further symmetry—a rotation not in ordinary space or spacetime, but in an abstract internal 'isotopic-spin' space, in which different directions correspond to different species of particles. One class of symmetries, known as gauge symmetries, actually require the existence of fields, as, for instance, the general principle of relativity requires the existence of the gravitational field. Theorists from 1954 on proposed new gauge symmetries, though not yet with any clear application to the real world. But by the end of the 1950s experiments had revealed a bewildering variety of other, non-gauge, symmetry principles, many of them (like isotopic-spin symmetry, and the symmetry between left and right) only approximate.

Given the importance of symmetry principles, it was exciting to discover that nature respects yet other symmetries that are 'broken'; they are not respected by individual particles, and are manifested instead in relations between processes involving different numbers of particles. Broken symmetry became a hot topic after the successful use of one of these broken symmetries in the mid-1960s to predict the properties of low-energy pi mesons.

Soon after, a broken exact internal gauge symmetry was introduced as the basis of a unified theory of the weak and electromagnetic forces. In 1971 it was proved that theories of this sort avoid the problems with infinities that had plagued the old Fermi theory. The predictions of the new 'electroweak' theory were dramatically confirmed in 1973, with the discovery of a new sort of weak force, and a decade later with the discovery of the particles that carry these forces.

This left the problem of the strong nuclear forces. One valuable clue was the surprising discovery in 1968 that, when probed by electrons of very short wavelength, neutrons and protons behave as if they are composed of particles that interact only weakly. In 1973 this phenomenon was clarified by a mathematical technique known as the 'renormalization group', which had previously been applied in quantum electrodynamics and the theory of phase transitions. It turned out that in a quantum field theory known as quantum chromodynamics the strong forces do become weaker at very small scales. Quantum chromodynamics is a theory of strongly interacting particles known as quarks and gluons (the constituents of neutrons, protons, pi mesons, etc.) based on an exact unbroken internal gauge symmetry. This weakening of the strong forces made it feasible to calculate reaction rates by the same techniques earlier used in quantum electrodynamics. Experiments at high energy (and on several types of quarks of large mass, discovered starting in 1974) probed these small scales, where calculations are possible, and confirmed that quantum chromodynamics does indeed describe the strong forces.

The electroweak theory and quantum chromodynamics together constitute what is known as the standard model. The structure of the model is strongly constrained by its exact spacetime and internal symmetries, and by the need to avoid infinities. Both Fermi's theory of beta decay and Yukawa's theory of nuclear forces are explained in the standard model as low-energy approximations. One happy by-product of the standard model, which contributed to its rapid acceptance, was that it also explained the known approximate symmetries as accidental consequences of the model's constrained structure.

The weakening of the strong forces at small scales makes it possible that the strong, weak, and electromagnetic forces should all become of the same strength at some very small scale. Calculations in 1974 showed that the strengths of these forces at accessible scales are consistent with this idea, and suggested that the scale at which the forces become of equal strength is about fifteen orders of magnitude smaller than the size of an atomic nucleus.

After the mid-1970s theoretical physics entered on a period of acute frustration. The standard model is clearly not the final answer; it incorporates some arbitrary features, and it leaves out gravitation. Another reduction is called for, that would explain the standard model and general relativity in terms of a simpler, more universal theory. Many theorists have tried to take this step, inventing attractive ideas of increasing mathematical sophistication—supersymmetry, supergravity, technicolor, string theory, etc.—but none of their efforts has been validated by experiment. At the same time, experimenters have continued to pile up evidence confirming the standard model, but, despite strong efforts, they have not discovered anything that would give theorists a clear clue to a deeper theory. Some help was expected from experiments that would clarify the one uncertainty left in the standard model—the detailed mechanism by which the electroweak gauge symmetry is broken—but a slowdown of research funding in the 1990s has put this off to the next century. It seems likely that a deeper, more unified theory will deal with structures at very small scales, perhaps sixteen to eighteen orders of magnitude smaller than an atomic nucleus, where all forces including gravitation may have similar strength. Unfortunately these scales seem hopelessly beyond the range of direct experimental study. For physicists, the twentieth century seems to be ending sadly, but perhaps this is only the price we must pay for having already come so far.

4 The Expansion of Knowledge

JOHN MADDOX

In the twentieth century, the mechanism of life itself has been explained in terms of physics and chemistry. That is the significance of the proposal, by James D. Watson and Francis H. C. Crick in April 1953, of what proved to be a correct atomic structure of the chemical material called DNA, technically deoxyribonucleic acid. Not since Copernicus, in 1545, put the sun rather than the earth at the centre of the solar system has a discovery so profoundly changed peoples' conception of the place they occupy in the world.

In the event, the twentieth century began with the rediscovery of a forgotten part of the legacy of the nineteenth century: the foundation of modern genetics (not so called until 1906 by William Bateson at Cambridge, England) by the Moravian monk Gregor Mendel, who in the 1850s had studied the inheritance of characteristics such as flower colour and height by pea plants of different varieties. One of those who, in 1990, rediscovered Mendel's work on inheritance was Hugo de Vries, originally a plant physiologist from the Netherlands, who had carried out plant-breeding experiments with the evening primrose at Amsterdam. His observations caused great excitement in Europe and the United States. There followed a long period of transatlantic tension over the significance of genetics. British biologists were uniformly adherents of Darwin's theory of evolution, with its assumption that the intergenerational variations that allow for the progressive evolution of species under the influence of natural selection are necessarily small variations. T. H. Morgan at Columbia University in New York was sceptical, suspecting that discrete changes of character were more likely to be at the root of evolution. Stimulated by a visit to de Vries (of whose results he was also sceptical), Morgan began breeding experiments with mice in 1908. Over the succeeding fifteen years and with the assistance of his academic recruits A. H. Sturtevant, J. B. Bridges, and H. J. Muller, Morgan showed that the physical seat of inheritance lies in the chromosomes which occur in pairs in most cells, but singly in the chromosomes of the nuclei of germ cells (sperm and ova in the case of animals), and that particular characters are determined by physical entities called genes at particular places on the chromosomes. Specifically, any gene may occur in several variant forms, called alleles of the gene, which are the physical embodiment of genetic variation, Darwinian or otherwise.

In 1911 Sturtevant (while still a graduate student) demonstrated that the arrangement of the genes must be linear, as if all the genes belonging to a particular chromosome could be laid out in order along some line. During this same productive period, between 1908 and 1920, the Columbia school was also able to establish the special role of sex chromosomes in sexual reproduction, both in determining the sex of individual offspring and in explaining why some genetic diseases (haemophilia in human beings, for example) become apparent only in individuals of one sex (males for human haemophilia). Morgan's suspicion that his research programme would uncover decisive evidence against Darwin's doctrine of imperceptible variation was not, however, fulfilled. Some genetic variations (haemophilia in people, for example) were far from small in their effects on individuals, but their relevance to past evolution was far from clear. Indeed, Morgan's school became the chief source of the still-accepted view that most genetic variations are harmful (and so will be eliminated by natural selection). There followed in the United States a reappraisal of Morgan's doubts about Darwinism, led principally by Theodosius Dobzhansky, a Russian immigrant to the USA and a recruit to the Columbia school. By the outbreak of the Second World War in 1939, the new synthesis was complete, largely because of the work of Dobzhansky and his fellow-American Sewell Wright in the United States and by R. A. Fisher and J. B. S. Haldane in Britain. The upshot of their work was the recognition that, while natural selection affects the survival of individuals, what changes in the course of evolution is the genetic make-up of the population to which the individual belongs. By ironic coincidence, opinions were shifting in a different direction in the Soviet Union. 'Mendel–Morganism' was denounced as heresy of a kind by the Central Committee of the Communist Party in 1937, apparently in protest at the idea that the genetic potential of an organism, or of a population, could be circumscribed by its genetic constitution. (Human perfectibility is, after all, a recurrent theme in Marxism.) T. D. Lysenko was supported by the Soviet Academy of Agricultural Sciences to embark on a series of large-scale experiments to adapt grain from southern Russia to the hostile conditions of western Siberia, and the distinguished biologist N. I. Vavilov was arrested in 1940 and died in prison three years later. The inevitable failure of Lysenko's efforts contributed to the fall of Nikita Khrushchev as Secretary-General of the Soviet Communist Party in 1964. The great controversies over genetics in the first half of the twentieth century typify the change there had been in the character of all scientific research. Mendel's early observations (published in a local naturalists' journal at Brno in Moravia) were understandably overlooked; no doubt his work gave great pleasure to Mendel himself, but he seems not to have appreciated its importance (especially in relation to Darwinism) and he had no band of students (or other acolytes) to whom to communicate whatever excitement he may have felt. Morgan's school at

Columbia, by contrast, was among the first to practise the belief that it is possible, even in the study of such phenomena as biological inheritance, to devise experimental conditions—breeding experiments in this case—in which the yield of meaningful information is optimized. At the same time, Columbia was recognized as the powerhouse of the new genetics; its methods and views were propagated through Western science by its recruitment of talented students, who eventually became professors at other institutions. In the twentieth century, this mechanism of rigorous recruitment and dispersal of talented people from centres of excellence became established as one of the most effective ways of making science grow and deepen.

Genetics is not, of course, the whole of biology. Thus the exploration of the structure of the nervous system was already under way when the century began, to a large extent under the impetus of the work of Charles Sherrington in Britain, who (with Michael Foster) recognized in 1897 that signals between nerve cells are conducted through microscopic structures they called synapses. By 1925 E. D. Adrian at the University of Cambridge was able to record the electrical impulses by means of which signals are transmitted within nerve cells, while Henry Dale demonstrated that nerve impulses trigger the action of the muscles they control by releasing the simple chemical acetylcholine.

Sherrington proved to be the founder of neurobiology, which by the end of the twentieth century had provided a detailed picture of the anatomy of the mammalian nervous system, and of the brain in particular. Significantly, Sherrington's goal was to relate the structure of an animal's nervous system to its behaviour, to which end a consistent theme in his own research was to study the degree to which reflex behaviour is determined by the spinal cord alone, with or without modification by the higher centres of the brain.

With the passage of the decades, techniques for mapping the anatomy of the animal nervous system improved enormously, notably with the development in the USA of means of making visible the often extensive ramifications in the human brain of nerve cells (called neurons). In the hands of David Hubel and Torsten Wiesel, whose collaboration at Harvard University began in 1958 and lasted for twenty years, they yielded a detailed account of the structure of the striate cortex, the primary seat of visual processing in the brains of primates. (Significantly, it emerged that information about the colour and the shape of a seen object is processed in different parts of the cortex.) Towards the end of the century, it had become plain where in the cortex information from the different senses is processed.

Partly stimulated by loose analogies between the functioning of the brain and electronic computers (whose development began during the Second World War and came to fruition only afterwards), the 1950s saw the beginning (and some would say the end) of a new science, that of cybernetics, or the study of information and its processing in telephone exchanges, computers, and even brains, for example. In many places, enthusiasm got the better of common sense. The schemes advocated in the 1950s for building electronic versions of the brain mostly came to nothing.

The explanation soon became clear. Neither the information stored in the brain nor the cognitive functions it performs are concentrated in single neurons or even in compact groups thereof, but rather are distributed among the billions of neurons in the adult human brain. The notion that widely separated neurons may function in concert, as developed in 1972 by John Hopfield at the California Institute of Technology, led to the development of electronic devices called neural networks that are able to simulate the process of learning, and which promise to be of great value in industrial and military applications.

Hopes that neural networks would lead to a deeper understanding of brain function have nevertheless been frustrated by continuing uncertainty about the manner in which learnt or remembered information is represented in networks of neurons. Similarly, questions such as mechanism of consciousness remain undecided in the closing years of the century, although, for the first time, neuroscientists have begun to acknowledge that this question will in due course deserve serious consideration. Has the twentieth century just failed to understand how the brain works? Or will another century have to pass?

By the end of the century, even the understanding of how the brain functions was both overshadowed and partly stimulated by the new knowledge of how cells function that derived from the discovery, to which we have already referred, of the structure of DNA put forward in 1953 by James D. Watson and Francis H. C. Crick, both then at the University of Cambridge. As the closing decades of the twentieth century have shown, the significance of this development cannot be overstated; seemingly extravagant claims of the explanatory power of DNA have repeatedly been discovered to have been over-modest. In retrospect, it is now clear that the roots of this discovery go back to the early decades of the century. H. J. Muller, from T. H. Morgan's school of genetics at Columbia, recognized the potential significance for genetics of a discovery in 1915, by Felix d'Herelle in Paris, of viruses that appear fatally to infect bacteria. Noting that the bacterial viruses (now called bacteriophage) are exceedingly small, Muller in 1921 raised at a scientific meeting in Toronto the question whether the viruses might be genes and asked, 'Must we geneticists become bacteriologists, physiological chemists and physicists? I hope so.' After the passage of half a century, his hope came true.

One chemist in Germany was already hard at work in this direction. Emil O. Fischer, then at Erlangen (but who later moved to Berlin), had laid the foundations of the chemistry of the substances called purines before the century began. His interest was stimulated by their relationship with uric acid, whose crystallization in the blood is responsible for gout. Fischer would not then, of course, have known that purines (together with another class of chemicals called pyrimidines) are the components of DNA that carry genetic information. In 1900 he turned his attention to two other classes of substances important in living things—proteins and carbohydrates—which usually occur as polymers (which means that similar chemical units are linked chemically together to form a long molecule). By 1907 Fischer had synthesized a small sample of a simple protein molecule in which eighteen of the essential building blocks (called amino-acids) were linked together.

Muller's guess that micro-organisms would provide a rapid route to the under-standing of genetics was confirmed when, in 1951, George Beadle and Edward Tatum at Stanford University in the USA concluded from a study of the bread mould Neurospora that the function of a gene is invariably to control the produc-tion of a single enzyme in the cells in which it is active. (Exactly that suggestion had been made in 1908, by the physician Archibald Garrod, a British physician working at St Bartholomew's Hospital Medical School in London, on the basis of his classic study of the genetic disease called alkaptonuria, but had been largely overlooked.) There followed in the United States a concerted study of the genetics of the bacte-rial virus called lambda, a naturally occurring infection of the common gut bac-terium Escherichia coli, from which Max Delbruck, a physicist turned biologist, and his colleagues were able in the early 1950s to unravel the processes by which genes are activated and inactivated.

By then, another line of enquiry bearing on the nature of the genetic material had been opened. In the 1930s chemists had shown that the material of which chromosomes are made consists of protein molecules and of material generically called nucleic acid. A remarkable experiment by O. T. Avery at the Rockefeller Institute (now the Rockefeller University) in 1944 clearly pointed to DNA as the seat of the genetic material: by introducing DNA from the virulent strain of pneu-monococcus bacteria into those not causing infection, Avery found that the defec-tive bacteria became virulent. In the modern idiom, DNA carrying the gene for virulence had 'transfected' the uninfectious strain. But Avery, aware that his con-clusion might be vitiated by contamination of the DNA, did not claim for his experiments the interpretation that hindsight shows it could have borne: that DNA is the stuff of genes.

DNA (the universal acronym for deoxyribonucleic acid) is the genetic material that ensures faithful inheritance in all creatures now alive and in many (but not all) viruses. The genes that T. H. Morgan and his colleagues concluded would lie lin-early along the chromosomes of organisms were quickly identified with con-nected (but not necessarily contiguous) stretches along the length of DNA molecules, which are long polymer molecules in the sense that chemists came to understand the term in the 1930s. The genetic information is coded chemically, and represented by the order in which four chemically different units are arranged. Crucially, the structure described by Crick and Watson for DNA is not that of a single polymer molecule, but of two geometrically complementary mol-ecules held together by molecular attraction and twisted into a helical structure (whence the term double helix); among other things, that allows the genetic infor-mation embodied in one strand, and which may become corrupted, to be faith-fully recovered by reference to the other.

The other crucial function of DNA is that of a chemical recipe by which all cells carry out the functions required of them. This is done by the physical transfer of information. In 1959 it was shown that the stretch of DNA corresponding to a gene is physically copied into an equivalent arrangement of chemical units in a molecule of the alternative genetic material called RNA (ribonucleic acid), which in turn directs the synthesis of protein molecules that function as enzymes in the cell. Thus the nature of inheritable diseases was for the first time explained: an aberrant version of a gene will direct the synthesis of enzymes which themselves differ from the standard, and which may be incapable of carrying out its intended function.

The decades after 1953 brought a sequence of important advances, both conceptual and technical. The mechanism by which genetic material embodied in DNA is translated into the structure of protein molecules was understood by 1960, the triplet character of the genetic code was established (by Crick and Sydney Brenner) in 1961, and soon afterwards it was possible to carry out most of the natural functions of DNA replication (as when cells divide) or transcription (into RNA, and then to protein) in test-tube experiments; larger quantities of genetic material could thus be obtained. In 1969 it became possible to turn genetic information embodied in RNA into the equivalent information in DNA (which viruses whose genes consist of RNA—HIV, for example—accomplish when they infect cells). That led, with the advent of other manipulations, to the feasibility of genetic engineering: the prospect of replacing particular genes by others, even genes from organisms other than the recipient.

On the initiative of Professor Paul Berg at Stanford University, who had by himself engineered a synthetic virus, the US National Academy of Sciences organized in 1973 an international conference at Asilomar in California on the potential dangers of these procedures; the outcome was a moratorium on genetic manipulation by researchers, supported by most of the research academies, pending the development of administrative guidelines for the avoidance of hazard, which was done at a second conference in 1974. From that point, research in genetic manipulation and its application have been licensed by national governments on the advice of committees whose members are not exclusively scientists. Despite these arrangements, industrial genetic manipulation has not won full-throated social approval, especially in countries such as Germany.

There seems less dispute about the eventual value of the Human Genome Project, so called because this loosely coordinated international research programme aims to determine the sequence in which all 3,000 million chemical units in the human complement of DNA are arranged. The project will be complete soon after the end of the century, certainly by 2005 but possibly two years before that. What value will the outcome be?

One obvious benefit will be the ease and, even more important, the certainty with which genes associated with human diseases can be identified. Even as early as the 1980s, diagnostic tests were being used to identify the individual carriers of some of these diseases, leading (at least in advanced societies) to the avoidance of genetically handicapped births associated with diseases such as haemophilia, the thalassaemias, cystic fibrosis, and so on. But the extension of programmes such as these to the whole range of inherited diseases is likely to be limited by practical considerations, notably cost and the complexity of the mode of inheritance of some diseases, as well as by ethical considerations, especially the difficulties of informing those likely to suffer from diseases such as Huntington's and Alzheimer's of their impending fate.

What the project will provide are means by which pharmaceutical companies and physicians can more confidently investigate the mechanisms of disease generally, thus pointing to novel drug therapies. By the 1980s, just such an approach had made it possible to provide preventative drug therapy for people liable to suffer heart attacks caused by congenitally high levels of cholesterol in the blood. The understanding of the nature of the genes has also made possible a better understanding of cancer. From the 1980s onwards, the occurrence of many kinds of tumours was associated with genetic changes in the cells of the body tissues in which tumours form, thus raising the possibility of drugs that would extirpate the tumours directly. It goes without saying that the completion of the Human Genome Project will also provide important clues to the evolution of the human species, at least in the past 5 million years of evolution from a common ancestor with the Great Apes.

Medicine began the twentieth century much as it had ended the nineteenth. Improvements on ether as an anaesthetic had made feasible novel surgical operations, while the recognition that infectious diseases are caused by micro-organisms of the kinds described by Pasteur in France and Koch in Germany engendered great interest in vaccination against infectious disease—a technique first developed in Britain at the end of the eighteenth century by the veterinary surgeon William Jenner and used successfully for the prevention of smallpox. But vaccines that were at once safe and effective reached the clinics only slowly; a prophylactic against diphtheria was introduced in the 1930s, for example.

By then, the foundations had been laid for the drug-based treatment of infectious disease that became the hallmark of medicine in the second half of the twentieth century. In 1931 Alexander Fleming at St Mary's Hospital in Paddington recognized that an airborne mould (or fungus) of the genus Penicillin had the previously unsuspected property of being lethal to bacteria. During the Second World War, the effective chemical (called penicillin) became the first of the generally used antibiotics. Many variants on the same theme were afterwards discovered chiefly as the result of systematic searches of the bacteriocidal properties of other moulds and funguses. As medicines go, these materials are relatively cheap. Their widespread use in the decades after the Second World War has markedly reduced early and mid-life mortality in developed countries and has contributed to changing demographic patterns elsewhere.

Infections caused by viruses (of which smallpox is one) are not directly susceptible to antibiotics, so that vaccines remain the chief source of defence against them. The developments in 1956 by the US immunologist Jonas Salk of a vaccine against poliomyelitis infection was a landmark in the improvement of public health internationally, especially after Albert Sabin (also from the USA) had developed a vaccine suitable for oral administration (and thus for easier use in poor countries). In 1995 the World Health Organization (WHO) adopted as a target for the early part of the following century the eradication of poliomyelitis from the whole world. (No cases of smallpox infection were reported after 1990.)

Despite these successes, expressions of optimism about the eradication of microbial infections, common in the 1950s, were moderated towards the end of the century, as it was recognized that most bacteria are capable of changing genetically so as not to be susceptible to antibiotics—the phenomenon is called resistance—and that viruses and bacteria in the environment (or cryptically infecting other species of animals) and whose existence may not even be catalogued could well emerge as serious threats to human well-being. It is notable that, in the closing decades of the century, there were recognized for the first time legionnaires disease and Lyme disease (both caused by previously unknown bacteria), Lassa fever, Eboli and Green-Monkey virus diseases, and, most seriously, Aids (acquired immune deficiency syndrome), all caused by previously unknown viruses. There was particular concern, at the end of the twentieth century, that bacteria such as that responsible for tuberculosis would re-emerge in virulent form. There is good reason to believe that the emergence of novel infections will continue as the demographic characteristics of the world's population changes and as foreign travel becomes more common.

As it happens, the treatment of Aids may well prove to be a model for dealing with forms of infection that have not yet arisen. The disease was first recognized as an infection in 1981 and as caused by a virus in 1984. (Probably the virus has evolved from a harmless parasite of African monkeys.) By 1990 the functions of its seven different genes has been largely understood, by 1995 the entire genetic structure of the virus was worked out, and by 1996 chemicals designed as drugs (called 'protease inhibitors') to interfere specifically with one of the genes has been administered to patients. The first results are encouraging, but even if they do not constitute a cure, they represent a considerable triumph for what was increasingly called 'molecular medicine'.

For the rest, twentieth-century medicine occupied itself chiefly with more or less successful attempts to control the function of the human body's organs by means of naturally occurring hormones or their synthetic equivalents. That was the spirit in which, in 1922, Frederick Banting and Charles Best at the University of Toronto treated diabetic patients with a material they called insulin extracted from the pancreas of the dog. By the end of the decade, animal insulin (usually obtained from pigs) was generally in use as a palliative medicine for the treatment of diabetes in rich countries of the world. Now the insulin is made synthetically, using the techniques of biotechnology.

The drug treatment of other conditions has similarly been extended (especially since the Second World War) to the regulation of blood pressure, various functions of the heart in general, and the improvement of the function of the kidneys. Some of the social consequences of these developments have been profound: for example, the use of analogues of the natural sex hormones to control the cycle of women's fertility, begun in the early 1960s. There are also drug treatments (palliatives, not cures) for the major psychiatric diseases, but even those whose design has been guided by the belief that the underlying mechanism of the disease is understood have turned out to be as perplexing in their mode of action as the conditions they are meant to treat. Even so, the effectiveness of these palliatives has encouraged many governments to dispense with asylum care for the psychiatrically disabled.

Meanwhile, the concept of the human body as a robust machine is embodied in the skills of late-twentieth-century surgery. You need a new kidney, or a heart? You shall have it if there is one to be found. Your blood is full of unwanted waste products? We'll clean it up! The prospect ahead is even more dazzling: supplementing genes that fail to do the job required of them by others that will (gene therapy is the name for that), regenerating organs such as muscle and the liver from the embryonic cells left over from ontogenesis—the process (whose recipe is in the same DNA) by which a single fertilized cell will yield an adult capable of manufacturing its own germ cells, and thus obviating the need for organ transplantation. All that, of course, lies a long way ahead. Perhaps a decade or so.

The distinction between science and technology needs clarification: science is the collective and cumulative attempt to understand the natural world, technology is the collection of techniques by which people and institutions (including commercial companies) seek to attain their objectives—curing the sick, growing food, and manufacturing machines, devices, and other products.

There is no necessary connection between science and technology: James Watt's steam engines, which transformed the technology of Western Europe in the first two decades of the nineteenth century, were designed in innocence of what would now be called science. But the first powered flying machine, built by Orville and Wilbur Wright and flown over a measured mile at Kitty Hawk in North Carolina in 1903, had been endlessly tested in a crude wind tunnel the brothers had built at their home base in Ohio. The science of aeronautics came only later, as a kind of rationalization of the phenomenon of flight.

The other striking innovation of the first decade of this century, however, was firmly rooted in science. In 1901 Guglielmo Marconi spanned the Atlantic with radio signals and, in doing so, built on the laboratory work of the German physicist Heinrich Hertz in the 1880s and on the earlier theories of James Clerk Maxwell. Similarly, the development in 1909 by Fritz Haber, an academic chemist at Karlsruhe, of an industrial process for the conversion of atmospheric nitrogen into ammonia became the chief source of agricultural fertilizers in succeeding decades—and a telling proof to the rest of Europe of the versatility of the German chemical industry.

During the course of the twentieth century, the mutual dependence of science and technology deepened markedly. By the end of the century, some entire industries (biotechnology, for example, and computer design) have sprung from

research laboratories, while the remarkable discoveries in the closing decades of
the century about the distant reaches of the universe were mostly made with techniques developed for military purposes between 1935 and 1970. There is every likelihood that the technologies of the decade ahead will be even more firmly rooted in
research laboratories than those of the recent past.

The four strands of the century's agenda for technology apparent in the first
decade of the century include almost everything that followed. Take power generation. In 1897 Charles Parsons, whose family engineering business was busily
competing for a share of the business to electrify Britain, understood that the efficiency of a steam engine would be remarkably increased if the hot steam were
made to lose its energy piecewise, through a series of stages. He thus invented the
steam turbine, installed one in a small vessel christened *Turbina* for the occasion,
and drove it at speeds exceeding 30 knots around Cowes harbour where a Royal
Regatta was being held to celebrate Queen Victoria's Diamond Jubilee. Since
Parsons's turbines were more compact sources of power than the old reciprocat-
ing steam engines, they were immediately favoured for the propulsion of naval
ships; by the outbreak of the First World War in 1914, several ships in the British
Navy, including the battleship HMS *Dreadnought,* had been so equipped. They
remain the most efficient ways of driving large ships of all kinds, commercial as
well as military. Steam turbines are also the standard sources for driving bulk electricity generators, largely because of their efficiency. Turbines capable of producing 1,000 megawatts of electricity with an efficiency of 40 per cent are in service at
the end of the century.

Because steam-raising equipment is necessarily bulky, Parsons's innovation
made no contribution to the great interest at the turn of the century in the propulsion of small vehicles, motor cars in particular. The four-stroke internal combustion engine invented by Nikolaus Otto in 1876 had become the workhorse of the US
automobile industry, whose growth was well under way by 1900. Then, in 1898,
Rudolf Diesel announced the development of a radical variation of Otto's design
which offered the benefits of improved efficiency and an escape from the need to
use as fuel a distilled fraction of crude petroleum (called gasoline in the USA,
petrol elsewhere). Diesel engines have, by the end of the century, become established as the preferred motor units of heavy road vehicles and small ships, as well
as in various immobile sources of power—stand-by electricity generators, for
example.

In the Parsons tradition, by the late 1930s, Frank Whittle in Britain began advocating another novel source of motive power—a turbine driven by hot compressed
air. The development was intended to reduce the weight of aircraft propulsion
units, and offered the attractiveness of increased efficiency at higher speeds
through the air. On this occasion, however, the British military were less welcoming
of the innovation, which came into its own only after the Second World War had
ended; the now huge civil air transport industry rests squarely on the technical
advantages of the jet engine. Rocket propulsion, by contrast, remains predomi-

nantly a military technology; its origins lie in the German programme of military missile development during the 1930s and an equivalent Russian programme.

Motive power requires fuel, traditionally wood or flowing water, coal since the late eighteenth century. The twentieth century has been ingenious in the exploitation of other sources of energy. The US automobile industry was founded on the discovery of petroleum in the oil-shales of Pennsylvania, whose importance was quickly dwarfed by new discoveries in Louisiana and Texas during the 1920s. But the world's oil economy came into its own only with the recognition that the oil reserves of the Middle East are at once larger and easier (and so cheaper) to extract than any other single oilfield. Since the 1970s the continental shelves have also proved prolific sources of crude petroleum.

The other major innovation of the twentieth century has been the exploitation of nuclear power, and specifically the fissile material uranium, as a source of energy; early optimism (in the 1950s) about the potential of this novel source of energy was moderated, in succeeding decades, by the high cost of safety precautions and by the accident at one of the four nuclear reactors at the Chernobyl nuclear plant in the Ukraine in April 1986. Even so, in the 1990s, both Japan and France were generating more than half of their electricity from nuclear sources, but it remains to be seen whether the nuclear industry will revive in the decades ahead.

The development of aircraft followed quickly on the first flights in North Carolina, but principally with military purpose. Britain, France, and Germany all established aircraft construction industries, and used them to some effect during the First World War. Neither the range nor the lifting capacity of the aircraft of the times was great enough to do much damage, with the result that the flying machines were most useful in gathering tactical intelligence. In any case, the performance of heavier-than-air machines continued to improve, steadily and inexorably, under the influence of both military and civilian demand. Speeds have increased fivefold, carrying capacities by twentyfold in half a century. In the closing quarter of the century, British and French airlines have even operated a commercial supersonic aircraft, Concorde, which can travel half as fast again as the speed of sound in air. It is not clear at present, however, whether the small fleet of aircraft in service will be replaced.

Marconi's venture at the beginning of the century had a more spectacular sequel. At the time, the electric telegraph had made the value of long-distance communications plain to potential users (and entrepreneurs), but the carrying capacity of the telegraph was very small. The telephone, invented in the 1870s, had shown how much greater benefit there would be in a system for transmitting speech over great distances—distances greater than could be spanned by the pairs of copper wires connecting telephones together.

Marconi's demonstration led to a great scramble, on both sides of the Atlantic, for an understanding of the mechanism of radio-wave propagation and for improvements in the means of detecting radio signals. The first led to the recognition of the electrified layers of gas high in the earth's atmosphere, now collectively called the ionosphere, which makes it possible for radio signals to be reflected, as if from a mirror in the sky, to very distant parts of the world. The second search led to the development of electronics, and was largely sustained by scientific discovery and ingenious engineering innovation.

Radio communication is based on the principle that an electromagnetic wave can carry a signal. The device developed for making such signals recognizable by their intended recipient was the thermionic valve (called a 'tube' in the United States)—perhaps the most ingenious invention of the entire twentieth century. Each initially cost roughly the equivalent of a week's wage in the countries where they were widely used, and were manufactured in millions each year as the international broadcasting industry grew. Then, early in the 1930s, the Radio Corporation of America began broadcasting signals corresponding to moving pictures (in monochrome), and television broadcasting began in earnest when the Second World War ended. Colour television began soon afterwards, when the problems of displaying the signals had been solved.

Meanwhile, in Britain in the 1930s, Robert Watson Watt had been advocating the use of pulses of radio waves for the detection of hostile aircraft, of which it was believed there would soon be a great many. Called *radar* (*r*adio *d*etection *a*nd *r*anging), the technique was the basis of a comprehensive system of aerial defence installed in Britain by 1940. It remains the chief means of regulating the flight of civil aircraft and has transformed maritime navigation, as well as being used for tracking objects in orbit about the earth. Microwaves are the preferred means of communicating between the surface of the earth and active objects in space, chiefly because of the compactness of the associated equipment—illustrated by the small size of the receiver dishes used for the reception of broadcasts from earth satellites.

Meanwhile the increasingly sophisticated design of electronic circuits during the 1930s had revived interest in a field neglected since the attempts by Charles Babbage almost exactly a century earlier to construct mechanical 'computing engines'. For one thing, it was appreciated that the properties of electronic circuits could be chosen so as to simulate directly the behaviour of other systems— whence the development of 'analogue' computers. Other devices were electro-mechanical, combining electronic circuits and mechanical linkages driven by small electric motors. But the true precursors of the now ubiquitous electronic computer were machines developed in the USA in the late 1930s, using paper cards punched with holes (called 'punched cards') both for representing data and for providing information about the way in which the data should be processed.

The significance of these machines, known as 'digital' since they manipulate the digits in numbers separately, is twofold. First, they rely on the 'binary code', or strings of the digits '0' and '1', for representing numerical information. Secondly, arbitrary mathematical operations to be carried out can also be represented in the same code and provided to the machine in what is called a 'program'.

The Second World War provided engineers with expertise in the accurate processing and transfer of signals, and by 1949 two prototype machines had been built independently and were operating at the Massachussets Institute of Technology and at the University of Manchester. Although more polished versions of these machines were built and sold for commercial and research purposes (notably for the design of nuclear weapons), their dependence on thermionic valves made them both slow and clumsy to use.

By marvellous coincidence a solution was at hand. In 1947 William Shockley, John Bardeen, and Walter Brattain at the Bell Telephone Research Laboratories in New Jersey invented a device called the transistor, which had by the end of the century almost entirely replaced the thermionic valve except where very high-powered signals were necessary. The advantages of these devices were readily apparent: they are intrinsically small, robust (even rugged), potentially cheap to manufacture, capable of operating at high frequencies, and consume very little electrical power. The immediate result was twofold: the production of mass-produced electronic devices (typified by the 'transistor radio' that swept the world in the 1960s) and the development of economical digital computers much more powerful than had previously been foreseen. In the 1960s and 1970s, companies such as IBM manufactured and sold thousands of 'mainframe' computers to commercial, defence, and research organizations, each capable of carrying through several millions of arithmetical operations a second.

Yet there remained many potential applications of computers to which these machines could not be conveniently applied, notably in aircraft and in the guidance of strategic missiles. In the late 1960s the Advanced Research Projects Agency of the US Department of Defense sponsored a research programme that led to the development of the *microprocessor*—nothing less than an electronic computer engraved on the surface of a piece of silicon (generally called a 'chip') with dimensions no greater than a millimetre. That, in turn, made possible the design and manufacture of the personal computer or PC, depending not only on the relatively low cost of microprocessors but on the development of programs allowing their use by people untrained in computer science.

The trend to personal computing was the driving force for another technical innovation: a global network (called the *Internet*) by means of which computers of all sizes could voluntarily (and sometimes involuntarily) exchange information. The feasibility of this system depends for the time being on the availability of spare capacity on global communications links via earth satellites and submarine cables. Whether it develops into a self-contained communications system, a publishing house, or both, and how its users will eventually pay for it, remains for the century ahead.

Haber's industrial plant for the synthesis of ammonia was important not merely because it provided a cheap source of nitrogenous fertilizer for the increasingly productive agricultural industry of Europe and North America, but because it gave the chemical industry of the twentieth century one of its conspicuous themes: how to accomplish in a factory chemical transformations of a kind ordinarily carried out by natural processes.

Recognizing that the natural textile fibres are chemically polymers, or molecules made from large numbers of identical chemical units strung together, chemists set about synthesizing structures of that kind. One of the first was an analogue of the fibres found in wood pulp used in the manufacture of paper, 'Rayon'. This was followed by the first successful synthetic rubber in 1929 and nylon in 1935. The foundations of the polyester textile industry were laid in Britain in 1941, and the process for developing polyethylene was developed at the same time. The foundation for Italy's 'economic miracle' of the 1950s was laid with the development there of the manufacture of the structurally regular version of polyethylene in 1954.

In the closing decades of the century, interest turned from the design of polymers simulating textile fibres to others with special properties. A polymer designed to be heat resistant, and used in the 1960s to shield nuclear warheads mounted on ballistic missiles from the frictional heat produced by rapid movement through the atmosphere, has important applications in general engineering (as well as producing 'Teflon' to coat domestic cooking utensils). Other polymers of organic chemicals have been designed to conduct electricity: some were even claimed to have the property of superconductivity, which means that they offer literally no resistance to the passage of electrical current.

By the end of the century the most direct imitation of life in the laboratory (and factory) is that represented by what is called *biotechnology*. Since the recognition in 1972 that what had been learnt about the constitution of living organisms was sufficient to enable genes to be manipulated artificially, the use of bacteria and other cells for making important medicines grew rapidly. Insulin (for the treatment of some forms of diabetes), Factor VIII for the treatment of haemophilia, and a variety of other biological materials were routinely made in this way from the 1980s onwards.

The economic impact of this new industry cannot easily be assessed. The annual market value of the genetically engineered products (mostly high-value pharmaceuticals) produced in 1995 is estimated to have exceeded $15,000 million, but that is probably an underestimate, given the high rate at which new products were due to be licensed for sale in the closing years of the century. Moreover, the application of the new techniques in the cultivation of improved crops had little effect before the end of the century, partly because of regulatory impediments to the growth of engineered organisms 'in the field', while *gene therapy*, canvassed in the 1980s as a treatment for human genetic disease and for some forms of cancer, awaits a technique for inserting healthy genes into human chromosomes at the places to which they naturally belong. The same difficulty affects the intended use of gene transplantation for the artificial improvement of the stock of domestic animals.

What these developments presage for the twenty-first century is unclear, but some present tendencies have enough momentum to ensure their influence on what lies ahead. Present ambitions to fashion novel materials by the manipulation and arrangements of atoms will not easily be extinguished; nor will the several schemes for simulating parts of the human nervous system for the design of computing systems capable of sensory and analytic power. The latter may yet give reality to one of the frustrated dreams of the twentieth century embodied in the phrase 'artificial intelligence'.

Biotechnology is also likely to be a powerful influence on medicine and agriculture in the decades ahead. Now that the molecular causes of many forms of cancer are understood, for example, it seems unlikely that effective treatments will be long delayed, while the genetic improvement of crop plants could have radical consequences for agriculture and food production world wide.

Finally, power production is bound to be a contentious issue. At the end of the century there were substantial grounds for fearing that the earth's climate would be changed for the worse by the continued consumption of fossil fuels, coal and petroleum especially. Nuclear power is the only alternative source of electricity in bulk, but is generally unpopular. Without it the choice seems to be that of being too hot (outdoors) and too cold (indoors). It seems improbable that the next century will settle for that uncomfortable choice.

5 The Growth of a World Economy

ROBERT SKIDELSKY

In the twentieth century, the world economy, measured by real income per person, has grown by 1.5 per cent a year. This is about two and a half times as fast as in the nineteenth century. As a result, absolute levels of real per capita income are three or four times higher at the century's end than at its beginning. However, these gains have been unevenly distributed. Although Asia and Latin America have grown faster than Western Europe and the United States, their incomes per head have grown more slowly, because their population growth has been three times as large. At the end of the century the average income per head of three-fifths of the world's population—3 billion people, mainly in sub-Saharan Africa, India, and China—is only about one-twentieth of that of the world's twenty-four richest countries. Over the century only a handful of poor countries have caught up with those who started rich.

Twentieth-century growth has not been continuous. Four phases may be identified, with three breaks in trend initiated by external 'shocks', which shifted the world economy onto lower or higher growth paths. Each phase is characterized by a different kind of political economy, as shocks triggered off changes in institutions and policy. We can identify the four phases of twentieth-century economic life by their political-economy characteristics: liberal market (1900–13), autarkic (1914–50), managed market (1950–73), and neo-liberal market (since 1973). Fig. 3 plots the salient features of these four phases, together with the main events which triggered the transition from one phase to the next.

The fact that the middle years of this century were a 'golden age' not just for the capitalist market, but also for the planned communist, economies suggests that planned systems, starting from a low base, can also accumulate wealth rapidly for a time, provided that they ruthlessly suppress the consumption demands of their populations. Since the early 1970s, the capitalist world has slowed down, and the communist world has collapsed. East Asia has been the main exception to the recent loss of economic dynamism, suggesting to many that the next century will be Asia's.

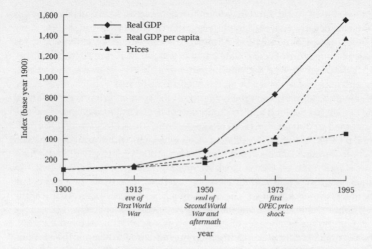

Figure 3. Indices of real GDP, real GDP per capita, and the price level, 1900–1995

Note: Countries are weighted according to relative GDP levels from Maddison. The index does not include the hyperinflations of Asia and Latin America. Africa is not included in any of the indices.

Sources: Angus Maddison, *The World Economy in the 20th Century* (OECD, 1990); B. R. Mitchell, *International Historical Statistics* (2nd edn, Basingstoke Publications, 1993).

The opening years of the twentieth century were a little-noticed coda to the liberal age. Keynes saw them as an 'economic eldorado', little affected by the 'projects and politics of militarism and imperialism, of racial and cultural rivalries, of monopolies, restrictions, and exclusion'. The world economic order still largely conformed to the tenets of classical liberalism: government spending and taxes were low, budgets were balanced, welfare states were in their infancy, domestic prices and exchange rates were stable, capital and labour were geographically mobile, and a mixed aristocratic–bourgeois ruling class manned all the leading states. The most disturbing premonition of things to come was the rise in tariffs after 1880. But, with some exceptions, they were still relatively low. Quantitative restrictions were unknown.

With economic recovery at the end of the 1890s came the longest and largest investment boom known hitherto, in which Western European savings flowed not just into their own domestic economies but into public utilities, railways, harbours, agriculture, and extractive industries all over the world. Rising real incomes and new inventions (the internal combustion engine, electricity, plastics, synthetics) gave birth to the new mass-production industries—particularly in the United States—which were to dominate the twentieth century. In the three years 1911–13 annual economic growth in Europe averaged 5 per cent.

These pre-war years were the culmination of the nineteenth-century pattern by which the growth of the advanced countries of Western Europe was diffused to the 'undeveloped' world through their import demand for food and raw materials and their export of capital and labour. Integration was extensive but shallow, since the bulk of the world's population still engaged in subsistence agriculture, and was achieved by a mixture of economic exchange and political control (colonialism), both made possible by a network of communications—railways, steamships, posts, and telegraphs—which by 1914 covered all continents.

Britain and Germany were the linchpins of the system. Britain, as the largest single market for the food and raw materials of overseas Europe, 'managed' the international gold standard which knit the trading nations of the world into a multilateral payments system. Its ability to offset its deficits with North America with its manufacturing surpluses with its Empire, particularly India, gave it a large margin for capital exports, whose stock by 1913 amounted to £4 billion, twice its national income. These capital exports, together with those of France and Germany, provided a fund for the development of Russia, Latin America, the British Empire, China, Japan, and the Middle East, while the central position of the City of London made it 'lender of the last resort' to countries in temporary balance-of-payments difficulties. Germany, more industrially dynamic than Britain, was the economic locomotive of Europe, supplying its neighbours with much of their manufactured goods and capital, and taking most of their imports.

Contrary to later Marxist argument, world capitalism was not in crisis in the pre-war period, and it is difficult to justify the argument that the First World War was caused by economic rivalries. What brought this first 'golden age' to an end were foreign-policy calculations, driven or reinforced by the political insecurity of the unelected rulers of the three great empires of Central and Eastern Europe.

The political economy of the inter-war years was dominated by the consequences of the First World War—the nearest thing to a genuine watershed this century. The main political economy characteristic of the period is the growth of government control over economic life. This proved incompatible with the attempt in the 1920s to restore the traditional 'disciplines of the market'. The clash between two systems of political economy, as well as the disruption of the pre-war equilibria between Europe and the USA, and Europe and its dependent peripheries, provide the indispensable context for the Great Depression of 1929–32 and the division of the world economy into quasi-autarkic blocs in the 1930s, as well as for the second great European war.

The First World War disclosed for the first time the techniques by which the economic and political life of a society might be effectively directed by the state. In the war economy, resources were allocated through state purchases and central planning rather than by markets and prices. Governments mobilized resources for the war effort by a combination of higher taxes, borrowing, and inflation. They used businessmen and trade-union leaders as agents of wartime coordination and wage control and deliberately strengthened their organizations.

These expedients were to have a profound effect on subsequent peacetime practice. The idea that a government might plan its country's economic development took root. The notion that a community's resources, human and capital, could be freely commandeered by governments replaced the earlier liberal idea that individually owned resources might be made available to governments only for certain limited purposes and under strict conditions. The corporatist or 'solidaristic' model of industrial relations replaced both the individual-contract model favoured by the Right and the class-struggle model of the Left.

These innovations were most eagerly seized on by the new dictatorships spawned by the war and used to justify them. When Lenin seized power in 1917 he applied the German war model to the task of making Russia a great industrial power: Communism, he said, was 'the Soviets plus electrification'. The Soviet planning system, started by Lenin and completed by Stalin, was to have enormous influence on the development policies of China and post-colonial India.

The war had taught the Italian leader Mussolini that nation is stronger than class, and that totalitarian control is feasible, as well as being necessary for an 'age of struggle'. Italian Fascism inspired National Socialism in Germany, Francoism in Spain, and Peronism in Argentina, as well as much of the theory of the authoritarian 'developmental state', so influential after the Second World War in Latin America and post-colonial Africa. Its rhetorical advantage over Leninism was that it left the system of private ownership intact, merely imposing state control over it.

But the First World War had a profound and long-lasting influence on the Western democracies as well. Why should the organizational powers shown by governments in war not be applied to the tasks of peace? The war killed off the idea of 'limited' government, of the 'nightwatchman state'. The idea of 'democratic planning', born in the First World War, reinforced by the Great Depression and the Second World War, lingered into the 1970s. The war undermined the classic liberal idea of budgets balanced at low levels of taxation and spending. In the twentieth century democratic governments have appropriated increasing shares of their countries' national incomes for welfare purposes and have often spent more than they could raise in taxes: state spending as a share of GDP rose in the main capitalist countries from 12 per cent in 1913 to 20–5 per cent between the wars, and to 45–50 per cent by the 1990s. The long twentieth-century experiment with incomes policies likewise has its roots in the First World War.

Wartime innovations could also be contrasted with the mediocre performance of post-war economies handed back to market forces. The demographic losses, physical devastation, and economic disorganization wrought by the First World War were compounded by huge policy mistakes in making peace. In the name of national self-determination and for the sake of weakening Germany and its Allies—both reasonable enough goals in themselves—the victors chopped up the empires of Germany and Austria–Hungary without giving a thought as to how to preserve the benefits of what had been, in effect, a single market with a population the size of North America's. Equally disastrous was the attempt by the French and the British to extract reparations from Germany, chiefly to pay back their wartime debts to the United States. The traditional logic of seizing resources from defeated enemies ran up against the economic logic of helping them back on to their feet.

What Europe needed was a net inflow of American money for its rebuilding, not a net outflow to service dead-weight debt. Instead of addressing the financial requirements of European reconstruction, the best brains of Europe and America spent four years trying to devise means of extracting tributes from Germany which would never be honestly paid because they could not be enforced.

The result of these mistakes of commission and omission was that peace started extremely badly. In lieu of official external finance for famine relief and reconstruction and, it must be said, adequate domestic revenue bases in the weak successor states of the defeated Central Empires, wartime inflation was allowed to continue and accelerate. A brief post-war boom based on pent-up demand rather than long-term prospects produced extravagant paper profits which in turn fed wild speculation in currencies, commodities, real estate, and companies. This was nature's way of getting rid of domestic debt and restarting industry. But the inflationary madness ruined millions of savers, while the collapse of the boom left a mass of unviable, overcapitalized firms. Capitalism started post-war life with a sullied reputation.

The characteristics of individual states dictated the financial policies pursued. Whereas 'strong' states such as the United States, Britain, and Sweden were soon able to impose austere stabilization policies, 'weak' states such as France, Italy, Germany, Austria, and Russia went on inflating, though at different rates, right through to 1924. The British state proved too strong for the health of the British economy. Not content with stable prices—achieved at the end of 1920—it persisted with a deflationary policy to bring down British prices and costs to the American level, so that the pound might regain its pre-war parity with the US dollar. The British economy in the 1920s never recovered from the double blow of a one-off increase in unit costs in 1919 and a prolonged dose of dear money in 1920–2. Elsewhere, hyperinflation was rampant in the weak successor states of Central and Eastern Europe: prices rose one trillion times in Germany. General currency stabilization in the area, backed by foreign loans and stringent budgetary policies, was not achieved till 1924 on the basis of new gold-backed currencies worth a tiny fraction of the pre-war ones. By contrast, France and Italy unwittingly came close to an 'optimum' rate of inflation—enough to allow reconstruction to continue without provoking a flight from domestic money. The lira and franc were stabilized between 1922 and 1924 at 20–30 per cent of their pre-war parities against the dollar. Italy (under Mussolini) made the fastest recovery from the war, and France did best of all European countries in the later 1920s.

More settled international conditions following the settlement of the reparations issue in 1924, the Locarno Treaty of 1925, and the general resumption of the gold standard between 1924 and 1927 brought a few years of patchy prosperity before the onset of the Great Depression in 1929. The enfeeblement of Britain and Germany was only partly offset by the steady expansion of mass consumption in the United States (more dramatic in headline images than cold statistics), and the impressive growth of Japan (from a very low base). On every measure, the *impact* of Britain and Germany on the world economy weakened, particularly their capacity to export. Britain's and Germany's manufacturing exports in the period 1926–9 were 88 and 78 per cent of their 1913 volumes respectively, although world exports of manufactured goods exceeded their pre-war volume. Surplus capacity in the old staple sectors of coal, iron, textiles, and shipbuilding, caused by the spread of overseas industrialization in the war, the proliferation of post-war tariffs, the switch in demand from coal to oil, and the slow growth of new products, produced heavy and persisting unemployment in the two countries. This reduced their ability to import food and raw materials from Eastern and overseas Europe. The downward pressure on primary product prices, which was misdiagnosed as a problem of oversupply, was really a problem of insufficient West European demand. The monetary expression of these trade imbalances was a set of misaligned exchange rates which led to a persistent drain of gold from Europe, Australasia, and Latin America to the United States, as well as to France in the later 1920s. A competitive scramble for gold replaced the British-managed gold standard of the pre-1914 era.

Apart from the disruption of the economic unity of Europe, first by a destructive war then by inept peacemaking, a serious inconsistency in political economy made impossible the return to normalcy craved by bourgeois Europe. After the war, the price mechanism was restored internationally, but the strengthened employers' and workers' organizations created by the war were left intact. The price of the bourgeois restoration of the 1920s was a corporatist immobilism, which greatly hindered the adjustment of the European economies to changed conditions. It left a highly rigid and artificial situation in which the avoidance of a severe decline in the real incomes of the leading European trading nations became dependent on capital exports from the USA whose own involvement in world trade was relatively small, which was largely self-sufficient in agriculture, and which excluded from its own shores the manufactured goods by which the Europeans—and especially the Germans—might hope to repay the huge sums they were borrowing. When the United States cut down on lending and imports at the same time between 1928 and 1930, the world economy collapsed.

The Great Depression of 1929–32 was the greatest peacetime breakdown of the world economy since the Industrial Revolution. It is estimated that world GDP fell almost 20 per cent by volume, with a 28 per cent fall in the United States. Unemployment rose to 22 per cent in the United States and 17 per cent in Germany. In the primary producing peripheries collapsing export prices shrank the incomes of the rural population. Under the strain of collapse, the world economy started to disintegrate. The gold-standard system was brought down in 1931, and with it the system of multilateral clearing. Tariffs, exchange controls, competitive devaluations, blocked accounts and defaults became standard as countries sought national escape, then recovery, from the economic holocaust.

The years 1929–32 encompassed a double catastrophe, because, contrary to much legend, the Soviet Union also experienced an economic as well as a demographic disaster in these years. Lenin's New Economic Policy (NEP) of 1921, which had sanctioned the revival of rural capitalism, was finally wound up in 1929, the collapse of the world wheat price destroying the possibility of financing industri-alization by exports. Stalin determined to make the peasants pay by confiscating their land. In January 1930 he decreed the incorporation of all peasant holdings into giant food-production 'factories'. Between 1930 and 1933 millions of peasants were murdered or died of starvation as agricultural output plummeted: according to revised estimates, there was a 20 per cent *decline* in Soviet national income under the first Five Year Plan (1928–32). These 'successes' of Stalinism led many Western intellectuals to embrace central planning as the only rational alternative to the 'anarchy' of market forces.

But it was the United States, not the Soviet Union, which decided the fate of the world economy, now as for the rest of the century. The diversion of US savings from foreign lending to the New York bull market in the second half of 1928 destroyed the financing of stocks of food and raw materials in Canada, Latin America, Australasia, as well as of the German municipalities which had borrowed heavily in the US market. Interacting with this deflationary shock was the American industrial recession which started before, but was greatly intensified by, the Wall Street Crash on 24 October 1929. The collapse of the US and German economies converted a world recession into a world depression.

Policy, far from offsetting the decline of activity, helped it. The Hawley–Smoot Act of 1930, raising the US tariff against manufactured imports to 48 per cent, and Britain's Import Duties Act of 1932, which abandoned almost a century-old tradi-tion of free trade, narrowed the world market at a time when it was already shrink-ing. Twenty-three countries raised their tariff levels, thirty-two applied import quotas, prohibitions, licences, and other quantitative restrictions. Fiscal policy was generally contractionary, as governments tried to balance budgets on the basis of falling revenues by raising taxes and reducing spending. Monetary policy was also contractionary. By failing to pump money into the US banking system during and after the first banking crisis of October 1930, the Federal Reserve Board allowed a massive wave of bank failures to proceed unchecked. Internationally, neither New York nor Paris, which held most of the world's gold reserves, would take over London's role as 'lender of last resort'. Britain's abandonment of the gold standard in 1931 transferred deflationary pressure to the United States and Germany. In 1933 President Roosevelt devalued the US dollar, transferring slump and deflation to the gold bloc headed by France. The leaders of the world economy broke it up to protect themselves.

The 1930s marked a general retrogression in economic life. Autarkic policies replaced economic mechanisms. International transactions were heavily con-trolled, prices and exchange rates deliberately manipulated, industries and agri-culture subsidized. Latin American primary producers, crippled by collapsing prices and debts, embarked on state-led industrialization policies, using the methods of quantitative restriction and bilateral trading agreements pioneered by Hitler's economic wizard, Hjalmar Schacht. In the fascist economies, recovery from depression was deliberately organized, most successfully in Germany and Japan. Hitler restored full employment in three years through a mixture of public works and subsidies; Roosevelt's 'New Deal' tried the same expedients, with less success, in the USA. Limited world recovery, based on nationalistic policies, gave way to renewed depression in 1937–8, once more starting in the USA. This confirmed some powers in their wisdom in cutting themselves off from the world economy. Germany, Italy, and Japan maintained and even increased their production, while Sweden, Britain, France, Canada went down. Tentative moves by the USA and Britain in mid-decade back towards currency stability and trade liberalization were promises of things to come. They had no influence on actual events.

One inevitable consequence of autarky was the attempt to enlarge political boundaries by those great powers who felt their existing ones too narrow to assure them a self-contained existence. In 1932 the Japanese occupied Manchuria and began their military expansion in East Asia. Three years later Italy attacked Abyssinia. In 1939 Germany invaded Poland, having absorbed Austria and Czechoslovakia peacefully. Ten years after the start of the Great Depression another great war started. It was the failure of the autarkic experiments of the 1930s to restore general prosperity or maintain peace which convinced the leaders of the democracies that they must rebuild a liberal economic order on an improved political and institutional basis.

Unlike the First World War, the Second World War led to a 'golden age'. The world boom, set going by the rebuilding of the industries of Europe and Japan, continued without interruption for over twenty years—a record. Between 1950 and 1973 world GDP per capita grew at 3 per cent a year, three times as fast as in the previous phase. In the developed world unemployment averaged 2.6 per cent between 1950 and 1973, as compared with 7.5 per cent between 1920 and 1938. Prices rose by 4.1 per cent a year in the same period, which was considered a tolerable trade-off for full employment. Central to the growth experience of developed countries were widespread opportunities to imitate American technology (promoted by direct American foreign investment in Western Europe); to contract low-productivity agriculture; and to exploit cheap energy. Opportunities for technological catch-up gave capital a high marginal productivity, leading to large increases in investment ratios. A high rate of productivity growth allowed a continuous transfer of low-skilled labour from rural occupations to industry and services, and a sufficient rise in real incomes to satisfy workers' aspirations, which, together with immigration, increasing international competition, and declining relative commodity prices, kept unit costs fairly stable. The rapid expansion in real incomes financed improvements in social services without recourse to inflationary financing.

Outside the West, Latin American countries also experienced high rates of input-led growth. The Communist bloc was able to achieve rapid growth in the 1950s and 1960s by mobilizing labour reserves, exploiting natural resources, and rigidly controlling consumption. But its gains from trade were not as large as those of the free world, since it could not import sophisticated technology, while its planning system prevented it from allocating production on the basis of competitive efficiency.

For once, secular forces making for strong growth were helped, rather than impeded, by the underlying policy regime and the course of post-war politics. Unlike after the First World War, much more explicit attention was paid to securing the 'public goods' of a market economy. The Bretton Woods Agreement of 1944 was a compromise between the United States' new economic internationalism and Britain's demand for national autonomy to pursue full employment policies. It accommodated the British desire for fiscal and monetary discretion within a framework of rules establishing currency convertibility at fixed, but adjustable exchange rates, guaranteed drawing rights on an International Monetary Fund (IMF) to smooth temporary balance-of-payments difficulties, an International Bank for Reconstruction and Development (World Bank), and retention of national controls on capital movements. A negotiating framework for freeing up trade—the General Agreement on Tariffs and Trade (GATT)—was added in 1947. Although these rules and institutions became operative only in the 1960s, they embodied the principle of centralized management of an international market order which had been lacking in the inter-war period.

In practice, the management was provided by the USA. Once the cold war had started in 1948, the United States assumed responsibility for underwriting the prosperity and security of the free world, its intervention in each region triggered off by the perceived threat of a Communist takeover. Marshall Aid to non-communist Europe in 1948–51 provided a model for US disbursements to Japan and (after the Communist takeover of China in 1949) to South Korea and Taiwan, as well as to Latin America in the 1960s, following Castro's revolution in Cuba. Under Marshall Aid the USA gave $13 billion conditional on the removal of trade and payments barriers. In this way it laid the foundations of the European Economic Community (EEC) (started in 1958), which went some way to restoring the single European market broken up by the First World War. The United States was also much more ready than in the past to open up its own market to foreign imports, exemplified by the 'Kennedy round' of GATT tariff negotiations in 1964–7. The combination of a fixed exchange-rate system and conservative fiscal and monetary policies in the United States (till the mid-1960s) provided the world with a reasonably secure anti-inflationary anchor. Nor should one ignore the stimulating effect of the United States' worldwide military expenditures *per se*, particularly in East Asia where the USA fought two short 'hot' wars against Communism—in Korea and Vietnam. Through a web of supranational institutions, as well as by direct action, the United States took over Britain's informal nineteenth-century role of energizing and stabilizing a liberal market order.

This was still far from being the integrated world market which had existed before 1914. The Soviet Union locked its East European satellites into its own autarkic planning system; Communist China and socialist India and Indonesia planned their economies with little reference to world conditions; authoritarian, import-substituting development policies in Latin America survived from the wreckage of European fascism. The positive effect of decolonization was offset, in large parts of sub-Saharan Africa, by state breakdown, with recurring wars, genocides, and famines. Basically, the core capitalist and communist countries integrated among themselves, with the rest of the world accommodated by *ad hoc* aid and trade packages dictated by strategic interests and traditional colonial ties.

The role of ideas in generating the 'golden age' of capitalism has been much disputed. The middle years of this century are sometimes called the 'Keynesian era', because of the explicit commitment of many developed-country governments (notably those of the United States and the United Kingdom) to pursue full employment policies based on the theories of John Maynard Keynes. The Keynesian influence can certainly be seen in the anti-deflationary design of the Bretton Woods system and the greater importance of state consumption and transfer payments in post-war national incomes. The declared willingness of governments to use fiscal and monetary policy to maintain full employment and stimulate growth may also have had a favourable effect on business expectations. However, 'national' management of economies was a minor factor compared to the 'international' management exercised by the United States. This, we have suggested, was based on the policies of the Cold War rather than economic theory, though we must not deny economic considerations their due influence on political choices. Politicians learnt from the economic mistakes of the inter-war years, and added new ones.

The influence of ideas on national policies was more obvious in the case of the development strategies pursued by poor countries in an effort to catch up with rich ones. These were based on pre-Keynesian notions (India's Nehru was a great devotee of Soviet planning), supplemented by neo-Keynesian 'growth models'. On the whole, these strategies either produced near zero per capita growth (in India) or growth that was so unsound that much of its results had to be scrapped in the 1980s and 1990s. Throughout the 'golden age' Latin American countries had double-digit annual inflation rates, with Argentina, Brazil, and Chile the worst offenders.

From the mid-1960s onwards, this system of precarious balances between the state and the market, American hegemony and national autonomy, started to crumble. The proximate cause of the upset was the inflationary financing of the Vietnam War by the USA in the late 1960s, followed by synchronized Western policy-induced booms in the early 1970s. These events destroyed the system of fixed exchange rates in 1971, leading to generalized currency floating, and triggered off a food and commodity price explosion which culminated in a threefold rise in oil prices in 1973–4. (As a result of two price hikes, the second in 1979–80, oil import prices rose from $3.73 a barrel in 1973 to $33.50 in 1980.) This oil-price shock brought the 'golden age' to an end in the West. The OECD rate of growth of real GDP per capita fell from 3.9 per cent in 1960–8 to 1.9 per cent in 1973–9. An important consequence of the growth slowdown was the 'fiscal crisis' of the state. Welfare expenditures went on growing, with the state becoming 'employer of the last resort', while the growth of state revenues slowed.

Apart from policy mistakes, the 'golden age' was undermined by faulty monetary arrangements. As early as 1957 the economist Robert Triffin had pointed to the self-destructive character of a gold-exchange standard based on dollar reserves—

namely, that it depended on a continuous increase in dollar liabilities which undermined confidence in the dollar. The emergence of a growing market in these liabilities (the Eurodollar market) weakened national control over money supplies while creating increasingly massive scope for currency speculation. Thus the cost shocks of the early 1970s were a predictable consequence of inflationary monetary conditions. A slowdown in economic growth was to be expected in any case, as some of the post-war sources of growth dried up. But over-expansionary financial policies, which reflected the hubristic mindset of the Keynesian macroeconomic managers, ensured that the slowdown would occur in conditions of accelerating inflation, which rendered Keynesian demand-stimulation policies unusable. Attempts to restrain wage costs by means of incomes policies (first used in the First World War) were overwhelmed by the inflationary impact of monetary policy, released, after 1971–3, from the constraints of fixed exchange rates. The rising 'misery index' (unemployment plus inflation) which ended the 'golden age' is captured in Table 1.

The widespread perception that misguided government policies were responsible for both the inflationary explosion and the growth slowdown of the early 1970s led to the revival of neo-liberal economics, proclaimed by Milton Friedman, and pursued by Ronald Reagan in the USA and Margaret Thatcher in Britain. In the face of the second oil shock in 1979–80, 'strong' states (the USA, Britain, Germany) tightened monetary, and in Britain and Germany also fiscal, policy, bringing about the worst slump since the 1930s. Latin American countries, which had been able to maintain their public-investment booms throughout the 1970s by borrowing recycled petrodollars at negative real interest rates, suddenly found themselves faced with crippling debt burdens as export earnings collapsed, real interest rates rose to punitive levels, and foreign investment dried up. Following the Mexican debt crisis in 1982, the IMF and the commercial banks stepped in, imposing tough

Table 1. Discomfort index: seven major countries

Year	Unemployment rate (%)	Increase in consumer prices (%)	Discomfort index	Year	Unemployment rate (%)	Increase in consumer prices (%)	Discomfort index
	1	2	1+2		1	2	3
1959	3.8	1.2	5.0	1969	2.6	4.9	7.5
1960	3.4	1.7	5.1	1970	3.1	5.6	8.7
1961	3.6	1.6	5.2	1971	3.7	5.0	8.7
1962	3.1	2.1	5.2	1972	3.7	4.4	8.1
1963	3.2	2.3	5.5	1973	3.2	7.7	10.9
1964	2.9	2.0	4.9	1974	3.7	13.4	17.1
1965	2.7	2.6	5.3	1975	5.4	11.1	16.5
1966	2.5	3.2	5.7	1976	5.3	8.1	13.4
1967	2.8	2.8	5.6				
1968	2.7	4.0	6.7	1980	(4)	(5)	(9)

Source: P. McCracken *et al.*, *Towards Full Employment and Stability* (OECD, 1977), 42.

stabilization policies in return for debt rescheduling. Soviet satellites such as Poland, Hungary, and Romania, which had also borrowed heavily from Western banks in the 1970s in a vain effort to develop hard-currency exports, likewise found themselves drowning in debt. The crisis of 'managed' capitalism had a far more dramatic counterpart in the Communist world, where growth stopped altogether. In 1978, the Chinese Communist leader, Deng Xiaoping, in a decisive reform, restored rural capitalism in China. Beset by the problem of negative growth and loosening grasp, Mikhail Gorbachev, who took over as First Secretary of the Soviet Communist Party in 1985, began to dismantle Stalin's central planning system.

Since it was widely accepted that the main cause of accelerating inflation was widening budget deficits, a central element of the new political economy was the commitment to reduce these deficits to 'sustainable' levels—levels which did not have to be financed by the 'inflation tax' or rising government debt—and maintain them there. Maximum government deficit and debt ratios were prescribed in the Maastricht Treaty of 1992, and accepted in principle by all its European signatories. This marks a notable repudiation of Keynesian 'discretionary' management and a return to the traditional philosophy of the balanced budget. However, the commitment to balanced budgets implies a shrinkage in the role of the state, since the macroeconomic imbalances of the 1970s had their source in expanding spending commitments which could not be covered by taxes. It was also widely argued that the undue expansion of the public sector (spending and taxes) slows down growth by squeezing profits and reducing the incentives to work, save, and take risks. The privatization of state industries, started by Margaret Thatcher in Britain in the early 1980s, spread over the whole world. It culminated in the restoration of capitalism in Russia and Central Europe. The 1980s also saw an attempt to reduce the tax burden and simplify the tax system, particularly in Britain and the United States, though this was partly reversed in the slump of the early 1990s. Deregulation, especially of financial services and capital movements, was another aspect of neo-liberal policy. The central theme of the neo-liberal revolution was that governments should give up trying to manage and control what had become unmanageable and uncontrollable.

This points to business and technological innovation as a crucial source of the neo-liberal policy revolution. Since the 1970s, the 'national economy' has been undermined from above by the spread of multinational enterprises with their ability to organize cross-border flows of information, capital, technology, and manufacturing capacity; and from below by miniaturized electronics which have brought the benefits of specialization within reach of the small producer. Spatially immobile entrepreneurs, financiers, firms, industries, and economies no longer exist to be regulated, managed, and milked for national aims. This means that governments have lost much of their old power to 'choose' exchange rates, inflation rates, wage rates, tax rates, and the social-security systems which these financed. Nor have supranational substitutes for vanishing national management yet been found. World economic conditions are no longer set by American policy; despite the ambitions of the European Union (EU), regional organizations are still far from plugging the growing gaps in state authority; international bodies such as the IMF and the newly created World Trade Organization (WTO) can do little without political support. As a result, market forces hit individuals and communities much more directly and painfully than they did in the 'golden age' when they were mediated by state and non-state institutions. Is this a good or bad thing? Collective choice is constricted, individual choice enlarged; the world is riskier, economies are more volatile, but opportunities for the enterprising are greater.

The historically minded will see in the remarketization of economic life a repetition of the technological changes which broke up the great mercantilist empires of the eighteenth century, ushering in the free trade age; or at least a modest movement back towards the world with which this century opened. The new global economy is certainly more of a single piece than at any time since 1913. Yet it is in some ways more anarchic, lacking a fixed exchange rate system (a new Bretton Woods is hardly in sight), a leading power to underwrite it, a stable security system, and a hegemonic class like the nineteenth-century bourgeoisie. Some bits of Russia and China resemble the nineteenth-century Wild West. Nor can late-twentieth-century Western conceptions of social protection be easily combined with the logic of global competition. This is the major inconsistency in the political economy of the highly taxed welfare states of Western Europe. How it will be resolved, or whether it needs to be resolved, will depend on the unpredictable dynamics of neo-liberalism. The East Asian economies of South Korea, Taiwan, Hong Kong, Singapore, Malaysia, Thailand, and Indonesia together with China, were the great exception to the slowdown of economic growth in the 1970s and 1980s. (Japanese growth, by contrast, has slowed to Western levels, confirming the catch-up approach to explaining economic growth.) Contrary to much belief, their successes have been largely due to opportunities for 'catch-up' rather than to spectacular technical progress. To this they added sound macroeconomic policies, flexible labour practices, and a strong export orientation. Their ability to sustain their 'miracles' will largely depend on whether they can raise the level of their technical efficiency and financial probity. Western Europe will have to invest more in 'human capital' and deregulate its product and labour markets if it is to remain competitive.

There is some evidence of 'growth fatigue' in Western Europe. It scarcely affects any other region of the world, even the United States, whose appetite for growth is constantly being replenished by successive waves of immigrants. In the countries of the EU there is increasing scepticism about whether growth of GDP is in any way an accurate measure of the growth of welfare, especially if it includes congestion, pollution, the destruction of natural beauty, the break-up of communities, the continual postponement of leisure and consumption—all in the name of faster growth! What growth is for, what kinds of growth are environmentally, psychologically, and socially sustainable and morally desirable, how privately wealthy societies should care for their 'sick, halt, and lame'—these questions are likely to offer a serious challenge to the hegemony of neo-liberalism as we move into the next century, at least in our part of the world.

6 The Growth of a Global Culture

ALAN RYAN

Discussions of 'culture' often display a multitude of sins—most strikingly, snobbery, affectation, and ill-temper. This is perhaps because 'culture' embraces two different topics, both of which can arouse strong feelings. This chapter discusses both; and although they are not wholly disconnected, it is important to keep them distinct. The first is the culture that a cultivated person possesses, the ability to appreciate 'the best that has been thought and written'. In Matthew Arnold's words, the purpose of culture is to bring 'sweetness and light' to our lives; this is what we often term 'high' culture, and, in this sense, we can all too easily imagine a society possessing *no* culture.

The other is culture in the anthropologist's sense: something that societies must possess almost by definition: the congeries of beliefs, values, and attachments that give those societies their character, and allow their members to make sense of their lives and aspirations. It is what one might call 'adjectival' culture, and it is in this sense that youth culture, drug culture, gang culture, or prison culture are cultures, however far their values may be from 'sweetness and light'.

High culture and adjectival culture involve different ideas of culture. Yet they have something in common. When we admire the temple carvings in which the religious culture of Balinese Hinduism expresses itself, we admire them both as art *and* as a vivid expression of a popular culture. Music is an important part of modern Western culture in the anthropologist's sense, but an ability to distinguish good and bad of its kind is the mark of a properly cultivated person—and all parents know that they and their children do not agree on just what it is. Novels, poetry, and detective fiction are all part of the literary culture of twentieth-century Western societies, but detective fiction is rarely thought of as part of high culture. When analysts ask us to take detective fiction seriously, it may be to remind us of the importance of outlets for the anarchic imagination in a tightly organized society or to ask us to see in the work of Raymond Chandler, Dashiel Hammett, or Arthur Conan Doyle the subtlety, imagination, and literary depth that we enjoy in the novels of Virginia Woolf or Faulkner—the first an exercise in showing their place in adjectival culture, the second recruiting them for high culture.

The standing fears of the nineteenth and twentieth centuries apply to both these senses of culture; many writers have thought that democratic societies cannot sustain high culture, while others have thought that democratic societies cannot sustain a single public culture at all, that they are doomed to be fissiparously, and self-destructively, multicultural. These anxieties have their global counterparts. Many critics fear that, as democratic politics and a high level of material well-being spread over the globe, a uniform culture (in the anthropologist's sense) that is wholly hostile to culture (in Matthew Arnold's sense) will infect the entire world: the world will become one vast suburb, filled with indistinguishable shopping malls supplying designer jeans and fast food. Many others fear that, far from becoming uniformly suburban, the world will erupt in endless wars between competing religious and ethnic groups. The American political scientist Benjamin Barber has memorably described these two visions as 'Jihad vs. McWorld'.

The central fact of the twentieth century is that the modern Western world has swept the rest of the world into its economic, technological, and, less straightforwardly, cultural orbit; the societies affected by this process have resisted, acquiesced, joined in with enthusiasm, and often all three in varying combinations. Almost every summary term for this process will give offence to somebody: 'Westernization' is not what a society such as Singapore has in mind when it seeks to preserve a Confucian respect for tradition, family, and community while gaining the benefits of advanced technology, sophisticated finance, and economic ties with the whole world. Even the more neutral 'modernization' rankles among many intellectuals from the developing world for its apparent implication that societies with simple technologies are in all ways 'primitive'. Still, the bleak truth is that the countries of the North Atlantic littoral have imposed on the rest of the world ideals of material prosperity and standards of economic rationality that have proved inescapable. It is an equally bleak truth that they have failed to export much else: a regard for human rights, the rule of law, representative political institutions, for instance; and that, in the process, much that was attractive and life-enhancing in the culture of non-Western societies has been destroyed.

An emphasis on the impact of the technologically advanced world on the rest of the globe may seem unduly ethnocentric. It is not, though it may come to seem so. It may certainly turn out that in the twenty-first century one of the societies thus dragged willy-nilly into the world of international capitalism will prove more attractive to other societies than its Western predecessors had been or more able to wield military and economic power than its predecessors have done. In the twentieth century, cultural change has reflected the twentieth-century global balance of military and financial power. The 'push' of Western power and the 'pull' of Western material prosperity are the central facts of the story, together with the hankering after them, or the resistance to them, that other societies have displayed, and the unpredictable effects of these interactions.

Most nineteenth-century thinkers believed that modernization would mean secularization: science would erode religion, modern medicine would put witch doctors and faith-healers out of business, and prayer would be replaced by technique. To some degree, they were right. Traditional religious allegiances have weakened in most industrial societies, and in these societies modernization has often meant secularization. Elsewhere, modernization has been more a matter of nationalization than secularization. Thus, tribal religions have been extirpated both by missionaries from the developed Christian world who have been intent on recruiting new adherents for a variety of Christian creeds, and by governments that have feared local religious and cultural loyalties as competitors to their own more narrowly political authority. The Soviet Union and the People's Republic of China (PRC) were unusual in espousing atheism as their official creed, and taking pains to suppress traditional religious attachments as such. How far this policy cut against the Russian grain, at any rate, was shown by the rapid growth of the Russian Orthodox Church after the dissolution of the Soviet Union in 1991. An even more striking testimony was offered by Stalin himself during the Second World War. Faced with the need to rally his reluctant population behind what was labelled 'the Great Patriotic War', Stalin called off the Communist Party's attacks on Christianity and happily accepted the Church's support.

The communist assault on Christian and other religious beliefs and practices was instigated and promoted by particular individuals and by the personnel of national Communist Parties. Yet much of the pressure on traditional religious allegiances and observances has come from impersonal and often unrecognized sources. Even in countries such as India where there is no national policy of hostility either to religion in general or to local religious allegiances in particular, local and tribal religious allegiances have weakened as the economy has developed and become more centralized. The dislocations suffered by workers from remote areas when they migrate to the cities in search of work does not result in the secularization that nineteenth-century theorists had in mind, however. Displaced illiterates do not adopt modern scientific habits of thought overnight. More often, they become easy prey for the preachers of assorted fanaticisms, as the example of India suggests.

The Indian government has adopted a policy of strict neutrality between its Hindu, Muslim, Sikh, and other subjects ever since India became independent in 1947. Memories of the horrific communal violence that led to the partitioning of the subcontinent and the creation of Pakistan as a separate and independent state have been sharp enough to sustain that policy for half a century. Even so, towards the end of the century India has witnessed a resurgent Hindu fundamentalism that threatens to undermine the secular state created at the time of independence in 1947, and after the 1984 assassination of Prime Minister Indira Gandhi by her Sikh bodyguards there were massacres of Sikhs in New Delhi and other cities.

The Indian example is not unique. Resentment at the social impact of economic change and resistance to it have been common reactions among socially, economically, and geographically marginalized groups within developing countries. On the world stage, whole societies have felt marginalized and have displayed similar patterns of resentment and resistance; both have fed into fundamentalism, sometimes with the paradoxical result that a national government is sustained by attitudes and beliefs that are almost anarchist in their hostility to government as such. The most spectacular political achievement of Islamic fundamentalism was the overthrow of the Shah of Iran in 1979. Although the Pahlevi regime was a brutal police state, its ambition was to join the circle of modern Western states. Its failure illustrates an important feature of adjectival culture—the difficulty of altering it in the desired direction by political action. The Shah of Iran had good reason to hope that prosperity and education would foster the political culture that a modern secular state needs; but the reality was quite different. It turned out, too, that the attractions of religious fundamentalism overlap with, but are quite distinct from, those of nationalism. Both give their adherents reason to dislike and resist the dominant powers of the modern world, the United States above all; but in Egypt and Algeria there is near civil war between nationalist governments and fundamentalist insurgents.

Some developed countries also have proved astonishingly resistant to the pressures that have weakened religious attachments. The nineteenth-century philosopher Friedrich Nietzsche declared that 'God is dead'; but 94 per cent of late-twentieth-century Americans tell pollsters that they believe in a personal God; over 40 per cent claim to have attended church within the previous two weeks, though a count of bodies in pews suggests they are not all telling the truth. Outside Eire, few Europeans show such enthusiasm. Just as, outside the developed industrial societies of the North Atlantic basin, fundamentalism has flourished, so, inside them, it is the evangelical and fundamentalist branches of Christianity that have flourished. Commentators have long expressed surprise that developing countries could so readily acquire Western technology without acquiring the attitudes with which it coexists in the West—but, seventy-five years before the Ayatollah Khomeini's overthrow of the Shah in 1979 was fuelled by tape recordings of the exiled leader's speeches, the Japanese believed both in the divinity of their emperor and in efficient naval gunnery. It is perhaps more surprising that secularization has made such slow headway in the West itself.

One reason is that many philosophers and social scientists have been extremely sceptical about the benefits of modernity. Before the end of the nineteenth century, it was clear that progress was a two-edged weapon. Even if they were generally healthier and better fed, working people who had left the country for the town often felt lost and unhappy. The benefits of peace were greater than ever, but the first mechanized wars, such as the American Civil War, had shown what mass slaughter on a scientific basis might look like and had foreshadowed the horrors of the First World War. The prospect of living in a secular society seemed to many critics to be a bleak and cold one. Max Weber, the greatest of modern sociologists, referred to the process of 'disenchantment'—better described by the original German term *Entzauberung*, or 'demagicalization'. In a non-magical world, rational calculation was the only way to survive, but calculation could tell us only how to achieve goals that reason alone could not choose for us.

There was in fact something of a revolt against reason, or, more exactly, a revolt against rationalism, in the social sciences and philosophy at the turn of the century. Weber was an irrationalist only to the extent of claiming that ultimate values are arbitrarily chosen; but, among his followers, Roberto Michels came in the end to embrace fascism as a more satisfying system for linking leaders to followers than any parliamentary regime could be. The French anarcho-syndicalist Georges Sorel, in his *Reflections on Violence* (1908), a work that both Lenin and Mussolini admired, argued for the importance of non-rational myths in forcing social and political change. A myth was not a rational blueprint for a future society, but a vague and indefinite picture around which revolutionary passions could form. In the work of Vilfredo Pareto and his followers, too, politics was understood, not as a way of accommodating interests so much as a terrain on which contenders for power fell and rose as they juggled irrational forces.

Marxism remained aloof from these arguments. A more philosophical, aesthetically oriented, humanist Marx was rediscovered after the Second World War, when his *Economic–Philosophical Manuscripts* (1843) provided ideas such as his theory of alienation that could attract radical social critics who had no time for Stalin's Russia and no taste for economics. For most of the century, Marxism appealed to its adherents as a scientific analysis of class conflict, and the basis of class conflict was the clash of economic interests between the owners of capital and the suppliers of labour. There were revolutionaries such as Leon Trotsky and Rosa Luxemburg—perhaps even Lenin himself—whose ability to infuse their followers with insurrectionary energy seemed to have rather little to do with the scientific validity of Marxian economics, but, in ambition at any rate, Marxism was a form of 'scientific socialism'.

The greatest assault on rationalism, so far as both the lay mind and sophisticated intellectuals were concerned, came from psychoanalytic theory. To say so is unfair to Sigmund Freud himself, who wanted to strengthen the role of reason in human life, and thought of his work with patients as allowing them to exercise an intelligent control of hitherto irrational and uncontrolled impulses. Freud was undoubtedly the most important figure of the movement. He was the first to startle his readers with the claim that our behaviour is to a great degree driven by desires of which we are systematically unaware, because those desires, frequently sexual and destructive in nature, are unavowable to other people and even to ourselves. Freud never claimed to have discovered the unconscious; rather, he claimed to have given a scientific account of its workings. That claim has worn badly over the past century, but poets, painters, novelists, and dramatists have all drawn inspiration from Freud's ideas. The analytic movement has always been a house divided, however. Alfred Adler thought a will to power rather than an urge for sexual satisfaction was fundamental, while Carl Jung attracted adherents who flinched at Freud's atheism and at his conviction that people who have not achieved psychic health when young will never achieve it. It is to Jung that we owe such ideas as that of the mid-life crisis as well as a good deal of New Age mysticism.

Marxism, psychoanalytic theory, and much of modern sociology are the somewhat estranged offspring of German philosophy. German philosophy had long displayed a tension between the ambitions of rationalists who followed Immanuel Kant in trying to give an account of the permanent structures of human reason and perception and the scepticism of anti-rationalists who thought that the modern world's hankering after reason and order was an act of bad faith. Friedrich Nietzsche died at the dawning of the century, and had been in a catatonic state for many years before he died, but his impact on literary and social critics if anything increased. The figure of the amoral Superman whose project of self-exploration took precedence over all social duties and institutional obligations took to the stage and the pages of the novel in every European country. In the twentieth century, the most important irrationalist philosophy was existentialism, forever associated with Jean-Paul Sartre and articulated not only in his *Being and Nothingness* of 1943, but in a series of plays and novels including the novel-trilogy, *Chemins de la liberté* (1945–50).

Sartre's master was the German philosopher Martin Heidegger, one of the two or three most influential philosophers of the century. In spite of his notorious readiness to ingratiate himself with the Nazis, few could resist the appeal of his vision. It was Heidegger who described us as 'thrown into the world', afflicted with *angst*, and cursed rather than blessed with freedom—for what makes us free is the knowledge that there are no rationally defensible answers to the questions 'who am I, what must I do?'. Heidegger's influence on modern theology as well as on what has come to be labelled postmodernism has been incalculable.

Not all German-speaking philosophers subscribed to such ideas. The 'Vienna Circle' that formed in the early 1920s and was forced to disband with the arrival of the Nazis in 1938 as its members fled to England, France, and the USA adhered to a positivism that in one form or another dictated what philosophers in the English-speaking world found interesting for many years after the Second World War. And Ludwig Wittgenstein was at the centre of two distinct philosophical revolutions; his *Tractatus Logico-Philosophicus* (1921) inspired the search for a logically and epistemologically pure account of the relationship between language and the world, while his posthumously published *Philosophical Investigations* (1958) showed why such a search was futile.

English-speaking philosophers generally agreed that the most persuasive accounts of the world were provided by science and mathematics rather than by poetry or religion. In England, Bertrand Russell was notorious for abandoning almost every position he adopted, but he never abandoned the view that the task of philosophy was to explain how we could know what we do know of the world. In the USA, pragmatism was a so far unique instance of an indigenous philosophical movement sprung from the fertile minds of C. S. Peirce, William James, and John Dewey. It was, as its adherents said, a form of 'radical empiricism', in as much as it did not take even the existence of the self and the mind for granted, but tried to give a naturalistic account of these, too. But pragmatists were confident that science was the royal road to truth, and thought the task of philosophy was to give an account of its working.

To the lay public, these forms of philosophy seemed unsatisfying; they did not readily yield a philosophy of life. Although Russell spent much of his life in a variety of radical good causes, he maintained that he did not do so as a philosopher; and John Dewey's impact on American education was not accompanied by any widespread understanding of his philosophy. The public's thirst for philosophical uplift was more likely to be slaked by such movements as Mme Blavatsky's Theosophy, or the ideas of popularizers of Indian mysticism such as Krishnamurti. To the present day successive waves of gurus have found a particularly warm welcome in the western USA.

The twentieth century has thus been a century in which modernizers and traditionalists, rationalists and mystics, have battled one another, both globally and within particular societies. It is in the natural sciences that modernization has met least resistance, and states have generally taken few pains to protect their citizens against new scientific ideas. This is true only in the broadest terms, however. In the USA the teaching of evolution was forbidden in the state of Tennessee as late as the 1920s; more impressively, Stalin all but wrecked Soviet biology by insisting that it must be consistent with the Marxist dialectic. As a result, the Soviet geneticist Trofim Lysenko (1898–1976) could suppress both his rivals and the evidence that disproved his claim that plants could pass on environmentally acquired characteristics. Only on the fall of Nikita Khrushchev in 1964 was Lysenko exposed as a charlatan. The damage this nonsense did to Soviet agriculture is incalculable. Before the Second World War, Nazi Germany drove many of its most distinguished scientists into exile, both Jewish scientists and non-Jewish liberals who sympathized with their persecuted colleagues; the damage this did to Germany's war efforts is hard to guess, but it certainly did no good. It certainly meant that the Allied powers could draw on some very distinguished refugee scientists to develop the atomic bomb.

One explanation for the relaxed attitude of those in authority to the diffusion of scientific knowledge is that the results of scientific research have become more and more inaccessible to the public. The broad idea of Darwinian evolution—that man was not created by God but evolved from primate ancestors he shares with gorillas and chimpanzees—was easy to understand and it caused pain as a result. The detailed analysis of the humane genome will have much more effect on our everyday lives, but is mostly impossible for non-experts to follow. It is, therefore, not as unsettling as it ought perhaps to be. The decoding of the DNA and RNA sequences that carry the information necessary for life to sustain itself by Francis Crick and James Watson, for which they received the Nobel Prize in 1962, struck the popular imagination because of the 'double-helix' shape that these long molecules adopt. But, apart from a vague fear of the potential hazards of genetic engineering, lay appreciation of the astonishing advances of molecular biology and associated sciences has gone no further.

The impact of Einstein's relativistic physics on intellectuals with only the slightest understanding of the natural sciences was an exception to this pattern, though its impact was not unlike that of Darwin's account of evolution. What affected the public was not the implications for *physics* but two thoughts. One was the wholly erroneous inference that relativistic physics somehow supported moral relativism, the idea that good and evil are a matter of perspective, relative to one's individual or social origins. The other was that, even in physics, the subjective standpoint of the observer made all the difference to what could be seen or understood. Heisenberg's Principle of Uncertainty, according to which we could not know both the position and the velocity of subatomic particles in orbit around a nucleus, perhaps had even more of an impact on intellectuals, who concluded that science had revealed that the world was at bottom not rationally explicable at all. Needless to say, the 'uncertainty' that critics and social commentators had in mind was very different from the uncertainty that had been introduced into physics.

Given the authority of the physical sciences, it seemed a striking thing that subjectivity and uncertainty had been reintroduced into the world by the scientific forces that previously appeared to have expelled them. Such ideas reinforced the anti-rationalist turn that had been taken by social scientists and psychologists at the end of the nineteenth century, and gave rise to the sense that Freud and Einstein had somehow allied to defend moral and cultural relativism. For the most part, however, science has been a culturally disturbing force more indirectly, by way of its technological impact. The cultural consequences of the automobile provide an obvious example. The motor car was a nineteenth-century invention, but its effect on the courtship rituals of American teenagers was first noticed in the 1920s, and these effects spread as its use spread.

The effect of the automobile on the cities of the rich countries of the world has been disastrous, and in poor countries seems likely to be much worse. This is not a matter of the noise and pollution it has brought, which are slighter than an equal number of horse-drawn vehicles would have created. Cities in which the motorists' need for easy access and speedy egress has prevailed over the pedestrians' and city-dwellers' needs have become much less attractive places in which to live. The culture of the city essentially needs to be enjoyed on foot, without the interference of motor traffic, but recapturing the city for pedestrian life has proved to be extremely difficult.

Among benign technologies, medicine made few advances until the 1920s, although antiseptics and anaesthetics had already made surgery less painful and less dangerous during the last half of the previous century. The impotence of medicine in the face of viral and bacterial infections was strikingly displayed in the influenza pandemic of the winter of 1918–19, which in a few months killed at least 20 million people in Europe alone, or rather more than twice the number of soldiers who had died of wounds and disease in the First World War. But, with the wide availability of antibiotics after 1945, doctors have much reduced deaths from diphtheria, tuberculosis, and a host of other infectious diseases. Once-familiar terrors, such as poliomyelitis, have been largely eliminated from well-off countries, and smallpox has been wholly eradicated. One profound cultural effect has been dramatically to reduce the infant mortality of poor countries; in due course, this will lead to a reduction of the birth rate, but over the past fifty years the effect has been to increase the numbers of children and of underemployed young people, with obvious consequences for the political volatility of such countries.

This volatility is an instance of a general phenomenon: so far from technological change painlessly carrying liberal, democratic values in its train, its effect has often been to increase the potency of illiberal, irrational, and anti-democratic forces. The radio broadcasts of Radio Free Europe and the Voice of America may have done something to weaken the former Soviet Union, and West German television did more to weaken the so-called German Democratic Republic; but the transistor radio has been a blessing to demagogues and those bent on stirring religious and ethnic strife.

Indeed, societies have been astonishingly apt at absorbing techniques without changing their cultural attachments. It is not surprising that they have adopted military technology in this fashion, though the Western mind still finds the *kamikaze* suicide pilots of the closing months of the last war as hard to comprehend as Islamic suicide bombers in the Middle East and Tamil suicide bombers in Sri Lanka. What is more surprising is the ways in which new artistic technologies have been given a local cultural twist. The Indian film industry is a striking example; the studios of Bombay turn out far more films than Hollywood, recently as many as 800 a year. Unlike the films made by Indian directors such as Satajayit Ray, which were instantly admired by Western film-goers used to the work of Federico Fellini and other realist directors of the 1950s, these mass-produced films have no counterpart in the Western cinema. In their mixture of melodrama, song, and the intervention of the gods, they are nearer to Homer on celluloid than to the offerings of Twentieth Century Fox. By the same token, the universal spread of television has seen the diffusion of American soap operas such as *Dallas* throughout the globe, the creation of programmes for local consumption that are unintelligible outside their immediate locality, together with some curious migrations, such as the smashing success of the Mexican soap opera *Wild Roses* in Russia.

The cultural impact of the new media on the Western societies in which they originated has been great, but not wholly easy to assess. Film offered quite novel ways of telling stories; some critics have said that directors of the silent-film era found ways of telling a story through visual means alone that the 'talkies' could not emulate for years. The sound track slowed viewers' visual response as they tried to make sure that they had heard what was going on. Only when audiences had come to terms with sound films could film-makers again play with the visual narrative as they had before. What is harder to know is how either the form or the content of the new medium of entertainment has affected its audiences.

The century's most famous, or notorious, theorist of the mass media, the Canadian philosopher and critic Marshall McLuhan, observed that mankind invents new tools and then the new tools change their makers. What is extremely hard to discern, however, is quite what effects the media have had on their creators. The fact that D. W. Griffith's masterpiece *The Birth of a Nation* (1915) was a racist celebration of the southern states' resistance to Reconstruction, and a glorification of the Ku Klux Klan, has long been a deep embarrassment to admirers of the great silent films, and their embarrassment is paralleled by the embarrassment caused by Leni Riefenstahl's *Triumph of the Will* (1935). All the same, it is not clear that the devotees of racial segregation or the admirers of Hitler were strengthened in their unfortunate faiths by these films. Similarly, Sergei Eisenstein's *Battleship Potemkin* (1925) probably did more to remind its audience of the Party's falling away from its revolutionary past than to inspire loyalty to the new Soviet state.

The effect of film, strengthened over the second half of the century by television, may well have been greatest at a subliminal level. Film and television may have done more to change the way people gain information and handle it than to move their thoughts in any particular direction. This is not a gain for rationality. Rationality demands that we stand back from first impressions, however strong they may be, but visual media rely on first impressions to carry conviction; in the USA especially, but everywhere else to a lesser extent, the effect on political discussion has been to reduce the exchange of opinion to 'sound bites'. Early fears—or hopes—that television would create a 'global village' have, therefore, not been realized, save in the sense that the world resembles a village of dysfunctional families who are not on speaking terms with each other.

Dictatorial governments find it easy enough to make sure that what appears on television is unthreatening to the regime. This is not because they find it easy to produce lively material supportive of their government. For instance, the military government of General Ershad in the mid-1980s reduced television in Bangladesh to spectacular dullness. In a country too poor and too puritanical to import frivolous and unthreatening entertainment such as *Dynasty* and *Dallas*—the soap operas with which the apartheid government of South Africa narcotized white citizens in its final decade—Bangladeshi television broadcast endless monologues by its notably uncharismatic rulers. Pirate television is not the threat that pirate radio is: it has been too dependent on bulky equipment to lend itself to pirate transmissions in the way radio does, and the television signal has too short a range.

This may change. Where dictatorial states border freer states, they cannot prevent their citizens from watching their neighbours' broadcasts. West German television did much to convince East Germans that their lives were needlessly drab and circumscribed. Satellite broadcasting, too, offers the prospect of beaming unwanted television programmes into any country whatever. This has not yet played a part in undermining the political leadership of any actual society, but the possibility that it might has already occurred to the government of China. The largest British commercial operator of satellite television dropped BBC World Service news programmes from its Asian programming at the behest of the Chinese Communist government.

Although the television and film industries have been spectacular commercial successes, the moving picture is by no means the only visual medium to make an impact on the twentieth century. Among the areas in which the interplay of colonial and colonized cultures has been most vivid, that of modern painting and sculpture is a very obvious one. In a curious reversal of effects, as modern art became increasingly divorced from popular culture, it also became more hospitable to forms that it acquired from alien cultures. This was not exactly a variation on what Paul Gauguin had done when he went to Tahiti in 1891 and painted local subjects. It was more nearly an acknowledgement that Oceanic sculptures and textiles, Benin bronzes, and other African artefacts satisfied a modern, Western, highly sophisticated taste for non-literalism—that is, for uncovering something about form or structure that the surface appearance obscures. It is thus not surprising that a constantly inventive painter like Picasso should have been both a Cubist and employed images from Oceania in his work.

The search for an authentically 'modern' style in art, architecture, music, poetry, and imaginative literature has not gone in one single direction. In architecture and industrial design, the principle that 'form follows function' has had some credibility; an aircraft built on Baroque or Victorian Gothic lines would suffer so badly from turbulence and wind resistance that it would be unflyable. Automobiles of a slippery design consume less fuel. All the same, the functionalist aesthetic was far from being a simple outgrowth of a search for efficiency; the most famous of all streamlined automobiles, the Chrysler Airflow of 1934, hardly needed the streamlining it was given. Even today few cars spend so much time at speeds above 75 miles an hour that their slipperiness matters very much. The Airflow's aesthetic properties were not an offshoot of its functional properties; rather, the streamlined appearance was deeply attractive in all sorts of settings from the Chrysler Building in New York onwards, and it became a decorative trope.

In something of the same way, modern painting could go in an almost infinite variety of directions just because a self-conscious modernity could mean among other things a search for the barest and thinnest structure beneath the visible world, an acknowledgement that, with the invention of photography, the purpose of art could not be literally representative and might therefore involve any amount of playful manipulation of appearances, or a happy luxuriating in the fact that the past could be exploited in innumerable ways, and so on indefinitely. Nothing else could explain why such different artistic movements as Surrealism, Cubism, the suprematist movement of the early Soviet Revolution, the Pop Art of Roy Lichtenstein and Claes Oldenburg, German Expressionism, and the aleatoric paintings of Jackson Pollock, and others are all properly described as 'modern'.

What is true of what are no longer the figurative arts has been true of literature and music as well. The early twentieth century was perhaps the high point of the realist novel, with George Gissing in Britain and Jack London in the USA. Yet the more characteristic 'high' culture product of the century has been the experimental novel; it is such names as Thomas Mann, whose most famous novel, *The Magic Mountain*, was published in 1924, James Joyce, whose *Ulysses* appeared in 1922, and Virginia Woolf, who published *To the Lighthouse* in 1927, that define the history of the novel in the earlier twentieth century. Although the novel began as a European art form, it has become thoroughly global; from Latin America there has come the 'magic realist' novel of which Gabriel García Márquez, the author of *One Hundred Years of Solitude* (1967), is perhaps the greatest exponent, while the list of prize winners of the Nobel Prize for Literature suggests the novel's appeal in Egypt, India, Japan, and elsewhere. The popular novel has been almost entirely untouched by experiment; changes there have been, but only in the same direction as the popular culture has taken—a greater tolerance of explicit sexual description, a greater acceptance of the existence of dysfunctional families, more rapid and violent action.

In poetry and the theatre, the same search for a self-consciously 'modern' mode has taken place. Once again, however, the interesting contrast has lain between the experimentation that has defined high culture and the conservatism of the popular stage. Western playwrights and directors have experimented with the techniques of the Japanese No play, the proscenium arch has been abandoned for theatre in the round, or the apron stage of Shakespeare's day, and even, on occasion, for performances in which the actors are interspersed among the spectators. To the consternation of experimentalists, however, it has been conventional drama that has drawn the crowds; Agatha Christie's *The Mousetrap* has been playing to London audiences since 1952, while the most successful musical comedies of the last three decades of the century have been the elaborately staged but intellectually and musically undemanding productions of Andrew Lloyd Webber.

It is more debatable where the important lines of cleavage have lain in the field of music. In the work of composers such as Arnold Schoenberg, Anton von Webern, Igor Stravinsky, and Alban Berg the old rules of harmony were discarded, and experiments with highly formalized musical structures such as twelve-tone composition took place. But experimenters took their inspiration from many places; Bela Bartók was influenced by Hungarian folk music as well as by atonalism, and Stravinsky, after scandalizing even the Parisians with *The Rite of Spring* (1913), later turned to Pergolesi for some of his most famous ballet scores. Folk musics of many different kinds continue to have a life of their own and to influence high art. Jazz, for instance, grew out of the songs of Black American field slaves, but by the time we arrive at Ornette Coleman it has lost its simple melodic line and its foot-stomping rhythms while remaining jazz rather than anything else.

The line between popular music and the music of the concert hall has curiously been both sharp and debatable. The reason, perhaps, is that popular music itself has constantly been subverted by alien influences; in the 1950s, rock and roll scandalized listeners, perhaps as much because it involved borrowings from Black rhythm and blues as because it was loud, raucous, and appealed to teenagers bent on destroying cinemas and concert halls. At all events, most popular music in the West is based on sentimental ballads that neither teenagers attracted to the latest version of grunge or heavy metal nor the audience for twentieth-century classical music can bear to listen to. The one thing we can say about all forms of popular music is that they have become a global cultural form; the Rolling Stones are a British band that sells out concerts in Tokyo as readily as in Los Angeles and Paris. The world of teenage consumer culture is very much McWorld.

In fact, modern cultural change seems to follow the course of demographic change. As the world's population has become younger and more mobile, an international youth culture has sprung up in which tastes in clothes, music, and leisure activities have become strikingly uniform while social and political allegiances have not. Serb snipers in the former Yugoslavia wear cheap copies of Levi jeans while avenging the Serbian defeat in the fourteenth-century Battle of Kosovo. In something of the same way, the youthful taste for experiment has fuelled the growth of an international drug culture. Until the early twentieth century narcotic and psychotropic drugs were not a source of great anxiety to governments or medical science. Opium dens feature prominently in Victorian thrillers, but heroin addiction was not a social problem. Only during the First World War did the United States discover that marijuana was a dangerous drug. Seventy years later, the paradox is that in the developed world much drug-taking is 'recreational' in the sense that it appeals to people who consume marijuana, cocaine, and various amphetamine derivatives casually, to heighten their experience of music, dance, or sex, and never become addicted, while at the other end of the spectrum lie the severely addicted whose need for their poison leads them to robbery and murder. All evidence suggests that, independently of their criminal status, psychotropic drugs, even including crack cocaine, do less medical damage and lead to less violence and to fewer deaths by accident than do legal drugs such as alcohol—responsible for some 40 per cent of all vehicular deaths in developed countries—and tobacco—which contributes to a quarter of all deaths from cancer and heart disease in those same countries. Quite what the effects of decriminalizing psychotropic drugs would be nobody knows. Estimates vary from a higher incidence of use but a lower incidence of addiction and crime to a vast increase in addiction. Once more, there is space here to do no more than gesture at the enormous difference between the cultural settings in which British and American teenagers take Ecstasy and a Peruvian peasant chews coca leaves while carrying heavy loads in the high Andes and what this means for anyone wanting to make such predictions.

In short, the twentieth century has seen cultural paradoxes galore. A popular culture spread by films, television, and popular music, and also today by the clothing styles attached to these, is as near as makes no difference universal; young people who are financially able to join this culture do so. Even regimes that disapprove and try to roll back its incursions have limited successes, as witness Saudi Arabia, Iran, and the PRC. Poverty rather than the vitality of traditional culture is the barrier to its spread in most countries, and it is hard to believe that the theocratic states that are its other great foe will be able to resist for ever. At the same time, our appetite for cultural difference and cultural variety is growing. American tourists gape at Mayan ruins and puzzle over their meaning. Indonesian hotels put on performances of the Ramayana for Australians. Prosperous Taiwanese tour Oxford and Cambridge colleges. And yet there may be no paradox. No two households in a village lead exactly the same lives as each other. As the world becomes truly a global village, we can expect its different national households to be as insistent as ever on what distinguishes each of them from all the others.

7 The Visual Arts

NORBERT LYNTON

From the vantage point of a century hence, twentieth-century art will certainly be seen as a phase in the continuing story of Romanticism, a climax in its programme of rejecting time-honoured models and authority in favour of relativism and individualism. It may appear a headlong phase, driven by a taste for change exceeding each generation's desire to disown its parents.

It will be seen as a period productive of great art. New work, thought destructive of artistic values, will come to be enjoyed for positive characteristics not acknowledged even by its champions. Just as Impressionism has turned out to be the most popular kind of art ever, so the charms of Cubism will soon be obvious to all, as will those of the broad category we call abstract painting in which the elements of picture-making are explored as self-sufficient means of visual poetry. It merely requires a shift of attention from the negatives signalling change to the positives it released. However radical the intention, however fierce the calls for destroying art's heritage (first heard in the name of Neoclassicism, around 1800), the result has been an art embodying positive, constructive passions. The arts do not destroy any heritage; they add.

In everyday life, images have become commonplace and transient. André Malraux recognized the 'imaginary museum' as a modern creation, by which we survey the art of all periods and places via illustrations. Today the computer promises even readier access to all known art. Ultimately this may prove what mass reproduction obscured, that art can be experienced only at first hand.

Change will be seen to have been accompanied by phases of concentration and expansion, all with their positive aspects. The quantity of artists and output leapt during the twentieth century, partly because the demotion of hard-won skills and the development of new techniques have made some art quicker to produce. While children have been encouraged to make art following their instincts, youngsters have been offered basic art training in schools, and professional training, once isolated in academies, flourishes in institutions of higher education. Neither gender nor class status blocks careers in art. Meanwhile Western art and architecture have absorbed influences from other cultures and in return become global. International exhibitions, arranged in national sections from almost every part of the world, have seen national characteristics shrink before the desire to be abreast the latest developments in the promotional centres of modern art. Competitions for major new buildings attract international submissions, and commissions go as often to foreigners as to natives. Whether the future will bring a further erosion of local idioms by the pull of the best promoted styles, or see regionalist reactions aided by deeper awareness, time will show. Early Modernism, essentially a Western event, showed an appetite for non-Western influences, and modern architecture has drawn on vernacular sources and then also on worldwide traditions for stylistic and at times functional reasons. There have been many indications that, especially, countries in cultural transition have felt the need to bring valued religious or other ethnic elements into the international mix—for example, in some Israeli, Indian, and African work. There is also growing attention to local needs, especially in architecture.

All this implies the instability of the centres of modern art. In 1900 Paris was the centre for the study and practice of modern art. After 1950, partly because of the disturbances wrought by war, New York, having made a relatively modest contribution to modern art except by collecting it, became the place to watch and be known in. Now some of the limelight has gone to such other centres as Berlin, Rome, and London. Plurality has taken over in this respect as in others.

Plurality was what modern architecture first had to escape from and to which, after a period of coherence that came to seem authoritarian, it has returned. Nineteenth-century architects were burdened with too much data, historical and technical, and developed the conviction that new kinds of architecture were needed to satisfy new requirements. Engineering offered dramatic new forms, but could these be adapted to become architecture? Could they themselves be architecture? One iron and glass Crystal Palace (1851, London) could not make an architectural summer, but the polarity it established was restated by bridges and such constructions as the Eiffel Tower, built to be a temporary exhibition feature (1889, Paris), and answered by more craft-like architectural design rooted in traditional needs and materials. Here was another way of eluding the pull of historical styles, to adopt and adapt vernacular idioms and building methods. Frank Lloyd Wright did this dramatically in America with his 'Prairie Houses' of the 1890s and after, at the same time as Charles Annesley Voysey and Charles Rennie Mackintosh and other British architects were designing their at once strikingly original and 'Olde World' houses. Their influence on Continental Europe was marked. The two poles, engineering and design without highbrow styles, were to some extent bridged, thanks to the urge towards a new architectural language, in Art Nouveau and *Jugendstil*. Much done then was too individualistic, but those years around 1900 saw also serious research into new building methods, notably the use of reinforced concrete and of standardized elements, and into the language of forms as such. Here design and art worked in tandem. On both sides there were efforts to bring analytical methods to bear in testing or developing first principles.

Named movements have shaped our knowledge of modern art. Some of these are represented as dominating certain periods—such as Cubism during 1910–20 and Abstract Expressionism from c. 1945. Abstract Expressionism, the work first of disparate New York artists in close contact, became an American and European movement and found adherents around the globe; though these shared some stylistic qualities, their purposes were too varied not to turn the pioneering movement into an international fashion. Almost instantly movements, narrow and relatively specific (Fauvism, Futurism, Dadaism, Constructivism, De Stijl, Op Art, Minimalism) or broad ranges of activity gathered under a slogan term (Expressionism, Surrealism, Conceptualism), became containers into which art was packaged for public consumption, with and without parallel activities in the other arts, and the story of twentieth-century art is still told as a succession of these. Many other groups and movements emerged to be quickly forgotten. Any historian knows that this story can at best be a mnemonic aid to what happened and that it was created by critics and curators whose first business was to promote and persuade. Recent formulations, such as Neo-Dada, Neo-Expressionist, Neo-Geometric, and Neo-Conceptual, as well as the notion of Postmodernism in art (in architecture it makes some sense), rely on culpable ignorance of the movements whose demise they assume. The vaunted rebirth of figurative painting around 1980 depended on ignorance of the significant (let alone conventional) figurative work done in the 1960s and 1970s; decades occupied, we were told by influential critics, by abstract painting and Conceptual art yet witnessing the figurative work of Pop and Photorealist artists, old modern masters such as Picasso (until 1973) and Balthus in France, Philip Guston (a senior Abstract Expressionist returning to figuration in 1970), Alex Katz and others in the United States, Francis Bacon, Lucien Freud, Frank Auerbach and others in Britain, as well as the emergence and first fame of the German Neo-Expressionists, including Anselm Kiefer and Sigmar Polke, during the 1960s.

More important than stylistic movements have been certain focal points of enquiry and achievement. The Symbolist movement of the end of the nineteenth century provided a basis for much that followed. Modernism (by which is meant here all twentieth-century non-reactionary art) at first eschewed art's attachment to literary content. It emulated Symbolism's focus on the communicative force of each art's essential constituents, as in Mallarmé's enrolment of the resonance of every word, and its quasi-religious ambition to engage and validate all experience, preached and demonstrated by Richard Wagner. The former made for economy and could ally itself to calls for primitivism and purity earlier voiced in Neoclassicism and then also in other aspects of Romanticism, such as the German Nazarenes' and the English Pre-Raphaelites' rejection of High Renaissance suaveties. The latter fitted the nineteenth century's taste for ample and inclusive work offering a total experience. Wagner wanted opera as a *Gesamtkunstwerk*, an interaction of verbal drama, musical drama, and new methods of theatrical presentation. This echoed the Baroque's desire to offer ecstasy. If the twentieth century could seem chary of emotional surrender, it in fact invited it by other means: in the overpowering experience of the cinema, the *Realpolitik* rallies of Nazi Germany, and soon in 'virtual reality' entertainment. This desire to involve spectators in a complex experience showed in Modernism's interest in Happenings and Performance Art (both from about 1950 on; performances of an often partly spontaneous sort in a prepared setting, at times calling for audience participation) and Installation Art (a prepared setting which the spectator enters; from about the same date on, but pioneered in late Surrealist exhibitions in which individual exhibits were subsumed by a dramatic environment). These propose the opposite to the Mallarméan quest for the succinct word, sound, or image, yet the succinct, severely distilled art of Mondrian and the Dutch *De Stijl* group (1917+) was offered as a model for a shining civilization of the future in which art itself would no longer be needed, while Minimalist Art (1965+) offered simple forms in two or three dimensions sensitizing viewers to the power of visual and haptic experience. *De Stijl* orthodoxy linked up with Neoclassicism's taste for clarity and economy to provide the basis of what became an International Style in architecture in the 1920s.

A related polarity is found in Modernism's desire both to assert the autonomy of each art form and to dissolve each art form's normative bounds. Painting, in 1900 unquestionably *the* Western art form, has continued as *a* major art form in spite of hearing its death announced many times. 'Remember that, more than being a battle horse, a nude woman or some anecdote, a painting is essentially a flat surface covered with colours arranged in a certain order.' This statement of 1890, by the painter Maurice Denis, made memorable a principle governing much of what later became known as Post-Impressionism: the work of painters developing out of and away from Impressionism, including such key figures as Gauguin and Redon (both directly associated with Symbolism), Van Gogh, Seurat, Cézanne, and then Munch, Matisse, and Bonnard. And it clearly led to abstract painting, mostly under Symbolist influence and with symbolical aims, as in Delaunay, Kandinsky, and Malevich (all around 1913). Yet this development owed much to quasi-religious tendencies pressing for attention to spiritual concerns and associated with cosmic speculations, as well as to the investigations of Art Nouveau and *Jugendstil*. Many Modernist artists have made finding the point of balance between exploiting artistic means and offering a legible subject the core of their work, outstanding amongst them Matisse, Mondrian, Brancusi, Giacometti, Moore, and De Kooning.

Rodin had called sculpture 'the art of the hole and the lump', yet manifested a Symbolist desire to move us through narrative and imprecise references; if much of his work explored expressive form at the expense of naturalism, most obviously his small, modelled pieces, his *Gates of Hell* (begun 1880; left incomplete at his death in 1917) was a sort of sculptural opera, influenced by Baroque painting and exceeding sculpture's normal remit. It was the thought of 'the hole and the lump' that has dominated Modernist sculpture, often in combination with another slogan, that of 'truth to materials'. Sculpture, like painting, had aimed at a technical perfection: stone (like paint) could seem to become flesh or paint sky, air, light. Carving was often done by specialist craftsmen armed with mechanical aids enabling them to make full-scale stone versions of the master sculptor's modelled clay or plaster maquette. Now 'truth to materials' called on sculptors to do their own carving but also to create in the process, responding to the nature of the particular piece of stone or wood. Historically the key event in this development was the hand-sized stone *The Kiss* carved by Brancusi in 1907–8 and left looking very much like a block of stone. Brancusi, of Rumanian peasant origin, had refused a place in Rodin's workshop. His dramatically primitive sculpture answered Rodin's large marble *The Kiss* (1898), widely admired but also censured for its explicit sexuality. Brancusi's inexplicit representation now seems the more passionate image. In other works that soon followed, modelled as well as carved, Brancusi showed how expression became fullest when form was most closely identified with the material. Moreover, in polishing his later bronzes he minimized their presence as solids, making them things of light and apparent transparency.

Le Corbusier's *Dom-ino* (1914–15), in its way as primitivist as Brancusi's *Kiss*, was logical in regard to function, material, and process. It was conceived as a way of building new houses partly from the rubble left by the war, but now looks like the first clear example of what became the International Style. The skeleton is functional and would in use disappear behind many sorts of walls and windows, but it proposed for housing a minimal aesthetic found in advanced factory design, as in Gropius's Fagus Factory (1911, Alfeld, Germany), with the same separation of structure from infilling and the same readiness to let style arise from rationally used materials. Here again design and art found a common principle, and with it moral overtones.

The combination of craftsmanlike care for the medium and a primitivist attention to its natural character found full expression in Klee's principle of letting images arise from a dialogue between the artist and the media and formal elements he was using. This genetic process is the opposite of the preparation required by traditional high art; it called instead for intimacy with the means of art and for trust in quasi-natural processes of development. In a period often associated with artists of more than normal arrogance and self-centredness, it implies yielding the controlling function. This is echoed in the other arts (e.g. Stravinsky's statement that he was the vessel through which *The Rite of Spring* reached us) and took many forms, serious and playful. Duchamp's 'readymades', things taken from the common world and designated as art by being offered for exhibition as art (1913+), cancelled the artist's role as inventor yet left him with the godlike one of working a sort of apotheosis by will alone. At much the same time Jean (Hans) Arp enrolled chance as his collaborator in making abstract collages.

The several kinds of stylistic primitivism found in art from the 1880s on, distinguishable from that in Neoclassicism and Pre-Raphaelitism in its attention to non-European sources, also implies a relinquishing of control. Imitation had long been a central academic principle, meaning learning from and quoting the great masters of the Renaissance and of antiquity. To imitate artefacts hitherto thought merely curious was a radical innovation. It was not Oriental art at its finest but cheap nineteenth-century Japanese woodblock prints that caught the attention of Manet and the Impressionists because of their non-perspectival design and flat colours and patterns. Gauguin turned from quoting Breton peasant art to adapting Javanese figures (as Rodin did) before abandoning civilization for the primitive life and culture of the South Seas. Derain's and Picasso's use of African and other tribal artefacts in their work of 1906+ was even more challenging, since Oriental culture was recognized as sophisticated. Russia's sudden enthusiasm for its own tradition of icon painting, affecting new art from about 1908 on, was equally surprising. Interest in folk art as well as in medieval practices had been made into a programme of craft and design reform by William Morris and others, but Modernism extended this radically by looking for instruction to the art of children and the insane, in other words to anyone untouched by conventional politenesses. Surrealism's attempt to penetrate to pre-civilized levels of the human psyche was an extension of this campaign. Modernism's interest in 'low' art, notably its urban forms from advertisements to comic strips and graffiti, stemmed from recognition that these have a proven power that 'high' art often lacks. Cubism and Futurism liked to dip into the 'low' art pool; Pop Art's exploitation of it, in the 1960s, was more exclusive, focusing often on the stylistic strengths and suavities of sophisticated consumer-society images.

Modernist architecture was able to deal with high and low demands, so to speak, with much the same means and forms. The same sort of design that Corbusier proposed for utilitarian mass housing was adapted by him, Mies van der Rohe, Gropius, Oud, and many others for the middle-class and cheaper units put up in Stuttgart in 1927 as the Weissenhof Siedlung, an exhibition of modern housing all in much the same idiom. It was used by Mies for the exquisite ephemeral Barcelona Pavilion (1929), intended to demonstrate the quality of which new German design was capable, its simplicity underlined by fine proportions and semi-precious materials. At the same time Corbusier was demonstrating his system's versatility by using it as the basis for such houses as the Villa Savoye (1928–9, Poissy, France), a white concrete box, partly raised on columns, with a range of slopes and curved elements inside it fitting the needs of well-to-do weekend and summer living. The 1920s were in many respects a period of consolidation, and the architecture of Corbusier, Gropius, Mies, and others, embracing the utopian aesthetic of Constructivism in Russia and the Dutch *De Stijl* movement led by Mondrian and Van Doesburg, became a world idiom, spreading to England, Scandinavia, and back to Russia, and flourishing in the United States partly through its kinship with aspects of the architecture of Louis Sullivan and Frank Lloyd Wright.

The start of this century saw Impressionism, in some circles still thought destructive of all idealism and skills, generally accepted as a way of describing the world. Its middle witnessed Abstract Expressionism sweeping the international board. Associated first with Jackson Pollock's large canvases articulated by swirls and drips of paint, and with Willem de Kooning's first apparently abstract, then aggressively figurative images in vehement brushstrokes and colours—both exhibited from about 1948 on—and then with the controlled, meditative colour compositions of older painters such as Mark Rothko, Barnett Newman, and Clyfford Still, the new American painting met with initial resistance in the United States but was soon promoted around the world as evidence of America's new cultural confidence. By the mid-1950s Europe had its own variants with such names as Tachism, *L'Art autre*, and *Art informel*. The American movement was associated with the size and old pioneering spirit of the United States, the European kind too often with a sort of visual Existentialism bred by the continuing threat of destruction. What they shared was not a style but an attitude to imagery and materials, and an appetite for intense personal expression combined with archetypal meanings. The headlong success of this art in the 1950s masked wide disparities in quality and modality. If some painters, such as Jackson Pollock and Willem de Kooning in the United States, Jean Fautrier in France and Roger Hilton in Britain, and Karel Appel, a Dutch member of the Cobra group, achieved dramatic new uses of paint, with and without figuration, leaving us in some doubt as to the emotions expressed, others, such as Clyfford Still and the Russian-born Mark Rothko in the United States and the Spaniard Antoni Tàpies, achieved remarkably strong and enduring statements with limited, controlled means. Their best works suggest sublime experiences before the face of nature akin to those of the great Romantics. The wide range of Abstract Expressionism demonstrated a general preference for emotional over intellectual content; it was justified by contemporary critics as a form of venturing 'into the unknown'. Under American influence, Japan contributed the lessons of traditional calligraphy to extend painting's expressive means.

Sculpture could contribute little directly to this development but sought to counter it. In several ways the sculpture of Picasso, and that of Henry Moore, developing impulses derived from Brancusi and Picasso as well as from ancient works seen in museums, had in the 1930s and 1940s given new life to the figurative tradition by involving it in bold metamorphoses. Subsequently their sculptures were to be set up in public places around the world, returning to sculpture some of the prominence it had lost since the seventeenth century. The 1950s saw much grim or elegant figurative sculpture, reflecting the war and a desire for pleasure, but also a turning to abstract sculpture, mostly in metal and built up by means of welding or bolting together—a significant extension of an art hitherto dependent on carving or on modelling and casting. David Smith the American and Anthony Caro the Briton were leaders in this, showing that here was another limitless field for exploration, not a style. Caro in particular proved the richness of his terrain, inventing images that at times felt like a sort of architecture, at others a kind of music; in his later work he brought in figurative suggestions, even, in the 1990s, specific references to Homer's time-honoured heroes. Attempts to make sculpture more directly associable with Abstract Expressionist painting generally failed; a more effective response was that of the Minimalists of the 1960s, who set up simple but monumental forms which impress viewers in the space of a gallery, and sharpen their perceptions, not unlike Rothko's dramatic juxtapositions of simple painted forms.

The International Style in architecture still flourished after the Second World War, partly in the continuing work of its originators. Yet one of them also produced mysterious new works that questioned its validity. In a sequence of buildings, most strikingly in his Chapel at Ronchamp (1950–4, France), a modelled thing of slopes and flowing curves, with scarcely a straight line or right angle in it, Le Corbusier became primitive and poetic, and monumental in his grandiose designs for the state buildings of a new capital city, Chandigarh (1951+, India) and the vast Unité d'Habitation outside Marseilles (1947–53, France). His example encouraged a more adventurous spirit resulting in buildings of pronounced individuality, each commission being seen as an occasion for a poetic response to its conditions. There have been many successful instances showing this new freedom and responsibility, including Louis I. Kahn's Richards Medical Laboratories in Philadelphia (1957–62, United States), and the Engineering Building of Leicester University by Stirling and Gowan (1959–63, Great Britain). The late 1950s and the 1960s also witnessed a return to radical city design, recalling architects' visions of the immediate post-First World War years, especially in Germany and Russia, where political upheaval created a false utopian dawn. The time had again come to grasp more fully the potentialities offered by technology and the world's need for better control of human and other natural resources. Dreams of a science-fiction sort hardened into ambitious projects for putting economic and ecological considerations first.

The same period brought a demand for intellectual content among young artists. The art situation needed disrupting, and it came through alternative forms, grouped under such labels as Conceptual Art, Land Art, Performance Art. The international success of what was still called avant-garde art, guaranteed by the well-financed interaction of galleries and museums and buoyed up by media interest and glossy art journals, rested on sophistries easily discerned by ambitious artists approaching maturity. Was there no contradiction between the saintly profundities claimed for Abstract Expressionism and all the accompanying hype? What had any of it to do with daily life in a world damaged by war and the possibility of renewed war, by economic spirals, by the threat of ecological disaster, by open racial hostility, with an art world blocked by the success of an ageing generation, leaving younger artists little chance of making their mark?

Artists operated as soothsayers, remote from questions of aesthetics. Marcel Duchamp had turned from painting to questioning the philosophical bases of art, extending the Symbolists' interest in esoteric learning in such works as his elaborate pictorial construction on the theme of sexual frustration, *The Bride Stripped Bare by her Bachelors, Even*, also known as the *Large Glass* (1915–23), a profoundly original work full of learned references and echoing the form of a Renaissance altarpiece. Exhibitions and publications from 1950 on drew attention to 'anti-art' tendencies in Modernism that had largely been forgotten, to Dada ideas and activities, and especially to Duchamp, offering an ironic response to the solemnity with which commentators (but not all practitioners) associated Abstract Expressionism. They were shocked at the coolness of what emerged: the disruptive attitudes and work of Jasper Johns and Robert Rauschenberg in the USA, the enrolment of commercial iconography in serious but often satirical art by Richard Hamilton, Eduardo Paolozzi, and others in Britain, both from the mid-1950s on, as well as an insistently inexpressive kind of abstract painting emerging at the close of the 1950s as Hard-Edge Painting or Post-Painterly Abstraction, and then the eruption of international Pop at the start of the 1960s. Remarkable articulateness and art–political awareness among artists was accompanied by a new sort of elaborately quasi-philosophical but also dictatorial art writing: the symbiosis of art and criticism attained unprecedented intimacy. By the end of the 1960s these alternative art forms and others under such unhelpful battle cries as the New Realism, were being promoted internationally. Mere cleverness seemed enthroned at the expense of sincere expression; the humanity and the poetry of much of what was being done by these artists in denying art-commerce's dependence on saleable art objects became evident only gradually. Many names press forward for notice, most obviously Robert Smithson, Joseph Kossuth, Bruce Naumann, and Jonathan Borofsky (USA), the partners Gilbert and George, Richard Long, Michael Craig-Martin (Britain), Yves Klein and Arman (France), the Bulgarian-born Christo, and the Germans, like Christo active internationally, Joseph Beuys and Hans Haacke. Haacke came to specialize in a campaign of rubbing art-establishment noses in board-of-trustees dirt, as when he proposed an exhibit tracing the hands through which a minor work by Manet had passed to enter Cologne's most prestigious museum collection, and found his exhibition at the museum cancelled. Events of this challenging sort signalled a new relationship between artists and the fat-cat world of major collectors and museums. Beuys made sculptures and installations referring symbolically to his own near-death in the Second World War, and these survive him, but he became famous through his teaching in Düsseldorf and his lectures everywhere on every individual's need to confront political systems. For him art was not a reserved occupation but the first step towards revolutionary action. Painting and assemblages or installations proved their social worth by reaching out to tackle similar issues through images, as in the work of Jannis Kounellis, Robert Longo, and David Salle. None the less, much painting from the late 1970s on confined itself to playing sophisticated games with the images and styles of the past whilst making ironic references to the contemporary world, as in the works of Francisco Clemente, Julian Schnabel, and Mimmo Paladino. The countries of origin of such artists are now irrelevant in view of their international lives, stance, and reputation.

In the 1980s the expression 'Postmodern' was used with increasing frequency to indicate the ending of prescriptions and inhibitions and the birth of a new phase in architecture promising stylistic freedom. A version of the International Style had been adopted by profit-hungry developers, but the games and historicist quotations of so-called Postmodernism have speedily bred their own banalities and routines. The living architecture of the last part of the twentieth century has been represented best in a new sort of Constructivism, involving an enthusiastic acceptance of technical services, of the informalities of the fairground and the temporary exhibition building, together with an outgoing conception of the social life of buildings. The Rogers and Piano Pompidou Centre in Paris (1974–6) was its first clear demonstration, Richard Rogers's Lloyd's Building in London (1979–86) its most sophisticated development; Adolf Krischanitz's Temporary Art Museum (1992) in Vienna's prestigious Karlsplatz, a factory-like structure providing beautiful galleries but stylistically offering only the absence of style, achieves the dignity of true functionalism.

Change shows in three other noteworthy respects. One is that, while there were few woman artists of note in 1900, in the 1990s there are many, though it remains true that the world makes it even more difficult for them than for men to make art their career. Few artists live wholly from their art. Many more women enter art schools than become professional artists or designers, yet many have become well known in the modern art world. This began to be noticeable in the 1910s and 1920s, notably in Germany and Russia, and has been more continuously the case since 1950: outstanding names include, from the early period, Käthe Kollwitz, Alexandra Exter, and Lyubov Popova, and, from the later, Germaine Richier, Bridget Riley, Agnes Martin, Marina Abramovic, and Eva Hesse. The second relates to a form of art and art-thinking developed in Russia about 1920 that divided soon after: Constructivism, either applying artistic inventiveness and knowledge to immediate practical needs in Productivism or exploring areas of ideas and methods close to those of mathematics and science as Constructive Art. Vladimir Tatlin was the key figure at the start; Naum Gabo and others brought Constructive Art to the West with immediate effect. Although this work has continued and spread, it has not had much fame, its often intelligent, impersonal products appearing insufficiently emotional for collectors and insufficiently vogueish for critics and museums. One of its heroes nearly spans the century: Max Bill (1908–95). Born in Switzerland and trained in craft and design, he studied at the German Bauhaus and perfectly embodied its desire to produce artist-designers capable of a full range of activities from painting to architecture. Bill's finest works are probably his sculptures: simple mathematical propositions given powerful, even monumental expression. The third is the need to point to one artist as the key figure of the century—a need not felt since Michelangelo. He is Pablo Picasso (1881–1973), whose fame, enormous in his lifetime, has grown further in spite of the usual urge to shelve and move on. It has been said that, wherever art goes, Picasso is already there, but in fact this is not so: his astounding productivity, driven by fears and doubts, closed to him less autobiographical kinds of art. Yet both his energy and restlessness fit the century, and his anxiety alternating with explosive joy well represents modern art. His acute awareness of art of the past and of other cultures, and his use of these amid great leaps of inventiveness, suggest a fusion of the classical and the Romantic and of the exotic with the Western, which may be art's principal gift to the twenty-first century.

So much of the past has remained, challenged and refreshed by Modernism, that perhaps the basic characteristic of twentieth-century art is growth, not change: growth in quantity, in the diversity of forms and purposes, in Western art's encircling the globe, in our capacity to engage with wide-ranging, often contradictory modes. Growth too in its systems of presentation and promotion. Educational programmes and devices loom larger year by year, while our newspapers place art with 'entertainment' and encourage reviewers to amuse rather than to guide the reader. If tomorrow we learn that admiring citizens have borne a great new work of art to its permanent location, presumably now a museum, as we are told that Florentines carried Cimabue's altarpiece 700 years ago to their cathedral, we shall immediately think first of the power of the media to stimulate events, not of the work's qualities. At the end of the twentieth century we are left with a situation in which ease of access forces us as individuals to make our own silent contact with art amid the hubbub that is now its normal habitat.

PART II

The Eurocentric World

1900–1945

8 The European Colonial Empires

WM. ROGER LOUIS

In the early twentieth century, colonial empires were associated with ideas of national greatness, competitiveness, and the survival of the fittest. The colours painted on maps over vast areas of Asia and Africa symbolized national power, prestige, and destiny. Colonies seemed to enrich national character and to encapsulate national glory. The 'natives' were to be civilized while the raw materials and other resources of the colonies would benefit the economy of the metropolitan country. But the popular view was not entirely optimistic or beneficent. Technological advance made it easy to believe in human progress throughout the world, yet at the same time humankind seemed trapped in an evolutionary struggle. Only the fittest nations and the fittest empires would survive. Great powers should possess great empires, if necessary, at the expense of lesser empires. Before 1914 the British Foreign Secretary, Sir Edward Grey, spoke of the Portuguese colonies as 'sinks of iniquity' and thought it would be merely a matter of time until they were partitioned between Germany and Britain. The possessions of the weaker colonial powers would be absorbed by the stronger, just as the territories of the 'dying' nations of Turkey and China would be annexed by the more virile European nations. The drive for empire contributed to a spirit of ruthless militarism.

Future historians writing a hundred years from now, when general interest in the details of the European empires may have faded, will continue to record the phantasmagoric significance attached to colonies in the years before 1914. They will also note the frenzied energy of the explorers, adventurers, soldiers, missionaries, traders, and administrators, who, for better or worse, tangibly extended European influence and affected the lives of non-Europeans throughout the world. Docks, roads, railways, plantations, and mines spread everywhere, at the same time as Western goods and money penetrated non-European societies. The beginning of the century in that sense represented a rubicon from which there could be no return. Indigenous societies would never be allowed to continue their own natural evolution. They would be modernized and, in some cases, assimilated. Imperialism would be the engine of social and economic change.

Each nation with colonial possessions large and small not only believed in the necessity of empire but also possessed a sense of superiority as a governing race and a divine mission to civilize the non-European world. This was perhaps a rationalization but it also became a galvanizing force. The ethic of empire created its own dynamic. Rudyard Kipling wrote of the British mission:

To us—to us, and not to others—a certain definite duty has been assigned. To carry light and civilization into the dark places of the world, to touch the mind of Asia and of Africa with the ethical ideas of Europe; to give to thronging millions, who would otherwise never know peace or security, these first conditions of human advance.

In similar vein, the most eloquent of British proconsuls, Lord Curzon, wrote of the British Empire as the greatest instrument for good that the world had seen.

The creation of the modern colonial empires was the work of a single generation whose lifetime extended from the last decades of the nineteenth century through the period of the First World War. The antecedents, of course, were historic. Fundamentally the empires were the product of the Industrial Revolution and Europe's consequent lead over the rest of the world in technology and weapons. Europe became a power house generating trade and commerce. In the last decades of the nineteenth century and until 1914, Europe expanded more rapidly than at any other time. Between 1800 and 1880, the colonial empires had added some 6,500,000 square miles to their domains. In the next three decades, the empires grew by another 8,655,000 square miles to increase European sway from 65 per cent of the land surface of the world to 85 per cent. The British Empire alone extended over one-quarter of the globe and over one-quarter of its population. The revolution in medicine as well as technology enabled explorers to penetrate into the African interior and allowed Christian missionaries to establish stations throughout the tropics. The Western advance appeared to be irreversible. In Africa railways reached Bamako in 1905, Katanga in 1910, Kano in 1911, and Tabora in 1912. Aeroplanes were used in the military campaigns in Libya in 1911 and Morocco in 1912.

With such a dramatic increase in territorial dominion, who made the profit? This was the principal question asked by John A. Hobson, the most outstanding writer on the subject of imperialism. Analysing the question of motive and profit during the period of the South African (Boer) War at the turn of the century, he speculated in his book *Imperialism* that Europe's expansion in tropical Africa must be accompanied by profit, but his interpretation erred. He and others confused political expansion with economic investment, which continued to flow elsewhere, not least to the Americas, to China, and to Russia. Africa remained the bottom of the imperialist's economic barrel. Hobson's criticism was nevertheless influential. All theories of imperialism, including those of Rosa Luxemburg and Lenin, can be traced to his work. Hobson expressed the moral outrage of hundreds of other writers. The colonial empires did not lack critics, either liberal or revolutionary.

The twentieth-century empires had more haphazard origins than most theorists would concede, but one aim was to prevent rivals from acquiring sources of national wealth. In the scramble for colonies there were a few lucky draws. Entrepreneurs and investors benefited from the diamonds and gold of South Africa, the copper of Katanga, the rubber of Malaya, the oil of the East Indies and the Middle East. Generally, however, the colonial possessions proved to be white elephants, not least in trade and commerce. In 1910 the German colonies accounted for less than 1 per cent of German trade and in 1912 the Belgian Congo contributed only 1 per cent of Belgian trade.

The smallest of the colonial empires in the twentieth century was the Spanish. The loss in 1898 of Cuba, Puerto Rico, and the Philippines to the United States, and the Pacific islands to Germany, reduced the Spanish Empire mainly to the Canary Islands, Spanish Sahara, a protectorate in part of Morocco, and Spanish Guinea in equatorial Africa (the only colony of any economic value, mainly in cocoa). The tradition of the old Spanish colonial system nevertheless proved to be significant. It was authoritarian, legalistic, and paternalistic—the forerunner of the twentieth-century colonial regimes. Of the lasting Spanish legacies, perhaps the most remarkable was the assimilation of the Filipinos to Catholicism and the Spanish way of life. The effective colonizers were not the Spanish sea captains and conquistadors but the friars and monks who built churches and created parishes and schools. The class structure of the Spanish era remained intact and the system of patronage continued into the era of independence.

The empires of the United States and Russia are beyond the scope of this chapter, but it is useful to bear in mind that, at the same time as the European colonial powers were expanding into Africa and the Pacific, the United States established a comparable empire on the remnant of the Spanish possessions; and that Russia continued to expand a vast land empire in central Asia and, by the turn of the century, had completed a huge railway network linking Siberia with Vladivostok, the major Russian port on the Pacific. The colonial domain of the United States included Guam as well as the Philippines and Puerto Rico as well as the Virgin Islands, which were purchased from Denmark in 1917. But the United States never described these colonial possessions as colonies but rather as 'territories' because of the American revolutionary and anti-imperial heritage. The acquisition of colonies in all but name caused ideological embarrassment. The United States and the Soviet Union were in this respect similar, each with a revolutionary heritage. Both consistently demonstrated an anti-colonial attitude though both had colonial empires of their own.

To contemporaries observing the fate of the Spanish Empire, it seemed inevitable that the weak had given way to the strong. No one anticipated that the lifespan of the great colonial empires would be relatively short. The preponderant view at the turn of the century held that the new empires would last for at least a thousand years. Yet within a hundred years of what the Spanish called the 'catastrophe' in 1898, even the great empire of the Soviet Union had disappeared.

The German Empire was the shortest lived. Born in 1884, it was extinguished in

1919. Most of it was concentrated in Africa. German East Africa extended over 384,000 square miles (nearly double that of Imperial Germany), South West Africa 322,000, Cameroon 305,000, and Togoland 34,000. In the Pacific, German New Guinea consisted of 93,000 square miles. Germany also possessed lesser territories in Asia and the Pacific, including Kiau-Chau in China, the Bismarck Archipelago, part of the Samoan group, and the Caroline, Mariana, and Marshall islands north of the equator. Only a few regions in South-West Africa and East Africa attracted settlers. Despite the brutal suppression of the Herero revolt in South-West Africa in 1904-7 and the Maji-Maji uprising in German East Africa in 1905-6, the Germans were no more, but no less, barbaric than the French in Algeria, the British in Kenya, or the Belgians in the Congo before 1908. A common fallacy held that colonies were vital to Germany's economic prosperity. Far from being an asset, however, all of the German colonies before 1914 except Togoland (productive in cocoa and rubber) and Samoa (copra) required subsidies. German financiers as well as emigrants demonstrated a distinct preference for Eastern Europe and the Americas rather than for the colonies. In 1919 Germany lost its place in the sun and with it an unprofitable empire. In the 1930s it seemed possible that some of the colonies might be restored (or other territory in Africa ceded to Germany at the expense of Belgium and Portugal). It remains debatable how the social engineering of the Third Reich might have affected black Africa and whether or not the Holocaust might have taken a slightly different direction with places such as East Africa available as a 'dumping ground' for Jews and Gypsies. The only thing that can be said with certainty is that after 1945 the Germans were spared the trauma of decolonization.

During the First World War, Britain and France emerged as major Middle Eastern powers and increased their colonial domains in Africa. The public mood changed. The European powers now paid lip-service, at least, to the ideal that colonies would be held in trust until the native peoples could stand on their own. Germany not only lost its colonies but, through British propaganda, unjustly acquired a reputation of a barbarous power unfit to govern native peoples. The German colonies were overrun by the British (with the help of Indian troops), and by French, Belgians, South Africans, Australians, New Zealanders, and Japanese. The Ottoman Empire was dismantled by the British and French, and to a lesser degree by the Italians. The smaller colonial empires of the Dutch, the Belgians, and the Portuguese remained intact. So also did the larger empires of France and Britain, but for the transcendent reason that Britain was an ally of Japan. Japan's policing of the eastern seas enabled the British fleet to concentrate in European waters and thereby contributed to Allied victory and the maintenance of the Allied empires.

After defeating China in 1894-5 and Russia in 1904-5, Japan had annexed Korea in 1910, thus gate-crashing the white man's club of imperial domination. During the First World War, Japanese influence increased both in China and in the Pacific. In 1919 the German islands north of the equator became Japanese-mandated territories. As in Germany in the 1930s, there emerged in Japan the doctrine that markets and raw materials were necessary for survival. After 1931 Japan occupied

Manchuria. To the south, the 'Greater Co-Prosperity Sphere' during the Second World War aimed to secure Japanese economic and political hegemony in South-East Asia. In the early part of the war, the Japanese conquest of the Philippines, Malaya, and the East Indies as well as the control of Indo-China demonstrated the vulnerability of the western regimes in Asia. Had the Japanese emerged undefeated from the Second World War, South-East Asia might have become part of an autarkic bloc not dissimilar from what the British had in mind with the sterling area. The islands north of the equator would probably have been swamped with Japanese immigrants and might have been assimilated as an outlying territory of Japan. As it transpired, the Japanese left no legacy in Micronesia, no tradition of language or education, no statues or parks. The most enduring feature of Japan's colonial experience was the profound bitterness of the Koreans for the violation of their 'national soul'. After 1945 the loss of colonial possessions demonstrated that Japan, like Germany, did not need tropical colonies to recover economically.

The Italian colonial empire was another casualty of the Second World War. At the turn of the century Ethiopia had not only remained free from European control but had inflicted a humiliating defeat on the Italians at the battle of Adowa in 1896. Mussolini's invasion of Ethiopia in 1935–6 aimed at revenge as well as the establishment of a 'neo-Roman' East African empire. Italy's domain in East Africa included Eritrea, 15,754 square miles with 4,188 Italians (according to the 1931 census); and Italian Somaliland, 194,000 square miles (over one and three-quarters the size of Italy) with 1,631 Italians. The numbers of Italians are significant because of the obsession with 'excess population' that characterized Italian public attitudes in the 1930s. The principal outlet for emigration was Libya, which Italy had won by conquest from Turkey in 1911. In the inter-war years Libya became Italy's 'Fourth Shore' and in 1938 had an Italian population of 89,098—a figure that bears comparison with 18,269 whites in Kenya, 386,084 Jews in Palestine, and 987,252 Europeans in Algeria. Libya under Italian rule became one of the most urbanized countries of North Africa with concentrations of population in Tripoli and Benghazi. Some 30,000 Italian peasants also settled on the Gefara Plain of Tripolitania. The Italian Fascist government built extensive harbours and roads but resettled the local Muslim nomads nearer the desert, thereby reducing their numbers drastically, perhaps by half. These projects were pursued for the greater glory of the Fascist state, but to the end they were a drain on the Italian budget and devastating to the indigenous population.

The Second World War destroyed another colonial system of much greater substance and longevity. The Dutch had held colonies since the seventeenth century. In the West Indies the colonial possessions included Surinam and Curaçao. In the East Indies, in the vast Indonesian archipelago of 13,000 islands extending 3,600 miles from east to west, the Dutch had developed a colonial economy producing tobacco, tea, coffee, sugar, copra, tin, coal, rubber, and oil. In neither the late nineteenth century nor the First World War did the Dutch Empire expand territorially. Its scope remained the same in 1939 as it had been in 1815. But from the late nineteenth century onwards the expansion of the economy brought to the East Indies a new

Dutch population of businessmen and civil servants. By 1939 there were 240,417 Dutch, many of whom regarded the East Indies as their home, who raised their children there, who retired there, and who later became embittered during the postwar struggle leading to Dutch eviction. The size of the indigenous population had risen from 6 million to 30 million in the nineteenth century and to 70 million by 1940. Dutch rule in part reflected the problem of how to govern such a vast and changing population. The Dutch from early on preserved native dynasties and ruled through them, though the expansion of European activities in the late nineteenth and twentieth centuries led increasingly to annexation. By the 1930s the Dutch held full sovereignty over 93 per cent of Java and more than half of the outer islands but gave the administrative districts considerable autonomy. Like the British system, and in contrast with the French, the Dutch system was characterized by decentralization and indirect rule. The extent of Dutch influence in densely populated areas such as Java as well as in the outlying areas was uneven. An indigenous bureaucracy buffered the peasant communities. The Japanese occupation after 1942 broke the continuity of Dutch rule. The Dutch were interned and the Indonesian élite assumed administrative positions that they had previously been denied. By enlisting the support of both nationalist and Islamic leaders, the Japanese fostered the nationalist movement. After the war the Dutch expected to reassert their control, but a long and acrimonious struggle ended when the United States sided with the nationalists. The new nation of Indonesia achieved independence in 1949. In the West it was regarded as one of the two great Asian events of the year, the other being the emergence of the Communist regime in China.

We now come to the empires that endured into the latter part of the twentieth century, the Belgian, the French, the British, and the Portuguese. There were basic similarities. Each colony had a 'steel frame' of military, police, and administrative officers who maintained order and defended the frontiers. A European outpost might consist merely of a district officer, a few interpreters, and a small military detachment. At the beginning of the century, the Portuguese, more than the others, lacked both military and administrative resources to go much beyond minimal occupation. Virtually all colonies developed revenue systems based on taxation of crops, which sometimes involved forced labour or its equivalent. Each colonial power exported a simplified form of its own system of government and law, and each colony possessed a system of justice, though this often amounted to unrestricted and arbitrary authority. As administrative units of the European powers, the colonies were also nascent states, each in the process of acquiring the modernizing characteristics of the states of Europe. Each colonial system invested in ports, roads, and railways as well as in education and health measures against, for example, sleeping sickness. By mid-century each had developed a network of government offices complete with files, typewriters, and telephones. Earlier it probably did not much matter whether an African, for example, happened to be under one regime or another. Later it mattered a great deal. Each colonial system came to possess distinctive characteristics that have endured in the post-colonial period to the end of the century.

By mid-century the Belgian Congo had acquired the reputation of a model colony. It had not always been so. Under the autocratic regime of King Leopold fifty years earlier, the Congo had been notorious. Leopold ruled in the Congo in his own right, not as King of the Belgians. His regime was exploitative and rapacious. Africans were compelled to collect a quota of wild rubber under penalty of punishment that sometimes led to atrocities. Part of the reason lay in the nature of the early *Force publique*, which resembled a mercenary army rather than a colonial police. In 1905 it consisted of 360 European officers of various nationalities and 16,000 Africans. Leopold demanded profits but his administrative apparatus proved too weak to prevent abuses. In 1908 Belgium annexed the Congo to remedy the evils of her king. The immense colony of the Congo extended over 902,082 square miles—eighty times larger than Belgium. The African population was relatively small, some 9 million at the beginning of Belgian rule and 13,540,182 in 1958. The Belgians in the Congo numbered only 17,536 in 1940 and 88,913 in 1958. The region provided a variety of rich resources, including copper, diamonds, and uranium as well as tropical agricultural products such as rubber, palm oil, and cotton. Mining was the most valuable part of the economy. The profits on Belgian investment, however, were not high, with an annual return of only 4 or 5 per cent. Before 1937 Belgium subsidized the colonial budget. By the standards of the time, Belgian rule was benevolent and efficient. No other colony had better labour conditions, health facilities, or primary education. No other perhaps was as paternalistic. Catholic missions provided for primary-school attendance of some 56 per cent, the highest in Africa, but few went on to secondary schools and fewer still to universities. By the time of independence the Belgian Congo had produced only 16 Congolese with university training. In December 1959 riots at Leopoldville shook the Belgian administration into a belated recognition of the strength of Congolese nationalism. The Belgians now made a fundamental miscalculation. Fearing that the troubles might escalate into the equivalent of the Algerian revolution, and nevertheless assuming that the Congolese could not manage without them, the Belgians decided in favour of immediate independence on 30 June 1960. The Congo quickly slid into anarchy. The summer of 1960 will always be remembered as the time of one of the great disasters in European decolonization. The phrases 'Congo' and 'post-colonial chaos' became synonymous.

Before the Second World War the French Empire stood as the only worldwide empire comparable to that of the British. In 1939 it extended over 4,617,579 square miles and had a population of 64,946,975. Algeria, administered directly as part of France, was the major colony of settlement and had nearly 1 million Europeans and over 6 million Muslims with one of the highest rates of population growth in the world. Other parts of the North African and Middle Eastern empire included the protectorates over Tunisia and Morocco and the mandated territories of Syria and Lebanon. In South-East Asia the French held sway over Indo-China. In the Pacific, France possessed Tahiti (Oceania) as well as New Caledonia and administered, with Britain, the condominium of the New Hebrides. In the Caribbean, France retained the sugar colonies of Guadeloupe, Martinique, and French

Guiana (but not Haiti, which had successfully revolted in 1804). Off Newfoundland, she held the fishing bases of St Pierre-et-Miquelon. In tropical Africa the French domain was larger than that of any other power, extending from southern Algeria to the Congo and east to the Anglo-Egyptian Sudan. There were two main administrative units. The Federation of French West Africa included the colonies of Mauritania, Senegal, the Ivory Coast, Dahomey, French Sudan, French Guinea, Upper Volta, and Niger. The other federal unit of French Equatorial Africa consisted of Chad, Gabon, the Middle Congo, and Ubangui Chari. France administered also the mandated territories of Cameroon and Togo. Nor is this long list exhaustive. French possessions further included French Somaliland, Madagascar, and island groups in the Indian ocean. In all of these territories the aim since the time of the French Revolution had remained the same. France's republican heritage and civilization would be offered to its subjects, allowing them to become assimilated as French citizens. The empire would be an integral part of France.

In the early part of the century it had already become clear to the French that it would be difficult, if not impossible, to assimilate entire societies in such places as Algeria, Indochina, and black Africa. In 1922 there were only ninety-six black French citizens in West Africa, though the figure rose to 2,000 by 1937. By 1936 there were only 7,817 citizens in Algeria who had qualified by renouncing Islam and traditional society. The project of transforming Arabs and black Africans into Frenchmen obviously had its limits. The idea of assimilation nevertheless did not disappear. The prominent French colonial minister after the First World War, Albert Sarraut, had called for investment to develop the colonies and to make the colonial economies interdependent with the metropolitan economy. This was significant because the French proved themselves consistently more willing to provide money and to commit military forces than any of the other colonial powers. The universalist assumptions of French republican philosophy and the *mission civiliatrice* might be impractical, but economic and military commitment helped the French to produce a small assimilated élite devoted to French civilization. Assimilation was as much cultural as political, and the Arab *évolués* were not strong enough to prevent Syrian nationalists from defending their independence in 1945. The demise of France as a Middle Eastern power was a result of the Second World War, which also sapped French strength in Indochina. The year 1954 marked a humiliating and decisive French defeat at Dienbienphu and effectively ended France's empire in Asia. In the same year the French government reinforced Algeria with 20,000 troops, a number that would grow to half a million by the end of the revolution in 1962. One of de Gaulle's supreme achievements, after his return to power in 1958, was the resolution of both the future of Algeria and the fate of the colonial empire. In 1958 he presented the Africans with a clear choice. They could decide in favour of independence and a privileged place within the French community with the continuation of economic and military assistance, or in favour of unfettered independence and the abrupt breaking of all links. Only Sekou Tourée of Guinea chose to sever the bond with France. The rest remained within the *Union Française*. In April 1961 de Gaulle survived a military revolt of the French army in Algeria and moved decisively towards *Algérie Algérienne*. It was Algeria that captured the world's imagination, in part because of the movie *The Battle of Algiers*, which dramatically conveyed the message that nearly half a million troops, sophisticated weapons, and torture could not destroy a revolution aiming at national freedom. On 3 July 1962 de Gaulle proclaimed Algeria independent.

The British Empire differed from the French colonial system above all by the possession of India and by the autonomous Dominions. At the turn of the century India constituted an empire in its own right with a territorial scope of 1,802,629 square miles and a population of 294,361,056. (India alone in 1900 had a population nearly five times that of the entire French colonial empire.) It is a measure not merely of fire power but of British confidence and prestige that India was administered by fewer than 1,000 members of the Indian Civil Service, almost exclusively British. By 1915 the percentage of Indians in the ICS had risen to 5 per cent and by 1935 to 32 per cent. The Indian army with a core of 250,000 troops made Britain the greatest military power in the East in the early part of the century. During that time the Dominions of Australia, New Zealand, Canada, and South Africa had become self-governing and virtually independent. By formally marking the birth of the Commonwealth, the Statute of Westminster of 1931 merely recognized the actuality of nations of kith and kin freely associating in self-interest. Until 1947 the Commonwealth remained an exclusive white man's club representing only a small part of a still vast empire that had reached its greatest territorial extent in the inter-war years. In 1939 in the Caribbean, British colonies included Jamaica, Trinidad, British Guiana, Honduras, the Leewards, the Windwards, the Bahamas, and Bermuda. In the Pacific, Britain administered Fiji, Tonga, and smaller island groups. In East and South-East Asia, British possessions included Hong Kong, Malaya, Burma, Singapore, and parts of Borneo. In the Middle East, Mediterranean, and Indian Ocean, Britain ruled over Gibraltar, Malta, Cyprus, Palestine, Jordan, Aden, the Persian Gulf protectorates, Ceylon, Mauritius, and the Seychelles. The African territories included the Gambia, Sierra Leone, the Gold Coast, Nigeria, Cameroon, the Anglo-Egyptian Sudan, British Somaliland, Kenya, Uganda, Tanganyika, Northern Rhodesia, Nyasaland, and Southern Rhodesia. Even this extensive list is not complete. The British Empire and Commonwealth was a complex, worldwide system stretching over 12.2 million square miles, roughly one quarter of the earth's surface, that included territories acquired during every stage of colonization since the sixteenth century.

In retrospect the inter-war years represent the golden age of British colonialism, at least in the imagination. The District Officer inspired trust in his subjects as well as in the British public that colonial rule was just and enlightened, as portrayed in the movie *Sanders of the River*. The reality was more complicated, but the fictional accounts usually conveyed the essential point that British rule depended on indigenous authority. The India Office as well as the Colonial Office monitored a decentralized and self-financing empire. The India Act of 1919 granted ministerial responsibility in the provinces and, through a system known as 'dyarchy', transferred to Indian hands authority in education, public health, public works, and agriculture while reserving to the British the crucial departments such as justice, police, finance, and foreign affairs. Part of the purpose was to win the loyalty and collaboration of the Indian leaders. The India Act of 1935 granted further autonomy to the provinces and created a federal structure including a Supreme Court, but, again, these measures were designed to prolong the Raj, not to end it, by consolidating British control at the centre of the Indian government. In Africa there emerged a similar design. In 1922 Sir Frederick Lugard's Dual Mandate developed the doctrine that local administration should be left to native authorities, preferably hereditary chiefs. As in India, the goal was to secure collaboration without weakening British control. The native authorities were self-supporting and therefore met the stringent fiscal requirement. Through indirect rule the British would act as trustees and the Africans would retain their own identity, thus solving both an ethnic and an ethical problem of empire. The difficulty was that the chiefs could not provide the leadership necessary for a modern colonial state. After the Second World War the Colonial Office began to dismantle indirect rule and to democratize the Empire by systems of local government, thereby providing an outlet for nationalist ambition. The aim was the same as in India, to win over the nationalists before they became irreconcilables. For a while it appeared that the strategy might succeed. In 1945 no one would have believed that the end would come so quickly, though it was already clear that India could not be held to the Empire. The Labour government was committed to India's freedom and in any event economic and military weakness dictated retrenchment.

The dismantling of the Empire began first in Asia by the granting of independence to India and Pakistan in 1947 and Ceylon and Burma in 1948. All except Burma remained in the Commonwealth, which provided a psychological cushion during the era of decolonization. In 1948 the British were driven out of Palestine, in part because of the intervention by the United States in favour of the Zionists and the creation of the State of Israel. It might be tempting to regard these events as the beginning of a preordained decline and fall, but it did not seem so to those at the time who hoped to rejuvenate the Empire in the Middle East and Africa. With India lost and Palestine shrugged aside, Africa would be developed as a replacement for India and the oil of the Middle East would sustain Britain as a great world power. The collapse of the Empire would be prevented by genuinely coming to terms with African and Middle Eastern nationalists as equals and not treating them as inferiors as in the earlier period. The Sudanese were among the first beneficiaries of this new approach, though they benefited as much if not more from the Egyptian support of their cause. The Sudan became independent in early 1956. It is interesting to speculate how the end of the British Empire might have come about had it not been for the Suez crisis later in the same year. Suez revealed the extent of British military and financial weakness as well as its dependence on the United States. In the wake of Suez, Harold Macmillan became Prime Minister and proceeded to liquidate the Empire as a questionable economic asset and a liability in Anglo-American relations. Above all Macmillan responded to the winds of African nationalism. He wanted to avert colonial wars and 'a British Algeria' in Central

Africa. Independence for the Gold Coast and Malaya had already been planned for 1957 and the goal already set for Nigerian independence in 1960. But it was Macmillan's Colonial Secretary, Iain Macleod, who now dramatically stepped up the pace in the years 1959–61. Largely as a result of Macleod's accelerated time-tables, Tanganyika, Cyprus, Sierra Leone, and Kuwait became independent in 1961, Uganda, Sierra Leone, Jamaica, and Trinidad in 1962, Kenya and Zanzibar in 1963, and Nyasaland (Malawi), Northern Rhodesia (Zambia), and Malta in 1964. There remained Aden and the protectorates in the Gulf; and the resolution of the Rhodesian problem was left to another generation twenty years later. But essentially the Empire—as represented by those great expanses of red on the map—had come to an end within a four-year period from 1960. The calculation was ruthless in the sense that it was based on British self-interest and not on humanitarian concern for the inhabitants. A prolonged British presence would end in colonial conflict. It was better to end colonial rule sooner, and hope for African goodwill and collaboration, rather than later with the certainty of ill will and bloodshed.

The Portuguese Empire was the last to be liquidated and it was in every sense an anachronism. Paradoxically, by the time that the other European colonial empires were in their death throes, the Portuguese had lost nothing until India seized Goa in 1961. The principal colonies were the immense territories of Angola (481,226 square miles) in western Africa, and Mozambique (297,654 square miles) in eastern Africa. These regions had been discovered by Vasco da Gama and others in the fifteenth century and held a vital place in the national psyche. Portugal's other colonies included Portuguese Guinea in western Africa, the Cape Verde islands, the islands of San Tomé and Principe in the Gulf of Guinea, Macao off Canton, and Timor in the Malay archipelago. In the first decade of the century the Portuguese were able to uphold their largely fictional claims to the vast hinter-lands of Angola and Mozambique only because the other colonial powers did not want to see the territories fall into the hands of their rivals. By 1910 no more than a tenth of either colony was under actual Portuguese control. The effective coloniz-ing instrument evolved in the shape of chartered companies or concessions dom-inated by British capital. To develop plantations the companies relied on forced labour, which roused international humanitarian protest until the reform of labour laws in 1926. Portugal acquired a reputation of a harsh and despotic colo-nial power almost rivalling that of King Leopold's regime in the Congo, but the rea-son lay in Portugal's own poverty and the carrying-over of nineteenth-century labour practices into the twentieth. Portugal itself was an underdeveloped coun-try. The Portuguese had not experienced an industrial revolution and did not have a humanitarian movement. The critical period of modernization began with Salazar's Estado Novo in 1928. In the renaissance of the Portuguese state, the mys-tique of empire held a prominent place. Salazar presided over a period of colonial development that included the introduction of telegraphs and telephones, ports and railways, hospitals and schools. By mid-century the Portuguese colonies had been brought into line with other European colonies, though observers com-mented on a twenty-year time lag. There was less of a colour bar than in any of the other European colonies. The Portuguese viewed Angola and Mozambique as multiracial societies on the model of Brazil. They regarded the colonies as an integral part of the Portuguese state. But despite public subsidies to Catholic missions for education, by 1950 there were only 30,089 *assimilados* in Angola and only 4,353 in Mozambique. In 1961 a nationalist rising began in Angola. Further insurrections occurred in Mozambique and Guinea in 1964. For another decade Portugal now fought rebel forces in all three of the African colonies. It is a measure of the vitality of the Portuguese colonial mission that the military commitment reached nearly 200,000 troops, which represented a huge number of soldiers for a country with a population of only 8 million. The Portuguese devoted half the national budget to the colonial war effort. In the end the Portuguese colonial empire in Africa died in 1974 as a result of revolution in Portugal, not defeat in the colonies.

In the aftermath of decolonization, the world has witnessed the rise and fall of such tyrants as Idi Amin of Uganda and Jean-Bedel Bokassa of the Central African Republic. It will long be debated how the European colonial powers might have better prepared the colonies for independence and the extent to which the new states are responsible for their own troubles. Many of the former colonies are hostages to the international economy, but the legacies of colonialism are carto-graphic, cultural, and aesthetic as well as economic and political. For better or worse the boundaries drawn by the colonial powers in Asia, the Middle East, and Africa 100 years ago have proved to be remarkably durable. So also have the French, English, Spanish, and Portuguese linguistic blocs of the non-European world. French cultural influence probably exceeds that of the British, though in the world of cricket and soccer the British have left a lasting legacy. The French have proved to be far more willing than the British and others to commit troops and economic assistance to the former colonies, not least to those torn by ethnic and religious strife. The political legacies, however, may in the long run prove to be less apparent than the aesthetic and even the culinary traditions. In the old French territories red wine is still mandatory at lunch and dinner. In former British colonies in the tropics one encounters mulligatawny soup, roast lamb, and steamed ginger pudding. Throughout the erstwhile world of French colonies from Senegal to Tahiti one of the most striking impressions is of French provincial houses and streets lined with trees. In Canada and South Africa as well as in India one is struck by the similarity of public buildings and especially by the magnificence of the former Viceroy's Palace designed by Lutyens in New Delhi. As we move into the twenty-first century, it could well be that architecture as well as language will serve as one of the conspicuous reminders of the colonial era.

9 Europe in the Age of the Two World Wars

MICHAEL HOWARD

At the turn of the century two events suggested that the days of European world hegemony were numbered. In 1898 the United States destroyed the crumbling empire of one European power, Spain. Six years later, in a far more serious conflict, Japan decisively humiliated another, the huge Russian Empire. In a world perspective, Europe already seemed to be shrinking. For decades political analysts had been suggesting that the historic states of Europe might be overshadowed in the coming century by a new league of 'World Powers', membership of which would be confined to continental-sized states such as the United States, Russia, and such European nations as could establish and exploit world empires. This fear, or expectation, was to explain much in the half-century of European conflict that was to follow.

The only European state that could claim such World Power status in 1900 was Britain, which had established itself as the world's first industrial nation and whose Empire covered a quarter of the habitable globe. But industrially and economically Britain was being fast overtaken by the recently united Germany. Germany's combined and growing population of 57 million surpassed the 37 million of Britain. Its coal, steel, and iron production (like that of the United States) had already overtaken that of the British; and it was pioneering a new technological revolution based on electricity, oil-derivatives, and industrial chemicals. By any criterion, many Germans believed that they deserved the status of *Weltmacht*, World Power, and were determined to achieve it.

The growth of German power was watched with particular concern by France, a country riven by social and ideological conflict and whose population, still consisting mainly of peasant smallholders, remained static at some 36 million. At a time when armies were based on universal conscription, population was still a primary indicator of military strength. For salvation the French looked to a Russian ally whose population in 1900 approached 133 million and by 1910 was to exceed 160 million. But this huge figure could not be made militarily effective without a substantial development of Russia's backward industry and railway system. Russia's defeat at the hands of the Japanese showed how far it still had to go before it could be regarded as a serious modernized military power, but that débâcle set in train a series of French-financed military and economic reforms that were observed in Germany with deep apprehension.

Domestic developments also gave German leaders cause for concern, for it was in Germany, where industrialization had been most rapid, that social conflict appeared most intense. The growing influence of the urban working classes, whose size increased *pari passu* with the development of German industry, alarmed the industrialists (largely in Western Germany) who employed them, the Catholic agrarian classes of the south who disliked the whole trend of urbanization, and above all the Junker landowners of the east—a class which retained its social dominance through the old Prussian monarchy in whose government it enjoyed a privileged position, and whose archaic militaristic ethos dominated the upper reaches of German society.

Anti-socialism was thus a good rallying-cry for the government to recruit potential political allies. So also, in 1900, was that of a 'forward' foreign policy. Assertiveness abroad appeared the best way of securing unity at home. None believed this more fervently than did the Kaiser Wilhelm II, who embodied in his own person the unstable combination of feudal archaism and aggressive modernity that characterized the country over which he ruled. In the view of the Kaiser and his most influential advisers there was no better way of asserting German power than to build a great navy, which would be both a symbol and an instrument of German determination to escape the traditional limits of European politics and to graduate into the new league of World Powers.

Given that Germany's formidable army already gave it dominance on the European continent, such a navy could only be seen as intended for war with Britain. There a Liberal government coming into power in 1906 pledged to a programme of radical domestic reform found itself forced to embark on an expensive naval competition with Germany, and to mend fences with its old imperial rivals France and Russia. With both powers Britain established ententes that fell far short of formal military alliances, but its diplomacy was seen in Germany as a deliberate attempt at encirclement in order to prevent the assertion of Germany's legitimate aspirations. By 1914 the mutual suspicion and dislike between the two countries had reached the intensity almost of a cold war.

But when war did come, it broke out at the other end of Europe. It arose from rivalry between the Habsburg Monarchy and Russia over the succession to the disintegrating empire of the Turks in the Balkan peninsula. There, for 100 years past, newly formed nations had, with Western support, been successively asserting their independence against Ottoman rule; Greece, Romania, Bulgaria, Montenegro, Albania, but above all Serbia. The Serbs saw themselves as the natural leaders of all the Slavic peoples in the region, destined to unite them into a great nation as Piedmont had united the Italian nation during the previous century. It was an analogy with alarming implications for the Habsburg Monarchy, itself an uneasy amalgam of nationalities, many of which were Slav. In Russia, on the contrary, the Serbs were seen as natural allies by powerful Pan-Slav elements who felt under a strong obligation to support them.

A precarious balance had subsisted between Russia and the Habsburg Monarchy during the last quarter of the nineteenth century, but it was badly shaken in 1903. In that year a Serb dynasty subservient to Vienna was brutally replaced by a nationalist regime that initiated a policy of confrontation with the Monarchy and explicitly aimed at liberating their brother Slavs over the frontier in Bosnia-Herzogovina—a Turkish province that the Austrians had 'administered' since 1879 and annexed outright to the Monarchy in 1908. That annexation sparked off a series of international crises culminating in the Balkan Wars of 1912–13, in which a League of the Balkan states, supported by Russia, drove the Turks out of the entire Balkan peninsula except for a small foothold in Eastern Thrace.

These wars doubled the territory, military potential, and aspirations of Serbia, and deepened Austrian apprehension to crisis point. The threat that Serbia posed to the cohesion of the Monarchy now appeared so great that the belief became widespread in Vienna that it could be dealt with only by the elimination of Serbia itself. In June 1914 the assassination in the Bosnian capital Sarajevo of the heir to the Habsburg throne, the Archduke Franz Ferdinand, by Bosnian terrorists covertly sponsored by elements in the Serb High Command, seemed to provide an ideal opportunity. Vienna presented the Serbs with an ultimatum that gave them no choice but to acknowledge Austrian hegemony or submit to a war of conquest.

In such a confrontation Russia felt bound to support Serbia, and Austria–Hungary needed German support to confront Russia. This was forthcoming. Germany could not afford to see its only ally disintegrate, and was increasingly alarmed by the growth of Russian power. War with Russia would certainly involve war with its ally, France; but since the beginning of the century the German General Staff had been perfecting a plan for a two-front war devised by Count Alfred von Schlieffen, by which German armies would initially stand on the defensive against Russia and destroy the French armies by a huge encircling movement through neutral Belgium. That this involved both an act of unprovoked aggression against France and the invasion of a small country whose neutrality had been guaranteed not only by Germany itself but by Britain, did not deter the ruling circles in Berlin. But considerations of international morality, of traditional balance of power, and ideological distaste for 'Prussian militarism' all combined to make the British government declare war on 4 August—thus transforming a quarrel in Central Europe into a worldwide war.

The Schlieffen Plan did not succeed. After an initial disastrous offensive of their own, the French armies fell back to avoid the German trap and counter-attacked on the Marne just as the Germans, finding themselves dangerously overextended, withdrew to defensive positions. Mutual attempts at outflanking failed, and by the end of the year the opposing armies had entrenched themselves along lines from which they were to move little, if at all, for the next four years.

Meanwhile the notional principals in the war, Russia and Austria–Hungary, rapidly became of secondary importance. In spite of ambitious offensives by both sides, logistical and administrative incompetence prevented either from gaining a military decision, and the course of the war on the Eastern Front was thereafter determined by the Germans. In 1914 they checked the Russian advance into East Prussia at the Battle of Tannenberg and cleared Russian armies from Western Poland. In 1915, taking increasing control of the exhausted Austrian armies, they drove the Russians back to their ethnic frontier. As for the Russians, although they were able to launch one last successful offensive against the Austrians in May 1916, in 1917 they collapsed, as much because of the inability of the Czarist government to solve the huge problems of total war as because of any specific defeats in the field.

Throughout 1915 the Germans focused on their Eastern Front and stood on the defensive in the west, where the French lost over a million men in repeated offensives in which the growing British armies had reluctantly to join—offensives justified largely on the grounds that without them the Russians were likely to make peace. Gradually a new and terrible form of war developed on the Western Front. The advantages provided to the defensive by deep trench-systems, protected by barbed-wire entanglements and covered by machine-guns and pre-registered artillery, meant that no attack could succeed without heavy artillery preparation. Initially neither the French nor the British had enough guns or sufficient ammunition of the right quality to force a breakthrough. When they mobilized their industrial resources to provide them, the result was to turn the battle area into a wasteland in which movement and communication proved almost impossible. This the Germans discovered in their turn when in February 1916 they themselves took the offensive at Verdun. There, in one of the most prolonged and terrible battles in recorded history, the French and Germans between them lost well over a million men, some 420,000 of them dead. When a few months later British and French forces launched a massive combined offensive on the Somme, they did little better. In a four-month battle they lost between them 600,000 men. Since they captured a few square miles of ground and inflicted approximately equal losses on the Germans, they claimed a Pyrrhic victory.

The Battles of Verdun and the Somme showed the German leadership that military successes could not by themselves win the war. Germany found itself involved in a long-drawn *Materielschlacht* that demanded the full mobilization of its economy. To achieve this the German High Command, backed by a powerful right-wing coalition, effectively took charge of the home front. But they could obtain results only with the willing cooperation of a people who were now beginning to suffer serious deprivation and malnourishment. The socialist opposition in the Reichstag had supported the war only so long as they believed that it was one of self-defence. Now they were beginning to press for the conclusion of a compromise peace. The High Command, however, under its leaders Generals Paul von Hindenburg and Erich Ludendorff, was determined that German victories should be crowned by a triumphant peace of widespread territorial annexations to justify

Germany's sacrifices and to ensure its future hegemony in Europe. The precarious domestic consensus was thus beginning to unravel at the moment when it was most needed.

It was this sense of political urgency that made the German High Command decide at the end of 1916 to launch unrestricted submarine warfare against Britain—the only adversary that its armies could not reach. Britain and France were by now almost wholly dependent on supplies from the United States, which, in spite of repeated declarations of neutrality by President Woodrow Wilson, had thus acquired a strong vested interest in Allied victory. The US government, already antagonized by earlier sinkings, made it clear that they would regard unrestricted submarine warfare as a *casus belli*; but the Germans hoped that by the time the United States had mobilized and deployed their forces the war in Europe would be over. In December 1916 they decided to take the risk.

Their gamble nearly paid off. The United States declared war in April 1917, but it was to take another year for it to put an army into Europe. Meanwhile Russia collapsed. In February 1917 food riots in St Petersburg escalated into a revolution that overthrew the Romanov dynasty and established a Provisional Government that staggered on with the war till it was overthrown in its turn by a second revolution in October, the leaders of which at once sued for peace. In April the French armies collapsed in mutiny and were unable to take the offensive for the rest of the year. Between August and November the British exhausted themselves in further fruitless attacks in Flanders. In November the Italians, who had been induced to join the Western Allies in April 1915 by the promise of territorial gains at the expense of Austria–Hungary and whose army had been decimated by repeated and mismanaged offensives, collapsed at Caporetto. By the end of the year it seemed to the Western Allies that the Germans were on the verge of total victory.

The Germans, on the contrary, saw themselves on the brink of total disintegration. Their Austrian ally was openly suing for peace; strikes were becoming common in German cities, and the Russian Revolution appeared as a sinister portent of what might happen in Germany itself unless peace was quickly made. By the Treaty of Brest-Litovsk in March 1918 Germany made huge paper annexations in the East, but was in no position to exploit them. Ludendorff saw his only chance lay in launching one final offensive in the West. Using techniques of breakthrough developed on the Eastern Front, the German armies smashed into the weakened British and French lines in a succession of attacks that opened in March 1918 and continued till July. But the Allies held firm. The German submarine campaign had failed, and US supplies and troops were coming across the Atlantic in increasing quantities. In August the Allies took the offensive. The German army retreated in good order, but its morale was disintegrating, and the domestic situation became so alarming that at the beginning of October Ludendorff approached President Wilson, hoping for lenient armistice terms.

None was forthcoming. The Allies demanded the virtual surrender of the German armed forces and the overthrow of the Hohenzollern Monarchy. Ludendorff refused these terms, but it was too late: Germany was becoming ungovernable. On 9 November a Republic was proclaimed in Berlin, and two days later its representatives accepted the Allied armistice terms.

Simultaneously the Habsburg Monarchy fell to pieces. The Emperor abdicated, and Hungary and a new Czechoslovak Republic declared their independence of Vienna. In Vienna itself an Austrian republic was established that proclaimed its union with Germany—a measure that the victorious Allies were to forbid. A Kingdom of South (Yugo-)Slavs was created, uniting the Serbs with their Croatian cousins from Hungary and the Slovenes from Austria. The Empires that had dominated Central Europe for 200 years disappeared in a matter of days, and the destiny of the Continent lay in the hands of the victors—France, Britain, and, above all, the United States.

When the representatives of the victorious Allies met in Paris in January 1919 with the task of reconstructing the shattered European order, they had very different ideas how to do it. The dominant figure was President Wilson, who was seen by many, not least himself, as a *deus ex machina* who would create a new world order in which the keywords would be 'self-determination' and 'collective security'. New, democratic states would be created out of the debris of the former empires, and their security would be mutually guaranteed under the aegis of a new League of Nations where open negotiation would replace the secret diplomacy of the discredited old order. But the French Premier Georges Clemenceau, speaking for all the French and initially for most of the British, was concerned primarily with preventing the revival of a Germany whose latent power had been left untouched by military defeat. And there was a third figure who was not present at the conference but of whose importance those who *were* present were very conscious: Lenin, the leader of the victorious Bolshevik regime in Moscow, who was now calling on the peoples of Western Europe to revolt in their turn. To many of the Allied leaders in the West, the containment of revolutionary Russia seemed quite as urgent as that of defeated Germany.

For the new regimes in Eastern Europe in particular, anti-Bolshevism seemed at least as important as democratic legitimacy. There after months of bloody confusion a *cordon sanitaire* of new states was created under Western patronage, extending from the Baltic to the Black Sea. Among these Poland was especially significant—a nation whose struggle for independence had commanded Western sympathy ever since its extinction in 1795, and which now reconstituted itself out of the ruins of the German, Russian, and Austrian Empires. The Allies watched approvingly as, after successfully defending themselves against a Russian attempt to reclaim their former Polish territories, the Poles counter-attacked and established their own rule in the East some way beyond their ethnic borders; while on their western frontier they received access to the sea by a corridor down the Vistula Valley that separated the province of East Prussia from the rest of Germany.

This inherently unstable settlement was clearly unlikely to survive once Russia and Germany were in a position to reverse it. The loss of its eastern territories to Poland was a major German grievance against the peace settlement. Others were the heavy burden of reparations, and the requirement to accept full responsiblity for the outbreak of the war. How far either demand was 'unjust' remains arguable; but they united Germans, almost regardless of party, in a common resentment that added to the precarious position of the government that had to sign the peace treaty at Versailles. The new left-of-centre Republic established at Weimar was besieged, on the one hand, by communists, until ferocious 'cleansing actions' by the Army and right-wing freelance military formations (*Freikorps*) destroyed their political effectiveness; and, on the other, by irreconcilable forces of the Right.

To contain Germany, France needed allies in the West as well as in the East, and initially hoped for security guarantees from the United States as well as from Britain. But Wilson failed to persuade Congress to undertake any commitments, either to individual European nations or even to the League of Nations on which his whole concept of 'collective security' was based. The League was thus left as a rump that excluded not only the United States but the two pariah European nations, Germany and Russia—whose rapprochement at Rapallo in 1922 provided a sinister indication of their joint capacity to destroy the settlement in Eastern Europe if they so wished.

The British followed the American lead in refusing to provide the French with any military guarantees. Since 1914 Britain had undergone a virtual social revolution, which culminated in 1918 in the enfranchisement of the whole adult male and the bulk of the female population. The priority for the government was now domestic tranquillity and welfare, while its main concern overseas was the increasing restiveness within its imperial possessions—a restiveness which in Ireland was only partly appeased by the recognition of a Free State excluding the largely Protestant counties of Ulster in 1922. So far as Europe was concerned, once wartime passions had died down, the British saw the best hope of peace and economic recovery as lying in the conciliation of Germany. They therefore distanced themselves from their former allies when in 1923 the French used an alleged default in the payment of reparations to occupy the Rhineland and to set up an 'independent' Rhineland Republic.

This latter step was so disastrous, leading as it did to total non-cooperation by the German population and deliberately induced hyperinflation within Germany, that the French reversed their policy. Conciliatory statesmen—Aristide Briand and Gustav von Stresemann—came into office in Paris and Berlin, and in 1925 Britain joined at Locarno in a mutual guarantee of the Franco–Belgian–German frontiers. 'The Spirit of Locarno' seemed to usher in a new era. In 1926 Germany joined the League, as in 1934 did the now-named Soviet Union. The Americans accepted a degree of economic if not political responsibility for the stability of Europe by initiating the Dawes Plan for the liquidation of mutual indebtedness. By 1928, ten years after the end of the war, Europe seemed at last to be at peace.

The 'Spirit of Locarno' barely survived the decade. The world economic collapse of 1929, and the massive unemployment that resulted, undermined the stability of all the newly established regimes in Europe, and shook confidence in the validity of liberal democracy itself. The alternative offered by communism increasingly attracted not only the organized working classes but many intellectuals in the West. The Soviet Union, in the carefully sanitized image it presented to the world, seemed to offer an alternative far preferable to a capitalism apparently unable to solve the systemic problems of widespread poverty and unemployment.

Yet equally significant were those elements in Western societies, among the possessing classes and the petty bourgeoisie, who saw in communism not a solution but a threat. Populist right-wing movements, generally known after their Italian progenitor as 'fascist', also began to proliferate throughout Europe, as hostile to liberal democracy as they were to communism. The Fascist regime established by Benito Mussolini in Italy in 1922 made only a superficial impact on Italian society and coexisted peacefully with the conservative institutions of Monarchy and Church. But its imitator in Germany, the National Socialist German Workers' Party (Nazis) which came to power in 1933, was a different matter. It drew enormous strength, not only from the general resentment at the Versailles settlement that Locarno had done little to appease, but from the despair of the middle classes who had seen themselves ruined twice within a decade. But its greatest asset was its charismatic leader, Adolf Hitler.

Hitler was not only a politician of machiavellian subtlety but an orator unmatched in his capacity to appeal to mass audiences in the theatrical surroundings that he so brilliantly stage-managed. He came to power by manipulating the conservative politicians who hoped to use his talents to gain a mass support that they could not command on their own. Once ensconced, Hitler dismantled the democratic scaffolding on which he had climbed to power and made himself invulnerable by a mixture of ruthless intimidation, skilful propaganda, and undeniable achievement. Within a few years he had created at least the appearance of economic stability, abolished unemployment, and above all restored German self-respect and prestige in international affairs. Nearly all sections of German society were momentarily satisfied except the Jews, against whom Hitler unleashed a persecution of a brutality unexampled in Western Europe, driving all who could escape into exile.

Few Western statesmen realized that Hitler was concerned not to readjust the balance in Europe but to destroy it, and on its ruins to re-create Germany as a World Power on a scale beyond the wildest dreams of his imperial predecessors. The weakness of 'collective security' had already been shown when the League failed to deal with a *prima facie* act of aggression—the Japanese seizure of Manchuria from China in 1931. It failed equally when Mussolini invaded Abyssinia in 1935—a last act of European colonial conquest which France and Britain would have found difficult to condemn if Abyssinia had not itself been a member of the League and vainly demanded that 'collective security' should be exercised on its behalf. A new German–Italian 'Axis' came into being—later to be joined by Japan—which, by posing as the paladins of anti-communism, was able to gain sympathizers in both France and Britain at a moment when the Soviet Union, alarmed at the rise of right-wing militarism in both Germany and Japan, had joined the League and was trying to close ranks with the 'bourgeois democracies' in a Popular Front against Fascism.

Throughout the West ideological divisions now began to transcend national loyalties. Those divisions were crystallized by the civil war that broke out in Spain in 1936, when a military junta with powerful clerical support attempted to overthrow a secularizing socialist regime. With the Axis powers supporting the rebels and the Soviet Union the Spanish government, Britain and France attempted to work through the League to insulate the crisis. Their failure further discredited the machinery of international cooperation.

Meanwhile Hitler had left the League, instituted a massive programme of rearmament, and begun step by step to destroy the servitudes imposed on Germany by the Treaty of Versailles. In 1936 he reoccupied the Rhineland, whose demilitarization had been one of the main security guarantees insisted on by the French. In the spring of 1938 he invaded and declared union with an acquiescent Austria. Later the same year he demanded that Czechoslovakia, now gripped between the upper jaw of Silesia and the lower of Austria, should abandon to Germany the Sudeten borderlands with an ethnic German population, whose possession alone made its frontiers strategically defensible.

Britain and France watched helplessly as the balance of power was thus reversed. In both countries public opinion dreaded the prospect of another war and welcomed any diplomatic initiative that might avert one. The dominant figure in the British government, Neville Chamberlain, who had become Prime Minister in 1937, believed that Hitler was a rational statesman with whom he could do business. He was therefore prepared to settle the Sudeten crisis at Munich in September 1938 by compelling the Czechs to grant all Hitler's demands on the understanding that he would make no more.

The British and French people greeted the Munich agreement with heartfelt relief. But by March 1939, when Hitler occupied what was left of Czechoslovakia, a revulsion of feeling had occurred in Britain, where war was now widely accepted as inevitable. Chamberlain was pressured by his colleagues into providing a military guarantee for the country widely seen as Hitler's next victim, Poland. It was a guarantee militarily almost impossible to fulfil without the cooperation of the Soviet Union, whose underlying ill-will towards the bourgeois democracies was no less than that towards Germany. But the Soviet leader, Josef Stalin, was even less ready for war than was the West. Concerned to postpone war rather than to provoke it, he was now anxious only to conciliate Hitler. *Raison d'état* overruled ideological hostility on both sides. On 23 August 1939 the German and Soviet governments announced the conclusion of a non-aggression pact. Hitler now knew that he could safely invade Poland. So did everyone else.

Hitler attacked Poland on 1 September 1939, and Britain and France declared war two days later. The German armies overran Poland in three weeks, the Soviets moving in on 17 September to claim their share of the spoils. Each totalitarian power then imposed its own version of a new world order. The Germans sealed the

Jews into their ghettoes and treated the rest of the population as *Untermensch*, 'sub-people'. Both eliminated all intellectuals and potential leaders, the Soviets massacring 4,400 Polish officers who fell into their hands in the Forest of Katyn. Shortly afterwards Stalin reoccupied the Baltic States and demanded territorial adjustments from Finland to make Leningrad less vulnerable. Rather than obey, the Finns fought a war of resistance, inflicting 200,000 casualties on the Soviets for the loss of 25,000 of their own men before they capitulated on 13 March 1940.

Finnish resistance achieved two things. First, it revealed the weakness of the Red Army to the Germans; secondly, it provided an opportunity for the Western Allies to widen the war. Under cover of providing help to Finland, they planned an invasion of northern Norway and Sweden to seize and deny to the Germans the iron-ore resources on which they believed the German economy to be largely dependent. Finnish capitulation put an end to this, but not before Hitler had decided to pre-empt the Allies. On 9 April 1940 he invaded Denmark and Norway with a speed and efficiency that made it impossible for the British to gain anything but toeholds from which they were rapidly ejected. Only in the far north did they gain any success, but before that was complete the Germans had opened an attack on France and the Low Countries on 10 May.

By the end of June the campaign in the West was over. The Low Countries had been overrun; the small British expeditionary force had escaped at Dunkirk abandoning all its equipment; and France had accepted armistice terms that involved German occupation of the whole of the north and the west coast, leaving only the centre and south under the administration of the subservient regime that Marshal Petain established at Vichy. By the end of 1940 the British were besieged on their island. Half-hearted German attempts to improvise an invasion were abandoned after the Royal Air Force successfully beat off the *Luftwaffe*'s attempt to gain the control over British airspace that both sides knew to be an essential preliminary to a successful attack. Hitler contented himself with stepping up submarine war and using the *Luftwaffe* against British cities to destroy British determination to continue the war.

The British in fact showed a determination that surprised everyone, including themselves. They were fortunate enough to find in Winston Churchill a leader who, however unreliable and erratic he may have been in peacetime, found war to be his true element. Initially he could do little except appeal for American aid, stand on the defensive at sea and in the air, and deliver token air attacks against Germany. But Mussolini's ill-judged entry into the war on Germany's side in June 1940 to reap rewards that he had done nothing to earn, and his clumsy attempt to invade Egypt, enabled the British and Commonwealth forces stationed in the Middle East to launch a counter-attack that swept Italian forces out of Cyrenaica and ultimately the whole of East Africa, thus safeguarding communications in the Indian Ocean.

But the British in their turn overreached themselves. Mussolini had also, in October 1940, attacked Greece, where his forces had suffered humiliating defeat. British diplomats were working to build an alliance between Greece, Yugoslavia, and Turkey to create a front against the Germans in South-East Europe. In March 1941 they scored a triumph when the pro-German Yugoslav government was overthrown by a *coup d'état*. German reaction was prompt and effective. German forces overran not only Yugoslavia but Greece, sweeping away the British forces that had belatedly gone to its help, and continuing, albeit at heavy cost, with an airborne conquest of Crete. To complete British humiliation, while the British were occupied in Greece, a small German force under General Erwin Rommel sent to stop the rot in Libya was able to counter-attack in the Western Desert and drive the British back to the Egyptian frontier.

By the summer of 1941 Hitler's triumph appeared complete, and won at astoundingly low cost. Apart from a few heroic cells, British efforts to spark resistance struck no fire among the peoples of Western Europe, who, much as they disliked German occupation, saw no practicable alternative to accepting it; and many of whom, it must be said, shared both Hitler's anti-Semitism and his contempt for democracy. In South-East Europe right-wing regimes in Hungary, Bulgaria, and Rumania preserved a shadow of independence by accepting German hegemony. The Czechs were stunned into submission by the brutal reprisals taken when the German governor Reinhard Heydrich was assassinated by a British-trained resistance group. Yugoslavia was divided into a Croatia whose leaders set about a campaign of racial extermination of their Serb population, and a Serbia where, although both geography and history kept alive a culture of resistance, the resistance leaders who did emerge were as concerned to use their weapons against one another as against their German and Italian occupiers. The same was, tragically, the case in Greece. If Hitler's boast that the Third Reich would last a thousand years seemed exaggerated, there was little reason to suppose that it would not survive well into the twenty-first century.

Then, on 22 June 1941, Hitler invaded the Soviet Union.

Historians still disagree as to why he took this step. German relations with the Soviet Union had certainly not been good, the Soviets in particular refusing to abandon their traditional interests in south-east Europe, but they had continued loyally to make the deliveries of oil and grain needed to fuel the German war economy. Some maintain that, faced with the prospect of a prolonged war against a Britain now openly supported by the United States, Hitler was no longer willing to rely on Stalin's goodwill to have access to the resources that he needed. Others argue that he believed, erroneously, that Stalin's neutrality was a factor in Britain's determination to continue the war. Be all this as it may, what is certain is that Hitler could not achieve his ultimate objectives without destroying the Soviet Union and embodying large swathes of its territories within the Third Reich: not only the industrial resources of the Donetz Basin and the oil of the Caucasus, but the great cornlands of the Ukraine and western Russia that would make the German economy self-sufficient, and on which he could settle and breed good German stock to correct the inbuilt decadence of West European industrial urban civilization.

But there was another, parallel step that had to be taken if Hitler was to fulfil all his goals. In his programme, the racial purity of the Third Reich was as important as its economic balance. He had tried before the war to solve the problem of the Jews by hounding them out of the country, but Germany's conquests left them nowhere to go. They could not be maintained indefinitely in concentration camps at home. Logic dictated, therefore, that they should be physically exterminated, and the process of extermination was given equal priority with the conduct of the war. From the beginning of 1942 the police forces of Occupied Europe were set to round up all Jews, regardless of class, age, or sex, and send them to Germany; whence they were transported to camps in a remote corner of Poland, to be either worked to death or killed in gas chambers, their bodies then being destroyed in large crematoria. The logistical expertise, industrial resources, and scientific brilliance of the technologically most advanced society of the twentieth century ensured that, by the time the war ended, some six million people had been disposed of in this fashion. From this ghastly self-inflicted wound, European civilization has never fully recovered.

The exterminators followed in the wake of the German armies as they penetrated deep into Soviet territory in the latter half of 1941. Entire communities of Jews were rounded up and shot as they were found—and not only Jews. Hitler had made it clear to his military commanders that this was not to be a war like others fought between European powers, but one of colonial conquest and racial extermination. Political commissars were to be shot on sight; all civil resistance was to be met with savage reprisals; prisoners of war were to be worked to death or left to starve. By the end of 1941 over a million of these had been taken, as German armour sliced through the bewildered and disorganized Soviet resistance, surrounding Leningrad in a siege in which a third of the population died, overrunning the Ukraine and the Donetz Basin and reaching, in the first days of December, the outskirts of Moscow.

Then in the course of forty-eight hours the course of the war was transformed by two interlinked events. On 6 December Soviet forces unexpectedly counterattacked north of Moscow; and the following day the Japanese attacked the US fleet at anchor in Pearl Harbor.

The link was this. After an initial panic, Stalin had kept his head. In spite of the immediate disasters, the Soviet Union was prepared for a long war. Its main war industries were located deep in the interior beyond the reach of the German invaders, and the reserve strength of its armies was far greater than German intelligence had revealed. An entire Army Group had been deployed in the Far East, to deal with an attack by Hitler's ally, Japan. But the Japanese had other plans, and Soviet intelligence discovered them. The collapse of the imperial powers of Western Europe—Britain, France, and the Netherlands—had left their possessions in South-East Asia virtually defenceless—possessions whose resources would enable Japan to build up an autarkic economy that would not be at the mercy of Western economic hegemony. In the late summer of 1941 the Japanese government took the decision to seize them, and to pre-empt American intervention by destroying their Pacific Fleet. The pacification of China was causing the

Japanese Army enough problems without adding the Soviet Union to its enemies. Once he discovered this, Stalin could concentrate all his resources on a single front against a Germany that was quite unprepared for a prolonged war—and which was simultaneously confronted in the West with a new adversary capable of waging war on a vastly different scale.

Until now, neither ideological hostility to Nazism nor Winston Churchill's powerful advocacy had been enough to bring the United States into the war. President Franklin D. Roosevelt had realized that it was in America's best interests to keep Britain fighting and provide help whether the British could pay for it or not, and for the past eighteen months he had been doing so in increasing quantities. There was still no wish on the part of the American people actively to enter the war; but they were left with no alternative when Hitler took the initiative and himself declared war on the United States in support of his Japanese allies on 11 December 1941.

Initially the American entry brought Britain little but disaster. As in 1917, American physical help could not be made available for the best part of a year, and material that the Americans had previously provided to the British was now needed to supply their own armies. German submarines could now freely sink American shipping; while in Asia the Japanese overran British and Dutch possessions, inflicting a humiliation from which the British Empire was never to recover. Nevertheless, Hitler saw the balance tilting inexorably against him. In June 1942 he launched one final offensive against the Soviet Union to seize the oil resources of the Caucasus that alone might enable him to fight a prolonged war.

It was not until the autumn of 1942 that the United States was able to throw its weight decisively into the scales in Europe. In November American forces made their first entry into the European theatre with an Anglo-American invasion of French North Africa. Simultaneously a careful build-up of naval, air, and armoured superiority enabled the British Eighth Army to inflict on Rommel a decisive defeat at el Alamein that made possible the clearing of the Mediterranean shoreline and restored British military self-confidence after three years of almost unbroken defeats. More important even than this, the Russians had trapped an entire German Army at Stalingrad, whose surrender in February 1943 made it clear to everyone—probably even to Hitler himself—that the war was now definitively lost. It was a message reinforced by the fleets of American and British bomber aircraft that in 1943 began systematically to destroy German cities.

In July 1943 Anglo-American forces landed in Sicily, precipitating the overthrow of Mussolini and an Italian surrender that compelled the Allies to improvise an invasion of the Italian mainland. At the same time Soviet Armies trapped and destroyed the bulk of German armoured forces at the Battle of Kursk, and began a series of unbroken advances that by the end of the year had cleared their entire territory of the invader. Involvement in the Mediterranean and the demands of the war in the Pacific delayed a major Anglo-American invasion of north-west Europe until June 1944, an operation then made possible only by the massive naval and air superiority provided by the resources of the United States. Skilful German resistance delayed the invasion of Germany itself for nearly a year, by which time allied air attacks had reduced every major German city to piles of rubble. On 29 April 1945 Hitler himself committed suicide in the ruins of Berlin as Soviet forces stormed into the city.

Four days earlier American and Soviet forces had met at Torgau on the Elbe, in the centre not only of a Germany but of an entire continent that lay in ruins. The age of the World Powers had indeed dawned, and the hegemony that the nations of Europe had exercised over the rest of the world for the previous hundred years could never be recreated.

10 The Russian Empire and the Soviet Union, 1900–1945

RICHARD STITES

The Russian Empire in 1900 was the largest land power in the world. Peopling its corners were Lutheran Finns, Orthodox Georgians, Muslim Tajiks, and animist Chukchi—each moving through life in ways vastly alien to the others. Between them lay 100 nations ruled by Russians who had built this huge state stretching from the Baltic to the Pacific. Outside the capitals old and new—Kiev, Moscow, St Petersburg—lay new industrial cities, garrison towns, and a sea of peasants and herders. Borderlands were settled and guarded by Cossack hosts and frontier regiments. The relative weakness of civil society, the recent history of serfdom, ethnic division, and the roiling underground movement that had assassinated a tsar two decades earlier—all in various ways contributed to the prominent role of the military and the police in administering the country. A big central bureaucracy, with long tentacles, did things that elsewhere in Europe were in private hands; its ruling style was arrogant and sometimes brutally indifferent to popular needs.

Crowning the system was an autocracy with power emanating from the tsar. In practice the imperial will was mediated by ministries and local governors, a tiny community of appointed, mostly Orthodox Russian males of the noble class; there was no parliament or national elections. The last tsar, Nicholas II (1894–1917), was a well-meaning politically blind incompetent possessed by a dangerous nostalgia—reinforced by his wife Alexandra—for mystical ties between throne and people. Their concern for the haemophiliac heir apparent led them into a deadly path of withdrawal from reality. Stubborn conservatism shielded Nicholas from the urging of reform-minded advisers and against liberal or lower-class aspirations.

The Revolution of 1905 resulted from a conjuncture of social unrest and an unpopular war—both tied to Russia's surge towards industrialization in the 1890s. Feeling the sting of economic backwardness, Finance Minister Sergei Witte supported new industry and rail lines—including the Trans-Siberian Railroad stretching to the Pacific. Paralleling it, investors and adventurers advanced steadily into East Asia, alarming Japan, a modernizing great power with its own interests there. In 1904 Japan had launched a surprise naval attack on the Russian fleet in Port Arthur and deployed ground forces in Manchuria. The skills of Russian commanders were not up to defeating Japan. In the midst of this costly war, revolution broke out. Student agitation, strikes, peasant jacqueries, terrorist acts, ethnic unrest, and ferment among intellectuals had led to the formation of organized protest groups: liberals, Marxists (including militant Bolsheviks under Vladimir Lenin and moderate Mensheviks), and peasant-and-worker-oriented Socialist Revolutionaries. A dreadful massacre on 9 January, Bloody Sunday, in which hundreds of peacefully demonstrating workers and their families were cut down by government troops in the capital St Petersburg, sparked a nationwide revolution that lasted through the year 1905, marked by unprecedented violence from every quarter. The repression of an uprising in Moscow ended the Revolution. In the meantime, Witte persuaded a reluctant tsar to summon a Duma (parliament) with real elections and legal parties. The first Dumas were riven by tension created by assertive opposition parties, a stubbornly resistant throne, and violence in the country. Subsequent Dumas were more tranquil, but less representative of the population.

The major achievement of the government was reform of peasants' landholding. To quench the peasants' thirst for land without dispossessing the landed gentry, the state began dismantling the village commune that periodically distributed land in small strips. Some peasants withdrew from it into consolidated family farms but this did not slake peasant land hunger. The proletariat displayed many signs of alienation. Small by European standards but concentrated in large factories under harsh conditions, it was easily accessible to radical agitation. Legal trade unionism made some headway after 1905, but, on the eve of the First World War, strike waves swept Russia, bringing pitched battles in July 1914 to the very heart of the capital. The Duma largely represented the conservative elements of educated society, and the landed gentry feared the renewed chaos of 1905 when many landed estates had been sacked. The urban élite ranged from anti-Semitic monarchists to conservative industrialists to liberal professionals. Public opinion was outraged by the ineptitude and callousness of throne and government, especially the rise to political influence of the faith-healer Grigory Rasputin, who could sooth the ailing tsarevich; by the shooting of Siberian gold miners protesting for better food; and by the framing of an innocent Jew for ritual murder. Was Russian society so torn by conflict as to make revolution inevitable even without the scourge of world war? Or was it sufficiently dynamic to develop along 'European' lines? Cultural clues point both ways. The high culture, a dark blend of eroticism, mysticism, and occult, was filled with apocalyptic premonitions. But its very vitality might be read as an index of political health; and mass culture contained few hints of impending doom.

Doom descended in a confluence of European diplomacy, tsarist foreign policy, and events in Bosnia and Serbia. Hesitant at first, Nicholas faced Germany and Austria in August 1914 with an army of immense size, but short on efficient commanders, trust between officers and civilians, and military–industrial sinew.

Millions of soldiers—mostly peasants—perished under machine-gun fire, artillery assaults, and gas attacks. Battle raged across Poland, occasional Russian victories giving way to the relentless advance of the German forces. Tragedy erupted along the front: enormous casualties, virtual death marches of an uprooted population, Jewish villages laid waste by Russian soldiery. Much of the horror was masked in the first months of the war by censorship, euphoria, and patriotism. Statesmen nursed dreams of inheriting Galicia—and later Turkish lands—as spoils of war. Poets spoke of the cleansing fire of battle. High and low culture demonized the enemy and glorified the Slavs. But the adoring crowd that cheered the tsar on the opening day of war represented a minute fraction of Petrograd (the renamed capital) but not the masses who felt the economic crunch. Peasant views ranged from indifferent to sullen. Even the heady war enthusiasm of upper classes and intelligentsia soon faded. The tsar stumbled ahead into fatal policies: taking personal command of the army, allowing the Empress and Rasputin undue influence at court, and displaying deafness to sensible advice from those who wished to win the war and preserve the monarchy. Duma figures, courtiers, foreign envoys, generals, and family members tried to reason with Nicholas. But he stubbornly ignored political society and growing mass disenchantment with the war.

After the murder of Rasputin by right-wing patriots and a series of disastrous appointments in the winter of 1916–17, the Revolution broke out in the capital, caused directly by a bread shortage. Within five days in February, strikers from the working-class districts, joined by other citizens, had invested the centre of the city, persuaded most of the troops to defect, and held the monarchy at bay. Duma members hastened to the tsar's train in Pskov and persuaded him to abdicate. Next day, his brother and appointed successor refused the Crown, thus ending a 300-year-old dynasty and a two-centuries-old empire. Duma leaders formed a Provisional Government that would rule Russia for the next eight months. It fired or arrested loyal monarchists, and disseminated news of the new order by wire and rail to the cities of the Empire. Russia was a *de facto* republic, although its final form was declared by the new Government to be the business of a soon-to-be-elected Constituent Assembly. The Provisional Government was dominated by liberal ministers who fervently desired to push the war to a victorious conclusion. But they were opposed by a variety of socialist leaders who wanted either peace at once or a strictly defensive war. As in 1905, the socialists formed a workers' council or soviet in Petrograd, soon emulated all over the nation. The radical lawyer Alexander Kerensky held posts in both Provisional Government and in the soviet. Government and soviet sparred constantly over who would make policy and wield unchallenged power. The soviet supported the 'bourgeois' Government only half-heartedly but declined to take power itself on ideological grounds.

The springtime of revolution, with its euphoric revelling in freedom, parades, and release of political prisoners, did not last long. Neither the moderate conservative Provisional Government nor the more radical soviet could govern the ungovernable. Peasants invested nearby estates, workers struck, factory owners responded with closures and lockouts, and non-Russians began organizing their future as autonomous or independent states. Continuation of the war, by far the most inflammatory political issue, evoked a dizzying display of nuanced positions from intellectuals and generalized discontent among the lower classes that was sharpened when they discovered Russia's imperialist war aims contained in wartime secret treaties. The soviets, heavily populated by soldier deputies, tried to democratize the army without attenuating its war-fighting capacity. But friction, indiscipline, and desertion ensued. The erosion of military authority disgusted the Provisional Government's War Minister and the war-aims revelations aroused the fury of the masses against the Foreign Minister, Pavel Milyukov, the strongest figure in the Government. These both resigned and the nearly all-liberal cabinet gave way to a series of coalition governments in which liberals shared power with moderate socialist leaders from the soviets. It was an uneasy mix, further spoiled by the fact that the socialist leaders—mostly Mensheviks and Socialist Revolutionaries—steadily lost political support among the masses whom they tried to keep in check. When the radical Bolshevik Lenin returned from European exile, he advanced an agenda of overthrowing the Provisional Government and establishing soviet power.

The Bolsheviks later took credit for radicalizing the masses and deploying their energies against the Provisional Government—and anti-Communists have agreed. But the masses were not radicalized in a vacuum. The violent summer of 1917 revealed that workers, sailors, and soldiers often outran the Bolsheviks in their desire to seize power. After the reshuffling of the Provisional Government, Kerensky became War Minister and launched an offensive in July that ended in disaster. The army began to melt away. Simultaneously, units of the garrison stormed the Provisional Government and the Petrograd Soviet demanding that the soviets take power. Although much of the initiative was out of their hands, the Bolsheviks were blamed for this and were arrested or forced underground. Kerensky, made Prime Minister in a new coalition, was besieged by urban unrest, rural outrages, army dissolution, and minority nationality demands. Seeking a broad base of support, he summoned a conference in Moscow of state leaders; but it backfired by displaying a vigorous wave of revulsion against the perceived weakness of central power. A patriotic counter-revolutionary movement of conservatives and moderate liberals rallied around the army commander-in-chief, General Kornilov, as one who could restore discipline in the ranks and order in society. Although Kornilov did not plan a *coup*, an unwise troop movement towards Petrograd was interpreted as such and Kerensky turned for support to workers and socialists, including the Bolsheviks. Kornilov was rebuffed and the resulting fear of counter-revolution amplified the radicalism of the masses and swung support from moderate socialists to the more responsive and militant Bolsheviks.

The steady weakening of Kerensky's Provisional Government was matched by an upswing of Bolshevik strength. The Party grew in numbers and was strengthened by an infusion of new leaders, the most important of whom was Lev Trotsky. Lenin managed to persuade the top leadership that time was ripe for a seizure of power. After a hot debate, the decision was taken and the uprising timed for the opening of a major Congress of Soviets in Petrograd. During 24–6 October (Old Style), armed workers led by Bolsheviks took over key points in the city and invested the Winter Palace, the last headquarters of the Provisional Government. Although many at the Congress protested, the Bolshevik-dominated regime was recognized as a Soviet government. Far-flung cities followed suit, though with a great deal of variation. The real Revolution now began: peasant land seizures were legalized, industry placed under worker surveillance, and a freely elected Constituent Assembly dispersed. A peace treaty signed with the Central Powers at Brest-Litovsk early in 1918 ceded all the western non-Russian borderlands— Finland, the Baltic, Poland, and parts of Belorussia and Ukraine. This, the Bolshevik publication of secret treaties, and the repudiation of foreign debts, angered the Allied powers and led them eventually to intervene to overthrow the new regime. The treaty also led the left wing of the Socialist Revolutionaries who had cooperated with the Bolsheviks for a while to launch an uprising against them. A notorious revolutionary police force, the Cheka, crushed the opposition, while Lenin, the Prime Minister or Chair of the Council of People's Commissars, settled into the new capital, Moscow, and regularized his state as the Russian Soviet Federated Socialist Republic.

The Russian Civil War was a devastating experience for all concerned, not least for the common people. The Bolshevik seizure of power and its radical measures prompted a 'White' movement—tsarist officers supported by a spectrum of conservatives, liberals, and socialists—to gather in the winter of 1917–18 to bring down Bolshevism. Limited help from Allied intervention forces was enough to taint them as imperialist puppets but not enough to let them win. The Whites' strength lay in their officer talent; their weakness in geographical dispersion on the southern, north-western, northern, and eastern fringes, their political division, and their fuzzy national and social policies—especially their refusal to recognize peasant land seizures. The Bolsheviks enjoyed inner lines of communication, a Red Army under the energetic leadership of Trotsky, and an effective propaganda machine. Both sides suffered from unpopularity caused by conscription, requisitions, and terror. Three years of bitter fighting brought Red victory and a mass emigration of about a million Russians. The non-Russian borderlands were re-won (in the west after the defeat of Germany and the nullification of Brest-Litovsk) largely by military conquest. The country was in ruins. An economic policy retrospectively called War Communism had virtually eliminated the market and private enterprise, imposed rationing, and subjected the peasants to food-requisitioning depredations. They rose up in numerous actions against the Bolsheviks—renamed Communists in 1918. Radical sailors of the Kronstadt naval base did likewise, arguing that the Communists had betrayed the revolution. All these were crushed in blood by Red Army units in one of the many tragic ironies of the Revolution.

Lenin's Russia was a one-party state ruled by a highly centralized revolutionary party, now a cadre administering and transforming the nation. Though Lenin was greatly revered within the Communist Party as its *de facto* head, he did not wear the trappings of a twentieth-century classical dictator. His policies were constantly challenged in the inner chambers by his comrades and he sent none of them to prison. On the other hand, Lenin brooked no organized opposition to his party's rule or policies—all 'factions' within the Communist Party were outlawed in 1921—and was happy to use the courts and the firing squad against enemies of the state. When he died in 1924, Lenin became the object of a national cult. In 1921 he had abandoned War Communism and introduced a New Economic Policy (NEP) that allowed limited private trade and business and a taxed agricultural market rather than state grain requisition for the peasantry. Banking, heavy industry, foreign trade, and economic policy remained in state hands, a novel landscape of private enterprise under the political hegemony of socialists. Few city folks were really satisfied with the arrangement. NEP capitalists wanted less state interference in business. Many factory workers grumbled under state management and wage scales and the co-optation of their unions by the state; and they resented the success of NEP businessmen. Party ideologues wondered what had happened to the socialist dream. Leftists among them, such as Trotsky, urged a rapid lunge into socialism in order to liquidate Russia's backwardness and deliver social justice. The economist Nikolai Bukharin envisioned a gradual evolution. This was a major issue in the power struggle of the 1920s.

Another one was world revolution. From the first moment, the Soviet regime and the outer world had greeted each other with mutual hostility. Shocked by 'red' extravagance, anti-capitalism, and anti-imperialism, the West had half-heartedly intervened in the Civil War. Lenin retaliated by inciting revolution everywhere he could. Revolutionary parties struck for power from Finland to Germany to Bulgaria in the years 1918–23. These failed attempts enraged the governing classes and helped give rise to fascist movements dedicated to wiping out Communists everywhere. Undaunted, the Soviets continued on into Asia, where they helped launch a major revolutionary struggle in China in the mid-1920s—a disaster that ended in a bloodbath. From 1919 onwards, the Moscow-based Communist International (Comintern) steered these attempts and seemed to pose a standing threat to the global order.

Yet by the early 1920s international accommodation was reached. Western governments wanted trade, investment, and the recovery of old debts—as well as a chance to 'civilize' the Soviets via normal diplomatic intercourse. Lenin was willing: Russia needed investment and technology of every sort. Following some smaller states, Britain and France extended recognition. Britain, mostly because of its own labour unrest and Comintern meddling in the British Empire, broke ties once during the 1920s and then renewed relations. In 1922 Germany signed a secret agreement at Rapallo on military cooperation with Russia, its fellow outcast from the Versailles system. Hotheads in Moscow led by Trotsky longed for aggressive worldwide revolution, believing it to be the only thing that could save revolutionary Russia. The emerging Stalin responded with the more cautious and nationalist-leaning slogan of 'socialism in one country'.

The 1920s were not only concerned with politics, economics, and diplomacy; nor were they merely an interval between revolution and Stalinism. They also saw an attempt to reshape art, society, and humanity itself. The revolution had wiped out the landed gentry and the big bourgeoisie, but among its unplanned consequences came famine, millions of homeless children, and female unemployment. Deeper maladies were seen by optimists as holdovers of an evil past: egoism, religion, patriarchy, ignorance, and illiteracy. Agitators sought to transform social values by teaching sexual and ethnic equality, science, efficiency, and a cult of the machine. The 1920s saw the birth of the Soviet Union, a federation of 100 nationalities—some organized into 'republics'—and a programme of 'nativizing' their governance and of uplifting—or even creating—local culture through alphabets and literacy campaigns. Best remembered in the world—though only partially appealing to the public—was the explosion of culture, both propaganda and avant-garde: literature, art, theatre, and cinema. While censorship interdicted oppositional currents and authorities repressed some writers, most creative artists who embraced the Revolution rose to its transformational challenge with spectacular and enduring works. The names of Vladimir Mayakosvky, Lyubov Popova, Vsévolod Meyerhold, and Sergei Eisenstein—trained or inspired in pre-revolutionary times—sparkled upon the cultural tapestry. On the eve of the revolution from above, there still flourished some spontaneity, social pluralism, artistic creativity, and even revolutionary goodwill—most of which would soon disappear.

One reason for the relative freedom of the 1920s was that the leadership was busy resolving whether to follow Lenin with a committee system or a new charismatic leader. If the latter, who would it be? By the decade's end, Stalin (Iosif Jugashvili) had answered both questions by emerging as undisputed leader. A Georgian by birth, he had served as a minor Bolshevik in the Caucasus. Energy and loyalty to Lenin won him key posts after 1917: as Commissar of Nationalities he designed the structure of the Soviet Union; as General Secretary of the Party, he built an organizational empire within it and kept a low profile in the early years after Lenin's death. The Party squabbled in the late 1920s over rural policy, rapid industrialization, world revolution, and—most of all—personal ambitions and animosities. Stalin changed sides (as did others) but amplified his bureaucratic network, even though the dying Lenin had urged his removal from the pivotal Party post. Stalin's extraordinary power of manœuvring, his patronage, his tough-guy charisma, and his internalized Russian nationalism, combined with the weakness of opponents such as Bukharin and Trotsky, brought him victory over various opposition groups. In 1929, on his fiftieth birthday, Stalin stood above Red Square in Moscow as dictator or *vozhd* of Party and state. During the agonies of collectivization, he held firm against real and imagined opposition; and when a high Party figure was assassinated under suspicious circumstances in 1934, Stalin used this—and later other murders—to attack all previous opponents. From 1936 to 1953 he ruled supreme over the Soviet Empire and became the most powerful and murderous leader in all of the twentieth century.

RICHARD STITES

Stalin launched a revolution from above in 1928–32. Industry and agriculture were transformed and the remnants of capitalism and civil society obliterated. Power at the top did not suffice for Stalin and his team. They wanted full social control, a powerful military, and what they understood as socialism—state ownership and control of the means of production and a planned economy. The first Five Year Plan was designed to increase national production dramatically in key infrastructural industries. Giant manufacturing complexes, hydroelectric dams, canals, and cities sprang up overnight—built by euphoric youth, by displaced peasants, and by convicts. Planners constantly increased already superhuman production goals. The results, sometimes falsified, were impressive. The system—later called a command economy—included successive plans, the absence of a legal market, the non-existence of private business, state pricing, subsidized services, a kind of full employment in which many were grossly underemployed, and a ruinous abuse of the environment. With all its distortions, this economy contributed to the country's victory over the German onslaught. But the costs of creating such a system were so terrible that one must take seriously the proposition that Russia could have won the war of 1941 with a different economy. The leaders' desire to control both food production and those who produced it drove the decision to collectivize the peasants against their will. The state took grain by force and arrested, deported, or shot resisters and herded villages into collective farms. A resulting famine, though not planned by the state, took millions of lives in Ukraine and Kazakhstan and in the Russian regions of the Volga and Northern Caucasus.

Opposition to Stalin's burgeoning power and his harsh policies never ceased throughout the period. Even if it had, Stalin—harbouring dark fantasies of treason, deep hatred of old rivals, and vast yearning for vengeance—would not have believed it. The terror began not in 1936 with the purge trials but in 1928 with massive assaults against the common people which surpassed the violence of the Civil War period. The wonder is not that Stalin would deploy his upgraded political police against intellectuals and politicians but that the terror was allowed to spin so dizzyingly close to the Kremlin palaces from whence Stalin ruled. No single cause can be invoked for the terror. A series of semi-public prosecutions in Moscow eliminated virtually all former comrades of Lenin and real or potential opponents of Stalin. Victims were forced to confess to heinous crimes against the state such as treason and collaboration with the Nazis and the Japanese. Trial scenarios—with their dastardly plots, dark villains, and folkloric heroes and martyrs—resembled the socialist realist fiction and art of the time. Violating the emerging cult of Stalin was not evil enough: the accused had to be demonized. Bukharin and other ex-oppositionists were liquidated, along with the cream of the military command, the diplomatic corps, foreign Communists, and vast reaches of Party, bureaucracy, intelligentsia, and the cultural community. Ordinary people were afflicted by false denunciations. Millions of innocents perished in jails, torture chambers, or in the satanic labour and death camps known as the Gulag. Most of those unpunished by the terror—and not only those millions reared and

educated under Soviet power—probably supported it; and thousands of its victims actually believed that Stalin was a blameless prisoner of 'dark forces'.

By 1939 Stalin had erected a political system and a political culture that would
last until his death—with many of its organizational and mental structures enduring down to the end of the century. Its written template was the Stalin constitution
of 1936 that ratified the Party's hegemonic role in the state, described the non-
Russian republics, and proclaimed its democratic essence. The potent myth of a
Soviet democracy and a socialist economy appealed widely to intellectuals all over
the world and to workers who migrated to the Soviet Union. Stalinism resembled
Hitlerism in function—terror, cultic leadership, shameless propaganda, a party-
state, and the fictions of popular rule masking a ruthless totalitarian behemoth.
But it differed in its ideological apparel which was not wholly cynical or mendacious: internationalism, outright atheism, social levelling, and class hatred
instead of racism. The Party was devastated by the purge and terror which not only
took victims but also reduced its once-vaunted role. The political police in turn
rose to ascendance, though its chiefs were periodically executed and replaced.
The army—gutted in the purges—could harbour no potential Bonapartes. Some
of the expressions of nationalism in the republics that were fostered in the 1920s
were repressed. Society was organized along corporate lines with mass organizations for women, youth, and workers, all trained in tightly controlled schools and
universities. Accommodating intellectuals and artists—true believers, cynics, and
survivors—constructed an elaborate cultural façade to legitimize ruler and system in the academy, the press, the temples of art, and the sites of popular culture.

The war between Hitler and Stalin was not inevitable; no war is. But given Hitler's
vaulting expansionist ambitions, far greater than Stalin's whose modesty was in no
way rooted in moral restraint, it is certainly understandable. Hitler hated
Bolsheviks, Russians, and Jews, whom he often conflated. All evidence points to
his long-held intention to invade Russia and subjugate its inhabitants. Historians
argue whether Stalin was a viable potential ally for the West against Nazi Germany
in the 1930s, some blaming appeasers for not seeking that alliance, others invok-
ing Stalin's utter cynicism and opportunism. But these do not conflict. If the cynics of Berlin and Moscow could ally—which they did in 1939-41—then Britain and
France could certainly have worked with Stalin against Hitler before 1939—as
Britain indeed would do in 1941-5. If that had happened, the Second World War
might have been rescheduled and reconfigured but probably not avoided. Stalin
supported collective security and anti-fascism through various international
bodies, treaties, and popular fronts. He also rearmed and intervened in the
Spanish Civil War of 1936-9. After German moves in Austria, Czechoslovakia, and
Memel it seemed to Stalin that the cards had been dealt. In 1939 he dismissed his
foreign commissar Maxim Litvinov, who was both Jewish and a spokesman for
collective security, thus paving the way for the talks with Germany that culminated in the Nazi–Soviet Pact, whose secret protocols arranged a partition of
Poland and other zones of Eastern Europe. This pact shocked Western Europe, as

did the Soviet war on Finland and the ruthless annexation in 1940 of the three Baltic republics.

Out of fear that they were in error, Stalin ignored the many warnings about the impending German invasion. It came in full force on 22 June 1941—a date treated in Soviet historiography as equivalent in infamy to Pearl Harbor day. The Germans and their allies crashed through the frontiers of Finland, the Baltic, Belorussia, and Ukraine. The northern salient sped to Leningrad and laid siege to it for nearly three years, subjecting its residents to hideous suffering and loss of life. The middle salient pushed up near Moscow but could not invest the city, partly because some of its forces were detached to help the conquest in the south, which proceeded with dazzling rapidity—through Kiev, the Don, Crimea, and eventually down into the Caucasus. In the summer of 1942, things looked bright for the Germans and their numerous foreign brigades of Romanians, Hungarians, Spaniards, Norwegians, and other anti-Communist volunteers. It was the darkest moment for the Soviet state and the armed forces. And much darker for most inhabitants of occupied areas. There the German forces—not only special detachments of SS but army soldiers and officers as well—inflicted unspeakable atrocities upon men, women, and children, sometimes with the assistance of the local anti-Communist population. Communists and Jews were summarily executed and bands of hostages or whole villages were hanged, shot, or incinerated. The Germans opened a few churches and closed down some hated collective farms, but not nearly enough to offset their brutal policies, including the deportation of forced labour to German factories and the starvation torture of Soviet prisoners of war.

Stalin, after some initial moments of panic, responded to the threat by reorganizing the command, firing some wilted generals, and mobilizing the population. Partisans were organized behind enemy lines to harass them, though these had more psychological than military effect. Whole industries, towns, and villages were evacuated to the rear and Soviet institutions—including much of the government—were relocated to cities on the Volga. Women were mobilized to replace men at the bench and on anti-aircraft batteries; a million of them also served in uniform as pilots, gunners, and tankers, as well as doctors and nurses. All of the arts were unleashed in a campaign of national defence and hatred of the enemy. A great emotional swelling of patriotism occurred based on attachment to home, homeland, and family, and containing little ideological content. Most important, like the Soviet system itself, the army held together in the midst of immense mismanagement at all levels. Great reserves were rolled in for the crucial battle of Stalingrad in 1942–3 to encircle and defeat a major German force. This defeat also ended the Wehrmacht's sally into the Caucasus to capture the oil centres there and spelled the beginning of a long retreat. The initial German armour and air superiority was reversed and was punctuated at the biggest battle in world history: Kursk in 1943. The siege of Leningrad was relieved in 1944 as the Red Army headed towards Poland. Some military historians have argued that the Soviet Union almost lost the war with Germany, and this may well be true. But 'almost' counts only in as much as it demystifies the heroic account of that war at the hands of official Soviet historians.

That account was mendacious on many levels. It downplayed the role of its allies in supplying lend-lease materials. More important, it ignored the Soviet war against its neighbours and its own people. Deportations in Polish Belorussia and Ukraine took place during the Soviet occupation under the Nazi-Soviet Pact. Thousands of captured Polish officers were executed in cold blood. Equally horrible were the sadistic murders and rapes during the Red Army's drive to Berlin which it took in May 1945. On the way, it paused outside Warsaw and allowed the Germans to crush the 1944 uprising there. Whatever previous expansionist plans Stalin had nursed, his diplomacy stiffened in proportion to his victories in the field. His takeover of Eastern Europe at the end of the war subjected its inhabitants to initial terror and then to decades of unwanted Soviet hegemony. At home, thousands of political prisoners were shot in the camps in the early days of the war as a security measure; thousands more were forced into punishment battalions and driven into suicide missions. Surviving Soviet prisoners of war and Russian residents of Central Europe were shipped back for incarceration or execution. Whole peoples were uprooted from historic homelands and transported for real or suspected collaboration with the invaders. The Volga Germans, resident in Russia since the eighteenth century, were among the innocent; Chechens and other Mountain People of the Caucasus and the Tatars of the Crimea—for example—produced some collaborators. But a vengeful state hauled the innocent away in cattle cars to perish with the guilty or live for decades in faraway exile. Finally, Stalin and the Party 'stole' the victory from the people by exalting their role and downplaying the spontaneous forces that had made victory possible.

11 The United States, 1900–1945

HUGH BROGAN

The twentieth century started early for Americans. It was in the nineteenth century that they began to experience such phenomena of modernity as industrial and agricultural revolutions, democratization, centralization, and urbanization. The net effect was that well before 1900 the United States was already equipped to meet every challenge which the new age would throw at it. It had not been an easy achievement, nor was it complete, and it was long before most Americans understood and accepted it; some have yet to do so. The story of the United States in the first half of the twentieth century is the story of the continuation of a process already well launched, yet still obstructed by formidable resistance. In the difficulties which the United States encountered it resembled other countries and continents; in its success in overcoming them it was unusual; and in the scale of its enterprise—the reward of success being world hegemony—it was unique.

Good fortune played its part, at any rate in the beginning, when what Mr Sherlock Holmes was to describe as 'the folly of a monarch and the blundering of a Minister' forced the Americans to tackle two of the classical problems of modernity early, while they were still manageable. They decolonized themselves in the American Revolution and in consequence had to invent a frame of government suitable to their new circumstances. The whole process took less than twenty years (1774–88), and was so successful that its outcome has never been successfully challenged. The success was possible because in 1774 a population of just over 2 million was scattered thinly along the East Coast from Maine to Georgia, and in that population the educated élite, while an unusually high proportion of the whole, was nevertheless sufficiently small and homogeneous to be of one mind on almost all important questions (they were, for instance, strongly committed to individualism and federalism). In consequence, the infant United States, benefiting from the best ideas of its age (Ralf Dahrendorf has called it 'the applied Enlightenment'), was able to face the onrushing tide of industrialization, urbanization and capitalism with the rationally designed institutions of a modern republic, including, as was to prove of central importance, a system of two-party politics.

Americans in the early nineteenth century made a fetish of their institutions, not without reason. For the first seventy years or so the republic was dominated politically by its most reactionary—indeed, its only reactionary—section, the slave-holding South. It took a civil war to throw off that ascendancy, save the union of states, and end slavery, when the slave-holders refused to abdicate gracefully; but the US government was strong enough to win. Industrialism brought with it industrial conflict on a scale, and occasionally of a violence, to match anything which Europe could show; but an alliance of financiers, industrialists, and lawyers captured the organs of state—particularly the US Senate and the Supreme Court—and by its selfish, intelligent single-mindedness ensured continuing political stability. By the end of the nineteenth century the United States stretched imperially from the Atlantic to the Pacific; thanks to the federal system (and to the transcontinental railroads) there was never, after the civil war, any question of fault-lines developing of the kind which were to split every other twentieth-century empire. A period of depression in the mid-1890s had been followed by renewed prosperity. By 1900 the only great modern test which the United States had not yet passed was that of a major international war, and to many, perhaps most, thinking Americans, this did not seem to matter, because they supposed that such wars were things of the past. They also believed that, even if such a war should break out, they would play no part in it. One of the strongest of all American traditions was that of isolationism, by which the United States saw it as its best, indeed its necessary policy, to remain aloof and neutral in any European conflict.

The United States also enjoyed a tradition of ever-increasing prosperity, generally diffused. So much was this the case that to most people, inside and outside the country, it seemed to be the whole point of America. The promise of American life was that every generation would be better off than its immediate predecessor. The United States was also rapidly emerging as the greatest industrial power in the world, and, technologically, as the most innovative. Most of the great inventions which were to transform society in the twentieth century—the telephone, the phonograph, the internal combustion engine—had been made in the nineteenth century (although only in 1903 did the Wright brothers make the first flight in a powered aeroplane), but Americans, led by Thomas Edison, showed themselves foremost in application and adaptation: perhaps Edison's greatest invention was the electricity industry. In 1908 Henry Ford began the production of his Model T car in what became the first assembly-line factory. America thus put its stamp on the twentieth century from the very first, and not only industrially. It was also the begetter of a highly original urban culture, of which baseball, ragtime, and vaudeville were perhaps the most obvious tokens.

Yet progress was never smooth, or easily accepted: it was too irregular and incomplete, and, for many, involved too much sacrifice. Public opinion in the first decade of the twentieth century was therefore confused and, on many points, contradictory. National problems might not be insoluble, but they were difficult and demanding, and grew more pressing as the country grew (its population in 1900 was 75.9 million; it would be more than 100 million by 1920), and these problems were not made any easier by the regional diversity of the United States, nor by the diversity of its many ethnic groups. The cities had enlarged with staggering speed in the previous half-century, too fast to be much more than ill-governed, ill-designed, incoherent agglomerations of humanity: urban reform was a pressing necessity, but it was hard to get agreement on what form it should take. Agriculture had recovered well from the crisis of the late nineteenth century, but its structural weaknesses (above all, too many farmers and too little capital) were surreptitiously intensifying. Social conflict, between classes, races, native and immigrant populations, religions, and regions, which categories often overlapped, was still intense, as Americans struggled to win or keep their share of the national wealth. Many manifestations of modern life, of which commercialized sex and excessive drinking were regarded as the most alarming, aroused deep anxiety in conservative souls. And the fourteen, fifteen, or sixteen states (depending on which you included) of the South exemplified all these problems, with the addition of a most un-American phenomenon, apparently permanently sluggish economic growth.

In retrospect it is clear enough that the agenda of domestic politics was set for the next half-century or more by these practical problems. The way in which that agenda was tackled was determined by the highly changeable impulses, ideas, and interests of the American people in all their variety, and by the enormous but unforeseen impact of two world wars. But the framework did not change: no matter what the challenge (the Great Depression of 1929–39 was to be the worst), the United States remained liberal, and responded to every crisis until 1945 and beyond, not by jettisoning its constitution or any part of it, but by extending its reach. By the standards of the end of the twentieth century, the United States was at its beginning a highly defective democracy: black citizens, and the poorest white ones, mostly could not vote in the South, and women in only four Western states. There were other defects; but Americans believe that the cure for the ills of democracy is more democracy. In 1913 two constitutional amendments respectively gave Congress the power to levy income taxes and required the election of US Senators by the people, not the legislatures, of the various states. Many of the states, at the same period, introduced the system of primary elections for the nomination of party candidates for office, and of referendums and recall elections to keep state politicans under popular control. In 1920, by another constitutional amendment—the nineteenth—the suffrage was extended to all adult women; and twenty years later the campaign, led by the National Association for the Advancement of Colored People, to strike down the various legal devices which restricted black suffrage, was well under way.

The glaring anomaly in this programme to increase the powers and enhance the legitimacy of republican government was the adoption in 1919 of the eighteenth, prohibition, amendment, which tried to stamp out the 'manufacture, sale or transportation of intoxicating liquors'. This was the culmination of an anti-drink campaign which, moved by the prospect of ruined families, drunken workmen, and political corruption associated with the saloon, was already very strong before the United States entered the war; after it had done so, compulsory abstinence seemed, to patriotic enthusiasts, to be a reasonable war measure. But in peacetime prohibition proved to be unenforceable and to foster organized crime. Realism reasserted itself, and the amendment was repealed in 1933.

The United States' effective and deepening commitment to democracy was of enormous importance to the history of the world; national traditions sustained it. But there can be no doubt that the stability of the political structure came about because of that structure's practical success. It delivered the goods; or, if it did not, the industrial system did, and democracy took the credit. Underlying all other themes of American politics in modern times has been a concern with the role that the state and federal governments might or should play in securing the prosperity of the people and in regulating its equitable distribution. Majority opinion has at times supported greater governmental activism, at times less. But it has always been the political system which has enabled majority opinion to make itself effective, and has sporadically protected the interests of minorities. The political and economic systems have supported each other, and the ceaseless competition of ideas and interests which both entail perhaps explains the comparative adaptability of the United States. Its wealth and its physical security, while they have often bred in the people a certain complacency and provincialism, have equally often mitigated the ill-effects of American divisiveness and self-deception: they have bought the time necessary for a democracy to make the right decisions. All in all, if the United States success in the twentieth century remains startling, it is hardly inexplicable.

Such was the burgeoning strength of the United States that many of its leaders in 1914 clearly foresaw that their country was going to enjoy pre-eminence in what, thirty-four years later, would be called, by Henry Luce of *Time* magazine, 'the American century'. The brisk, effective way in which the US government had shouldered aside the British Empire and taken upon itself alone the enterprise of building the Panama Canal (1904–14) had been one illustration of the emergence of American power; another had been the suppression of the revolt of the Philippines which had followed the annexation of those islands after the Spanish–American War of 1898. And if Americans were isolationists, they were not isolated: being a bi-oceanic people they were neighbours to all the world, not just to the Latin American republics south of their border, the dominion of Canada to their north, or the Russian Empire just across the water from their remote territory of Alaska. They looked east and west—particularly east, to the countries where most of them originated. Commercially, from their earliest beginnings, they had provided the most important foreign market for Britain, the mother country and the first industrialized nation. British subjects—English, Welsh, Scots, and Irish (both Protestant and Catholic)—had provided the main stock of the American people. During the nineteenth century they had been joined by emigrants from every other European state and nation, and this process was continuing: between 1903 and 1914 annual immigration was never less than three-quarters of a million.

In 1914 itself total immigration was 1,218,480, the largest such figure ever recorded; 284,000 of the arrivals were Italians, 256,000, Poles. Remittances flowed back across the Atlantic and sustained the economy of many a Calabrian village; there was a substantial amount of return migration, and with the development of large, fast, comfortable, and cheap ocean liners there was substantial seasonal migration too, workers arriving in the New World in the spring and leaving after the last harvest. The rich did not migrate, but they travelled a lot, and European musicians (Dvořák, Mahler), actors, writers, and artists (1913 was the year of the New York Armory show, which introduced the School of Paris to America) were more and more aware of the opportunities offered by the United States. The financier J. P. Morgan was merely the greatest collector among the multimillionaires who despoiled the palaces and churches of Europe to the benefit of American museums, and many a European lordling married a multimillionaire's daughter (and her fortune). Between 1900 and 1913, the last full year of peace, US exports to Europe went up by nearly half, and imports more than doubled. On the whole, it is probable that connections between the Old World and the New had never been tighter than on the eve of the First World War.

The impact of that war on the United States was immense, appalling, and is still felt today. It was experienced not only in America's own brief period of belligerency (war on Germany was declared on 6 April 1917), although the economic and military effort of those eighteen months was unequalled in previous American history: in that time an army of 4 million men was raised, deployed, and supplied. The American state passed its test triumphantly: it organized for war and victory in exemplary fashion, and valuable experience was gained by young officers such as George C. Marshall and Dwight D. Eisenhower, by young officials such as Franklin D. Roosevelt, Assistant Secretary of the Navy, and by business and government leaders who collaborated in organizing the war effort. But to most Americans the experience was on the whole purely hateful. The casualties were bad enough, though not comparable to European losses: 110,000 men died. In this and in other ways the war seemed to be not only a personal disaster and an intolerable inversion of normality: it seemed to break the promise of American life. The cost of living doubled, and, although wages on the whole kept up with this inflation, salaries did not. Wartime boom was followed by a brief but painful post-war slump. The draft took the young men from the farms: women and preachers worried about the effect on their morals. It took white workers from Northern factories: the bosses filled their places with women and black migrants from the South, and when the soldiers returned there was trouble. Wartime rage and patriotism were expressed in a wave of jingoism, directed especially against the large German–American community, but spilling over into attacks on all 'hyphenated Americans' and all who, for whatever reasons, questioned the righteousness of the war or of wartime measures (Eugene V. Debs, the socialist leader, was sent to prison for ten years for defying the Espionage Act of 1917). News of the Bolshevik Revolution reactivated a long-standing dread of socialism and of anything that might be labelled foreign subversion, which resulted in the notorious 'Red Scare' of 1920. War's end was marked by various episodes, from race riots in Chicago to the rejection of the League of Nations, from the adoption of the prohibition amendment to a Republican landslide in the presidential election of 1920 (the Democrats had been the party of wartime government) which cumulatively demonstrated the United States' rejection of the path into which it had wandered. The reaction continued deep into the 1920s, as was shown by the mushroom growth of the second Ku Klux Klan and the Immigration Act of 1924; under that Act the total immigration to the United States was sharply reduced, Japanese immigration was stopped altogether, and a quota system discriminated heavily against all nationalities which had not been substantial parts of the US population in 1890.

But from the moment that the war began, in August 1914, decision-makers in Washington, New York, and elsewhere had been confronted with problems that could never be wished away, even temporarily. In its very first months the war had nearly ruined the cotton-growing South, dependent as it was on exports; and although in the end the United States had done tremendously well out of the war—manufacturing capital doubled in value between 1914 and 1919, so did farm income, the surplus on international payments went from $56 million to $352 million, and by 1919 the United States was for the first time a creditor nation, exporting more capital than it imported—the post-war contraction plunged the farm sector into difficulties from which it was not finally to be rescued until the Second World War. More than that, the ruin or weakening of all other advanced economies during the war left the United States in a position of dangerous pre-eminence, for which it was both politically and institutionally unprepared: its economic power gave it new, global responsibilities which it did not completely accept until, during the Second World War, it made the Bretton Woods Agreements. Above all, as Woodrow Wilson (President, 1913–21) painfully discovered, in the modern world a foreign policy composed of such shibboleths as isolationism, the Open Door, and the Monroe Doctrine was no longer adequate: the United States needed an active foreign policy with a global reach. Wilson believed that free trade and free institutions would bring about the peace and betterment of all mankind, and whether as the leader of the world's greatest neutral power, as the commander-in-chief of the United States at war, or as the chief peace-maker in 1919, he tried to shape his course according to those principles. But although the United States fought, in Wilson's phrase, 'to make the world safe for democracy', it had gone to war because Germany had been sinking American merchant ships, and threatening to form an alliance with Mexico to seize Arizona and California, and bringing France, Britain, and Russia nearly to their knees. The world was not as safe a place for Americans as they had thought. Even in the period of neutrality Wilson had discovered that to make his policy effective the United States would have to arm itself on a scale unprecedented in peacetime. This requirement was not made obsolete by victory in 1918; but it was one which many Americans—especially in Wilson's own Democratic Party—would find it impossible to accept in the 1920s and 1930s. Appropriations for the army and the navy were sharply reduced.

Yet the reaction against the war and what it stood for was not long in provoking its own counter-reaction. The 1920s are remembered as a decade of prosperity and youthful high spirits. Although the conservative Republican Party won all the national elections, at state level the practical reforming spirit that had been so much a feature of the pre-war United States continued to operate, most conspicuously in New York state, where Alfred E. Smith was elected governor four times—the first Irish–American Catholic to hold the post. Herbert Hoover as Secretary of Commerce worked in the same spirit in the cabinet, and when he defeated Smith for the presidency in 1928 he promised America a new era of permanent prosperity. It seemed plausible, for the great consumer transformation of the twentieth-century economy was beginning to make itself felt. The Model T is usually taken as a symbol of the decade, but in fact Ford was losing ground to his chief competititor, General Motors (and the Model T was discontinued in 1927). Between them the great motor manufacturers put what had been a luxury item within the reach of millions, and placed the national economy on a quite new footing: from now on automobiles, not steel, coal, or railways, would be the most important sector of industry. The equally rapid rise of the movies was almost as powerful a note of the 1920s. It seemed to the sterner moralists that the quest for pleasure was now all in all; they exaggerated, but in such a time it is no wonder that prohibition failed. The business of booze simply went underground; Americans eagerly sought out the speakeasies, and in those shady dives made other exciting discoveries, such as the jazz of black musicians which soon modified the Jewish traditions of Tin Pan Alley. Popular music began to assume a new importance, both cultural and economic, especially after sound came to the movies with *The Jazz Singer* in 1927. New methods of birth control, though not yet legal, began to make sex a somewhat less risky pastime. The spirit of 'the Jazz Age' is still wonderfully fresh in F. Scott Fitzgerald's *The Great Gatsby* (1925).

Motorized transport was an economic stimulus in many ways—for instance, to the building of bridges and highways to accommodate it. Palpably shaped by so much innovation and enterprise, it is hardly surprising that the 1920s seemed to be a decade of vast economic success, and vaster promise. Yet America was still the prey of social dislocations and economic problems, which might be thought to require national action. The difficulties of the agricultural sector in particular needed and attracted attention: the problem was of agreeing on what to do about them. As late as 1940 half the American people lived on the land or in small country towns; but farming could no longer support them all. Technological innovation was coming (in 1918 there were 80,000 tractors on the farms, in 1929 850,000) but not fast enough; demand for American produce had fallen steeply as Europe returned to production after 1918; farm income dropped steadily behind expenses, and was not helped by efforts to grow yet larger crops: glut merely forced prices down. Partly because of this, the overwhelmingly rural South remained sunk in racism and poverty. Even in the booming industrial sector too many workers did not receive the high wages which were creating the mass market to absorb American goods. Management was not particularly enlightened: the war had touched off a business reaction as well as a popular one, its chief objective being lower taxes and the freeing of business as much as possible from governmental interference, which had gone pretty far during the war: the railways had even been temporarily nationalized. Profits were pursued at all costs, and when realized were invested in the stock market. It was not understood that production was out-running consumption even in the United States, or that the rest of the post-war world was in no condition to take up the slack (a weakness not made any better by short-sighted protectionist US tariffs). Far too many leaders on Wall Street were reckless, when not outright swindlers. Inert and feeble national government completed the recipe for disaster. Yet the Crash of 1929, which nearly wiped out the savings of a generation, would not have had such catastrophic results if the United States had not for years been the only truly prosperous economy in the world. All the other nations depended on American success, and went down when it ended. This too was a new thing: another consequence of the war. The world could not afford any mistakes by Americans; but what set of human beings does not from time to time make mistakes?

The Great Depression was worldwide, and may well have been the biggest single factor bringing about the Second World War. It brought in its train evils of many kinds, including famine and tyranny. In the United States in 1932-3, when things were worst, unemployment stood at 24 per cent of the labour force of 53.2 million people. It was the sort of challenge which simultaneously brought down the Weimar Republic in Germany, making way for Nazi dictatorship; but the immense and ancient structure of American party democracy was not to be swept aside in a year or two, however long the breadlines. There were serious disturbances in the mining areas and the farm states, but as a whole the Americans stood fast. As the Depression deepened, they did not entirely despair or turn to communism; simply, they abandoned President Herbert Hoover and his Republicans, who had shown themselves unable to attack the country's problems effectively, and in 1932 elected Franklin D. Roosevelt to the White House, and a large Democratic majority to Congress.

It was the sensible thing to do, but superficially neither Roosevelt nor his party was obviously right for the job they had to do. He was the distant cousin and nephew-by-marriage of Theodore Roosevelt, who had been the most famous Republican president since Lincoln. FDR was a landed gentleman from upstate New York, at the head of the party of the white South and the big city machines, such as Tammany Hall; crippled by poliomyelitis, he yet inspired almost everyone he met with his infectious humour, courage, and energy. His party was even more anomalous. 'I'm not a member of any organized political party,' said a famous wag, 'I'm a Democrat'. Until 1912 its dominant tradition had been agrarian, isola-tionist, and bigoted. Woodrow Wilson had begun to change that. The demo-graphic facts did the rest, as the urban, immigrant, Catholic electorate rapidly increased—an electorate to which the overwhelmingly middle-class, conserva-tive, rural, and Protestant Republican party made little appeal. Under another leader the Democratic Party might easily have fumbled its opportunity; under Roosevelt, who was as cheerfully bold as most of his rivals, Republican or Democrat, were conservative and cautious, it seized the dominant position in American politics which it was to maintain for nearly fifty years, and made over the United States in the process.

Roosevelt promised 'a new deal for the American people'. 'Relief, recovery and reform' was the mantra by which the New Deal justified itself, and according to which its many critics judged it. Its success in bringing relief to the desperate millions can hardly be denied: through a string of emergency programmes, federal help was administered to the unemployed, the young, the farmers, the bankers, the industrialists, the state governments—to all the groups and agencies of American life which the Depression had brought to the end of their tether. The Democrats' reward was their crushing victories in the elections of 1934 and 1936. Recovery was much more problematic. GNP slumped from a high of $103.8 billion in 1929 to $55.8 billion in 1933; only crawled upwards after that; and sustained a severe setback ('the Roosevelt recession') in 1937–8. It did not pass the 1929 mark until 1941. Unemployment followed a similar curve, and had not got down to the 1929 level (1.55 million) by 1942. The problem of confidence was not solved: the country had no confidence in business, and business had none in the New Deal. 'Reform' is a tendentious term: undoubtedly the New Deal gave new strength to previously slighted groups in American society, such as labour unions and American Indians; it brought Catholics and Jews fully into the political mainstream; it brought the stock exchanges under government regulation; it outlawed child labour and somewhat increased black American participation in government. But not all citizens approved of these changes, and others felt that they did not go far enough: for instance, Roosevelt never saw his way to getting an anti-lynching law through Congress.

The New Deal's fundamental achievement, it may be, lay elsewhere, in what might be called (were the word not consecrated, in American usage, to the battles for civil rights) a reconstruction of American society and government. The 1930s were a decade of immense public works, which were undertaken to create employment, but which also accelerated the modernization of America. The Tennessee Valley Authority harnessed the waters of the south-east to generate electricity; at Roosevelt's personal insistence what was then the biggest dam in the world, Grand Coulee, was built on the River Columbia. The Reconstruction Finance Corporation spent $8 billion in as many years to refinance and stabilize the national economic structure. The Public Works Administration built bridges, airports, roads, government buildings. The Agricultural Adjustment Administration and its successor agencies put federal finance behind commercial farming, though it was unable to do much for small farmers and nothing for Southern sharecroppers. The federal government began to grow to meet its responsiblities: in 1932 there had been fewer than half a million civil servants, in 1940 there were 727,000—more than had been employed at the height of the First World War. In 1939, after a great political battle, Roosevelt was able to get through Congress an

act reorganizing the presidency itself, and previously, in an even more bitter struggle, which cost him dear, he drove the Supreme Court out of the shaping of economic policy, in which it had frequently meddled since the civil war. Roosevelt
tended to the view that the Court and Congress should take distinctly subordinate
roles, leaving power and initiative to the President. This was too radical: by 1940
Roosevelt had been decisively defeated by Congress, where a coalition between
Republicans and conservative (mostly Southern) Democrats was going to impede
presidential policies for the next twenty-four years; nevertheless, taken as a whole,
the sweep of his restructuring remains staggering. He had revived organized
labour and, with the Social Security Act of 1935, founded an American welfare
state. With less fanfare he had begun to rebuild the US navy and air force. The years
of the locust were far behind in 1939: even if Germany and Japan did not realize it,
the United States had collected its strength.

It was a notable achievement, but it represented less of a breach with the past
than either conservatives or radicals admitted. Before Grand Coulee there had
been Hoover Dam, on the Colorado, started in 1928, and the Reconstruction
Finance Corporation had been launched, in smaller, less effective form, by the
Hoover administration. Federal assistance in building up the economy was a
practice that had been customary right through the railroad age and as far back as
Alexander Hamilton's report on manufactures (1791). Military preparedness and a
strong national government were Republican ideas rather more than Democratic
ones. Modernization, in short, was as much an American tradition as was conservatism. Franklin Roosevelt never saw himself as a revolutionary.

The pay-off came with the Second World War, for which the First World War and
the New Deal might almost seem to have been mere rehearsals. The Japanese
attack on the US naval base at Pearl Harbor in Hawaii (7 December 1941) put an end
to the passionate controversy between isolationists and internationalists as to
whether the United States should enter the war—a controversy which, fifty years
later, survivors would remember as the bitterest in their long lives. The attack united the country as it had never been in its other wars, and it now had the strength
and organization to achieve victory on its own account while supplying the sinews
of victory to its allies. The reconciliation between government and business for
which Roosevelt had hoped in 1933 came about. Taxation soared, but so did GNP
(from $125.3 billion in 1941 to $213.1 billion in 1945), profits, and pay. Unemployment vanished. By 1945 12 million citizens were in uniform. Even more than the
First, the Second World War moved the population about with a giant hand, calling
up women, stimulating black migration from Southern fields to cities north and
south, and launching new industries in new places, of which the most ominous
was the development of nuclear power (made possible in part by TVA electricity)
and nuclear weapons. Wartime investment stimulated, at long last, the economic
resurrection of the South. Rationing, severe by American standards, was imposed;
nevertheless the foundations were laid solidly for that new consumer society of
which the 1920s had afforded a tantalizing glimpse, and for the longest period of
general prosperity in American history.

Americans at war had little faith in such a future; they thought that peace would bring back depression. It was not to happen, for various reasons, one of which was less a legacy of the New Deal than of the Great Depression itself. The government in Washington now accepted that it had entered into a contract with the citizens; it was not only that their wartime services and sacrifices must be acknowledged, but that the government was obliged to see to their well-being at all times. America was also accepting its destiny as the world's first superpower, with momentous consequences for its national history. It was becoming what Anthony Badger has called 'a business–warfare–welfare state'. Like the New Deal, this development was as much a fulfilment of earlier patterns as an innovation; but the New Deal was one of those patterns, and it was remembered, not quite accurately, for having come successfully to the rescue of the people in their worst crisis.

So there was a convergence of ideas, best perhaps symbolized by the Servicemen's Readjustment Act of 1944, better known as the GI Bill of Rights. It was designed to guarantee jobs, homes, and education for returning soldiers who claimed its benefits; it was a triumphant success, assisting millions of veterans and pumping consumer expenditure into the economy; it was thus a foundation stone of post-war prosperity; and no law better demonstrated the mixture of tradition and innovation with which the American people and their leaders had learnt to meet the challenge of the twentieth century.

12 East Asia and the Emergence of Japan, 1900–1945

AKIRA IRIYE

World history entered a new phase at the turn of the twentieth century, when Japan emerged as a new power, the first of a series of non-Western nations that would, in the course of the century, steadily make their appearance and challenge, individually or collectively, the hegemonic position held by the European powers in global political, economic, and cultural affairs. If the nineteenth century had been a Eurocentric age, the twentieth was to be one in which the United States would develop as the strongest member of the international community. At the same time, non-Western peoples made themselves steadily conspicuous, to such an extent that not just American power but also multicultural consciousness were to characterize the century's history as it drew to a close.

Not that the non-West existed as a self-defined entity from the outset, or that Japan consciously pursued a policy of challenging Western supremacy. Actually, it might have seemed, when Japan went to war against China in 1894 and acquired, upon its victory, the island of Taiwan as its first overseas colony, that the nation was merely following the imperialistic example set by the European powers and was further undermining the position of China and other Asian countries. Few would have foreseen then that Japan would in time decide to fight against the West in the name of Asian liberation, and still fewer would have predicted the rise of Asian military and economic power which would turn the whole region into a centre of gravity of international military and economic affairs. In retrospect, however, it seems clear that the Age of Imperialism which saw European (and later US) control over the globe's peoples and resources steadily extending itself was also paving the way for Asian development, politically, economically, and culturally. Whether East Asia would have so developed without Western imperialism is impossible to say. What is less disputable is that Japan played a dual role, as a Western-style imperialist and as a non-Western power whose policies and activities came to challenge the West, while at the same time spurring nationalistic responses in the rest of Asia. While much of Asian nationalism was directed against Japanese imperialism, it could also develop as a force for nation-building whose ultimate objective was liberation from all imperialism, Japanese as well as Western.

Japanese imperialism, however, differed in important respects from European and US imperialism. For one thing, Japan could hardly be said to be at an advanced stage of economic development when it undertook overseas expansion. Its overall per capita income, estimated at about $20 in 1900, put the nation at the bottom of all colonial powers. The European nations as well as the United States had already gone through their 'first' industrial revolution, characterized by the textile industry, and they were now carrying through the 'second' industrial revolution, in which iron, steel, and petroleum were among the main symbols. These countries did not really need new colonies in connection with industrialization, although apologists for their imperialism often made that argument. For Japan, on the other hand, carrying out the two industrial revolutions simultaneously, colonies with abundant raw materials, foodstuffs, and space were of obvious importance. Taiwan, for instance: the Japanese could utilize its sugar and its markets for the fledgling Japanese manufactures. Although it cost money to establish a military stronghold—the army of occupation faced an organized resistance movement by the indigenous population—and to develop an administrative machinery, from the beginning the island's relevance to the nation's economic interests was taken for granted.

Secondly, Japanese imperialism differed from European or American in that its immediate targets were neighbouring lands, inhabited by people who were very much like the Japanese ethnically and culturally. In fact, Chinese and Koreans considered themselves superior to Japanese; after all, they had given the latter much of their civilization, including the written characters and traditional religions. To come under Japanese control, therefore, was a real affront, an indignity far beyond any sense of outrage they felt toward the Western imperialists. From the Asian point of view, Japanese imperialism was more odious than Western in this regard. Instead of joining them in a struggle against imperialism, it seemed that the Japanese had joined Westerners in subjugating their lands.

This, however, did no more endear the Japanese to Westerners than to other Asians, for the West was immensely suspicious of Japanese designs, attributing to them some pan-Asianist conspiracies even when such did not exist. Some in the West began to see the rising power of Japan as a menace not only to their position in Asia, but also to Western cultural supremacy.

For these reasons, neither Asia nor the world would ever be the same again after the Sino-Japanese war. For the next fifty years, 1895–1945, the themes that emerged during the war and its aftermath were to play themselves out in such a way as to engulf the entire globe. Wittingly or unwittingly, Japan became an agent of drastic change in international affairs.

Japan's colonial expansion was continued after the Sino-Japanese war, thereby inevitably bringing the nation face to face with other imperialist powers. As Japan consolidated its control over Taiwan, sought to bring Korea into its imperial domain, and continued to eye the southern part of Manchuria as its sphere of influence, Russia emerged as the major threat to its ambitions. An interest in countering this threat brought Japan and Britain together. The two island nations signed an alliance in 1902, and two years later Japan attacked Russian forces in north-east Asia. Japan's victory in the Russo-Japanese war (1904–5) solved, at least for the moment, the problem of the two nations' respective spheres of influence, and henceforth they steadily came together so as to defend the post-war status quo. As Britain and France were also at that time forging an entente in Europe in which Russia became incorporated after 1907, there effectively developed a pattern of imperialist collusion among Japan, Britain, France, and Russia in East Asia. The only major powers excluded from this entente were Germany and the United States. These two might have organized a rival alliance system, but they failed to do so, in part because their navies viewed one another as potential antagonists. More fundamentally, the United States at that time was trying to develop an alternative pattern of international relations, in Asia as well as elsewhere.

The critical importance of the emergence of the United States as an Asian power in the wake of the war with Spain (1898) lies in the fact that the nation sought to use its power, not simply to uphold its security interests but also to define an alternative to power politics, or geopolitics, as the key to foreign policy. Even as geopolitically-oriented a leader as President Theodore Roosevelt was interested in assisting Caribbean countries in modernizing their economies, thereby raising their inhabitants' standards of living. Roosevelt's successors, William Howard Taft and Woodrow Wilson, went further and developed what historians have called a liberal (or capitalist) internationalist agenda, according to which nations were to promote an economically interdependent world order where international law, rather than armed force, would arbitrate differences. To these ideas Wilson added a vision of democratic transformation throughout the world, in which peace and harmony would be promoted through 'world public opinion', a product of democratization.

Certainly, none of these ideas was unique to Americans. Since the seventeenth century, European statesmen and publicists had sought to envision a pattern of interstate relations that went beyond military power and geopolitical considerations. What made the new US initiatives important was their application to non-Western parts of the world, what were then called 'uncivilized' areas, those that had not begun the process of modern transformation. And none attracted the attention of Americans at this time more than China, a country that was characterized by a weak central government, a military establishment demoralized by a series of defeats in foreign wars, and a growingly radical public opinion demanding drastic change. Such a country was a fit candidate for US interest, for it seemed to exemplify all the ills of a premodern society but at the same time held out promise for significant transformation. If China, with its rich resources and a teeming population of over 400 million, could be modernized, it would add immeasurably to the well-being of the people and to the peace of Asia. American prestige would soar, and its commercial interests would be amply served.

China's destiny, in other words, was being affected both by Japanese imperialism and by American internationalism, the former supported by most of the European powers. Because the latter's attention was shifting away from Asia, to focus on rivalries closer to home, it was inevitable that Japan and the United States would emerge as major rivals over China's development. Not that the Chinese were entirely at the mercy of foreign powers. They sought to determine their own fate, but they lacked a national consensus as to the best strategy. Modernization began at many provincial levels, but this did not add up to national strengthening or national movements. The one symbol of national unity, the Ch'ing dynasty, tried desperately to prolong its life by last-minute attempts at administrative and educational reform, but these came too late and were too insufficient to make a difference. Under the circumstances, foreigners could play major roles in the story. And it was unfortunate that the powers, above all Japan and the United States, developed conflicting strategies towards late-Ch'ing.

This became particularly evident during the First World War, which coincided with the period of turmoil in China following the downfall of the Ch'ing dynasty in 1911. The European powers were in no position to pursue an active policy in East Asia, thus leaving the field to Japan and the United States. Japan sought to take advantage both of the Chinese upheaval and the European war by entrenching its influence in various parts of China, while the United States was intent upon preserving the latter's territorial integrity and promoting its economic transformation. Although Japan was successful in the short run—for instance, in 1915 it imposed a series of demands on the new republican regime in Peking, the so-called 'twenty-one demands', including the cession of Shantung province—American influence grew among China's political, economic, and cultural leaders. Many of them turned to Washington to check Tokyo's ambitions. And President Wilson obliged by sending advisers to the Chinese government and encouraging US banks to invest in China's nascent industry. Even with such assistance, China was unable to reduce Japanese power on the continent, which grew in proportion as European interests diminished. Still, to the extent that China underwent transformation, it was due to a considerable extent to American influence. Certainly, most of 'young China', the reformers intent upon modernizing their country, turned to the United States for inspiration and support.

The First World War was a landmark in the history of East Asia and of the United States in many ways. While the Europeans concentrated their resources on their war, Japan, China, and the United States vastly expanded their trade. Japan's share in world trade, for instance, grew from slightly over 1 per cent in 1913 to nearly 5 per cent in 1918, while America's grew from 10 per cent to more than 20. With their huge trade surpluses, which could be utilized for foreign loans as well as for domestic investment, Japan and the United States emerged as creditor nations for the first time in modern history. In the meantime, both Japan and China took advantage of the temporary absence of European imports by undertaking industrialization.

Even more important was the self-assertiveness on the part of Japanese,

Chinese, and other Asians, reflecting their perception of Europe's loss of prestige. That the world's presumed centre of civilization should have witnessed a carnage of unprecedented proportions was enough to disillusion Asians about the West. Few dared to assert that the war signalled the end of the age of European suprem- acy; Asian observers remembered that the European nations had time and again regained their strength after lengthy conflicts. Still, Europeans themselves were talking about the passing of their dominance in the world, a sentiment that was also expressed in the United States. Even after US involvement in the war, American leaders attributed the origins of the conflict to inherent deficiencies in the European state system. Moreover, after 1917, Russia, too, turned against the West under its Bolshevik leaders, who argued that the war had been an inevitable consequence of the capitalist states' competition for markets. These attacks could not but impress Asians, who now turned to the United States and, to a lesser extent, Russia as the new centre of world power.

The Paris Peace Conference, convened in 1919, was of historic significance not just for Europe but for Asia, for there, for the first time, China and Japan sat on the side of the victors to pass judgment on German war guilt. (Japan had declared war on Germany in 1914, China in 1917.) The new League of Nations, designed as an alternative to the pre-war system of balance of power, had, from its inception, a large number of non-European members. Japan was given a seat on the Council as one of the five permanent members, along with Britain, France, Italy, and the United States. China was not among the permanent members, but it actively sup- ported the League and identified itself with the new international system. Although the Chinese delegates at the Peace Conference were disappointed that the Japanese would not restore Shantung to China, this did not prevent both of them from insisting on the inclusion of a racial equality clause in the preamble of the League's Covenant. It was as striking an example of Asian self-consciousness as any, for it was the first time in modern history that non-European states got together to insist on equal treatment. Their initiative bore no fruit at this time— the British delegates, under pressure from Canada and Australia, were adamantly opposed to the inclusion of a racial equality principle—but the Chinese and the Japanese were serving notice that henceforth they would be much more vocal in protesting against instances of discrimination.

An awakened Asia, however, did not turn collectively against the West. Rather, both China and Japan focused their energies on domestic reform and develop- ment, and in this process their leaders often found it desirable to undertake co- operation.

Certainly, the basic structure of Japanese imperialism on the Asian continent remained. Although China was finally successful in dislodging Japan from Shantung, in 1923, Japanese forces returned to the province in 1927 and again in 1928 to protect nationals. The Japanese, moreover, were adamant about retaining their rights in Manchuria. Japan's colonial rule in Taiwan and Korea did not change, although there was more readiness than earlier in accommodating the cultural nationalism of the indigenous populations. (Newspapers and magazines in the Korean language, for instance, were allowed for the first time since 1910, when Japan had annexed Korea as a colony.) Still, Japanese policy after 1919 was more moderate than earlier, as can best be seen in Japan's signing of a number of treaties and agreements at the Washington Conference of 1921–2, which upheld the principles of China's integrity and the Open Door, and denounced unilateral action on the part of any power at the expense of China. As typically specified in the nine-power treaty, Japan, China, and seven other countries (including the United States and Britain) pledged to cooperate with one another to maintain those principles and to assist in the establishment of a unified government in China. The importance of this and other agreements at Washington was symbolic; for the first time, the powers would cooperate with one another and with China to bring about a new regional order in East Asia.

The basic reason for Japan's acceptance of the Washington Conference treaties was domestic politics. After the war the political parties as well as governmental leaders came under the strong influence of Wilsonianism, and they recognized the 'trends of the times' that appeared to be pushing more and more countries along liberal, democratic paths. Voices of protest against oligarchic rule became louder, many of which coalesced in what came to be called 'Taisho democracy', after the reign title of the emperor who had come to the throne in 1912. Although he was a weak monarch, physically infirm and mentally deficient, his son, Hirohito, was sympathetic towards the idea of a constitutional monarchy, especially after his European tour in 1921. With most of the Meiji oligarchs now dead, Japanese government fell into the hands of younger politicians and bureacrats who were more attuned to public opinion. Industrial, financial, and commercial interests, strengthened during the war, demanded a say in state decisions. Japanese foreign policy reflected such a trend.

Instead of overt military and imperialistic activity, Japan concentrated on economic and cultural diplomacy in China. The 1920s saw Japan emerge as China's top trading partner as well as a major investor. Japanese factories in such cities as Shanghai and Canton were as numerous as British or American, employing thousands of Chinese workers. Often factory managers and workers collided, as the latter, increasingly class conscious in addition to being nationalistic, resorted to strikes and boycotts. Even so, Japan did not rely on military force to protect its investments. The support of a moderately nationalistic China, as exemplified by the Nationalist regime established in Nanking in 1928, was meant to indicate Japanese understanding of Chinese nationalism so that even labour disputes could be settled peacefully. This was not always the case, but in Japan there was much interest in cultural communication and exchange between the two countries. The idea was that, by bringing Chinese students to Japan, or by inviting Chinese intellectuals to come into contact with their Japanese counterparts, the nation could generate an atmosphere of better understanding, which in the long run would ensure a more stable relationship. Thousands of Japanese tourists, intellectuals, journalists, and students in turn went to China.

In Japan, the influence of the United States rose to unprecedented heights. This was the case even if Japanese–US relations were seriously damaged by the passage of a new immigration act in 1924 which forbade the immigration of all nationality groups that were denied the right of naturalization. Japan was a main target of the law, and its passage embittered many Japanese and worried even more numerous Americans. Still, the episode did not prevent Americans from enlarging their investment opportunities in Japan. They had given the citizens of Tokyo and Yokohama substantial amounts of aid when these were devastated by earthquake in 1923, and they would continue to purchase Japanese municipal bonds and securities. There was a vogue of 'Fordism' and 'Taylorism' in Japan, just as in Europe; the mass productive system of the Ford Motor Company, and the theory of efficient management–labour relations expounded upon by Edwin Taylor, symbolized American capitalism, and it was assumed that Japan had nothing to lose but everything to gain by inviting further American investment and learning from American philosophies of mass production. All this was matched by the influence of American culture, ranging from Hollywood films and radio programmes to jazz music and skyscrapers. America's popular and material culture appeared to spread all over the world, making inhabitants of different continents interchangeable. Japan was no exception. As its increasingly urban and educated population embraced American culture, its intellectuals echoed the words of one of their American counterparts that 'a single world community' was emerging.

The promising development of East Asian affairs in the framework of the Washington Conference treaties proved to be short-lived, as Japan violated those treaties in the 1930s and began acting unilaterally in China and ultimately in the whole of Asia, thereby incurring the opposition not only of China but of the United States and several European powers as well.

The story of Japan's renewed aggression in China and the latter's ultimately successful resistance constitutes a part of the history of the Second World War. Its origins differed in Asia from those in Europe. Unlike Germany, where an aggrieved public opinion, resentful of the harsh terms imposed on the nation at the Peace Conference, fell easy prey to the extremist rhetoric of the National Socialist Party, the Japanese had no reason to complain of its international position during the 1920s. Apart from the immigration dispute with the United States, there had been few crises in Japanese foreign affairs, and the nation had prospered along with the other capitalist countries. Even after 1929, when the spreading worldwide Depression produced an appalling level of unemployment in Germany, the Japanese economy suffered relatively little, as it was much less industrialized than Germany. Both Germany and Japan, however, had one thing in common: the rise to positions of influence of those ideologically opposed to capitalist liberalism and internationalism. Anti-bourgeois and anti-liberal forces had always existed, but the Depression, of whatever scale, gave them a pretext to denounce capitalism and its political manifestation, parliamentary democracy. In Japan, as in Germany, violence frequently accompanied political agitation. Between 1930 and 1936 two prime ministers, one finance minister, and one prominent banker were assassinated. Even those who escaped such attacks were driven to silence, or else they began parroting the language of the extremists in order to save their skin.

Even so, Japan might have been spared the fate of militarism and totalitarianism if China's nationalism had remained quiet or only moderately active. However, the Nanking regime of Chiang Kai-shek found it impossible to moderate nationalistic public opinion. After all, the Chinese were engaged in a serious task of nation-building, a task in which nationalistic opinion provided the glue. Although its administration did not cover the entire country, with communists and other dissidents challenging its authority, the Nationalist government from its inception was eager to negotiate an end to all existing foreign treaties so as to increase tariff revenue and promote economic modernization. In Manchuria (or the Three Eastern Provinces, as the Chinese called the region), in particular, they were determined to undermine Japan's special interests by such means as building railways parallel to the Japan-controlled South Manchuria Railway and driving out Japanese and Korean farmers who had come in search of farmland. It was the fear of China becoming more and more unified, strong, and nationalistic that alarmed those in Japan—the military, the colonial administrators, merchants, and other nationals in Manchuria—and inclined them to take action to preserve their interests before it was too late. There was nothing new about such imperialistic designs. But this time the military activists had to surmount the opposition or at least the lack of enthusiasm on the part of the civilian leaders, including the emperor, who had come to accept the Washington Conference framework as the best strategy for the nation's welfare. The military activists and their supporters—right-wing ideologues and politicians, as well as representatives of Japanese organizations in China—thus considered it imperative to undermine, if not eliminate altogether, the civilian leadership as they undertook an aggressive strategy in Manchuria.

The civilian leadership proved too weak to meet the challenge. The emperor provides a good example. In 1928, when some officers of the Kwantung army (the Japanese army in Manchuria) assassinated Chang Tso-lin, the warlord, in order to create chaos in the region, the emperor was adamant about punishing the offenders. In the 1930s, however, he became less willing to interfere in such matters. Such reluctance was shared by some of his trusted civilian leaders, who were cowed by nationalists and militarists as the latter berated them for their lack of initiative in the face of the rising tide of Chinese nationalism. Undoubtedly, the economic crisis at home, although by no means as severe as in Germany or the United States, played into the hands of the activists, for they could appeal to the masses by using anti-capitalist, anti-liberal rhetoric. Capitalism had failed in the West and in Japan, they argued, and those leaders identified with it were in no position to conduct national affairs.

This was anti-Western rhetoric, something new in the vocabulary of Japanese imperialism. Earlier, Japan's imperialistic expansionism had been couched in the same vocabulary as Western imperialism, with the implication that Japan was becoming like one of them. But now the prevailing view was that of Western civilization in crisis: not a temporary loss of prestige as during the First World War but a permanent damage as exemplified by the unprecedented Depression and the challenge to liberal democracy throughout Europe and even in the United States. With the Western powers in crisis, Japan's nationalists argued, there was no point in basing the nation's foreign policy on cooperation with them. Indeed, the European nations and the United States seemed themselves to be engaged in self-centred policies, as witness their prohibitive tariff policies and trading blocs. Japan must do likewise, abandoning any pretence of cooperation and, further-more, weakening the Western powers' position in Asia. A new order in East Asia must be established from which ultimately European and American influence would be removed.

This was a pan-Asianist agenda, taken quite seriously by the military activists, who resorted to drastic action in September 1931 to detach Manchuria from the rest of China. From then on, their ambitions extended to north China and envisioned an eventual establishment of a new East Asia in which Japan, China, and Manchuria (now renamed Manchukuo) would cooperate—that is, the latter would provide Japan with space and resources, while Japanese arms would protect the region against possible attack, from the Soviet Union or any other source. Not only the mil-itarists but others eventually came to uphold such a vision. After an easy military victory in Manchuria, the government in Tokyo was reluctant to go back to the pre-1931 status quo but, on the contrary, came to give such a forward strategy active sup-port. The best example of this civilian acquiescence was the decision to withdraw from the League of Nations when the latter, in 1932, made public a report on the Manchurian crisis in which it exhorted Japan to restore the pre-conflict status quo. Japan was defying the League and the principle of international cooperation.

The basic problem with Japan's pan-Asianism, of course, was that it was not accepted by other Asians, least of all by Chinese. Instead of unifying Asians to gen-erate their collective power, the Japanese were dividing them, between a minority of collaborators and the majority who either passively acquiesced in Japanese rule or actively opposed it. Asians were fighting against one another, with casualties in the hundreds of thousands even before the conflict became merged into the Second World War in 1941. Particularly galling was Japanese aggression after July 1937, when a clash between Japanese and Chinese forces outside Peking devel-oped into a full-scale war. With the Japanese army bent on the conquest of China, it assaulted Chinese cities and railways, frequently murdering civilians along the way. The 'rape of Nanking' occurring in December 1937 as Japanese troops entered the Nationalist capital, resulted in Chinese casualties of 300,000, according to standard Chinese estimates. From then on, Japan's thrust turned inland, pushing Chinese forces to the mid-Yangtze city of Wuhan and then further back to Chungking. The strategic bombing of Chungking which commenced in 1940 pre-saged attacks on civilian populations during the Second World War.

Of course, the Chinese were not just passive victims but fought back directly and indirectly, through underground resistance, propaganda, and appeals to for-eign governments for support. Initially, it is true, the Nationalist leadership under

Chiang Kai-shek did not want to engage the Japanese in war, giving up the Three Eastern Provinces for lost for the time being. Instead, the Nationalists concentrated on nation-building, an unusually difficult task as they could not count on much foreign investment and other support during the worldwide Depression. Still, they made some impressive gains. For instance, agricultural production rose during the first half of the 1930s, as did the production of iron and steel. Road construction went apace. By the beginning of 1937, less than ten years after the Nationalists had taken over the reins of government, even the Japanese military were impressed with the growing strength and self-confidence of China. Some of them for that reason argued for an accommodation with the Chinese instead of perpetually antagonizing them, while others insisted, just as the Kwantung army had done in 1931, that Japan should strike before China became even stronger.

When Japan did strike, China was more ready than ever. Nationalists and communists combined their forces, factories and universities were moved inland to continue their production and education, and, particularly important, the Chinese succeeded in obtaining foreign assistance against Japan. This came first from the Soviet Union and then from Britain and the United States, all of them supplying China with weapons, military vehicles, and loans to such an extent that the Chinese–Japanese war became steadily more international. Certainly, Germany gave Japan diplomatic support, and, when the Soviet Union signed a neutrality treaty with Japan in April 1941, its support of China diminished. Nevertheless, China was no longer fighting alone, as best revealed in the fact that the Japanese themselves began to see Western powers as obstacles to victory. They talked of their country's being 'encircled' by an ABCD combination consisting of America, Britain, China, and the Dutch East Indies.

That the ABCD coalition had been formed indicated the division of Asia between Japan and its empire, on the one hand, and the rest, consisting of 'Free China' and the Western colonies in South-East Asia as well as Australia and New Zealand, on the other. The Soviet Union stood in between, with its position shifting from time to time. The coming of the Second World War in Europe in 1939 confirmed the division of Asia, as Japan sought to take advantage of the European war to extend its power to French Indochina and, eventually, to the Dutch East Indies, attempts that brought a strong reaction on the part of the colonial powers as well as of the United States. They were determined to preserve the status quo and to prevent the rich resources of South-East Asia from falling into Japanese hands. Hence the formation of the ABD coalition, to which China was added in early 1941 as an inevitable step, for, in order to prevent Japanese penetration of South-East Asia, it was imperative to keep Japanese forces bogged down on the continent.

Japan was all alone except for its partnership with Germany. This, however, served only to solidify the alliance among the USA, Britain, and the Soviet Union (after the latter was invaded by Germany in June 1941). It was the desperate feeling that all paths to expansion were closed, while the war in China had stalemated, that led the Japanese military to gamble on a war against the ABCD coalition. Why they should have thought there was any chance of success in such a gamble, when they had not been successful against one country, China, cannot be explained in terms of rational logic or geopolitical calculations. In what must have been a good example of wishful thinking combined with a fanatical belief in the superiority of the Japanese spirit over the West's material resources, Tokyo's leaders, including the emperor, decided to strike at US, British, and Dutch possessions on 8 December 1941 (7 December east of the international dateline).

That move brought the Asian and the European wars into one. Only the Soviet Union, of the major powers, was uninvolved in the Asian theatre of the Second World War, as neither Tokyo nor Moscow wished overtly to violate the neutrality treaty. Even so, both the Japanese and their opponents expected that sooner or later the Soviets would enter the war. Indeed, by the time Japan surrendered in August 1945, over fifty countries had declared war against the aggressor.

It is ironic that, despite such a suicidal act on their part, the Japanese intensified their pan-Asianist rhetoric. Obviously, it was imperative to obtain the collaboration, passive if not active, of Asians whose lands they occupied, so that they would help drive out European and American interests from the region. The war was officially named the Great East Asian War, indicating Tokyo's propaganda that Japan was fighting for Asian liberation from Western domination. Few Asians took the rhetoric seriously, least of all the leaders of national liberation movements, who had begun their activities long before 1941. The Japanese occupiers initially did not encourage their movements, fearing that they might be turned against them. South East Asian lands were to be fully incorporated into the war effort, providing raw materials, foodstuffs, and manpower for the occupiers. Japanese civilian bureaucrats, journalists, and businessmen were sent to the region to supplement army and navy personnel. They replaced European and American rulers but behaved in much the same way. Indeed, for the native populations, Japanese rule was more odious because it was combined with the rhetoric of Asian liberation which had little content.

From 1944 onwards, with the tides of war definitely shifting, the emperor and his court circle, as well as some senior statesmen and retired military leaders, groped for ways to end the war short of a humiliating surrender. That it took them more than a year to take decisive steps for bringing the war to its end was due mostly to domestic factors: the concern over incurring the army's displeasure; the fear, on the other hand, of inciting a radical political change as a result of a defeat; and the structure of decision-making which mandated that all influential people be consulted before anything important was agreed upon and obtained the emperor's sanction. The delay was to cost Japan dearly. The nation could have been spared most of the devastating air raids, including the atomic bombings of Hiroshima and Nagasaki, if it had approached the enemy nations for a surrender negotiation in early 1945. Certainly, the allied powers' unconditional surrender principle, which was recapitulated in the Potsdam declaration of July 1945 calling on Japan to surrender, complicated the matter. But Japan did not even try, until it was too late, to see if the emperor institution could be spared in the event of its surrender. The United States and its Allies in the end agreed to this condition, thus paving the way for the emperor's radio announcement on 15 August that Japan was accepting the Potsdam declaration.

The war drastically altered the shape of Asia. Causing anywhere between 15 and 30 million deaths, it brought about untold suffering in China, South-East Asia, and Japan itself. In contrast, the war had the effect of extending the power of the United States to the western Pacific and even to the Asian continent, in sharp contrast to the further erosion of European prestige and influence. For the European nations, Japan's defeat was but the beginning of long-drawn-out fighting against native populations demanding a greater measure of autonomy, or in some instances outright independence. The struggle against Japan had provided an opportunity to Chinese nationalists to develop administrative skills and economic capabilities. Anticipating Japan's ultimate defeat, Koreans, too, prepared themselves for independence. In short, even as Japan's power suffered an apparently fatal setback, other Asian countries were emerging as significant factors in the regional drama.

This, and the newly acquired power and prestige of the United States, were to be two of the main themes of post-war history in Asia, and indeed in other corners of the world. Non-Western parts of the globe underwent major changes during the war, with the result that they were more than ever visible and insistent that their voices be heard. That the new world organization, the United Nations (UN), which was established in San Francisco in June 1945, should have contained a ringing endorsement of the principle of racial equality, whereas a mere twenty-six years earlier the Western powers had refused to approve such a statement as part of the League covenant, was a good indication of the rising assertiveness of the non-West, as was the willingness on the part of the Western governments to make China a permanent member of the Security Council.

The rise of the United States as the major Asian–Pacific power was foreordained once the nation determined to defend a forceful alteration of the regional status quo against Japanese aggression. It played a key role in the defeat of Japan, primarily through its 'island-hopping' campaigns in the Pacific but also through the military and economic assistance it gave to China. The dropping of atomic bombs symbolized the new power of the United States. Henceforth, no development in Asia or anywhere else would proceed without some input from the United States.

Whether the new power of the United States and the new assertiveness of Asian peoples were mutually compatible was a question few asked then, but its significance in post-1945 history is obvious. The history of East Asia after the Second World War was to unfold around the dialectic of the twin themes. In a sense it had been Japan's historical mission to bring about both the more awakened and better organized Asian nationalism and the emergence of the United States as the principal world power. Few Japanese were aware of the mission, and still fewer realized their responsibility for the uncivilized warfare they had begun and continued for so long, a warfare which was a fitting climax to some of the main themes of the history of the first half of the twentieth century.

PART III

The Cold War

1945–1990

13 The Confrontation of the Superpowers, 1945–1990

LAWRENCE FREEDMAN

The years 1945 and 1990 offer two punctuation points in international history. The first marks the end of the Second World War and a German defeat which left its European ambitions shattered and the country divided; the second marks the reunification of Germany and a new stage in its relations with its neighbours. In 1945 the Soviet Union emerged as the most powerful country in Europe; 1990 saw the Soviet Empire in Europe dissolved. The period in between constitutes the 'cold war', a confrontation between two ideological blocs, each led by a superpower, which touched all parts of the globe.

Confrontation between the Soviet Union and its American and British Allies was developing before the close of the Second World War and had been evident at the 'big-three' summits at Yalta and Potsdam in 1945 intended to design the post-war world. It came to dominate international politics immediately thereafter. In terms of military preparedness, the organization of alliances, and competitive diplomacy, the antagonism continued until the breach in the Berlin Wall on 9 November 1989. In early December 1989, Presidents George Bush and Mikhail Gorbachev had an informal meeting off Malta and announced the cold war concluded. As Gorbachev's spokesman, Gennady Gerasimov, quipped, it had lasted from Yalta to Malta. A more formal end came a year later, in the November 1990 Paris summit of the Conference on Security and Cooperation in Europe, which helped manage the break-up of the Warsaw Pact. A year after that the Soviet Union itself broke up into fifteen separate states.

There are three types of explanation for the cold war. The first we can describe as 'power politics as usual'. According to this view, there was nothing unusual about the cold war. Major powers are fated to distrust each other, for what they must do for their own security can seem threatening to their neighbours. The Soviet Union was impelled by the same expansionist urge that led old Russia to spread its boundaries. Its size rendered it overbearing, and smaller countries to its west not yet in its orbit would have been intimidated whoever was in power. Their only recourse was to band together for comfort and/or draw on the strength of the alternative super-power. This is what happened in 1949, when the European democracies came together to encourage the United States to accept a permanent security commitment to the continent under the North Atlantic Treaty. After the communist takeover in China that same year, the same pattern was followed in Asia.

The second explanation identifies ideological antagonism as the wellspring of the cold war. Here were two opposing concepts of how to organize society and the economy, and the political organization necessary for this task. This gave to power politics an unusually harsh edge—the mutual threat was not only external aggression but internal subversion. From the Soviet perspective, the American orchestrated alliance system reflected a strategy of capitalist encirclement designed to squash a socialist experiment; the West saw international communism seeking to impose a socialist order that would otherwise have been rejected by those in whose name this was done.

The third explanation, but one which might properly be seen as a consequence, lies in the arms race. Along the front lines of the cold war substantial military establishments were sustained, backed by the unprecedented and awesome power of nuclear weapons. While the origins of the cold war might lie in fundamental conflicts of interest, those stressing this factor claim that the competitive acquisition of ever-more deadly armaments militarized political relations and reinforced mistrust and suspicion.

It will be argued in this chapter that ideological antagonism was at the heart of the cold war, for this gave the power politics of this period its distinctive flavour. This is why the cold war's conclusion came with the defeat of Soviet-style state socialism. However, long before this time, the ideological factor had been on the wane, along with the relevance of the superpower confrontation for much international activity. For this reason the cold war was by no means the sole, nor necessarily the most important, distinguishing feature of this period. Much of its drama stemmed from the interaction between those strategic imperatives which flowed from the East–West confrontation, and those associated with the even more profound and lasting upheavals set in motion by the processes of post-war decolonization.

In 1945 the supreme power of the United States was undoubted. Its military strength had been decisive in concluding the war—during which its economy had grown to the point where it accounted for some 50 per cent of the total world GNP. The war's grim finale—the detonation of two atomic bombs over Japan—confirmed both its technical prowess and its military superiority.

However, Britain, exhausted by the war and unable to sustain its Empire, had already come to recognize that future influence depended on sustaining a close relationship with the United States and then encouraging it to watch over European security. After the First World War the Americans had retreated back into isolationism. The British and the French were determined that this time the United States should accept its international responsibilities.

The concern was with the new threat posed by the Soviet Union. Though the Soviet Union had been devastated by the war, suffering enormous casualties, which themselves followed those resulting from collectivization and Stalin's purges, its armies controlled the territory stretching from the Soviet border into the centre of Germany and down to the Balkans. The scale of the Soviet sacrifice, as well as the awesome determination of its victorious armies, contributed to the prestige of communism, which was further reinforced by the conviction that this was the ideology of true progress as well as social justice.

As Stalin worked to bring the states of Eastern Europe under his control, the Truman administration soon needed little persuading that, unless it became an active participant in European politics, it would be conniving in the imposition of a new totalitarianism. So 'containment' became the prime foreign-policy objective of the United States. When, in March 1947, the administration picked up from Britain the costs of opposing communism in Greece and Turkey, President Truman described his country's policy as one of supporting 'free peoples who are resisting attempted subjugation by armed minorities or outside pressure'. In June of that year Secretary of State George Marshall unveiled the plan forever afterwards associated with his name to inject substantial sums into the European economy to restore prosperity, and thus reduce the political opportunities for communism in Western Europe.

Some of Josef Stalin's advisers would have welcomed access to Western credits, but the supreme Soviet leader saw a plot to revive Germany as an anti-Soviet instrument and undermine his hold on Eastern Europe. He rejected the Marshall Plan and mobilized such an uncompromising campaign against it throughout Europe that non-communists were obliged to accept that the time had come to take sides and accept the polarization of the continent. The next year Czechoslovakia was brought firmly into the Soviet sphere, while the division of Germany according to the post-war occupation zones acquired a permanence. West Berlin, now the responsibility of the Western Allies, stuck out as the sole capitalist enclave in socialist Europe; it survived a Soviet siege only through a massive airlift which continued from June 1948 to September 1949, when Stalin gave up. By this time, the North Atlantic Treaty had been signed (4 April 1949), committing the United States to come to the aid of the Western democracies if they were attacked.

By now the possibility of a third world war was being taken seriously, though neither side yet had major rearmament programmes in place. The United States had expected to be able to hold on to its nuclear monopoly for some time, but this was lost in August 1949 when the Soviet Union exploded its first nuclear device. This event in itself prompted the United States to review its conventional military capabilities, but the resources to fund rearmament were only released after communist North Korea invaded the South in the summer of 1950. This, coming on top of the communist takeover in China the previous year, convinced the Truman Administration not only that a confrontation was developing in Asia as serious as that in Europe, but also that cold wars could turn very hot.

The first response in Washington to the Soviet atomic test had been to move to the next stage of nuclear power and develop thermonuclear (hydrogen) bombs. This had been bitterly contested by those who feared the consequences of a move to weapons of virtually unlimited power, whose explosive yield would be measured in terms of their equivalence to millions of tons of TNT (megatons), rather than the thousands of tons (kilotons) of atomic bombs. Proponents argued that the United States dare not wait for the Soviet Union to take the first step, but nor did they assume that successful development would do anything more than extend the period of a meaningful American superiority until this was neutralized by a comparable Soviet capability. They believed that the breathing space provided would be best used rebuilding the West's conventional military strength, and, at great expense, this was set in motion.

The Republican administration which took office at the start of 1953 with the election to the presidency of Dwight D. Eisenhower, had a different strategic perspective from that of its Democrat predecessor. It was aware of the unpopularity of the deadlocked war in Korea and the economic harm caused by conventional rearmament. After flirting during the election campaign with the idea of 'rolling back' communism, it accepted that the only realistic objective was to contain further Soviet advances, and that therefore the West had to plan for a 'long haul' in its confrontation with the East. It also concluded that this might not be as difficult as its predecessors had supposed if more reliance was put on the fear of nuclear war, which would make it unnecessary to match the conventional strength of China and the Soviet Union. In 1954 John Foster Dulles, Eisenhower's Secretary of State, warned Moscow that any further Soviet advances risked 'massive retaliation', and to give this credibility he sought to establish a series of alliances on the NATO model around the periphery of what was now known as the 'Sino-Soviet bloc'. Winston Churchill observed that, as a result of a shared fear of nuclear war, 'peace' might become the 'sturdy child of terror'.

There were many reasons why contemporary commentators judged 'massive retaliation' to be an extremely foolhardy strategy. It apparently allowed for the possibility of a minor Soviet incursion in some distant territory triggering a nuclear Armageddon or else forcing a humiliating climbdown because of a lack of available and usable conventional strength. The idea of a nuclear stalemate was challenged by strategic analysts, who described how a well-executed surprise attack might remove the victim's capacity to retaliate and so leave the perpetrator in a commanding position. If one side achieved this sort of first-strike capability, then its hand in future crises would be strengthened immeasurably. If both sides moved in this direction, then future crises could become extraordinarily fraught as both kept their nuclear arsenals on a hair-trigger to avoid being caught by surprise. On the other hand, if both gained confidence in their ability to withstand a first strike and then retaliate, how could either threaten nuclear war with confidence? To rely on this sort of threat for purposes of deterrence risked the bluff being called.

In different ways these lines of criticism sustained strategic debate for a further thirty-five years. Each new technological development—intercontinental missiles, early warning radars, missile-carrying submarines, anti-missile missiles, multiple warheads atop missiles—was examined as to whether it would either make possible or frustrate a decisive first strike. By the mid-1960s the consensus view had become that the two sides had reached a condition of 'mutual assured destruction'—effectively a stalemate. The difficulty of finding and then attacking missile-carrying submarines, and of tracking and intercepting incoming missiles, meant that it was impossible to design a strike that could guarantee that the enemy would not retaliate.

This view was continually challenged through descriptions of complicated nuclear strikes which might paralyse the opponent's decision-making or forms of deadly bargaining based on limited strikes against politically significant targets. The influence of such ideas waxed and waned but none ever really took such a grip of policy-makers that they were tempted to carry them out in a real crisis.

The risks that such temptations might none the less arise and so cause an East–West war to escalate almost uncontrollably into a nuclear catastrophe were large enough (and they did not have to be very large) to inject a large dose of caution into the decision-making of both East and West. Viewed logically it made sense to prepare to fight on the assumption that the two nuclear arsenals had neutralized each other. A deliberate policy of mutual restraint, perhaps even reinforced by formal pledges not to be the first to use nuclear weapons, might allow hostilities to proceed on a conventional basis. In practice, the assumption seemed a dangerous one upon which to rely, especially when contemplating any war being fought over non-trivial stakes.

The logic of basing deterrence on the prospect of an extended conventional war rather than a short, convulsive nuclear war was also expensive. So long as deterrence appeared to be working, few governments were anxious to push conventional force levels beyond those necessary to ensure a range of available options sufficient to manage crises and conduct low-level hostilities without resort to nuclear war. At times of crisis and generally tense relations, the dependence on nuclear deterrence, the resources expended on keeping the relevant arsenals updated and the intellectual energies put into refining the doctrines could appear frightening and reckless. From the late 1950s, there were occasional waves of protest, especially in Western Europe, against the nuclear arms race and the dreadful conclusion to which it seemed destined to lead. As the communist order in Eastern Europe consolidated then stagnated, the 'nuclear threat' often appeared more dangerous than any 'Soviet threat'.

The two superpowers, both uncertain as to exactly what it was about their nuclear forces that helped deter the other, managed to acquire a great surplus capacity in their arsenals. Eventually, they recognized a shared interest in capping their nuclear arsenals, and configuring them in such a way to ease fears of surprise attacks. This provided the basis for a twenty-year effort in nuclear arms control that produced some successes, but was always hampered by the technical complexity of the subject matter and the consequently arduous nature of the negotiations. This was despite the fact that, in practice, the destructive power needed for deterrence was probably quite small, and the strategic calculations involved rather crude and simple.

Nuclear deterrence worked better and more safely in practice than in theory in part because the East–West confrontation it was intended to steady was stabilizing on its own. The division of Europe was so sharp that the two ideological blocs could develop their own distinctive economic, political, and military systems. By the end of the 1950s Stalin's successor, Nikita Khrushchev, was talking of 'peaceful coexistence' whereby two systems could survive and even flourish without attempting to destroy the other. At the time, following Soviet successes with the first artificial earth satellite and the first man in space, Khrushchev felt confident that the system over which he presided was as technologically dynamic and had as golden a future as the capitalist one. When in 1959 he told the West 'we will bury you', it was not because he expected to defeat it in war, but because he saw communism outliving capitalism.

Yet, with the limited exception of France and Italy, communism was already a spent political force within Western Europe. Khrushchev himself had done much to undermine it, by confirming in a speech to the Communist Party Congress of 1956 that Stalin had indeed been the dreadful monster portrayed by the capitalists, and then later that year by his own brutal suppression of the uprising in Hungary which confirmed that it was Soviet tanks rather than the loyalty of the working classes which had become the mainstay of the communist order. By now it was becoming apparent that, if the cold war was going to turn hot, it was likely to be as much because of upheavals within the Warsaw Pact as because of a Soviet offensive against the West.

The obvious flashpoint was Berlin, which came increasingly to be seen by Khrushchev as a Western jewel tarnishing an Eastern crown. It became an even greater irritant at the beginning of the 1960s, as the freedom of movement within the city provided an escape route for tens of thousands of East Germans anxious for a better life in the West. This haemorrhage threatened to destabilize the East German regime. In August 1961 the flow was stemmed when the Berlin Wall was constructed overnight.

This was a stark demonstration of communism's repressive character, and it led for a while to heightened tensions. But it was also a defensive move. The response indicated that there was little enthusiasm in the West to risk war in the name of a united Berlin, let alone a united Germany, but the allies were prepared to be firm on maintaining the status quo. Now the division of Europe had become even starker, but yet there was no particular dynamic to the cold war in Europe. For the rest of the decade the West Germans digested the implications of this, eventually deciding, by the late 1960s, to start to prise open the Iron Curtain through dialogue and economic cooperation. There would be no external challenge to the Soviet sphere of interest in Europe. Even an internal challenge, as subsequently mounted in Czechoslovakia during the 'Prague Spring' of 1968, could be suppressed in a 'fraternal' Warsaw Pact invasion with only a minimal Western response.

This restraint encouraged Moscow to feel secure enough to push for the consolidation of the status quo. This was the starting point for a European *détente* that came to be marked in the early 1970s with a series of agreements which served to establish West Germany's relations with East Germany and the other communist states, and regularize the status of Berlin. In 1975 all European states came together, with the United States and Canada, for the Conference on Security and Cooperation in Europe (CSCE), where they all signed up to the status quo.

The so-called 'Final Act' of the CSCE, which was in general a hymn to stability, also contained the seeds of future change. In addition to declarations on the inviolability of borders and non-interference in internal affairs, there were provisions on human rights that were used increasingly within the Soviet bloc to legitimize dissent, and provisions for economic cooperation which reflected little understanding of the consequences of the interplay between two economic systems, one of which was as dynamic as the other was stagnant.

The consequences of this were not fully played out until a decade later. Before that the soothing words of *détente* had been replaced with an altogether harsher rhetoric. The reasons for this lay outside Europe and in the Third World.

At first the old European powers sought to justify their Empires and then their resistance to anti-colonial movements as part of a general response to a communist threat. Eventually, they were obliged to recognize the irresistability of the anti-colonial tide. During the 1950s and the 1960s, as the former colonies received their independence, it was widely assumed that they would follow either the Eastern or the Western ideological models. It was in response to this presumption that the 'Non-Aligned Movement' was established at Bandung in 1955 to demonstrate the possibility of alternative forms of political development. The term 'Third World' captured the idea of entities quite distinct from those of the first and second, capitalist and communist, worlds.

In practice the newly independent states saw in the superpower confrontation both a threat and an opportunity. They did not want to lose their independence, yet they could see advantages in appearing as anti-communist or anti-capitalist as required to gain support in conflicts with local enemies. The two superpowers often succumbed to such ploys more than was prudent, on the negative basis of preventing the other side gaining strategic advantage through the acquisition of Third World clients as much as the positive basis of promoting their core values. Because the regions of the Third World turned out to be far less stable than Europe, the opportunities for conflict were many and some became quite dangerous.

The most dangerous crisis of all occurred in October 1962 when the Soviet Union attempted to insert missiles into the Caribbean island of Cuba. US–Cuban relations had deteriorated progressively after the overthrow of the Batista regime at the end of 1958, to the point where the new leader, Fidel Castro, declared his revolution to be Marxist-Leninist, and John Kennedy, in one of the first acts of his presidency, had backed a failed landing by emigrés. Castro wanted Soviet protection against a full American invasion; Khrushchev saw an opportunity to redress an unfavourable shift in the military balance as US intercontinental ballistic missile production outstripped that of the Soviet Union. When Kennedy, having warned Khrushchev against such a move, discovered the Soviet deception, he was furious and demanded the removal of the missile bases. After some extremely tense days, Khrushchev complied, saving some face by extracting an American promise not to invade Cuba and an understanding that comparable US missiles (which were supposed to be leaving anyway) would be removed from Turkey.

The Cuban crisis had been too close for comfort for Khrushchev and Kennedy. It led to a series of measures, including an agreement on a 'hotline' for instant communications in similar situations, together with moves to ease the nuclear threat. The first of these was the Partial Nuclear Test Ban Treaty of 1963 which ended atmospheric nuclear testing. After Cuba the two superpowers never again got themselves into a position where they risked direct confrontation. This did not mean that they eschewed participation in Third World conflicts, but their participation was confined either to providing training and material for clients or, at most, to fighting the clients of the other side.

The most serious example of this was the American involvement in South Vietnam, which grew during the late 1950s and early 1960s as the American-sponsored anti-communist regime wobbled in the face of an insurgency backed by North Vietnam. In early 1965, as the South Vietnamese government appeared on the brink of collapse, the Americans launched a major air campaign against the North and then, when this failed to make much difference to the situation on the ground, introduced large numbers of combat troops. The impact of the air campaign was limited by a desire not to provoke war with China. The ground campaign was undermined by the US army's lack of grasp of guerrilla warfare and by the growing impatience of the American people as casualties mounted to no evident purpose.

The lesson drawn by President Richard M. Nixon when he assumed office at the beginning of 1969 was that America's clients should expect to fight their own wars, but could expect substantial logistical support. On this basis, he had extracted American troops from Vietnam by 1973 and arranged a peace settlement which failed to protect the South from a Communist takeover. The same approach was followed in the Middle East, with more success, in 1973 when the Israelis reeled under a surprise attack mounted by Egypt and Syria. The United States would not intervene directly but mounted a massive airlift to help the Israelis recover.

While the Americans had been getting themselves bogged down and demoralized in Vietnam, the Soviet Union had been investing in all forms of military power and the ability to project this power throughout the globe. A significant part of this build-up could be traced to the split with China, which had been simmering since the late 1950s, turning it into open ideological warfare in 1963 and almost leading to war in 1969 when there were skirmishes over the two communist giants' long and disputed border. The Americans used the split to improve relations with China and the Soviet Union, and to help ease their way out of Vietnam.

As the 1970s progressed, however, American opinion became alarmed at the implications of a pattern of Soviet activity designed to exploit Third World conflicts so as to enhance its global influence. This involved airlifting Cubans or East Germans into strife-torn African countries (Angola, Ethiopia) and assisting Vietnam in expanding its hegemony in Indochina. Nervousness about Soviet intentions came to a head in December 1979 when Soviet troops moved *en masse* into Afghanistan. There a chaotic situation had developed the previous year following a *coup* by a Marxist faction. The Soviet move was geared to the local situation, although it was given more lurid interpretations in the West, where some saw it as part of a drive towards the Gulf. This interpretation reflected Western anxieties rather than Soviet objectives, since steep rises in the price of oil over the previous decade had created an acute awareness of dependence on the Gulf for supplies. There had recently been yet another oil crisis following the overthrow of the Shah of Iran in 1979 by Islamic fundamentalists.

The invasion of Afghanistan introduced a new freeze into US–Soviet relations. When Ronald Reagan became President in 1981 he showed scant interest in *détente* and pushed major new military expenditures through Congress. Anti-communist guerrillas in Afghanistan were armed. America's European allies became nervous lest the complex web of East–West agreements through which a degree of stability had been brought to Europe be lost. When yet another liberation movement in Eastern Europe was squashed, this time by the imposition of martial law in Poland, they urged moderation in response, still accepting this as part of the Soviet sphere of influence. They did accept the introduction of new intermediate missiles into Western Europe, in part in response to a formidable enhancement of Soviet missile capability, despite vociferous Soviet protests and mass demonstrations organized by local disarmament campaigns, but encouraged Reagan to couple this with serious initiatives on arms control. We now know that this period was one of great anxiety in Moscow, with real fears that the Americans were preparing for war.

The Soviet fear represented a growing sense of weakness in Moscow. Soviet forces were making little progress in Afghanistan and casualties were starting to mount. The limited returns on all the other interventions mounted in the 1970s were leading to a reassessment of the value of this sort of global role. Meanwhile the new American build-up, including some highly imaginative plans for space-based defences against missile attack, were exposing just how far ahead of the East the West was technologically. Since the mid-1960s the Soviet economy had been stagnating, and attempts to use the *détente* of the early 1970s to import Western technology had generated more debts than dynamism. In the ideological struggle communism was clearly losing ground. The West's standard of living posed a challenge to the faltering economies of the Soviet bloc. The leadership had grown old with the economy. Three leaders—Leonid Brezhnev, Yuri Andropov, and Konstantin Chernenko—died in office in quick succession.

In early 1985 the Soviet leadership made a last desperate attempt to save its system. Chernenko was succeeded by the much younger Mikhail Gorbachev.

Gorbachev sought to modernize the Soviet system under the slogans of *perestroika* (reconstruction) and *glasnost* (openness) and spoke honestly of the need for political reform to make possible economic reform. These tasks required calming Soviet relations with the West through arms-control agreements and a campaign of political reassurance. His readiness to cut back Soviet military strength impressed itself even on the conservative governments of Ronald Reagan in the United States and Margaret Thatcher in Britain.

Gorbachev apparently believed that the Communist Party could still be an agency of radical change, but to be effective there had to be a direct confrontation with Party privilege and its supporting ideology. It also required a similar confrontation in Eastern Europe, despite the fact that hardliners were still so firmly in charge there that the alternative was not a reformist Party but no Party at all. Already Poland, under martial law but with the dissident Trade Union Solidarity Movement exercising substantial power, and liberal Hungary were edging out of the old communist order. It all came to the crunch in 1989 when Gorbachev had to decide whether to acquiesce in the end of Communist rule or to sustain it at the risk of undoing all the goodwill obtained from the West and reinforcing his own hardliners. To his credit he chose acquiescence.

As Hungary opened its border with Austria, East Germans began to take advantage to escape to the West. Unlike 1961, this time the loss of population was coupled with mass demonstrations in cities such as Leipzig. The East German government lost its nerve, hoping that a more moderate image, symbolized by the end of the Berlin Wall, would allow it to survive. It was a forlorn hope.

The year 1990 opened with communism in retreat throughout Eastern Europe and pressures building up for the unification of Germany, largely through the mass movement of population from East to West and despite misgivings in the West as well as the East. There no longer appeared to be any geopolitical or ideological basis for a separate East German state. The first months of the year were taken up with the effort to discover how to manage this unification without alarming the Soviet Union, even though the result was inevitably to strengthen NATO even as the Warsaw Pact was collapsing. To achieve this the West had to demonstrate that it would not seek to exploit Moscow's weakness, and would help the political and economic reform process. However, by this time the rot within the Soviet system was too great to reverse through mere reform. After he had survived an inept *coup* attempt by old Communist hardliners, Gorbachev made the mistake of failing to recognize that this meant the end of Communist Party rule. There was nothing left to hold the Soviet Union together. The Baltic States had been clamouring for independence. Now their wish was granted and soon Russia found itself without territories laboriously acquired over centuries. As part of the deal of 1990 the West continued to flatter the Russians, recognizing their continuing great power status and consulting them on all manner of crises. After all Russia still possessed a substantial nuclear arsenal.

The international agenda had, however, by now moved on. At the same time as the euphoria of the end of the cold war and the unification of Germany, in October 1990, there was Iraq's crude act of aggression against Kuwait in the Gulf of August 1990 and then the bloody break-up of Yugoslavia which began in the summer of 1991. While the Gulf allowed for a coherent and robust response in the face of a challenge well understood in terms of an established framework of international politics, Yugoslavia found the old great powers disoriented in the face of disruptive and intractable conflicts infused with ethnic nationalism. For some the cold war even began to appear as a period of calm and stability in Europe's turbulent twentieth-century history.

The stark bipolarity of the cold-war years did lend itself to a sort of order in Europe, but it was not one that could last indefinitely because it was based on an ideological division that was inevitably competitive. As one side clearly prospered and relished freedom, the other was marred by stagnation and repression. Outside Europe neither the strategic nor the ideological bipolarity was ever so stark, and the cross currents produced by the disparate local conditions and histories produced a greater variety in regional politics. The influence of East–West antagonism could therefore be a source of great violence, as in East Asia, as much as of stability. The cold war was also accompanied by a constant fear that, should the superpowers collide, the consequences would be truly apocalyptic. The fact that this was avoided, so that the formal conclusion came with comparative grace, and that liberal political values triumphed, allows us to say that, as much as any war can be, this was a 'good' one.

14 The United States since 1945

JAMES PATTERSON

The domestic history of the United States between 1945 and 1995 may be divided roughly into two different eras, each of approximately twenty-five years. The first, between the end of the Second World War and the late 1960s, featured economic growth and affluence that were unprecedented in the history of the world. A vibrant economy based heavily on the production of consumer goods enabled people to live at levels of comfort that could scarcely have been imagined in the Great Depression of the 1930s and that far outpaced standards elsewhere in the world. Economic progress, in turn, seemed to be eroding social divisions of religion, region, ethnicity, and class. Some intellectuals by the mid-1950s imagined that the nation was becoming a consensual, 'post-industrial' society. Dwight Eisenhower, President from 1953 to early 1961, enjoyed an extraordinary popularity throughout his tenure. 'Ike' resisted major changes. To many Americans he represented an anchor of stability and prosperity in an otherwise stormy world.

The affluence of the era incited enormous expectations about the capacity of the United States to promote a Good Life for individuals, a Great Society for previously disadvantaged groups, especially African Americans, and a democratic, non-communist world order. By the mid-1960s, when optimism peaked, the majority of the American people felt extraordinarily hopeful about the future and confident about the further expansion of their personal and civil rights.

The rise of rights' consciousness made the 1960s an unusually turbulent decade of social and political change. The Supreme Court, dominated by Chief Justice Earl Warren and other liberals, greatly widened the civil rights and liberties of aggrieved groups, including blacks, women, welfare recipients, political leftists, and alleged criminals. John F. Kennedy, who succeeded Eisenhower, heightened hopes by calling for a 'New Frontier' that would transform American life. Lyndon Johnson took over after Kennedy's assassination in November 1963 and proclaimed his commitment to what he called a Great Society. Elected in a landslide in 1964, he helped persuade Congress to approve a huge burst of liberal legislation in 1965. By then reformers were more expectant than ever. They anticipated the virtual abolition of poverty and an ever more egalitarian social order. Johnson was equally optimistic about America's power to protect democracy and capitalism in the world. That included faraway areas such as South-East Asia. No task, it seemed to Americans at the time, was beyond the capacity of the United States, incomparably the richest and most powerful nation in world history.

Even before 1970, however, the relentless revolution of expectations began to outrun the capacity of economic and political institutions to deliver change. This was most obvious concerning Vietnam, which mired the nation in ten years of fighting, the longest war in US history, and fomented great acrimony at home. Expectant advocates of rights confronted other obstacles as well. Militant blacks, having achieved legal rights at last, demanded social and economic equality. Inspired by their example, other groups—women, Indians, Mexican-Americans—also struggled for greater social justice. The majority of Americans, however, believed in equality of opportunity for individuals, not governmentally sanctioned mandates of equality of condition for groups. They resisted further guarantees of rights, especially following a spate of riots that ravaged central cities in the late 1960s. By 1968 a backlash against demands for rights shook American politics and culture. Divisions of race, ethnicity, gender, region, and social class rent the nation.

The turbulence of the late 1960s and early 1970s did much to smear the image of government among the American people. Johnson misled the nation about what he was doing in Vietnam and promised far more than he could deliver in the realm of domestic affairs. When his popularity plummeted in 1968, he decided not to run again. His Republican successor, Richard Nixon, further misled the people concerning Vietnam and lied about the involvement of his aides in a burglary of Democratic National Committee headquarters at the Watergate building in Washington. When his cover-up was exposed, the scandal of 'Watergate' forced him to resign in 1974. He was the first American President in history to do so.

The massive deceptions of Johnson and Nixon shocked millions of Americans and helped to benefit aspirants for high office who rejected governmental solutions to public problems. Jimmy Carter, a Democrat, won the presidential election of 1976 against President Gerald Ford in a campaign that emphasized his distrust of Washington. Ronald Reagan, President from 1981 to 1989, proclaimed that government *was* the problem. His successor, George Bush, was almost as conservative as Reagan. Bill Clinton, who broke the Republican hold on the White House in the election of 1992, ran one of the most conservative Democratic presidential campaigns of the post-war era.

The greatest blow to the post-war age of optimism was the unsettled state of the economy. This began in the late 1960s, when inflationary pressures caused primarily by military spending began to mount. Other forces added to economic instability: weaknesses in America's manufacturing sector, especially steel and automobiles, rising competition from nations such as Germany and Japan, and an oil embargo that shook much of the industrialized world in 1973–4. By then millions of younger Americans, born in the 'baby boom' of the 1940s and 1950s, were entering the labour market and finding it difficult to get secure, well-paying jobs. So were women, who by then were working for pay in unprecedented numbers: the percentage of adult women in the labour market shot upward from 26 per cent in 1940 to 42 per cent in 1970, and kept rising throughout the 1970s and 1980s.

The economy grew especially shaky in the late 1970s and early 1980s. 'Stagflation' featuring double-digit unemployment and double-digit inflation rattled the people as well as government leaders, who seemed powerless to restore stability and growth. Conditions improved during the mid-1980s, but economic growth remained sluggish, and another recession jolted the nation in the early 1990s. Increasing percentages of people worked in the service sector, where many jobs offered low pay and poor benefits. (As of 1996 the United States and South Africa were the only two industrialized nations lacking a comprehensive public system of health insurance.)

The unsteadiness of the economy exacerbated the social tensions that had intensified in the late 1960s. The poverty rate, which had fallen from 22 per cent of the population in 1959 to 11 per cent in 1973, began to rise again and remained at between 13 and 15 per cent for the next two decades. Income inequality increased, whether during the relatively good times of the mid-1980s or the shakier times of the late 1970s and early 1990s. Widely reported accounts of the millions amassed by corporate magnates and speculators heightened class antagonisms. Out-of-wedlock pregnancy and divorce, having started to rise in the early 1960s, skyrocketed to record highs in the 1970s and 1980s. So did levels of violent crime, which far exceeded those of other Western nations. Inner-city ghettos peopled by African-Americans featured especially high rates of unemployment, family break-up, and crime. Race relations seemed more acrimonious in the 1980s and 1990s than at any time since 1945. Other groups—women, Indians, recent immigrants—complained angrily of discrimination and asserted their group identities in an ever more self-consciously multicultural society. Fundamentalist religious groups came out in the open, boldly challenged secular values, and opposed such causes as the right of women to abortions. By the 1980s and 1990s the Religious Right had considerable political influence, especially in the South and the West.

Some observers insisted that the rise of backlash and fragmentation after the 1960s need not create too much alarm. The United States, after all, was a geographically vast and populous nation where disagreements were to be expected. (The population rose from roughly 140 million in 1945 to more than 250 million in the early 1990s.) The United States was also very heterogeneous. Blacks, numbering 30 million in 1990, were around 12 per cent of the population. A total of 22 million people at that time told the Census Bureau that they were Hispanic; this was 9 per cent of the population, a percentage that was rapidly increasing. Legal immigrants, most of them Asian or Latin American, were arriving by the 1990s at a rate of close to a million per year. Many others came illegally. In these circumstances, it was hardly surprising that multicultural conflicts abounded, especially in an age of rights consciousness and mass-media coverage where instances of exploitation received widespread attention.

Those who counselled calm also reminded alarmists that the United States remained a remarkably stable nation politically. Despite the excesses of leaders such as Johnson and Nixon, the centre had held. The nation remained committed to a Constitution that had been ratified in 1789 and to electoral practices that were the envy of much of the world. Far-reaching Civil Rights Acts passed in 1964 and 1965 remained the law of the land in the 1990s, as did most of the liberal decisions of the Warren Court. The rights consciousness that peaked in the 1960s had left a significant mark on American life, widening the civil rights and liberties of the people.

Even the economy managed to sputter along at modest rates of growth in most years after 1982. The majority of families were a little better off in terms of real income than they had been in the 1970s—in part because so many wives and mothers were in the workforce. By the mid-1990s American rates of inflation and unemployment were moderate by comparison to those of many other industrialized nations. And the so-called American Dream that people could work hard and rise in a free and democratic society—retained some of its magnetism, especially for the millions of foreigners who continued to perceive the United States as a beacon of economic and political opportunity.

Still, the rising optimism that had characterized the 1940s, 1950s, and early 1960s had diminished. Backlash and fragmentation seemed endemic. The self-centredness of interest groups appeared to be unyielding. The noise of cultural antagonisms sometimes seemed deafening. Although the United States remained a wealthy and powerful nation, it was far from resolving its internal divisions.

The strong performance of the US economy between 1945 and the late 1960s owed much to the vast expansion of production during the Second World War and to enormous increases in the spending of governments—federal, state, and local—at all levels. The war pulled the United States out of the Great Depression, virtually eradicated unemployment, and enabled millions of Americans to gather savings. It also left the nation in an amazingly dominant position. In the late 1940s the United States, with 7 per cent of the world's population, possessed 42 per cent of the world's income and accounted for half of the world's manufacturing output. It had three-quarters of the world's gold supplies. The per capita income of US citizens in mid-1949, at $1,450, was much higher than that in the next group of nations (Canada, Britain, New Zealand, Switzerland, and Sweden), at between $700 and $900. Urban Americans at that time consumed more than 3,000 calories of food per day. This intake was approximately 50 per cent higher than that of people in Western Europe.

Many developments in the late 1940s and 1950s accelerated economic growth in the United States. One, which lasted until the 1970s, was the remarkably low price of energy, especially oil. Another was the lack of foreign competition from nations that had been ravaged by the war. Congress also abetted economic expansion. In 1944 it had passed the so-called GI Bill of Rights (GI meant 'Government Issue' for military personnel), which offered returning veterans valuable cash benefits enabling them to go to colleges and universities. The Veterans Administration and Federal Housing Administration provided veterans and others with unprecedentedly low-cost mortgages. Higher education and home-building enjoyed fantastic growth in the post-war era.

Wartime savings further spurred a boom in the production of consumer goods, especially automobiles. As early as 1950 there were 49.3 million cars registered in a nation that then had only 39.3 million families. By 1960 registrations numbered 73.8 million. This was a level of automobile ownership that staggered visitors from overseas. The boom in automobiles energized a host of other important economic activities: oil and gasoline consumption, suburbanization and mall construction, highway-building, and the motel and restaurant businesses.

A baby boom accompanied this quickening of economic progress. In 1946—the year following the return to the United States of military personnel—the number of births jumped to 3.4 million, 20 per cent more than in 1945. Surprising demographers, the boom persisted into the early 1960s. Birth rates (estimated live births per thousand population) had ranged between 18 and 19 per annum during the Depression years; from 1946 through to 1959 they were always 24 or higher. The total number of babies born between 1946 and 1964 was 76.4 million, or two-fifths of the population in 1964 of 192 million.

Demographers have offered many explanations for this extraordinary boom in babies. The causes, indeed, varied considerably. But one reason was the psychology of many young adults in the post-war era. Americans, living in a much more affluent age, were optimistic about the future. They sensed that they could afford to get married—the average age of marriage dropped at the time—buy a house, and raise a family of three or four children. The baby boom, moreover, had enormous economic consequences, fuelling a dynamic 'juvenile market' for consumption of toys, sweets, records, children's clothes, washing machines, furniture, and all manner of so-called labour-saving devices in the home. It also accelerated the spread of television, which reached virtually all American homes by the mid-1960s. The construction and staffing of schools became a major economic activity in the 1950s and 1960s.

The response of many Americans to such prosperity evoked considerable contemporary criticism. The economist John Kenneth Galbraith, in *The Affluent Society* (1958), deplored the extent to which Americans threw money into glitzy consumer goods while starving public services. There was indeed a baroque character—huge, flaring tail fins on cars, for example—to the eager consumerism of the era. Other books, notably Michael Harrington's *The Other America* (1962), lamented the persistence of poverty amid abundance. More than 20 per cent of the population at the time lived in households that did not have enough income to meet governmental 'poverty lines'. As the turmoil of the 1960s revealed with special clarity, sharp class distinctions continued to rankle millions of people in the United States. Socio-economic consensus in the 1950s had been much exaggerated.

Still, economic progress was significant, and it greatly excited the optimism of the ever more numerous middle classes who were advancing between 1945 and the late 1960s. Many people, after all, remembered the terrors of the Depression years, when unemployment had afflicted 25 per cent or more of the labour force and the percentage of Americans in poverty (officially unmeasured at that time) may have been as high as 50 per cent. By contrast, most years of the 1950s and 1960s witnessed relatively low unemployment (usually around 4–6 per cent), stable prices, and substantial economic growth. Government social programmes, most of them inaugurated in the 1930s, grew slowly but steadily. The number of elderly people who received social-security cheques increased from 1.2 million in 1950 to 5.7 million in 1960; the total paid in such benefits during those years jumped from $960 million to $10.7 billion.

Social indicators seemed especially promising during the 1950s and early 1960s. Divorce rates between 1947 and 1963 remained unusually low; crime was not a major concern; young people completed more years of school and were more likely to go on to college. Thanks in part to low levels of immigration (the result of restrictive laws dating to the 1920s), contemporaries also imagined that ethnic distinctions would gradually diminish: the melting pot seemed to be bubbling with special vigour. Conservatives (and others) took special heart from statistics on church membership, which reached an all-time high of 69 per cent of the population in 1959. Evangelists like the Revd Billy Graham attracted enormous audiences. President Eisenhower signed legislation in 1954 that added the phrase 'one nation under God' to the Pledge of Allegiance recited by schoolchildren. A year later Congress approved legislation that added the words 'In God We Trust' to American coins and bills.

The economic progress and apparent social stability of the late 1940s and 1950s promoted a political complacency that played into the hands of moderate and conservative public officials. Harry Truman, who succeeded to the presidency on the death of Franklin D. Roosevelt in April 1945, attempted to extend many of Roosevelt's liberal social programmes and to secure passage of federally supported health insurance and aid to education. Although he had enough popularity to win re-election in 1948, he was repeatedly foiled by a bipartisan conservative coalition that dominated Congress. Eisenhower, scoring a clear victory in 1952, did not try to repeal social measures on the books, but he resisted further liberal efforts. Excepting a Highway Act in 1956 that pumped billions into road-building, no significant domestic legislation emerged from Congress between 1945 and the early 1960s.

The rise of the cold war, moreover, dominated American politics in these years, especially after the United States became embroiled in the Korean War between 1950 and 1953. Both Truman and Eisenhower devoted much more time and effort to foreign policies than they did to domestic matters. Indeed, political leaders did not dare to seem 'soft' on communism or to back advanced progressive programmes: the Left in the United States was far weaker than in most other nations. Senator Joseph McCarthy, a demagogic Republican Senator from Wisconsin, achieved great attention between 1950 and 1954 by accusing Truman, State Department officials, and liberals in general of harbouring subversives in government. In 1954 he even assailed the army, thereby overreaching himself and falling from respectability. Before then, however, a post-war Red Scare poisoned much of American political life and forced liberals to the defensive. They remained there into the early 1960s, when turbulence unsettled American society and politics.

In retrospect it is easy to see that some of the roots of this turbulence lay in social and cultural developments that were gathering strength in the 1950s. By the end of that decade scattered groups of young people, many calling themselves 'beats', were deliberately rejecting what they considered to be the crass materialism and conformity of American society. Much larger numbers of the young avidly followed Elvis ('the Pelvis') Presley and other rock 'n' roll musicians. Worried conservatives grew frightened about the rise of an irreverent youth culture. They also fretted that some American women were beginning to demand more than the nurturant and home-building roles that the culture had prescribed for them.

Blacks grew especially restive. In a vast and important migration, millions left the South in the 1940s and 1950s (and later) for jobs and better treatment in the urban North and Midwest. Those who stayed in the South, however, continued to confront legally sanctioned discrimination and segregation. The Supreme Court in 1954, ruling unanimously in the landmark case of Brown v. Board of Education, attempted to end racial segregation in the public schools, but the Court could not force compliance, and separate schools for whites and blacks remained the norm in the Deep South until the 1970s. Blacks also resented discrimination and segregation in public accommodations and transportation. In 1955 Rosa Parks, a black seamstress, refused to give up her seat to a white person on a public bus in Montgomery, Alabama. Her act of resistance ignited a dramatic, year-long black boycott of the city's buses and established the reputation of the Revd Martin Luther King, Jr., a young and charismatic advocate of civil rights and non-violence who became leader of the movement. The boycott ended in a partial victory for civil rights (the buses changed their regulations) but did not otherwise affect segregation in Montgomery or anywhere else in the South.

These and other manifestations of unrest in the late 1950s, however, were mostly unrelated, and they did not seem to change much of the substance at the time. Civil-rights activism, indeed, seemed relatively quiet in 1958 and 1959. And Congress remained resistant to change until the mid-1960s. Although Kennedy's call for a New Frontier may have helped him win the presidential election of 1960, his triumph was extraordinarily narrow, and the conservative coalition in Congress blocked his efforts for federal aid to education and health insurance. Kennedy, like his predecessors, spent most of his political capital on efforts to bolster the USA against communism in the world, not on domestic concerns.

While politicians were fighting the cold war in the early 1960s, however, signs of dramatic change were appearing. In 1960 the Food and Drug Administration authorized the sale of Enovid, a birth-control pill, thereby giving further impetus to an already ongoing revolution in sexual behaviour. In the same year radical young people founded the Students for a Democratic Society (SDS), which later in the decade became the best known of many left-wing organizations. Most significant, young activists in the South, the majority of them black, started 'sit-ins' in 1960 to protest against the racial segregation of lunch counters, restaurants, and other facilities. Their boldness unleashed a much more activist phase of the civil-rights movement. Over the next few years King and others engaged in thousands of demonstrations, most of them in the South. These produced an irresistible moral force that excited not only advocates of civil rights but also, in time, activists for many other disadvantaged groups in American society, including women, Mexican-Americans, Indians, gay people, and the handicapped. No social development of post-war US history was more significant than the civil-rights movement.

Many other events of the early 1960s also revealed the existence of ascending pressures for a freer, more egalitarian society. In 1962 the folk singer Bob Dylan wrote 'The Times They Are a-Changin', a prophecy of forthcoming cultural change. In the same year Rachel Carson, a biologist, published *Silent Spring*, a moving condemnation of environmental pollution. It served as a gospel for an environmental movement that peaked in the 1970s. Harrington's *The Other America* did the same for critics of poverty. In 1963 James Baldwin, a leading African American writer, published *The Fire Next Time*, an angry warning about racial confrontation, and Betty Friedan produced *The Feminine Mystique*, a resounding, widely read call to arms for women's rights. In 1964 Malcolm X, a dynamic black leader, broke with the Black Muslims, formed the Organization of Afro-American Unity, and set about mobilizing blacks in the ghettos of the North. In California César Chávez and others organized farm labourers and proceeded to lead highly publicized strikes and boycotts to improve the working conditions of exploited agricultural labourers, many of them Filipino and Mexican-American.

Although these and other developments of the early 1960s hardly added up to a coherent movement, they came hard and fast on one another. Many of them, especially the often bloody civil-rights confrontations, received wide coverage on television, which came of age as a medium of communication. The times indeed were a-changin', witnessing blow after blow to the standards and pieties of the 1940s and 1950s. By the mid- and late 1960s hundreds of thousands of college and university students were demanding liberalization of curricula and rules concerning social relations between male and female students. Some young people, including self-identified members of a 'counterculture', joined communes where they defiantly abused drugs and flaunted their sexual freedom. Magazines and motion pictures abandoned long-established strictures against the display of sex and violence. 'Acid rock' music—loud and only dimly comprehensible to many people—made the sounds of pioneers like Presley seem tame and dated. In 1969 homosexuals at the Stonewall Inn in New York City's Greenwich Village fought back against police harassment, setting off five days of rioting and arousing greater group consciousness among the gay population.

Some of this activity, notably the civil-rights movement, placed formidable pressures on American politics, which shifted briefly to left of centre in 1964 and 1965. Johnson, a consummate legislative leader, drew on pressures, as well as on widespread yearnings for redemption of Kennedy's aspirations, to press for passage of domestic reforms. In doing so he was fortunate that the economy was booming as never before—the 1960s were the longest period of uninterrupted economic growth in US history. The growth further fuelled already great expectations and made social programmes affordable. It also made it seem as if Johnson and his liberal advisers, presiding over a healthy economy, knew what they were doing.

For these and other reasons Johnson was able to drive significant legislation through Congress in those two years. The lawmakers approved a 'war on poverty', federal aid to elementary and secondary education, Medicare (a system of contributory health insurance for the elderly), Medicaid (a tax-supported programme of healthcare for the welfare poor), and an immigration reform act that ended a four-decades-old system based on bogus racial classifications. Most important, Congress enacted two Civil Rights Acts. The first, approved in 1964, abolished *de jure* discrimination and segregation in public life. The second, passed following dramatic demonstrations in Selma, Alabama, in early 1965, established federal enforcement of voting rights, thereby dramatically cutting down on racial discrimination in politics in the South. These two laws were the most important pieces of US domestic legislation passed in the twentieth century.

When the Voting Rights Act was signed in August 1965, many liberals rejoiced, anticipating a new, more egalitarian age to come. Five days later, however, blacks rioted in Watts, a ghetto in Los Angeles. This outburst was followed by a spate of racial riots, the worst of them in 1967, that revealed the continuing rage of many African Americans. The rioters, like other people, had been swept up in the revolution of greater expectations and of rights' consciousness. They demanded not only equality before the law—the civil-rights acts had provided that—but also greater social and economic justice. At the same time the civil-rights movement, until then proudly interracial, broke apart along racial lines and renounced nonviolence. The divisions that befell the movement, the most important engine of change in the 1960s, damaged the quest for social reform that had seemed so promising by 1965.

Much of the liberal legislation approved in 1964 and 1965, moreover, fell well short of the expectations that Johnson and others had aroused for it. The 'war on poverty' was poorly funded and for other reasons had far less impact on the diminution of poverty in the 1960s than did economic growth. Its 'community-action' programmes fomented antagonism between poor people, who demanded to run the programmes, and city officials, who resisted challenges to their authority. Aid to education, which had been heralded as a means of improving the schooling of the poor, seemed to make no substantial difference, partly because school administrators siphoned off a good deal of the money to wealthier suburban districts. Inner-city schools attended primarily by minority groups appeared to get worse, not better. Medicare and Medicaid did improve healthcare for millions of Americans, but both initiatives lacked effective controls on costs, which escalated enormously over the years. The limitations of these and other programmes stemmed largely from the power of special-interest groups—municipal leaders, school administrators, corporations, the medical profession—which did much to shape the nature of the laws. The limitations also contrasted sharply with the hyperbole that Johnson and other liberals had used to get them enacted. The contrast badly hurt the standing of liberals and by extension the reputation of government. From the late 1960s on, conservatives maintained the offensive in American political debate and practice.

Most damaging of all to reformers was American involvement in the Vietnam War, which Johnson escalated significantly in 1965. By the end of his administration in early 1969 there were more than 500,000 American military personnel in South-East Asia. As escalation mounted, money for domestic programmes became harder to find. And, as casualty figures grew more alarming, Americans began to understand that Johnson had misled them about the military and political situation in Vietnam. Furious anti-war protests, many of them led by college and university students (and by radical organizations such as Students for a Democratic Society (SDS)), broke out across the nation. These did not make much of an impression on the President, who adhered stubbornly to his course, but they did serve as constant reminders of domestic turmoil. Contemporaries complained of a 'credibility gap'—between what government said it was doing and what in fact it was doing. This gap persisted long after the war—indeed, into the 1990s.

It happened also that indicators of social stability, so important to the optimism of the 1940s and 1950s, changed dramatically in the mid- and late 1960s. Divorce rates began to rise, as did illegitimacy, welfare rolls, and violent crime. Average test scores of high-school students started to fall. The reasons for these developments were complex. Some people blamed the sexual revolution, television, films, or permissive child-rearing. Others lamented the role of inequality and relative deprivation—the most alarming social statistics involved the poor. Still others concluded that the sources of rising crime rates were at least partly demographic. Starting around 1963 unprecedented numbers of baby boomers reached their late teens, the age group most likely to engage in crime and other forms of unruly behaviour. No theory, however, explained all. Many Americans, confused and angry at what was happening, blamed the young and the activists—blacks, Mexican-Americans, feminists, students, anti-war protestors, welfare 'bums', counterculturalists, rock musicians—for what appeared to them to be the fragmentation of civilized society.

Class resentments grew especially open by the late 1960s. When African Americans and other groups demanded 'affirmative action' or related forms of federal protection, many working-class and lower-middle-class whites dug in their heels to protest against what they considered to be favoured treatment for others. Working-class people (including blacks) also resented what they regarded as the hypocrisy of middle-class student anti-war protestors, most of whom enjoyed deferments from the military draft. 'Here were those kids, those rich kids who could go to college, didn't have to fight,' a construction worker railed. 'They are telling you your son died in vain. It makes you feel your whole life is shit, just nothing.'

This was a classic expression of 'backlash', as contemporary commentators called it. Some of it was racial in origin, some of it based on class antagonisms. Whatever the reason, the backlash assisted the political aspirations of conservative and reactionary political leaders after 1964, including Alabama Governor George Wallace, a presidential contender in 1968 who proved remarkably popular in many working-class wards of northern cities as well as in the South. That was in many respects a terrible year in American history—both King and Jack Kennedy's brother Robert, another presidential contender, were assassinated. Nixon, who rivalled Wallace in his courtship of the backlash vote, ultimately won the election on a platform that expressed no enthusiasm for domestic reform and offered only a vague 'secret plan' to end US involvement in the Vietnam War.

Many of the social changes that shook people in the 1960s, a pivotal decade, persisted in the years that followed. Distrust of government, already strong, expanded when Nixon carried on the war in Vietnam for four more years and tried to cover up the role of his top aides in the scandal of Watergate. Gerald Ford, who replaced him, had no mandate for change. By then, moreover, the economy had fallen into the unsettled state that persisted for much of the next twenty years. Neither he nor Jimmy Carter, his successor, managed to pull the nation out of the doldrums. Ronald Reagan rode to victory in 1980 by castigating Carter for the state of the economy and by promising to be tougher than ever against the Soviet Union. The Cold War was still alive and well in American politics.

Reagan was in many ways an extraordinary figure. Deeply conservative, he appealed to Americans who distrusted government by claiming that he would downsize it. He also gained support from many members of the revitalized Religious Right and from determined anti-communists. A former movie actor, he appeared to good advantage on television, which had become a vital part of campaigning. Reagan's most valuable political asset, apart from the rebounding of the economy after 1982, may have been his infectious optimism. Americans, having suffered through the turmoil of the 1960s and the doldrums of the 1970s, seemed eager for a leader who would tell them—again and again—that all was right with the United States and the world. He swept to re-election in 1984 and, despite scandals in his second term, remained popular until he left office in 1989.

George Bush, who assumed the presidency in 1989, had been Reagan's Vice-President. While he was more moderate than his predecessor, he shared Reagan's lack of interest in domestic affairs. Although he secured temporary popularity by waging a brief and successful war against Iraq early in 1991, voters blamed him for a sharp recession that descended during his term and chose Bill Clinton over him in 1992. Clinton proved to be the first post-war President since Johnson to focus on liberalizing domestic policies, especially healthcare. Some liberals hoped that he could break the legislative logjam that, apart from the break in 1964–5, had deadlocked American national politics since 1945.

Polls in the early 1990s, however, continued to reveal powerful anti-government feelings among the people, and in 1994 the Republicans regained control of both houses of Congress for the first time since 1954. They threatened to roll back many of the social and environmental laws that liberals had enacted in the 1960s and succeeded (with Clinton's assent) in ending welfare rights established in 1935. Although Clinton managed to win again in 1996, he confronted Republican majorities in both houses of Congress and seemed unlikely to promote liberal causes. There was little, moreover, to suggest that America's social divisions could soon be repaired. The conflicts of class, region, gender, race, ethnicity, and religion seemed as sharp as ever, perhaps sharper. Interest groups retained substantial political power. In many ways the American people were better off than they had been in 1950, or even in 1975. But their expectations and rights consciousness, whetted by the affluence and optimism of the post-war era, were in many cases higher than their institutions could satisfy. In the late 1990s, as in much of the time since the late 1960s, a great many people are doing a little better but feeling a little worse.

15 The Soviet Union and Beyond

ARCHIE BROWN

The Soviet Union suffered enormous losses, both human and material, during the Second World War, but emerged from it with its prestige enhanced. Although, however, no state had made a greater contribution to the defeat of Nazi Germany than the USSR, the gratitude of its Western allies soon changed to apprehension and hostility when Stalin turned the new Russian sphere of influence in Eastern Europe into a tightly controlled Soviet bloc and reimposed a totalitarian regime at home which was no less oppressive than that of the pre-war period.

While the peoples of the newly incorporated territories of the Soviet Union, such as the Baltic republics (which had earlier been part of the Russian Empire but were independent states between the First and Second World Wars) and parts of western Ukraine, were well aware of the extent to which they were being repressed, a majority of Russians were not. A combination of extreme state control over the educational system and the means of communication, the ubiquitous presence of the secret police, and uncritical support for Stalin, whose name was now linked, above all, with victory in the 'Great Patriotic War', meant that the Soviet leader had little difficulty in re-establishing a peacetime dictatorship. It was one in which most of his subjects, taking a patriotic pride in rebuilding their war-shattered country, also sincerely believed that they were living in a society more just than any to be found in the West.

A mendacious but successful propaganda machine played its part in producing this outlook, whereby suppression of freedom and individuality and the presence of economic hardship were accompanied by patriotic support for the Soviet state on the part of a large proportion of the population. The post-war Stalin years reached their grim culmination in the early 1950s. The already severe repression was selectively stepped up, with vicious attacks on 'rootless cosmopolitans' (which, in Soviet coded language, meant Jews), and it is likely that only Stalin's death in March 1953 saved the country from domestic blood-letting on a scale reminiscent of the late 1930s.

Though the Soviet Union was eventually to become increasingly influenced by the world around it, for as long as Stalin was alive it was able to insulate itself from foreign influences to a remarkable extent. Indeed, even in the generation following Stalin's death (up until the mid-1980s) Soviet citizens' knowledge of the West remained limited as a result of strict censorship, by the jamming for most of that period of Russian-language foreign broadcasts and, though less rigorously than in Stalin's time, by surveillance of contacts with foreigners.

So much power was concentrated at the apex of the Communist Party—in the Politburo (the Political Bureau of the Central Committee) and, above all, the General Secretaryship—that the tone of political life continued to be set to a surprising degree by the top party leader (the General Secretary, or First Secretary of the Central Committee, as he was known from 1953 until 1966). Initially, however, it was not clear that the new Soviet supreme leader was, indeed, Stalin's successor as party chief, Nikita Khrushchev. In his later years Stalin had ruled as much through the government machine, as Chairman of the Council of Ministers, and the secret police as through the Communist Party, thus obscuring the fact that the person who headed the Communist Party Secretariat commanded more political resources than any other.

During the first year after Stalin's death the new Chairman of the Council of Ministers, Georgy Malenkov, wielded powers which rivalled Khrushchev's and he was regarded in the West as *the* number one Soviet leader. A struggle for power ensued in which Khrushchev's opponents were mainly people who were closer to Stalin than he had been, although all (including Khrushchev) had been Stalinists and none had clean hands. Some, however, such as Malenkov (who lost his position as Chairman of the Council of Ministers to Nikolai Bulganin in 1955), were prepared in the earliest post-Stalin years to take a softer line—one manifestation of which was support for faster development of the consumer-goods industry—whereas others, including Lazar Kaganovich and Vyacheslav Molotov, remained ultra-hardliners, albeit loosely allied with the devious Malenkov on the basis of their suspicion of the ebullient and unpredictable Khrushchev.

The latter made life more dangerous for them—and, indeed, for Communists everywhere—when he set about acknowledging the crimes of Stalin. In his 'secret speech' to a closed session of the Twentieth Congress of the Soviet Communist Party in early 1956, Khrushchev made a scathing attack on Stalin's terrorization and murder of members of the ruling party (although he remained silent on the repression of non-Communists). The leader who had until recently been treated as a god-like figure was revealed as a cruel despot.

Many sincere, albeit hitherto gullible, Communists both in the Soviet Union and, still more, abroad were devastated by the information Khrushchev revealed. Some details apart, most of what Khrushchev divulged was not new to objective Western observers, but it had been easy for both Russian and Western Communists to dismiss it as lies when it came from tainted 'bourgeois' sources. Nothing had prepared them for the psychological shock of learning from the leader of the Soviet Communist Party that Stalin had been personally responsible for the deaths of many of their revolutionary heroes. Most dangerously for Khrushchev, his denunciation of Stalin stimulated some dissent and the beginnings of reformist movements within the East-Central European Communist Parties and helped to trigger serious unrest in Poland and Hungary. Even though he was capable at other times of displaying a humanity which was entirely foreign to Stalin, Khrushchev was enough of an unreconstructed Communist not to hesitate to send Soviet tanks to put a stop in the autumn of 1956 to what had turned into a revolution in Hungary and a potential threat to Soviet hegemony in the satellite countries as a whole.

Khrushchev's enemies within the Soviet leadership believed, not without reason, that it was he who had shattered the myth of the infallibility of the Soviet Communist Party by his exposé of Stalin and they joined together in 1957 in an attempt to overthrow him. Faced by opposition from what he described as 'a so-called arithmetical majority' in the Politburo (or the Presidium of the Central Committee, as the Politburo was known at that time), Khrushchev enlisted the support of the Central Committee—a body which had hitherto obediently followed the edicts of the Politburo. Nevertheless, according to the Party Statutes it was the Central Committee which elected the Politburo and which possessed, in principle, a still higher authority than that smaller inner committee of the party leadership. Khrushchev had already made skilful use of his powers as Communist Party leader, revitalizing the party organization and making sweeping personnel changes, so that many members of the Central Committee owed their preferment to him. Forced to choose between their patron, Khrushchev, and his enemies within the Politburo, a majority in the Central Committee backed Khrushchev, who, over the next few years, was able to dismiss from political life those other heirs of Stalin who had tried to overthrow him. He labelled them 'the anti-Party group', and so they became known in the official histories of the Soviet Communist Party, although they had spent long decades in that Party and were, more strictly, an anti-Khrushchev group, united only by their fear that Khrushchev was becoming over-powerful and by their desire to preserve the essentials of the system that Stalin had built on foundations laid by Lenin.

It was highly significant, however, that Khrushchev's defeated opponents were given minor jobs or allowed to retire on pensions rather than being executed— their certain fate in Stalin's time. Khrushchev was himself aware of the extent to which his political beliefs and reflexes had been moulded during the Stalin years, yet he had the capacity to transcend that experience. Ill-educated but intelligent, Khrushchev was capable of ruthlessness, but also of responding to the material needs of the average Soviet citizen. A true believer in the ideals of the Soviet 'founding fathers', he was probably the last Russian leader seriously to imagine that he was engaged in building a self-governing communist society in which the state would eventually 'wither away'. Yet, Khrushchev was a pragmatist rather than a theoretician—his response to Mao, whose pretensions in the latter direction profoundly irritated him, was to say that 'you can't make soup out of an idea'—and taking the first steps towards de-Stalinization was not the only achievement of the Khrushchev era.

A vast house-building programme enabled millions of Soviet citizens to move out of communal flats into self-contained apartments, and the conditions of everyday life improved for the average family. Moreover, having their own homes—most of them municipally owned—had more than material significance. The greater privacy was a stimulus to a growing freedom of speech in private which only some three decades later was matched by freedom of speech in public, but the former was a vital precondition of the latter.

The Soviet economy was still growing in quantitative terms—although not so fast as the official statistics claimed—and when political priorities and economic resources were concentrated on a particular area of development, spectacular results could be achieved. The one which most impressed the outside world, and which succeeded in creating the illusion in the minds of Western leaders that the Soviet economy might actually be outperforming the West, was the technological feat of launching the first *sputnik* in October 1957 and putting the first person in space with Yury Gagarin's flight in April 1961. The Soviet Union also devoted great resources to the build-up of its military strength, with a new emphasis on rocketry, although it was not until the Brezhnev years—more specifically, the first half of the 1970s—that a rough military parity with the United States was attained.

Although, taken as a whole, Khrushchev's period of rule was far less inhumane than Stalin's, it was marked by inconsistency in many spheres, including cultural life. Thus, on the one hand, Boris Pasternak was vilified for the publication abroad of his novel, *Doctor Zhivago*, and forbidden to accept the 1958 Nobel Prize for Literature, while, on the other, Alexander Solzhenitsyn was permitted in 1962 to publish his powerful short story, *One Day in the Life of Ivan Denisovich*, which broke the silence on the appallingly harsh treatment of political prisoners in Stalin's labour camps. Again contradictorily, Khrushchev played a decisive role in having several millions of Stalin's victims released from those camps, and yet he vigorously persecuted religion, closing many thousands of churches, especially during his last years in power.

Khrushchev's style of rule—which included frequent administrative reorganizations and great insecurity of tenure for party and state officials (even if loss of office was a mild sanction compared with loss of life under Stalin)—increasingly alienated his comrades and subordinates. From 1958 Khrushchev combined his party leadership with the Chairmanship of the Council of Ministers and pushed through many decisions, including the placing of nuclear missiles in Cuba in 1962, which struck his colleagues as rash and dangerous. When they conspired to remove him from office in October 1964, there was no repeat of the 'anti-party group' crisis of 1957. By this time a majority of the Central Committee was glad to see Khrushchev go, and the population as a whole, believing that political changes at the top were no more subject to their influence or control than the weather, went about their business as if nothing had happened. It was not until the late 1980s that balanced assessments of Khrushchev could be published in Russia;

only then was he given due credit for breaking the taboo on criticism of Stalin, notwithstanding his unwillingness to change the Soviet system fundamentally.

Resistance to fundamental systemic change was, however, even more characteristic of Khrushchev's immediate successors. A more collective leadership was established after Khrushchev's fall with Leonid Brezhnev chosen as party leader and Aleksei Kosygin appointed Chairman of the Council of Ministers. Brezhnev held on to the General Secretaryship for almost two decades, until his death in office in late 1982. Kosygin remained head of the government until a few months before his death in 1980, but during the 1970s, as distinct from the second half of the 1960s, he wielded substantially less power than Brezhnev, who demonstrated once again the potential of the office of party General Secretary. A cautious and conservative Communist, Brezhnev was content to increase his power gradually and to take few risks either in domestic or foreign policy. Even the relative freedom to attack the crimes of Stalin was brought to an end, for Khrushchev's successors realized that unfettered investigation of Soviet history would undermine their own authority. The senior Politburo members—Brezhnev, Kosygin, Suslov, Kirilenko, and (from 1973) Gromyko, Ustinov, and Andropov—had all advanced their careers in Stalin's time in ways which would not withstand close scrutiny; although some, such as Ustinov, who had played an important part in the war effort, and Kosygin, an efficient economic administrator, had solid achievements behind them.

Putting an end to de-Stalinization was deeply troubling for that part of the intelligentsia which had started to think in terms of reforming the Soviet system, and the bolder among them began in the second half of the 1960s to engage in overt dissent. The Soviet leadership, however, took severe and successful measures to ensure that dissidence would not develop into a mass movement. An early sign of their determination to tolerate not the slightest opposition was the trial and imprisonment in 1966 of the writers Yuly Daniel and Andrei Sinyavsky for publishing abroad under pseudonyms works deemed to be anti-Soviet. It was around the same time that Alexander Solzhenitsyn's work was no longer accepted for publication within Russia, and this turned him from a covert into an overt opponent of the regime. As a result he was kept under constant surveillance and subjected to harassment. He was eventually forced into exile abroad in 1974, from which he did not return to Russia until 1994. The other Soviet dissident of comparable international prestige, the distinguished physicist Andrei Sakharov, was banished from Moscow at the beginning of 1980 and forced to live in administrative exile for the next seven years in the provincial city of Gorky (now restored to its old name of Nizhny Novgorod). Less famous dissidents were treated still more harshly and a number of them died in labour camps; albeit a small number compared with those who had perished during the mass terror of Stalin's time.

For the majority of the population, the Brezhnev years were, however, the most stable and predictable period of twentieth-century Russian history—the time which attracted most nostalgia in Russian public-opinion surveys of the mid-

1990s, even though Brezhnev personally was not highly esteemed either then or when he was still in power. Whereas Stalin's terror was arbitrary and could strike anywhere without warning, there were rules of the game in Brezhnev's Soviet Union. Conformist political behaviour and total loyalty in public could reasonably safely be combined with criticism in private. The extreme atomization of Soviet society and fear of expressing heterodox political views even within a circle of friends, characteristic of the Stalin era, began to be replaced under Khrushchev, in a process which continued under Brezhnev, by a sharper dichotomy between the ways people would speak at home and at work. The USSR was still a highly authoritarian state but it was gradually becoming post-totalitarian.

It remained, however, far from possessing a civil society, for informal groupings and networks were one thing, organized groups quite another. Apart from the dissident circles, numerically small and constantly persecuted, no autonomous groups capable of criticizing the party-state authorities were allowed to emerge until the Gorbachev era. In so far as the Soviet Union had developed some of the elements of a civil society in the last years of its existence, this was a *result* of Gorbachev's reforms and *not* the precondition of them. There were, however, gradual social changes during the Khrushchev and Brezhnev years which meant that by the mid-1980s the society was more prepared for liberalizing reform than it had been at the time of Stalin's death. In spite of ideological constraints, the educational system had reached standards which compared not unfavourably with those of Western countries and the expansion of higher education produced a large social stratum of professional people, a significant number of whom came increasingly to resent the denial of freedom to travel abroad or to read books deemed politically unsuitable by the authorities. They formed a potential constituency for change, even though many of them had lapsed into cynicism in the Brezhnev years and became politicized only when Gorbachev made the Soviet Union safe for dissent.

Brezhnev's health deteriorated in the later 1970s, and though the Soviet mass media attempted to compensate for his increasing frailty by manufacturing a 'mini-cult' (in comparison with Stalin's) of his personality, in reality key decisions were taken by an inner oligarchy within the Politburo in which, apart from Brezhnev himself, the most influential voices were those of Suslov, Gromyko, Ustinov, Andropov, and (except on foreign affairs) Chernenko. One decision taken by Brezhnev, together with that narrow group, was to send Soviet troops into Afghanistan in December 1979, a move which exacerbated already worsening relations with the USA and led the Soviet Union into a military quagmire comparable in some ways with the American war in Vietnam.

Domestically, Brezhnev's policy of 'stability of cadres' had allowed the top leadership team to grow old together, while many fundamental problems—including those of an economic growth rate which had declined by the beginning of the 1980s to zero, a deterioration in health and mortality indicators, worsening environmental pollution, and a growth of alcoholism and in corruption—remained untackled. The age structure of the leadership was such that Brezhnev's demise turned out to be the first of three deaths of a General Secretary within the space of two and a half years. His successor, Yury Andropov, who had headed the KGB for fifteen years, attempted to get the Soviet economy moving again and to tackle corruption, but there were strict limits to his reformism as well as to his physical capacity. Within a few months of succeeding Brezhnev in November 1982 Andropov's health began to decline and he died in February 1984. His successor, Konstantin Chernenko, lasted only thirteen months before he, too, died. A loyal subordinate of Brezhnev for many years, Chernenko achieved nothing of note during his term of office. Given Chernenko's lack of experience of international affairs, Andrei Gromyko had more leeway than ever in the conduct of Soviet foreign policy and neither the style nor the content of Soviet policy towards the outside world changed so long as he headed the Foreign Ministry. Relations with the West remained tense at the point at which the Soviet leadership finally made a generational change and chose the 54-year-old Mikhail Gorbachev to succeed Chernenko.

Ever since he had entered the Soviet top leadership group at the early age (by the standards of Brezhnev's Russia) of 47 in 1978, Gorbachev had been by far the youngest member of that team. His comparative youth at first counted against him, but when Chernenko, following (as had been the case with Brezhnev and Andropov) a long period of very visible decline, died in March 1985, the ruling oligarchs were aware that the annual ritual of state funerals was becoming a sick joke. That factor, together with the solid power base which Gorbachev had by this time acquired in the Central Committee Secretariat, made him the natural successor— the sixth and, as it turned out, the last General Secretary of the Communist Party of the Soviet Union.

The suggestion sometimes made in the West that the Politburo chose a 'soft-liner', Gorbachev, in response to the 'hardline' policies of the American President, Ronald Reagan, is totally fanciful. Foreign policy was not at issue when Gorbachev was chosen and neither in public nor at Politburo meetings (including the one which voted unanimously to recommend him to the Central Committee as General Secretary) did Gorbachev give the slightest indication that he would take a conciliatory line with the West. Nor was it clear to most of his Politburo colleagues that they were electing a serious reformer, still less someone who would shake the foundations of the Soviet system.

Gorbachev's coming to power was, nevertheless, a turning point in Russian and European history. His relative open-mindedness meant that his views developed during his years as Soviet leader, but from early on he recognized the need for economic reform and political change. At first this was reform within the limits of the existing system, involving a restructuring (*perestroika*) of the Soviet economy which would lead to an acceleration (*uskorenie*) of economic growth. A greater openness (*glasnost*) was advocated both as something desirable in itself and for instrumental reasons—as a means of revitalizing and mobilizing an inert society. From the outset of his leadership Gorbachev spoke also about the need for democratization (*demokratizatsiya*) of Soviet society, although during the first three years of his General Secretaryship the political change could more aptly be described as liberalization than as democratization. It was at the Nineteenth Conference of the Soviet Communist Party in the summer of 1988 that Gorbachev assumed responsibility for the crucial breakthrough, which was to turn the Soviet system into something different in kind, when he not only accepted the principle of contested elections for a new legislature but also proposed that the appropriate laws should be drawn up that very year and that the new assembly should be in place by the first half of 1989.

In each successive year in the second half of the 1980s the limits of *glasnost* were broadened until this openness became virtually indistinguishable from freedom of speech and of publication. One taboo after another was removed as the political evolution of the Soviet Union gathered pace. Criticism of Stalin preceded criticism of Lenin, but by the end of the decade even the principal founder of the Soviet state, along with the current Communist Party leadership and even the fundamentals of the Soviet political and economic system, could be attacked in print. Works, previously banned, such as Alexander Solzhenitsyn's *Gulag Archipelago*, Varlam Shalamov's *Kolyma Tales* (which exposed the lower depths of Soviet labour camp life), the works of Daniel and Sinyavsky, George Orwell's *Nineteen Eighty-Four* and *Animal Farm*, and Arthur Koestler's *Darkness at Noon* were published in substantial editions and had a profound effect on public opinion. Tens of millions of Russians, who had previously taken the Communist system for granted, became increasingly anti-Communist.

If *perestroika* was initially a 'revolution from above', albeit one which, in its more radical aspects, was supported only by a minority within the party leadership (but including, crucially, Gorbachev), it had become, by 1989–90, increasingly a movement from below. The contested elections which took place in March 1989 saw the defeat of a number of Communist Party functionaries and brought into the legislature nationalists from the Baltic and Caucasian republics as well as a number of Russian liberals and radicals, including Sakharov. Gorbachev himself had moved from being a would-be reformer of the Soviet system to a leader who recognized the need for its comprehensive transformation. By 1988 in private and by 1990 in public he had accepted that it was necessary to replace authoritarian single-party rule by political pluralism, whereby contested elections would in due course produce a competitive party system, while a command economy, totally state-owned, would be replaced by a mixed ownership and predominantly market economy.

By temperament and political conviction, however, Gorbachev was an evolutionary rather than revolutionary and his position became extraordinarily difficult as the former artificial, yet effective, unity of the Soviet system gave way to a high degree of polarization. On the one hand, Gorbachev found himself by 1990 increasingly outflanked by radicals such as Boris Yeltsin, whose speedy transformation from local Communist Party boss to democratic tribune of the people had been made possible by the political space for independent political action which

Gorbachev's reforms had opened up. On the other hand, Gorbachev was subjected to at least as intense pressures from the defenders of the Soviet system within the party and state apparatus, including the military and the KGB, who feared that the far-reaching changes he had introduced were endangering both the Soviet system as they had known it and the integrity of the Soviet state.

Gorbachev had been not only ready to see the Soviet system transformed but had also played the most decisive role in the breakthrough to political pluralism. It was no part of his developing project, however, to countenance the break-up of the Soviet state. He, and the reformist wing of the Communist Party leadership, attempted instead to replace a unitary state which had falsely claimed to be a federal system with a genuine federation. By 1991 he even embraced as a fallback position the idea of the Soviet Union becoming a looser confederation, but he was firmly opposed to the complete break-up of the union. Pressure for full independent statehood was especially strong in the Baltic republics and, increasingly, in Ukraine, Georgia, and Armenia. The most surprising advocate of independence from the union was, however, the Russian Republic. In his desire for power, Yeltsin played the Russian card, and, notwithstanding the dominant role historically of Russia and Russians in the Soviet Union, argued by 1990 that Russian laws had supremacy over Soviet law. On 8 December 1991, along with the presidents of Ukraine and Belorussia (now Belarus), he applied the *coup de grâce* by announcing unilaterally that the USSR was ceasing to exist and would be replaced by a Commonwealth of Independent States (CIS).

Yeltsin's stature had been enhanced by his success in three successive elections—to the Congress of People's Deputies of the USSR in 1989, to the Congress of People's Deputies of Russia in 1990 (following which Yeltsin was elected Chairman of the inner-legislative body, the Supreme Soviet), and, above all, by his election to the Presidency of Russia in June 1991. A huge, although unintentional, contribution to the break-up of the Soviet Union and the enhancement of Yeltsin's authority was made by the hardline *coup* plotters who attempted to overthrow Gorbachev in August 1991. The Prime Minister (Valentin Pavlov), the KGB chief (Vladimir Kryuchkov), the head of Soviet military industry (Oleg Baklanov), and the Minister of Defence (Dmitry Yazov) were among those who formed a self-appointed State Committee for the State of Emergency, put Gorbachev under house arrest in his Crimean holiday home on 18 August, and attempted to return the Soviet Union to the *status quo ante*.

Gorbachev's refusal to provide any fig leaf of constitutionality for the action of the plotters played an important part in the failure of their action, although the focus of international attention was on the Moscow 'White House', the home of the Russian parliament where Boris Yeltsin, strongly supported by tens of thousands of Muscovites who formed a protective ring around the building (thus raising the political costs of its storming) and by the great majority of world leaders, led the resistance to the takeover. By 22 August the *coup* had failed, Yeltsin's prestige had been further enhanced, and Gorbachev returned to Moscow seriously weakened. The fact that the *coup* leaders had been Gorbachev's appointees to high office was fully exploited by Yeltsin, who lost no opportunity to underline that in the new situation of 'dual power' in Moscow (Soviet and Russian) it was he who was now by far the stronger partner.

These last months of the existence of the Soviet Union were the high point of Yeltsin's popularity. In contrast, Gorbachev, who had been the most popular politician in Russia and the USSR for the five years between his selection as General Secretary of the CPSU in March 1985 and his election as President of the USSR by the Congress of People's Deputies in March 1990, now enjoyed far less support than hitherto and was held in lower esteem than Yeltsin. Nevertheless, it was Gorbachev who had been the key mover and facilitator in the dismantling of the Communist system. Freedom of speech, publication, and religion, contested elections, a legislature which could and did criticize the executive, and autonomous political organization (including the emergence of pressure groups, broad political movements, and embryonic political parties) had all come into being under the aegis of Gorbachev and, for the most part, as a result of his crucial support. What this meant was that Russia by the end of the 1980s had acquired many of the features of a civil society and of political pluralism. Indeed, the essentials of Communism had been discarded at least two years before the Communist Party of the Soviet Union was suspended in the wake of the failed August *coup* and long before the red flag, with its hammer and sickle, was lowered from the Kremlin on 25 December 1991.

The Gorbachev era saw also the end of the Cold War and it was the new thinking espoused by Gorbachev and the new Soviet behaviour which accompanied it that made this possible. The military–industrial complexes in both the Soviet Union and the United States had reached bloated levels, but the cost of keeping up with the rival superpower was a greater strain on the Soviet than on the American economy, given the superior level both of American GNP and of American technology. Yet, it took a bold Soviet leader to give a higher priority to stilling the fears of the West than of his own military–security apparatus. Having, however, established good personal and political relations with the major Western leaders—most crucially, with successive US presidents Ronald Reagan and George Bush, but also with Margaret Thatcher, François Mitterrand, Helmut Kohl, and Felipe González—Gorbachev was able to reach agreement with those counterparts on a wide range of issues.

Even more important than arms control treaties in demonstrating that the much-trumpeted new thinking presaged a new political reality was the changed Soviet behaviour towards Eastern Europe. When the East-Central European countries tested the Gorbachevian new thinking which proclaimed that each country had a right to choose its own political and economic system, this turned out to be matched by Soviet actions—or, more precisely, inaction, for as one country after another in the Soviet bloc became independent and non-Communist in the course of 1989–90, there was no attempt at military intervention. The most difficult change of all for the Soviet leadership to accept (and one which caused dissension within the ruling circles) was the unification of Germany as a member of NATO. With this, too, Gorbachev ultimately acquiesced.

Although Gorbachev's attitude to what was sometimes called the 'inner empire' of the USSR, as compared with the East European 'outer empire', was different, there, too, he refrained from resorting to what was by 1990–1 the only means possible of holding the entire Soviet Union together—namely, harsh and sustained repression. Instead, he tried, somewhat belatedly, to negotiate a new Union Treaty which would keep all or most of the union together on a voluntary basis. That failed, but not primarily as a result of the mistakes of the post-1985 Soviet leadership but as a legacy of the entire Soviet period and even of Imperial Russian history. Once liberalization and democratization had been introduced, providing the opportunity, first, for the airing of numerous national grievances concerning past oppression and injustice and, secondly, for the election of politicians who, far from being controlled by Moscow, would espouse the Estonian, Lithuanian, Latvian, Ukrainian, or Georgian nationalist cause, the odds were stacked heavily against the preservation of a political union covering the entire territory of the former USSR.

There were parts of the Soviet Union in which national élites did not agitate for full independence—in particular, Kazakhstan, under the leadership of Nursultan Nazarbayev, and the Central Asian republics. In an important sense they had independence thrust upon them in December 1991. One reason for the hesitation of the local élites was that they had attained their positions of power through service to Moscow and either belief in or, increasingly, lip-service to Marxism-Leninism. Since it seemed more than probable that in post-Soviet Central Asia the official state ideology would be Islam, it was not entirely obvious that those who had formed the ruling stratum in the late Soviet period would be able to hold on to their positions of power and privilege. In fact, the turnover of élites was on an extremely modest scale. Throughout the former Soviet Union, including not least the Central Asian states, former Communist Party officials became the principal political office-holders and economic beneficiaries of post-Communism.

This was true also of Russia itself, where in the summer of 1996 the former Secretary of the Central Committee, Boris Yeltsin, was elected for a further four-year term as President, following which he retained until 1998 the services of the former head of a Central Committee department, Viktor Chernomyrdin, as Prime Minister. Yeltsin's political outlook had, however, developed radically over the previous decade and in the one area of transition from Communism where only modest progress had occurred under Gorbachev—the marketization and partial privatization of the Soviet economy—dramatic change occurred between 1992 (the year in which the pro-market economist, Yegor Gaidar, was acting Russian Prime Minister) and 1995. While it was clear to most well-informed Russian citizens that there could be no return to a Soviet-style economy and the world of - five-year-plans, the costs of the economic transition were, however, high. The gap between rich and poor widened dramatically, inflation wiped out savings, production plummeted, job insecurity loomed, and organized crime burgeoned.

Whereas democracy and the market had been embraced by a wide section of the Russian population in 1991, they were seen as panaceas which would lead quite rapidly to West European standards of living and styles of life. For a majority nothing of the kind transpired, nor could it have done on the basis of the wrongly developed (rather than underdeveloped) Soviet economy. Growing hostility to the Yeltsin presidency and the policies pursued by his government led to a showdown between the President and the Russian Supreme Soviet in 1993 which ended with Yeltsin forcibly disbanding the legislature he had formerly headed. The Moscow White House which Yeltsin had defended in August 1991 became the site of resistance of the legislature to Yeltsin which was ended only when Yeltsin, not without difficulty, persuaded the army to end the deadlock. The assault on the White House left scores of people dead but paved the way for the adoption of a new Constitution and elections to a new legislature—a State Duma and Federation Council—in December 1993. This parliament had substantially fewer powers than its predecessor, which was just as well for Yeltsin, since the shift in public opinion was reflected in substantial electoral support for the nationalist movement, the oddly-named Liberal Democratic Party led by the cynical populist Vladimir Zhirinovsky, and for the Communists and their allies. In the election to the Duma exactly two years later Communists and nationalists emerged with a similarly large share of the popular vote and of seats, but with the difference in 1995 that the Communists did better than the nationalists.

If the losers in post-Soviet Russia were now making their voices heard, the winners, who included many formerly senior officials in the Communist party-state who had now become the owners of property they formerly administered, were unlikely to give up their gains without a fierce struggle. It seemed likely that some kind of capitalist economy, however distorted, would continue because of the strength of the vested interests supporting it and also because no viable alternative to an essentially market economy had been found. Soviet experience over seventy years had eloquently illustrated that latter point. It seemed that a majority of citizens of Russia wished for a form of social democracy in which the new freedoms would be combined with a welfare state and social security. Since, however, the scope for economic manoeuvre in conditions of political pluralism and of industrial decline was extremely limited, and since social democrats had bickered amongst themselves and failed to cohere in a strong political party, a substantial minority of Russians were tempted once again by Communists and their allies, even though (or in some cases because) those who had remained Communist Party members were the people who had bitterly opposed Gorbachev's introduction of political and intellectual freedom and Yeltsin's privatization programme.

It seemed highly unlikely that Russia would revert to a classical Communist system of the kind which prevailed in the Soviet Union until the late 1980s. The revolution in communications was one factor making this more difficult. While, prior to the Gorbachevian liberalization, even photocopying machines had been kept under strict lock and key and the regime had largely maintained its informational monopoly, this had changed dramatically by the late 1980s and especially the

1990s. By the last decade of the century electronic mail, fax machines, and satellite television had taken off in Russia. The desire of the new business élite to enjoy at least as many advantages as their Western counterparts and of post-Soviet governments to integrate Russia more fully in the world economy militated against a return to the closed society. More generally, it is harder to take away freedoms once granted than to withhold freedoms which have never been experienced. Yet the authoritarian temptation continued to loom large and Russia in the last years of the century had not only a mixed economy but also a mixed polity—one in which authoritarian and democratic elements were combined, sometimes in the head of the same person. Great power had once again been placed in the hands of the executive and although it was still possible to criticize the President and government, it was less easy to call them to account in between elections and only partially through the electoral process.

One reason for this was the great power wielded by financial interests. An ironical remark which gained some currency in post-Soviet Russia was that 'Everything the Communists told us about socialism was a lie and everything they told us about capitalism was true'. In a curious way, old Soviet propaganda about capitalist systems—which downplayed the significance of Western democratic institutions and overstated the power of financiers—would not have been so far off the mark if framed as a prediction about Russian capitalism. Since orthodox Soviet Communists had not for a moment believed that a transition in *that* direction was possible, they do not deserve any particular credit for prescience. But Russian politics in the 1990s was characterized by the emergence of golden triangles which saw close links between particular bankers, leading politicians, and the profitable parts of Russian industry (especially the energy sector). Even as industrial production declined, vast profits were made by unscrupulous businessmen who either had friends at court or themselves acquired a seat at court; several of them were appointed to high positions within the Yeltsin administration.

A capitalist economy, with some corporatist characteristics, had been consolidated surprisingly quickly, while democracy remained far from consolidated. Faced with the threat of a return to power by unreconstructed Communists, there were those in Boris Yeltsin's entourage who wished to avoid holding the Russian presidential election when it was due in June 1996. Yeltsin resisted that temptation, but relied heavily during the campaign on the mobilization of bias in his favour by the mass media, especially television. Among the problems he faced was that he had embarked on an unpopular war in late 1994 to bring Chechnya, a republic of the Russian Federation which had asserted its independence, back within the Russian fold. In the run-up to the election Yeltsin declared that war to be over, adding that Russia had won it. This was far from the truth. With the election battle won, Russian forces attempted to secure the military victory in Chechnya which had consistently eluded them, launching a new, and unsuccessful, offensive.

Although Yeltsin did not (as in 1991) secure an overall majority in the first ballot, he defeated his principal opponent, the Communist leader Gennady Zyuganov, comfortably enough in the July run-off, although this nationalistic Communist and voice from the past secured over 40 per cent of the vote. Between the two rounds of the election Yeltsin had strengthened his position by co-opting former army general Alexander Lebed—who had come a strong third in the first round—and appointing him to be his National Security Adviser. It was Lebed who, in late August–early September 1996, negotiated a settlement of the Chechen dispute and appeared to have ended a bloody and unnecessary war which, on his plausible estimate, had cost some 80,000 lives. Predictably, the ambitious Lebed soon clashed with senior members of the presidential administration and with Boris Yeltsin himself. Yeltsin removed him from office shortly after he had served his electoral purpose. The Constitution decreed that Yeltsin could not serve a third term as President, and his failing health also ruled out a further four years in office. Yeltsin underwent major heart surgery in 1997 and thereafter was frequently unwell and sometimes a public embarrassment. He appointed as Prime Minister and dismissed in quick succession Sergei Kirienko, Sergei Stepashin, and Yevgeny Primakov after sacking Viktor Chernomyrdin. Finally, in the person of former KGB officer Vladimir Putin, Yeltsin found a Prime Minister to whom he believed he could safely entrust the fate of his family and country. On the eve of a new millennium Yeltsin announced his resignation from the Presidency which meant that Prime Minister Putin—who in autumn 1999 had launched a new war in Chechnya—became acting President with immediate effect and the firm favourite to win presidential elections brought forward from June to March 2000.

What has made the Soviet and Russian transition uniquely difficult is that both the political system and the economic system had to be transformed simultaneously, while at the same time an empire of sorts (whether that of the Soviet Union or of the Russian Federation) had to be converted into a genuine federation if a transition to democracy was to have a real chance of success. These momentous changes were further complicated by the need for Russian rulers and citizens to accept the international standing of a major power rather than superpower status and by the difficult psychological adjustment involved in fully recognizing the independence of territories which, in some instances, had been part of a greater Russian state since the eighteenth century or earlier.

In the light of these historic obstacles to a transition to liberty and democracy in Russia, it is the extent of the achievement in the second half of the 1980s and, to a lesser extent, in the 1990s, above all in the realm of human freedom, which impresses itself on the outside observer more than the failures and setbacks. Yet for millions of Russians the pain of the transition was such that freedom came lower on their scale of values at the end of the 1990s than it had at the beginning of the decade. The older generation in particular expressed, both in voting behaviour and in answer to surveys, an attraction to the security and predictability which they associated with the last decades of Communist rule. Moreover, the self-proclaimed democrats—among them Yeltsin and his associates—had frequently acted in ways which accorded higher priority to safeguarding their power and property than to safeguarding the norms of democracy. As a new century began genuine Russian democrats were once again on the defensive and highly conscious of the difficulties and dangers ahead.

16 The Remaking of Europe

ANNE DEIGHTON

In many respects, the history of Cold War Europe has been one of spectacular success. There has been general peace in a continent which had experienced devastating warfare twice in the twentieth century. After a short period of economic and political reconstruction, Western Europe experienced a phenomenal economic boom that lasted until the 1970s. Technological changes influenced every part of society, from jobs to communications systems, consumer products to transport. The 'magnet' effect of Western Europe has been striking, and the European Union's membership has risen from six to fifteen, with the prospect of twenty members after the turn of the century. Welfare provisions for citizens across Europe have been matched by spreading democratization, secularization, greater personal freedoms, a rapid breakdown of restrictive class structures, and increased educational opportunities.

In 1945, to forecast such success would have seemed bizarre. 'What is Europe now?', Winston Churchill once asked. 'It is a rubble heap, a charnel house, a breeding ground of pestilence and hate.' As the war ended, Europe was in a desperate state. Industry, commerce, and trading patterns were disrupted, and production was only 20 per cent of pre-war levels. Bombing had destroyed cities and transport systems. Relief, not reconstruction, was the order of the day. Huge numbers of refugees and displaced persons were on the move across the continent: as many as eight million moved westwards from Poland and other Soviet-occupied areas, while millions were also forcibly repatriated to the east. Acute shortages of food, fuel, and commodities were commonplace, and 100 million Europeans were living on less than 1,500 calories a day, despite the best efforts of the UN Relief and Rehabilitation Administration. Financial disaster threatened, Britain was bankrupt. While discredited wartime puppet regimes had been ousted, there were grave political uncertainties across the continent. There was no German government at all. The debilitating psychological after-effects of dictatorship and war in

Europe were fuelled by information about Nazi war crimes which had accounted for the lives of over five million people.

Ironically, it was the nature of the wartime victory against Nazism and Fascism that became the determining geo-strategic feature of post-war Europe. The United States, the Soviet Union, and Britain finally met on the battlefields of a defeated Germany, to try to forge a peace settlement. But the 'Grand Alliance' had been sustained by the struggle against a common enemy, and, now victorious, there was little to hold it together. The shape of post-war Europe had been endlessly debated at the summit conferences of Teheran, Yalta, and Potsdam, but in reality there was little idea of the enormity of the problems that confronted the post-war world.

The West's fear of German power remained even after military victory, but fear of communism and the intentions of the Soviet Union quickly became more pressing. It was principally over Germany, the geo-strategic and economic heart of Europe, that the breakdown with the Soviet Union came. Germany (and Berlin) had been divided into American, Soviet, British, and French zones of military occupation soon after the heads of state meeting at Yalta in February 1945. The four-power system of control broke down almost as soon as it had been set up, as it proved impossible to run the country by mutual agreement. The struggle to defeat Germany quickly became the new struggle for Germany. Western money was poured in to prevent economic collapse, and a new political system was established to ensure that at least the western part of the country would not succumb to communism but would become part of the newly invented 'West'.

By 1955, the territorial division of Germany, and the disappearance of central Europe behind Stalin's 'Iron Curtain' clearly reflected the global bipolarity between West and East. The two superpowers, the United States and the Soviet Union, were the new hegemons which largely determined the ordering of Europe. Even as democracy was re-established in Western Europe, and economic reconstruction got under way, Stalinist regimes were being set up in most of the central European countries which had been 'liberated' in 1945. Agriculture was usually collectivized, and political opposition to Moscow was crushed, often forcibly. The disappearance of central Europe under the skirts of Stalinism was a slow but relentless process, engulfing the eastern zone of Germany, Czechoslovakia, Poland, Hungary, Bulgaria, Romania, Albania, and the Baltic States. Thus, Berlin, Germany, and the continent of Europe was slowly divided into ideologically hostile camps. The only country to ward off Eastern—and Western—pressures was Yugoslavia, where popular support was very strong for the communist leader Tito, who had masterminded Yogoslav wartime resistance against the Nazis.

Two competing reconstruction programmes—Marshall Aid (the Economic Reconstruction Programme) and the Council of Mutual Economic Assistance (Comecon)—emerged in the late 1940s. By 1947 US President Harry Truman had realized that Europe's economy—and the United States' trading markets—needed more than short-term palliatives, and twelve billion dollars were given or loaned by the United States to sixteen participating countries between 1948 and 1952. It is hard to overestimate the psychological, political, and economic significance of this aid for Western Europe. The United States was a model of success, and in terms of growth, investment and innovation, had benefited from the war. Although the US population was roughly the same as that of Europe, its standard of living was far higher. But with the help of Marshall Aid, Western European economies—including the Western German zones—quickly recovered from the wartime losses, grew beyond their pre-war levels, and were encouraged towards further integration. The Soviet Union, its German zone, and the countries of central Europe did not participate in the programme, and it is hard in retrospect to imagine that the Americans would have been so generous if Marshall Aid had not been perceived as containing the spread of communism. So both the territorial and ideological division of Cold War Europe, and the roots of Western post-war economic integration are to be found in Marshall Aid. The Soviets' first reaction to Marshall Aid had been to step up the propaganda war. Their subsequent introduction of the Council of Mutual Economic Assistance was less well funded and less effective. However, by the 1950s there existed a real competitive edge between West and East European economies, fuelled, for example, by the Soviet Union's spectacular triumph with the Sputnik satellite in 1957.

As well as economic rivalry in Europe, two competing security systems developed—the North Atlantic Treaty Organization (NATO) in 1949 and the Warsaw Pact in 1955. NATO has remained the overarching organization that exemplifies what has been meant, in Europe, by the West: it represented the commitment of the US to the military and political security of Western Europe, by upgrading American security to include that of the West Europeans. The underlying notion was that of the tripwire: the death of one American soldier on European soil would trigger an overwhelming American response against the Soviet Union. Yet NATO also represented a political commitment to West Europeans, with massive financial transfers and continuing transatlantic planning and diplomacy. New members —Greece and Turkey in 1952, West Germany in 1955, Spain in 1986—reinforced the organization's appeal. In a dreadful symmetry, fear of Western capitalism and the NATO alliance helped to shape Soviet military policy with the creation of the Warsaw Pact, composed of the major central European countries and led by the Soviet Union. Both sides probably overestimated the aggressive intentions and capabilities of the other, but at the time the dangers seemed real enough, and the bipolar alliance system completely dwarfed any other European security arrangement throughout the period.

Ideological competition between socialism and capitalism was also found in a propaganda war waged through channels such as Cominform and 'The Voice of America', and ideological hegemony was endlessly reinforced in both blocs. Europe was a politically divided region in a global setting, with only a few small states remaining technically, if not emotionally, neutral (Sweden, Finland, Switzerland, Austria), or outside the new bipolar setting (Spain).

The first thirty years after the war brought phenomenal prosperity to economically developed states. On both sides of the Iron Curtain, industrial progress and technological advances were paralleled by a remarkable increase in standards of living, and raised expectations about what every state should deliver to its peoples. The advances achieved in the first forty years of the twentieth century were extended, with child benefits, elaborate pensions and unemployment schemes, free health provision, and a massive expansion in the length and richness of state educational provision. Although the scope of welfare provision varied between the countries of Europe, common patterns emerge which show that welfare expectations were continually rising, and that economic growth coupled with extensive taxation dramatically increased the role of public authority and public policy over the lives of Europe's citizens. The 'Golden Years' were characterized by dramatic, and perhaps unique, growth for developed economies, based upon rising GDP, full employment, steadily falling mortality rates, technological developments, and the internationalization of economic enterprises. The widespread application of computers, of new research in chemicals' applications ranging from nylon to fertilizers, and of oil and nuclear-based industries, as well as the commercial expansion of automobile production, television, and telecommunications, all transformed public, industrial, and private life. As these new industries developed, employment in traditional industries such as agriculture, shipbuilding, coal, and manufacturing production declined, bringing changes in employment patterns and expectations. In Western Europe, a Golden Triangle of industrialized regions (roughly between Paris, Hamburg, and Milan) became the core of the new European prosperity. Why this boom came about is not fully understood, but can be explained in part by the Bretton Woods system of fixed exchange rates, the Marshall Aid programme, and by the low base line from which the continental economies were operating after the war.

Across Western Europe there was a general commitment to Keynesian principles of intervention, although the instruments used varied between countries. The social-market economy in Germany was based upon market liberalization and fiscal encouragement for investment in industry. Italian policy stressed a preference for stimulating consumer-goods production and the service sector. In France, a more *dirigiste* line prevailed, characterized by the Monnet Plan. By the advent of the Fifth Republic in 1958, with the end of France's imperial preoccupations in Indo-China and North Africa, and the creation of the European Economic Community (EEC), French growth rates really took off. After the war, British GDP was already higher than that of its continental neighbours, and, while the British economy did continue to grow, it did so relatively more slowly than the continental economies. British economic strategy was based upon import-led growth, but because of factors including an over-attachment to the psychological importance of sterling, growth was uneven, and policy was marked by stop–go measures, inflation, and rapidly changing interest-rate levels.

Yet by the 1970s, all European economies were forced to react to the end of dollar convertibility, which was then followed by the oil crises of 1973–4, and 1979–80.

The inglorious end of the 'Golden Years' brought inflation, slump, and recession, and rising unemployment across the continent. Britain—although possessing her own oil in the North Sea—was keenly affected, and it was the Conservative Thatcher governments (1979–90) which led the way to a fundamental shift in governmental economic priorities, with a policy of reducing trade-union power, privatization, and the scaling-down of welfare provision. Privatization was also followed by French Prime Minister Chirac after 1986. Despite a short-term recovery in the mid-1980s, European economies have generally been unable to find the steady growth, economic security, and prosperity that marked earlier post-war decades. Immigration, which was largely acceptable when the employment market was booming (Europe received 8 million immigrants between 1950 and 1980), became an increasingly serious social issue during the 1970s, with Turkish guest workers in West Germany, North African migration into France, and post-imperial immigration into Britain all attracting alarmist reactions. Events in the economic arena from the mid-1970s have underscored the interdependence and potential fragility of each state's economic system, and the need for policy-makers to be able to secure growth in order to make social legislation viable, and to retain outward-looking and open societies.

Coupled with the growth in national economies during the Golden Years, Europeans also witnessed the 'Europeanization' of their economies, and, notably, the development of supranational institutions of economic and political integration in the Western part of the Continent. This phenomenon is probably the most striking feature of the period. It owes its genesis to the convergence of a number of quite different factors. The bloody inheritance of the European nation-state after two wars, and the radical idea that the balance of power in Western Europe could be managed through institutions of integration rather than by antagonistic military alliances, were powerful motivators. The comfort of military protection provided by the USA in the face of communist pressures was also important. The demand of rapidly developing national and transnational enterprises for larger markets unimpeded by restrictive practices and tariffs was yet another consideration.

Decolonization was also an important factor in the drive towards integration. The move away from colonial to regional status represented a seismic shift in the international standing of Europe. As British, French, Italian, Belgian, and Dutch colonial markets (and later those of Portugal) began to diminish in size and importance, the European colonial core needed to seek a new economic as well as strategic power base. The Suez fiasco of 1956 provided a powerful spur to the French in their tortured route from global to regional status. The failed Suez invasion was to have the same effect upon British thinking, but this was to take a few years longer. The European Common Commercial Policy with former colonies and overseas areas of interest, particularly through the Lomé and ACP Agreements, provided a worldwide trading mechanism.

The predecessor to the EEC was the European Coal and Steel Community

(ECSC) of 1952, which had an overtly political message: another war between Germany and her neighbours—especially France—must be made impossible. This would be achieved by the integration of coal and steel industries which were traditionally key war-making industries. But it was the more wide-reaching EEC (set up by the Treaty of Rome in 1957) that, coupled with the European Atomic Community, promised freedom of goods, capital, services, and people between the member states, and which looked forward to the future management of changing economies, rather than back to the traditional industries of coal and steel. The EEC's most startling characteristic was its supranationality, epitomized by a non-elected executive, the Commission, and by a preparedness of the member states to accept some decision-making by majority voting. As well as ending tariffs and restrictive practices, a common external tariff against other countries was introduced between the member states, and agriculture was protected through the Common Agricultural Policy. The Community was dominated politically by France, which saw the organization as a mechanism for its new entente with West Germany. But the EEC was always vigorously supported by its other founder members, Italy, Belgium, the Netherlands, and tiny Luxembourg, whose international standing all rose because of their membership. The United Kingdom rashly rejected the opportunity to become a founding member of the Community, while the United States consistently supported West Europe's efforts to integrate.

The Community was to become the bedrock of Western Europe's economic integration, and the EEC (or European Community (EC), as it was called after 1967), remained the focal point of Europe's economic development. The original Rome Treaty was revised in 1987 by the Single European Act which sought completion of a single market in Europe as envisaged by the signatories of the Rome Treaty, and to do this by the end of 1992. The Maastricht revisions of 1993 (which again renamed the Community, this time as the European Union (EU)), went even further by creating new policy areas and a more efficient decision-making system. These treaties all reflect the place in European economic thinking of free-market ideas alongside a certain degree of planning and state (or Community) intervention. Thus regional policies, structural adjustment funds, and special dispensations for backward economies coexist with a commitment to a 'level playing field', free and genuine industrial and commercial competition, and Europe-wide markets. Part of the Community's success stemmed from the realization of its limitations, at least until the end of the cold war. It was quite unsuited to managing a common foreign or defence policy, which was left to NATO. It did not, in practice, try to destroy European nation-states, despite taking away some of their sovereign powers. Nevertheless, a greater uniformity of habits and life-style has emerged in Europe, through trade, travel, and mass communications.

Since 1958, non-members have continually sought to join or to be associated with the Community, and many countries have association agreements and special trading agreements. In 1973, the United Kingdom, Ireland, and Denmark joined, unfortunately just as the post-war economic boom was ending. In 1981 Greece was admitted, in 1986, Spain and Portugal, in 1990, the former East

Germany was absorbed into the EU when Germany was unified. In 1995, Sweden, Finland, and Austria also secured admission. The EC had been a symbol of democracy for Greece, Spain, and Portugal when they were ruled by dictators, and after 1989 the EU also became the symbol of central European countries' desire for a 'return to Europe' after they had thrown off communist rule. The newly created democracies of central Europe—Poland, Hungary, the Czech Republic, Estonia, Slovenia, and Slovakia—still await membership of the Community club. Indeed, the perceived political and economic advantages of Community membership outweigh the erosion of national sovereignty and autonomy that membership involves. For countries like Turkey, whose membership of NATO since 1952 has been crucial in defending the organization's southern flank, Community membership has remained an unobtainable target, and its subsequent increasing instability may yet become an example of the political costs of discouraging new applicants.

In the east, post-war modernization was achieved by very different means. Integration in the West has been driven by a voluntary wish to combine, backed by strong political and economic pressure from the United States. Unity in central Europe was, by contrast, largely imposed from above upon reluctant, if not recalcitrant, peoples. Political, economic, and military integration, with an overt ideological dimension, squeezed central European states into a Soviet-style mould of post-war socialism. Economic structures clearly existed to ensure the development of the Soviet Union, and, although considerable sums of money were pumped into the region, the race with the West for technological competitiveness and consumer satisfaction was soon lost, although statistical information about the former Soviet European empire is notoriously unreliable. Political and economic integration in Eastern Europe produced some macabre regimes, and, indeed, revolt against the Soviet Union flared up in 1953 in East Germany, in 1956 in Hungary and Poland, and in 1968 in Czechoslovakia, even before the cumulative effects of Polish-instigated opposition to Moscow from 1981 led the way to the breakdown of the Soviet Union's European empire.

The bipolar divide that forced Europeans into joint security arrangements with their respective hegemons, and the drive to economic modernization that edged them into supranational integration, may seem to indicate that, after the Second World War, the days of the nation state were numbered. But this is not the case. In 1955 there were roughly twenty-two more or less autonomous European states (of which fifteen were, broadly speaking, in the Western camp); in 1995 there were nearly thirty European states. Western European states, economies, and societies share many common features, yet they retain national distinctiveness, be it in social and political culture, organization, religious make-up, or language.

Within Western European states, two major seams of political thinking have dominated: one largely conservative and often Catholic, and the other socialist in outlook. The practical differences between parties in power have largely been of emphasis and priority, rather than of core principles. Christian Democratic parties have been most closely associated with the drive to European unity, characterized particularly by West German Chancellor Konrad Adenauer, while Social Democratic parties have traditionally been identified with labour, and the poorer and less privileged sectors of society. In domestic affairs, for example, in Britain, the Beveridge Report of 1942 urged public protection for the individual and the family 'from the cradle to the grave', against sickness, poverty, unemployment, and ignorance. It struck a chord all over Europe, and its ideals both reflected and underpinned much of the social legislation in health, housing, education, and benefits that have been common to European countries until the 1980s.

Constitutional reform was one of the most urgent post-war problems for continental Europe, and the eventual establishment of democratic regimes, effective party systems, and sophisticated administrative structures in Western Europe was one of the period's greatest success stories. The need to create political stability immediately after the war was made more difficult by hard-fought political struggles in countries which were also coping with the economic and social transition from war to peace. Until 1947, indigenous communist parties reflected a general European shift to the left, particularly in France and Italy. In Italy in 1946, the Constituent Assembly voted in support of a new constitution, and abolished the monarchy, which had played an inglorious role during the Fascist period. The skills of Alcide de Gasperi were to ensure that for the whole cold war period the Christian Democrats were dominant, although the governmental system was inherently unstable, with constantly changing coalition governments, and became endemically corrupt. In France, where the Third Republic had collapsed in 1940, the wartime Vichy regime was replaced (in 1946) by a new constitution which heralded the Fourth Republic. However, this was after a year of crisis in which Gaullists, Communists, Catholics, and former Resistance leaders were pitted against each other, and public support for the new constitution remained weak. As in Italy, governments changed with alarming frequency, which created an atmosphere of insecurity and instability.

The political dilemma of politics in France was resolved by General Charles de Gaulle's success in driving through a new constitution in 1958. The Fifth Republic brought a more presidential—and more autocratic—constitution, but has proved far more durable than its predecessor. De Gaulle dominated French national life and European politics between 1958 and 1969, doggedly pushing forward a programme that reinforced the image of French grandeur. The active role played by the Americans in Western European politics, as well as the much vaunted Anglo-American 'Special Relationship', encouraged him to build upon earlier French efforts at reconciliation with West Germany, and to pursue a wide, all-Europe and intrinsically anti-Anglo-Saxon strategy. Although he withdrew France from the integrated command structure of NATO, and unilaterally rejected Britain's application to the EEC in 1963 and 1967, de Gaulle never risked undermining the Western Alliance unduly, but combined rhetorical flourishes with a considered pragmatism about France's real capacities and national interest. This dual approach to international politics remained constant through subsequent presidencies. In domestic politics, centralization also remained a central feature of the Fifth Republic, with an elaborate cobweb of political and administrative structures which looked to Paris. It was not until the 1980s that measures of decentralization were seriously undertaken by the Socialist President François Mitterrand (1981–95), ironically at the very time that centralization of governmental power was increasing dramatically in Britain.

For Germany, 1945 was Year Zero, and the new Germanys that emerged by 1955 were the two twins of the cold war. Divided into four zones, a common programme of constitutional reform quickly appeared impossible. An Anglo-American Bizone was created by 1947, which was expanded to a Trizone with the French, and plans were made for a common currency, and a new provisional constitution for the three Western zones. The Basic Law was introduced in 1949, when the capital of the newly created Federal German Republic was also moved to Bonn. The Basic Law emphasized the federalist traditions of Weimar Germany, encouraged the growth of democracy 'from below' through the Länder, and restrained the powers of the President relative to those of the Chancellor. While the Basic Law retained a commitment to the eventual unification of Germany, its new Western democracy was 'monitored' by the Western Allies until it joined NATO. In 1949 the Soviet-inspired German Democratic Republic was also established, with its very different interpretation of democracy.

Berlin, deep inside the Eastern zone, had also been divided into four zones in 1945. In 1948–9 its land access routes were blocked by the Soviets for nearly a year, and then in 1961 a wall across the city was rapidly erected to stop the flow of Germans from east to west. The wall became the major symbol of a divided Germany and a divided Europe until it was breached in November 1989.

Therefore West Germany and East Germany were both 'invented' states of the Cold War. For the aged but tenacious West German Chancellor Konrad Adenauer (1949–63), national political and economic recovery required first of all a commitment to West European integration and to the Atlantic Alliance: an effective *Westpolitik*. *Westpolitik* would strengthen his country's legitimacy, and this might, in the distant future, provide a basis for German unification. Meanwhile, it provided West Germany with the 'golden handcuffs' that would prevent revanchism.

It was under the Social Democratic leadership of Willi Brandt (1969–74), that the extraordinarily complicated and subtle policy of *Ostpolitik* was most vigorously pursued. German unification as an immediate aim was not explicitly made public, or perhaps even consistently envisaged by *Ostpolitik*. It was rather a process of easement of tensions within Berlin, with East Germany, with the relevant states of Eastern Europe, and with the Soviet Union. This had to be undertaken without disturbing the structure of the Western Alliance. The content of *Ostpolitik* ranged from new treaties (acknowledging, for example, the 'two states in one nation' of the German status quo), to official visits, financial transfers to East Germany, and provision for Germans to cross the border between them. It was a policy that survived shifts in superpower relations, particularly through the tense years of superpower animosity in the early 1980s, and it did much to keep alive a notion of a non-divided Germany and Europe.

'Exceptionalism' in Britain emerged even as the war ended. British institutions had been preserved during the war, though many democratic rights had been suspended throughout the period of hostilities. Parliament, the Monarchy and the British system of Common Law were held up in 1945 as models of flexibility and effectiveness in a country that had not been invaded, and that had fought on the European front from start to finish. The surprise victory of the Labour Party in the general election of 1945 threw Winston Churchill out of office, but brought back many men (Clement Attlee, the new Prime Minister and Ernest Bevin, the new Foreign Secretary, for example) who had already experienced high office in the wartime coalition government. Labour introduced a radical programme of economic and social changes, including a national health service and national social-security scheme, and many key sectors of the economy were nationalized. For thirty years the underlying assumptions of these changes were not seriously challenged by subsequent Labour or Conservative administrations. It was not until the early 1980s that privatization and the dismemberment of a universal welfare state became an issue.

Bipartisanship was also a characteristic of British foreign policy. Winston Churchill's schema of the three great interlocking circles of Empire/Commonwealth, United States, and Europe, in each of which Britain was the only country to have an interest, was an apt assessment of Britain's place in the world in 1945. But the schema soon changed, as the Empire/Commonwealth rapidly waned, and the United States began to turn its attentions to the burgeoning strength of Western Europe. British policy after the mid-1950s became one of damage limitation under Conservatives and Labour alike, as membership of the EEC was, humilitatingly, twice refused to them by de Gaulle (in 1963 under Harold Macmillan's premiership, and in 1967 when Harold Wilson was Prime Minister). When Britain was finally admitted to the Community in 1973, recession, not growth, was dominant, and it proved more difficult to integrate the country fully into the political culture of the European Community. The end of global commitments in the Indian subcontinent and east of Suez inevitably reinforced the country's declining imperial role. The so-called 'Special Relationship' with the United States, which was based upon common strategic, political, and intelligence interests, was always more important to the British, as the lesser power, than to the Americans. Although Britain remained a global power (highlighted by the Falklands War in 1982), a member of the United Nations Security Council, and an occupying power in West Germany until 1990, her ability to 'punch above her weight' in the arenas of European and world power became an increasingly hard task.

In the Iberian peninsula constitutional reform was not a dominant issue as the war ended. In Spain, the civil war of the 1930s and Franco's subsequent autocratic regime meant that the country was largely excluded from general European politics until the General died, and until both Spain and Portugal had transformed their constitutions to democracies in the mid 1970s. By 1989, both countries, as

ANNE DEIGHTON

well as a democratized Greece, had been admitted to the EC; the Iberian economies were experiencing a rapid development; Spain had joined Greece (1952) and Portugal (1949) in NATO, and all three were well embedded into the Western system.

The drama of 9–10 November 1989, when Germans danced on the wall that divided Berlin between East and West, has little, if any, parallel in Europe's history. These events presaged not only the end of a divided city, but also the end of a forced division of Europe's most powerful country, and of a divided Europe itself, whose multiplicity of Cold War international institutions highlighted the artificial barriers that now cut across Europe's geographic borders.

In 1985, when Gorbachev came to power in the Soviet Union, the country was engaged in a debilitating war in Afghanistan, had lost three leaders in rapid succession, had an economy that was stagnant, and faced disrupting discontent in Poland. Gorbachev's attempts to revive and to modernize the Soviet Union through *perestroika* and *glasnost* showed the perils of attempting to reform a seriously rotten system. By 1989 the government was beginning to lose control over the pace of change, although it had initially wanted the region to reform whilst retaining the cohesion of the Soviet European empire. The Solidarity party, with its strong record of opposition to the Communist regime in Poland, swept to power in free elections; Hungary moved towards political plurality; massive demonstrations took place in Czechoslovakia and East Germany, although both had politically conservative leaderships; dissident activity increased in Bulgaria and even in Romania. It was the demonstrations by huge crowds of ordinary people, and the movement of peoples over borders, that created a bottleneck of pressure for change in the Soviet Union's European empire. First, Hungary began to open its borders: East Germans moved through the country into Austria and thence to West Germany, creating extraordinary scenes as embassies were besieged by escaping populations. By November, after mass demonstrations in East Germany, the government finally decided to open border posts in Berlin. The Wall was breached: the Iron Curtain across the continent was effectively drawn back. Over the next two years, Christian Democrat Chancellor Helmut Kohl led a diplomatic revolution which culminated in West Germany absorbing East Germany while still, with the blessing of the Soviet Union, remaining a member of NATO. The Warsaw Pact was dismantled, communist regimes collapsed across central Europe, and war broke out in Yugoslavia. By December 1991, the Soviet Communist Party had been dissolved, and the Soviet Union disintegrated.

It seemed as if everything that the West stood for had, in the end, triumphed. The Soviet system had imploded, and its leaders had given up the struggle against the comparatively richer, more inventive, and more open societies of Western Europe and the USA. It was not clear whether the constant pressure upon the Soviet system in the 1940s and early 1950s, and again in the early 1980s, had convinced the Soviet leadership of the futility of their cause, or whether it was *détente*, conducted at both a superpower, and a Western European level through *Ostpolitik* and the multilateral process of the Conference on Security and Cooperation in

Europe, that had eroded the capacity of the Soviet Empire to remain isolated from the global community of trade and ideas. But it was certainly clear that Europe could now be redesigned, and that its central lands could 'return' to the fold. Only slowly did Western Europeans begin to realize that change in the eastern part of Europe might also destabilize accepted Western structures, and undermine the status quo in the west of the Continent as well.

Nationalism had been a continual irritant to governments in Britain (with Irish, Scottish, and Welsh nationalism); Spain (the Basques and Catalans); France (Algeria and Corsica); and Belgium (Flemings and Walloons), for example. But after 1989 nationalism made a more serious and ugly appearance in Yugoslavia, which collapsed into war, and in Czechoslovakia, which divided. Political instability produced a wave of immigration from the east and from North Africa which unsettled many Western European countries. The security structure of NATO began to appear anachronistic: it had done its job against the Soviet Union. The *raison d'être* of the US interest in the future of Europe would have to be reinvented, while, within the continent, a new European balance of power system was emerging. The cosy European Community, which had embarked upon its Single Market programme, could no longer rely upon the vague ambiguities of 'ever closer union' as a long-term aim between the twelve members. Citizens in France, Britain, Denmark, and even Germany began to challenge the rationale of supranational integration, of more of the same. Yet outside the EU the newly democratized countries of central Europe were making demands for political support, money, and, eventually membership of a new, wider 'Europe'.

The pressures of a global economy and global competition, of the imperatives of large-scale economic management, and of a European regional presence on the world political stage, on the one hand, and nationalism, social fragmentation, and disillusionment with integration, on the other, have never been more acute. Further, new issues of concern, ranging from uncontrolled nuclear proliferation to environmental hazards and social disaffection, present challenges of a quite different nature. Europeans are now trying to resolve the problems of defining their borders, especially to the east and south, without the presence of cold war superpower hegemons, and to map out afresh the security, political, and social characteristics of a 'European' identity in the post-Cold War world.

PART IV
The Wider World

17 East Asia

AKIRA IRIYE

As seen in Chapter 12 on East Asia and the emergence of Japan, the Second World War had brought about three important consequences for the region: Japan's destruction and loss of influence as a major definer of regional affairs; the rise of China and other Asian countries to positions of influence; and the emergence of the United States as the major Asian–Pacific power. These themes would continue to shape post-war East Asia, but the region was to be characterized by cataclysmic changes which neither the victors nor the vanquished visualized in 1945.

In China, which was to have emerged as the one non-Western great power, even before victory over Japan was celebrated, the conflict between Nationalists and Communists intensified, nullifying any attempt by both of them jointly to deal with the former occupiers and their collaborators. (Indeed, some collaborators as well as Japanese military and civilian personnel were utilized in the domestic struggle.) In Korea, which was to have been placed under a joint trusteeship by the great powers, the Chinese did not become actively involved, instead leaving the occupation of the peninsula to Soviet and US forces. Matters were even more fluid in South-East Asia, where returning European forces and officials were greeted with insistent demands on the part of indigenous people for freedom, autonomy, and ultimate independence. The Philippines were an exception, as the islands had already been promised independence by the United States, and as Filipino leaders, wartime collaborators and resisters alike, were able on the whole to work together to prepare for independence, which came in 1946. But elsewhere, from the Dutch East Indies to French Indochina, from British Malaya to Burma and India, national liberation movements picked up momentum in the wake of Japan's defeat. Hundreds of thousands of Japanese personnel were expatriated, if they had not been tried and punished for their war crimes. Europeans trying to regain their lost positions in the colonies found it increasingly difficult to do so. Some countries, like Indochina, declared independence outright as soon as Japan formally surrendered, while others were willing to negotiate with the European governments only on their own terms. Underneath the political drama, there was a profound social and cultural transformation brought about by the unsettling circumstances of the war. All over Asia there were voices demanding economic well-being. Many leaders in South-East Asia shared a distinct sense of regional identity which had little to do with big-power politics.

Ironically, in Japan, in contrast to other parts of Asia, the USA pursued a set of clearly articulated policies which, while by no means always internally consistent, provided a solid framework for the defeated nation's post-war destiny. The US occupation authorities under General Douglas MacArthur initiated a number of measures designed to eradicate Japanese militarism, such as war crimes trials and the purge of over 200,000 Japanese leaders from governmental, business, and educational positions. They encouraged labour union activities, emancipated women, and imposed a constitution on Japan that was vastly different in character from the Meiji antecedent. In the meantime, the occupation authorities distributed food from their stock and from shipments from the United States to starved millions in Japan. Agrarian reforms were carried out, enabling the majority of Japanese farmers to own plots of land for the first time in modern history. Business concentration and combination were prohibited so as to encourage the sharing of capital and to foster individual entrepreneurship. School textbooks were rewritten to correct the Japan-centric interpretations of history, geography, philosophy, and literature.

Since the situation in the rest of Asia was much more fluid, the US occupation of Japan served, almost by default, to define a new structure of East Asian international relations. That is, the United States came to look to Japan as a principal success story and as the key to its Asian policy after the war. More and more, Japan, rather than China, assumed importance as America's potential partner in defining a new regional order.

The Japanese, on their part, eagerly fitted themselves into the picture. They would rather be occupied by the United States than any other power. Americans had done their homework during the war to identify 'cooperative Japanese' who would assist in easing the burden of occupying the country. Japanese officials below the top leadership levels were not purged, and the bureaucratic structure was kept intact by the occupation authorities primarily to facilitate the governing of more than 100 million people. It is important to note that a close relationship between the USA and Japan was developing even before the cold war came to Asia in the late 1940s.

The story was very different in Korea. Soviet troops, fighting Japanese forces in Manchuria, rushed into northern Korea as soon as Japan surrendered, in the process assisting some Korean leaders to emerge to shape what they hoped would be a new government for the former Japanese colony. The United States, for its part, did not welcome the prospect of the Soviet occupation of the entire peninsula and hastily proposed a division along the thirty-eighth parallel, the area south of which would be designated the American zone of occupation. (No zone was earmarked for either Chinese or British forces.) But Americans were far from ready to occupy southern Korea. In sharp contrast to their painstaking plans for the occupation of Japan, they had not really anticipated such a development in Korea. And it was not till early September that the first contingents arrived, under the command of General John Hodge.

Unlike MacArthur, Hodge did not have at his disposal either a carefully worked-out set of directives or a well-qualified staff. Many Korean individuals and groups were contending for authority in a new government, and Hodge was reluctant to choose among them. Instead, he kept the wartime Japanese machinery of administration for the time being to maintain law and order. Moreover, he tended to retain in positions of power those Koreans who had collaborated with the colonial regime. The inevitable result was administrative and political chaos in the Korean peninsula. It was to have come under a United Nations trusteeship, but no such arrangement was established in the immediate aftermath of the war.

Had such a machinery been organized in 1945, the peninsula might have remained at least as an administrative unit. As it was, it was divided from the beginning. All efforts at establishing a unified government failed for the simple reason that neither the United States nor the Soviet Union, the occupying powers, was willing to back up a Korean leader's pretensions to speak for the whole country. In 1948 the United Nations belatedly stepped into the fray, sending a commission to Korea to supervise national elections as a basis for the establishment of a unified, independent republic of Korea. But the election was boycotted by politicians in Northern Korea as an interference in a domestic question. So elections were held only in the south, resulting in the formation of a national assembly which chose Syngman Rhee as the first president of the Republic of Korea. The northerners responded by holding their own elections and establishing the Democratic People's Republic of Korea under Kim Il Sung.

Both the Democratic People's Republic of Korea and the Republic of Korea claimed to speak for the whole country and sought diplomatic recognition on that basis. Indeed, the Soviet Union, the United States, and most other countries recognized only one of the two governments as the government of Korea, so that in principle there remained just one Korea under one government, although in reality there were two Koreas under their respective governments. Soviet troops were withdrawn from North Korea in 1948, and American in 1949 from the South, thus creating a highly explosive situation in which the stability of either regime depended on authoritarian rule, often bordering on terror, and on the presumed willingness of the outside powers to step in at a moment's notice.

Still, there might have been no international crisis over the Korean question but for the spread of the Cold War (defined simply as US–Soviet confrontation) to East Asia. Historians differ as to when this happened, some arguing that from the very beginning the region was considered by the superpowers in the context of their global struggle for power. As seen above, however, misgivings and tensions between the United States and the Soviet Union were only some of the many themes and developments in Asia after the war, and to comprehend them all in the monolithic framework of the Cold War would be a mistake, no matter how persuasive such an argument might be for Europe or the Middle East. Neither Moscow nor Washington had a systematic Cold War strategy for Asia for several years after 1945.

It was not until 1949–50 that the Cold War came to define many aspects of Asian affairs. The division of Vietnam into the communist-ruled North and the anti-communist South, the establishment of the People's Republic of China (PRC), its recognition by the Democratic People's Republic of Korea and by North Vietnam, and the thirty-year treaty of alliance between China and the Soviet Union—after the latter had successfully carried out its first nuclear tests—unmistakably suggested the spread, even preponderance, of Soviet influence in the region and provoked a systematic response on the part of the United States. As developed by the National Security Council—which had been established in 1947 but which had thus far tended to focus on issues in Europe and the Middle East—the Cold War had now assumed global proportions, and it was imperative to defend forces of 'freedom' in Asia as well as elsewhere. Specifically, Japan should be turned into a forward base for US forces, South Korea, and South Vietnam should be assisted militarily and economically, and a flexible approach should be undertaken towards the PRC so as to prevent it from coming totally under Soviet control.

The new policy had enormous implications for Japan and Korea. The American occupation of Japan would end, to be replaced by a new security arrangement in which the United States would retain military bases throughout Japan, especially Okinawa. In order to effect these moves, a peace conference would first have to be convened to put an end to the state of war with Japan. But it was highly unlikely that either Moscow or Peking would agree to a peace treaty which was a product of American Cold War calculations. Indeed, the San Francisco Peace Conference, convened in September 1951, proved to be just as divisive as anticipated. The Soviet Union and its 'satellites' refused to accept a treaty that did not have the unanimous support of all wartime allies, especially China. But China was not even invited to the Peace Conference because the United States had not recognized the PRC, and there was strong domestic pressure to support the Republic of China in Taiwan, where the Nationalists had fled, as the legitimate government of China. Moreover, two Asian countries, India and Burma, rejected the peace treaty as inadequate for the same reason. But the overwhelming majority of the delegates accepted the treaty, which was duly signed by the Japanese Prime Minister, Yoshida Shigeru, and representatives of most of Japan's former enemies on 8 September 1951.

By then, however, the Cold War in Asia had become militarized, triggered by the North Korean invasion of the South on 25 June 1950. When the Korean War broke out, the US response to the North Korean invasion was so decisive that Yoshida was convinced that the United States was showing its willingness to defend the status quo in East Asia, an essential condition for Japan's own security. The fact that US forces under General MacArthur were able to repulse North Korean troops back to the thirty-eighth parallel seemed to suggest that Japan could count on US support in case of a similar threat. American officials, in the meantime, were impressed anew with the strategic importance of Japan in the Cold War and speeded up the process of ending the occupation of that country, coupled with the establishment of a new security arrangement. Events in Korea and Japan were thus closely connected, and in the early 1950s there was being established in East Asia what may be termed a 'San Francisco system' in which the USA and its security partners (initially Japan and the Philippines, later joined by South Korea and Taiwan) were to be pitted against the Soviet Union, China, and North Korea.

For the Koreans, these developments meant that the division of the peninsula would be a very prolonged one, even that intercourse between the two Koreas would become more difficult than ever, now that they were fighting against each other. Just as US forces, weapons, and goods poured into South Korea to sustain its existence, Chinese and Soviet aid became an important source of support for North Korea. Both regimes took on a more authoritarian character than ever before, in order to cope with the military crisis. Both had to spend larger portions of their resources on the war. Even when stalemate developed along the thirty-eighth parallel in the middle of 1951, a stalemate that eventually led to a ceasefire agreement of 1953, neither could relax their military preparedness. Thus Korea, which was to have emerged as a winner in the Second World War, liberated from Japanese colonial rule, plunged into a period of profound uncertainty, political authoritarianism, and material hardship.

Japan, in contrast, had, by the mid-1950s, regained the pre-war level of industrial production and become a full-fledged member of the US alliance system. What came to be known as the '1955 system' in domestic politics, referring to the emergence of the Liberal Democratic Party (LDP) as the party in power and the Socialist Party as the major party in opposition, had an intimate connection with Japan's foreign affairs. The LDP, working closely with the bureaucracies, banks, and the business community, especially manufacturers of goods for export, developed a strategy for quick economic recovery and growth through an export-oriented industrial policy. The policy included the encouragement of savings so that domestic capital could be made available, at low interest rates, to manufacturers of strategic goods, as well as tax incentives and foreign-exchange policies that favoured exporters. The other side of the coin was that, in order to concentrate on economic objectives, defence expenditures were kept low. In 1953, for instance, the first full year of the newly acquired sovereignty, Japan's total defence spending amounted to 117 billion yen, or roughly 2.6 per cent of the national income. Five years later, the figures were 151 billion yen and 1.6 per cent, respectively. In other words, the economy grew much faster than defence expenditure, the underlying assumption being that the nation would be protected by the United States, by its bases as well as its 'nuclear umbrella', so that Japan's modest armed forces would be used primarily in domestic contingencies.

Having established a basic orientation of its economic and security policies, the Japanese government at that time focused its attention on normalizing relations with other Asian countries. Of course, no normalization was possible with China so long as the United States continued to ostracize Beijing. But this did not prevent Tokyo from vigorously promoting bilateral trade. Under the principle of 'the separation of politics from economics', succeeding Japanese cabinets encouraged business missions to China to negotiate trade agreements. Trade between Japan and China grew considerably, reaching the high of $140 million in 1957. This was still only about 2 per cent of Japan's total trade, a meagre figure in contrast to the pre-war pattern of its foreign commerce, but even this was considered important, especially as China provided an important market for post-war Japan's fledgling industry in such consumer goods as bicycles and sewing machines. China needed these commodities, for which it paid mostly through barter, shipping to Japan coal, iron, and other materials. The promising bilateral trade received a blow in 1958, when the Beijing regime, increasingly self-confident and critical of Tokyo's continued unwillingness to recognize it, abruptly terminated talks for another trade agreement. This, however, proved to be a brief interlude, and the momentum, once started, could not be reversed artificially.

Japan's relations with Korea were even more beset with problems. It might have seemed much easier for Japan to establish a normal relationship with its former colony, but neither the regime of Syngman Rhee in South Korea nor public opinion there would accept anything less than an explicit apology for Japanese colonial rule and a huge reparations payment as conditions for establishing relations. Despite prodding from Washington, Seoul stood its ground, while the Japanese countered with their own conditions, such as restitution of property owned by Japanese in Korea but confiscated after the war. Numerous meetings between officials of the two governments produced little progress, and in the meantime commercial relations were carried on only on an *ad hoc* basis. In the meantime, Japan's relations with North Korea were virtually non-existent, except for the repatriation of a large number of Koreans from Japan, to which most of them had been brought during the war for compulsory labour service. But many Koreans remained in Japan, numbering over half a million in the mid-1950s, down from 2.3 million at the end of the war. Their status was another sore spot in Japanese–Korean relations, the Korean government insisting that they be granted a special status because of their long suffering as forced labourers, whereas the Japanese did not want to establish a special category of alien residents.

In retrospect, the 1960s sowed the seeds for the future development of an Asian–Pacific community. This may not appear so clear so long as one focuses on the Vietnam War in the discussion of the decade. But Vietnam was only one of many developments in the region which were enhancing the relative power and influence of Asian countries and bringing at least some of them closer together.

This can be seen, for instance, in the *rapprochement* between Japan and South Korea, culminating in the treaty of normalization, signed in 1965. The two countries now established a diplomatic relationship for the first time since Korea was liberated from Japanese colonialism. The thorny issue of reparations and property restitution was solved through a compromise; the two sides agreed essentially to cancel these matters out, and Japan offered Korea an outright credit of $300 million, along with a loan of an additional $200 million. While not called reparations, these amounted to recognition on Japan's part that it had done much damage to Korea during its thirty-five-year rule. As for the Koreans residing in Japan, they were given the status of permanent residents, who would retain their Korean citizenship but would be distinguished from other foreigners in the country.

The normalization agreement was achieved only after Rhee was overthrown in a wave of demonstrations in 1961. By then his autocratic rule had become extremely unpopular, not only among student radicals and left-leaning intellectuals who questioned his uncompromisingly anti-communist stance, but also among politicians, businessmen, and even the military. Many of them believed the country's political instability and Rhee's staunchly anti-North policy were making it difficult to achieve economic successes of the kind that were taking place in Japan. A wave of mass demonstrations finally brought down Rhee's leadership, and, after an interlude of attempts by some democratic politicians to organize an effective government, political power was seized by Park Chung Hee, a young officer who had exhibited leftist leanings earlier but was known for his efficient, disciplined command of forces under him. The Park era, lasting from 1961 to 1979, when he was assassinated, was not much more democratic than the Rhee period, but he understood the need for economic development and pushed energetically for industrialization. The credits and loans extended by Japan fitted into such a scheme.

The year 1965 was also important for Japan in that it was only then that its foreign trade recorded an export surplus. At a modest $285 million, it nevertheless was a harbinger of things to come, for it reflected the government's and the business community's almost singled-minded devotion to the expansion of Japanese export trade. By then Japan was exporting transistor radios, television sets, and other electronic products, with high 'value-added' components. Prime Minister Ikeda Hayato (1960–4) believed that, by developing Japan's industrialization in these areas, it should be possible to expand export trade without holding down wages. Instead, wages would rise, which in turn would stimulate domestic demand for more manufactured goods. The fact that the 1960s saw a worldwide trend toward liberalization of trade policies—witness the successful negotiations for the 'Kennedy Round'—was a fortunate circumstance for Japan. It benefited from, and became part of, the impressive growth in world trade, whose value increased by 150 per cent in the decade.

It is interesting to recall that it was also in the 1960s—1967—that several South-East Asian countries came together to form the Association of South-East Asian Nations (ASEAN). Intended for mutual cooperation in both security and economic affairs, it was a clear signal that South-East Asia, too, was partaking of the global trend towards economic growth. At the very moment that the Vietnam War was escalating, Thailand, Malaysia, Singapore, the Philippines, and Indonesia were turning their attention elsewhere, for regional economic development. And this undertaking fitted in rather nicely with Japan's economic objectives. By the mid-1960s Japan had paid most of the reparations to the countries it had occupied during the war, and fresh loans and credits were extended to them. These funds enabled them to purchase Japanese manufactured items, while at the same time encouraging them to produce goods—fish, pulp, oil—that were in increasing demand in Japan. The economic connection between Japan and South-East Asia became so close that some even recalled the wartime Great East Asian Co-Prosperity Sphere. Whether that pattern of Japanese domination would return ultimately depended on the attitudes and perceptions of the countries in South-East Asia. For the Japanese, there was certainly the widespread view that this sort of 'peaceful' penetration of Asian markets was far better than the military alternative. Indeed, the success of its Asian economic policies may have strengthened Japanese pacifism. Towards the Vietnam War, for instance, it showed little sympathy or support. While its ally, the United States, was flying bombing missions on Vietnam from its bases in Okinawa, the Japanese government under Satô Eisaku (1964–71) was even demanding the return of the islands to Japanese sovereignty. Clearly, Asian affairs were developing with their own momentum.

By the end of the 1960s, signs were everywhere that post-war East Asian history was entering a new phase. The United States, having stretched its power as far as it could in the war with Vietnam, reversed course and, instead, announced the policy of 'Asianization'. As enunciated by Richard M. Nixon in Guam shortly after he became President in 1969, henceforth US ground forces would not involve themselves in Asian conflicts. Instead, Asians would be left to their own devices, while the United States would continue to provide air and sea power, including, of course, nuclear weapons, to maintain regional order. The American withdrawal from Vietnam, completed by 1975, was clear evidence that the alliance system designed to contain the Soviet Union, China, North Vietnam, and North Korea was breaking down. To take its place, a new geopolitical arrangement was worked out by the Nixon administration. Its architects, Nixon and Henry Kissinger, believed that American power could be used, not to contain Soviet and Chinese power, but to complement the latter against the former. The *rapprochement* between the United States and the People's Republic of China, effected when Nixon went to Beijing and Shanghai in early 1972, resulted in a redefinition of Asian international affairs.

For Japan and Korea, these developments had enormous implications, but more in the economic than in the strategic realm. Japan had not been a principal player in the containment strategy, so that the US–PRC *rapprochement* did not necessitate a reorientation of its military policy. It did sanctify, as it were, Japan's post-war policy of economic growth, for, in the new alignment of forces in East Asia, the likelihood of a regional military conflict would become less likely than earlier. The nation could continue to devote its energies to achieving economic objectives. For South Korea, too, the easing of tensions between Washington and Beijing was welcome news, as it suggested that Beijing would use its influence to restrain North Korean belligerence, and that Seoul's leaders could reinforce the business community's interest in economic development through rapid indus-trialization.

It is a remarkable fact that during the 1970s, a decade that was beset by oil shocks, a worldwide recession, and the collapse of the Bretton Woods system which had been built on stable rates of exchange among major currencies, Japan, South Korea, and most other Asian economies recorded impressive rates of growth. As importers of petroleum, they suffered from the steep rise in its price, but the industrialists in Japan, and to a degree in South Korea and elsewhere, suc-ceeded in absorbing the costs through rationalizing the process of production and through their willingness to receive relatively less profit than during the 1960s. Japanese and South Korean export trade grew faster than that of most Western nations, and Japan even began to export some capital. Domestically, there was a boom brought about by ambitious plans for building national infrastructures.

Economic successes inevitably produced political consequences. In Japan, political scandal, involving connections between politicians and businessmen eager for government contracts, forced a prime minister to resign in disgrace and to face trial. In South Korea, an increasingly affluent middle class began demand-ing more say in political decisions. The long-simmering dissatisfaction with the military rule of Park Chung Hee ended abruptly in 1979, when he was brutally assassinated by one of his trusted aides. He was succeeded by Chun Doo Hwan, another military figure, but the latter was more sensitive to public opinion. Even so, he suffered from movements and demonstrations both from radicals and also from moderates. Many of the latter were American-educated politicians, officials, businessmen, and intellectuals who found it unacceptable that Korea, going through rapid economic change, should still suffer from autocratic rule. They wel-comed President Jimmy Carter's human-rights diplomacy, as it was aimed not only at communist totalitarianism but also at non-democratic non-Western countries.

Economically underdeveloped non-Western countries were collectively known as the Third World. Before the 1970s they had shared a sense of identity as victims of Western colonialism and capitalism. But the economic successes of South Korea and other Asian countries such as Taiwan, Hong Kong, and Singapore were creating a division in the Third World, and by the 1980s Asian economies had clearly distanced themselves from those in the Middle East, Africa, and Latin America as being the most rapidly developing. Indeed, the decade, which saw cat-aclysmic changes in the world arena culminating in the collapse of East European Communist dictatorships, was also notable because of the spectacular rise of Asian economies. Most of them grew much faster than even European economies, to such an extent that by the end of the decade the per capita incomes of some Asian countries surpassed those of several European nations such as Portugal and Greece.

It was in such an environment that Japan emerged as an economic super-power. Its GNP became the second largest in the world, after that of the United States, and in terms of per capita income Japan even surpassed the latter. Much, of course, depended on how one translated one currency into another, but the fact that by the end of the decade a dollar was being exchanged for a little over 120 yen, whereas twenty years earlier the rate of exchange had been one dollar to 360 yen, indicated the growing strength of the Japanese economy. Its trade always showed an export surplus over imports, and the foreign exchange thus earned was shipped abroad in search of investment and real-estate opportunities. Japanese-owned mansions and country clubs became a familiar sight everywhere. What was less clear at that time was that Japanese trade and investment were increasingly aimed at Asian markets. In part this was necessitated by the growing trade friction with the United States. As the latter complained, with increasing bitterness, about Japan's industrial policy and cumbersome distribution system that hampered the growth of foreign imports into the country, Japanese businessmen began building factories in Asian countries, from which to export to the United States. But the shift also reflected the increasing cost of labour in Japan as a result of its affluence. Looking for cheaper (but well-educated and disciplined) labour, Japanese businessmen inevitably turned to Korea, China, and elsewhere in Asia. The fact that Asian economies were growing fast facilitated the process, for there were ready markets for Japanese investment and production.

If Japan's emergence as an economic giant was an impressive development, even more so was the rise of South Korea as a formidable economic power. More or less approximating the story of Japan's post-war economic recovery, but abbreviating the process in many ways, the South Korean economy grew by over 7 per cent annually. Its exports now included cars, ships, and computers, often competing successfully with Japanese products. Politically, Chun's successor, Roh Tae Woo, also a military figure, was willing to make concessions to public opinion, to such an extent that free elections were held and, in 1993, the first civilian president in thirty-two years assumed office. As if to celebrate Korea's coming of age, the Seoul Olympics, held in 1988, impressed the entire world with South Korea's modernization. And South Korea, too, was keen on exporting its capital to other Asian countries, even to China, for many decades South Korea's arch-enemy because of its support of North Korea. But in 1992 Seoul and Beijing recognized each other, and the official liaison was immediately reinforced by economic ties.

Were these developments creating a new order in East Asia? Certainly, there were obvious obstacles in the way. Memories of the war were still very fresh in the minds of Asians, especially Chinese and Koreans, who, according to periodic opinion surveys, continued to distrust the Japanese. Some Asian countries, South Korea, Taiwan, and Singapore in particular, were beginning to compete with Japan economically, and quite successfully. The kind of complaint the Japanese were accustomed to hearing from Americans and Europeans about their country's unfair trade practices was now often hurled by them at other Asians. More fundamentally, unlike the European countries which to a considerable extent shared a common culture and a common historical background, Asia consisted of more divergent ethnic, religious, and cultural traditions. There was no common past to share.

At the same time, however, there were more promising signs suggestive of some new trends in the region. As the world looked upon the economic achievements of the newly industrialized economies (NIES) (South Korea, Taiwan, Hong Kong, Singapore), China, ASEAN, and other Asian countries as 'economic miracles', there was regional pride that transcended national identities. The spread of democracy, however painfully slow it may have seemed to many in the region, was another encouraging sign, for the various countries could say that they shared the common vocabulary of human rights. Above all, the end of the Cold War provided an opportunity for Asians to consider, perhaps for the first time, whether there was something they could collectively aim for as a regional objective. It was far from certain if they would opt for a regional, as against a national, definition of their objectives, but at least they all recognized the opportunity. For the alternative could only be intra-regional division, with perhaps China, steadily gaining in economic and military power, emerging as the new hegemon. Moreover all countries in the region shared such by-products of rapid industrialization as environmental degradation, urban crime, gaps between rich and poor, and an increase in the old-age population. These problems were not susceptible of national solution, but called for regional, indeed international cooperation. In that sense, too, Asians were facing an uncharted future.

As the twentieth century draws towards its close, it is obvious that Asian countries have, collectively and individually, played important roles in the making of contemporary history. Whether through imperialism and war, through revolution and reform, or through democratization and economic development, they have done away with the kind of Asia that had existed in 1900 and brought about an entirely different region a century later, one that the rest of the world has come to take more and more seriously. The history of Japan and South Korea since 1945 is symbolic in many ways. Starting virtually from ground zero—Japan because of the devastation it had brought upon itself through its wars, and South Korea because it had just been liberated from colonialism—the two countries together have come to account for almost 15 per cent of the world's income and about 10 per cent of its trade. This is no mean achievement for two countries whose combined population barely accounted for 3 per cent of the world's total. How they will make use of the wealth and influence is the question they are bequeathing to the next century.

18 China

JONATHAN SPENCE

China entered the twentieth century on a wave of reactionary terror, as the loose affiliation of north-east Chinese Secret Society groups known as the 'Boxers' began a protracted attempt to destroy all Chinese Christian converts, and the missionaries who preached to them. Openly encouraged by a number of conservative officials, most of them from the ruling Manchu minority, which had controlled the Chinese government since the seventeenth century, the Boxers entered Peking in the summer of 1900 and laid siege to the foreign legation quarter. Only after a large multinational foreign expeditionary force had fought its way through to Peking did the Boxers raise the siege, and the ruling Empress-Dowager and her court fled to the rural hinterland of Xi'an, on the Yellow River. In the meantime, pro-Boxer generals and their followers in Shanxi and other northern provinces had conducted a brutal round-up and massacre of missionary families and their converts. By the terms of the vindictive Treaty Settlement that followed, several senior pro-Boxer Qing dynasty officials were executed, pro-Boxer areas were penalized, and the Chinese government was compelled to promise to pay a colossal indemnity for the lives and property destroyed.

The sequel to the Boxer Uprising was not however without some benefits. The shock of defeat and the experience of flight through desperately poor parts of China made the Empress-Dowager and her advisers more sympathetic to the needs of China's peasants, and more conscious of the need for dramatic reforms. The powerful provincial governors of central and southern China, who had refused the court's demands to come to the Boxers' aid, had now tasted a measure of independence, and grew bolder in their own attempts at radical change. And the catastrophe served as a final blow to the old Confucian educational and examination system that had endured for over a millennium, and was officially abolished on orders of the court in 1905.

The end of the old examination system had a number of unanticipated effects: students, both male and female, now felt freer to enter the missionary schools in

China, with their semi-Westernized curricula, where they encountered new ideas about society, geography, science, and ethics; a sizeable number chose to go to Japan, which, though hated by many for its humiliating defeat of China in the brief war of 1894–5, was also admired for the effectiveness of its constitutional, military, and economic reforms under the Meiji emperors, and for its defeat of Russia in the war of 1904–5; while others chose to adopt a military career, formerly despised by Confucian-educated youth, but now seen as a possible means for ending China's cycles of humiliation and defeat.

In Japan, the young Chinese were free from the omnipresent scrutiny of the moral watchdogs of the Manchu dynasty; they read voraciously in the new journals that their compatriots founded, listened enraptured to the bold demands of exiled radicals like Liang Qichao or Sun Yatsen that the Qing adapt to the modern world by shifting to a Republican form of government; and they joined the various politically radical Secret Societies pledged to overthrow the dynasty that found eager recruits both among Chinese in Japan and those in the 'Chinatowns' of Canada and the United States.

In an effort to stem the tide of disaffection, the Qing leaders purchased modern arms and equipment and reformed their army command and training structures along Western lines. They made significant strides in suppressing the opium trade that had ravaged China for decades, and also promoted a centralized railroad system and broadened the state's tax base to pay for the military expansion. And in 1906 they began actively to study the structures of foreign governments, with a particular eye to seeing if they might not be able to perpetuate their power through some form of constitutional monarchy. The momentum thus begun could not be checked, and by 1908 plans were implemented for the formation of provincial assemblies with elected representatives, which would in turn select delegates for a central parliament or national assembly in Peking.

Sporadic uprisings against the Qing had begun even before the Boxer movement, and by 1911 were becoming common all over China. In October of that year one such movement among disaffected troops at the garrison barracks in Wuhan spread from a local mutiny into a full-fledged insurrection. To the court's bewilderment, the unrest and uprisings spread to other provinces, often directly fostered by members of the various provincial assemblies. Many Manchu troops and their families were massacred in their garrisons as the chaos spread. Abandoned by many of the most important generals in the New Armies that they had tried to foster, the regents for the child emperor Puyi (the formidable Empress-Dowager having died in 1908) saw no alternative but to abdicate the throne. This they did in February of 1912, on favourable terms that left the former Manchu ruling house the palaces and treasures of the Forbidden City in Peking, along with a sizeable annual stipend, but at the same time ended the period of centralized Chinese Imperial rule that had endured in largely unbroken succession since 221 BC.

A group of provincial assembly delegates selected Sun Yatsen as the first provisional president of the Republic. The choice seemed logical in many ways, since

Sun, though born to a poor south China rural family, was a symbol of the new and restless 'modern' age. He had been raised by emigrant relatives in Hawaii, baptized a Christian, trained in medicine in Hong Kong, had also travelled and lived in Japan, the United States and England, and was the founder of a successful anti-Manchu Secret Society with many influential members, and had also been an impassioned spokesman for the values of a Chinese republic for more than fifteen years. But Sun had two fatal flaws for the post: he lacked strong organizational political skills, and he had only weak support among the new professional military men of China. Thus he felt compelled to relinquish the provisional presidency almost at once to the general with the strongest military following, Yuan Shikai.

Yuan Shikai initially impressed the foreign powers by the apparent sincerity of his support for democracy. But Yuan was consistently jealous of his own emerging prerogatives, and when the party that had grown out of Sun Yatsen's previously illegal underground organization, now renamed the 'National People's Party' or 'Guomindang', won a near majority of the seats in parliament, with a platform that urged limitations to the executive powers of the presidency, Yuan secretly arranged to have the Guomindang's most brilliant young politician assassinated. When the Guomindang members sought to reassert themselves, he had them banned as a political party, and drove many of their members, including Sun Yatsen, into exile. Yuan's attempts, in 1915, to reassert central control over China by having himself named Emperor brought an element of tragic farce to the proceedings. He was apparently genuinely surprised by the rejections of his pretensions that came from both the provinces and many of his 'own' generals and he died a disappointed man in 1916, leaving the central government in shambles.

Despite the disruptions at the centre, however, China in the early years of the century was comparatively prosperous. Mounting foreign investment, especially in the 'concession' areas of the main coastal cities, but also in newly emerging industrial areas such as Wuhan on the Yangtze River or Shenyang in southern Manchuria, gave China the beginnings of a modern industrial infrastructure. Foreign firms, their work eased by the entrepreneurial skills of the Chinese middlemen known as compradors, were beginning to bring new products and sales techniques to China, most spectacularly in such areas as electric-power generation, tobacco, kerosene, sewing machines, firearms, looms for both cotton and silk production, and steam-powered ships for riverine and coastal transportation.

Symptomatic of this change was the growth of a number of universities in China, deliberately developed on the Western pattern, with faculty staffed by both foreign scholars and by Chinese Ph.D.s returned from overseas. On 4 May 1919 the university students of Peking staged major demonstrations against their own inept politicians and the foreign powers that exploited them, giving birth to modern Chinese nationalism. It was to the intellectual leaders in these universities that the first Comintern agents dispatched to China by Lenin in 1920 naturally turned and found their first eager recruits. With Comintern help a small group of delegates, meeting secretly in Shanghai in 1921, founded the Communist Party of China.

Even while some Comintern agents were working successfully to form a disciplined Chinese Communist Party that would be obedient to Moscow, others were negotiating with Sun Yatsen, who had set up a separatist regime in the Canton region, in cooperation with the local warlords. Comintern agents and Soviet military advisers helped Sun to develop a major military academy on the island of Whampoa, downriver from Canton. At the same time, they infiltrated the Guomindang Party and the Whampoa Academy with their own party members, until in 1923 a formal 'United Front' was established between the two Chinese organizations. Since a majority of China's major modern factories in the key industrial cities such as Wuhan and Shanghai were foreign-owned, clashes with foreign managers and foreign troops in the 'concession areas' were frequent, and in 1925 in both Shanghai and Canton foreign police and troops opened fire on angry Chinese civilian demonstrators, killing scores and fanning the flames of revolutionary activism.

By 1926, under the aggressive leadership of one of Sun's key disciples, the commandant of Whampoa Chiang Kai-shek (Sun having died in 1925), the United Front forces drove their way northwards, routing a succession of warlord armies and entering Shanghai in April 1927. But, despite the apparent unity preserved during this savage warfare, major splits had emerged between the Guomindang forces and the Communists. In 1927 these tensions broke into the open, as the Guomindang won three struggles with the Communists, one in each of the three key urban centres of Canton, Shanghai, and Wuhan. By early 1928, as the Guomindang forces once more pushed northwards, entered Peking, and established a nominal 'unified government' over the country, the Communists either went underground in the major cities, or retreated to isolated regions of the countryside to regroup among the peasantry.

Despite his apparently brilliant successes, Chiang Kai-shek's power base was in fact a flawed one. Ideologically, though he claimed to be the true heir to Sun Yatsen, espoused the Three Peoples' Principles, and continued the tradition of demanding strong personal loyalty to the Guomindang party leader, he had numerous opponents within the leadership ranks of his own Party. Economically, Chiang was always short of funds for his growing armies. In Shanghai, to break the hold of the Communist-dominated labour unions, he had formed secret understandings with some of the most important Chinese leaders of the criminal underworld, especially those in the so-called 'Green Gang', who controlled much of the opium and heroin traffic which once again plagued China, along with prostitution and gambling. These racketeers gave Chiang an effective source of strike-breakers, but the 'alliance' had obvious costs, compounded by the fact that many of the racketeers lived in the foreign concession areas of the major cities, and so were effectively beyond the law.

Perhaps most importantly, Chiang's claim to power was constantly and visibly undercut by the growing strength of Japan on China's soil. In Manchuria the Japanese were especially aggressive, controlling the major railway networks and industrial enterprises, which they protected initially with their own special police forces, and from the late 1920s onwards with their regular armed forces. In 1931 Japanese forces moved openly to seize the key Manchurian city of Mukden, claiming 'provocation' by Chinese troops stationed there. In 1932 they launched a major assault on Shanghai, to protest alleged violations of their economic rights there. And in the mid-1930s they not only forced the Chinese to establish a 'demilitarized zone' in north China, between Peking and the sea, but also formed an allegedly 'independent' state in Manchuria, now renamed 'Manchukuo'. Chiang Kai-shek could do little about these acts of aggression, given his own weak military base, and the continuing threat to his own leadership from the Chinese Communists.

That the Party survived at all was due largely to the policy of a few members who retreated to poverty-stricken areas of the countryside, far from industrial cities with their proletarian masses, but also far from Chiang's or his warlord allies' troops and secret police. By 1930 there were about a dozen rural Soviet areas in China, where the Communists organized peasants against their landlords, gave them rudimentary military training and ideological indoctrination, and pursued various policies of land reform, land redistribution, or confiscation. The emergence of Mao Zedong into the leadership echelons of the Chinese Party occurred in this context. Mao, born in 1893 in rural Hunan, was a largely self-taught man who participated briefly in the 1911 anti-Manchu risings in Hunan, and studied informally in Peking in 1918, where he attended Marxist study groups and had some introduction to revolutionary theory. Active in organizing workers in 1921, he attended the Shanghai founding Party Conference in 1921, and worked on peasant organizations under the United Front. After the purges and *coups* of 1927, he retreated to the impoverished and mountainous borders of Jiangxi and Fujian provinces, where he established a regime that came to be known as the 'Jiangxi Soviet'. This Soviet survived a series of four vigorous attacks by Chiang Kai-shek, but the fifth, coordinated for Chiang by the tactical skills of hired German military advisers, forced Mao and about 150,000 of his rural followers into a disastrous year-long retreat through western and northern China, till some 30,000 survivors reached at last a comparatively secure base in another Soviet that had been formed in the Yan'an region in the eroded land inside the bend of the Yellow River. Chinese propaganda and sympathetic Western journalists swiftly transmuted this disaster into the triumphant epic of 'The Long March'.

Chiang Kai-shek, desperately trying to break the Communists before he turned his troops to try and halt the Japanese, flew in person to Xi'an near Mao's new base area to supervise a final 'extermination campaign'. But his own troops mutinied, and held Chiang captive in December 1936, demanding that the internecine fighting end, and that all Chinese unite to curb the Japanese aggression. Chiang was released after grudgingly agreeing to form a new United Front against the common enemy. Thus when in the summer of 1937 Japanese troops on manœuvre in north China were once again embroiled in a number of provocative confrontations with Chinese troops, they were met for the first time since their 1932 attack on

Shanghai by a decisive show of force. But by December 1937 the Chinese troops, having suffered immense losses to Japanese artillery and bombs, were routed. In their headlong flight they also abandoned Nanking, the Guomindang capital, where the Japanese mutilated and murdered tens of thousands of the civilian population in an orgy of destruction that had not previously been seen in the war.

Chiang Kai-shek made the strategic decision to move his own wartime capital to Chongqing, far up the Yangtze, leaving the Communists to defend their Yan'an base area against the northern Japanese armies. Before the collapse of Shanghai, the machinery from a number of factories had been moved inland by river to Chongqing, and other war industries were soon developed there by refugee workers. After Pearl Harbor, the wider spread of the war acted to China's advantage by bringing in the Americans as China's allies, though Chiang's problems were compounded rather than eased by President Roosevelt's choice of General Joseph Stilwell to be his liaison with Chiang, supervisor of lend-lease, and field commander of the American forces in the China–Burma–India theatre. Though Stilwell was a courageous man, with long experience of China and good knowledge of the language, he was intemperate in speech, quick-tempered, and prone to bitter denunciations of the cowardice of other less bold officers commanding Chiang's field forces. When Japan's major 'second front' in China in 1944 led to the capture of many of Chiang's airfields and most of his stockpiled fuel and munitions, Stilwell was at once bitter and jubilant. But his response so outraged Chiang that he successfully persuaded Roosevelt to have Stilwell recalled.

Thus, when the war ended in August 1945, China was in a curiously stalemated situation, with several of Chiang's divisions retrained by Stilwell and his successors, and with American advisers working in small groups to upgrade the military effectiveness of the Communist forces in their struggles with Japan in the north. The Americans airlifted many of Chiang's troops so they could accept the Japanese surrender in east and north China. But, seizing their opportunity, the Communists had in the meantime raced many of their best troops into Manchuria, where they linked up with the Soviet forces who had just entered the same area under the terms of the Yalta agreements. Thus was China poised for renewed conflict in the now twenty-year-old Civil War.

In the years between 1946 and 1949 the base of Chiang Kai-shek's power steadily eroded. Chiang was unable to dislodge the Communist forces entrenched in Manchuria, while in many other parts of the Chinese countryside the Communists also dominated large areas, and even pushed through new programmes of land reform. The Guomindang officials sent to retake control over the east-coast municipalities were often inept, ruthless, or corrupt, and their rapacity in reasserting control over Taiwan (which had been a Japanese colony since 1895) led to a large-scale uprising followed by a bloody massacre of the Taiwanese in February 1947. Inflation, already serious in the early 1940s, reached disastrous proportions by 1947. The country was exhausted by long years of vicious warfare, and the Guomindang seemed to have no solutions, while the Communists, even if harshly disciplinarian themselves, seemed at least to have a meangingful vision of China's future and offered the promise of a reassertion of national dignity. In 1948 and 1949 the Guomindang forces steadily disintegrated and the Communist field armies advanced south from Manchuria, occupying Peking and Shanghai. On 1 October 1949, Mao Zedong, as Chairman of the Party, from a reviewing stand atop the great archway at the entrance to the Forbidden City, declared the inauguration of the People's Republic of China (PRC).

During 1950 the Communists moved vigorously to assert their political control. A massive programme of land confiscation and redistribution brought small plots of land to almost every peasant family in China. Former nationalist officials were encouraged to stay in their posts if they acknowledged the error of their former ways. Plans for state control of heavy industry and raw material supply were initiated, the hold of organized crime over the larger cities and such occupations as dockworkers, seamen, and transport workers was broken, along with main sources of income that had flowed from prostitution and the heroin and opium trades, which were all now forbidden. Foreign enterprises were limited in scale, foreign personnel repatriated, and nationalization of many once-foreign companies initiated. From Moscow, Mao gained loans and credits to help with reconstruction, and thousands of Soviet technical experts were sent to China to help develop hydroelectric power and expand the railway system. Triumvirates, each composed of a senior civilian governor, a ranking Party secretary, and a military commander, were set up in China's newly redesigned regions. A vigorous programme of Party recruitment and indoctrination was undertaken. New marriage laws promised greater freedom to women. And Chinese armies moved into Tibet and assembled on the Fujian coast to launch an amphibious assault against Taiwan.

It was at this apparently promising stage of development that the Korean War erupted in the summer of 1950, and the United Nations' energetic counter-attack through North Korea towards the Chinese border at the Yalu River prompted China to send her own armies—under the guise of 'volunteers'—into Korea in October. China suffered almost a million casualties (one of the dead was Mao's own son); the US fleet began to patrol the Taiwan Straits, making recapture of the island impossible; and a wave of anger and paranoia gripped the country. Foreigners were arrested and in many cases terribly mistreated before being released after issuing abject 'confessions'. The whole former professional élite of China now began to come under suspicion, with corresponding collapse in confidence and efficiency in business, government, and education. After the armistice had been signed in 1953, the Party continued to use mass campaigns as a way to control its own people, leading to a constant fear of being branded a 'rightist' of some kind, which could lead to disaster for oneself and one's family. In 1954 Mao ordered the cooperativization of agriculture, which by 1956 became collectivization, with the peasantry forced to yield up the ownership of the private plots that had been granted them in the first phases of land reform.

In a different kind of mass campaign, that to 'Make a Hundred Flowers Bloom' in 1956 and 1957, Mao Zedong, apparently convinced the intelligentsia were now cowed, urged them to speak out boldly against abuses in the bureaucracy or the Party. But when the expected polite criticism turned into a storm of abusive complaint against Party ideology, the leaders, and even Marxism itself, Mao reacted vigorously, and hundreds of thousands were dismissed from their posts and sent to remote rural areas to be 'reformed through labour'.

The Hundred Flowers movement coincided with Khruschev's denunciations of Stalin, which were seen in turn by many in China as an indirect critique of Mao Zedong and the Chinese Party. When the Soviets harshly criticized the 'adventurism' and 'utopianism' of Mao Zedong's next venture—the 'Great Leap Forward' of 1958 and 1959, which was meant, through even higher levels of collective organization and mass participation in industrial and agricultural production, to rush China into a truly 'Communist' society—the break between the two countries became final. The aid programmes were cancelled, all Soviet technicians were recalled from China, and the Chinese studying with the army or universities in the Soviet Union were called home. By 1960, as the Great Leap was followed by a catastrophic famine that may have cost as many as twenty million lives, China's isolation was virtually total.

It was this isolation from the Soviet Union, Japan, Western European powers, and the United States that helps explain the remarkable and terrifying period of Maoist excess known as the Cultural Revolution, which was at its zenith between 1966 and 1970. Fostered by the ideological leftist wing of the People's Liberation Army under Defence Minister Lin Biao, and encouraged by Mao's wife Jiang Qing and a number of extreme radicals from Shanghai, the movement extolled every aspect of Mao's thought as the country's highest inspiration, and launched mass campaigns of young so-called 'Red Guards' against all the institutions of the country—governmental, economic, educational, social—that could be shown to have any 'rightist' taint. The nightmarish pressures brought death to hundreds of thousands, perhaps millions, and a renewed forced exodus from the cities down to the countryside. Only in 1971, when in a mysterious and still unexplained series of events Lin Biao apparently tried to oust Mao Zedong from power, did the country begin to return to a more realistic view of government. In a startling turn of events this new direction was ratified in 1972, when, despite the Vietnam War then raging, President Nixon was invited to China, and at a meeting with Mao Zedong announced the beginnings of a new era of Sino-American cooperation and understanding.

One of the many victims of the Cultural Revolution in 1967 had been Deng Xiaoping, for many years the Party General Secretary, who was branded as a rightist and dismissed from his numerous powerful positions. But in September 1976 Mao Zedong, who had long been ill with the palsy known in the West as Lou Gehrig's Disease, died. The next month Mao's widow and the three chief Cultural Revolution radicals—now branded as 'The Gang of Four'—were all arrested, and

JONATHAN SPENCE

Deng Xiaoping returned to power, becoming by 1978 the *de facto* ruler of the country. Deng moved energetically to foster ties with the United States, announcing a new era of 'modernizations' for China in the fields of industry, education, the army, and the sciences. He also ordered the rehabilitation of hundreds of thousands of intellectuals who had lost their posts in the Hundred Flowers or the Cultural Revolution, and declared a new era of openness in the general world of culture. But when this resulted once again in an outpouring of Chinese emotion and criticism of the Communist system, most dramatically at the 'Democracy Wall' in Beijing during late 1978 and early 1979, Deng soon showed the limits of his tolerance. The most articulate of the dissenters were arrested and given long jail sentences, while numerous small magazines and newspapers were suppressed.

From this time onwards, Deng Xiaoping pragmatically and on the whole successfully separated out the Chinese people's new opportunities for economic growth—which were given ever greater openness—from their opportunities for intellectual self-expression, which continued to be closely monitored. He effectively dismantled much of the structure of state-planned subsidization and wage guarantees that had existed in China since the early 1950s. Except for some of the largest complexes of heavy industry in key cities, most other companies were decontrolled, and forced to turn a profit if they were to survive. Their former Party overseers were replaced by managers. Raw materials had to be bought competitively, and products sold on the open market. Workers lost their guarantees of lifetime job security, and could be dismissed for inefficiency or absenteeism. The so-called 'iron rice bowl' was broken. In the countryside, the vast communes that had existed since the late 1950s were broken up. Though individual farmers were still not allowed to purchase land, they and their families were allowed to buy contracts to work a given plot of land, and, once a stated agricultural quota of basic food materials had been met and turned over to the government, all surplus production was the possession of the family unit, to consume or to sell on the open market. The impact of these changes was threefold. A new wealthy group of independent consumers began to emerge in the cities; life in the countryside changed as families bought contracts to work the land and divided their labour power, leaving some to till the land intensively while others worked in new food-processing plants and small industries which sprang up all over China; and a large new group of rootless labourers slowly emerged, no longer tied to the commune but free to roam at will to the cities in search of work.

Culture itself adjusted to meet these new tendencies and markets. A young group of talented film-makers, popularly known as 'The Fifth Generation' began to explore China's imperial legacy and recent past in films of great technical maturity and emotional intensity. A new generation of poets, teenagers in the Cultural Revolution, began to write poetry—branded by the government as 'misty' or 'ghost' poetry—that used imagery and allegory to explore the sense of wasted past and wasted lives that they had all experienced. And home-grown rock singers, adjusting swiftly to styles, dress, and even diction of the West, shocked and thrilled their contemporaries with their heavy beat and their frankly erotic or political lyrics.

By 1987 the surviving older Party leaders around Deng Xiaoping felt the society was slipping entirely out of their control. Their first scapegoat was Hu Yaobang, the popular former head of the Communist youth league and recently appointed general secretary of the Party, who was dismissed from his post on the grounds that he had been too lenient to political dissenters. His death from a stroke in April 1989 brought students and townspeople of Beijing out into Tiananmen Square in homage. Clumsy government attempts to dispel the demonstrators backfired, and by May a vast movement of political protest had developed, which was given worldwide publicity by the international camera crews gathered in Beijing to record the arrival of President Gorbachev of the Soviet Union, a solemn event designed to highlight the formal ending of the thirty-year-old Sino–Soviet rift. Repeatedly breaking through police cordons, and closing ranks to prevent army units approaching, by mid-May close to a million people were in the Square, demonstrating for democracy. When workers in some of Beijing's largest factories also began to organize, forming a 'worker's federation' and demanding the right to negotiate and even strike for better wages and work conditions, Deng Xiaoping decided the time for decisive action had come. Apparently backed by most of his senior leadership, he ordered veteran units of the People's Liberation Army— backed by tanks and armoured cars—to smash their way into Tiananmen and clear the demonstrators. After imposing a television blackout on the foreign cameramen, the troops stormed the Square before dawn on 4 June. Within the next dozen hours many hundreds of Chinese citizens, perhaps far more, were shot and killed, or crushed by the treads of the tanks. The toll will never be known, for the government ordered hospitals not to receive or treat the crucially wounded, there was no official listing of the dead, and individual families were forbidden to mourn in public for their children who had died. Though anger in Beijing was high and world outrage profound, the Party had calculated correctly: no foreign government imposed any significant forms of sanctions against China—however strong that government's public stance on human rights might be—and sympathy protests that erupted in other major cities were swiftly quelled.

After June 1989, political life in China returned to a quiescent state, while Deng concentrated on economic growth. A population that had risen in the 1980s past the one billion mark now poured its energies into making money. The union of China with Hong Kong, negotiated by the British in 1984 and effected in 1997, brought vast new Hong Kong investments into China, and Taiwan also, at last moving to adopt a democratic structure of its own, followed suit. The People's Liberation Army itself became a major seller on the world arms market, netting billions of dollars from the war between Iraq and Iran, and invested its newfound gains either in high-technology purchases from the United States, or in luxury hotels, apartment buildings, and other business ventures. A boom in housing benefited both the travelling workers and the big construction companies, while a new rage to own automobiles led China to embark on a vast road-building programme. Thwarted by a close international vote from the chance to host the

Olympic Games in the symbolically important year of 2000—the honour went to Sydney—the Chinese government pressed aggressively for membership in international bodies, in GATT, and to be a charter member of the new World Trade Organization (WTO) scheduled to commence in 1995.

The profits of capitalist expansion also brought its perils, as most would have predicted: a growing drug problem; rising numbers of prostitutes; violent robberies in the streets and on trains; corruption throughout the bureaucracy and most visibly among the children or grandchildren of the senior Party leaders who carved out their own economic empires; environmental pollution so serious that many cities were perpetually shrouded in industrial smog. Available arable land shrank steadily as new roads and building projects swallowed it up; water tables fell by fifty feet or more on the north China plain; soil grew exhausted from overuse in market gardens or by improper use of chemical fertilizer. But, despite the growing lawlessness visible in so many realms of society, the political structure held firm as the Chinese watched the Soviet Union collapse. The lesson of Gorbachev's fall taught Chinese leaders only that political freedoms brought chaos and disintegration. As long as they possibly could, accordingly, they would hold off from allowing such freedoms to their own people, and cling as tightly as possible to their own reins of power.

The death of Deng Xiaoping in early 1997 was received calmly by the Chinese people, and the successors whom he had put in place after the crisis of 1989 moved effectively to continue his legacy. It was Deng's choice as China's new president, Jiang Zemin, who presided over the return of Hong Kong to Chinese control on 1 July 1997. And it was Jiang who decided, in late summer of that year, that the last of the huge collectivized factories should be privatized. China's revolutionary century had apparently ended with a move from all the principal elements that had once been taken to give it meaning.

19 South-East Asia

MICHAEL LEIFER

South-East Asia comprises ten states: Myanmar (formerly Burma), Thailand, Vietnam, Laos, Cambodia, Malaysia, Singapore, Brunei, Indonesia, and the Philippines. They are diverse in human and physical geography, their territorial boundaries a legacy of colonial interventions and accommodations.

At the outset of the twentieth century, the term South-East Asia did not enjoy common currency; its disparate territories were objects of empire and not subjects of international relations, with Thailand, known as Siam until 1939, as the sole exception. They did not begin to enjoy international status until after the end of the Pacific War in 1945.

The term South-East Asia came into effective usage only during the Pacific War. It was employed by the Western Allies as a military–administrative arrangement for dispossessing Japan of wartime gains. A South-East Asia Command (SEAC) was created in August 1943. Based in Ceylon (now Sri Lanka), its responsibilities were confined initially to Burma, Thailand, Malaya including Singapore, and the island of Sumatra. In July 1945, at the Potsdam Conference, SEAC's domain was enlarged to include British northern Borneo, the whole of the Netherlands East Indies (except western Timor), and French Indochina south of the sixteenth parallel of latitude but not the whole of South-East Asia. When SEAC was disbanded in November 1946, a common understanding of South-East Asia's bounds still did not exist.

South-East Asia began to assume a geopolitical coherence only during the last quarter of the twentieth century. That coherence came to be registered through the activities of the Association of South-East Asian Nations (ASEAN) established in August 1967 by Thailand, Malaysia, Singapore, Indonesia, and the Philippines. Brunei became a member on resuming sovereignty in January 1984. But it was only at the end of the cold war from the early 1990s that the three states of Indochina (Vietnam, Laos, and Cambodia) as well as Myanmar acknowledged ASEAN's regional credentials, attracted partly by the economic achievement of most of its member states. Vietnam became its first communist member in July 1995.

Colonialism was imposed on South-East Asia from the sixteenth century but its consolidation was not completed until the early years of the twentieth century concurrent with the first stirrings of nationalism. By 1900 the British were ensconced in Burma, in Malaya, including Singapore, and northern Borneo, as were the Dutch in their East Indies archipelago incorporating in the main Java, Sumatra, Sulawesi (Celebes), and the major part of Borneo. The French had established dominion over Indochina, while the USA had just succeeded to Spanish rule in the Philippines. The Portuguese retained a vestige of empire in the eastern half of the island of Timor. Only Thailand enjoyed an independent status as a buffer zone between British and French colonial domains.

Colonial rule disrupted and changed traditional society. For example, kingship was either removed, as in Burma and Vietnam, or remodelled to lend legitimacy to the machinery of colonial government, as in Malaya, Cambodia, and parts of the Netherlands East Indies. Colonialism also made an impact through promoting plantation agriculture and extractive industry. Metropolitan economies profited from exchanging their manufactures for tropical products. This kind of economic development was accompanied and stimulated by flows of migrant workers from southern China and to a lesser extent from southern India and Ceylon. These migrants served the colonial economic design in filling the roles of labouring and economic middlemen and in consequence stirred up local resentments which were a factor in the emergence of modern nationalism. Nationalism was stimulated also through educational provision for indigenous élites to service the needs of colonial society.

Modern nationalism developed in urban centres where Western-educated indigenous élites who had assimilated liberal ideas experienced frustration and humiliation because of the racialist structure of colonial societies. Nationalism proved to be a containable challenge until Japan overthrew the colonial orders within a matter of months from December 1941.

The first major expression of nationalism took place in the Philippines when a short-lived independence was declared in June 1898 in the political vacuum created by the Spanish–American War. The United States decided to retain possession. It crushed all resistance but then coopted the mestizo élite which had evolved during Spanish dominion. Political accommodation with this landed oligarchy was sealed with the establishment of civil government on the American democratic model in July 1901. National independence was never in contention but a matter of timing, which was agreed during the 1930s and upheld after the Pacific War, despite a brutal and destructive Japanese interregnum.

Collaboration was also a feature of colonial experience in Vietnam but in tandem with strong élite resistance to French rule inspired partly by Japan's modernization and China's republican revolution. Nationalist parties modelled on Chinese example were crushed by French repression which provided scope for the clandestine Communist Party of Indochina which the Vietnamese exile Ho Chi Minh founded in Hong Kong in 1930.

Elsewhere, nationalism arose from a religious source. In Burma, Buddhism was a vehicle for anti-colonial resistance after the First World War but was overtaken during the 1930s by a radical student-based movement influenced by Marxist ideas. Led by Aung San, this movement established a military link with the Japanese before the Pacific War and took part in their invasion of Burma. Buddhism played a corresponding role in Cambodia during the 1930s.

In the Netherlands East Indies, Islam provided an organizational frame for nationalism stimulated by resentment of alien Chinese competition in traditional textiles. The *Sarekat Islam* (Islamic Union) was set up in 1912 and attracted a mass following and also a Marxist affiliate which developed in 1920 into the Communist Party of Indonesia. Internal division and governmental repression destroyed its viability, while a Communist revolt in 1926 was put down ruthlessly. A distinctive Indonesian political identity crystallized nevertheless during the late 1920s from a secular base. Leadership was provided by a young architect named Sukarno, who was confined to internal exile by the Dutch before collaborating with the Japanese during their occupation in the nationalist interest. In Malaya, nationalism also had an Islamic source as a basis for upholding an indigenous Malay identity threatened by alien migration. Religious nationalism, however, did not gain the support of the Sultans or rulers of the Malay states, who enjoyed a privileged role under British rule.

Thailand was not subject to colonial rule but registered an anti-Western nationalism under a military regime which had come to power through overthrowing the absolute monarchy in 1932. Modernizing reforms introduced during the late nineteenth century by King Chulalongkorn had generated tensions between the court and the bureaucracy over political prerogatives which were resolved in the latter's favour. Japan provided a model for emulation which was employed by the military leader Marshal Phibun Songkhram, who pursued irredentism at French colonial expense. After the fall of France in June 1940, Thailand went to war to recover territory in western Laos and Cambodia, securing its ends through Japan's mediation, which foreshadowed its subsequent aggression in December 1941. From June 1940, Japan secured military access to Indochina, from which its forces were able to strike at colonial South-East Asia.

Japan launched airborne attacks on the US naval base at Pearl Harbor on 7 December 1941. Concurrent attacks were launched within South-East Asia, beginning with an air raid on Clark airfield in the Philippines and a sea-based assault on southern Thailand, from which the invasion of Malaya, Singapore, the Netherlands East Indies, and Burma proceeded. By May 1942, with the fall of Corregidor in the Philippines, the Japanese conquest of colonial South-East Asia was complete. The superiority of Europe was exposed as a hollow myth as its surviving soldiers and colonial civil servants were herded like cattle into prison camps.

With Japan's displacement of the colonial orders, the pace of political change was strictly controlled to serve its war effort. A nominal independence only was conferred on Burma and the Philippines in August and October 1943 respectively, and in Indochina in March 1945, when the French Vichy administration was removed in favour of local nominees. The human effect of Japan's occupation was profound, with economies devastated and subject peoples and colonial captives treated with great brutality. Japan was driven forcibly from South-East Asia by Allied forces only in Burma and in part in the Philippines, which meant that there was minimal opportunity to redeem a shattered colonial reputation. Elsewhere, Japan's dispossession followed from the atomic bombing of Hiroshima and Nagasaki.

Returning colonial powers divided into the compliant and the dogged. The United States was the most compliant, honouring a promise made in the 1930s by according independence symbolically on 4 July 1946 to the Philippines. Manuel Roxas, a nominee of General Douglas MacArthur and a collaborator of the Japanese, was elected as the first President of an independent Republic. Britain made concessions in the face of an assertive and popular Burmese nationalism organized through the Anti-Fascist People's Freedom League led by Aung San. An agreement on independence was concluded in January 1947. The assassination of Aung San by a political rival in July did not interrupt the timetable for the transfer of sovereignty, which took place on 4 January 1948, with U Nu as Burma's first Prime Minister.

In Malaya, including Singapore, Britain did not face pressing demands for independence. The indigenous Malay majority were apprehensive of the large ethnic-Chinese community which had provided most recruits for armed resistance to the Japanese through the vehicle of the Malayan Communist Party. A Malay nationalism emerged with the formation of the United Malays National Organization (UMNO) in March 1946 in reaction to a British proposal for a Malayan Union, excluding Singapore, in which non-Malays would enjoy ready access to citizenship, while the Sultans, the symbols of Malay rule, would lose their constitutional status. In the event, Singapore remained a separate British colony and naval base, while Malaya was reorganized into a Federation with the status of the Sultans restored in return for a more gradual acquisition of citizenship by non-Malays.

The eruption of Communist insurrection in Malaya in June 1948 delayed Malaya's progress to independence. The transfer of sovereignty occurred on 31 August 1957 with Tunku Abdul Rahman as Prime Minister after a Malay–Chinese political accommodation at élite level which has been the basis for political rule ever since. Singapore became self-governing in June 1959. British possessions in northern Borneo had reverted to direct colonial control for reasons of good government. Sarawak was transferred from the personal rule of the Brooke family and North Borneo (now Sabah) from that of a chartered company, while Brunei was restored as a protected state. Portugal resumed control over the eastern half of the island of Timor.

Fierce struggles for independence took place in the Netherlands East Indies and Indochina. The Republic of Indonesia was the first new state to assert independence, proclaimed by nationalist leaders Sukarno and Hatta on 17 August 1945 just two days after Japan's surrender. Indonesia's independence was achieved through a combination of armed struggle and negotiations, with the embryonic Republic being accorded quasi-international status and representation at the United Nations from August 1947. The Dutch were obliged to transfer sovereignty in December 1949, but relations with Indonesia remained strained by their unwillingness to concede the western half of the island of New Guinea. Indonesia's struggle for independence was aided by Cold War considerations. Initial US support for the Dutch was withdrawn after the Republic had put down a communist-supported revolt in Madiun in East Java in September 1948.

In the case of Indochina, however, and in particular Vietnam, US Cold War calculations served French interests. Unlike Indonesia, Vietnam had declared independence under the aegis of the Communist Party. In July 1941 Ho Chi Minh, operating from southern China, had established the League for the Independence of Vietnam or *Viet Minh* which attracted nationalist support. In August 1945 it took advantage of Japan's surrender by seizing Hanoi and forcing the abdication in its favour of the Emperor Bao Dai. The proclamation of the Democratic Republic of Vietnam took place in Hanoi on 2 September 1945, with Ho Chi Minh employing the idiom of the United States' declaration of independence in an abortive attempt to secure international recognition.

Indochina had been divided along the line of the sixteenth parallel of latitude with responsibility for taking the Japanese surrender shared between the Nationalist Chinese forces of Chiang Kai Shek to the north and those of SEAC to the south. The Chinese dispossessed the *Viet Minh* in North Vietnam, while SEAC enabled the return of French administration to South Vietnam, Laos and Cambodia. A *modus vivendi* between the French and the *Viet Minh* against a background of Chinese withdrawal broke down at the end of 1946. The political future of Vietnam, as well as of Laos and Cambodia, was then to be decided by force of arms in two stages.

Thailand was an exception to the regional pattern. It was an independent state but had become tainted politically through association with Japan's aggressive design. The United States sought Thailand's international rehabilitation, however. Bangkok's declaration of war had not been communicated by the Thai legation in Washington nor accepted by the US government, while Britain's and France's wish for retribution was interpreted as an expression of an abiding colonialism. With a civilian government restored, Thailand was treated little differently from any other country liberated from Japan's tyranny, albeit obliged to return its wartime territorial gains. But when that government was overthrown by a military *coup* in the wake of the unexplained violent death of the young King Ananda in June 1946, cold-war priorities interposed to sustain American patronage.

The post-colonial states of South-East Asia began their independent existence with two legacies: the colonial political boundaries and the parliamentary democracy deemed a necessary symbol of international legitimacy, given the global dominance of the United States. Those state boundaries contained fissile social diversities which were not readily willing to accept the cultural and economic imperatives of alien political centres. For example, Burma was afflicted with ethno-regional dissent and challenge which has persisted for over half a century. Neighbouring Thailand also experienced a separatist pull from its mainly Muslim south stimulated by the rise of Malay nationalism. Indonesia in its archipelagic condition was most vulnerable to centrifugal political forces, encouraged by Dutch policy before the transfer of sovereignty.

Communist insurrection was another endemic feature of South-East Asia in the wake of the Pacific War. It made a major impact in Burma and the Philippines shortly after independence and in Malaya and Indonesia before the transfers of sovereignty, although ultimately failing. In the important case of Vietnam, the communist movement assumed the mantle of nationalism to attain ultimate military and political success.

Despite an endemic separatism aggravated by communist insurrection, none of South-East Asia's post-colonial states have experienced involuntary dismemberment. The Federation of Malaysia took a conscious decision to eject Singapore to independence in August 1965. Irredentism has enjoyed greater regional import, for example, in Indonesia's recovery of the western half of the island of New Guinea (known now as Irian Jaya) in May 1963 and in the unification of Vietnam in April 1975. With minor exceptions, the territorial inheritance of colonialism has been transferred intact. But Indonesia's annexation of the eastern half of the island of Timor in December 1975 was inconsistent with the nationalist *raison d'être* based on the Dutch colonial domain.

The political inheritance of the West has been much less durable. Parliamentary systems have experienced a chequered record and were placed under great strain in Burma and Indonesia during the 1950s as tensions between polity and society were aggravated by economic difficulties. Both states opted for authoritarian solutions, as did Thailand. The Philippines maintained the form of democracy into the early 1970s, but then President Ferdinand Marcos assumed dictatorial powers for over a decade. Malaya/Malaysia and then Singapore sustained their initial parliamentary practices on independence but increasingly employed legislatures as rubber stamps for one-party government.

The post-colonial era coincided with and was affected deeply by the Cold War and the determination of the United States to contain international communism. In Indochina, France's confrontation with the *Viet Minh* was represented as a theatre of global conflict. Its failure to contain the *Viet Minh's* advance by early 1954, however, prompted the United States to contemplate direct military intervention, which caused alarm among regional states of a neutralist disposition. The governments of Burma and Indonesia combined with those of three South Asian states in Ceylon's capital Colombo to appeal for moderation. That meeting led on to a wider Asian–African Conference in the Indonesian city of Bandung in April 1955, which registered for the first time the international agenda of post-colonial states.

The historic Bandung Conference convened in the wake of the First Indochina

War. France had suffered a devastating military reverse at the hands of *Viet Minh* at the battle of Dien Bien Phu in the north-west of Vietnam close to the border with Laos. The surrender of the French position took place on 7 April 1954, one day before an international conference convened in Geneva to address the Indochina conflict. Ceasefire agreements were concluded for Vietnam, Laos, and Cambodia, together with an unsigned Final Declaration endorsing their terms. Vietnam was divided along the line of the seventeenth parallel of latitude for the purpose of regrouping military units. That line solidified into a *de facto* international boundary enduring for over twenty years. A communist government led by Ho Chi Minh took power to its north; to its south an anti-communist administration headed by former exile Ngo Dinh Diem was installed. Under the terms of the Geneva agreements, nationwide elections were to be held in Vietnam within two years, but they never took place as the country became the locus of the Cold War in Asia.

Communist-supported revolutionary movements in Laos and Cambodia were not recognized at the Geneva Conference. Cambodia was restored to independence under the leadership of King Norodom Sihanouk, who abdicated in favour of his father in March 1955 to set up a Vichy-style organization through which he dominated politics for a decade and a half. Laos was also restored to a fragile independence; two of its provinces abutting China and Vietnam remained under control of *Viet Minh*-controlled Laotian forces. The United States sought to hold the line against further communist advance in Indochina through a Collective Defence Treaty for South-East Asia concluded in Manila on 8 September 1954 whose members assumed unilateral obligations to Cambodia, Laos, and South Vietnam. Within South-East Asia, only Thailand and the Philippines signed up. A South-East Asia Treaty Organization (SEATO) was set up in Bangkok in February 1955 but without a military command. From the early 1960s, the south of Vietnam reverted to armed struggle, with Laos drawn into that conflict because of the importance of its eastern uplands as an infiltration route into South Vietnam—which achieved notoriety as the Ho Chi Minh Trail.

In Indonesia, President Sukarno replaced Indonesia's parliamentary system with an authoritarian Guided Democracy in July 1959 in the wake of abortive regional uprisings. He commanded the country's political heights through remarkable oratorical skills and by playing off the armed forces and the large Communist Party. He also exploited nationalist issues—in particular, Holland's refusal to transfer the western half of the island of New Guinea. Fear of Communist advantage attracted US support for this irredentist cause, but its realization encouraged Sukarno's engagement in external diversion as a way of maintaining political control in deteriorating economic circumstances. A revolt in the British-protected Sultanate of Brunei in North Borneo in December 1962 provided a pretext for challenging the formation of the Federation of Malaysia.

In May 1961 the Prime Minister of Malaya, Tunku Abdul Rahman, proposed unifying the Malay Peninsula with self-governing Singapore and British possessions in North Borneo as a way of containing local communist and Chinese influence in Singapore seen as synonymous. Indonesia's challenge to the legitimacy of

Malaysia from January 1963 was distinguished by the term *Konfrontasi* (Confrontation)—a form of coercive diplomacy which had been used against the Dutch over West New Guinea. Malaysia was established on 16 September 1963 but without Brunei's adherence. Indonesia's 'Confrontation' and Sukarno's 'Guided Democracy' collapsed in the wake of an abortive *coup* in October 1965 attributed to the country's Communist Party. On 11 March 1966 power was assumed by Lieutenant-General (later President) Suharto, whose military-based administration embarked on economic development and regional cooperation involving reconciliation with Malaysia and a newly independent Singapore.

Political crisis and change in Indonesia occurred concurrently with political decay and military confrontation in South Vietnam. The leadership of President Ngo Dinh Diem had failed to prise the nationalist standard from the grasp of the *Viet Minh*, who were reconstituted under the leadership of the Communist Party as the National Liberation Front of South Vietnam (NLF) in December 1960. Buddhist protest against the government in Saigon, seen as dominated by Catholics, as well as the lamentable military performance of its army against a rural insurgency, led to a withdrawal of American support for Diem who was murdered during a military *coup* in November 1963, just days before the assassination of President Kennedy. A series of juntas then exercised power but without any grasp of the requirements for political victory which led the United States to assume growing responsibility for the conduct of the widening war. By March 1965 the United States had changed its nature by embarking on the sustained aerial bombardment of North Vietnam. When this attempt to impose an unacceptable cost on the ruling party in Hanoi failed, more than half a million combat troops were introduced progressively into the south but without inflicting the desired military reverse on the communist army increasingly stiffened by infiltration from the north.

The turning point in the conflict came at the end of January 1968 during the Tet festival for the Vietnamese lunar new year when the NLF launched coordinated attacks against urban targets. Although a military failure, the Tet Offensive proved to be a historical turning point because of its political impact within the United States where popular protest was rising in opposition to the heavy price in lives and casualties being paid by American servicemen. A peace agreement concluded in Paris in January 1973 left the government in Saigon in place but not for long. A Vietnamese communist military offensive in March 1975 in the central highlands set off a rout among the southern army, with northern forces seizing Saigon on 30 April. Formal reunification took place on 2 July 1976 with the promulgation of the Socialist Republic of Vietnam.

A communist victory had also occurred in neighbouring Cambodia on 17 April when Phnom Penh was invested by a revolutionary movement known as the Khmer Rouge. This movement had its roots in a nationalist–communist alternative to the neighbouring Vietnamese party but had acquired military and political significance only in the wake of Prince Norodom Sihanouk's overthrow by a right-wing *coup* on 18 March 1970. The restoration of the royal government in April 1975 was short-lived, to be replaced on 5 January 1976 by an ironically termed 'Democratic' Kampuchea and Prince Sihanouk's resignation and house arrest. Under the leadership of the fearsome Pol Pot, a gruesome social experiment was inaugurated. Cambodia was transformed into a primitive agricultural work camp combining the worst excesses of Stalin and Mao in which around a million people died from execution, starvation, and disease. An attempt to conceal the failings of economic dogma through xenophobic nationalism led on to military confrontation with Vietnam. Laos, subject to a fragile coalition, also succumbed to communist control during the course of 1975. In December, the constitutional monarchy was removed and the Lao People's Democratic Republic was established in a close relationship with Vietnam.

As the Vietnam War intensified, a group of non-communist states began an experiment in regional cooperation. Thailand, Malaya and the Philippines set up the Association of South-East Asia (ASA) in Bangkok in July 1961, based on the rationale that economic progress through regional cooperation would provide a foundation for national security. ASA fell victim to Indonesia's 'Confrontation' and the claim by the Philippines to the part of North Borneo incorporated into the Federation of Malaysia as Sabah. ASA was superseded in August 1967 in Bangkok by ASEAN, with the additional membership of Indonesia and Singapore.

ASEAN was an attempt to provide a framework for regional reconciliation. Its declaratory goals were economic and cultural cooperation but security was uppermost in mind among governments which shared a common experience of resisting internal revolutionary challenge and which also had misgivings about the regional staying power of the United States. A progressive willingness to cooperate in avoiding and managing conflict served to engender external business confidence in regional economies which, beginning with Singapore under the dynamic leadership of Lee Kuan Yew, came to emulate Japan's example of export-led growth.

In February 1976, after the success of revolutionary communism in Indochina, ASEAN demonstrated its collective nerve by holding the first meeting of its heads of government in Indonesia. A political agenda was set and an agreement reached to establish a secretariat in Jakarta. Moreover, Japan began to take ASEAN seriously. Prime Minister Takeo Fukuda with his Australian and New Zealand counterparts attended the next meeting of heads of governments convened in August 1977 to commemorate the tenth anniversary of ASEAN's formation. Japan had returned to South-East Asia in an economic role during the 1950s through the vehicle of reparations agreements. That role expanded over the years as access to raw materials and market opportunities was succeeded by capital investment to take advantage of cheaper labour and land, pointing the way for burgeoning multinational enterprise.

The Third Indochina War marked the final occasion in the twentieth century when a local conflict within South-East Asia would serve as a focus for global conflict. It began in December 1978, when Vietnamese forces invaded and occupied Cambodia. The belligerent Khmer Rouge regime was driven out to find active sanctuary in Thailand, and a People's Republic of Kampuchea was established in January 1979 in a special relationship with Vietnam. China responded by launching a punitive expedition into North Vietnam in February. The United States and Japan applied economic pressure on Vietnam while the ASEAN states played an active diplomatic role, with the alignment supporting an armed resistance against the Vietnamese occupation, including the Khmer Rouge.

The burden of the Third Indochina War broke the back of Vietnam's resolve to engage concurrently in socialist development and to uphold a special relationship with neighbouring states in Indochina. In the event, Vietnam lost the countervailing support of the Soviet Union and was obliged to appease China in particular by withdrawing its forces from Cambodia from the end of September 1989. ASEAN then took a back seat diplomatically, as the permanent members of the Security Council assumed the initiative for a peace settlement through the vehicle of a United Nations Transitional Authority in Cambodia (UNTAC) provided for at an international conference in Paris in October 1991. UNTAC conducted nationwide elections in Cambodia in May 1993, despite the recalcitrance of the Khmer Rouge, leading to the restoration of the constitutional monarchy under Norodom Sihanouk in September and the formation of a fragile coalition government in October. Complete peace was not restored, however, as a diminished Khmer Rouge continued to fight for a share of power as a basis for resuming its exclusive exercise.

The end of the Cambodian conflict registered the regional impact of changes in global politics at the end of the century. It also registered an acknowledgement by the ruling party in Hanoi that it had lost its way economically and had placed its legitimacy at risk. During the Third Indochina War, the members of ASEAN, augmented by an independent Brunei from January 1984 and with the exception of the Philippines, continued to prosper as they benefited from concentrating on comparative advantage in manufactures. Vietnam faced penury as the cost of prosecuting the Cambodia war compounded the failings of the rigid application of socialist doctrine. Revision in Hanoi came in December 1986 at the Third National Congress of the Communist Party which appointed the economic reformer Nguyen Van Linh as General Secretary. A new doctrine of *Doi Moi*, meaning renovation or renewal of the economy through free-market practice, was promulgated and applied progressively, despite resistance from party diehards.

Doi Moi registered the need to encourage free-market economics and inward investment if Vietnam was to raise standards of living to match those of its regional neighbours. Such a repudiation of economic doctrine, replicated in Laos, was not matched by a revision of the political system. On the contrary, economic change was undertaken in order to protect the leading role of the Communist Party. To that extent, a convergence of a kind emerged in political systems with some other regional states which had pioneered successful economic growth through a practice of developmental authoritarianism whereby the state intervened to ensure political demobilization in the interest of social stability and economic progress. Such a practice had been demonstrated in the case of Indonesia under the leadership of President Suharto and Malaysia under Dr Mahathir Mohamad, and strikingly so in the case of Singapore, whose Senior Minister and former Prime Minister, Lee Kuan Yew, was invited to Vietnam to offer economic advice.

In the wake of the Cold War, the astounding economic successes of a number of South-East Asian states provided a source of self-confidence in rebutting attempts by the West to impose its own democratic values. The issue of democratization within the region had arisen well before the end of the Cold War in the Philippines, where the venal rule of President Marcos had provided a political opening for the insurgent Communist Party. Against a background of political and economic decay Marcos called a snap election in February 1986. He was challenged by Mrs Corazon Aquino, the widow of his one-time principal political opponent, Benigno Aquino, who had been murdered at Manila Airport in August 1983 on his return from exile in the United States. Fraudulent conduct of that election served as the context for a military revolt in Manila led by Fidel Ramos, the deputy Chief of Staff of the Armed Forces, and Juan Ponce Enrile, the Defence Minister. Marcos loyalists were prevented from crushing that revolt in support of Mrs Aquino by the physical interposition of civilian demonstrators encouraged by the Catholic Church. That display of so-called 'people power' persuaded the United States to withdraw its longstanding support for Marcos, who, with his family, went into exile in Hawaii, leaving Mrs Aquino to be inaugurated as President. She restored the democratic process, but a stable political order had to await the election in June 1992 of her successor Fidel Ramos, whose loyalty as Defence Minister had thwarted a series of military *coups*.

Democracy triumphed also in Thailand. A false start had been made in October 1973 when student revolt and intervention by King Bhumibol restored the parliamentary system, but it was soon overturned by another military *coup* three years later. During the 1980s benign military rule and respect for constitutionalism ensued under Prime Minister General Prem Tinsulanond. When the military removed his elected successor, Chatichai Choonhavan, by a *coup* in February 1991, King Bhumibol distanced himself from the junta, who chose a civilian caretaker, Anand Panyarachun, as Prime Minister. Fresh elections were held in March 1992, but the appointment of an unelected former army commander, General Suchinda Krapayoon, provoked angry demonstrations in Bangkok reminiscent of Manila in February 1986 but culminating in a bloody confrontation. The King intervened to restore democratic order, with further elections in September 1992 giving rise to an elected government with a civilian base which has been sustained. In both the Philippines and Thailand, popular protest but in contrasting economic circumstances had served the democratic interest. Corresponding protest in Burma, however, resulted in the flowering of democracy being ruthlessly crushed.

Burma had been ruled by a military regime headed by General Ne Win ever since the armed forces had seized power in a *coup* which displaced the democratic regime in March 1962. A mixture of Marxist and Buddhist nostrums provided a doctrinal basis for a so-called 'Burmese Road to Socialism' under the monopoly rule of the Burma Socialist Programme Party (BSPP). The outcome by the late 1980s was a condition of national penury indicated by application to the United Nations for Burma to be accorded the status of 'least developed country' in order to secure grants in aid. Demonetization of larger currency notes in circulation in September 1987 provoked student unrest which rose to a crescendo during August and September 1988, to be met with ruthless military repression. Ne Win had resigned as head of government in 1981 and gave up the leadership of the BSPP in July 1987, but he retained a dominant political influence despite his ailing physical condition. In the face of popular protest which was inspired by the presence in the country of Aung San Suu Kyi, the daughter of the revered nationalist martyr Aung San, the armed forces launched an 'incumbency *coup*'. All state and party organs were abolished by the new junta, which styled itself the State Law and Order Restoration Council (SLORC) and which in June 1989 changed the name of the country to Myanmar.

Elections were held in May 1990 in which the National League for Democracy—led by Aung San Suu Kyi, who had been placed under house arrest in July 1989—won an overwhelming majority over the National Unity Party, which was the political vehicle of the military junta. That electoral outcome was not honoured and the SLORC went ahead with drafting a new constitution designed to entrench the political role of the armed forces along the lines of the Indonesian model as well as to exclude Aung San Suu Kyi from power.

Through its diplomatic performance and economic accomplishments, ASEAN had become increasingly attractive to non-members, giving the region a historically unprecedented coherence. The prospect seemed good for realizing the aspiration of transforming South-East Asia into a Zone of Peace, Freedom, and Neutrality (ZOPFAN) which had been articulated at a meeting of ASEAN's foreign ministers in November 1971. In fact, with the end of the cold war, the strategic environment in East Asia, including South-East Asia, changed in a way that did not permit the members of ASEAN to shape regional order in a prerogative manner. South-East Asia did not enjoy a self-contained condition but was linked by land, water, and politics to a more extensive East Asia. This geopolitical linkage was pointed up in contention over the Spratly Islands in the South China Sea, which had not been dominated or delimited by colonial powers.

The People's Republic of China had pressed a claim to all the islands of the South China Sea from its establishment, had employed force to secure the northerly Paracel Islands at Vietnam's expense in the mid-1970s, and had seized a limited number of the southerly Spratly Islands in the late 1980s with a further armed occupation in the mid-1990s. Claims to partial jurisdiction in the Spratly Islands had been asserted also by Malaysia, the Philippines, and Brunei—all members of ASEAN—while Vietnam, which joined the Association in July 1995, sought jurisdiction over both the Paracel and Spratly Islands. China's irredentist disposition was displayed at a time when it had come to enjoy an unprecedented regional strategic latitude free from any major adversary and had begun to modernize its armed forces with an increasing ability to project naval and air power southwards. Moreover, the United States had conceded nationalist demands and had withdrawn its once formidable military presence from the Philippines by the end of 1992.

Despite a sustained commitment to a ZOPFAN, ASEAN governments have never shared a common perspective of external threat; nor has the Association been willing to engage in defence cooperation. In the circumstances, ASEAN opted to extend its approach to regional security based on multilateral dialogue to a wider East Asia in order to cope with an assertive China and a retreating United States. In July 1993 in Singapore, the annual meeting of ASEAN's foreign ministers was used to host an inaugural dinner for eighteen foreign ministers to launch the ASEAN Regional Forum (ARF) intended to promote a predictable and constructive pattern of relationships in Asia–Pacific. Apart from the six ASEAN states, and their seven dialogue partners from the United States, Japan, Australia, New Zealand, Canada, South Korea, and the EU, there were Papua New Guinea, Vietnam, and Laos as well as China and Russia. The first working meeting of the ARF convened in Bangkok in July 1994.

South-East Asian governments have also found themselves obliged to accept a wider framework for economic cooperation. ASEAN has long had a formal commitment to economic cooperation but it was only in January 1992 that a decision was taken by its governments to set up a free trade area. By this juncture, however, through Australian initiative in 1989, a wider consultative forum for Asia–Pacific Economic Cooperation (APEC) was established which has assumed a growing importance through annual meetings between its heads of government.

By the end of the twentieth century, the governments of an expanding ASEAN have given coherence to the concept of a South-East Asia. Ironically, just as this coherence has been registered, they have been obliged to expand their regional horizons in order to cope with changing strategic and economic environments in a way which casts doubt on the very viability of the concept of South-East Asia.

Postscript: By the end of the century, ASEAN had expanded to coincide with geographic South-East Asia. That expansion was controversial, with Myanmar (as well as Laos) joining in July 1997 and Cambodia in April 1999. ASEAN's greater political diversity aggravated the problem of managing consensus and further diminished the Association's standing, which had been reduced by a regional economic crisis, precipitated by the devaluation of the Thai currency in July 1997. In Indonesia, political turbulence ended the authoritarian rule of President Suharto in May 1998. He was succeeded in October 1999, after an interim presidency, by President Abdurrahman Wahid who was faced with upholding the Republic's territorial integrity after an overwhelming vote for independence in a UN-supervised referendum in East Timor in the previous August. Regional economic recovery was soon in train, but the crisis punctured confidence about continuous development, while altering the political pattern in favour of greater democratization.

20 South Asia

JUDITH M. BROWN

Few areas of the world have experienced such great change in the twentieth century as the Indian subcontinent. Changes have transformed life for many of its peoples, as well as its relations with the wider world and its international public image. In 1900 it was the 'jewel in the crown' of the late-Victorian British Empire and vital to Britain's worldwide influence. Within fifty years it was South Asia, a subcontinent of several independent states. At the start of the century South Asians lived in predominantly agrarian societies, despite the existence of towns and cities built on trade, administration, and religious observance. Now their grandchildren live in environments powerfully moulded by mega-cities, modern industry, and commercial agriculture, and the growth of a sizeable middle class. In very practical ways South Asians have been drawn together by road, rail, and air transport, and into easy contact with other continents. In 1900 it could take up to three weeks to travel by sea between Britain and India: in the 1990s the journey is nine hours' flying time. This has led to major movements of people both ways as migrants, students, businessmen, and tourists.

This spectrum of changes occurred in the context of one of the most profound political transformations of the century, the erosion of Western imperial influence in Asia and Africa, and subsequent decolonization. Such radical change in government and politics has had implications for virtually every aspect of life—from mortality and health, to education and employment, economic conditions, and people's expectations of life and of their governments. So discussion of the area in this century must start with changes in relation to the nature and use of public power.

The Indian Empire was twenty times larger than Britain itself—the size of Europe without Russia. (This excluded the island of Ceylon to the south-west, itself as large as a sizeable Indian province.) Given the long timescale of established civilization and government on the subcontinent, the British Empire was a recent phenomenon, British rule having been consolidated only in the early nineteenth century. However this rule (*Raj*) and its consequences rapidly became of great consequence not only for its Asian subjects but also for Britain. India became a reservoir of fighting power, paid for by Indians, which the British could and did deploy around the globe for imperial purposes—from China, through the Middle East to the Western front in the First World War. It was also a major trading partner, taking manufactured goods and exporting raw materials like many colonial countries in relation to the industrial core of empire. Its trade and public finance supported sterling as an international currency; and it was, with Ceylon, a major area of British overseas investment, receiving about one-tenth of the total, around £365 million, at the beginning of the twentieth century.

The mechanisms of government reflected British goals: to maintain the area's capacity to service these broader imperial needs, to guarantee domestic security and tranquility, to collect revenue (particularly from land), and to prevent disruptive social change. The rationale of government was static and conservative, and the administration was designed to perform these minimum functions. In two-thirds of India, directly under the British, the élite Indian Civil Service (ICS), composed largely of expatriates, formed the core of the thinly spread administration, organized in provinces headed by governors, under the Viceroy, whose secretariat was the connecting link with the Secretary of State for India and his India Office in Whitehall. Ceylon, by contrast, was a Crown Colony, under the jurisdiction of the Colonial Office. Beneath this élite level local people in their thousands performed the basic functions of government. Indians also formed the bulk of the police and the army, though both were officered by Europeans until after the First World War. One-third of the subcontinent, however, remained under the control of the remaining Indian princes, as subordinate allies of the British. Government priorities were clear in its expenditure patterns. By the early twentieth century defence was the single largest item of government expenditure in India—nearly one-third of the total revenue: and the provinces spent almost double on police, jails, and justice than on education. 'Human investment' was far smaller than in Britain itself and in the white colonies. Only in Ceylon at the very end of colonial rule did welfare expenditure rise significantly.

However, South Asian society could not be mothballed or preserved in a mould Europeans considered traditional and unchanging. Forces were working to create new political ideas, identities, and demands, which culminated in articulate nationalist movements, pushing for constitutional reform and eventually for independence. Earliest of these forces was modern education, in English for a privileged few. It was the Western-educated who were exposed to new political and social ideals, who became anxious about their employment prospects in the modern professions and in government service, and began to press for wider opportunities, and ultimately to articulate political nationalism and to form new political associations to press their claims. This process was most advanced in areas longest exposed to Western influence: the Indian National Congress had emerged in the 1880s, through the efforts of educated men from Bengal, Bombay, and Madras. However the great nationalist organizers and idealists, men such as M. K. Gandhi, S. C. Bose, or the Nehru father and son, were not just spokesmen of a 'microscopic minority', as the British claimed at the start of the century. Their sense of 'national' identity was far broader than the vested interest of an élite. Often it was sharpened by the force of religious reawakening in response to Western pressure, in India in the Hindu and Muslim traditions, or in Ceylon in the context of resurgent Buddhism. Gandhi, for example, spoke of true independence as a moral and social, as well as a political transformation, which had to benefit those at the base of Indian society. Economic forces were also creating new concerns and discontents which generated wider support for these early English-speaking nationalists. Commercial agriculture, for example, in some areas of India and particularly in Ceylon, and the development of modern business and industry in Asian hands, produced economic groups with financial muscle and a new awareness of the constraints on expansion and on profits imposed by imperial rule. In India economic dislocation in the wake of the First World War and the international depression, which hit primary producers particularly hard, created wide social and economic distress which in turn fed into articulate nationalism—for example, into Gandhi's populist movements of non-cooperation with British rule.

The British were pragmatic imperialists, and extremely cost-conscious. They moved down the road of constitutional reform for their South Asian dependencies, not primarily out of idealism but as a mode of placating significant local opinion and maintaining cheap government. Although they had the power to crush what they considered to be disaffection (and did not hesitate to use it, as against the 'Quit India' movement of 1942), they recognized that this was too expensive and too destructive of their public image in Asia and at home to be permanent policy. So Ceylon achieved universal suffrage and the assurance of imminent self-government in 1931. British India saw a progressive devolution of power to Indian politicians in the provinces through constitutional reform in 1919 and 1935, though the franchise still excluded most women and the poor. However, these devices for ensuring local cooperation and cheap government meant that local rather than imperial priorities shaped government policy; and the area as a whole became less supportive of broader imperial interests. (For example, from the 1920s it was accepted that the Indian army could no longer be used outside India at Indian expense: from the 1930s it became apparent that India was of declining economic importance to Britain.) The Second World War completed this process, leaving India, for example, with major sterling balances in London, a creditor rather than a debtor of Britain. Independence, carefully negotiated and timed, creating allies within an evolving British Commonwealth, thus seemed the most practical way of securing Britain's reduced interests in South Asia. Suppression of nationalism would have been intolerable for the British (in terms of money, manpower, and repute), who were now impoverished by war, anxious for domestic reconstruction, and dependent on American support. However, in India independence was fraught with problems caused by the emergence of a specifically Muslim sense of political identity which culminated in the Muslim League under M. A. Jinnah, demanding special status and eventually a state for a distinctive Muslim 'nation'. The escalating violence which accompanied this demand as the war ended and it was clear that the British were going, and the failure of Indian politicians to reach a settlement among themselves, led the British to partition the subcontinent as they left, thus creating a predominantly Hindu India (though leaving in India a sizeable Muslim minority constituting about 11 per cent of the population), and Pakistan, including what is now Bangladesh. The process of partition was violent and bitter, and its legacy in memory and suspicion remains. Figures for deaths, abduction and rape of women, and migrations across the new borders will never be accurately known, so intense was the disruption and the pressures on administration. But the migrants numbered many millions— probably around 7 million in each direction.

India and Pakistan gained independence in 1947, followed by Ceylon in 1948. (The island was renamed Sri Lanka in 1972.) The new political shape of the subcontinent was completed in 1971 when the eastern wing of Pakistan broke away in a bloody civil war to become Bangladesh. These were the giant states of the region, in terms of area, population, and influence, compared with such tiny states as Nepal, Bhutan, and the Maldives. The nature of these new governments was to affect the experience of their peoples as profoundly as had the presence of colonial rulers.

In external relations the major countries of the region have sought to protect what they see as their interests and to give substance internationally to their new political independence. But the area has been marked by intense conflicts among neighbours, often exacerbated by the ambitions and fears of the world's great powers, particularly during the Cold War, which sucked arms and finance into the area. Despite the policy of non-alignment with any power bloc set in place as the cornerstone of Indian foreign policy by Jawaharlal Nehru, India's first Prime Minister, local tensions and external pressures pushed India for long periods into cooperation with the Soviet Union, while Pakistan has received military aid from the United States and has at times allied with China. The major intra-regional conflict has been that between India and Pakistan on border issues and in particular over Kashmir, which has been disputed territory between them since the partition. The two countries have locked in armed conflict on several occasions. In 1962 India was also subjected to humiliating if brief invasion by China. India itself has intervened in other regional conflicts. It supported the Pakistani dissidents in 1971; and in the 1980s became embroiled in Sri Lanka's domestic civil war between the Sinhala population and sections of the Tamil population, many of whom were Indian in origin. The main impact on ordinary South Asians of these conflicts has been, apart from heightened senses of distinct national identity, the very high government expenditure on defence (and advance to nuclear power status by India and Pakistan) to the detriment of social investment. By the 1990s India's army of 1,100,000 was the third largest in the world, and her defence budget of $6.75 billion was 15 per cent of the total budget. Pakistan's army is about half that size; but in 1984 its defence expenditure was running at nearly 40 per cent of government spending.

The new governments of South Asia have also been intent on internal political reconstruction, to make new nation states into national political communities, and to make good nationalist claims by doing for their peoples what colonial rulers could or would not do. Their proclaimed objectives have been partly socio-economic—to encourage broader economic development in order to raise the standard of living to acceptable levels, to generate sufficient national wealth to pay for defence and major social investment—in transport, education, medicine, and welfare. It was clear that only this sort of transformed socio-economic under-pinning in new states would turn colonial subjects into participant citizens with a clear stake in the new political order. However, as will become clear from the discussion below of changes in economy and society, these efforts were often thwarted by a dramatic rise in population, the sheer dimensions of poverty, and the difficulties in the context of the international economy of turning a primary-export-dominated economy into a more balanced economy where agricultural development and industrialization would work together to produce self-sustaining economic growth.

The overtly political aspect of internal reconstruction was the establishment of mass democracy. This ideal was a legacy of British rule, for it was in the name of 'the people' that nationalists had challenged the legitimacy of colonialism. All the successor states of the British Empire in South Asia started the new era with demo-cratic constitutions and institutions, either in place or in the making. Despite the common British legacies of democratic ideals, an independent civil service and an apolitical army, and independent judiciaries and the press, the experience and sustainability of democratic government and politics have varied greatly between the countries of the region. At one end of the spectrum are Pakistan and Bangladesh, whose politics and government have been marked by lengthy peri-ods of military rule, and in the Pakistani case by experiments in controlled forms of 'basic democracy'. In the middle lies Sri Lanka, where British patterns of gov-ernment were replaced in the 1970s by a more French style. At the other end is India, where democratic institutions, often direct descendants of those created in 1935, have flourished, where there has never been military intervention to replace civil government, and where there is an open and at times chaotic party system, and regular elections. Even the 'emergency' under Indira Gandhi (1975-7) was autocratic, repressive government within the civil and democratic framework. But it showed how much of the colonial system of civil control was still available to democratic politicians. The reasons for this political divergence and the extreme fragility of democracy outside the Indian heartland are complex, and deeply rooted in the area's differing social structures and political history, despite the for-mer colonial power in common. The presence of the Indian National Congress as an integrative force with deep social roots has been vital in the Indian capacity to establish democratic practice over a long period, and to manage diversity, poverty, and increasing public demand for rights, goods, and services. In what became Pakistan and Bangladesh, Congress had never had such roots, but neither had the Muslim League, whose growth and support were restricted to the years between the end of the war and partition. Nor has Islam provided a solid foundation for democratic management of public power, despite the claims of a Muslim national identity. What is common to the whole region, including those countries most 'democratic' in their politics, is the high level of violence in public and political life. The most extreme instances of this are military *coups*, civil wars, and political assassinations. But even in democratic India the army has increasingly been used to control internal dissent; and two Prime Ministers, Indira and Rajiv Gandhi, have been assassinated. More generally, violence between citizens is increasing, indicating the profound problems democratic institutions face in containing the tensions in society and resolving its urgent problems.

A major problem common to all the larger states in the region is the fact that they are plural societies, including several markedly different religious, ethnic, and regional groups. Although they emerged as states out of nationalist movements and in the name of 'nations', they do not have homogeneous social foundations. This has made the construction of national political communities particularly problematic, as the meaning of national identity has been disputed by people with very deep and often very different senses of public identity, grounded in religion, language, culture, and ethnicity. Most national leaders have recognized this problem and have sought a slogan or a genuine ideology which would integrate or overcome these other identities. Jawaharlal Nehru, for example, was a passionate exponent of the vision of a secular, inclusive India, where India's minorities (particularly the millions of Muslims remaining after partition) would be secure; and where the dominant identity would be a common citizenship in a country dedicated to forging a better and more equal society for all. Pakistan's leaders have struggled with the possible role of Islam as a unifying force, as have Sri Lanka's politicians with the place of Buddhism in national identity. Western observers once tended to see subnational identities as one of a range of primordial loyalties which would disappear under the impact of 'modernization'. What is now clear is that many of these loyalties are neither traditional nor static: they are dynamic and often feed on new economic and educational opportunities, particularly where these are unevenly available.

A few examples indicate the destructive power of these loyalties, and the urgent need for sensitive political management of them if they are not to tear apart South Asian states. In India identities rooted in region, language, and local culture found political expression in the demand for linguistic states within the Indian Union— the objective being to secure political and cultural recognition for these identities, and to ensure employment, using the regional language, for local men and women. Although he considered such movements divisive of the nation, Nehru agreed to the redistribution of state boundaries on linguistic lines within a decade of independence. India's religious diversity has proved harder to manage, and several religious minorities have remained concerned about their status and future as equal citizens. The crucial frontier province of Punjab has been convulsed for a decade by terrorism and official repression, as some Sikhs have demanded special political status, if not independence. Indian Muslims, the largest national group of Muslims in the world except for Indonesian Muslims, have become increasingly impoverished and under-represented in government service of all kinds. While Congress was without dispute the major political party in India, Muslims drew some security from supporting it. But in the 1990s Congress no longer has that dominance, and there has been a resurgence of a Hindu revivalist politics which disputes the secular, composite nature of the Indian state. Muslims have suffered violent attacks at various times since 1947, but a wave of violence followed the destruction by Hindus of a mosque at Ayodyah in December 1992, menacing Muslims even in the traditionally cosmopolitan city of Bombay. Pakistan's major problems of national identity have resulted from the strength of provincial regionalism and from the reaction among non-Punjabis to the dominance of Punjabis in the army and civil service. This lay behind the Bengali resistance to incorporation into Pakistan in 1971. Regional loyalties are now made even more complex by the articulation of a further identity by representatives of Pakistan's Urdu-speaking community, who originated as migrants and refugees after partition, and now feel excluded from the benefits of the nation their parents chose to join. Sri Lanka, though so much smaller, has its own deep ethnic division between Tamils and the Sinhala Buddhist population: this erupted in the 1980s into violent conflict which is still continuing as overt civil war in the final years of the century.

The resolution of these problems of identity is made more difficult by the incidence of social and economic change. There is huge pressure on all resources and they are unevenly spread: yet people are learning to expect more from their life experiences and particularly from their governments.

The major fact of social life in South Asia has been a dramatic rise in population since mid-century—largely as a result of modern medicine to combat killer diseases (such as cholera, malaria, typhoid, and plague), of increasing awareness of public hygiene, and of control of famine. In the recent past disease and famine had taken a devastating toll of the vulnerable, particularly mothers, babies, and the very old. (For example, over 17 million South Asians died from influenza in the 1918 pandemic.) Birth rates have remained fairly constant, but death rates have dropped sharply. In particular, maternal and infant mortality has plummeted, letting more children live to maturity and more women live through their childbearing years. In India population grew annually by 0.6 per cent over the decade 1901–11, from the 1950s the annual percentage per decade has been over 2 per cent. This means that a population of just over 300 million at independence had become one of around 900 million by the 1990s. Family size is a complex issue. In South Asia it reflects in part the lack of public social security, which makes families the provider of income and care, particularly in old age; and also the comparative lack of female education. Where women are more educated, as in Sri Lanka or the south Indian state of Kerala, women tend to marry later, and to have the skill and incentive to manage their own fertility. Without female education and basic provision for children's health, the huge sums now being spent by governments on family planning may well be wasted. As a result of population trends, South Asian society is now much younger in profile than Western societies, with 40 per cent now under 15 in some countries, compared with 20 per cent in Britain. This means huge pressure from a more demanding citizenry on all resources—from water and food, to land, housing, jobs, education, and medical care.

South Asian states all recognized that education would be a crucial factor in their political and economic development as well as in the quality of their citizens' lives. They determined to provide free, mass education in place of the élitist education available to those who could pay for it under colonial rule. Since independence, literacy has increased very markedly in the region. In 1951 literacy rates for Indian males were 29 per cent and for Pakistani men 21 per cent. Within thirty years Indian male literacy had risen to 47 per cent and Pakistani male literacy to 30 per cent (the lowest in the region). Sri Lankan male literacy was by then over 90 per cent: its educational achievement reflected political commitment even before independence and its subsequent ability to control population increase. In most rural areas literacy is far lower than in urban areas. The urban–rural difference is nearly 30 per cent in Pakistan and over 33 per cent in India: only in Sri Lanka is the difference less than 10 per cent. Moreover, women in general have had less access to education than men. The lowest literacy rate for women taken as one group towards the end of the century was 6 per cent in Bangladesh, and the highest 81 per cent in Sri Lanka. But virtually 97 per cent of *rural* women in Bangladesh were illiterate, as were 87 per cent of rural Indian women. Thus, despite new policy priorities and rising expenditure on education there remain millions of uneducated, illiterate people in the subcontinent—with all the implications of that for barriers to social betterment and the growth of a skilled labour force. Women's educational backwardness is a particular constraint on social and economic dynamism. What can happen where women are given new freedom and skills through education is evident in certain areas such as Sri Lanka and Kerala.

The creation of new national political communities also required major economic transformation—to take South Asians out of deep poverty and improve living standards above bare subsistence, and to enable governments to raise the taxes necessary for social provision. In order to achieve self-sustaining economic growth, Asian leaders were determined to get out of the trap of being primary producers for an unpredictable world market. All have endeavoured to encourage industrialization and have realized (though often after a significant time lag) that agricultural transformation through new technology, enabling more intensive land use, is vital if South Asians are to feed themselves and generate sufficient rural income to create a market for industrial goods, as well as a surplus for ongoing economic investment. As a result, South Asian countries now all have more vibrant and diverse economies, linked to the wider world by more varied trading patterns and by the receipt of considerable sums in aid. (India has over time received the largest amount of aid; but Bangladesh has the economy most dependent on aid.) Nor has the region suffered economic problems on the scale of some African and Latin American countries. However, economic development has occurred slowly and very unevenly through the region. Bangladesh has the poorest economy, for reasons of geography, climate, demography, and the nature of government. India, Pakistan, and Sri Lanka by contrast have all managed to increase their food production and feed their rising populations. India and Pakistan have achieved a small but sustained rate of economic growth, but there is great disparity in each country within regions and between social groups. The Green Revolution of the 1970s in wheat production and to a lesser extent in rice, by using new seeds, fertilizers, and copious irrigation, and then using increased profits for mechanization, has benefited certain areas of the subcontinent only, particularly Punjab, and the southern Indian states of Andhra Pradesh and Tamil Nadu. By contrast, Bihar remains a devastatingly poor relation, barely touched by agrarian dynamism. Early industrial growth in India was also geographically localized—bringing new wealth and employment to a range of cities and their hinterlands, such as Calcutta and Bombay. Gradually the energy consumption between Indian states has begun to even out, indicating that modern industry is becoming more widespread. But still there are key states such as Punjab, Maharashtra, or Tamil Nadu which are clearly forging ahead economically by contrast with others.

Some South Asians have done very well out of economic development—the prosperous peasant farmer producing for a vast domestic market who can now build a brick house with modern conveniences, farm with sophisticated machinery, and send his son to college; the modern businessman; the technologically literate who are leading the South Asian computer revolution. But others have little to distinguish them from their parents and grandparents, and live precarious lives as agricultural labourers without land, or as urban menials with a toehold in an urban slum. In India the number of landless labourers and marginal farmers is increasing, and nearly half the population lives in absolute poverty, suffering malnutrition and ill health. Famines and flu may no longer kill millions, but people die in destitution, as the late Mother Teresa's sisters discover nightly on the streets of Calcutta. Some comparisons put South Asia's experience into perspective. Observers of worldwide economic change use an index of the quality of life rather than measuring incomes or GNP in an attempt to understand the extent and meaning of economic change for real people. In the mid-1980s the UK's score in this index was 97. In Asia the highest figure was for Hong Kong (95). The main South Asian countries scored as follows: Sri Lanka (87), India (55), Pakistan and Bangladesh (both 43).

Economic changes and new educational opportunities, however limited given the size of South Asia's population, have begun swifter and more radical processes of social change, and certainly of social expectation, than were possible under colonial rule. It is certainly true that some old social formations and traditions are still present, and powerfully resistant to change, even where the state has engaged in social reform from above. In India, for example, the practice of 'untouchability', discriminating against those at the base of the Hindu ritual hierarchy, is still evident, despite legislation in 1955 to ban the practice in public places. Ultimately only access to new resources such as education, land, or capital (all of which are in short supply) can alter the situation of untouchables and give them new life chances. Similarly landlords have evaded laws designed to limit their holdings, because they have the knowledge and skills to use the state legislatures and courts to their own advantage. In Pakistan, too, landlord power is still a major force in rural life and has extended into politics and government. Across South Asia the position of women has been slow to change. Education and medical care go first to men and boys; and modern medical technology even plays into the hands of families who prefer to abort female foetuses. (Indeed there is now concern about a growing and serious imbalance between the sexes as a result of females 'lost' through different sorts of medical discrimination.) The presence of powerful women in South Asian politics, and the irony that all the major states of the region have had female prime ministers at some time, says virtually nothing about the chances of ordinary women. (Women like Indira Gandhi achieved power through highly privileged access to education and to male familial connections: she was educated in India and Europe—including an Oxford college—and was the daughter of India's first Prime Minister.) It is only in families with adequate resources that girls receive significant levels of education, can engage in paid professional work outside the home, and enjoy more equal relations with men.

However, change in the economy and educational provision, and increasing contact with a wider world, is beginning to create new social groups and identities. There is a significantly higher urban population in South Asia than there was at the beginning of the century. Of the major states in the region in the 1980s Bangladesh has the lowest urban percentage (15.2), followed by Sri Lanka (21.5), India (23.3), and Pakistan (28.3). But, in spite of lowish percentages, the sheer numbers of South Asians in total mean that there are by the end of this century many millions who are townspeople. Generations of South Asians have been born and have grown up in towns and cities such as Calcutta, Bombay, Kanpur, Karachi, or Dhaka. At one end of the urban spectrum there are the truly urban poor, lacking proper housing, sanitation, and water, or any prospect of permanent work. Far above them in terms of social and economic status and stability are a genuine working class, though they are poorly organized and protected compared with their Western counterparts. Higher again are educated urban people, who have benefited from higher education, professional opportunities, government service, modern business, and increasingly service-sector careers. This broad swathe of urban men and women are becoming a new middle class, a process of social formation leaping ahead in the 1990s, in India particularly, as a result of economic liberalization and the freeing-up of private enterprise. The urban members of the new middle class are being joined by a group of upwardly mobile rural people, climbing on the back of the Green Revolution. Here are the new consumers of everything from computers and televisions, the goods and services of fashion boutiques and Western-style beauty parlours, to higher education for their children in England and the United States. One observer has written of 'bourgeois revolution' in India: there is truth in his observations, but he ignores those South Asians who have barely entered the modern world in their capacity to consume, or to engage in social and economic self-improvement, and whose priority is survival.

British colonial rulers conceived an 'orientalist' vision of India, as a land locked in tradition, and culturally stagnant, whose peoples were trapped in a social and economic order from which they could not even choose to escape because of the power of religion. Half a century after the ending of the Raj it is abundantly clear that South Asia is a culturally vibrant region, displaying great creativity which results from interaction between indigenous forces and external influences. Probably the region has never been so open to a wider cultural world, through education, travel, and mass communications, including the press, radio, and television. (Satellite television means that world news comes into richer Indian homes as quickly as it does to American or British homes; and often provides more accurate news of Asian affairs than is available on national channels. This is a revolution in horizons even greater than that produced by the emergence of a popular press in the nineteenth century.)

This creative interaction is visible in a broad sweep of activities and concerns. Most obviously there has been considerable Westernization or internationalization of clothes and life style among the wealthier and more educated. This is seen in household equipment and decor, in dress, or in participation in international sport such as cricket, hockey, and tennis, which is followed with a passionate public fervour. (India and Pakistan have for decades fielded formidable international cricket teams: in 1996 tiny Sri Lanka joined its giant neighbours by winning the cricket world cup.) Indian domestic and international tourism, a new cultural phenomenon, has also expanded rapidly. The advertisements in an international magazine, *India Today*, show the appeal of Western clothes, five-star hotels, and modern housing developments built to international standards. The intended consumers are not just resident Indians but also non-resident Indians, now living and working abroad, whose investment and tastes are highly significant in the development of India's economy and modern culture. Yet such Westernization is often selective; and can be combined with traditional behaviour patterns in certain areas of life. The businessman who is equally at ease in a Western suit for work and a *dhoti* at home is not uncommon: nor is the girl who changes from jeans into a sari for a special social occasion: nor is the apparently secular middle-class family which chooses Hindu rites to mark death or marriage.

In the world of religion the vitality of Asian culture is particularly clear. Despite the modern life styles of many South Asians, there has been no long-term or fundamental secularization of minds and hearts such as historians have noted in parts of the Western world. All South Asia's religious traditions have seen processes and movements of redefinition, modernization, and revivalism: these were plain in the previous century as Asians responded to Western and specifically Christian influences, and to changes in their environments. Sri Lanka has seen a Buddhist revival; and in Pakistan Islamic fundamentalism opposed to Western culture has taken form in the *Jamaat-e-Islami*. In the Hindu world the Ramakrishna Mission is just one example of a movement which has made a rational, reformed, and socially responsible Hinduism highly attractive to many of its well-educated followers. Religious interaction between East and West is also clear in the numerous other Hindu groups which have gained followers in India and the West by prizing Hindu beliefs out of their specifically Indian social context. More dramatically, religious identity and passion have given a violent edge to much political activity in South Asia, underlining the power of religion in society, particularly when it is used to harden lines of social division in a world marked by scarcity and inequality.

In a whole range of artistic and literary activities there has been a great flowering of creativity, not least as methods of communication have developed. There has been throughout South Asia a literary explosion, feeding on developments in cheap printing and rising literacy. Using English and regional vernacular languages, many of which have been transformed through linguistic renaissances, publications now cover every conceivable genre, from political and religious analysis, to poetry and novels, the political press, women's magazines, and children's stories. In India alone the twentieth century has seen authors of international stature. Rabindranath Tagore, Bengali educationalist, novelist and poet, is one example, or Prem Chand, writing in modern Hindi and famous for his sensitive descriptions of rural life. More well known to contemporary Western audiences are such writers in English as the ironic non-fiction writer on India, Nirad C. Chaudhuri, R. K. Narayan (author of the Malgudi stories), and such portrayers of middle-class Indian life as Ruth Prawer Jhabwala and Anita Desai. There have also been developments in art and renewals of interest in Asian classical painting and dance; and, at the other end of the cultural spectrum the emergence of a local pop culture and of Asian film, the latter based primarily in Bombay. Film remains one of the most popular forms of mass entertainment on the subcontinent: its stars have great media exposure and in several instances have used their film careers as political launching pads. The growth in disposable income means that there are new patrons and consumers of art in various forms on a scale inconceivable in colonial times.

Finally, the creativity and ability of South Asians to undertake major life changes have been most apparent in their great movements outside their subcontinent in this century. South Asians had long been traders and travelling scholars, and in the nineteenth century had moved in significant numbers as indentured labourers to South Africa and the islands of the Caribbean. Later, in the mid-twentieth century, there occurred a major shift in this pattern of migration—the growth of substantial Asian settler populations in Britain and in North America particularly, as a result of movements of free people in search of jobs and better life chances for themselves and their children. People from Pakistan and Bangladesh who have settled in Britain have tended to be unskilled labourers, while Indians have been professionals or self-employed. Indians moving across the Atlantic have also been highly educated and skilled people, able to gain entry and residence visas as a result of their qualifications and potential contribution to American and Canadian society. In Britain Asian migration has been radically curtailed in the last quarter of this century but even so there are now far more South Asians in Britain than there ever were Britons in India. In 1991 out of a total British population of nearly 55 millions, about one and a half million were South Asians, among them Indians being the largest group. For British Asians, Britain is their home, particularly for those in the ethnic community (now over one half) who were born in Britain, for whom Britain has been their childhood world and English their major language of education and communication. South Asians are some of the major consumers of the state education system, they are increasingly forming an ethnic middle class, and their shops and services have changed the landscape, culture, and the public and political arena of many British cities. It is a process which demands cultural and political adaptation, as Asians evolve new British Asian identities, and as ethnically white Britons learn what it means to have Asian neighbours and colleagues, and for South Asia's domestic political and religious tensions to impinge on British life. Britain has since its imperial days become a plural society. At the close of the twentieth century the British can no longer afford an orientalist view of Asians: nor can they ignore events on the subcontinent as separate and distinct from their own Western world.

21 North Africa and the Middle East

ROGER OWEN

The use of the term 'Middle East' to cover the wide belt of countries ranging from Egypt to Iran derives from the strategic necessities of the Second World War, when the whole region was managed by the British, Free French, and Americans as a single military theatre for operational and supply purposes. From then on, the region was found to have sufficient cohesion to justify continued usage of the term, at least as far as the Arab countries were concerned, all of which shared a common language, a common history, and, to a large extent, a common religion. To this we can add the historical ties which linked the Arab world to the two major non-Arab, but largely Muslim, countries of the region, Turkey and Iran, and the fact that the predominantly Jewish State of Israel was founded there in 1948. The states of North Africa, from Libya to Morocco, are also considered to be part of the Arab world and shared many of its basic features such as Islam and the possession of oil.

At the beginning of the twentieth century the Middle East and North Africa contained a population of some 60 million to 65 million people, the majority living in lands controlled by the remnants of three empires, the Moroccan in the west, the Ottoman Turkish in the centre, and the Persian (Iranian) in the east. However, it had also become subject to increasing measures of European political control, whether in terms of the spheres of economic and cultural influence established by the British and French in the territories later to become Syria and Iraq or the more direct rule established by the French over Algeria and Tunisia and the British over Egypt, northern Somalia, and Sudan during the previous century. To this should be added the Anglo-Russian division of Iran into rival zones of influence institutionalized in 1907, the British treaties of protection over Kuwait, Bahrain, and a number of the tiny sheikhdoms along the Arab side of the Persian Gulf, and the beginnings of Italian colonization of southern Somalia in the 1880s and then the Libyan coast in 1911.

The First World War was the first of a number of defining events which led to new patterns of foreign control and the creation of the modern state system in the region. After the collapse of the Ottoman Empire under Allied military pressure, the Arab provinces were divided up into newly created Mandated territories, Syria and Lebanon passing under French control and Iraq, Palestine and Trans-Jordan (later Jordan) under British. These Mandates were run largely as colonies but with some international constraints imposed by the League of Nations, notably the British obligation to facilitate the establishment of a 'Jewish National Home' in Palestine. Elsewhere, Allied attempts to impose tighter political control over what remained of the Ottoman Empire in Anatolia and over Iran were thwarted by anti-colonial nationalist movements led by two forceful military commanders, Mustafa Kamal (later Ataturk) in the new state of Turkey (established in 1923) and Reza Khan (later Reza Shah), who seized power in Teheran in 1921. A third independent state then emerged in Egypt as a result of the British decision to withdraw from direct control in 1922, and a fourth in Saudi Arabia in 1926.

The next two defining events were the Second World War, followed quickly by the build-up of oil revenues in the states along the Persian Gulf. As far as the war was concerned, although the Anglo-French position finally held firm against the German military threat, post-war weakness and the strengthening of the US position in the region set in train a rapid process of independence, beginning with Syria, Lebanon, and Jordan in 1945–6, then moving to North Africa, with Italy's Libyan provinces in 1951, Tunisia in 1954, Sudan and Morocco in 1956, and a united Somalia in 1960. For the most part this transfer of power was accomplished with relatively little violence, but in three other cases, Palestine, Algeria and what was to become South Yemen, it was the subject of prolonged and bitter conflict.

The revelation of the extent of the Nazi Holocaust during the Second World War and the existence of large numbers of Jewish 'Displaced Persons' at the war's end meant that the drive for a Jewish state in Palestine became virtually unstoppable, particularly after it received strong American support. This put paid to British, and then international, efforts to find a way of peacefully partitioning the country between its Palestinian Arab and Jewish inhabitants, leading to a brief period of fighting between the two communities followed by a military attack on the new state of Israel by some of its Arab neighbours in May 1948. The result was an enforced partition of Palestine between Israel, Jordan—which was left in control of the hill country round Jerusalem or what was to become known as the 'West Bank'—and Egypt, which occupied the narrow Gaza Strip. Israel's military victories were also to result in the flight of nearly three-quarters of a million Palestinians, the majority to hastily constructed camps in Syria, Lebanon, Gaza, the West Bank, and Jordan. There they stayed, barred from return by an Israeli policy decision to readmit only a small portion of their number and unwilling or unable to be absorbed into the surrounding Arab societies.

The fighting in Algeria had more of the character of an anti-colonial insurrection, pitting the forces of the Front de Libération Nationale (FLN) against a large French military presence. This same character can also be seen in the way in which France largely succeeded in winning the war on the military front only to lose it politically when President de Gaulle decided that the struggle was imposing too great a strain on French society itself. What gave this struggle its particular intensity was the existence of a large community of French settlers in Algeria, the majority of whom chose, reluctantly, to leave in 1962. It also produced deep divisions within Algerian society itself which remained largely latent during the period of state-building by the FLN élite in the 1960s and 1970s, only to surface once again when political life began to open up in the late 1980s.

The withdrawal of the British from their colony in Aden and its surrounding protectorates was also a bloody affair ending in the seizure of power in 1967 by the National Liberation Front (NLF), which then proceeded to establish the one Marxist-inspired regime in the Middle East under its new name of the People's Democratic Republic of Yemen.

The impact of oil revenues can be seen in a second process of state-making and independence in the Persian Gulf. Beginning with the Al-Sabahs in Kuwait, the ruling families concluded that the best way to secure their own, as well as their people's, welfare was to use the money to create modern infrastructures and modern welfare services. This in turn demanded the import of large numbers of foreigners to carry out most of the necessary work. Fear that these foreign workers would swamp local interest led to a division of Gulf societies into those people with local nationality, who were given near monopoly control over industry, commerce, and the ownership of fixed assets, and the permanent outsiders, who were simply there to provide the services they required. Then, as the Gulf states developed, they also obtained their independence from British tutelage and control, beginning with Kuwait in 1961 followed by Bahrain and the states of the newly formed United Arab Emirates (Abu Dhabi, Dubai, and five others) as Britain withdrew its military forces from the region in 1971.

Once established in the decades after the Second World War, the newly independent regimes found themselves in a region which, though sharing many common features with the rest of the non-European world, also contained certain specific features of its own. Three were of particular importance. The first was the close ties which connected the Arab states of the region, a factor which created contradictory forces making for both unity and disunity in about equal measure. To begin with, Arab efforts concentrated on utilizing the institutional mechanisms of the League of Arab States (founded in 1945) to promote schemes for mutual cooperation. However, this was then made more difficult by the rise to power and influence of Abdul Nasser's Egypt, which gave a great boost to popular Arab nationalism while, at the same time, causing considerable concern among the leaders of weaker regimes, such as those in Lebanon and Saudi Arabia, who felt threatened by the new phenomenon. The one undoubted success of the movement was the brief experiment in union between Egypt and Syria between 1958 and 1961. But similar attempts between other states were even more short-lived and gave way to an atmosphere in which regimes were prepared to consider only those schemes for cooperation that left all of their own sovereignty and control intact.

The second factor was the continuing hostility between Israel and its Arab neighbours. This was not only responsible for major wars in 1956, 1967, and 1973 but also provided another unsurmountable challenge to Arab diplomacy, producing as much disunity as unity and allowing only fitful support for the Palestinians, most notably the decision to allow the formation of the Palestine Liberation Organization (PLO) in 1964.

The third and final factor was the rapid increase in oil wealth among the Gulf states and Libya, particularly after the considerable increase in its price in 1973–4. Some of this wealth was then spread to the other Arab states of the region by a combination of direct aid and the remittances sent home by the some 4 million Egyptians, Jordanians, Lebanese, Palestinians, Yemanis, and others who had found work there by the early 1980s.

One consequence of these three factors was that the cold-war competition between the USA and the Soviet Union for power and influence in the non-European world had a particularly strong impact in the Middle East, with the USA supporting Turkey and Iran against a possible Soviet threat, as well as Israel, Morocco, and the important oil state of Saudi Arabia. The Soviet Union responded with its own economic and military support for Egypt, beginning in 1955, followed by Syria, Iraq, Libya, and South Yemen. This was to create a situation which was of some short-term benefit to those states which, like Egypt, were able to play off one side against the other. However in the longer run it helped to fuel a Middle Eastern arms race which absorbed a growing proportion of local resources in military expenditure as well as producing a significant increase in the tension between Israel and its Arab neighbours, a vital factor contributing to the outbreak of the June war of 1967.

Such was the context in which the newly independent Middle Eastern regimes began that general process of state- and nation-building which they shared with most of the rest of the non-European world. This process had begun in the 1920s with Ataturk's attempt to create a homogeneous Turkish nation following the death or expulsion of the vast majority of the Greek and Armenian inhabitants of Anatolia during and after the First World War, a process which we would now term 'ethnic cleansing'. It was started at the same time in Iran as well, where Reza Shah used his army to create a strongly centralized state for the first time in modern Iranian history. In addition, both rulers also began to use their newly built state machinery to direct schemes for national economic development, a process which gained added impetus in the 1930s in response to the collapse of their export prices and the enforced decline in their international trade as a result of the Great Depression. The Depression was also responsible for Reza Shah's challenge to the monopoly position enjoyed by the Anglo-Persian Oil Company in 1932, a confrontation which produced a small increase in royalty payments from 16 to 20 per cent of total profits.

The few nominally independent Arab states—Saudi Arabia, North Yemen, Iraq after the British Mandate came to an end in 1931—lacked both the freedom and the resources to follow along the same path during the inter-war period. By 1945, however, the promise of large oil revenues as well as the progressive retreat of the colonial powers seemed to offer more hopeful prospects for state-building. But the first steps towards the creation of new national institutions were largely undermined by the shock which followed the Arab defeat by the Israelis in 1948–9 as well as by the failure of their politicians to cope with what were identified as the pressing political, economic, and social problems of the day. The result was a series of military *coups*, in Syria in 1949, Egypt in 1952, Sudan and Iraq in 1958, North Yemen in 1962, and Libya and Somalia in 1969, which began the process of replacing the governments dominated by landlords or by tribal chiefs with powerful authoritarian regimes focusing on populist policies of rapid economic and social development, usually in the name of what came to be known as Arab Socialism.

Even those regimes where family rule managed to survive—Morocco, Jordan, Saudi Arabia, and the Gulf—adopted similar strategies of state-led development with little tolerance of opposition. The same was also true of Tunisia and Algeria, where the groups which came out on top in the struggle for independence proceeded to entrench themselves in power at the centre of what was virtually a one-party state. In these circumstances, the existence of parliaments and party politics was confined only to those Arab states such as Lebanon, where it was an essential component of its system of balancing the interests of its major Christian and Muslim communities, or Morocco, Jordan, and Kuwait, where the rulers made intermittent use of a form of limited democracy as an adjunct to their own power.

This left Turkey, Israel, and Iran—for a brief period during and after the Second World War—to attempt to institutionalize systems of multi-party politics. In Turkey this stage was ushered in by the decisive defeat of Ataturk's Republican People's Party in the hotly disputed national election of 1950 and its replacement by the rival Democrat Party. However, progress was not smooth and in 1960 allegations that the Democrats were going to establish their own system of one-party rule led to the first of a series of three military interventions which punctuated Turkish political life at regular intervals until 1980. As might be expected, the officers who made these *coups* tended to blame the civilian politicians for the frequent crises. But this can just as easily be put down to the difficulties of trying to maintain a system of representational democracy in a country undergoing a rapid process of economic and social transformation marked by successful industrialization and a huge movement of the rural population into the towns.

In Israel the practice of party politics had begun in the pre-state period in Palestine and proved resilient enough to cope with the huge problems of the early independence period, notably the near-doubling of the population during the first four years as a result of Jewish immigration from Europe and the Middle East. Much of the success of these early efforts must be attributed to the role played by the Mapai (later Labour) Party under David Ben Gurion, which not only led the government coalition which remained in power until 1977 but was also instrumental in creating a general consensus among the majority of Israelis as to the priorities to be pursued by the new state. These included, at home, state management of a mixed economy and a compromise with the orthodox religious parties in matters of education and personal status and, regionally, a policy of immediate military response to any Arab cross-border attacks or armed infiltration. The small Palestinian Arab population which had resisted flight occupied an uneasy position within these new arrangements, being given the vote but kept under a harsh military law until 1965 and forbidden from serving in the Israeli armed forces.

Lastly, in Iran, the brief hope that democracy might revive after the Allied decision to depose Reza Shah in 1941 soon foundered on a combination of fractious party politics, repeated foreign interference, and the growing assertion of authority by the new Shah, Mohamed Reza, who used his control over the army to rebuild royal power. The one setback to this process was the skilful use of the widespread popular resentment at the privileged position of the British Oil Company (renamed the Anglo-Iranian Oil Company (AIOC), in 1935) by a group of politicians led by Muhammad Mossadeq, who obtained sufficient support in parliament to nationalize Anglo-Iranian's Iranian assets in 1950. There then followed a protracted series of negotiations brought to a premature end by the US-assisted anti-Mossadeq *coup* in 1953, after which the Shah was able to establish a virtual dictatorship helped by the ever-increasing oil revenues that flowed into the country once an agreement to replace AIOC by an international consortium had been completed.

By the 1960s it looked as though the existing Middle Eastern state system had been reasonably well established, with strong governments either firmly entrenched or in the process of becoming so throughout the region. However, it then experienced a number of shocks which posed a severe challenge to the existing order while encouraging a variety of oppositional forces to express themselves. The first of these was the Six Day War (1967), which not only produced a staggering military defeat for Egypt, Jordan, and Syria, but also led to the loss of a considerable amount of Arab land to the Israelis, including Egypt's Sinai peninsula and the Jordan-controlled West Bank. Even though Egypt and Syria were able to perform better in the second round of fighting in 1973, the prestige and authority attached to their Arab nationalist, Arab socialist, policies were much reduced, and they soon began to experience real pressure from two different directions: from exponents of more open, more liberal economic policies, on the one hand, and from religious forces, on the other.

The 1967 war also had a profound impact on Israel and the Palestinians. In the case of Israel, the nature of its huge military victory combined with the capture of the West Bank, which many Israelis regarded as the heartland of Jewish history, produced a mood of religious fervour that found practical expression among a number of groups determined to establish settlements there as quickly as possible. It also contributed to the undermining of the old Labour-inspired consensus and so paved the way for the victory of the Likud opposition in the 1977 national elections.

The comprehensive Arab defeat produced a new mood among the Palestinians as well, bringing huge numbers of volunteers to Yasser Arafat's newly organized Fateh organization dedicated to the concept of armed struggle against Israel. This both allowed Arafat and his group to take over the main institutions of the PLO in 1969 and then to begin the long process of creating a new Palestinian political élite able to guide the national movement towards its goal of establishing a state on any part of liberated Palestinian land. However, the first attempts to organize attacks on Israel, first from Jordan, then from Lebanon, were largely ineffective and had the side effect of drawing the PLO into violent confrontation with the Jordanian army and subsequently with the largely Christian Lebanese militias, which saw it as a threat to their own position and their country's sovereignty. Then, as the ability of the PLO to inflict significant military damage waned, the role played by those Palestinians on the inside, under Israeli occupation, began to assume a much greater importance, culminating in the largely unarmed act of collective resistance which began in December 1987 under the general name of the Intifada.

The second shock to the Middle Eastern state system was the sharp rise in oil prices following the 1973 Yom Kippur War. This had contradictory effects. For those states such as Iran, Iraq, and Algeria with big oil exports, the increased revenues were used to push on with ambitious programmes of economic and social development. Similar policies were also pursued in the less well-populated states such as Libya, Saudia Arabia, and the Gulf sheikhdoms, although with a smaller emphasis on industrialization and a much greater reliance on foreign labour. As for the states with little or no oil of their own, the impact was more varied. Whereas Arab regimes such as Egypt, Syria, and Jordan could hope for a share of the new wealth through aid and workers' remittances, Israel and Turkey experienced real difficulty in paying for their oil imports; one of the factors which forced them to begin a long and painful process of economic retrenchment.

The stresses and strains produced by these events led to a number of outbreaks of fierce domestic conflict. One was the Lebanese Civil War, which raged from 1975 to 1990, fuelled by repeated interventions from outside, notably by the Syrians and the Israelis. Another was the increasing factional violence in Turkey, which was only brought to an end by the country's third episode of military intervention in 1980. But certainly the most spectacular development was the overthrow of the Shah of Iran by a long process of civil disobedience which found its eventual leader in the Ayatollah Khomeini, a Shiite Muslim cleric, who provided the inspiration for an unyielding drive for political power. Once the Shah had been forced to leave the country in January 1979, the revolutionaries set about creating a modern Islamic state run increasingly by clerical personnel.

The impact of these dramatic events in Iran was felt throughout the Middle East. Religious radicals everywhere felt emboldened to try to imitate a movement which had managed to overthrow so powerful a dictator and posed brief but serious military challenges to the regimes in Syria and Saudi Arabia as well as carrying out the spectacular assassination of President Sadat of Egypt at a military parade in 1981. Meanwhile, the influence of the revolution encouraged a rise in Shiite militancy which found expression in the creation of new militias and movements in

Lebanon and also produced a major response in the invasion of Iran in September 1980 by the forces of the new Iraqi leader, Saddam Hussein, determined to topple the revolutionary regime before it managed to undermine him. But this was a war which neither side could win, dragging on for eight years at a cost of perhaps a million dead, causing consternation and fear among the rulers of the small Arab sheikhdoms and bringing large numbers of US forces back to the Gulf for the first time since the Second World War.

Developments in the 1980s produced two new sets of related challenges. One was economic. As far as the Arab states were concerned, a share of the oil wealth had allowed a number of them such as Egypt, Tunisia, and Morocco to postpone necessary economic reform. But, once prices began to decline sharply in real terms, many of them were forced to seek financial support from the World Bank and the International Monetary Fund (IMF) in exchange for promises to open up their economies to outside forces, to reduce state control, and to encourage private-sector activity. Turkey followed the same path with greater success, due in part to the fact that the military intervention produced a period of strong and reasonably effective government, and in part to the fact that the oil boom and the Iran–Iraq War opened up huge markets for Turkish exports. Israel, on the other hand, suffered greatly from a number of ill-thought-out attempts at economic deregulation, while its long series of coalition governments from 1984 to 1992 lacked the strength to tackle the more deep-rooted structural problems posed by decades of statist control.

The second challenge came from increasingly vocal religious forces like those behind the military *coup* which led to the establishment of an Islamic regime in Sudan in 1989. Other religious groups were quick to establish themselves as the main opponents of many of the existing Arab regimes. Attempts to cope with this situation took a number of forms. Some regimes, such as the Syrian and the Saudi, were forced to repress serious armed challenges to their authority while, at the same time, taking care to stress their own credentials as good Muslim rulers. Others sought to accommodate what they identified as the more moderate religious elements within a revived party system, either directly, as in Jordan after 1989, or indirectly, as in Egypt, Tunisia, and Morocco.

The century's last great challenge was provided by the combination of the collapse of the Soviet Union and then the Gulf War of January–February 1991 in which the United States, Britain, and France, together with a range of Arab allies, were successful in expelling the Iraq forces which had occupied Kuwait the previous August. Most regimes were quick to position themselves to try to take advantage of these events. Some, like the rulers of the Gulf states, hastened to place themselves under a permanent US security umbrella. Others, like those in Egypt and Syria, sought to derive financial advantage by obtaining large sums of money for protecting the oil producers from attack or, in the case of Egypt, by securing sufficient debt relief from its grateful foreign creditors to embark on its programme of economic structural adjustment in earnest. In contrast, the few regimes which supported Iraq suffered a dramatic loss of aid as well as the expulsion of most of their labour migrants from the Gulf state, a crisis situation which helped to promote the union between the two Yemens, beginning in 1990 as both sides sought to bolster their battered political positions.

But for many of the Arab peoples it was quite another matter. The spectacle of Muslim Arab states fighting each other, and of foreign military intervention on such a large scale, aroused popular feelings throughout the region, fuelling existing resentments against their governments and their alliance with the West. Attempts to head off such criticism led the Al-Sabah family in Kuwait to revive parliamentary life once it returned from exile, while even the King of Saudi Arabia was persuaded, reluctantly, to appoint a small Consultative Council. Elsewhere, the intensification of armed Islamic opposition in Egypt and Tunisia helped to blur the division which the regimes had sought to maintain between religious moderates and extremists, placing them in a position in which they often seemed to be at war with religion itself.

An even more spectacular example of the power of Islamic militants to obtain a large popular following was provided by Algeria, where President Chadli's decision to allow the main religious grouping, the Front Islamique de Salut (FIS), to contest the 1991 elections led the army to intervene just when the Islamicists looked like winning a majority, sparking off a violent response by armed extremists against the security forces and the more secular elements in Algerian society.

A last result of the new situation produced by the Gulf War was an intensification of the claims of the region's two main stateless peoples, the Palestinians and the Kurds, for accommodation within the existing state system. In the case of the Palestinians, the breakthrough came with the US government's efforts to solve the Arab–Israeli dispute once and for all by persuading all sides to attend a conference in Madrid in October–November 1991. Further progress was made as a result of the replacement of the Likud government by Labour after the June 1992 elections. The result was the beginning of a long-drawn-out series of bilateral negotiations culminating in the 'Oslo Accords' followed by the Israeli–Palestine Agreement of September 1993 which led to the establishment of a Palestinian National Authority in Gaza and parts of the West Bank.

Kurdish pressure for recognition of their national rights in Turkey and Iraq was not so rewarded. The result was an intensification of the armed campaign conducted by the guerrilla movement known as the PKK (Turkish Workers' Party) against the Turkish security forces in the mountainous region of the East. In neighbouring Iraq the local Kurdish people enjoyed an uneasy coexistence with Saddam Hussein's regime, protected by an Allied air umbrella but divided among themselves and subject to increasing outside pressure from the Turks, the Iranians, and the leadership of the PKK.

The mixed reactions of the Gulf War provided a graphic illustration of some of the basic features of the Middle East at the end of the twentieth century. On the one hand, the fact that almost all the peoples and governments across the region were involved, directly or indirectly, in the struggle provided testimony to the continued existence of those ties of religion, sentiment, and sheer proximity which had always given it cohesion. On the other, the war also revealed fissures and divisions which suggested that the important processes leading to ever greater fragmentation were also becoming more strong. These included the various attempts to create viable subregional groupings such as the Gulf Cooperation Council, the Maghrib Union in North Africa, and a common market or customs union uniting Israel, the Palestinians, and Jordan with some of their Arab neighbours. But, increasingly, such attempts were cross-cut by considerations of domestic political advantage which led the Gulf States, for example, to vie with each other for US protection or those of North Africa, such as Tunisia and Morocco, to seek bilateral economic arrangements with the European Union (EU) under the umbrella of the proposed Euro-Mediterranean Free Trade Area announced in Barcelona in November 1995.

Another trend was the process by which interstate conflict had been replaced by internal struggles which pitted governments against various types of domestic opposition, whether religious, liberal, or separatist. In some cases, this resulted in either the destruction of the central government itself, as in Somalia after 1991, or the loss of control of large sections of the national territory, as in Sudan. In others, regimes were forced to devote a huge security effort simply to stay in power, leaving little space for political, as opposed to economic, reform.

What made domestic situations even more complex and fluid was the breakdown of most of the old consensuses which had been built up around the statebuilding projects of the founding fathers, whether an Ataturk, a Nasser, or a Ben Gurion, or founding élites such as Algeria's FLN or the military members of the Syrian Ba'th. Such projects had many achievements to their name in terms of welfare and general economic progress. But, increasingly, the founding élites and their successors had been unable to manage the task of combining steady economic progress with the creation of the institutions required to encourage new and more appropriate forms of accountability and popular participation. The result was a vacuum, to be filled in some cases by religious forces, in others by a more discordant set of ideologies and interests in which women's groups, minorities, community associations, and others all vied for popular attention and support. Some spoke the language of civil society, others of human rights, others again of the need for authenticity and cultural renewal in the face of a triumphant Westernization.

To the first Middle Eastern nationalists, independence had seemed to offer the possibility of national revival coupled with the opportunity to compete as equals in a world of nation states. But the reality, as elsewhere, was somewhat more complex. The vast majority of the region's now 400 million people are certainly better off, better educated, and longer-lived than they were when the century began. In the Arab states, for example, infant mortality rates were cut in half between 1965 and 1991, while a child born in 1990 could expect to live thirteen years longer than his or her parents. But, on the debit side, the states they inhabit have often been built on the forced expulsion or enforced inclusion of various minority groups. Wars, either local or imposed from without, have created added misery while producing major economic dislocations and new floods of refugees. National consensuses have only been maintained by authoritarian regimes which have relied on torture and fear to keep their citizens in line.

Few Middle Eastern families can have been untouched by these events in the twentieth century. For the majority, many of the promises which accompanied independence, whether in terms of dignity or development, freedom or justice, still remain unfulfilled. It is true that the beginning of the twenty-first century contains some promise of improvement in terms of an Arab/Israeli peace agreement and greater liberalization of the Islamic revolution in Iran. There will also be Middle Easterners who are well positioned to benefit from the opportunities provided by eonomic globalization. Nevertheless, the century just past will certainly be remembered as one in which pain and disappointment were among its most dominant themes.

As often happens, it is the novelists and poets, rather than the historians, whose independent voices provide a sharper testimony to this aspect of twentieth-century life. Those who search for such themes will certainly find them forcefully recorded in the novels of writers such as the Egyptians Naguib Mahfouz and Yusuf Idris, the Iraqi Abdel-Rahman Munif, the Israelis, A. B. Yehoshua and Amos Oz, and the Turk, Yasha Kamal. But for clarity of vision there has been nothing like the work of the century's outstanding Arabic language poets such as Abd al-Wahhab al-Bayyati, Mahmoud Darwish, and Muhammad al-Maghut whose poem, 'An Arab Traveller in a Space Ship' seems to say it all:

> Scientists and technicians!
> Give me a ticket to space
> I've been sent by my sad country
> In the name of its widows, its children and its aged
> To ask for the price of a free ticket to the sky
> I don't bear money in my hands . . . but tears
>
> No place for me?
> Put me at the rear of the ship
> Outside on top
> I'm a peasant, used to all that
> I'm a peasant and used to all that
> I shall not offend a single cloud
> All I want is to reach God
> In the quickest possible way
> To put a whip in His hand
> That he may rouse us to revolt!*

* Translated by May Jayyusi and John Heath Stubbs, quoted from Salma Khadra Jayyusi, *Modern Arabic Poetry: An Anthology* (New York: Columbia University Press, 1987).

22 Africa

TERENCE RANGER

It would be impossible to provide a full or accurate narrative for black Africa's twentieth-century history. Africa is much larger than Europe; its environment is much more varied (from desert to rainforest); before colonialism it was divided into dozens of polities and after it into more than fifty territories. The colonial period itself offered a misleading simplicity. One could then talk about Portuguese, French, German, and British Africa, about British 'Indirect Rule' as contrasted to French 'Direct Rule', or about German militarism and Portuguese assimilation. But these generalizations thinly concealed an enormous variety. In 'British Africa' the Sudan could hardly have been more differently administered than Kenya; in 'French Africa' Senegal was a complete contrast to Gabon. When colonialism gave way to independent African states, the diversity of Africa persistently burst through such positive assertions as 'African personality' or such negative ones as 'African despotism'. Given the outrageous simplification of Africa's realities offered in the European and North American media today, the first duty of any historian is to differentiate and complicate.

Of course, there *has* been a process of simplification going on during the twentieth century, as black Africa has been further 'integrated' into the world economy; as millions more Africans have been brought into the world religions of Islam and Christianity; as states have emerged with recognizable bureaucracies, presidencies, and foreign ministries. Territorial African nationalism, though much criticized by both enemies and friends of African emancipation, has created new units of administration, patronage, and loyalty. These processes have often been described as 'modernization', a theme implicit in much of this book as a whole, and one to which I shall repeatedly return as a way into the complexities of black Africa in the twentieth century. I shall do so within a narrative which roughly relates to the modern history of much of black Africa, though probably fitting exactly to the experience of none of its constituent territories.

The twentieth century dawned with black Africa neatly divided on the map into colonial territories. Relatively little of it, however, was effectively administered by its notional rulers. The conquest of Africa was a long-drawn-out process. Its final achievement can be dated only to the 1920s when what has been described as the flexible and living 'tradition' of equatorial cultural and political systems was finally broken, to be replaced by colonial bureaucracy and invented tribal 'custom'. In many parts of black Africa the pitched battles and wars which marked the late-nineteenth-century European invasion—Omdurman, the French wars against Samory, the Zulu wars, the 1893 Matabele War, and so on—gave way in the twentieth century to piecemeal local conquests, village by village. This process was disrupted by African uprisings against the new colonial order: the *Menelamba* rising in Madagascar in 1896 and the Ndebele and Shona risings of the same year; the 1905 Maji-Maji rising in the south of German East Africa; the 1904–7 Herero and Nama risings in German South-West Africa; the 1905 Bambatha rising in Zululand, and many others.

Colonial conquest was accompanied by two great and interconnected processes, one ecological and the other ideological. Almost everywhere, colonial conquest was simultaneous with epidemic human and cattle disease and with large population losses. It was also accompanied by the spread of mission Christianity and of Islam. Both of these great faiths had been in Africa long before colonialism, of course. Islam had existed on the East African coast for many centuries and had long interacted with states in the interior of West Africa; Christianity had been a North African faith, had flourished in Nubia and Ethiopia, and had taken on a Roman Catholic coloration in the first European missionary movement of the sixteenth and seventeenth centuries. In the nineteenth century the second great Protestant wave of European and North American missions had often established a presence in the interior of Africa before formal colonial occupation. But the great expansion of both faiths began at the end of the nineteenth century. At the same time there were striking changes in African 'traditional' religions primarily as a response to disease, drought, and the perception of alien ideas and cultures and only secondarily as resistance to Christianity, Islam, and colonialism.

These religious changes can be seen as various approaches to modernization. This is clearest in the case of missionary Christianity, which responded to David Livingstone's slogan of 'Christianity, Commerce, and Civilization'. Before the imposition of colonial rule, there were modernizing alliances between white and black missionaries and African élites. In the Merina state of nineteenth-century Madagascar aristocrats seized upon the congregationalist patterns of the London Missionary Society to construct a centralized 'Christian' state, with a national system of education and with congregations used as units for taxation, conscription, and forced labour. In the Bamangwato state of late-nineteenth-century Bechuanaland, Khama the Great carried through a Tudor-style revolution, reducing the powers of the aristocracy, creating a Protestant state church; asserting royal control over a 'liberalized' economy. His biographer has written without irony of Khama's 'personal puritan–capitalistic ethic'. On the coast of West Africa

Christian intellectuals were inspired by the modernizing yet traditionalist example of Japan—as the Gold Coast intellectual historian of the Fanti Confederation of 1871, J. M. Sarbah, put it, Japan had 'shown it possible to retain one's national costume and excel in wisdom and knowledge'.

Others of the West Coast intellectuals were inspired by Islam, which they saw as more African and hence more able to produce a truly African modernization than Christianity. Indeed, in East Africa, where the expansion of Islam was most marked in the late nineteenth and early twentieth centuries, the Sufi brotherhoods represented an alternative way of responding to social and economic change. Christian missionaries proclaimed the emancipation of slaves but condoned the exploitation of 'free' labour. Sufi teachers brought ex-slaves and women into a new community, announcing the purity and superiority of the poor and oppressed. Even the developments within African religion can be seen as modernizing, with the emergence of prophets and with systematic conceptual change along the axes of ecology, time, community, and definitions of evil.

All these were ideas and developments which did not necessarily imply European rule. In the event, of course, the colonial invasion pre-empted any autonomous modernization. Many missionaries, uneasy at their exploitation by chiefs and aristocrats in responsive societies, or resentful at their exclusion from unresponsive ones, welcomed the colonial conquest. It was certainly possible for German missionaries in South-West Africa to believe that German imperial rule was the best means to civilize Africans.

These South-West African missionaries were profoundly shaken by the brutalities and land seizures which provoked the Herero and Nama risings, and by the virtual genocide which followed them. This was, of course, an exceptional case. But everywhere early colonialism as a method of modernizing Africa was very imperfect, distorting in practice and half-hearted in ideology. None of the colonial powers invested heavily in Africa. The Portuguese had to farm out great regions of their colonial territories to chartered companies; much more British capital was invested in the infrastructure and manufacturing of Latin American countries than in their own colonies in Africa. Colonial economies, whether extractive, agricultural, or mineral, were exploitative and depended on forced labour or on lowly paid migrants. The roots not so much of development as of underdevelopment can be traced to this early colonial period. Worse was to come.

The complex colonial incursion and conquest was mostly achieved without war between European interests. To this there were two great exceptions—European wars fought amongst and profoundly affecting African populations. The first exception was the South African (Boer) War of 1899–1902, which pitched Imperial and South African British against Afrikaners. The second exception was the First World War of 1914–18, which brought to German East Africa and the territories bordering it four years of extreme violence, disruption and death.

In the German East African campaign, Africans were soldiers and porters—and suffered terrible casualties; they were also spies, as the German and imperial forces staggered about in the bush, desperately needing intelligence; they were barking dogs, as they took the opportunity to harry retreating Europeans, and they were sheep as they suffered the reprisals of returning Europeans.

The East African Campaign affected most of black Africa. Troops from the Gold Coast and from the Belgian Congo and Southern Rhodesia and South Africa were deployed there; porters from Kenya and Nyasaland and northern Rhodesia and Mozambique. It was the climax of European violence. Forced recruitment for porters triggered off a series of African uprisings, varying from the dignified protest and utopian uprising of the frustrated modernizer John Chilembwe in Nyasaland in 1915 to the rallying of chiefs and spirit mediums in the 1917 Makombe rising in central Mozambique. It did much to discredit original missionary hopes of an imperial civilizing mission. 'The war has taught the natives', wrote a German missionary, to see 'the white man from a point of view from which he never knew him before. The native has seen him in his hatred, his hypocrisy, brutality, dishonesty and immorality. He could often justly say "The blacks are better men".'

It was a dreadful irony that the experience which most tied black Africa to world history was the influenza epidemic of late 1918, which fell with savagery on prisoner-of-war camps, demobilization centres, urban locations, and mining compounds alike. In a few weeks influenza killed between 2 and 5 per cent of the population in every colony in Africa.

After the First World War the victorious powers parcelled out the 'trusteeship' of the German colonies between themselves, but hardly had the energy to pretend to develop them. The war was followed by a series of economic depressions which forced administrations to cut expenditure to the bone and missionary societies to close down schools and churches. In the 1930s producer prices fell by more than 60 per cent; markets and employment collapsed; in settler colonies savagely discriminatory measures were instituted to subsidize white farmers and cattle ranchers at the expense of the black. Across Africa there were tax riots, rural revolts, and boycotts of the market by cash-crop producers.

The colonial powers responded with introversion and conservatism. Earlier optimistic hopes of modernizing change were abandoned. In settler colonies there was a movement from 'civilization to segregation'. At best, the whites thought, Africans could occupy a 'different sort of civilization from our own'. In the rest of British Africa there was resort to the alliance with 'traditional' authorities dignified by the name of Indirect Rule. There was much appeal to the mystique of the Imperial Monarchy. Colonial administrators behaved—and were expected to behave—with autocratic paternalism. British colonies might be run in the now somewhat sluggish interests of metropolitan and settler capital, but administrators had to hold the ring between these and the interests of the African peasantry. In Africa senior administrators had to behave more like gentlemen than it was any longer possible to do in Britain itself.

Africans related to them in familiar aristocratic subordinate roles—as house servants, as foot soldiers, as honest peasants. Administrators came to dislike indigenous modernizers: mission-educated clerks and teachers; chiefs who aspired to transform their societies rather than merely play their role in the

Indirect Rule system; aristocrats who wanted to achieve constitutional reform. They came to glorify—and largely to invent—African 'tradition'; to define Africans as 'tribesmen' rather than as citizens. Appeals by African Christian would-be modernizers to the progressive connotations of Imperial Monarchy were increasingly made in vain.

With variations these patterns were replicated in the rest of colonial Africa. Belgian ethnographers, it has been said, 'provided the blueprint of a spurious, segmentary, hierarchized, patrilineal society for use in the Congo', and the French saw local peoples as 'families, grouped in villages'.

Yet, despite all this self-conscious conservatism there *were* changes between the two world wars. The opening-up of the copper mines in Katanga and Northern Rhodesia attracted large labour forces and created new urban centres. Colonial administrators strove as hard as they could to prevent these African miners from being 'detribalized', ignoring the long history of pre-colonial urbanization, but they could not prevent many Africans from moving to and fro between one mine or town and another.

Despite schools closing down, numbers of educated Africans grew. But newly literate African men and women had to develop ideas about the modern world on the basis of a very narrow intellectual provision. Missionary responsibility for African education meant that the books which dominated African imaginations up to the Second World War were those which had shaped Europe before the twentieth century—the Bible pre-eminently, but also *The Pilgrim's Progress*, together with simple histories of the Reformation or of the Protestant nations. For some Catholics even these texts were dangerously modernizing. 'Both as a Catholic and a colonial', wrote a Rwandan white in 1925, 'I cannot see any value in Protestant education . . . it ignores the special character of our primitive races and hands out spiritual food which revolutionizes their way of thinking, creates anarchy . . . and gives rise to extreme individualism.' African Catholics were reared on a diet of nineteenth-century devotional literature.

Most Africans themselves joined in readily with further imagining the ethnic identities which missionary language work and administrative convenience had done much to invent. For many of them, however, 'tribes' had a modernizing rather than a conservative potential. The foremost ethnic imaginers were the most educated rather than the most 'traditional'. Africans who were content to work within the limitations of missionary education, or unable to escape them, nevertheless made their own innovative and sometimes revolutionary uses of the Bible or even of *The Pilgrim's Progress*. Some African proto-intellectuals eagerly devoured the prophetic and anti-imperial literature of the North American inspired Watch Tower Bible and Tract Society. Some passed Garveyite and other black American publications from hand to hand. Yet others experimented with religious innovations—with Apostolic and Ethiopian independent churches or with great movements of renewal and cleansing within African religion. A small minority had access to the world outside Africa and aspired to equality of opportunity within modern nations. It was quite mistaken to suppose that the great majority of Africans were locked in customary stasis between the world wars.

The Second World War of 1939–45 had a very different impact upon both colonialism and black Africa than the first. There was very little fighting in black Africa itself. In the First World War it was only the Senegalese *tirailleurs* who served outside black Africa. Now members of African regiments and Labour Brigades saw service in North Africa, in Italy, in Germany itself, and in the Burma Campaign. These men were recruited in the name of a war for democracy and against racist dictatorship. Grandiose declarations like the Atlantic Charter raised the hopes of African intellectuals. All over Africa they declared that the price of African loyalty to the Empire must be development and democracy. In this way, the dream of modernization revived among Africans.

It revived among Europeans too. Africa was plainly coming out of recession. Instead of the great population losses of early colonialism which climaxed in the First World War, the 1940s saw the first realization of Africa's rapid population growth. Between 1920 and the late 1940s the population of the whole of Africa increased from some 142 million to 200 million. This did not alarm administrators, who once again wanted African labour for industrial growth and rural development. The war was accompanied by greatly increased demand for agricultural and industrial products. It was followed, not by the usual post-war slump, but by continuing high prices for African products. Settlers began to believe that the long-awaited golden age was at hand.

The metropolitan governments, too, put their hopes in Africa. Exploitation of the French African colonies had been critical to both the Vichy and the de Gaulle regimes. Britain planned to recoup in Africa the opportunities lost with the inevitable independence of India. Even the Portuguese began to stir and to plan for more rational and less coercive cash-crop production. In Mozambique by the 1940s food shortages, peasant flight and environmental degradation had produced a crisis in rural areas. Allen Isaacman has described how a 'new cotton policy began to take shape immediately after World War II . . . a combination of social engineering, scientific farming and nutritional science'.

The war had stimulated state planning and direction of the economy in Europe and this was now extended to Africa. What historians have come to call 'the second colonial invasion' took place almost everywhere in black Africa. This invasion took many forms. In settler Africa it took the form of eviction of tenants and 'squatters' from land so that white farmers could exploit the new opportunities. In the zones allocated to African peasant food or cash-crop production it took the form of an incursion of thousands of technical experts, determined to reallocate land more efficiently, to insist on labour-expensive conservation methods, to issue commands on how to farm intensively on irrigation schemes. Interventions of this sort had already begun in West Africa before the Second World War, but after it they became almost universal. The French invested public funds to develop infrastructure and primary production in their African colonies; for the first time the

Belgians produced a development plan for the Congo in 1948 which aimed to 'stabilize' both urban and rural classes.

The impact of this 'second invasion' can be illustrated by one case—that of the sleepy mandated territory, Tanganyika. Suddenly in the late 1940s the whole range of colonial interventions took place there. There was direct state farming in the notorious and disastrous Groundnut Scheme. There was alienation to whites in the Meru ranching scheme. There was intervention in African production in the Mbulu Development Scheme, the Usukuma Development Scheme, the Mlalo Rehabilitation Scheme, the Uluguru Land Usage Scheme, the Iringa Dipping Scheme, and many others. The terminology is eloquent. Development was back on the agenda and this time was not left to private investment or missionary philanthropy but was the direct concern of the modernizing state.

This new colonial policy needed more capital than Europe had invested in Africa ever before. It also needed 'new men', both on the white and on the black side. The old-style aristocratic conservatives in colonial administration gave way to men who could work with and coordinate a team of interventionist experts. The 'customary' authority of chiefs was now less relevant than the entrepreneurial zeal of African master-farmers and businessmen. In the north-eastern province of Northern Rhodesia the government encouraged settlement by entrepreneurial black farmers—including returning soldiers—on land outside registered chiefly villages. Even in West Africa, where opportunities for 'new men' had long existed, the post-war years gave new incentives.

There were many Africans ready to take part in this renewed push to modernization. Even in the inter-war years many Africans had obtained a functional education; had struggled hard to maintain 'the peasant option'; had established themselves and their families in the towns. Nor were these would-be African modernizers merely a small minority, working against the apathy or resistance of the masses. They had a great resource in the continuing flexibility of pre-colonial African institutions and ideas. Thus twentieth-century African urban culture was based on the associational forms of rural Africa. African Christian pioneers combined their literacy with command of powerful oral modes. Master farmers and business grew out of pre-colonial 'Big Men'. African teachers, evangelists, and entrepreneurs debated along with chiefs and elders about the meanings of 'tribe' and 'tradition'.

So all over Africa there were people ready to respond to development opportunities. In north-eastern Northern Rhodesia the young Kenneth Kaunda and other ex-teachers and clerks at first tried to take advantage of government rural development schemes. The Chinsali Youngmen's Farming Association, of which he was Treasurer, aimed 'to set a practical example to our fellow Africans . . . by applying modern methods of farming and thereby helping to uplift the area . . . [and] to work in collaboration with Development Officers, following their methods of doing things and doing all in our power to enlighten their work in our district by advising them as to how Africans should be approached'. In the Limpopo Valley of southern Mozambique there developed a group of *Machambeiros* large farmers, some of whom had saved up their wages as labour migrants in the South African mines to invest in alluvial land. In northern Mozambique Lazaro Kavandame, who returned from working as a labour recruiter in Tanganyika in 1950, began with a small shop and a banana field but ended up as chairman of the Mozambique African Voluntary Cotton Society and one of the most prosperous Africans in the territory. In Tanganyika entrepreneurial cotton farmers like Daudi Kabeya Murangira founded powerful producer cooperatives.

For a brief period it looked as though real prosperity might come to colonial Africa. The 'Central African Federation' of the Rhodesias and Nyasaland, created in 1953, was proclaimed as a potential United States. Its official ideology of 'partnership' could have been the slogan of many colonial regimes who hoped to produce reliable entrepreneurial allies in development and, if necessary, in controlled decolonization. Policies of 'stabilization' in towns and land reallocation in the countryside were designed to produce productive African workers and contented African peasants.

None of this came to pass. African intellectuals were embittered by the betrayal of both promises of democracy and promises of development. Everywhere in settler Africa whites fought to frustrate African advance. In South Africa, where there was more industrial and urban growth, more African modernizers, more semi-skilled workers, and more Africans with post-primary education than anywhere else on the continent, the policies of apartheid after 1948 were a doomed attempt to lock Africans back into invented traditional identities and into all too modern inequalities. The Central African Federation seemed more like an attempt to frustrate African development in Northern Rhodesia and Nyasaland than a project of shared prosperity. Kenyan settlers obstructed constitutional and economic change. Meanwhile the metropoles were not convincing developers either. Britain drew some £140 million from its African colonies between 1945 and 1951, and used surpluses accrued by state marketing boards in Africa for local projects, while investing only £40 million of metropolitan funds.

The 'new men' in Northern Mozambique, Northern Rhodesia, Tanganyika, and elsewhere, rapidly became frustrated by the limitations imposed on their activities. In much of colonial Africa the structures and attitudes of the Indirect Rule period remained. Chiefs opposed the emergence of a group free from their control; white administrators feared the rise of a nationalist middle class. They dreamed instead of 'controlled' peasant farming schemes, of a 'platonic communism' which would allow for economic advancement without the evils of individualism. Initially cooperative modernizers, like Kenneth Kaunda, soon turned to opposition. By the early 1960s they were leading campaigns of rural sabotage and defiance of agricultural rules. In a typical colonial irony, by the 1960s administrators espoused 'development' as 'the probable solution to any subversive political action', and as a euphemism for government control of the economy, while the aspirant African modernizers were stigmatized as the enemies of development. Kavandame and Daudi Kabeya also became important nationalist mobilizers.

As for African workers and peasants, they too reaped few of the fruits of post-war modernizations. Poor housing and declining real wages in the towns gave rise to a rash of post-war strikes. In settler Africa peasants were evicted from the best land so as to allow white farmers to take advantage of the boom. Within African peasant societies themselves authoritarian interventions in agricultural production produced yet more widespread campaigns of rural sabotage and defiance of agricultural rules. In much of East and Central Africa it was widely complained that whites loved contour ridges, dams, and roads but were never to be seen actually building any. 'Sir', wrote one rural protestor against compulsory conservation labour, 'as far as we are concerned we hate everything in force. We appreciate with pleasure everything free will.' 'Smoke in the hills'—to quote the title of one account of a Tanganyikan rural resistance—spread throughout peasant Africa.

The post-war period produced violent uprisings to match any that had gone before. The largest of these, and the one suppressed with the most casualties, was the 1947 nationalist insurrection in Madagascar, whose leaders invoked the memories of the 1896 *Menelamba* insurrection. The most notorious was the Mau Mau Emergency of 1952–6. Both the Madagascan revolt and Mau Mau seemed to many observers to be atavistic protests against modernization, but in fact were rather civil wars between different kinds of modernizers and different definitions of 'tradition'.

Elsewhere such civil wars were avoided and a loose but effective nationalist coalition built. Of course, African modernizers had developed class interests which divided them from the majority of the urban and rural poor and which were to become yet more apparent after the overthrow or the withdrawal of colonialism. There was no automatic unity of all classes under the leadership of the modernizers as the nationalist myth suggests. Nevertheless, there were enough connections between them and black urban and rural society and its discontents to enable them to create nationalist movements and to challenge colonial rule.

As for the colonial powers, Britain, France, and Belgium came to realize that the second colonial modernization thrust had failed. They prepared either to bale out or to hand over to more or less reliable élites. The Portuguese, lacking other bases of national wealth or significance, clung on until it became too costly to do so. In settler societies there was a retreat from the heady ambitions of the late 1940s and 1950s; a focus on the development of the white sector alone; and a return to a sort of Indirect Rule combination of support for 'tradition' and a cutting of costs.

Anti-colonial nationalism had a paradoxical relationship to the idea of modernization. It was partly about the recovery and glorification of pre-colonial African values and achievements; it was partly a sustained critique of the failures of colonial modernization—the limited provision of health and education facilities, the immiserated labour reserves, the grossly unequal rewards allocated to white settlers and international capital; it was partly a resistance to compelled rural transformation; it was partly a claim that a legitimate indigenous leadership would be able to modernize and transform more thoroughly. Majority rule, it was promised, would achieve the ambition of the many, who had always wanted modernization on their own terms and by their own definition.

In some parts of Africa the withdrawal of the colonial power was smooth and peaceful. In others—in Angola, Mozambique, and the British settler colonies— independence had to be fought for, with much destruction and death. South Africa, long a post-colonial nation, had a different trajectory but in the end the same result. From Ghana in 1957 to South Africa in 1993 there was a sequence of achieved 'majority-rule' regimes, the main cluster coming in the 1960s, with the Congo, Nigeria, Ivory Coast, Senegal, Gabon, and Guinea in 1960, Sierra Leone and Tanzania in 1961, Uganda in 1962, Kenya, Zambia, and Malawi in 1963. The Portuguese colonies did not attain independence until 1974, Zimbabwe until 1980.

During this long period of transition from colonial to African control of the state, analysts often made distinctions between 'reformist nationalism', which had come to power as a result of a compromise with the metropole, and 'liberation movements', whose victory on the battlefield would enable them to transform colonial social, political, and economic institutions. A longer perspective has shown that all the successor regimes have faced the same problems and constraints.

A more compelling periodization of 'post-colonial' Africa—an epoch which has since continued for nearly forty years in many places—divides the initial decades of independence from the recent years of structural adjustment and the withdrawal of the state. In many ways this sequence is reminiscent of the constant colonial pattern of a push towards development followed by emphasis on 'tradition' and economy. The condition of Africa since the 1960s, in short, is less the result of some 'African' cultural characteristic and more the result of the continent's whole twentieth-century history.

In the first period there were very substantial continuities with late colonialism. This was disguised by the attempts of all post colonial regimes to break away from an exclusively European view of world history. They looked to North Africa in the Organization of African Unity; they looked to Asia in the Non-Aligned Movement; they looked to Eastern Europe or to China for models of the commandist socialist state. But they shared the late-colonial belief that development could spring only from the state itself and they shared its top-down authoritarianism and contempt for grass-roots African modernizers.

The adoption of socialist models merely took these tendencies to an extreme. Socialist state bureaucracies were manned by the small African educated élites, who soon separated themselves not only from the 'masses' but from non-bureaucratic African modernizers. They resolved the ambiguities within nationalism by opting unequivocally for modernization over 'tradition', and for modernization through commandism rather than through participation. They aspired to be different from colonial rulers not in the sense that they were more sensitive to indigenous dynamics of development but in the sense that they were more 'legitimate' and hence could be stronger and more effective. The new leaders knew that colonialism had retarded African economic progress. They aimed now to plan and effect it.

Nyerere's Tanzania provides a case-study of the consequence of a 'coercive state' overriding local ecological knowledge in the name of scientific agriculture. 'The sub-species of high modernism driving Nyerere and TANU bore (not excluding their "socialism" and infatuation with the Chinese communes of the day) a distinct Western intellectual lineage. The logic behind the *ujamaa* villages was that large-scale farms were inherently superior to small farms, that the more mechanised the enterprise the better, and that concentrated "town" living was inherently superior to rural dispersal.' The 'more tragic' outcome of Tanzanian—and other African state—high modernizations was the product of greater ideological belief. Colonial administrators had often suggested similar concentrations of people but had never had the will to carry them out. There is still a hidden history in Tanzania of peasant resistance to villagization, but Tanzania has remained remarkably stable compared to other examples of failed high modernism, such as Frelimo's policies in Mozambique which gave South Africa the opportunity to exploit rural unrest and to throw the country into a destructive civil war. In many other countries the increasing alienation of the centre from the localities gave rise to a politics based on those artificial units of 'tradition', tribal, or ethnic groups.

Much of the rest of the world was lazily content to explain independent Africa's development failures and consequent disorders as the inevitable result of atavistic tradition. What were really the discontents of modernity—the skewed and dysfunctional modernization brought about by colonialism; the excessive confidence placed in modernization from above by the successor regimes—were seen as ethnic wars. In Zimbabwe in the 1980s a majority-rule regime, legitimated by two-thirds of the vote, sought to develop African rural areas by central bureaucratic planning. In western Zimbabwe the Mugabe regime encountered the suspicion of peasants who had every reason to be sceptical of state modernization plans, and who had historically supported the party and army of Mugabe's rival, Joshua Nkomo. Scepticism, opposition, and even armed dissidence might have been overcome, but ministers could not tolerate such a repudiation of their modernizing intent. 'We worship the majority as Christians worship Jesus,' declared one. Soon the Fifth Brigade was attacking all local leaders, whether 'Ndebele' or not. Zimbabwe's violent disorders in the mid-1980s came to be viewed by the world as yet another retreat from modern politics into tribal strife, although the Zimbabwean state had not then withered away nor abandoned its project of modernization.

Nevertheless, these modernizations failed and these post-colonial states did eventually falter and withdraw. They were operating in a hostile international environment. Since independence, as before it, Africa has remained subject to the crises experienced or generated by the Western world—the cold war, the rise in the price of oil, the fall in commodity prices, Aids. By the 1970s the combined effect of these crises and the lack of interest shown by the ex-colonial powers in resolving them, have led to the virtual collapse of Africa's economic relations with the industrial world. Mineral and agricultural prices fell by two-thirds; the burden of debt grew. The World Bank abandoned its high modernist assumption that African agricultural production was so inefficient that technical intervention in it was bound to be vastly profitable. Instead it demanded that the state cut back its machinery.

All this was accompanied by the explosive growth of Africa's population. In the forty years between 1950 and the general fall of birth rates in the early 1990s, Africa has experienced the most rapid population expansion in history. Such explosive growth, which might have powered expanding economies, has strained and shattered declining ones.

So we are in another period of state retreat. Many countries, even including the recently commandist Mozambique and Zimbabwe, are returning powers to chiefs. In Zaire scholars have proclaimed a 'return of the kings'. In Somalia the state seems to have given way to factional strife between clan-heads. Even in Nigeria, that huge country held together by a patronage system which amounts to loot, the units of local government are being constantly multiplied.

Cynics maintain that African majority rule has made little difference to the continent's underdevelopment. Africans now have the capacity to make war on each other and to spread their own diseases, but there is little evidence of a sustained ability for internally generated modernization. Meanwhile, despite the development failures of colonialism, the self-confidence of the West that it knows best how to modernize Africa remains unshaken. Given all this, many observers, both inside and outside Africa, have come to denounce the nation state as the worst of all the distortions imposed by colonialism on Africa.

To all this many people believed that majority-rule South Africa would prove an exception. The African National Congress (ANC), which has overwhelming popular support, has long been devoted to a policy of state intervention in the interest of redistributive modernization. South Africa's industrial, commercial, and financial strength dwarfs the economies of the rest of Africa. Its new constitution is uniquely progressive. Nelson Mandela is a statesman of world stature. Many Western countries hope that they can hand over the 'modernizer's burden' of developing Africa to the new South Africa. The *Independent* published a cartoon showing Mandela's face filling up the map of the whole of Africa. On the other hand, many South Africans, black as well as white, do not think of themselves as part of the chaotic and impoverished African continent at all, but as part of a First World country.

Yet South Africa has always been part of the general twentieth century of the continent. South African segregation inspired Indirect Rule; apartheid was an extreme and reactionary form of the same policy. The problems facing the new South Africa are those of the rest of Africa writ large. African skills have been grossly underdeveloped; global capital demands a non-interventionist state as the price for investment; prospects of significant redistribution seem remote. Immiseration and the legacy of 'ungovernability' in the townships ensure a high level of violence. South Africa is not a First World country but a country combining a minority more privileged than almost anywhere else in the world with a majority more deprived than almost anywhere else in Africa. Far from being able to resolve the continent's problems as a whole, South Africa will be totally preoccupied with seeking to resolve its own.

Yet if it seems sensible to adopt a cautious pessimism even towards South Africa, we can nevertheless risk some optimistic concluding generalizations for the continent at the end of the twentieth century. Africa shares a common predicament, but its constituent nations are not equally affected by it. If there are areas of chaos, there are also regions of effective governance or of newly self-confident civil society. The nation state cannot be jettisoned. African thinkers everywhere are seeking to work out how it can coexist with civil society and with strong local institutions. It seems certain that one day there will be yet another thrust towards modernization. But one may have a qualified optimism. After decades of suppression, peasants and workers and entrepreneurs are finding their various voices. The development failures of colonialism and of the post-colonial state have ushered in a more modest, gradual, and promising approach to change. There is reason to suppose that Africa in the twenty-first century can do more than relive in some yet more extreme form the calamities of the twentieth.

23 Latin America

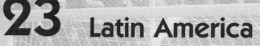

ALAN KNIGHT

At the end of the nineteenth century Latin America consisted of seventeen sovereign republics and two Spanish colonies, Puerto Rico and Cuba, the latter locked in a bitter struggle with its declining imperial metropolis. These republics had enjoyed two generations of political independence; only a tiny nonagenarian minority retained infant memories of Spanish or, in the case of Brazil, Portuguese rule. But Iberian colonialism had left an enduring legacy. Spanish and Portuguese were linguistically dominant, although a sizeable minority in the Andean and Middle American highlands spoke Indian languages; the Catholic Church remained culturally powerful, even where it had been stripped of its swollen land-holdings by Jacobin governments; and Iberian systems of law and land tenure had favoured the creation of large private estates which underwrote a dominant landlord class. But independent Latin America was no mere cultural extension of Iberia. Although the nomadic frontier Indians of the Mexican north and the Argentine and Chilean south had been crushed, dense Indian peasantries survived—spatially corralled, economically exploited, and culturally denigrated by Europhile, usually racist, élites. Indigestible lumps within the body politic, the Indians of Mexico and Guatemala, Peru and Bolivia, were seen as obstacles to progress, symptoms of an imperfect nationhood.

Though internally fragmented, the Latin American states were externally coherent, possessing generally stable borders (dangerous *irredenta* were rare); they also shared a common attachment to republican government, expressed in constitutions—some fly-by-night, some remarkably enduring—which prescribed civil rights, regular elections, representative assemblies, and the division of powers. Since independence, however, civil conflict had vitiated constitutional rule, as 'ins' fought against 'outs', federalists against conservatives, liberals against conservatives, clericals against Jacobins. Thus—in a marked departure from colonial rule—independent Latin America developed a praetorian style of politics, typified by the caudillo: the man on horseback who ruled on the basis of personal clienteles, charismatic appeal, and politico-military prowess, sometimes in formal compliance with the letter of the constitution, often in defiance of its spirit. The caudillo—who survived vigorously into the twentieth century—was a Protean figure, capable of contrasting political incarnations: progressive, conservative, élitist, popular, clerical, Jacobin. The sole common denominator was a high degree of discretionary power and a corresponding reliance on personal clienteles: political attributes which circumvented constitutional rules but which—many have argued—represented pragmatic concessions to reality in societies where orderly, rule-bound, representative civilian government had tenuous roots.

The end of colonialism left the Latin American landlord class socially supreme and, with time, economically buoyant. Republican government reflected landlord interests; the law favoured the landed élite to the disadvantage of peasant, Indian, and cowboy. The middle class and artisans of the cities could make their voices heard—in battles over tariff and currency reform—but they lacked the wealth, numbers, and organization to challenge the landlord interest. The peasantry, denied political representation by *de jure* franchise restrictions or *de facto* landlord power, resorted to sporadic protest, rebellion, or, more often, sullen footdragging. Political supremacy did not, however, guarantee economic spoils. Most Latin American landed classes ruled poor, unproductive countries; like H. G. Wells's Napoleon, they were cockerels on dungheaps. Hence they envied and emulated European or North American manners, lamenting the degeneracy of their inferior peoples.

During the later nineteenth and early twentieth centuries, however, Latin America was increasingly integrated into world trade, as countries experienced lucrative—though often fluctuating—export booms: beef and grain in the temperate southern cone, from Brazil's Rio Grande do Sul to the pampas hinterland of Buenos Aires, which would prove the pacemaker of the continent's new externally oriented development pattern (*desarrollo hacia afuera*); coffee in Guatemala, Colombia, and central Brazil, where, after 1888, the Paulista planters successfully weathered the final abolition of slavery; guano, later copper, cotton, and sugar in Peru; nitrates and copper in Chile; silver, then tin, in Bolivia; rubber—briefly and euphorically—in the Amazon basin; sugar in the Spanish colony—soon to be the US protectorate—of Cuba; petroleum in Mexico, later Venezuela. Foreign investors, leery of Latin America for decades, financed the railways which made these export booms possible; by 1914 the continent had absorbed some $10 billion of foreign capital, over half of it British. Export-led growth required not only railroads and ports, but also an abundant labour supply. Employers, facing unprecedented market opportunities, got workers as best they could, frequently complaining—like their colonial counterparts—of the fecklessness of lazy natives. Slavery had been killed off by British pressure, but forms of coerced labour remained, or were revived: debt-peonage in southern Mexico, corvée labour in Guatemala and the Andes, a horrendous neo-slavery in the upper Amazon. Where labour was more abundant—central Mexico, the central valley of Chile—landlords could rely on quasi-feudal tenancies. Where it was not—and where demand was buoyant—they resorted to free wage labour, including European migrant labour, which flowed in a mighty torrent to the farms and cities of the southern cone. Latin America's already complex ethnic make-up was further enriched: by 1914 the population of Buenos Aires was 60 per cent foreign born (and 30 per cent Italian). With European migrants came skills and some capital; the migrants, drawn by the promise of better pay, formed the basis for a deeper domestic market; they also brought new words, accents, music, and culinary tastes. (Pasta supplemented the abundant beef of Buenos Aires, and the city attuned its ears to the new Italianate argot, *lunfardo*.) But immigrants also brought subversive ideas, like the anarchism of Malatesta, which took root among the infant—but precociously militant—labour movement of the southern cone. Though the new export wealth derived from farming—or, in Bolivia, Peru, and Mexico, mining—it stimulated the growth of cities. Buenos Aires in 1914 had a population of 1.6 million; Rio of one million; São Paulo and Mexico City around half a million each. Provincial towns, too, changed from sleepy backwaters to bustling local entrepots. Paved roads, drains, electric or gaslight, and broad avenues à la Haussmann now graced the major metropolises. But the cities—though still far removed from the teeming megalopolises of post-1945—also sheltered a growing proletariat, packed into insalubrious downtown tenements, where their presence—threatening crime, disease, and riot—alarmed respectable folk (the *gente decente*)and set them pondering the new 'social question': the unforeseen price of economic progress.

Since the bulk of government revenue derived from foreign trade, export growth boosted income. Budgets—chronically precarious for much of the nineteenth century—were more easily balanced; states found themselves with resources which, like other 'late-industrializers', they could devote to infrastructural investments (ports, railways) or, in some cases, to direct economic interventionism, as with Uruguay's national development bank or Brazil's coffee valorization scheme. *Laissez-faire*, though admired in theory, was often eschewed in practice; in Latin America, the 'active state' had a long history. Although no simple correlation between economy and politics emerged, economic buoyancy tended to favour stable, solvent, and increasingly civilian government. Suave financiers began to supplant the craggy caudillos of the nineteenth century. In some countries, this retreat from praetorianism assumed politically liberal—though not necessarily democratic—forms. That is to say, a decorous civilian polity was established, under the aegis of a cosmopolitan landed oligarchy, committed to foreign trade, a restricted (often rigged) franchise, a relatively free press, and an orderly distribution of political spoils among the élite. Such a system characterized Chile's parliamentary republic (1891–1924); oligarchic Argentina (1880–1916); and Brazil's old republic (1889–1930), which was dominated by the *cafe-com-leite* ('coffee-with-milk') alliance of the São Paulo planters and the ranchers of Minas Gerais. Oligarchic rule, by promoting growth and affording qualified forms of political expression, eventually spawned its antithesis, which, at the time, appeared more radical and challenging than it really was: a species of petty-bourgeois democratic reformism—not unlike French Radicalism—which welled up in the major cities, marshalling middle-class and (some) working-class support, calling for free elections, social welfare, and white-collar jobs, while voicing, to a degree, nationalist critiques of oligarchic cosmopolitanism. This reformism coloured Balmaceda's abortive challenge to Chilean parliamentary rule in 1891 and Rui Barbosa's similarly unsuccessful confrontation with Brazil's oligarchs in 1910; but it also powered successful political movements, such as Irigoyen's Radicals, who took power in Argentina (1916–22, 1928–30), and Batlle's Colorados, who twice governed Uruguay (1903–7, 1911–15).

If, in the southern cone, the skewed prosperity of export-led growth tended to consolidate liberal, civilian, oligarchic rule, further north the outcome was different. In the Andean Republics and Middle America minerals were more important than staple crops; the demand for labour was less, the supply of (often indigenous) labour ample; hence the political economy of mining generated neither mass immigration, nor rapid urbanization, nor an incipient domestic market. It did, however, help consolidate more durable and solvent regimes, less liberal than their southern-cone counterparts, often frankly dictatorial. But the authoritarian presidents of Middle America and northern South America—Porfirio Díaz in Mexico (1876–1911), Estrada Cabrera in Guatemala (1898–1920), Cipriano Castro and Juan Vicente Gómez in Venezuela (1899–35)—were not old-style caudillos; or, if they began like that, as Díaz and Castro did, they changed with the times. Rather, they constituted 'order-and-progress' dictatorships, wedded to a species of Comtean positivism which stressed economic development over constitutional niceties; which promoted material development—railways, ports, telegraph—in the interests not only of economic growth but also of political stability and centralization; and which, while offering a secure haven for foreign investment, justified draconian repression of popular protest. Positivism became the leitmotiv and slogan of Díaz's Mexico and his élite technocracy, the Científicos; stitched into the Brazilian flag, the positivist motto 'Order and Progress' waved over a continental society, in which the dynamic immigrant south, focused on São Paulo, followed the southern-cone model, while the impoverished north-east and interior more resembled authoritarian northern South America. Thus, from the Andes to the US border, oligarchic rule lacked the civilized veneer of Argentina's élite; the Argentine—and US—models attracted wistful gazes from governments which, because of prevailing wage levels and work conditions, failed to attract European migrants. Political openings, too, were more constricted. The cities were smaller (Caracas and La Paz were well under 100,000 in 1914); the urban middle and working class weaker. Middle-class democratic parties could not mount the successful challenge of Argentina's radicals. Beyond the cities, there was no shortage of protest: social banditry and messianic movements flourished in arid poverty of the Brazilian backlands; sporadic Indian revolts shook the Bolivian and Peruvian highlands. But neither could crack the carapace of oligarchic rule.

The great exception was Mexico. Here, liberal oligarchic development came late, fast, and furious. Díaz rescued Mexico from endemic instability, balanced the budget, and boosted exports. The old vicious circle of insolvency and instability gave way to a new virtuous circle of solvency and stability, which foreign observers—and beneficiaries—extolled. Political rights, enshrined in the 1857 liberal constitution, were infringed, elections were fixed. But the chickens of Porfirian development came home to roost in 1910. In Mexico as elsewhere, the cities began to generate a new brand of middle-class liberal opposition, which rallied behind Francisco Madero, when he challenged the octogenarian Díaz for the presidency in 1909–10, demanding an open politics along the lines of Republican France or Progressive America and harking back to Mexico's glorious traditions of patriotic liberalism. Pragmatically accommodated in Argentina, Chile, and Uruguay, where middle-class parties gained access to power in loose conjunction with oligarchic interests; thwarted in Brazil, where the entrenched oligarchs refused to cede ground to Rui Barbosa in 1910 or the Democratic Party in 1926, middle-class democratic protest was initially stymied in Mexico. A Brazilian outcome was averted, however, when Madero quixotically called for a popular uprising and, to general surprise, got one. The victims of Porfirian progress—dispossessed peasants, exploited peons, impoverished artisans, and some dissident élites—rallied to the revolutionary cause and ousted Díaz in 1911. For the rest of that turbulent decade Mexico experienced Latin America's first and greatest social revolution, during which central government collapsed and a congeries of revolutionary forces contended for power. Madero's liberal centre was squeezed between an alarmed oligarchy, which sought salvation by means of a draconian military dictatorship, briefly realized during the presidency of Victoriano Huerto (1913–14), and heterogeneous popular forces, including the dashing Francisco Villa's Division of the North and the dogged agrarian rebels of Emiliano Zapata. Madero's democratic experiment ended with his assassination in 1913, but his military killers were bloodily ousted by a new revolutionary coalition in 1914. Mexico now descended into decentralized factional chaos. The final outcome—the Constitutionalist regime of 1915–20—represented a loose synthesis of progressive northern leaders, a small but strategically placed labour movement, and an admixture of popular leaders who placed agrarian reform on the national agenda. Reformist goals—nationalist, pro-labour and pro-peasant—were embodied in the 1917 Constitution, which conferred on the nascent revolutionary state a key mediating role in what, nevertheless, remained a capitalist society. Perhaps more important—and ensuring that these goals would not remain mere paper proposals—Mexican society had been transformed by the decade of revolution: the old regular army was replaced by a fractious revolutionary host; the erstwhile dominant landlord class was decisively weakened; the infant labour movement acquired a political voice out of proportion to its numbers; and—uniquely in Latin America at this time—the peasantry, now coalescing in regional leagues and parties, acquired both a foothold in national politics and a constitutional guarantee of its right to land.

With the Revolution Mexico violently parted company with the rest of Latin America and, in consequence, became a source of inspiration for the continent's emerging nationalist left, and of consternation for conservatives, business, and—especially in the circum-Caribbean region—US interests. But, prior to the 1950s, no other country experienced a comparable social revolution or ventured a major agrarian reform. Peasant protest remained recurrent, but localized and relatively ineffectual; in countries whose socio-economic profile roughly paralleled Mexico—such as Brazil, Peru, or Colombia—oligarchic parties clung to power and the labour movement remained weak, more liable to repression than co-option. Even in those southern-cone countries where democratic advance was more apparent, and where the labour movement enjoyed greater leverage, the chief beneficiaries of oligarchic concessions were the urban middle class and their political caudillos.

Conjuncturally, too, what for Mexico was the decade of revolution—a period of traumatic but transforming introversion—was for most of Latin America the decade of world war, when events in Europe not only hogged the headlines of the new mass press, but also had a direct impact on the societies of the region. Thus, Latin Americans, now more firmly integrated than ever into a global economy that, they were told, offered the high road to prosperity, experienced the first of three successive external shocks—1914–18, 1929–30, and 1939–45—and became painfully aware of the perils as well as the privileges of 'dependent' development.

The First World War sliced through the intricate web of international trade and finance which radiated from London and enveloped much of Latin America. Investment ceased; imports dried up; some exports ground to a halt, as markets were closed off, some, stimulated by the war, experienced an unhealthy and unsustainable boom. British pre-eminence faltered, as capital was repatriated and US business, already dominant in the Caribbean and Middle America, surged into South America, particularly Venezuela, Peru, and Brazil. Deprived of manufactured imports, the major Latin American economies—notably Brazil and Argentina—embarked on an incipient phase of import substitution industrialization (ISI). Smaller economies, cut off from markets and suppliers, tended to languish. The old boom-and-bust export cycles—which had affected Peruvian guano and Brazilian rubber before the war—were now repeated with greater intensity. As the war ended, the Latin American economies experienced a final, brief, euphoric boom (1918–19), followed by a traumatic bust, especially severe for economies which exported industrial raw materials for which demand was unusually elastic: Chilean copper, Bolivian tin. Wartime inflation stoked the fires of labour militancy, which peaked in 1919—a 'red year', in Latin America, as in Europe and the USA, when strikes and demonstrations came thick and fast, especially in Chile and Argentina. In 1918, too, nationalist students met in Córdoba, Argentina, and initiated a university reform movement that would spread throughout the continent. Such mobilization, coupled with the distant threat of the Bolshevik Revolution, alarmed élites; and, as boom gave way to bust, a reaction—in the full sense of the word—set in. Governments connived at lockouts, deported aliens, and resorted to repression. During the 'Tragic Week' of January 1919, right-wing mobs, Argentine counterparts of Italy's squadristi, hunted down leftists and Jews on the streets of Buenos Aires.

If, during this dramatic conjuncture, bourgeois Europe was recast, so, in its way, was oligarchic Latin America—or, in the southern cone, petty-bourgeois Latin America, where the *fin-de-siècle* reformists now faced serious threats on their left flank. For, while the forces of the left were generally defeated, they were not eliminated. The student movement grew; unions regrouped and retrenched; anarchist and anarcho-syndicalist organizations, briefly hegemonic in some Latin American labour movements, gave way to socialist and communist parties, who sought to capture—rather than to abolish—the newly 'active' Latin American state. In Peru, José Carlos Mariátegui blended indigenous radicalism with Marxism, while Haya de la Torre's Alianza Popular Revolucionaria Americana (APRA) (1924), pioneering a mass, reformist nationalism, redolent of the Mexican revolution, put down deep roots among the middle and working classes of Peru's coastal north. More generally, post-war Latin America evinced new cultural forms: some, such as São Paulo's avant-garde, closely attuned to 1920s Europe; others, like Mexico's revolutionary muralists, combining European influence with a didactic radical nationalism.

During the 1920s—that brief hiatus between the shocks of world war and the global Depression—governments sought to recover external stability, while confronting fresh domestic challenges. Even in 'revolutionary' Mexico, the regime of the Sonoran dynasty (1920–34), while it skirmished with the over-mighty oil companies, patched up its relations with foreign business and the USA; US investment in Mexico grew during the 1920s, as it did throughout Latin America, supplanting Britain's economic hegemony north of Argentina. The most notable innovations of Mexico's revolutionary regime were domestic: the start of an unprecedented agrarian reform; state promotion of secular education; an onslaught on the Catholic Church, which provoked a serious civil war in 1926–9; and a close alliance with the new 'official' labour confederation, the Confederación Regional Obrera Mexicana (CROM), which foreshadowed state–labour alliances elsewhere. *A fortiori*, regimes in the rest of Latin America—whether of continued oligarchic or more recent petty-bourgeois make-up—tended to combine domestic caution (if not outright conservatism) with vain attempts to revive the old external relations of the *belle époque*; in which sense many found themselves assuming the same wistful retrospective stance as their old economic partner, Great Britain. But—even if it took over a decade to become clear—the old pre-war free trading system was as irretrievably cracked as Humpty Dumpty. Latin American trade never recovered its 1914 level; outside Argentina, British finance irretrievably lost its hegemonic role; and the USA—which, compared to Britain, enjoyed a less cosily complementary relationship with the continent—could not or would not assume that role in Britain's stead. The Latin American economies, too, had changed. Some faced structural crises of war-induced overproduction, which 1929 exacerbated: hence the alarming premonitory gluts of Brazilian coffee and Cuban sugar. More positively, the major economies had undergone significant industrialization, which engendered new social interests demanding political attention and, in some cases, economic protection. The liberal *belle époque* had gone for good.

Latin American politics in the 1920s were fluid, effervescent, and scarcely amenable to neat generalizations. In Brazil, Paraguay, and the Andean republic, oligarchic parties clung to power, despite fresh challenges, ruling in the landlord interest. The petty-bourgeois parties of the southern cone, themselves products of pre-war prosperity, tended to shift right, fearful of working-class radicalism and committed to free trade. Erstwhile crusading parties of reform—like Irigoyen's Radicals—metamorphosed into political machines run by hard-headed urban bosses. In such countries, where pre-war growth had spawned a sizeable urban population and encouraged a degree of democratic mobilization, a chronic dilemma emerged and set its stamp on Latin American politics: voters expected and demanded material rewards; but economies required domestic investment if growth—including industrial growth—was to be sustained as Britain wilted and what Coolidge inelegantly termed the 'return to normalcy' proved frustratingly elusive. Consumption vied with investment and the state—more interventionist than before, but still lacking the tools and techniques of economic management— tacked between the two, as politicians bought votes, printed money, squabbled among themselves, and—even in erstwhile civilian polities—proved vulnerable to military *coups*. Under these pressures, Irigoyen's Radicals and Batlle's Colorados split; by the mid-1920s the military emerged as the arbiter of Chilean politics. Elsewhere in South America the shift towards authoritarianism, though less of a break with the past, was clearly evident during the 1920s, as countries fell under the sway of authoritarian modernizers who, spurning constitutional niceties, sought to solve the consumption/investment dilemma—and its associated polit- ical challenges—by executive action, combining economic developmentalism, outright repression, and, sometimes, a veneer of populism: Peru's Leguía (1919–30); Cuba's Machado (1924–33); Venezuela's Gómez (1909–35); Chile's Carlos Ibáñez (1927–31); Ecuador's Isidro Ayora (1925–30).

Thus, the world Depression of the early 1930s, traumatic though it was for Latin America, did not strike with the same sudden and devastating consequences as in Germany or the United States. It did not overturn mature democracy or buoyant industrial capitalism. As in Britain, the 1920s had been years of economic travails and fluctuations; the slump was signalled in advance, and its effects were more incremental than in the United States. And Latin American politics were already in flux; the Depression, while it cut a swathe through existing regimes, tended to reinforce existing trends: a vocal nationalism; a diffuse radicalism; a rising author- itarianism; an already waning liberal oligarchic order.

As exports slumped, government revenue and foreign credit evaporated, and governments faced insolvency and social protest. Six governments were toppled by force in 1930, four more in 1931. Since the victims were often dictators—Cuba's Machado, Chile's Ibáñez, Peru's Leguía—the immediate outcome could seem deceptively democratic (in which respect the 1930s recession bears comparison with that of the 1980s). But, in the medium term, as the shock of the Depression was followed by the Second World War, both political and economic liberalism foundered; the old liberal oligarchic order—always more oligarchic than liberal—now went into terminal decline. The depression triggered an understandable critique of *laissez-faire* economics and quickened interest in alternative models: fascism, corporatism, Soviet planning, the New Deal. Latin America's old reliance on external markets as the motor of development seemed mistaken; circumstances dictated a shift from *desarrollo hacia afuera* ('outward-oriented development') to *desarrollo hacia adentro* ('inward-oriented development'). In the larger countries, already possessed of an industrial base and a domestic market, the ISI process accelerated, with state actors—central banks, development agencies, labour ministries—playing an increased role. In Brazil, Mexico, and Argentina, industrial growth helped offset the fall in foreign-exchange earnings; but, in the process, the domestic political economy underwent substantial change, with political consequences. Agro-exporters lost ground to industrialists; urban labour expanded in number and influence; and the state came to play a regulatory and mediating role.

Forms of corporatism flourished: often pragmatically, sometimes—as with Cárdenas's Partido de la Revolución Mexicana (PRM) (1938–46) or Vargas's Estado Nôvo (1937–45)—in accord with official blueprints. Meanwhile, tariffs rose, as they did around the world; and external trade assumed a more managed, bilateral character. Cuba signed a Reciprocity Treaty with the United States (1934); Argentina struck a similar deal with the United Kingdom (the Roca–Runciman Pact, 1933), becoming, for the purposes of trade, an honorary member of the British Empire. Nationalist opinion was offended, but the pact helped preserve the old agrarian–exporting economic order along with a modicum of prosperity. Meanwhile, the economic fortunes of individual countries varied according to the vagaries of the 'commodity lottery' of the 1930s. Where exports enjoyed relatively inelastic demand (e.g. for basic foodstuffs such as grain), economies recovered; Argentina, favoured by the lottery and—contrary to nationalist opinion—shielded by her inclusion in the imperial preference system, fared relatively well. Brazil suffered from a profound and prolonged fall in coffee prices, but the metropolis of the coffee zone, São Paulo, experienced brisk industrial growth. A similar concatenation of coffee and industrialization was evident, on a lesser scale, in Colombia. Mexico, too, emerged from the depression relatively quickly and positively: the country possessed an industrial base, did not rely on a single major export (Mexico's chief export, silver, was buoyed by US government purchases), and benefited from presciently Keynesian fiscal policies, coupled with structural social reform. President Cárdenas (1934–40) promoted organized labour, nationalized the Anglo-American oil companies, and sponsored a massive agrarian reform. Divisive and contentious at the time, the Cárdenas reforms laid the basis of the modern Mexican state, and afforded an example to reformist nationalists elsewhere.

ALAN KNIGHT

Milder versions of nationalist social reform proliferated: some, such as the Chilean and Peruvian Popular Front governments of the late 1930s, were short-lived civilian experiments; others, such as Bolivia's 'military socialist' regime (1936–9) or Brazil's Estado Nôvo (1937–45), combined state intervention with authoritarian rule. Superficially resembling—and often consciously copying—European fascism, such fascistoid regimes, spawned by societies very different from Italy or Germany, in fact performed a more 'progressive', popular, and mobilizing role than their European counterparts; hence, for some analysts, the catch-all term 'populist' is preferred. Nationalist opponents of conservative oligarchs easily assumed 'fascist' trappings: they mobilized mass support, especially among the infant labour movement, they repudiated 'neocolonial' subservience to Britain or the USA, and they looked to the state to promote 'inward-oriented' development, especially of industry. In smaller countries, however, especially in the circum-Caribbean region, where US armed interventions had been frequent prior to 1930, the louring presence of the *coloso del norte* inhibited nationalist reform; in the eyes of Central American dictators, the export agriculture enclaves of Central America—classically, the banana plantations of United Fruit—were assets to be protected and communities to be controlled—not populations to be mobilized. With the exception of Costa Rica, whose smallholding coffee economy permitted a happier trend towards democracy and social reform, Central America remained under the sway of strong-arm caudillos who combined longevity and tyranny—proof that 'development' did not necessarily promote democracy. In Nicaragua the Somoza dynasty (1937–79), initially mildly nationalist and reformist, became increasingly conservative and corrupt. Similarly, the wily Cuban army sergeant Fulgencio Batista, architect of a reformist regime in the 1930s, returned to power in the 1950s, capitalizing on the disgrace of Cuba's factionalized parties, but now an older, fatter, more conservative and corrupt Cold Warrior. The extremes of such 'Sultanism'—idiosyncratic personal dictatorships—were reached in Guatemala under Ubico (1930–44); in Trujillo's Dominican Republic (1930–61); and in the El Salvador of Maximiliano Hernández (1931–44), who inaugurated his regime with the slaughter of 20,000 insurgent peasants in 1933. Neither economic growth, nor US tutelage, served to promote democracy; rather, they helped entrench narrowly personal—hence 'Sultanistic'—autocracies throughout Central America and the Spanish-speaking Caribbean.

The Second World War—a renewed external shock, which blighted some markets, while boosting others—tended to confirm existing trends towards dirigisme and import substitution industrialization. But it also imposed a new lattice on the fractious politics of the continent. Even before 1939 global alignments were gaining influence: a crop of minor fascist parties, each with their chosen coloured shirt, sprang up; Catholic elements, like Mexico's Sinarquistas, aped Franco's Falange; and the Spanish Civil War became the defining external conflict for domestic politics, especially in Mexico, whose government staunchly supported the Republic. Communist parties—strong in Cuba and Chile—espoused popular frontism and, after a brief but politically costly tergiversation during 1939–41, became strenuous supporters of the Allied war effort. Since the natural allies of the Allies tended to be the old oligarchic exporting élites (Argentina's ranchers, Bolivia's tin magnates, Brazil's coffee planters), odd alliances resulted, in which the Stalinist left aligned itself, usually as junior partner, with its old conservative opponents. In reaction, middle-class nationalist parties—such as Bolivia's infant Movimento Nacionalista Revolucionario (MNR)—or radical right groups in the military veered towards the Axis, in part out of ideological sympathy, in part because of the odd logic of domestic politics. Yet 'fascistoid' regimes like Villaroel's in Bolivia (1943–6) were, in terms of domestic policy, usually more reformist, popular, and 'mobilizing' than their pro-Ally, Stalinist-conservative rivals.

The relative weight of these shifting forces varied by country. Mexico, ruled by a staunchly anti-fascist 'revolutionary' regime, was strong for the Allied cause; the Roosevelt administration—pursuing the non-interventionist principles of the Good Neighbour Policy—took a soft line following the oil expropriation of 1938 and strove successfully to achieve a close economic alliance with Mexico during the war. Mexico collaborated; its government shifted briskly to the right; and wartime inflation benefited the rich at the expense of the poor. The regime of the Mexican revolution was never the same again. In Brazil, too, Vargas shed his fascistoid feathers and collaborated with the USA; as did the majority of lesser South American powers. Argentina, however, broke ranks: while the conservative-military regime of the 1940s stuck to its pro-British line, a radical wing of the army dissented; the young, canny, charismatic Colonel Perón weaned the labour movement from its inchoate leftism and built a powerful nationalist and reformist coalition which, in the teeth of US opposition, won power through the ballot box in 1946. Backed by his charismatic wife, Evita, Perón led a nationalist, populist government until his ouster, at the hands of the conservative military, in 1955.

Argentina's trajectory was distinctive, since the conclusion of the war generally marked the discrediting of 'fascist' regimes, and signalled a brief—and often skin-deep—democratic opening. Dictators fell and democratic governments were installed. But electoral origins did not necessarily denote deep democratic commitments. Many democratic regimes were controlled by well-to-do élites who found in Cold War anti-communism a fresh justification for their old exclusionary politics. Even in democratic states such as Chile and Costa Rica, communist parties were banned, proscribed, and broken up. Communist leaders were purged from the unions. Electoral politics still tended to remain an urban phenomenon: outside Mexico, peasants were spurned by mainstream parties, who preferred to focus on the cities, wooing the beneficiaries of ISI: business, the urban middle class, and organized labour, whose numbers and influence had grown apace during the war. Departures from this trend were few and risky. When Guatemala's democratic revolution of 1944 moved to the left and, under the leadership of Jacobo Arbenz, began to distribute land—including United Fruit land—to the Indian peasantry, the United States raised the spectre of Communism (the Guatemalan Communist Party, though small, was influential); the CIA orchestrated Arbenz's overthrow and replacement by a conservative, counter-revolutionary regime (1954).

Throughout Latin America, the old consumption/investment dilemma became more acute in the wake of wartime inflation and urbanization. Electorates grew; rival parties competed for votes; and the beneficiaries of ISI lobbied to maintain their interests. Business confronted states that were powerful in terms of their interventionist powers, but often weak in respect of their institutional structures and stability. However much business might laud *laissez-faire*, it depended on protection (tariffs, quotas, overvalued currencies), in order to cheapen wage goods and to avoid competition from an industrially dominant United States and a resurgent post-war Europe; urban workers—not, of course, urban consumers—had a similar vested interest; and the economic doctrine of the UN Economic Commission on Latin America (ECLA), pioneered by the Argentine economist Raúl Prebisch, afforded a powerful and sophisticated rationale of the need for continued protection and ISI. The USA, negotiating from strength, favoured an open, free-trading hemisphere; but it also sought to cultivate Latin American goodwill in the crusade against Communism. Politically, Latin America played along: the Rio Treaty (1947) committed Latin American states to joint defence against Communist subversion from within and without; the Organization of American States (OAS) (1948) obeyed a similar geopolitical rationale. But the United States, for its part, failed to dismantle Latin America's protectionist apparatus. Instead, US capital vaulted the tariff walls and began a massive spree of direct investment in Latin America, especially in new manufacturing plants, serving the domestic market. The traditional forms of foreign investment—pioneered by Britain and typified by mines, railways, and plantations—gave way to car factories, cement plants, and a host of enterprises catering to the new 'Americanized' consumerism of affluent urban populations. Hollywood films—actively promoted by the wartime US government—paralleled and promoted the new consumer tastes for Palmolive, Colgate, aspirin, radios, and Ford trucks.

The state played a prominent part in post-war industrialization: it took over and ran some of the traditional sectors—Mexican oil, the Argentine railways—and it invested in new capital goods plants, such as Brazil's massive Volta Redonda steel plant. But the motor of post-war development was private capital, much of it foreign, most of it geared towards the upper end of a growing domestic market. Meantime, as industry throve—and agriculture, both subsistence and commercial, tended to wilt—the flow of population to the cities accelerated, at a time when the logic of the job market and the advances of medicine boosted the rate of population increase. Metropolises became megalopolises: gleaming skyscrapers commanded city centres that were ringed by swelling shanty towns and pockets of affluent suburbia. By the 1980s Mexico City—with its population nudging 20 million—was the biggest city in the world, with traffic and pollution problems to match.

The economics of ISI—by the end of the century the object of much retrospective criticism—were remarkably successful. During the 1950s and 1960s GDP grew at 5–6 per cent p. a. in Mexico, Brazil, Peru, Venezuela, and Colombia. In contrast, the once prosperous southern cone—Chile, Uruguay, Argentina—lagged behind. Indeed, Argentina, the economic showcase of the early twentieth century, now became a (relative) economic sluggard—even, it was said, 'a drop-out from the First World', the victim of a particularly acute investment/consumption dilemma, which the rise and fall of Peronism had both exemplified and exacerbated. If ISI brought growth, it also implied certain rough socio-political correlates, particularly in the major countries: benefits for big business and organized labour; a relative neglect of both export and subsistence agriculture; an indifference to the teeming 'marginal' populations of the shanty towns, except in as much as they presented a threat to public order or, occasionally, an opportunity for populist politicians, such as Peru's President Manuel Odría (1948–56).

But these rough correlates did not dictate any specific political system. During the post-war era, Latin America displayed a bewildering range of regimes, although a clear tendency towards authoritarianism emerged after the mid-1960s. There were some consistent—though not necessarily democratic—patterns. In Paraguay, General Alfredo Stroessner's grimly efficient tyranny lasted over forty years (1954–89). Mexico under the PRI remained solidly civilian and semi-authoritarian; Colombia, having weathered the bloody, confused civil war known as the Violencia (1946–58), remained civilian and semi-democratic. In Venezuela, oil revenue underpinned democracy after 1958; while Costa Rica stood as a democratic—even mildly social democratic—beacon in a Sultanistic and counter-revolutionary Central America, where the reformist challenge of Sandinismo was broken by US pressure. Chile, too, retained a vigorous but ideologically polarized democracy down to 1973. Elsewhere, however, change was the norm, and democracy frequently the victim. Urbanization, industrialization, literacy—the whole ragbag of 'modernization' and 'development'—far from promoting democracy, seemed often to doom it. Following the military's ouster of Perón in 1955, Argentina oscillated between unstable democratic and transient military governments, neither of which could come to terms with the enduring Peronist constituency. Peruvian politics were similarly compromised by the old enmity between APRA and the army. Bolivia experienced a democratic and nationalist revolution, led by the MNR, in 1952; the United States, which would soon quash Guatemala's reformist project, chose to recognize, restrain, and deradicalize Bolivia's; thus, although the reforms of the MNR—universal suffrage, land reform, and tin nationalization—endured, the revolution soon lost steam and, in 1964, the MNR were ousted by a new US-trained Bolivian military. In the same year, Brazil's fragile democracy was replaced by a harsh military government which held power—albeit with a certain flexible pragmatism—down to 1985. Peru acquired an unusually radical and nationalist military government in 1968; and two bastions of civilian rule—Uruguay and Chile—succumbed in 1973. By the mid-1970s, therefore, the bulk of Latin America languished under military government, which—in the cases of

Brazil, Chile, Uruguay, and Argentina—combined high technology, systematic repression, and an arrogant claim to power premissed on anti-communism, 'Christian' values, and the providential mission of the military.

The causes of this 'new bureaucratic authoritarianism'—which particularly affected the more rich and developed nations of the southern cone—are contentious and multiple. For some, these regimes were the political consequence of an economic cul-de-sac. The domestic market, constrained by poverty, was saturated, industry had lost its dynamism, ISI therefore reached an impasse from which military rule offered an escape. If this was a conscious rationale, it proved erroneous, since military rule compounded rather than solved such problems. More likely, the new authoritarianism—like the fascism of interwar Europe— reflected mounting fears of the left: of leftist governments, like Allende's Popular Unity (1970–3); of leftist political mobilization, notably of the peasantry in Brazil and Chile; of leftist urban guerrilla movements (Uruguay's Tupumaros and Argentina's Montoneros); and of the leftist challenge of socialist Cuba, which, following the triumph of Castro's Revolution in 1959, not only offered a radical example, but also plotted the subversion of the mainland, notably with Che Guevara's—abortive—guerrilla campaign in the jungles of Bolivia. Military takeovers could also—witness the case of Peru—reflect frustration at the failure of civilian politics and the military's promise to put the country to rights—and not simply by shooting leftists.

Whatever the motives, military rule failed. Economic difficulties mounted: inflation in the 1970s; a build-up of debt coupled with recession in the 1980s. Popular pressure, now channelled through new 'social movements'—churches, civic groups, human-rights activists, independent unions, neighbourhood associations—played an important part, seconded by radical Catholic priests and intermittent US pressure. In response, Latin America's armies began a collective retreat to barracks—gradual and controlled in the case of Brazil, more precipitate following Argentina's defeat in the Falklands War (1982).

Meanwhile, the continent as a whole—north and south, democratic and authoritarian—was affected by that sea-change in macroeconomic fashion which is conveniently labelled 'neo-liberalism'. States shrank their economic activities; nationalized enterprises were sold off; trade was liberalized inside and across borders; the neo-liberal ethic of the free market was seen as the cornerstone of growth and the natural partner of liberal democracy. For Latin America, this meant an economic volte-face: a rejection of the structures, institutions, and practice of ISI and a return, *mutatis mutandis*, to the old, liberal, exporting project of pre-1914; a return to the past that was hailed as a leap into the future, and that was justified by an incessant rhetoric of first-worldism, revamped modernization theory, and warmed-over anti-communism. (The existence of a sclerotic socialist Cuba— bled dry by the US blockade and bereft of its Soviet sponsor—was now providential rather than threatening: if Castro had not existed, it would have been necessary to invent him.) Latin America's neo-liberal élites—without, no doubt, realizing it—thus proclaimed an updated version of the old positivistic developmentalism of the early twentieth century.

These élites spanned a wide range of political actors and countries. Neo-liberal policies were pioneered by Chile's military government and its 'Chicago boys'; they were implemented, sporadically, by the Argentine military; but they also became the chosen policies of civilian parties—some of whom, like Mexico's PRI under Salinas and Argentina's Peronists under Menem, broke with older party traditions of dirigisme and economic nationalism and, with the zeal of converts, auctioned off state enterprises, broke the power of the unions, and took their countries into regional free-trade blocs (Mexico into NAFTA, (North American Free Trade Agreement), Argentina into Mercosur). Remarkably, these neo-liberal policies—usually and knowingly associated with higher unemployment and lower real incomes—did not spell electoral disaster; the smack of firm government, coupled with the decline of inflation and— in Mexico's case—the calculated provision of public works, enabled these populist-turned-neo-liberal leaders to retain, at least for the time being, a measure of electoral support.

But for how long? Whereas the old ISI model had formed around a protected national market and state patronage of favoured groups, the new neo-liberal project made a virtue of external dependency and cut back the networks of traditional patronage. National economies found themselves at the mercy of volatile world markets; and a new generation of neo-liberal leaders—Mexico's Salinas, Peru's Fujimori, Argentina's Menem, Brazil's Collor, practitioners of a brash 'neo-populist' political style tailored to the new mass medium of television—played fast and loose with traditional constituents, especially small business and organized labour. Success varied: despite scares in Argentina and Venezuela, the military have remained in barracks; and, in Chile and Uruguay at least, today's democracy appears to draw strength from historic traditions. But more generally the supposed union of neo-liberal economics and democratic politics—an article of faith for some—remains shaky, contradicted by the authoritarian tendencies of several neo-liberal administrations and contested by radical opponents: Brazil's PT, the Zapatista rebels of southern Mexico, and—the most extreme and violent case— Peru's Sendero Luminoso. The inherent instabilities of the neo-liberal project scarcely promise a stable and prosperous future for the continent; yet if, as the mantra states, 'there is no alternative' to neo-liberalism, what will happen if and when neo-liberalism fails?

24 The Old Commonwealth: The First Four Dominions

PETER LYON

Today the Commonwealth has fifty-four members, spread over every continent. At the beginning of the century almost all belonged to a British Empire that sprawled splendidly red over the world map. All have now gone their separate ways, most of which are described in other chapters of this volume. But at their heart lay the self-governing colonies of white settlement termed 'Dominions' to distinguish them from the rest, many of whose inhabitants at the turn of the century still regarded Britain as 'home': Canada, Australia, New Zealand, and South Africa. It is with these original dominions that this chapter primarily deals.

In 1900 the British Empire appeared to be at its zenith, straddling the world and sustaining a global *Pax Britannica* regarded by its votaries as greater and more glorious even than the original *Pax Romana*. Since it projected a pre-eminently navalist notion of international order based on Britain's maritime and mercantile ascendency, it was actually Greek rather than Roman in its pedigree. Ironically it was only as strong threats of Britain's naval eclipse were foreshadowed in the German naval bills of the 1890s that Roman ideas of a greater and tighter organization of the heterogeneous British Empire gathered pace and achieved some small degree of practical realization; not by means of Imperial Federation or an Imperial Parliament or a Customs Union, an Imperial *Zollverein*—these proved to be too grandiose and impractical ideas—but by the launching of a Committee of Imperial Defence, by conference diplomacy, and by the sharper differentiation of the Empire into Dominions and the rest—as indicated by the creation of a separate Dominions department within the Colonial Office in 1907, embryonic precursor of the full-fledged Dominions Office whose life cycle ran from 1925 to 1947.

The navalist conception of the *Pax Britannica* was expressed classically in the British Admiralty's nostrums of an all-ocean capability and of a 'two-power standard': that Britain's navy should be all-oceans in capability, and with a size and strength equal to those of the next two largest naval powers. At the turn of the century both of these requirements were quietly modified. Britain, by *détente* with the

United States (in two Hay–Pauncefote agreements) and in the Anglo-Japanese alliance of 1902 (but especially in the extended versions of 1905 and 1911), drew in its naval resources to concentrate on home waters, the British seas, and the Indian Ocean—trends which were watched warily and apprehensively, for local reasons particularly, by Canada, Australia, and New Zealand.

During the first decade of the twentieth century, and afterwards, what exactly Dominion status involved was less clear and standardized than has often been supposed. Canada, as the first Dominion, from the time of the British North America Act of 1867, had not only assumed and demonstrated that it meant full internal autonomy, including powers of taxation, responsibility for law and order, and all domestic legislation (save fundamental constitutional change), but had in fact obtained British recognition that there should be Canadian plenipotentiaries present when fundamental Canadian external interests, such as halibut fishing, or demarcating maritime or land boundaries, were at stake. Even so, British garrisons remained on Canadian soil until 1906 and Canadian troops served under British generals up to the First World War. None the less, Canada had led the way in defining and enlarging Dominion competence in external affairs matters, whilst not disputing in principle British primacy in imperial foreign policy and defence.

It was not Australians or New Zealanders who first followed the Canadian lead in this respect. Among the Dominions it was Irish Catholics, Afrikaans-speaking South Africans, and French-Canadians who dissented from, or at least differentiated themselves from, the broad Anglophone, Protestant, Westminster- and Whitehall-led Imperial Commonwealth of the early twentieth century. Sizeable majorities among the ruling élites of these Dominions, right up to the First World War, considered, or at least spoke of, Britain as 'home' even though there were articulate minorities who dissented from what they regarded as this form of political dependency and immaturity. These were then in terms of their ruling classes and political and administrative systems predominantly white man's Dominions. Each was an embryonic national society, a carrier and embodiment of 'Britishness' but with distinctive local variations. The Commonwealth of Australia became a Dominion in 1901, New Zealand in 1907, and the Union of South Africa in 1910.

These four 'British' Dominions, for they were widely thought of as such, regarded themselves, whether country or townsfolk, as in the forefront of modern agricultural (and, for New Zealand, of dairying) economies, pioneering in the application and adaptation of the world's most up-to-date agricultural technology to their use of the land. Theirs were capital- and machine-intensive rather than labour-intensive agricultural economies, somewhat sluggishly recovering from the protracted world agricultural depression of the 1880s. By the beginning of the twentieth century, furthermore, all four of these para-national societies, of white man's rule, were tampering drastically with their environment and further subjugating their indigenous peoples. Much—in New Zealand's case, most—accessible forest had fallen to the axe or the match, many of the native fauna were on the brink of extinction, and indigenous peoples—'Red Indians' and Eskimos (as they were then called—Dike and Inuit today), Aborigines or Maoris, or the extensive non-white peoples of South Africa—had either just reached or just passed their demographic nadirs. These indigenous peoples owned only marginal, relatively unproductive land. The Maoris, for instance, owned virtually none of the South Island and only the less fertile parts of the North.

In the late nineteenth and early twentieth centuries general trade relations with other countries, shipping, immigration, and treaty rights were the chief spheres of continuing British imperial control. The doctrine of free trade was still espoused by British governments, but the Dominions, or proto-Dominions, showed increasing protectionist tendencies and a desire to impose stringent immigration controls against 'Asiatics', meaning Chinese and Indians especially. In 1903 New Zealand began discrimination against certain foreign imports. In 1906 it made a reciprocity treaty with the South African Customs Union, but attempts at reciprocity with Australia failed.

Treaty-making power rested absolutely with the Imperial government, but the 'advanced' colonies were allowed a voice in the mode of executing the provisions of treaties affecting them. It was also an accepted convention that no treaty imposing obligations on the Dominions should be made without their concurrence. A distinction was made between commercial and political treaties. In respect of the former, the Dominions already had considerable powers. From 1882 they could adhere to a commercial treaty within a certain time; from 1899 they could withdraw separately.

Even so, a Dominion could not offer to a foreign power tariff concessions which were not at the same time given to all other powers entitled to most-favoured-nation treatment. Any concession made to a foreign power had to be extended also to the rest of the British Dominions. A Dominion by itself could not enter into any arrangements deemed prejudicial to the interests of any other part of the Empire, as construed by British authorities. If a Dominion made a commercial treaty with a foreign power, as Canada did with France in 1907, it had to negotiate not directly but through the Imperial government.

In the matter of political treaties, the Dominions as yet had no power. There was consultation with a Dominion on questions especially affecting it, as with New Zealand on several occasions in regard to treaties affecting the New Hebrides. Advantage was taken of the Imperial Conference of 1911 to expound and discuss British foreign policy in a conclave of Imperial and Dominion Ministers. However, it was still with the Imperial government that final decisions rested, as was assumed to be true in regard to all foreign relations of the Empire.

The first four Dominions were not supine puppets of the British government of the day. They had patriotic—albeit often very parochial—politicians representing their own countries and constituents, and their attitudes and policies have to be construed in this light. By 1910 the idealistic schemes for Imperial Federation, last flutters of a movement which in Britain at least had peaked between 1885 and 1895, were shattered and scattered by the realities of colonial nationalism—Canadian,

Australian, Kiwi, and last, but not least, Afrikaner South African. The South Africa Act of Union 1910 (a political formula which rejected federation) inspired many enthusiasts for empire with a naïve optimism and led to Round Table groups being formed in each of the Dominions. These groups were ostensibly devoted to promoting 'organic union' throughout the Empire, a phrase which had a convenient ambiguity and elasticity, given that national particularisms actually came to dominate over ideas of imperial solidarity, and despite the fact that onlookers from outside the Empire often exaggerated its coherence and unity.

If the prospect of impending imminent German naval rivalry sent shivers down the spines of the British Admiralty and supporting navalists, it soon also alarmed distant Dominions as to the credibility of claims that the British fleet afforded them security and protection. The second South African (Boer) War (1899–1902)—a quintessential example of Kipling's phrase about 'savage wars of peace'—had repeatedly demonstrated the inadequacies of the British army. The War Office in London was chastened by the failure of many would-be recruits from northern industrial towns to pass the far from onerous physical tests for entry into the ranks, and the deadly accuracy of horse-borne Afrikaner sharp-shooters devastated British troops, who were still using close-order tactics that had been effective in earlier colonial wars. The Boers of the Transvaal and the Orange Free State acknowledged overall British sovereignty in the Peace of Vereeniging, signed in May 1902, and were in return promised self-rule. Subsequently, the former Boer generals—Botha, Smuts, and Hertzog—shaped the changing fortunes of South Africa. Politically, as the importance of farming declined in the economic structure of southern Africa, the use of the term 'Boer' was replaced by the linguistic and ethnic concept of 'Afrikaner'.

Canadians, Australians, and New Zealanders served as 'volunteers' on the British side during the South African War, during which time they acquired, or conferred on themselves, the reputation of being superior to the British in waging counter-insurgency warfare. The Second Boer War was the first occasion when volunteers from Britain's overseas Empire fought alongside troops from the United Kingdom. Some 16,500 men came from the Australian colonies (588 were killed or died), Canada sent 8,500 volunteers, and 8,000 came from New Zealand.

The First World War greatly stimulated national sentiment. During fighting at Gallipoli and later in France, troops from the Dominions eventually proved themselves to be excellent soldiers. The costs were, however, terribly high. Canadian troops distinguished themselves, while suffering heavy losses, at the Second Battle of Ypres, Vimy Ridge, Passchendaele, the Somme, and Cambrai. During the First World War Australia enlisted almost 420,000 volunteers—out of a total population of about 5 million—of whom 330,000 served overseas. As a result of war service, just under 60,000 were killed. New Zealand was the first to base military service on conscription. Nearly one of every three men in New Zealand between the ages of 20 and 40 was killed or wounded. The loss in leadership for the immediate post-war years was considerable.

From 1910 to 1924 Smuts was Minister of Defence and created the South African Army, with which he conquered German South-West Africa (now Namibia) in 1915. He commanded the allied armies in East Africa in 1916–17 before coming to Britain for the Imperial War Conference and serving in the War Cabinet in London (June 1917 to December 1918). After playing a leading role in the post-war Peace Conference and in setting up the League of Nations, he returned home as successor to Botha and henceforth was treated by successive British governments as a wise counsellor.

The end of the First World War saw the USA recoil from the Versailles peace settlement and from the League of Nations, thus rejecting any formal long-term commitments, especially in Europe. Canada, South Africa, Australia, and New Zealand officially attended the Peace Conference as part of the British Empire delegation, but played distinctive national roles, with South Africa, Australia and New Zealand assuming responsibilities as Mandatory Powers—for South-West Africa, Papua New Guinea, and Western Samoa, respectively. Each of them became founder-members of the League of Nations, thus signalling their growing international personalities and interests. Canada eschewed any overt or quasi-colonializing role.

Post-war American isolationism did not extend to the Pacific. At the Washington Conference in 1921–2, the three Dominions with Pacific coastlines combined with the United States in bringing about an end to the Anglo-Japanese treaty of alliance, in being since 1902, whilst officially enveloping it in wider arrangements regarding the territorial integrity of China, Open Door trading policies, and some naval arms control of the capital ships of the world's main navies. The Washington Settlement advertised that naval and commercial primacy in the Pacific had passed to the United States, a fact which three of the four Dominions took close note of (South Africa, naturally, being uninvolved in these Pacific Ocean matters), though many ambiguities remained within American policy right up until the Japanese assault on Pearl Harbor on 7 December 1941.

There are two peculiarly tenacious myths about the inter-war Commonwealth: (1) that the Balfour imperial committee report of 1926 and its expression in the Statute of Westminster of 1931 marked the constitutional and international coming of age for the Dominions; and (2) that the Imperial Economic Conference held in Ottawa in 1932 introduced a strongly comprehensive system of imperial protectionism for the first time.

The Statute of Westminster—by abrogating the Colonial Laws Validity Act of 1865—ended the automatic superiority of the Westminster parliament over all Dominion parliaments and thus registered a major change from Empire to Commonwealth. Ireland's and South Africa's governments of the day particularly favoured this. For Canada, William Lyon Mackenzie King wanted to reduce the powers of the Governor-General and favoured some general discussion of such matters, though in fact the Canadian provinces opposed any final patriation of Canadian constitutional matters from Westminster to Ottawa, as was to be the case several times in the next five decades. South Africa and Canada ratified the Statute immediately, though both Dominions subsequently clarified their relationship to the 'mother country' by the Status of the Union Act (1934) and the Canada Act (1982). Australia did not ratify the Statute until 1942, and New Zealand not until 1947, as both Dominions regarded the issue as an ultimate constitutional matter primarily for the United Kingdom, rather than for themselves.

The Imperial Economic Conference in Ottawa in July–August 1932 was a desperate attempt by Britain and the Dominions to erect economic shelters in the face of the raging blizzard of the world economic depression. Although ostensibly a collective occasion, the main substance was a series of bilateral, preferential agreements made between Britain and various Dominions. It was a rather ill-tempered conference. The hopes of the Canadian prime minister of the day, Richard Bennett, of securing guarantees of wheat prices were not realized. The Ottawa agreements were a series of bilateral undertakings whereby the United Kingdom would allow the import of goods, food, and raw materials from the Empire either without tariffs or at preferential rates. In return, the Dominions would give preference to exports from each other or from Britain, provided always that they did not harm native industries. (The Ottawa agreement was extended in 1933 to cover the colonies as well as the Dominions.) It is important to remember, however, that these protectionist devices were frankly confessions of weakness brought in at a time of unprecedented shrinkages in world trade. Henceforth, every Dominion was acutely conscious of its role, and vulnerabilities, as a world, not merely an imperial, trader.

As the menace of fascism mounted in Europe, especially in the second half of the 1930s, the Dominions showed themselves initially to be strongly in favour of 'appeasement' and, with some reservations, to follow British predilections about security. The Imperial Conference of 1937 gave a ringing endorsement to the term and notion of 'appeasement'. Averting conflict in Europe whilst avoiding being sucked again into Europe's, and especially Britain's, quarrels were understandable hopes and preferences—though Canada, Australia, and New Zealand each looked with increasing unease at Japanese militarism and expansionism, from the invasion of Manchuria in 1931 onwards.

In South Africa, during an uneasy coalition partnership from 1933 to 1939 between Hertzog's wing of the nationalist movement and Smuts's United Party, racial segregation was intensified by a series of 'status' bills (including the Status of the Union Act, June 1934) and a Representation of Natives Act (April 1936). Hertzog's failure to keep South Africa neutral in 1939 and the subsequent wartime leadership of Smuts (lasting until his electoral defeat and political eclipse in 1948) pushed the 'native problem' into the background.

The great Depression hit each of the Dominions hard. In New Zealand, for instance, the collapse of wool prices and the withdrawal of overseas funding for major public-works projects meant that 80,000 New Zealanders were unemployed by October 1933. Even in the Depression years of the mid-1930s, however, New Zealanders were modernizing in significant ways which affected their life styles. By 1935, for example, there were 7.6 New Zealanders to each motor vehicle, close to the American figure for that year of 4.8, and there were telephones, radios, and electricity for country as well as town.

The alacrity with which Canada, Australia, and New Zealand went to war in 1939 (whilst the South African parliament, and then thanks to the leadership of Jan Christiaan Smuts, only voted to go to war against Germany by a narrow majority and after a fierce debate) showed that for these three dominions their undoubted independence had not removed their sense of close ties with Britain. At first the war resembled that of 1914. Canadian troops came to Britain (and soon Canada provided bases for the training of pilots under the Commonwealth Air Training Scheme). Australians and New Zealanders were sent out to Egypt to train for the European conflict. Soon too they were in combat because of enemy advances, and eventually they were involved in action in Greece, Crete, North Africa, and Italy.

South African forces also played significant parts in the Second World War. About 200,000 white men (more than half of them Afrikaners) and 125,000 non-whites (mainly Africans and Coloured men) joined South Africa's forces and many of them served with distinction in the Ethiopian, Mediterranean, and Madagascan war theatres. The non-whites were not allowed to bear arms but were distributed among the combatant units, for whom they performed vital work as stretcher-bearers, labourers, etc. Industry was efficiently switched to the production of munitions and clothing for military purposes. South Africa's military achievements were impressive, considering the strength of the domestic opposition to the war, though, fortunately for Smuts's government, this opposition splintered into fragments during the critical phases of the war.

The Japanese attack on Pearl Harbor in early December 1941 was followed within months by rapid Japanese advances in South-East Asia and the Pacific which engaged (and captured) tens of thousands of Commonwealth and Imperial troops, including Canadian forces in Hong Kong. Anzac forces fought alongside British, Imperial, and American troops, experiencing together the setbacks and successes of changing military fortunes. The Pacific theatre was dominated by the United States, as were the latter stages of the North Atlantic and Mediterranean theatres. The fact that disaster was averted by American much more than British strength strongly influenced changes in Dominion attitudes to their future security. Henceforth, all four original Dominions sought to define their international positions in relation to what was in effect a post-war *Pax Americana*, which was an international economic as well as a diplomatic and military order, because the Bretton Woods system of 1944–7 in effect recognized and institutionalized the emphatic primacy of the US economy in world economic matters.

The Second World War was a demonstration of the truth of a thesis expounded by the British historian Jack Gallagher, to the effect that in the twentieth century the British Empire did not straightforwardly experience decline and fall but that in two world wars it proved to be a remarkably resilient coalition of interests, so that one should more accurately write of a decline and rise (in effect, two rises, 1914–18 and 1939–45) and only then of an eventual fall of the British Empire. Furthermore, throughout the Second World War (and in some respects replaying Anglo-American debates during the latter stages of the First World War), whilst British and other West European imperialisms were at bay, there was sharp debate and disagreement between Britain and the United States (albeit behind closed doors) as to the desirable nature of the post-war colonial order, with President Roosevelt favouring a post-war international regime for all colonies, whereas Britain, Australia, New Zealand, and South Africa (all Mandatory Powers under Article 22 of the League of Nations Covenant) preferring—and in effect succeeding—in getting an international regime, the UN Trusteeship system, which, as in 1919, only stipulated provisions for the disposal of the colonies of the defeated powers.

All four Dominions played active roles at the launching of the UN system at San Francisco in 1945. Canada, propelled to unprecedented and relatively short-lived significance as a prominent power, was an advocate of international functionalism and of middle-power status. Australia, whose delegation was headed by the irascibly articulate Dr Evatt, advocated anti-colonialism and the interests of smaller powers, meaning Australia especially. Smuts, from South Africa, by now a veteran international statesman, drafted the noble-sounding preamble to the UN Charter—a somewhat ironical contribution, considering that within three years he was in political eclipse and his country, led by Afrikaner racists, was hell-bent on institutionalizing apartheid.

As the aftermath of the Second World War shaded into Cold War, the four Dominions all sought to reorientate themselves, in distinctive ways, in a world dominated by the Cold War in which the United States and the Soviet Union were the principals, and in which they, each and all, broadly identified themselves, albeit with some reservations, with US policies. Incidentally, as India, Pakistan, and Sri Lanka gained independence in the late 1940s, initially as Dominions, the four original Dominions gradually and without fuss dropped the term Dominion from their own official descriptions, as being now incompatible with their undoubted independence. De-dominionization thus either preceded or accompanied the high tide of British disimperialism.

As Cold War confrontations intensified in the late 1940s, Canada joined the North Atlantic Treaty Organisation (NATO) at its inception in April 1949, thereby accepting a commitment to maintain troops on the continent of Europe, at a time when there was no hot war raging there. Joining NATO was just as much a revolution in Canada's strategy as it was for the United States and for Britain. Article 2 of the founding NATO treaty is sometimes referred to as Canada's clause because the idea that the signatories should work towards creating a NATO political and economic community was put there at Canadian insistence. After involvement in the Korean War, Canada remained (like Britain) cautious of being involved as a junior military ally of the United States in Asia and the Pacific, preferring economic involvement (as in its membership of the Colombo Plan, from the early 1950s, and in association with the Association of South-East Asian Nations (ASEAN), from the late 1970s onwards). Even so, economic imperatives ensured that Canada's closeness, in many senses, to the United States was demonstrated by her international economic affiliations—as co-members with the United States of the G7, of Asia–Pacific Economic Cooperation (APEC), and especially in the North Atlantic Free Trade Agreement (NAFTA), concluded in the early 1990s. As well over 70 per cent of Canada's trade in the 1990s is with the USA, these economic factors have their own logic and compulsions.

The first two decades of the post-Second World War era were marked, for Australians and New Zealanders, by active partisanship in the Cold War in support of the regional aims of both London and Washington, notably in diplomacy and defence. Forces from Australia and New Zealand participated in the Korean War, the Malayan Emergency, Indonesia's 'Confrontation' against Malaysia, and in support of the USA in Vietnam: the latter commitment seriously divided the publics in both countries. The United Kingdom's accession to the European Community (EC) in the early 1970s substantially emphasized these processes, so that subsequently Australian and New Zealand governments defined their countries as part of the Asian–Pacific region, even whilst maintaining strong links with the industrialized West and especially still with Britain.

The Suez crisis, which basically lasted from late July to November 1956, with its climacteric in a few days of warfare in early November, sent shock waves throughout what was still very much a UK-led Commonwealth. The Prime Ministers of Australia and New Zealand sided emphatically with Britain's Sir Anthony Eden and carried their cabinet colleagues with them, despite the muffled misgivings of a few of them and cross-currents of contradictory reactions from their electorates. Canada, notably through the efforts and skilled diplomacy of Lester Pearson, helped to get Britain and France off their self-impaled hooks, and, by inventing the United Nations Emergency Force (UNEF), pioneered peacekeeping as a prominent *leitmotif* in that country's internationalist policies. The South African government's rather aloof attitude to the whole Suez misadventure was summed up in a statement made by its Prime Minister, Mr Johannes Strijdom, on 27 July 1956, when he said: 'It is best to keep our heads out of the beehive. But the Middle East, which has always been a dangerous spot, is of the utmost importance to South Africa as geographically it is the gateway to this continent.' The Commonwealth was rather swiftly recomposed in 1957; but decolonization soon led to a rapid expansion of its membership, the dilution of its 'British-ness', and its considerable transformation in the 1960s and thereafter.

The growing preoccupations of Australians and New Zealanders with the regional affairs of the Pacific were partly due to their changing economies, but also to Britain's withdrawal from an imperial role in this vast region, leaving the two antipodean ex-Dominions to accept larger responsibilities and yet making them more dependent on American power. In the 1950s and 1960s the foreign policies of both Australia and New Zealand became deeply coloured by anti-communism, culminating in their participation in the Vietnam War, a commitment which proved to be deeply controversial and politically divisive for both countries.

In 1974 the Whitlam government in Australia disavowed a 'white-Australia' policy and henceforth all subsequent Australian governments adopted an ostensibly liberal, non-racial immigration policy, though the liberality in practice of such policies depended critically on the state of the economy, and especially of the labour market, at a particular time. Roger Douglas, as New Zealand's Minister of Finance in the Labour government led by David Lange, which was elected in 1984, was the driving force responsible for the attempt to convert his country's stalled protectionist economy into a free-trading, market-led economy (policies dubbed 'Rogernomics' by New Zealand's media).

American cultural influences (television, films, magazines) tended to standardize the increasingly suburbanized aspects of Canadians', Australians', and New Zealanders' life styles. In South Africa, even after the ending of apartheid, its structural deformities in terms of highly contrasting standards of living generally as between whites and non-whites seemed to replicate the differences between what, in the idiom of the 1960s and 1970s (still serviceable in this particular sense for South Africa in the late 1990s), were called contrasts between the First and Third Worlds.

In South Africa, the power of the Nationalist Party was promoted by legislative enactment and the strong leadership of three successive Prime Ministers—Malan (1948–54), Strijdom (1954–8) and Verwoerd (1958–66). Their formal policy of political and social racial segregation became known as apartheid. Thus, these Nationalist governments brought in a mass of racial legislation to enforce their ideas of white supremacy. They created a population register to fix the racial category of every South African. They made marriages as well as unions out of wedlock between whites and non-whites unlawful. They rigorously divided towns as well as rural areas into zones in which members of only one race could own or occupy property or conduct business. They assumed control over African and Coloured school education, eliminating the mission schools. They excluded non-whites from the established universities and founded separate colleges. They intervened in the labour-union movement to separate white from non-white. They gave officials sweeping powers to remove 'undesirable' Africans from towns. They extended the practice of reserving particular types of jobs for whites. They enforced segregation where it did not previously apply, as in buses, trains, post offices, libraries, cinemas, and theatres. White and non-white South Africans could thus rarely meet, except as masters and servants, or rulers and subjects.

The Nationalists also changed South Africa into a republic. In a referendum in 1960 a small majority of the white voters expressed a preference for a republic. In March 1961, Verwoerd asked the Commonwealth Prime Ministers' Conference, meeting in London, whether South Africa might remain a member of the Commonwealth when the change took place. He withdrew his request when other members criticized his government's racial policies: Canada, led by Diefenbaker, was strongly outspoken; only the Australian government, headed by Menzies, and the host government, led by Harold Macmillan, seemed keen to keep South Africa in the Commonwealth. Consequently, when South Africa became a republic on 31 May 1961, it left the Commonwealth.

For a mixture of geopolitical and ideological reasons—to do with South Africa's location on the world map and the white man's exclusivism and hegemony embodied in the apartheid state—South Africa was only peripherally involved in Cold War commitments and crises. The anti-communist rhetoric of the regime (throughout changes of government, 1948 to 1994) was in practice much more part of the sustained campaign against domestic opponents (the proscribed South African Communist Party, the African National Congress, and other challengers) than an indication of its international partisanship in the Cold War. Apartheid virtually prescribed if not autarky then reluctant but defiant acceptance of the status of a pariah state and a high degree of isolationism and unilateralism.

The next thirty years saw successive South African governments acting defiantly towards the international community, which treated the apartheid-practising regime as an international pariah. It was not until 1989 (coincidental, but not causally linked, with the collapse of the Soviet Union) that, as a consequence of internal opposition, economic strains, and international sanctions, the restrictions of apartheid began to be removed, and the government announced its willingness to extend political rights to all adult South Africans. In February 1990, a thirty-year ban on the African National Congress (ANC) was lifted and its leader, Nelson Mandela, released from prison. On 22 December 1993 parliament approved (by 237 votes to 45) a Transitional Constitution, paving the way for a new multiracial parliament which was elected in late April 1994.

Whereas at the end of the nineteenth century New Zealand was a social laboratory for the world in its pioneering of welfare policies, in the last decade or so of the twentieth it was widely seen as an initiator of privatization, an open, deregulated economy and far-reaching reconstruction. Towards the end of the century, too, these erstwhile Dominions were actively debating the nature of their respective national identities, the place to be accorded to their aboriginal indigenous peoples, to environmental and ecological concerns, matters of human rights, and constitutional revision. These reappraisals meant considering the case for or against republicanism in Australia, redefining Quebec's place inside or outside Canada, applying for a new system of proportional representation within its unicameral parliament for New Zealand, or devising a new, post-apartheid, political, socio-cultural, and economic order for what its President, Nelson Mandela, has called the 'rainbow nation' of the 'new' South Africa, which returned to the Commonwealth in June 1994.

The United Nations Development Programme (UNDP) has annually published a Human Development Report since 1990, which seeks to supplant 'the mismeasure of human progress by economic growth alone' and to replace it in favour of a measure of 'sustainable human development', thereby providing both a 'mirror reflecting present patterns of global imbalance and a telescope, showing the more positive futures possible'. In the six years 1990–6 Canada has always featured in the top three of this index of 170-plus countries, and in 1996 was first again. In 1996 Australia was rated eleventh and New Zealand fourteenth (above the United Kingdom which was sixteenth, but below France which was seventh, and above Germany which was eighteenth). South Africa, with its startling contrasts between rich and poor, was not characterized among the first fifty-seven countries which were said to enjoy 'high human development' but was placed exactly one hundredth, two-thirds down in the second category, 'medium human development', and well clear of the third and final category, of the forty or more countries classified as of 'low human development'. Thus three of the four original Dominions of 1910 were by 1995 not only modern but continuously modernizing, whilst post-apartheid South Africa is energetically embarked on belated modernizing for the vast majority of its population.

At the close of the century, three of these four countries are indubitably modern (even postmodern) in the sense that they are *au fait* with the world's most advanced technologies and seek continuously to utilize and upgrade these within their national life. All three have citizens enjoying, in world terms, high standards of living in peaceful countries. Many tourists and would-be immigrants regard these three as desirable, even enviable, countries to holiday or settle in—as they may again so come to regard South Africa, vested with a new democratic constitution in 1996, if it can also produce both political stability and enough prosperity to entice tourists and new immigrants.

At the beginning and for the first half of the century there had been fairly consistent attitudes to the British Empire and its transmuted successor, the British Commonwealth. For most Canadians, Australians, and New Zealanders, the Empire–Commonwealth was an association entwined with their own history and a part at least of their own traditions. White South Africans generally were divided, mostly as between the Anglophones and the Afrikaners, as to its merits. The Imperial existence had involved a complex heritage of pride and humiliation. In the mid-1960s Britain gave up the permanent chairmanship of the Commonwealth and a pan-Commonwealth Secretariat was set up with a Canadian, Arnold Smith, as its first Secretary-General. The British Commonwealth indubitably had now become simply 'the Commonwealth'.

The post-1965 Commonwealth seemed to many outsiders to suffer both from rather fuzzy, benign sentiment and from the legacies of old suspicions and hostilities of earlier generations. Canada, Australia, and New Zealand took a much stronger line than Britain against apartheid-practising South Africa, especially in Commonwealth conclaves in the 1980s. The older, guardedly negative emotions vanished and no longer is there any marked suspicion that someone is trying to draw his country back into an imperial womb. The dominant feeling is rather that the Commonwealth affirms fine values but that it probably does not matter much since it appears to be outside the mainstream of contemporary international life—a view which, naturally enough, would be strongly contested by its votaries.

After all, the Commonwealth of the 1990s provided no common defence, did not supply substantial amounts of capital on a multilateral basis, and did not pack punches equal in impact to those of the World Bank, the European Union (EU), the G7, or a number of other international institutions and associations. Even so, each of these four original Dominions plays an active part in Commonwealth affairs. Canada, Australia, and New Zealand each hosted Commonwealth Heads of Government Meetings (CHOGMs)—Canada in 1973 and 1987, Australia in 1981, and New Zealand in 1995. The Auckland CHOGM of November 1995 was significant for the return of South Africa to the Commonwealth, with Nelson Mandela as its President, and South Africa is to host the CHOGM in 1999. Canada and Australia, with Britain, provided most of the working funds for all official pan-Commonwealth organizations—for example, the Commonwealth Secretariat and the Commonwealth Fund for Technical Cooperation (CFTC) from the 1960s to the 1990s—even though by the latter dates Malaysia and Singapore in particular, and some others potentially, had rendered obsolete the notion that Britain and the former Dominions were the only rich members and the rest of the Commonwealth was poor.

The Commonwealth at the end of the twentieth century may seem to outsiders to be an anachronism, but to those who follow its actions closely it is a remarkably active and persisting post-imperial association of governments and peoples.

25 Towards a World Community? The United Nations and International Law

ADAM ROBERTS

The twentieth century, often called 'the century of total war', could also be called the century of international law and global organization. From 1899 onwards, and especially in the wake of the two world wars, there was a series of efforts to bring the anarchic and war-prone system of sovereign states under an effective over-arching framework. Practical necessities, as well as idealistic desires to create a better world, contributed to unprecedented developments in the fields of law and organization. The idea that the states of the world constitute in some sense a 'community' or 'society'—or at least that they ought to do so—gradually became a commonplace. Yet the development of international relations in the twentieth century was not a straightforward progression from war to law, nor was it a total transformation from the anarchy of sovereign states to the framework of the United Nations.

Ever since the modern system of sovereign states emerged in Europe in the seventeenth century, there has been some degree of acceptance that the relations between states had to be governed by law. There could be, and frequently were, disputes about what the law was, how it was created, how it was applied to particular situations, and how it was enforced. More fundamentally, there was enduring tension between the idea of the state as sovereign and its supposed obligation to observe international rules.

Up to at least the mid-nineteenth century, most law was codified in treaties between two or at most a very few states, or in the writings of legal experts. Only in the second half of the nineteenth century did the multilateral treaty, open to any state to accept, become a principal mode of international law-making. The landmark development was the 1856 Paris Declaration on Maritime Law, which was concluded at the end of the Crimean War and laid down general rules on the tangled problem of relations between belligerents and neutral shipping in wartime. Within a year forty-nine states—as far apart as Japan, Peru, and Sweden—had become parties. The idea of treaty-based rules which applied equally to all states was to become a mainstay of international law in the twentieth century.

The second half of the nineteenth century also witnessed an astonishing increase in the number of international organizations. States established functional organizations to deal with practical matters such as navigation on the Rhine and other major European rivers. In 1868 the oldest intergovernmental organization still in existence was established: the International Telegraph Bureau (since 1932, International Telecommunication Union). In 1874 the General (since 1878, Universal) Postal Union was set up. Similar bodies were created to deal with everything from weights and measures to health.

These nineteenth-century beginnings of a new intergovernmental system of law and organization had obvious limits. Such international law as existed was mainly European in origins and character. Its application in large parts of Africa and Asia, especially where the inhabitants were deemed by Westerners to be 'backward' or 'barbarian', was at best problematical. There remained deep ambiguities as to whether any international community that was emerging was European or global. There were no permanent international institutions in the security field, and relatively few legal restraints on the resort to force. Yet the emergence of international legal instruments and functional organizations did open up visions of a future in which states would be part of a larger framework of law and organization.

The Hague Peace Conferences of 1899 and 1907 were the last major effort of the nineteenth century, and the first of the twentieth, to tackle in a general way the problem of war. They were summoned by Tsar Nicholas the Second of Russia, who was concerned about the possibility of major war, about new weaponry which might undermine Russia's advantage in manpower, and about the sheer cost of armaments. These conferences, in which an unprecedentedly wide range of states took part, were precursors of the worldwide diplomatic gatherings which were to be a notable feature of twentieth-century international relations.

At the First Hague Peace Conference, held in May–July 1899, there were representatives of twenty-six states, including such non-Europeans as China, Japan, Mexico, Persia, and the United States. They failed, as would often happen in the twentieth century, to reach any general agreement limiting possession of major armaments. However, they did adopt three conventions and three declarations. The first two conventions were of pioneering importance in establishing, respectively, a new international legal institution, and a new legal codification of the laws of war:

- *Convention I for the Peaceful Adjustment of International Differences.* This established the Permanent Court of Arbitration, consisting of a standing panel of arbitrators who could be selected by states for each specific dispute.

Between 1900 and 1932 it dealt with twenty cases. It has been moribund since then, but still exists. This might seem all too symbolic of the restricted role of international law in the twentieth century, but a principal reason for this court's disuse is the emergence of several other more satisfactory mechanisms for settling disputes, including the Permanent Court of International Justice (now International Court of Justice) mentioned further below.

• *Convention II on the Laws and Customs of War on Land.* This developed, and codified for the first time in multilateral treaty form, a series of rules (most of which were already broadly familiar to well-trained armies in what were at that time called 'civilized states') covering such matters as treatment of prisoners of war, protection of hospitals, truce negotiations, and the conduct of armies in occupied territories. The basic provisions of this convention, which was modified only very slightly by 1907 Hague Convention IV, remains, battered but intact, still formally in force at the end of the twentieth century.

The Second Hague Peace Conference, held in June–October 1907, had stronger participation than the first: forty-four states, of which no less than seventeen were from South and Central America. Again, no general agreement on arms limitation was reached, but the conference did adopt thirteen conventions (ten in the field of the laws of war) and one declaration. An interesting innovation was the attempt to restrict the use of force in the recovery of debts. Thenceforward, acts of intervention having the character of debt collection had a cloud of opprobrium over them.

The final act of the 1907 Hague Peace Conference had envisaged that a Third Peace Conference might be held within seven or eight years. By then the 'Great War' was being fought, and many of the hopes raised at The Hague had died. The more critical views of the Hague Peace Conferences seemed to be vindicated. Joseph Conrad had said that the 1899 conference constituted 'solemnly official recognition of the Earth as a House of Strife', and the German historian Theodor Mommsen had called it 'a misprint of world history'. Although these views were too dismissive—some parts of Hague legacy did endure in the twentieth century—they were uncomfortably near the truth.

The disaster of the First World War decisively strengthened the view that it was not enough to limit or humanize war (which was what the Hague Conferences were seen as having tried and failed to achieve): it was necessary to prevent it altogether. The victorious allied powers, meeting in Paris in 1919, established the first-ever global international organization of general competence, the League of Nations. Its founding document, called the 'Covenant' to dignify it with almost religious significance, contained a number of provisions intended to discourage states from resorting to force. Three main approaches were embodied in the Covenant: the reduction of national armaments, the judicial settlement of disputes, and collective responses to acts of aggression. Article 10 was typical of the Covenant as a whole in its status quo assumptions, its grand promises, and its lack of precision about means of enforcement:

The Members of the League undertake to respect and preserve as against external aggression the territorial integrity and existing political independence of all Members of the League. In case of any such aggression or in case of any threat or danger of such aggression, the Council shall advise upon the means by which this obligation shall be fulfilled.

The League of Nations, established in 1920 with its headquarters in Geneva, failed to live up to the hopes invested in it. Partly this was because, although it did gain some sixty members, several great powers remained outside, and others undermined it from within. The USA, which had done more than any other country to bring it into being, refused to join: Congress was nervous about taking on commitments to tackle distant conflicts, and reluctant to see its own constitutional powers, and US sovereignty, weakened in any way by a transfer of decision-making power to an international body. Japan and Germany announced their withdrawal in 1933, and the Soviet Union, having previously denounced it as 'a coalition of the victor Powers who wish to impose their will on other States', joined only in 1934.

The League failed partly because its proposed mechanisms for achieving security were inherently flawed. The idea of collective responses to acts of aggression could not work when there was no agreement among states as to whether particular acts constituted aggression; when there were arguments about whether economic sanctions or military force were appropriate responses to such acts; and when the League's decision-making procedures required unanimity, which was simply not attainable on most security issues in the 1920s and 1930s. The League did earnestly discuss major crises—and it heard powerful pleas for action against Japanese, Italian, and German uses of force in the 1930s—but its responses were ineffective.

The League era witnessed many attempts to bring the possession and use of force under international legal control. Some endured better than others. The 1925 Geneva Protocol prohibiting the use of gas and bacteriological weapons in war was violated by Italy in Abyssinia in 1935–6, but it may have played some part, along with threats of retaliation in kind, in limiting the resort to these weapons in major international conflicts, including the Second World War; and it has remained in force since. However, there were many expensive failures. In the 1928 General Treaty for the Renunciation of War as an Instrument of National Policy, otherwise known as the Kellogg-Briand Pact, the major powers of the day stated that they renounced war 'as an instrument of national policy in their relations with one another'. Subsequent experience showed that this paper promise was of little or no worth. The centrepiece of the League's disarmament efforts, the Conference for the Reduction and Limitation of Armaments 1932–4, failed to achieve any significant measures of disarmament, and was overshadowed by Germany's departure from the League.

Even before the outbreak of the Second World War, the League had failed in its security functions, and was effectively dead. It was formally wound up in April 1946. Yet it left some enduring legacies. In the 1920s it did dampen some incipient conflicts, and it helped to settle a few international disputes. Under its wing several international organizations were created which survived their ailing parent: these included the International Labour Organization (ILO), and also the Permanent Court of International Justice (since 1945–6, the International Court of Justice, or ICJ), to which states can bring interstate disputes for judicial settlement. Perhaps the League's most important legacy was a negative one: it exemplified mistakes which statesmen were anxious not to repeat next time round.

The post-1945 international organizational and legal order was shaped powerfully, not just by the perceived lessons of the inter-war years, but also by the events of the Second World War. The anti-Axis wartime military alliance, which from 1942 onwards called itself the 'United Nations', had not only seen itself as expressing the collective will of states to resist aggression, but had also proclaimed as central purposes the punishment of war crimes and the establishment of a new international organization. As a direct reaction to the events of the war, there were to be numerous war-crimes trials and a new stream of human-rights law: the impact of these and other international legal developments is discussed further below. The wartime alliance was also the chrysalis out of which emerged the new international organization of the same name, the 'United Nations'.

The UN Charter—signed in San Francisco on 26 June 1945 by the representatives of fifty states, and entering into force on 24 October 1945—was intended by its framers to provide a more imaginative, complex, and realistic framework for collective controls over the use of force than that of the League Covenant. This interstate treaty opened with the words 'We, the Peoples', which would have made the state-minded framers of the League Covenant turn in their graves. At the same time, in a change symptomatic of its greater acceptance of the facts of power, the UN had its main headquarters, not in Geneva in neutral Switzerland (though it did establish offices in the old League building there), but in New York, on the territory of one of the two major victorious Allies of the Second World War—the USA.

The UN Charter followed the League Covenant in some matters: it established a plenary body (the General Assembly), a smaller executive body (the Security Council), and a Secretariat; it further developed the League precedent by providing for a network of specialist functional organizations as part of a system with the UN itself at the centre; and, like the Covenant, it was centrally preoccupied with the prevention of war. However, apart from being much longer and more detailed, it differed from the Covenant in three vital respects. The first, and most crucial, difference owed much to the US input into the Charter, which was far more extensive than it had been into the League Covenant: by stressing fundamental human rights, the importance of economic and social issues, and 'the principle of equal rights and self-determination of peoples', the Charter established that the UN was not just a trade union of governments or a cartel of European empires. Secondly, by saying relatively little about disarmament it avoided setting aspirations so high as to lose touch with reality. Thirdly, in its provisions for the Security Council it established a basis for decision-making that did not depend on complete unanimity of all the members, and therefore had at least a chance of leading to action.

The Charter provisions for the Security Council represented an interesting compromise between the principle of the equality of states and the facts of power. The Council had eleven members, increased in 1965 to fifteen. Of these, five (Britain, China, France, the Soviet Union, and the United States) were permanent members, while the rest were to be elected for two-year terms by the General Assembly. A resolution on anything other than a procedural matter needed a three-fifths majority 'including the concurring votes of the permanent members'. These delicate words of the Charter have been interpreted in practice to mean that any one of the permanent five can, by voting against, veto any resolution on a substantive matter. The number of vetoes cast in the first fifty years of the UN was 236. Although the veto provisions are often seen as having prevented the UN from taking effective action in many crises, they were necessary if great powers were to join, and stay in, the UN.

The UN Charter envisaged elements of collective security, which were spelt out in more detail than in the League Covenant. In particular, Chapter VII provided for economic sanctions and military action, all organized under the leadership of the Security Council, as methods of countering what were termed 'threats to the peace, breaches of the peace, and acts of aggression'. This was not a perfect system of collective security, even in theory, as it could not work if one of the five permanent members of the Security Council opposed action; and it was based on an acceptance that states retained a right of self-defence if the Security Council was unable to act.

The UN, unlike its predecessor, has attracted almost universal membership. At any given time it has had as members the great majority of existing states. Their number has grown owing to successive waves of decolonization, and the disintegration of large federal states. In 1945 the UN had 51 original members; by September 1961, 100; by the end of 1984, 159; and by September 1999, 188. The most conspicuous case of non-membership of the UN was the result of exclusion rather than unwillingness to join: from the Communist revolution in 1949 until 1971 the Chinese government was kept out, China being represented at the UN by the regime in Taiwan. Since 1971 the UN's claims to near-universalism have had real substance. By a perverse paradox, the UN, identified in so many minds with internationalism, presided over the global triumph of the idea of the sovereign state.

The greatest achievements of the UN in its first fifty years were probably not in the field of international security narrowly conceived, but rather in providing a framework for the most fundamental change in international relations since 1945: European decolonization, and the emergence of a global international society. The UN sometimes assisted the process of decolonization through referenda, and also through General Assembly resolutions—most notably the 1960 Declaration on the Granting of Independence to Colonial Countries and Peoples. But its most important contribution was in providing a framework for entry into international society of the numerous new and reconstituted states, many of which were intensely vulnerable. For them, the UN was not just the main means of securing diplomatic recognition, but also a world stage, a negotiating forum, a provider of well-paid jobs, and a source of symbolic protection. The UN embodied principles, including racial equality and the sovereign equality of states, that were vital to the decolonization process. It also assisted in addressing numerous post-colonial crises. Virtually all UN peacekeeping operations up to the late 1980s were in recently decolonized territories. Thereafter some were also concerned with the post-communist equivalent of decolonization.

From its earliest years, the UN Security Council was not able to operate as effectively as the Charter might have suggested. Provisions whereby states were to put forces at the general disposal of the Security Council were never implemented. The Cold War, characterized at its height by the division of the world into blocs and attempts by each to subvert the other, was the almost complete antithesis of the Charter vision of states living together 'in peace with one another as good neighbours'. The UN had a peripheral role in many situations threatening international peace and security, including the Berlin crisis in 1948, the Soviet invasions of Hungary in 1956 and Czechoslovakia in 1968, the US intervention in Vietnam in the 1960s and early 1970s, the Indonesian invasion of the former Portuguese colony of East Timor in 1975, and the Iraqi attack on Iran in 1980 which led to eight years of war. Similarly, the UN was peripheral to many important peacemaking and arms-control efforts, including the development of an arms-control regime between the USA and the Soviet Union from the 1960s onwards. In Europe, the key East–West diplomatic process based on the 1975 Helsinki Final Act took place outside a UN framework.

Although the UN has never even come close to setting up a general system of collective security, the UN era has seen three striking variations on the collective security theme, each of which is discussed in turn below: regional alliances; UN authorizations of the use of force; and international peacekeeping forces.

Regional alliances became a central feature of the international security arrangements that did emerge in the first decades of the UN's existence. Regional arrangements had been foreseen in the Charter, and in turn many of the post-1945 treaties setting up regional security arrangements referred explicitly to UN Charter principles and procedures. This was true of the 1949 North Atlantic Treaty, establishing NATO; and the 1955 Warsaw Treaty, establishing the Warsaw Pact. These arrangements reflected the reality that states are generally willing to commit their forces for serious military action, not on a universal basis, but in their own region, or in defence of countries with which there are strong ties of interest or feeling.

UN authorizations of the use of force by states, only dimly envisaged in the Charter, became a significant form of UN action. In June 1950, after communist North Korea attacked the non-communist South Korea, the Security Council approved a resolution recommending member states to assist South Korea in repelling the invasion. It was only able to do so because the Soviet Union had unwisely walked out of the Security Council shortly before, in protest at its refusal to seat the People's Republic of China (PRC). The ensuing UN role in the Korean War (1950–3) was widely viewed as exceptional, and the huge losses in the war acted as a further discouragement to viewing it as a prototype international enforcement action.

After the end of the cold war, and following a dramatic decline in the use of the veto, the Security Council acquired a critically important role as a legitimizer of certain uses of force. It gave authorizations to US-led military operations to reverse Iraq's 1990 attack on Kuwait, to intervene in Somalia in 1992, and to topple the military government in Haiti in 1994. Also in 1994, it authorized the French-led 'Operation Turquoise' in Rwanda. In 1995 the NATO 'Operation Deliberate Force' in Bosnia had a legal basis in earlier Security Council resolutions. In many of these cases, the interventions were in response to the collapse of civil institutions, accompanied by famine and huge refugee flows—situations far removed from the international aggression which had been the principal concern of those who framed the UN Charter.

Peacekeeping—the use of lightly armed forces drawn from many countries, and acting in an essentially impartial role to ensure implementation of agreements—is the third major variation on traditional collective security ideas. There was no explicit provision for it in the Charter, which was based on the idea of collective military enforcement actions in support of states which are victims of aggression. However, in practice there are many other military tasks to perform, including assisting in the implementation of ceasefires. Peacekeeping developed thanks partly to innovative thinking by the second UN Secretary-General, Dag Hammarskjöld (1953–61). Most member states were willing to see the organization take on such new tasks, but the Soviet Union objected to some early peacekeeping efforts, and to paying for them.

Peacekeeping forces are an appropriate symbol of the UN because they have, like the UN itself, an extraordinarily mixed record of failure and success. In Cyprus and Kashmir large peacekeeping forces, operating for decades, have proved unable to resolve deep underlying conflicts, and have at best preserved an armed truce. Similarly, the heavy involvement of UN peacekeepers in communal conflicts in Lebanon and former Yugoslavia stretched the UN's resources but was probably not the decisive factor in bringing peace. In Egypt in 1967 and Somalia in 1995 UN peacekeeping forces had to stage humiliating withdrawals. Yet some of these forces achieved impressive results: they did help isolate many conflicts from competitive foreign interventions; and, starting in the late 1980s, with the cold war winding down, they helped in the implementation of agreements for the withdrawal of external forces in Afghanistan, Cambodia, Mozambique, and Namibia. In the 1990s they became increasingly associated with efforts to monitor and even organize elections as a means of ending prolonged conflicts.

The end of the Cold War, culminating in the collapse of communist regimes in Eastern Europe in 1989, and of the Soviet Union itself in December 1991, cannot be ascribed simply to multilateralism in general or the UN in particular. However, it did reflect well on these approaches. East–West confrontation was scaled down through major arms-control treaties on intermediate nuclear forces (1987), conventional forces in Europe (1990), and strategic nuclear weapons (1991). The UN, especially through the good offices of its Secretary-General Javier Pérez de Cuéllar (1982–91), assisted the end of the Cold War by helping to wind down numerous regional conflicts with an East–West dimension. UN peacekeeping operations also played a vital part in this process. Further, the Soviet leadership under Gorbachev repeatedly emphasized UN principles and procedures as a basis for modifying existing Soviet policies. Well before the Soviet Union's final collapse, its policies had changed sufficiently for the Security Council to be able to operate effectively on a wide range of issues, as it did, for example, in authorizing force to end the Iraqi occupation of Kuwait in 1990–1. When the Soviet Union ceased to exist in December 1991, Russia's succession to its permanent seat on the Security Council was handled smoothly.

There were many visions of the UN's role in the post-Cold War world. The Security Council summit of January 1992, and Secretary-General Boutros-Ghali's report *An Agenda for Peace* issued the following June, held out the prospect of a world in which the UN would have a central role not only in matters of international security, but also in diplomacy and standard-setting worldwide. There were even prognoses that the UN could make inroads into state sovereignty, not just in extreme cases where fundamental human rights were being violated, but also by helping to develop a global civil society.

In a few cases, where the human-rights situation was exceptionally bad and the regime strikingly weak, the UN did tolerate or even authorize so-called 'humanitarian intervention': this happened, for example, in northern Iraq in 1991, Somalia in 1992, and Haiti in 1994. More routinely, UN financial agencies attached conditions about human rights, democratic practices, and good government generally to their loans or investments, imposing thereby controversial limits on the freedom of action of many governments.

If the end of the Cold War offered opportunities for the UN, it also posed severe problems. It led to new wars, particularly in the collapsing federal states of Yugoslavia and the Soviet Union, cases which themselves constituted a warning of what can happen to overambitious attempts at multinational organization. Faced with a variety of challenges, old and new, it rapidly became apparent that the use of the veto (mainly by the Soviet Union and the United States) during the Cold War had not been the sole cause of the UN's failures. The Security Council was now able to take decisions on a wide range of matters, but was not always effective. There were doubts about the quality of its actions in many crises from 1992 onwards, especially regarding former Yugoslavia, Somalia, and Rwanda. The incapacity of the UN (or, rather, the unwillingness of states) to back up Security Council guarantees was cruelly exposed by the fall of two UN-declared 'safe areas' in Bosnia in July 1995. In a few cases—most conspicuously over Rwanda in May 1994—the Security Council authorized increased peacekeeping activity, but states refused to provide troops for it. Even states which had voted for resolutions often failed to provide the resources which were necessary for their implementation. The USA defaulted massively on its financial obligations. Repeated attempts to improve the UN's hand-to-mouth financing of peacekeeping operations failed. Many countries were nervous about the huge demands that might be placed on them through the UN, and about its lack of capacity to develop strategic goals. Over some conflicts, including several in the former Soviet Union, the UN, suffering from its own version of 'imperial overstretch', declined to get involved. There was a strong sense that the UN needed fundamental reform, but less agreement about what exactly was needed or how it was to be achieved.

The UN system comprised, not just the UN itself, but also sixteen specialized agencies, each with its own constitution, budget, and membership. The two big financial agencies—the International Monetary Fund (IMF) and the World Bank—were much more than talking shops: they played an important and frequently controversial role in regulating the world economy. The other specialized agencies provided a focus for international cooperation in fields as diverse as agriculture, civil aviation, copyright protection, environmental protection, health, labour, and scientific cooperation. Other intergovernmental organizations closely associated with the UN included the International Atomic Energy Agency, founded in 1957, and the General Agreement on Tariffs and Trade (GATT), reincarnated in 1994 as the World Trade Organization (WTO). One or two specialized agencies came to resemble overblown bureaucracies, even baronial fiefdoms, satisfying some member states but otherwise unresponsive to outside demands. For the most part this huge network of functional bodies did reinforce the interest of states in the UN system.

After 1945, many powers viewed international law with a degree of healthy scepticism. The experience of the inter-war years had left them doubtful about grand general pronouncements which were not enforceable, or which lacked firm foundations in the real interests of states. Hence the careful wording of the Charter's preamble when it specified one of the UN's purposes as 'to establish conditions under which justice and respect for the obligations arising from treaties and other sources of international law can be maintained'. The UN era has in fact seen a vast increase in the number and scope of international legal agreements. Some of these have emerged outside a UN framework—testimony to the complexity of a legal system which is overlaid, but not dominated, by the UN.

One of the first tasks undertaken by the Allies at the end of the Second World War was the trial of major Axis war criminals. Allied declarations in London (13 January 1942) and Moscow (1 November 1943), declaring the prosecution of war crimes to be one of the Allies' principal war aims, were followed by a vast number of trials in national courts, and also by the creation of international military tribunals at Nuremberg (1945–6) and Tokyo (1946–8). In these tribunals, systematic Axis atrocities against prisoners and against civilians in occupied territories were one major focus of attention. At Nuremberg, nineteen of the twenty-two defendants were found guilty, and twelve were sentenced to death. At Tokyo twenty-five of the twenty-eight defendants were found guilty, and seven were sentenced to death. The Nuremberg and Tokyo tribunals have notoriously been a subject of controversy, and they have been criticized as victor's justice. Yet they did help to establish the idea that there are some standards of behaviour so basic that they must apply to all states and their citizens, in peacetime and in wartime, irrespective of whether or not those standards had been clearly spelt out in treaties to which the state in question has subscribed, and irrespective of claims that the criminal acts were carried out on orders from superiors. This idea, which challenges exclusively state-based conceptions of the rules of international society, powerfully influenced subsequent law-making in two key fields: human-rights law, and the laws of war.

Of all the areas of law-making in the UN era, the one with the most complex effects for the system of sovereign states was human rights. The UN Charter laid emphasis on human rights partly because of a belief, reinforced by the events of the Second World War, that dictatorial states which threatened the lives of their own citizens were also likely to commit acts of international aggression. In 1948 the General Assembly approved the Universal Declaration of Human Rights, a document which, while not technically in the binding form of an international treaty, was given great sanctity as an authoritative exposition of the UN Charter. In 1966 two formal treaties on the subject were adopted—one on economic, social, and cultural rights, the other on civil and political rights. Their negotiation was particularly tortuous as many of the states involved were themselves dictatorial. The emphasis on the rights of individuals and groups within states meant that various UN meetings became rhetorical battlegrounds. There were also accusations of double standards: states were quicker to criticize their adversaries than themselves or their allies. In the end, the formal powers of the international community to bring about change within criticized states proved to be limited, but the capacity to put human rights at the centre of international and even national debates had huge ramifications.

After the Second World War, development of the laws of armed conflict took place largely outside a UN framework—partly because the UN, being committed to the prevention of war, did not want to be seen to be drawing up detailed rules of conduct in possible future wars. The four 1949 Geneva Conventions, dealing with the protection of victims of war, were negotiated by states under the auspices of the Swiss-based body with expertise in the subject, the International Committee of the Red Cross. These agreements gained almost universal formal adherence from states: in 1998 there were 188 parties. Implementation of these and other agreements was uneven, contributing to further attempts to develop the law, in some of which the UN became involved.

The general process of law-making that has taken place directly under UN auspices has emerged mainly from the deliberations of the UN General Assembly and its specialist committees; and also from large UN conferences on key topics of the day. The resulting international agreements have addressed such varied matters as genocide; civil aviation; diplomatic relations and treaties; protection of the environment; law of the sea; and the non-proliferation of nuclear weapons.

In addition to this law-making, the UN had an important role in standard-setting. Along with various other institutions (some outside the UN system), it played some part in establishing international priorities and principles. General Assembly resolutions and special conferences convened by the UN sometimes helped to establish, or keep alive, such norms as respect for the independence and integrity of states, observance of the rules of armed conflict, human rights, population control, and the equality of women. Although the UN consisted of states of all kinds, dictatorial as well as democratic, in the 1990s it became increasingly associated with processes of democratization. Further, UN pronouncements stressed the value of plural and multicultural societies, and expressed support for minority rights within states, as distinct from the fragmentation that might result from an extreme application of the principle of self-determination.

Human rights law has presented peculiarly complex problems of enforcement. The UN has established a vast array of committees, commissions, subcommissions and working groups, yet their powers are limited. By contrast, the judgments of the European Court of Human Rights (which is not a UN creation) have been more or less routinely accepted by the states which are parties to the European Human Rights Convention.

Implementation of the laws of war has presented a similarly mixed picture, with some states observing such basic rules as proper treatment of prisoners of war, while others have neglected them. In the 1970s and 1980s the UN General Assembly frequently passed resolutions calling for better implementation of such rules, but it was sometimes criticized for selectivity, even bias, in its choice of issues to address and in its manner of doing so. In the post-Cold War era the Security Council has attempted to strengthen respect for the laws of war, including through the establishment of international criminal tribunals for former Yugoslavia (1993) and Rwanda (1994), but it has also learned the limits of its own power against recalcitrant states and warlords. There was no chance of a single grand trial of major leaders, as happened after the Second World War, when the victorious allies actually controlled Germany. In general, the implementation of international law, including the law of war, presents a paradox: it is in fact largely through the agency of states that international rules are actually transformed into practice. If states need international law and institutions, it is also true that the latter need states.

Many aspects of the international system have changed radically in the course of the twentieth century. International law and organization were far from being the only agencies of this transformation. As some nineteenth-century visionaries had already foreseen, a new global community of shared activities and values was created by business and global communications. A degree of interdependence emerged, even a new cosmopolitanism among élites, reinforcing ideas of a world society. However, increased interchange of various kinds did not remove causes of international tension, nor did it undermine nationalism or the state in the way that some had hoped and others feared. It did lead to attempts to bring the process of economic development under institutional control, whether through the interventionism of national governments or through demands for a new international and social order. Although much was done, the regulation of trade and business practices is still, archaically, almost entirely at the national (and, in Europe at least, regional) level: the establishment of effective international standards in this area remains a challenge for the international community, and the World Trade Organization (WTO).

International law and organization have often been envisaged as transforming the system of states completely. Yet they have also had to adapt to the very system they are thought to challenge—not least because the UN has, through supporting decolonization, assisted the emergence of new states which jealously defend their hard-won sovereignty. Despite predictions that the state would decline into irrelevance in an era of transnational processes and rapid advances in worldwide communications, the state as a unit of political organization has remained fundamentally important. Many familiar features of the international system have shown no signs of disappearing: traditional diplomacy; the balance of power; and spheres of influence. The old society of states has been overlaid with, but not replaced by, elements of a more uniform and structured world of international law and organization. As the Italian international lawyer Antonio Cassese has put it: 'The features of the world community are quite unique. Failure to grasp this crucial fact would inevitably entail a serious misrepresentation of the impact of law on this community.'

At the time of its foundation, the UN was often envisaged as the focus of a new era of harmony and human rights, enabling mankind to march towards a better future. It was so depicted in some of the more dated parts of its curious art collection in New York and Geneva. It has developed differently. In many of the issue areas it covers, the UN is perhaps best seen, not as a prototype executive body, nor as the centre of a completely new order, but as a provider of services to a still divided world. Sometimes it has merely served as a scapegoat, enabling states to deflect attention from their own failures to take action.

Despite all its limits, and its perennially parlous financial situation, the UN achieved in its first fifty years a quality of permanence and universality that had eluded all its predecessors. It had played a positive part in the great international transformations which flowed from the two great challenges of decolonization and the end of the cold war. At the end of the century there is no shortage of new challenges: among them, global economic, environmental, and population problems; failed states; democratization; and the need to reconcile the right of self-determination with the stability of states and of the international system.

Throughout the twentieth century, there has been an underlying tension between two logically incompatible sets of ideas: the sovereignty of states, on the one hand, and the creation of a supranational order through international law and organization on the other. Sovereignty implies the right of each state to have its own rules and institutions. International law and organization, especially when covering the vast range of matters which they now encompass, imply a serious limitation of sovereignty. The experience of the twentieth century is that neither approach can triumph over its opponent. If some kind of ordered and law-based international society has emerged, it has done so on a curious basis: it is founded on two logically incompatible sets of ideas, each of which needs the other in order to remedy its own inherent limitations.

PART V

Envoi

26 The Close of the Twentieth Century

WM. ROGER LOUIS

Each phase of twentieth-century history has reflected the anxieties and hopes of the previous decade. Those living in the closing years of the century still pondered, with a sense of awe, the exhilarating events of the fall of the Berlin Wall, the collapse of the Soviet Union, and the overthrow of the apartheid regime in South Africa. But the collective memory of the darker side of human affairs also recalls massacre at Tiananmen Square, ethnic cleansing in the Balkans, and mass slaughter in Rwanda. No one now dreams, as did writers a hundred years ago, of utopias in which such atrocities would no longer characterize human society. But the ends of the two centuries do share much in common, including millenarian visions of the universe. At the close of the nineteenth century H. G. Wells wrote *The War of the Worlds*, an apocalyptic account of the world invaded by Martians. In 1997 the Earth spacecraft *Pathfinder* landed on Mars on the Fourth of July, thus ending the twentieth century with a distinctly American celebration of the future of the universe.

During the First World War, the Four Horsemen of the Apocalypse captured the public imagination. They are as appropriate an image for the 1990s as they have been throughout history. From the time of their appearance in the Book of Revelation to that of the novel by Vicente Blasco Ibáñez in 1916, the riders terrorizing the world were variously represented by the white horse of war, the red horse of slaughter, the black horse of famine, and the pale horse of death, more recently of the death of the planet as well as its inhabitants. Some of these issues, such as those of environment, the clash of civilizations, and certain global trends, both good and evil, are considered by Ralf Dahrendorf in the next chapter. This chapter in its concluding part will deal with the Four Horsemen as they appeared in the 1990s in slightly altered guise on the horses of civil war, genocide, terrorism, and famine and disease. What events in the last decade of the century will be recalled as having tilted the balance one way or another for or against those agents of destruction? As a preliminary question, what of the struggle for a better life in Europe, the Americas, the Middle East, Africa, and Asia? Or, to put it less extravagantly as a major theme, how will the years in the run-up to the turn of the century be remembered?

Certain events reveal the temper of the times. It is appropriate for an *Oxford History* of the Twentieth Century to comment at the outset that, to many who witnessed the Labour Party's landslide victory in May 1997, Britain almost over night seemed a different place. With the Tories in disarray over Europe, the new Prime Minister, Tony Blair, offered a vision of the future comparable to that of Clement Attlee in 1945, though with a post-socialist outlook that the old Labour Party would scarcely have recognized. Sceptics wondered how long the new Labour era would last before degenerating into something similar to Harold Wilson's administration in the 1960s. Hardly before the Blair regime got underway, however, there occurred an event that brought Britain to the centre of world attention. Early on the morning of 31 August 1997, Diana, Princess of Wales, was killed in an automobile accident in Paris. The image of a young princess was instantly frozen in time, just as John F. Kennedy's had been at the time of his assassination. Diana's marriage to Prince Charles in 1981 had brought revitalized pageantry to the British monarchy. She lived in a world of glamour and fashion, but people throughout the world sympathized with her because of her intense personal struggles. The grief over her death struck a genuine chord throughout the British Isles. To some it verged on national hysteria. Together with the advent of Tony Blair as Prime Minister, the death of Princess Diana did give the impression, however momentary, of a cultural tectonic shift in Britain, not so much the passing of an old order but the ascendancy of a new one with which the old had yet to come to terms. Another significant point about Diana's death affirms one of the major themes of the present volume: the global reaction to the event revealed the existence of an integrated global culture. It was a time of international as well as national mourning and reflection.

A similar moment of national stocktaking occurred in France on the death of François Mitterrand in January 1996. Mitterrand had served as President of France for fourteen years and left an imprint on post-1945 French politics second only to that of Charles de Gaulle. A champion of European unity, Mitterrand in 1990 sent troops to the Gulf War and drew France closer to the North Atlantic Treaty Organization. Though he feared the consequences of German reunification, he championed good relations between France and Germany as the foundation for a strong and united Europe. Yet by the mid-1990s the dream of a unified Europe seemed to be fading. In the summer of 1997 France's conservative Prime Minister, Alain Juppé, met defeat, and in Germany the worst budget crisis in decades paralysed the coalition under Chancellor Helmut Kohl. The 'Euro', the celebrated single currency envisioned as the last major step towards a fully united Europe, threatened to rupture the European Union (EU). Kohl staked his political career on Germany joining Europe's single currency on time in January 1999. If the plan for monetary union were to be derailed, would the will for closer political integration survive? In the run-up to 1999 there was no clear answer to that question, but, against considerable odds, the timetable for the Euro seemed to remain intact.

Not the least of the surprises of the mid-1990s was the recovery of President Boris Yeltsin of Russia. As late as 1996 he had teetered on the verge of a third heart attack, faltered on economic reform, and faced an unremitting and fierce battle against the old Communists. By mid-1997 he had defeated the Communists, survived a difficult heart operation, accelerated privatization, and steered Russia increasingly towards the West. Yeltsin was still widely portrayed as a drunkard, though perhaps slightly reformed, who had held office during a rise in crime, spiralling inflation, a collapse in living standards, and a disastrous civil war in Chechnya. Drugs, alcoholism, and corruption continued to plague Russian society. Nevertheless Yeltsin appeared to be back in control of internal and external policy. Although George F. Kennan, the American doyen of Russian history and culture, warned that NATO's expansion would be 'the most fateful error of American policy in the entire post-cold war era', Yeltsin took a relatively conciliatory attitude. His acceptance that Poland, Hungary, and the Czech Republic would be new members of NATO proved to be a turning point in the European defence structure of the 1990s. NATO itself, in contrast to the EU, faced a robust future. Though the threat of a Soviet invasion had all but disappeared, NATO acquired two new functions. One was to respond immediately to local crises, as in Bosnia by launching a massive aerial bombardment and then deploying peacekeepers. The other new function was the attempt to make the Eastern European states more stable and secure by granting membership to some and strengthening ties with others. Without Yeltsin's acquiescence NATO's new life would have taken a different direction.

If NATO had been resuscitated, the United Nations in the 1990s sank to a low point in its history. The ghost of the Somalia operation, 1992–3, rose to haunt and challenge its image of an impartial and moral world body. Not only did the UN fail in its mission to rebuild the country, but charges of atrocities were raised against the blue-helmeted peacekeepers. More than 140 UN troops died in Somalia, one of the highest casualty rates in a UN operation since the Congo in the 1960s. Confidence in UN peacekeeping operations was shaken. Nor were the reasons for plummeting morale confined to peacekeeping. Despite anniversary celebrations after fifty years of its founding, the United Nations had troubled relations with the United States, which owed back dues and assessments of $1.3 billion. Jesse Helms, the Republican Chairman of the Senate Foreign Relations Committee, sought a 50 per cent cut in the UN's bureaucracy and a 75 per cent cut in the secretariat's budget, promising American payment of $819 million over three years in return for specific 'benchmarks' of UN performance. The US unilateral imposition of reforms flouted the collective procedures that the United States had accepted upon joining the United Nations. A slimmer and ultimately more efficient UN bureaucracy might paradoxically owe a debt to isolationist sentiment in the United States. Perhaps the recognition of the vital but limited function of the

United Nations in resolving international conflict will be a lasting legacy of the 1990s.

In the Americas the salient event in Canada was the referendum in October 1995 in Quebec, where voters narrowly rejected independence. The event of hemispheric proportion was the conclusion of the North American Free Trade Agreement (NAFTA) in 1993 linking Canada, the United States, and Mexico. NAFTA was the pre-eminent achievement of Bill Clinton's first term in office. Trade liberalization emerged as one of his few core convictions. After his re-election in 1996 he convened a 'Summit of the Americas' in Miami and pledged to achieve a free trade area in the Western Hemisphere by the year 2005. By the middle of the 1990s NAFTA had become a byword for Mexican corruption, a weak peso, illegal immigration, and drugs flooding into the United States.

Bill Clinton may be remembered in popular lore for dalliances reminiscent of John F. Kennedy, but at the time of his re-election in November 1996 he presided over the most remarkable economic performances in a generation. Unemployment was at its lowest in a quarter century, and the record against inflation was almost as impressive. The key to the recovery had been the austerity measures of deficit cutting. Many Americans were certainly richer than ever before, and many were able to take advantage of the technological wonders of the information age. Nevertheless there was widespread discontent in the mid-1990s at the inequities in American society, as well as a sense of alienation expressed in one of its most extreme forms by the 'Unabomber' Theodore J. Kaczynski, who was arrested in Montana in April 1996 and charged with sending exploding packages and letters to university professors including a sixty-two page manifesto denouncing the industrial revolution. Most people regarded Kaczynski as a lunatic, though a Luddite lunatic who exploited in different ways the resistance to technology found in the writings of Emerson, Thoreau, and E. F. Schumacher, the author of *Small is Beautiful*. Discontent with American society seemed to provide at least part of the explanation for the continued flowering of fundamentalist and religious groups. The Unabomber did not stir much interest beyond American shores. Nor did the ordeal of O. J. Simpson, the former football hero. For Americans themselves, however, his two trials were probably the singular episode of the mid-1990s. In the first, a criminal trial, Simpson was acquitted of the killing of his ex-wife Nicole Brown Simpson and her friend Ronald Goldman in 1994; in the second, a civil trial in February 1997, a jury found him guilty of the same charges. The televised courtroom drama touched everyone, black and white. The first verdict outraged white Americans because it seemed to demonstrate that wealth and clever lawyers could obstruct justice. Whites cheered when the verdict was reversed—but there was no cheering from blacks, who had regarded the first verdict as a defeat of a judicial system biased in favour of whites, and who believed the Los Angeles Police Department had rigged the evidence. The Simpson trials brought to the light of day the underlying reality of uneasy and ambivalent relations between whites and blacks in America. Especially in the inner cities, race relations were exacerbated by the related problems of drugs and crime, which remained the foremost American malaise.

In the Middle East the Israeli Prime Minister Yitzhak Rabin was assassinated in 1995. This was the assassination of the decade, of an order of magnitude approaching that of the slaying of John F. Kennedy. Every Israeli, at least, will remember where he or she was on 4 November when Rabin was shot by a Jewish extremist gunman, Yigal Amir, in a peace rally at Tel Aviv. Amir was a student of religion who believed that God had given the Land of Israel between the River Jordan and the Mediterranean to the Jews and that retreat from the land was synonymous with treason. Rabin had been Chief of Staff in the Six Day War of 1967 when Israel captured East Jerusalem and all of the land to the west of the River Jordan as well as the Sinai Peninsula from Egypt and the Golan Heights from Syria. He had eventually concluded that, despite military superiority, 5.5 million Jews could not indefinitely confront 3.25 million Palestinians in a sea of hostile Arab states. He accepted the idea of an autonomous Palestinian state, and he concluded that he would have to deal with Yasser Arafat and the Palestine Liberation Organization (PLO). Rabin proved to be one of the giants of our times by providing both the leadership and the vision of a compromise peace between two obdurate peoples. His philosophy was not shared by his successor, Binyanin Netanyahu, whose advent as Prime Minister marked a turn towards the traditional idea of permanent confrontation. The peace process in the Middle East in the mid-1990s suffered a severe setback.

Throughout the Middle East, the aftermath of the Gulf War of 1991 continued to be felt in the last years of the century, in part because of the scale of American intervention. The coalition of forces led by the United States and deployed in 'Desert Storm' surpassed the mark of half a million personnel, thus in a sense establishing the Iraqi war along with those of Korea and Vietnam as one of the major conflicts in the post-Second World War era. The miscalculation that Saddam Hussein might be toppled from within Iraq had profound consequences, but what might have been the alternative? The American occupation of Iraq? Though the war proved to be more of an improvised operation than people generally believed at the time, with less of a precise weapons-system than portrayed by the Pentagon, it made clear to the world at large that the United States would go to war to protect access to oil in the Middle East, and that Arab states would attempt to benefit from the American presence as well as to oppose it. Popular resentment against Middle Eastern governments for allying themselves with the West contributed to the dynamism of militant Islam and raised the great question for the end of the century and beyond: what is the future of Islamic fundamentalism? In Iran in May 1997 the election of the moderate cleric Mohammed Khatame as President seemed to indicate that there would be social reforms, including women in his cabinet, but the landslide vote in favour of Khatame also endorsed the Islamic Republic and affirmed its vitality. Over the years, however, revolutionary Iran has become less savage. One could paint a different picture by dwelling on Islamic militants in Algeria, but the general trend in the late 1990s seems to point to one of the remarkable books of the decade, the best-selling *The History of the Arab Peoples* by Albert Hourani, who argues that Islamic fundamentalism is a passing phase: the appeal of militant Islam will be overcome by a reconciliation of secular public law and morality with the principles of social justice of the Koran.

In Africa the two memorable points of focus were South Africa and the Congo. In South Africa the public mood had shifted from the euphoria of post-apartheid liberation, when the world in the early 1990s marvelled at the South Africans' ability to bury the past and to hail a common future, to more worrying concerns of unemployment and violence. The threats to the new South African state no longer came from the white far right, or from Zulu secession, but in the transition from the tight controls of apartheid. Violent crime was on the rise—not only robberies and car-hijacking but outright murders. The dismantling of apartheid, among other things, seemed to turn the country into a trans-shipment point for drugs from Latin America and Asia to Europe. South Africa's banks became a shelter for money launderers. President Nelson Mandela continued to stand as the embodiment of hope for the future and a moral authority recognized by virtually everyone in the country. In June 1995, in one of the remarkable images of our time, he donned the green and gold jersey of the Springboks, the mainly white rugby team that had symbolized diehard Afrikaner nationalism, thus sending a message that reverberated around the world: South Africa would continue the miracle of transformation from apartheid to a democratic and egalitarian society. The whites had not been driven into the sea, nor had their homes been invaded. Black South Africans had proved to be remarkably forgiving. Public confidence remained generally high despite dark clouds of unemployment and violence.

In the heart of Africa in June 1997 the cry resounded, 'Zaire is dead! Long live Congo!' The fall of Mobutu Sese Seko's corrupt and rapacious dictatorship of more than three decades marked the end of the post-colonial era in the Congo. The summer of 1997 will be remembered as the end of a crisis that began in the summer of 1960 with the abrupt departure of the Belgians. Propped up by the CIA during the period of the Cold War, Zaire had experienced not merely corruption but wholesale looting and systematic theft from the state, with Mobutu's bank account indistinguishable from the national treasury. As Mobutu's army melted away before the sweeping advances by rebel forces from the eastern provinces, it became clear that the Zairian state was a hollow shell, with state organizations such as health clinics and schools hardly extant. The standard of living was lower than that in the time of the Belgians. The rebels of Laurent Kabila's Alliance of Democratic Forces met virtually no resistance. A radical from the 1960s, Kabila had spent his formative years in the Lumumbist pan-African movement. Backed by Uganda, Burundi, and especially Rwanda in the mid-1990s, he launched an alliance against Mobutu in exchange for clearing eastern Zaire of Hutu refugees from Rwanda. It became clear in the summer of 1997 that Kabila had given a free hand to Rwandan and Ugandan security units to gun down the refugees, who numbered nearly a million. It will probably never be known how many were killed and how many have survived. The massacres did not augur well for the beginning of the post-Mobutu state.

In South Asia on 15 August 1997 India and Pakistan celebrated their fiftieth year of independence, but the year 1997 had a much more important significance: the two countries, which had fought three wars against each other, moved towards peace. The breakthrough came when senior officials from both countries agreed to negotiate on Kashmir, which since 1947 has been the permanent point of conflict. If a settlement is reached, the economic as well as the defence ramifications could be significant. Kashmir has been the main obstacle in cutting defence expenditure, with 30 per cent of Pakistan's and 15 per cent of India's government spending dedicated to defence. More generally the 1990s in India will probably be remembered for the lifting of socialist controls, a move that might eventually push India's economy into becoming one of the largest in the world. Sustained economic growth and a more equitable distribution of the nation's wealth, however, will require statecraft that has not characterized Indian politics in the 1990s. The decade began violently, with the assassination of the Prime Minister, Rajiv Gandhi, on 21 May 1991. The son of Indira Gandhi, who had been assassinated by extremists seeking a Sikh state in the Punjab, Rajiv was killed by Sri Lankan Tamils. As a national leader he had been faint-hearted and his regime was tainted with corruption. Nor have the successor Prime Ministers managed to approach the level of vision and statesmanship of the first Prime Minister, Jawaharlal Nehru. As Judith Brown has explained in this volume, the principal image of the decade was the destruction in December 1992 of the sixteenth-century mosque in Ayodhya by Hindu nationalists, who plunged India into the worst outbreak of communal violence since partition in 1947. Of the 2,000 people killed, two-thirds were Muslims. In the wake of the Ayodhya incident, the Indian government forfeited the trust of the Muslims and failed to measure up to Nehru's challenge to reconcile all religious faiths in Indian society.

In South-East Asia the dramatic set of events of the decade was the currency crisis that began in Thailand in July 1997 and swept through the Philippines, Indonesia, Malaysia, and Hong Kong. Previously the 'Asian Tigers' had given the impression of sovereign though authoritarian states cooperating within a regional framework to produce astounding economic growth. The miracle of South-East Asian development had been exaggerated. No one perhaps knew of the deficiencies of planning and policy better than those who lived in urban shanties and slums, or worked as labourers in the countryside, and who harboured a sense of resentment against those who had become rich and powerful. The financial crisis will probably have profound social as well as political consequences. Beyond the phenomenon of economic instability, two personalities continued to catch world attention. Aung San Suu Kyi of Myanmar (Burma) in 1991 received the Nobel Peace Prize for her non-violent struggle for democracy and human rights. Under house arrest, Aung San Suu Kyi remained buoyant, a person of intellectual depth and integrity and a beacon of light in a dark and tyrannous state. The other figure in South-East Asia to attract international comment was of an entirely different sort and had a good claim to a place alongside Stalin and Hitler as one of the mass murderers of the century. Pol Pot, who was responsible for the deaths of perhaps nearly 2 million of his countrymen, was found in the summer of 1997 to be alive in a remote jungle in Cambodia. He was sentenced, ironically, merely to life imprisonment after a show trial conducted by his party comrades. Pol Pot had been the central figure in the Khmer Rouge, a radical Maoist group that reduced the already poor nation of Cambodia to a primitive society where education, commerce, culture, and religion were forbidden. From the mid-1970s, one quarter or more of the population was executed or died of torture or forced labour. Pol Pot thus achieved notoriety as the leader of one of the most murderous revolutionary regimes in modern history. His resurfacing in the waning years of the century revived lurid memories.

Certainly one of the most dramatic events of the closing years of the century was the transfer of power in Hong Kong on 1 July 1997. What will be the future of the former colony? The answer probably lies in Chou En-Lai's remark frequently quoted in the weeks before the handover. When asked whether the French Revolution was a good thing or not, Chou said: 'It is too early to tell'. It is possible, however, to discern China's interests in Hong Kong, which are threefold, and which in turn serve as a comment on China in the last decade of the century. First, ideas about democracy and freedom would not be allowed to spread to the rest of China; secondly, the notion of 'one country two systems' if workable in Hong Kong might also be made to work for Taiwan, which has always been a greater Chinese priority; and, thirdly, Hong Kong might become an engine for the further creation of wealth in China without adversarial politics or democratic confrontation. The spectre of Tiananmen Square continued to haunt all speculation on the future of China. As Jonathan Spence has written in this volume, the patriarchal leader Deng Xiaoping had personally ordered troops to smash the pro-democracy demonstrations in Tiananmen Square. But Deng Xiaoping had also initiated sweeping changes throughout China by letting the regions experiment economically. Can China make the leap towards a modern economy without democratization? There are many tensions beneath the surface as Chinese leaders attempt to direct a vast country in a state of change: a profound sense of national pride, rising living standards, but also a deep anxiety about instability. It would be risky to single out any one event by which China in the 1990s will be remembered, but if one is chosen apart from the aftermath of Tiananmen Square, then it would be the funeral in February 1997 of Deng Xiaoping, the last of the great leaders of the Chinese Communist revolution. His death marked the end of an era.

In Japan the event of the decade may well be still to come: the 'Big Bang' that will free the Japanese financial system from rigid regulation. On the model of the London Stock Exchange being thrown open to all comers, the Japanese plan will aim even more ambitiously to introduce fundamental reforms in the banking system. By the mid-1990s economic regeneration and a revival of political purpose seemed to be increasingly urgent. The dominant image of Japan in the last decade of the century was that of a nation retreating from technological ingenuity and economic vitality into political sleaze and government-business collusion—in short into a corrupt system extending into all areas of Japanese life, not least shipping, aviation, and agriculture. Preoccupation in Japan in the 1990s, however, seemed to be with the past as much as with contemporary problems. On the fiftieth anniversary of the surrender at the end of the Second World War, the Japanese Prime Minister offered 'heartfelt' apologies for the suffering caused by his country. And on the fiftieth anniversary of the bombing of Nagasaki, President Clinton announced a halt to nuclear testing by the United States. This did not prevent the French from exploding a nuclear bomb in the Pacific, but Clinton's declaration did serve as a reminder that the world had somehow managed to get through the cold war without the use of nuclear weapons and at least expressed the hope that Nagasaki might never again occur.

What of the four agents of destruction, one riding the white horse of civil war, another on the red horse of genocide, still another on the black horse of terrorism, and the last on the pale horse of famine and disease? Some regions of the world managed to stay more or less out of their path, but the Balkans were especially ravaged by civil war, Rwanda by genocide, Oklahoma City by terrorism, and North Korea by famine. And no place in the world seemed to be immune from disease, notably the plague of Aids. Nor did the Four Horsemen fail to have a grotesque sense of humour associated with them. After the trial of two environmental activists, who claimed, among other things, that the fast-food company McDonald's had damaged the global environment, a writer in the *International Herald Tribune* commented that the pace as well as the gravity of the charges 'put McDonald's right up there with the Four Horsemen of the Apocalypse, accusing it of responsibility for starvation in the Third World, aiding and abetting the destruction of the Central American rain forests, serving food that could cause cancer, heart disease and food poisoning, exploiting children in its advertising, cruelty to animals, lousy treatment of employees and lying about its use of recycled paper and nutrition'. In June 1997 McDonald's was acquitted, but only after the longest libel case in British history consuming 314 days of trial. It was a legal defeat, at least, for the Four Horsemen.

How did the Four Horsemen fare in the four different parts of the world? One of the most conspicuous sites was the Balkans, beginning with the civil war that broke out when Yugoslavia fell apart in 1990–1. Consisting of six republics, the multi-ethnic Yugoslavia had been a country in which nations and nascent states did not coincide. Serbs and Croats, above all, held ancient and enduring animosities. Under Tito and the pressures of the cold war, ethnic tensions had been held in check; but when Communism began to falter, Serbia's President, Slobodan Milosevic, aimed at creating a Greater Serbia. Armed Serb raiding bands terrorized Croatia and Bosnia to drive out the non-Serbs, especially

Muslims. The civil war produced 'ethnic cleansing', a chilling phrase that continues to reverberate around the world in places of ethnic tension. The massacre of some 6,000 Bosnians at Srebrenica in 1995 was probably Europe's worst war crime since 1945. NATO aircraft began sustained attacks on Serb targets until subsequent negotiations at Dayton, Ohio, secured a precarious peace. After the end of hostilities the international war crimes tribunal at The Hague charged Bosnian Serb leaders with crimes against humanity, denouncing the atrocities at Srebrenica as 'scenes from hell, written on the darkest pages of human history'—a triumph for the first of the Four Horsemen.

In Rwanda the slaughter surpassed that in the Balkans, with some 800,000 people in the period of April and May 1994 beaten, stabbed, chopped to pieces, or shot by organized gangs. Rwanda and its twin state of Burundi had been ruled traditionally by the minority Tutsi, about 15 per cent of the population, over the majority of Hutu people. Though the divide between the two groups is often referred to as ethnic and cultural, it is in fact extremely complex, with political and economic roots stretching back some 400 years when Tutsi cattle herders settled among local farming people, most of whom were Hutu. Tutsi and Hutu became part of the same culture, sometimes intermarrying; but politically and socially the Tutsi were reinforced by the colonial rulers, first the Germans and then the Belgians, who used ethnic classification for their own purposes and supported the Tutsi by allowing them to hold positions of authority. The underlying tension concerned land. Tutsi and Hutu did not have separate areas but had lived together for centuries on the same hills and in the same communities, both believing that the land was theirs. By 1962, at the time of independence, majority rule threatened Tutsi supremacy. In Burundi the Tutsi lashed out first, killing off the Hutu political leadership. In Rwanda the Hutu mounted an offensive before independence and killed thousands of Tutsi, securing a Hutu regime but one fearful of vengeance from Tutsi exiles. In 1994, after four years of civil war, extremist Hutu groups organized the mass slaughter of nearly all Tutsi still living in Rwanda. This was the genocide of the 800,000 referred to above, by no means the largest single killing of the century but probably the quickest, within two months—a triumph for the second of the Four Horsemen. In the end the Tutsi prevailed and some 2 million Hutu fled to the Congo and Tanzania. Donald Cameron Watt, a leading historian of the twentieth century, has summed up the general significance of genocide, not merely for Rwanda, but for the world: 'No society, so far, has shown itself to be completely invulnerable to the political encouragement of racial or social enmities within the body politic. That is the lesson of this century.'

In Oklahoma City on 19 April 1995 a gigantic truck bomb exploded and destroyed the Alfred P. Murrah Federal Building; 168 people were killed. It was an act of calculated terrorism with the fuse set not during the middle of the night, when the building would have been nearly empty, but for a time during the day when the maximum number would be murdered. At first the American public suspected terrorists from the Middle East, but after the almost immediate arrest of Timothy McVeigh, everything pointed to terrorism of the home-grown American variety. In June 1997 a Federal jury found McVeigh guilty and sentenced him to death by lethal injection. McVeigh had had a troubled but unremarkable background. He was a veteran of the Gulf War. In the army he had met companions who shared his conviction that the federal government represented an evil force in American society—a belief driven home by the death of eighty-four people during the 1993 federal crackdown on the Branch Davidian sect near Waco, Texas. McVeigh had become associated with the militia movement in the USA. In some twenty-three states militiamen upheld Ku Klux Klan white supremacist views, combining them with gun obsessions of the John Birch Society and with the belief that the CIA had assassinated John F. Kennedy. Perhaps the general point is that, after the end of the cold war, conspiracy theories of international communism now turned inward on the US government. McVeigh may become a martyr for those who believe that the Oklahoma City bombing was carried out by the FBI to subvert American liberty. The Oklahoma City bombing drew on ideas with deep roots in American history and society. It was the most appalling act of terrorism ever to take place on American soil—undeniably a triumph for the Third Horseman.

The Fourth Horseman, famine and disease, had a qualified success in North Korea. Though the famine was a disaster of sweeping magnitude, it was mitigated by the ingenuity of the Korean peasants, who demonstrated tenacious methods of survival. It is not entirely clear whether the famine was a natural disaster or whether it was political in origin, whether it was caused not so much by food shortages as by political decisions. The immediate origins arose in the regime of Kim Il Sung, whose death in July 1994 represented as much of a landmark for North Korea as Deng Xiaoping's did for China. North Korea under Kim Il Sung was an aggressive, authoritarian state with a personality cult rivalling that of Stalin or Mao. But famine was not one of North Korea's characteristics. Until the early 1980s its rice fields were probably more productive than those in South Korea because of large subsidies, chemical fertilizers, and large-scale irrigation works. In the early 1990s, however, support from Russia and China evaporated. Tractors and fertilizer factories fell into disrepair. There was no fuel for transport. North Korea's command economy began to crack. Hills had been stripped of trees and shrubs and reshaped into terraces to provide extra rice paddies. The countryside thus became vulnerable to floods, which devastated the region in 1995 and 1996. Nevertheless the North Koreans demonstrated great fortitude in coping with food shortages. External aid made hunger in the country less desperate even though the long-term prognosis remained dire. There seemed to be no prospect that the regime would decollectivize the country's farms or make serious reforms, in part because reform would acknowledge that there existed no rational reason for not joining the capitalist south. In any event, the long-term famine in North Korea did not seem beyond the power of human ingenuity to solve. In other parts of the world, notably in Africa, the Fourth Horseman still rides, but in Africa as in North Korea biotechnology and the breakthroughs in agricultural techniques (such as the use of artificial fertilizers and high-yielding seeds in India's 'Green Revolution') may eventually help to prevent or at least diminish the severity of famine. Hunger and food scarcity no longer seem to be as implacable an enemy as in earlier decades, certainly not as in earlier centuries.

The Fourth Horseman wielded two swords, one of famine, the other of disease, with the latter taking a deadly toll throughout the world in Aids, though the impact was blunted by advances in medical technology. The access to treatment was uneven. Some 26 million people in the world suffered from the disease. In the West the chances of survival were much greater than, for example, in Africa, where those afflicted often died within two years. In the USA in the 1990s rates of HIV and Aids began to decline among white homosexuals but rose among intravenous drug users and the poor black and Hispanic men and women, heterosexual as well as homosexual. Perhaps more than any other modern medical disaster, Aids intensified more general problems of poverty and drugs, which cast long shadows over the 1990s. But the devastation of the Fourth Horseman was not unqualified and the closing years of the twentieth century should be seen in the perspective of the long-term demographic and disease record. In the past hundred years the population has quadrupled and medical advances have very substantially reduced the virulence of infectious diseases.

Despite civil war, genocide, terrorism, famine, disease, and other catastrophes, the record of the 1990s is emphatically positive. The lesson of the allegory of the Four Horsemen is that they can be kept at bay if not defeated. Human folly and natural disaster, if nothing else, will ensure their survival, but in assessing their significance for the 1990s there is an estimate emphasized by Ralf Dahrendorf in the next chapter that is important: perhaps 20 per cent of the world's population may be worse off than previously, but some 80 per cent are better off. In the former category the Russians are a conspicuous case. In the wake of economic and social dislocations since the dissolution of the Soviet Union, there has been a drop in life expectancy. Indeed the death rate among working-age Russians is higher than a century ago. There is a national pattern of too much smoking and too much vodka—and thus a high rate of death from lung disease and alcoholism—but part of the underlying problem is that the Russian government spends less than 2.6 per cent of the gross national product on health care, far below the levels of other industrial nations. This is a dismal statistic but not one beyond human agency to improve.

The expectation of life throughout the world has risen in the last 100 years from forty-five to seventy-five. In the 1990s the risk of dying in childbirth is at least forty times less than it was fifty years ago. In Britain in 1951 there were 271 people who had lived to be 100. In 1991 there were 4,400. The provision of cleaner water, more adequate sanitation, and better diet is probably just as important as advances in medical treatment, but, by any standard, an assessment of the 1990s reveals remarkable human advance over the course of the last 100 years. And the traditional ravages of the Four Horsemen also pale in relation to one of the greatest successes of our century. We have survived the cold war. Looking back from the vantage point of the 1990s, we now live not only in a time when world war no longer looms on the horizon but generally, despite wide areas of poverty and instability in the world, in an era of emotional and material well-being unimaginable in earlier decades. For many living in the closing years of the twentieth century, especially in the West, the decade may well appear at a later time to have been a golden age.

27 Towards the Twenty-First Century

RALF DAHRENDORF

As the twentieth century draws to a close, one seemingly irresistible force has come to dominate people's lives, hopes, and fears: globalization. Signals of this force have accompanied the century throughout, from the 'world economy' as Robert Skidelsky has written in one chapter in this volume, to a 'universal culture' as Alan Ryan has written in another. But only now, as the year 2000 approaches, has the human life world become truly global. Few things can be understood without the context of the entire globe. We have to think globally to respond to an increasingly global reality.

Perhaps this new experience started in earnest when the first astronauts stepped out onto the sandy surface of the moon. The rest of the world watched their pantomime with bated breath on television: virtual reality along with actual reality. They had, after all, left the globe and thereby emphasized its discrete wholeness. They had also seen the globe; we now have photographs, and even films of it turning as Copernicus told us it would.

The discovery had its less enchanting side when the human habitat on this globe caught the attention first of scientists and then of a growing number of threatened inhabitants. Not only is the the globe real; we also change it by our behaviour, above all those who live a privileged existence of prosperity. Perhaps it was the authors of the first Club of Rome report on *Limits to Growth* (1973), mistaken as they may have been in many details, who made us aware of the consequences of man's quest for subjugating nature. In the end the globe may become uninhabitable: too many people; too much poisonous CO_2 produced by them; too many chemicals altogether in the soil and the air and the waters, even the oceans. Holes in the protective ozone layer over the poles were discovered which let in deadly rays. There are signs that the climage changes; 'global warming' may make the seas rise to swamp whole countries. At the same time, we are eradicating a growing number of species. Will humans be one of those on the death list before long?

The risk of extinction is not just a by-product of economic advancement for large numbers, it is also a result of the destructive potential of modern weapons, whether nuclear, biological, or chemical. The atom bombs of Hiroshima and Nagasaki may still have been fairly localized death weapons (though they may also have had unknown global effects, as did the thermonuclear tests of the 1950s and 1960s), but later nuclear weapons could, and can, wipe out large parts, perhaps the whole of mankind. The Chernobyl accident of 1986 gave many in Russia, Europe, and beyond a foretaste of risks.

Globalization is not just an ecological, military, or technical idea; it is above all used as an economic concept. Information provides its base. By virtue of technical developments, notably in electronics, information has become ubiquitous and instant. The moment a news item—the death of a statesman, the price of a share, the discovery of a new drug—is entered into a computer in Tokyo or San Diego or Dublin, it is available everywhere, twenty-four hours a day, every day of the year.

The most immediate economic effect of the globalization of information was on financial markets. Gone are the days in which people in the City of London could go home once the first trend figures from Wall Street were telephoned through. They can never go home nowadays. Shares and bonds and many derivatives from them are quoted at all times; funds are 'moved' through the virtual world of markets day and night. Other information has followed the change. A London travel agency can have a computer system in Bombay; a Japanese car company can have components produced in Mexico. The price of goods and their parts is no longer burdened by transport costs and local constraints; competition, fair as well as foul, keeps the information varied and different. People speak of Singapore and Honolulu, Santiago de Chile and Vancouver, Glasgow and Istanbul as if these places were just next door, especially if they 'speak' on the Internet, the global computer network which seems to belong to nobody.

Globalization—the entire world of humans as an instant and permanent reality—has many effects, and in one way or another these effects will determine the future. It may be useful to distinguish between some consequences, which are worrying in terms of the values defended by the enlightened minority in the twentieth century, and other consequences which give hope.

The twentieth century has been largely, if not throughout, determined by divisions which led to wars, hot and cold, but which also provided sources of identity: alliances of nations, democracies versus dictatorships, the free world versus the kingdom of evil. Globalization became the dominant theme at precisely the moment at which these notions—and notably that of a First and Second World, the US-dominated world of capitalism and the Soviet Union-dominated world of communism—had lost their force. As it progressed, even the Third World of developing countries became a less and less relevant category. Nation states re-emerged but they were also weakened by global trends. Norway cannot close the ozone hole over the North Pole, and even the United States cannot control world financial markets. So who is in charge? And where do people belong in the global-ized habitat of the twenty-first century?

Some answers that are given both in theory and in fact are worrying. One is that the cold war between capitalism and communism will, and even should be, replaced by powerful regional blocs. Asia, Europe, and America are most often quoted. At times they are identified with organizations, APEC, EU, NAFTA (acronyms thrive in this period!). These are economic alliances, though one way of viewing them in the global market place is that they make little or no economic sense other than to protect their members from the rest. This purpose is even more explicit when wider political considerations enter the scene, as in the case of NATO and its expansion eastward. The Eurasian 'heartland' (as Halford Mackinder described Russia and Europe at the beginning of the twentieth cen-tury) once again leads the way, though in doing so it raises as many questions as it answers.

What exactly is the reason behind the drive for an 'ever closer union' of the small and medium-sized countries assembled in the EU? Who are they guarding against, and what instruments do they want to play in the concert of blocs? Where does an enlarged NATO leave those at its margin, the new in-between countries such as the Ukraine, even perhaps the Baltic States and nations of South-Eastern Europe? What, above all, will the place and the role of post-Soviet Russia be? Where does China fit into the picture? Where does India? Must South America support NAFTA, which may lead to a new Monroe Doctrine? These are explosive questions in a kaleidoscopic world in which new shapes of alliances are forming without clear pattern or purpose.

Or is the purpose going to be provided by new ideological divisions? The American political scientist Samual Huntington has certainly found many readers for his book on *The Clash of Civilizations* (1996). His thesis is that the great world religions, notably Christianity and Islam, form the basis of new cleavages which have the potential of political and even armed conflict. At the turn of the millenni-um the contrast if not the clash between a largely secular Christianity and a newly orthodox Islam is clearly evident. The former is strong in Europe, North and South America, and some other parts of the world, the latter in the Middle East, in impor-tant parts of West and South-East Asia, and increasingly in Africa. A number of vio-lent clashes with Islamic forces involve not just Christianity but other religions such as Judaism and Hinduism.

Another way of looking at this new conflict is to contrast secular and funda-mentalist creeds. The issue then is modernity itself, with the secular religious groups granting Caesar what is Caesar's and reserving merely the spiritual life for God, whereas fundamentalists are *intégriste* (to use their French description) in that they want one law to apply to all spheres of life. While in secular societies indi-viduals benefit from the world economy, fundamentalist societies want to save older patterns of cohesion and domination even at the risk of economic disad-vantage.

Such divergences are closely related to new political divisions which also carry with them the seeds of future conflicts. What is called democracy is by no means an undisputed value among those who have the choice. Democracy and the rule of law are in fact denounced as neo-imperialist values of the European and American world. The 'Asia that can say no' is one of authoritarianism, of the allegedly benevolent rule by élites which claim moral as well as political authority while leaving the people alone as long as they respect authority and do not demand free speech and political participation. As in the case of religion, the conflict between democracy and authoritarianism is not just one between countries but occurs within them too. The temptations of authoritarianism are considerable in Europe and North America as well, whereas many Asians believe in democracy and the rule of law. Thus the new struggles are as much intra-national as international, and who will prevail where remains an open question.

As new divisions emerge and new lines of conflict are drawn, another more profound set of problems begins to affect ordinary life. What of those excluded from the brave new world of globalization? There are many who either feel or are left out, and they tell a story of anomie—the disintegration and absence of binding norms.

Exclusion has an international aspect. When the notion of a Third World is used at the end of the twentieth century, it usually applies to Africa. That variegated and in many parts unhappy continent may have fewer inhabitants already than it did twenty and thirty years ago. War and civil war, famine and illness, epidemics such as Aids have devastated it. Africa has become a symbol of exclusion everywhere. There are 'Africans' in Asia and Latin America, indeed in the cities of Europe and North America. The globalized world has an underside of destitution and death.

International experience is mirrored within societies. In the United States of the 1980s authors like William Julius Wilson first identified what they called an 'underclass' of the 'truly disadvantaged'. Since then the phenomenon has migrated to the rest of the developed world and beyond. There is some dispute about its size—10 per cent? 30 per cent?—but agreement that a sizeable proportion of people have lost touch with the labour market, with the political community, and with social participation more generally. They live a life of poverty and often crime at the margin of society, and there seems to be little economic incentive to integrate them. In the global economy businesses can grow with declining numbers of workers. A new contrast emerges between macro-wealth and micro-misery, thus aggravating already serious issues of social cohesion. The modern road 'from status to contract'—that is, from a firm place for everyone within the social order to individual choice in a wide-open market place—has brought great freedom but also great strains on the texture of societies. 'Belonging' becomes an issue which remains unresolved for many.

The consequences of this process are numerous and serious. For the major part of the twentieth century the notion of a struggle of 'the poor against the rich' dominated people's thinking and determined organized action. This seemed to apply within countries as a class struggle as it did internationally. The proletariat was regarded by some as the harbinger of the future, tomorrow's dominant class, and the international 'proletariat' of the Third World was praised as the source of true values. Along with other certainties, however, this pattern has crumbled at the end of the century.

The social conflict of the twenty-first century will thus be different in nature. It will be an individualized version of the old struggles. Within countries, problems of 'law and order' will dominate the agenda. Internationally, terrorism will threaten assumptions of security. Social conflicts are transposed into individual actions. They do not involve organized social groups, but activists who may or may not represent larger groups. This means that in substance the new conflicts are moral rather than economic; they are about the values which make societies cohere rather than about their wealth and its distribution.

There is a common theme to the new problems which the twenty-first century is going to inherit from the twentieth century. Many of these problems arise from what may well be an emotional reaction against globalization. Compared to the family or the village, the globe is a lonely place in which people easily lose their bearings. Thus they look for bearings and are more likely to find them in smaller groups. The blossoming of para-religious groups which claim people's hearts and minds is one striking example. Total openness seems to give rise to the call for total involvement, for closure.

The philosopher Karl Popper called this the 'return to the tribe'. A new regionalism is rapidly gaining ground at the end of the twentieth century, and it is tribal in character. People look for homogeneous units and thereby turn their backs on the larger heterogeneous nation states which the nineteenth century created. Sometimes they claim that their Catalonia, Slovakia, or Wallonia will connect more easily with the global network of a new age; but the probability must be high that these allegedly homogeneous regions will in fact resemble Chechnya or Bosnia or other war-torn areas. Intolerance within and aggressiveness without are a frequent concomitant of nationalism.

Will history now come to an end? Such a notion was first advanced in this form by Hegel at the beginning of the nineteenth century, and was recently repeated and applied to the late twentieth century. History according to this theory is the unfolding of one great principle through conflicts and pendulum swings, thesis and antithesis. Once such antagonisms are all resolved in the final—global—synthesis, 'normal' life will dominate everything and there is no great story to tell any more.

Not everyone shares such a Wagnerian view of history. Those who believe that history has no meaning other than that which humans give it will be less concerned. But philosophy of history apart, the great conflicts of the twentieth century have certainly run their course. Whether one describes them in social terms as class struggles, in economic terms as conflicts between market and plan, in political terms as battles between modern and pre-modern forms of governance, or indeed in international terms as wars between the First and the Second (and perhaps the Third) Worlds, they no longer describe the new reality of a globalized world. The drama of history is likely to have other themes in the century ahead.

Ordinary people will not care much about a new history of struggles, conflicts, and wars, nor does the author of this postscript to a volume about a murderous century. Moreover, the list of problems drawn up here gives more than enough ammunition to potential warlords. For the great, often violent, struggles of the time are not like earthquakes which no one can control. They do not arise from some deep emotional lava in which people are mired without being able to resist. On the contrary, they are the result of the mobilization of emotions by leaders—or seducers, as they should be called. The two most obvious dangers, nationalism and fundamentalism, which often go hand in hand, would not exist as risks to liberty and security were it not for those who exploit them to satisfy their own lust for power.

If we assume for a moment that history need not go down the slippery slope of violent antagonisms, globalization offers the great opportunity of a competition of compatible responses. Capitalism and socialism were mutually exclusive and therefore at war with each other. Versions of capitalism are not mutually exclusive. The American version of 'pure capitalism' as well as the several variants of the social market economies of Continental Europe, and the Asian capitalism of social cohesion and traditional values, can coexist without war. The world can benefit from the fact that there is no longer an irreconcilable conflict of 'systems'.

Globalization may seem a harsh and unfriendly force to some, but it is also a source of unheard-of opportunities for many. Another scenario for the twenty-first century can, therefore, be drawn which looks at the potential for increasing the life chances of hundreds of millions of people. Early theories of economic development sometimes assumed that the wealth of the few would gradually 'trickle down' to the many. It did not. The capacity of the few to guard their privilege and exclude others is great. But development has turned out to be a bushfire in an age of globalization. China, with its more than one billion people, shows both the ravages and the new life chances which arise from development once it has caught on. At the turn of the century, some 20 per cent of all humans live in destitution; but the other side of this figure is that 80 per cent have stepped on the ladder which leads to greater prosperity. Increasingly, the whole world is becoming one OECD, an Organization for Economic Cooperation and Development.

Prosperity fails to reach above all those who actively resist it. As Mario Varga Llosa put it when he was a candidate for the presidency of Peru, countries can now decide whether they want to be rich. All they have to do is to accept the challenges of globalization and create a degree of institutional stability. Not surprisingly, most countries have done so. Some of those which have not are likely to follow soon.

The road to prosperity is always hard. A valley of tears precedes the ascent to greater welfare and well-being. Several of the authors in *The Oxford History of the Twentieth Century* have described the travails of this valley in vivid terms. Yet it could be argued that the trek through the valley of tears need not take as long as it did when Britain, the United States and a succession of European countries opted for industrialization and modernization. While uprooting people from their traditional habitat seems inevitable, new opportunities are often available, if not immediately, then very soon. With the help of information technology, the road from take-off to full development can be completed in one generation.

Full development itself opens up new opportunities for millions of people. The experience of the old industrial countries may well point the way. Life is no longer all work and little time for other endeavours. Work itself has become easier; working hours have been reduced; working lives are interspersed with holidays, sabbaticals, periods of educational renewal. Through extended initial education and several decades of 'retirement' experience, a new balance of paid employment and other activities is emerging, at least for some. The transition is, like all transitions, painful—for example in the United States where many women as well as men have to hold two jobs to make ends meet. In the late 1990s most societies are still organized around paid employment. Both the earnings and the entitlements of individuals depend on jobs. Unemployment is for many a curse. But this may be no more than a transitional phenomenon. Globalization demands flexibility; it also makes flexibility easier to bear. Once the imagination of social institutions catches up with that of people, societies may emerge in which individuals enjoy much greater life chances.

At the beginning of the twentieth century, the American author Thorstein Veblen wrote *The Theory of the Leisure Class*, and assumed that its privileges would not be available to the vast majority of the working class. At the beginning of the twenty-first century the picture is about to be reversed. A small ruling class (if such exists in the old sense of the term) will insist on remaining busy at one set of tasks for many hours each day; the majority, however, have become a more flexible multitude which combines work with leisure, education, and family life in a kaleidoscope of activity. People have what Charles Handy called 'portfolios of work' rather than old-style jobs, or, as Jeremy Rifkin put it in *The End of Work*, they can move between the wealth-generating, the public, and the voluntary sphere of activity.

The globalized world of the coming decades offers new opportunities of participation. In the nineteenth and twentieth centuries the market place of old, where active citizens debated and decided their affairs, gave way to institutions in which a limited number of representatives—or activists—derived their legitimacy from regular expressions of view by the many who remained otherwise fairly passive. Now direct democracy is virtually dead, but representative democracy too is increasingly replaced by wider participation. This can take the form of referenda, but also of civic initiatives of many kinds, and of course of the interactive use of new media and information systems. The boundary between activists and passive, part-time, even occasional citizens becomes blurred. Potentially at least, we are all active citizens now.

As in other respects, systems of governance bear the traces of transition; old patterns no longer work, but new ones have not yet been established. This is notably true when it comes to the issue of appropriate governance. The nation state is still the most effective frame within which people of different cultures and orientations can find their civil rights guaranteed. In the more enlightened parts of the world, at least in the view of this author, people are citizens of nation states. But the winds of globalization have dented national borders. Nation states cannot introduce effective rules for financial transactions, indeed for economic processes more generally. They cannot prevent their citizens from making use of information of many kinds, whether desirable or not. They cannot guarantee a sustainable natural environment. They cannot safeguard peace. Larger units of governance are needed even for the elementary functions of minimal governance.

The twentieth century may come to be seen as a time of experimentation in this regard. In this volume Adam Roberts has described the trials and errors of this process and also the contradictions involved in the attempt to combine the sovereignty of states with a supranational order based on the rule of law. He has also argued that logical incompatibility need not rule out practical viability. For the latter, the habit of international cooperation is as important as the charters of international organizations. With respect to the future world order, as in other respects, the crystal ball is clouded. One may hope, however, that the twenty-first century will see a greater congruence of real or pragmatic action and institutional arrangements. This involves, above all, a new combination of the local and the global, with appropriate though possibly less important alliances and arrangements in between.

The problems and the opportunities of an age of globalization are finely balanced. Whether mankind will succumb to the problems or grasp the opportunities one dare not predict. Perhaps the safest prognosis is a bit of both. Even so, one crucial task has to be resolved. Put in terms of domestic affairs, it is to square the circle of making use of the economic opportunities in a global market place while preserving and perhaps recreating cohesive civil societies, and achieving those aims within liberal political institutions. Prosperity, civility, and liberty all have to be secured. Put in terms of international affairs, the same task involves a combination of creating conditions of economic growth while respecting cultural differences and establishing rules of peaceful cooperation for the world as a whole.

The circle cannot be squared perfectly, but it is possible to come close. In the economy, the removal of obstacles to human endeavour is critical. Entrepreneurs must be encouraged and all those involved in the creation of wealth must show—and be able to show—flexibility. But the other side of such freedom is one of rules which safeguard opportunities of access and prevent abuse of the market place. This is the minimal function of a social policy of inclusion and citizenship. Beyond policy, both the creation of wealth and the rules of fairness have to be anchored in buoyant civil societies. By their associations people will construct the safety net holding those who are weak or threatened. They will also engender that sense of belonging which is so hard to maintain in an age of globalization. Deregulating the economy, rethinking the welfare state, promoting social cohesion, and reasserting democracy and the rule of law are major tasks ahead.

The international equivalent to this set of tasks can be put in similar language. Traces of a world civil society have already emerged. It is hard to exaggerate the importance of the role of non-governmental organizations and the growing signs of international justice. The trials of war criminals from former Yugoslavia may be awkward and inconclusive but they set an example, as do Truth Commissions or their equivalents in South Africa and elsewhere. From the annual meetings of public and private financial institutions under the auspices of the IMF and the World Bank as well as the Group of 30, the signals of new rules have emerged. The recently created World Trade Organization (WTO) can help. Serious peacekeeping and effective environmental protection are lagging behind but at least attempts have been made. The UN Environmental Summit at Rio in 1992 was followed by one on Social Development in Copenhagen in 1995.

Thus there is much to build on. There are also hints at the spirit in which the construction of a world of opportunities should be approached. Indeed as the twentieth century draws to a close there is a great debate on moral values and their role in business, in politics, and in everyday life. Morals are not an exact science; different people have different preferences; but perhaps it is useful to point to three elements of an approach to the future which have emerged.

The first is that few are now looking for a perfect world. Utopia is one of the casualties of the twentieth century. Not only can it not be found, but the attempt to create it leads to disaster, totalitarianism, and war at its worst. As we try to square the circle we realize that we cannot fully achieve the ideal. There will be lapses; there will be no shortage of problems; conflicts remain a source of progress which needs to be channelled, not closed. Only open societies can be good societies.

The second and most difficult element of the new morals has to do with future generations. Mankind has a disconcerting way of dealing with problems only when the clock has begun to strike twelve. It solves problems which are upon us, not those which experts anticipate for the future. Yet once some of the problems cited here are upon us, it will be too late. This is notably the case with respect to nuclear war and environmental destruction. Some have spoken of the 'responsibility principle' which is necessary in the 'risk society' in which we are living. We must think ahead to what we are doing to our grandchildren, yet we do not want to allow anyone to tell the rest of us precisely what needs to be done. How can we act responsibly without inviting an allegedly benevolent dictator? The unanswerable question has to be answered somehow. What is more, it will be answered, if only by deadly silence.

Thirdly, there is the matter of underlying attitudes. Ernest Gellner, in his sermon on *The Uniqueness of Truth*, categorized them as those of the Relativist, the Fundamentalist, and the Enlightenment Puritan. Certainly, a wave of relativism is sweeping the world, especially the old developed world. Anything goes, either because it serves the self-interest of those who do not want to be told by others what not to do, or because it seems the logical end of the road from liberal to libertine predilections. Such relativism, however, will not help us square the circle in an age of globalization. It will make things too easy for those who believe that two of the three objectives are enough, wealth and cohesion without liberty, wealth and liberty without social cohesion, solidarity and liberty without prosperity.

Fundamentalism—or *intégrisme*, as we have described it—is the worst of all answers. Its enforced cohesion robs people of basic liberties and in the end is bound to impair economic opportunities as well. Protectionism, ethnic cleansing, and tyranny are not only bad prescriptions for squaring the circle of goals to attain, but destroy both civil society and the strength of markets as sources of wealth creation.

There remains what to many now seems a rather old-fashioned view. We are living in a horizon of uncertainty; we do not know for sure what is right and good and just, but we can try to find out; trying means erring, and our institutions must provide for correcting error; above all, we must never give up trying to enhance the quality of life. Such enlightened values have not done very well in the twentieth century, which has seen them extolled and violated in equal measure. Their mixed fortunes in the past are, however, no argument against their validity. After all, they may do better in the twenty-first century.

FURTHER READING

1. The Dawn of the Century

BULL, HEDLEY, and WATSON, ADAM (eds.), *The Expansion of International Society* (Oxford, 1984). Excellent articles on the diffusion of European ideas.

HOBSBAWM, E. J., *The Age of Empire, 1795–1914* (London, 1987). The best general account.

KIERNAN, V. G., *The Lords of Human Kind* (London, 1972). Lively account of European supremacism.

MAYER, ARNO, *The Persistence of the Old Regime, 1890–1914* (London, 1981). Lively but uneven account of the survival of feudalism in Europe into the new century.

ROMEIN, JAN, *The Watershed of Two Eras: Europe in 1900*, trans. A. J. Pomerans (Middleton, Conn., 1982).

TANNENBAUM, EDWARD R., *1900: The Generation before the Great War* (New York, 1976). Two excellent studies of intellectual trends at the turn of the century.

2. Demography and Urbanization

BAIROCH, PAUL, *Cities and Economic Development from the Dawn of History to the Present* (Chicago, 1988). European focus; quantitative emphasis.

CRITCHFIELD, RICHARD, *The Villagers: Changed Values, Altered Lives: The Closing of the Urban–Rural Gap* (New York, 1994). Field studies of rural change in different continents and cultures.

EHRLICH, PAUL R., *The Population Bomb* (New York, 1978). Alarmist view, emphasis on impact on environment of population growth.

HAUSER, PHILIP M. (ed.), *World Population and Development: Challenges and Prospects* (Syracuse, NY, 1979). UN studies, quasi-official views.

HUNT, R. DOUGLAS, *Agricultural Technology in the Twentieth Century* (Manchester, Kan., 1991). Narrowly US focus; but that country was the technological leader.

QUALE, G. ROBINA, *Families in Context: A World History of Population* (Westport, Conn., 1992). Emphasis on role of women; impact of urbanization on demography.

SEITZ, JOHN L., *The Politics of Development: An Introduction to Global Issues* (New York, 1988). How to manage population growth and pollution.

SHANIN, TEODOR (ed.), *Peasants and Peasant Societies: Selected Readings* (Oxford, 1987). Exactly what the title says.

TAPINOS, GEORGE, and PIOTROW, PHYLLIS T., *Six Billion People: Demographic Dilemmas and World Politics* (New York, 1978). What governments can do and are doing.

TODARO, MICHAEL P., *Internal Migration in Developing Countries: A Review of Theory, Evidence, Methodology and Research Priorities* (Geneva, 1976). An official study by the ILO.

WOLF, ERIC, *Peasants* (Englewood Cliffs, NJ, 1966). Textbook by a famous anthropologist.

WRIGLEY, E. A., *Population and History* (New York, 1969). Popular presentation by a leading historical demographer.

3. The Great Reduction: Physics in the Twentieth Century

Compiled by Thomas Fink

CREASE, ROBERT P., and MANN, CHARLES C., *The Second Creation* (New York, 1986). A very readable account of the major players in twentieth-century physics.

DAVIES, PAUL C. W., and BETTS, DAVID S., *Quantum Mechanics* (London, 1994). Clear and compact technical introduction to quantum mechanics.

FEYNMAN, RICHARD P., *The Character of Physical Law* (London, 1965). Lectures on the character of Newtonian to twentieth-century physics.

FEYNMAN, RICHARD P., LEIGHTON, ROBERT B., and SANDS, MATTHEW, *The Feynman Lectures on Physics, Vol. III* (New York, 1996). Feynman's insightful and highly entertaining undergraduate lectures on quantum mechanics.

PAIS, ABRAHAM, *Inward Bound* (New York, 1986). A physicist's account of the developments in twentieth-century physics.

——, '*Subtle is the Lord . . .*' (New York, 1982). Biography (as much of the science as of the life) of Albert Einstein.

PENROSE, ROGER, *The Emperor's New Mind* (Oxford, 1989). A fascinating and lucid tour of computers, minds, and the laws of physics.

RHODES, RICHARD, *The Making of the Atomic Bomb* (London, 1988). Authoritative Pulitzer Prize-winning history of the bomb.

PAULI, WOLFGANG, *Theory of Relativity* (London, 1958). Classic technical text on Einstein's special and general theories of relativity.

SCHWEBER, SILVAN S, *QED and the Men Who Made It* (New Jersey, 1994). The development of quantum electrodynamics and its principal actors: Dyson, Feynman, Schwinger, and Tomonaga.

WEINBERG, STEVEN, *Dreams of a Final Theory* (New York, 1958). The idea of, progress towards, and implications of a final unified theory, written for the general reader.

4. The Expansion of Knowledge

BOORSE, Henry A., and MOTZ, LLOYD, *The World of the Atom* (New York, 1966).

JUDSON, HORACE, *The Eighth Day of Creation* (Harmondsworth, 1995).

OLDBY, ROBERT, *The Path to the Double Helix* (Macmillan, 1974).

TATON, R., *Science in the Twentieth Century* (London, 1966).

WILLIAMS, T. I., *A Short History of British Technology* (Oxford, 1982).

—— *Biographical Dictionary of Scientists* (HarperCollins, 1996).

5. The Growth of a World Economy

BHAGWATI, JAGDISH, *India in Transition: Freeing the Economy* (Oxford, 1993). A trenchant critique of Indian central planning.

CALLEO, DAVID P., *The Bankrupting of America: How the Federal Budget is Impoverishing the Nation* (New York, 1992). An excellent analysis of the impact of US budgetary policy on world economics since the 1960s.

CARR, E. H., *The Russian Revolution from Lenin to Stalin 1917–1929* (London, 1979). The best short summary of early Soviet economic policy.

HIRSCHMAN, ALBERT O., *Essays in Trespassing: Economics to Politics and Beyond* (Cambridge, 1981). Contains some of his best writing on development economics, Latin American experiences, European integration, and other matters.

KEYNES, JOHN MAYNARD, *The Economic Consequences of the Peace* (1st edn., London, 1919; Collected Writings edn., London, 1971). Remains the classic account of the folly of the peacemakers at Versailles, and the economic effects of their handiwork.

KINDLEBERGER, CHARLES P., *The World in Depression 1929–1939* (London, 1973). A characteristically authoritative, but also racy, economist's account of the inter-war years.

KRUGMAN, PAUL, 'The Myth of Asia's Economic Miracle', *Foreign Affairs*, Nov.–Dec. 1994. For a sceptical view of it.

McCRACKEN, P., *et al.*, *Towards Full Employment and Price Stability* (Paris, 1977). A sophisticated economic analysis of 'what went wrong' in the early 1970s.

MADDISON, ANGUS, *The World Economy in the Twentieth Century* (Paris, 1989). The best short survey of the whole field.

MAIER, CHARLES S., *Recasting Bourgeois Europe: Stabilization in France, Germany, and Italy in the Decade after World War I* (Princeton, 1975). A densely argued account of how political and economic élites retained their power by institutionalizing 'corporatism'.

SKIDELSKY, ROBERT, *The World after Communism* (London, 1995). An attempt to understand the shifts in political economy over this century.

STEWART, MICHAEL, *Keynes and After* (3rd edn., London, 1986). An accessible survey of twentieth-century economic theory and policy from a Keynesian point of view.

VAN DER WEE, HERMAN, *Prosperity and Upheaval in the World Economy 1945–1980* (London, 1986). A solid account of the 'golden age'.

6. The Growth of a Global Culture

CAMUS, ALBERT, *The Rebel* (Paris, 1958). A riposte to the gloom and despair of post-war existentialism by John-Paul Sartre's most distinguished rival for the attention of European intellectuals.

DE BEAUVOIR, SIMONE, *The Second Sex* (London, 1953 [Paris, 1952]). A somewhat two-edged feminist statement, since its argument is that women can gain their independence only by being like men.

DEWEY, JOHN, *Experience and Nature* (New York, 1925). Aptly described by Justice Holmes as a book that God might have written to tell mankind how things truly were—if he had found himself at a loss for words.

FREUD, SIGMUND, *Civilization and its Discontents* (London, 1930). The German title, *Unbehagen in dem Kultur*—or 'Anxiety in Culture'—better catches the thought that humanity resists the civilization it so much needs.

GISH, LILLIAN, *Mr Griffith, The Movies, and Me* (Englewood Cliffs, NJ, 1969).

HEIDEGGER, MARTIN, *Sein und Zeit* (Halle, 1927). The seminal work in the existentialist tradition.

JUNG, C. G., *Modern Man in Search of a Soul* (London, 1933). The spiritual response to Freud's bleakly materialist account of our religious aspirations in *The Future of an Illusion*.

OSBORNE, HAROLD, *The Oxford Companion to Twentieth Century Art* (Oxford, 1981). An exhaustive, but far from exhausting account of an enormous variety of persons, movements, and objects.

RAWLS, JOHN, *A Theory of Justice* (Cambridge, Mass., 1971). One of the most distinguished analytical philosophers of post-war years revives the philosophical discussion of issues of social justice.

RIESMAN, DAVID, *The Lonely Crowd* (New York, 1953). An updated account of Tocqueville's anxieties about the American tendency to 'go along to get along'. It introduced the now-famous idea of 'other-directed man' to sociology.

RUSSELL, BERTRAND, *Autobiography* (London, 1966–7). The first volume especially is a wonderfully vivid and highly personal account of the origins of modern logic and philosophy.

TRILLING, LIONEL, *The Liberal Imagination* (London, 1951). America's most distinguished literary critic's reflections on the achievements—and limitations—of modernism.

WEBER, MAX, *The Protestant Ethic and the Spirit of Capitalism* (London, 1930). The classical discussion of secularization and modernity.

WITTGENSTEIN, LUDWIG, *Tractatus Logico-Philosophicus* (London, 1922). Enigmatic, and oddly poetic, but a crucial work in the growth of analytical philosophy.

7. The Visual Arts

ARNASON, H. H., *A History of Modern Art, Painting, Sculpture, Architecture* (London, 1969). An efficient survey of two-thirds of this century, starting with Impressionism.

ASHTON, DORE, *A Fable of Modern Art* (London, 1980).

CURTIS, WILLIAM J. R., *Modern Architecture since 1900* (Oxford, 1982). A selective yet searching and intelligently critical account of its subject.

HAMILTON, GEORGE HEARD, *Painting and Sculpture 1880–1940* (Harmondsworth, 1967). A thoughtful account of modern art but sparsely illustrated.

HUGHES, ROBERT, *The Shock of the New* (London, 1980). In spite of its journalistic title, an intelligent and refreshing narrative of modern art history by a critic whose views are clear and vividly expressed.

HUNTER, SAM, and JACOBS, JOHN, *Modern Art: Painting, Sculpture, Architecture* (New York, 1985). A spirited survey of modern art history since Post-Impressionism, with extra attention given to America's contribution since the 1940s.

KLOTZ, ROBERT, *Twentieth Century Architecture* (London, 1989). A lively and informative discussion of a sequence of key works and issues.

LYNTON, NORBERT, *The Story of Modern Art* (Oxford, 1980) (2nd edn, with additional material, 1989). Invites a questioning approach to art from 1900 to the 1980s.

RICHARDSON, JOHN, *A Life of Picasso* (2 vols.; London, 1991–6).

SMITH, EDWARD LUCIE, *Artoday* (London, 1996). A well-organized survey of international Western and Westernized art since 1960.

8. The European Colonial Empires

FERRO, MARC, *Colonization: A Global History* (London, 1997; French edn. Paris, 1994). Especially useful for the French perspective on empire.

FIELDHOUSE, D. K., *The Colonial Empires: A Comparative Survey from the Eighteenth Century* (London, 1966). The best general account.

LOUIS, WM. ROGER, *Imperialism at Bay* (Oxford, 1978). A study of American influence on the European colonial system during the Second World War.

McCLINTOCK, ANNE, *Imperial Leather: Race, Gender and Sexuality in the Colonial Context* (London, 1995). An inquiry into feminist, post-colonial, psychoanalytic and socialist theories as an explanation of European imperialism.

MACQUEEN, NORRIE, *The Decolonization of Portuguese Africa* (London, 1997). Useful summary of Portuguese colonial rule as well as decolonization.

MORRIS, JAMES, *Heaven's Command; Pax Britannica;* and *Farewell the Trumpets* (London, 1968–78). A famous and readable trilogy on the rise, decline, and fall of the British Empire.

Scott, Paul, *The Raj Quartet* (London, 1976). A saga of a British military family in India. Perhaps the greatest novel on the British Empire ever written.

von Lettow-Vorbeck, Paul, *My Reminiscences of East Africa* (London, n.d. (*c.* 1920)). The riveting and classic account of the battle for German East Africa during the First World War.

Weinstein, Brian, *Éboué* (Oxford, 1972). A biography of Felix Éboué, the black colonial administrator who rallied the French Forces of General de Gaulle in the Second World War. Throws much light on the inner workings of French colonial administration as well as on the colonial mystique.

Young, Crawford, *The African Colonial State in Comparative Perspective* (New Haven, 1994). Especially strong on the Belgian Congo, this is a seminal study on the general problem of colonial rule and its consequences.

9. Europe in the Age of the Two World Wars

Bell, P. M. H., *The Origins of the Second World War in Europe* (London, 1986). A worthy companion volume to Joll (see below).

Calvocoressi, Peter, and Wint, Guy, *Total War* (2nd edn., London, 1988). A superb survey of both the military and the political aspects of the Second World War.

Falls, Cyril, *The First World War* (London, 1960, repr. 1989). Still the best brief military history of the conflict.

Fest, Joachim, *Hitler* (London, 1974). The most accessible biography.

Fischer, Fritz, *Griff nach der Weltmacht*, trans. as *Germany's War Aims in the First World War* (London, 1967). A controversial restatement of the thesis that Germany bore prime responsibility for the First World War.

Herwig, Holge, *The First World War, Germany and Austria–Hungary* (London, 1996). A Central European perspective that corrects the Anglocentrism of Cyril Falls.

Hitler, Adolf, *Mein Kampf*, ed. with an introduction by Donald Cameron Watt (London, 1969). Indispensible for an understanding of Hitler's world view.

Joll, James, *The Origins of the First World War* (London, 1984). A balanced analysis of the different schools of thought.

Parker, R. A. C., *Europe, 1919–1945* (London, 1969). The best brief survey.

Rich, Norman, *Hitler's War Aims* (2 vols.; London, 1973). The best account of the creation and administration of Hitler's 'New Europe'.

Taylor, A. J. P., *The Origins of the Second World War* (London, 1961). A controversial interpretation that questions Germany's primary responsibility for the Second World War.

Weinberg, Gerhard, *A World at Arms: A Global History of World War II* (Cambridge, 1994). More detailed and comprehensive but less readable than Calvocoressi and Wint.

10. The Russian Empire and the Soviet Union, 1900–1945

The Guide to Historical Literature (3rd edn., 2 vols., New York, 1994).

Ascher, Abraham, *The Russian Revolution of 1905* (2 vols.; Stanford, Calif., 1989–1992). An incomparable account of the political forces in the first Russian Revolution.

Carr, E. H., *History of Soviet Russia* (14 vols., some co-authored by R. W. Davies; London, 1950–78). A magisterial account of early Soviet political and economic history.

Chamberlin, William Henry, *The Russian Revolution* (1935; Princeton, 1987). An older lively and detailed narrative that covers both the 1917 Revolution and the Civil War.

CLARKE, KATERINA, *The Soviet Novel: History as Ritual* (Chicago, 1981). A brilliant introduction to Stalinist cultural mythology.

CONQUEST, ROBERT, *The Great Terror: A Reassessment* (New York, 1990). A harrowing and painstaking reconstruction.

ERICKSON, JOHN, *Stalin's War with Germany* (2 vols.; New York, 1975–83). Published separately as *The Road to Stalingrad* and *The Road to Berlin.* The authoritative work.

FIGES, ORLANDO, *Peasant Russia, Civil War: The Volga Countryside, 1917–1921* (Oxford, 1989). A masterly study that makes the minute facts of social history illuminate the broad sweep of the revolution.

—— *A People's Tragedy: The Russian Revolution, 1891–1924* (New York, 1996). Balanced and moving, this riveting account is now the best work on the subject.

KENEZ, PETER, *Civil War in South Russia* (2 vols.; Berkeley and Los Angeles, 1971–7). A deep probe into the causes of the White defeat.

LINCOLN, W. BRUCE, *Passage through Armageddon: The Russians in War and Revolution, 1914–1918* (New York, 1986). A skilful blend of vivid detail, scholarship, and readability.

NATION, R. CRAIG, *Black Earth, Red Star: A History of Soviet Security Policy, 1917–1991* (Ithaca, NY, 1992). A succinct and fair-minded synthesis that puts diplomacy properly in the context of national security.

NOVE, ALEC, *Economic History of the USSR* (3rd edn., London, 1992). The final edition that brings the historical account to completion.

SCHAPIRO, LEONARD, *The Communist Party of the Soviet Union* (2nd rev. edn., London, 1970). The classic study of Soviet power politics.

TUCKER, ROBERT, *Stalin in Power: The Revolution from Above* (New York, 1990). The second volume in the monumental Stalin trilogy.

WERTH, ALEXANDER, *Russia at War, 1914–1945* (New York, 1964). Soviet life at the front and on the home front.

11. The United States, 1900–1945

BROCK, WILLIAM R., *Welfare, Democracy and the New Deal* (Cambridge, 1988). A searching, scholarly treatment of what was perhaps the central achievement of the New Deal.

FERRELL, ROBERT H., *Woodrow Wilson and World War I* (New York, 1985). A study which concentrates at least as much on the experience of the American people between 1917 and 1921 as on the strategy of war and peacemaking.

GALBRAITH, J. K., *The Great Crash: 1929* (London, 1955). A superbly lucid, witty account of one of the period's defining episodes.

HOFSTADTER, RICHARD, *The Age of Reform: From Bryan to F.D.R.* (New York, 1955). Is still the most thoughtful, if not entirely persuasive, introduction to the period, by a master historian.

LEUCHTENBURG, WILLIAM E., *Franklin Roosevelt and the New Deal 1932–1940* (New York, 1963). Still the best one-volume treatment of its subject.

LINDGREN, RICHARD B., *Don't You Know There's a War On? The American Home Front, 1914–1945* (New York, 1970). A vivid evocation of its subject.

POLENBERG, RICHARD, *One Nation Divisible: Class, Race, and Ethnicity in the United States since 1938* (New York, 1980). Carries the story brilliantly forward from the last days of the New Deal to the 1970s.

SINCLAIR, ANDREW, *Prohibition: The Era of Excess* (London, 1962). A lively, comprehensive treatment.

SULLIVAN, MARK, *Our Times* (6 vols.; New York, 1926–35). A journalistic but rewarding chronicle of the USA between 1900 and the 1920s, which recounts what happened and conveys what it all felt like. Best read nowadays as a primary source, for the early twentieth-century mentality.

TERKEL, STUDS, *Hard Times: An Oral History of the Great Depression* (New York, 1970). Conveys, better than any other book, what the Depression meant to the American people.

THOMPSON, J. A., *Progressivism* (British Association of American Studies, 1979). An excellent introductory pamphlet, with a first-rate bibliography thrown in.

TINDALL, GEORGE B., *The Emergence of the New South, 1913–1945* (Baton Rouge, La., 1967). An indispensable work on an essential subject.

12. East Asia and the Emergence of Japan, 1900–1945

BEASLEY, W. G., *Japanese Imperialism, 1894–1945* (Oxford, 1987). A judicious interpretation of the history of Japanese overseas expansion, with an occasional comparison to other empires in Asia.

DOWER, JOHN, *Japan in War and Peace* (New York, 1993). The book emphasizes continuities in Japanese politics, business, and culture between the 1930s and the post-1945 years.

DUUS, PETER, *The Abacus and the Sword* (Stanford, Calif., 1995). The best study of the establishment of Japanese control over Korea, leading to the latter's annexation in 1910. Especially useful are the descriptions of what went on in the peninsula prior to the formal annexation.

HOWE, CHRISTOPHER, *The Origins of Modern Japanese Trade Supremacy* (London, 1995). An excellent analysis of how Japan accomplished a successful drive for export trade expansion, which was becoming apparent by the 1930s.

IRIYE, AKIRA, *After Imperialism* (Cambridge, Mass., 1965). A study of the Washington Conference (1921–2) and its aftermath, describing the foreign policies of the powers during the 1920s as they sought to cope with modern Chinese nationalism.

—— *Power and Culture* (Cambridge, Mass., 1981). A comparison of Japanese and US wartime perceptions and visions of the post-war world.

—— *The Origins of the Second World War in Asia and the Pacific* (London, 1987). A survey of Asian–Pacific international affairs during 1931–41, a period which began with Japanese aggression in Manchuria and ended with Japan's struggle against the combination of China, the United States, Great Britain, and, ultimately, the Soviet Union.

IRIYE AKIRA *China and Japan in the Global Context* (Cambridge, Mass., 1992). A brief history of Chinese–Japanese relations since the late nineteenth century. The discussion of post-1945 affairs stresses the growth of economic ties even while the two nations were still formally at war.

JANSEN, MARIUS, *The Japanese and Sun Yat-sen* (Cambridge, Mass., 1951). A fascinating account of how the Chinese revolutionary leader was aided by a vast assortment of Japanese, many of them with their own ambitions.

MORLEY, JAMES W., *The Japanese Thrust into Siberia* (New York, 1957). A careful analysis of Japan's Siberian expedition in 1918, a military and political fiasco that soured Japanese relations not only with the Bolsheviks but also with the Americans, who sent a small-scale expedition of their own.

13. The Confrontation of the Superpowers, 1945–1990

ACHESON, DEAN, *Present at the Creation* (New York, 1969). An unusually rich memoir.

FREEDMAN, LAWRENCE, *The Evolution of Nuclear Strategy* (London, 1989). On the influence of the theories of nuclear deterrence.

GADDIS, JOHN, *Strategy of Containment* (New York, 1982). American policy after the Second World War.

—— *We Now Know: Rethinking Cold War History* (Oxford, 1997). A judicious account, based on documents from both sides, of the Cold War, up to the Cuba Missile Crisis of 1962.

GARTHOFF, RAYMOND, *Detente and Confrontation* (rev. edn., Washington, 1994).

—— *The Great Transition: American Soviet Relations and the End of the Cold War* (Washington, 1994). Essential histories for the last two decades of the cold war, drawing on both Russian and American sources.

HALLE, LOUIS, *The Cold War as History* (New York, 1967). One of the first attempts at a historical approach to the cold war.

KISSINGER, HENRY, *The White House Years* and *Years of Upheaval* (2 vols.; Boston, 1979, 1982). Memoir of the Nixon years.

LOTH, WILFRIED, *The Division of the World, 1941–1955* (London, 1988). A useful survey of the origins of the cold war from a German perspective.

PARTOS, GABRIEL, *The World that Came in from the Cold* (London, 1993).

ULAM, ADAM, *The Rivals: America and Russia since World War II* (New York, 1972).

—— *Dangerous Relations* (New York, 1983).

WALKER, MARTIN, *The Cold War* (London, 1993).

YERGIN, DANIEL, *Shattered Peace: The Origins of the Cold War and the National Security State* (Boston, 1977). One of the more impressive 'revisionist' discussions of the early years.

ZELIKOW, PHILIP, and RICE, CONDOLEZZA, *Germany Unified and Europe Transformed: A Study in Statecraft* (Cambridge, Mass., 1995). An eyewitness account of the negotiations that ended the Cold War.

14. The United States since 1945

BAUGHMAN, JAMES, *The Republic of Mass Culture: Journalism, Film-Making and Broadcasting in America since 1941* (Baltimore, 1992). A concise, well-conceived study.

BRANCH, TAYLOR, *Parting the Waters: America in the King Years, 1954–63* (New York, 1988). A well-written and thorough narrative of race relations, with considerable focus on Martin Luther King, Jr.

CHAFE, WILLIAM, *The Unfinished Century: America since World War II* (New York, 1991). A well-written, wide-reading survey.

—— *The Paradox of Change: American Women in the Twentieth Century* (New York, 1991). A well-researched and readable interpretation of the subject.

GADDIS, JOHN, *Strategies of Containment: A Critical Appraisal of Post-war American National Security Policy* (New York, 1982). Wide-ranging interpretative survey.

GARTHOFF, RAYMOND, *Detente and Confrontation: American–Soviet Relations from Nixon to Reagan* (Washington, 1994). Detailed study of diplomatic relations.

HAMBY, ALONZO, *Liberalism and its Challengers: From F. D. R. to Bush* (New York, 1992). Interpretative essays about leading political figures.

HERRING, GEORGE, *America's Longest War: The United States and Vietnam* (2nd edn., Philadelphia, 1986). A balanced, solid account.

HUNTER, JAMES, *Culture Wars: The Struggle to Define America* (New York, 1991). Focuses on religious divisions and their cultural manifestations, especially 1970–90.

JONES, LANDON, *Great Expectations: America and the Baby Boom Generation* (New York, 1980). Well-written social history.

LACEY, MICHAEL (ed.), *Government and Environmental Politics: Essays on Historical Developments since World War Two* (Washington, 1989). Well-researched scholarly essays.

LEMANN, NICHOLAS, *The Promised Land: The Great Migration and How It Changed America* (New York, 1991). A moving account of African–American life in Mississippi and Chicago, and of the nation's 'war on poverty'.

LEVY, FRANK, *Dollars and Dreams: The Changing American Income Distribution* (New York, 1987). A clear, jargon-free study of the subject.

PATTERSON, JAMES, *America's Struggle against Poverty, 1900–1994* (Cambridge, Mass., 1994). An interpretative survey of social trends and public policies.

—— *Grand Expectations: The United States, 1945–1974* (Oxford, 1996). Narrative and interpretation focusing on politics and social change.

POLENBERG, RICHARD, *One Nation Divisible: Class, Race, and Ethnicity in the United States since 1938* (New York, 1980). A concise and balanced interpretative survey.

RAVITCH, DIANE, *The Troubled Crusade: American Education, 1945–1980* (New York, 1983). A shrewd and careful account of a controversial subject.

WEISBROT, ROBERT, *Freedom Bound: A History of America's Civil Rights Movement* (New York, 1990). A readable survey.

WHITFIELD, STEPHEN, *The Culture of the Cold War* (Baltimore, 1991). Emphasizes the role of domestic anti-communism, especially in the 1940s and 1950s.

ZIEGER, ROBERT, *American Workers, American Unions, 1920–1985* (Baltimore, 1986). A balanced and brief account of the rise and decline of the labour movement.

15. The Soviet Union and Beyond

BREMNER, IAN, and TARAS, RAY (eds.), *New States, New Politics: Building the Post-Soviet Nations* (Cambridge, 1997). A substantial volume containing well-informed discussion by a variety of specialists on the successor states to the USSR.

BROWN, ARCHIE, *The Gorbachev Factor* (Oxford, 1996). The most comprehensive analysis, drawing on fresh sources, of the part played by Mikhail Gorbachev in changing both the Soviet system and Russia's relations with the outside world.

—— KASER, MICHAEL and SMITH, GERALD S., (eds.), *The Cambridge Encyclopaedia of Russia and the Former Soviet Union* (Cambridge, 1994). A wide-ranging and lavishly illustrated reference book covering the history, culture, environment, peoples, politics, military, and science of Russia and the former Soviet Union written by over 130 specialist contributors.

COLTON, TIMOTHY J. and TUCKER, ROBERT C., (eds.), *Patterns in Post-Soviet Leadership* (Boulder, Colo., 1995). A useful survey by prominent specialists of early post-Soviet politics.

DALLIN, ALEXANDER, and LAPIDUS, GAIL, (eds.), *The Soviet System: From Crisis to Collapse* (rev. edn., Boulder, Colo., 1995). A collection of some of the best articles from Western and Russian journals analysing politics and society in the last years of the Soviet Union.

GRACHEV, ANDREI, *Final Days: The Inside Story of the Collapse of the Soviet Union* (Boulder, Colo., 1995). A perceptive narrative by a Kremlin insider—Gorbachev's presidential press secretary and adviser—of the final months of the Soviet Union.

Nove, Alec, *Glasnost in Action: Cultural Renaissance in Russia* (London, 1989). An informative and readable account of the fruits of the new openness in the Soviet Union after 1985.

Palazchenko, Pavel, *My Years with Gorbachev and Shevardnadze: The Memoir of a Soviet Interpreter* (University Park, Pa., 1997). Gorbachev's and Shevardnadze's English-language interpreter participated in many of the most important encounters of the years, 1985–91. In his depiction of those years Palazchenko demonstrates independence of judgement and analytical as well as linguistic talent.

Remnick, David, *Lenin's Tomb: The Last Days of the Soviet Empire* (London, 1993). A highly readable account by an observant journalist (Remnick was *Washington Post* correspondent in Moscow) of Russia in transition.

Rigby, T. H., *The Changing Soviet System: Mono-Organizational Socialism from its Origins to Gorbachev's Restructuring* (Aldershot, 1990). A shrewd historical view of Soviet politics by one of the most distinguished students of the former USSR.

Schapiro, Leonard, *The Communist Party of the Soviet Union* (2nd edn., London, 1970). The most thorough study in any language of the CPSU from its origins to the Brezhnev era.

Suny, Ronald Gregor, *The Revenge of the Past: Nationalism, Revolution, and the Collapse of the Soviet Union* (Stanford, Calif., 1993). A concise historical survey of the 'national question' in Soviet history by a leading specialist on the subject.

Tompson, William J., *Khrushchev: A Political Life* (London, 1995). The best account to date of the political career of one of the most colourful and important of Soviet leaders.

White, Stephen, Rose, Richard and McAllister, Ian, *How Russia Votes* (Chatham, NJ, 1997). A valuable study of Russian elections and referendums from the advent of pluralist politics in the Gorbachev era to the re-election of President Yeltsin in 1996.

16. The Remaking of Europe

Ash, Timothy Garton, *In Europe's Name: Germany and the Divided Continent* (London, 1993). A provocative and closely argued account using many new sources.

Bark, Dennis L. and Gress, David R., *A History of West Germany* (2 vols.; Oxford, 1993). Domestic and international politics are closely interwoven in this general history.

Bartlett, C. J., *A History of Postwar Britain, 1945–74* (London, 1977). A political history of Britain up to accession to the European Communities.

Bell, P. M. H., *France and Britain, 1940–1994: The Long Separation* (London, 1997). A comprehensive overview of bilateral relations.

Deighton, Anne, *Building Postwar Europe, 1948–1963* (Basingstoke, 1995). National perspectives on early European integration.

de Porte, Anton, *Europe between the Superpowers* (New Haven, Conn., 1987). A magisterial general account.

Hanrieder, Wolfram F., *Germany, America, Europe: Forty Years of German Foreign Policy* (New Haven, Conn., 1989). Explores the re-emergence of Germany in a European, and Atlantic context.

Middlemas, Keith, *Orchestrating Europe: The Informal Politics of European Union, 1973–1995*, (London, 1995). A wide-ranging but detailed survey that explores economic as well as political developments.

Milward, Alan S., *The Reconstruction of Western Europe, 1945–1952* (London, 1984). A dense but path-breaking account of early post-war economic developments.

REYNOLDS, DAVID, *Britannia Overruled: British Policy and World Power in the 20th Century* (London, 1991). A stimulating survey, written with great clarity.

RIOUX, J.-P., *The Fourth Republic, 1944–1958* (Cambridge, 1987). Covers the complex period of France's post-war recovery before de Gaulle's accession to power.

URWIN, DEREK, *Western Europe since 1945* (London, 1989). The standard introduction to the history and politics of Western Europe.

YOUNG, JOHN W., *Cold War Europe, 1945–1989: A Political History* (London, 1991). Useful introductory text.

17. East Asia (see also Chapter 12)

ECKERT, CARTER (ed.), *Korea: Old and New* (Cambridge, Mass., 1990). A reliable guide to the past and present of Korean society, politics, and culture.

GIBNEY, FRANK, *The Pacific Century* (New York, 1992). A comprehensive survey of the recent past as well as the future prospects of the Asian countries and of their relationship with the United States and Europe.

SCHALLER, MICHAEL, *The Altered States* (New York, 1997). An excellent study of post-war Japanese politics and foreign policy as they were profoundly affected by the US security treaty.

SCHONBERGER, HOWARD, *The Aftermath of War* (New York, 1990). A discussion of US policies towards occupied Japan, some of which aimed at social reform, while others were interested in restoring Japan as a bulwark against radical forces.

STUECK, WILLIAM, *The Korean War: An International History* (Princeton, 1995). The best history of the Korean war in a multinational framework.

VOGEL, EZRA, *The Four Little Dragons* (Cambridge, Mass., 1991). A brief but insightful analysis of how South Korea, Taiwan, Hong Kong, and Singapore have achieved amazing economic successes.

18. China

BERGÈRE, MARIE-CLAIRE, *The Golden Age of the Chinese Bourgeoisie* (Stanford, Calif., 1989). Shows how the end of the dynasty led to burst of business initiative and economic expansion.

BILLINGSLEY, PHIL, *Bandits in Republican China* (Stanford, Calif., 1988). The organization, recruitment, life style, and argot of China's dispossessed.

ESHERICK, JOSEPH, *The Origins of the Boxer Uprising* (Berkeley and Los Angeles, 1987). Combines ecology of the region where the Boxers flourished with local and religious factors.

FU, POSHEK, *Passivity, Resistance, and Collaboration: Intellectual Choices in Occupied Shanghai, 1937–1945* (Stanford, Calif., 1993). Survival patterns for those who joined neither the nationalists in Chongqing nor the communists in Yanan.

LEVINE, MARILYN, *The Found Generation: Chinese Communists in Europe during the Twenties* (Seattle, 1993). Shows how Chinese youth in France became communists and learned to organize for revolution.

LIEBERTHAL, KENNETH, *Governing China, from Revolution through Reform* (New York, 1995). Careful background on Party history, and full details of bureaucratic institutions and the nature of Communist decision-making.

McCord, Edward, *The Power of the Gun: The Emergence of Modern Chinese Warlordism* (Berkeley and Los Angeles, 1993). Growth of military structures and their relationship to local élites and political groupings in central China.

Pomeranz, Kenneth, *The Making of a Hinterland: State, Society, and Economy in Inland North China, 1853–1937* (Berkeley and Los Angeles, 1993). How a rural area loses out economically, socially, and politically, as others develop and modernize.

Saich, Anthony, *The Origins of the First United Front in China: The Role of Sneevliet (alias Maring)* (2 vols.; Leiden, 1991). Secret Comintern activities in China illuminated through archives and an agent's secret papers.

Smil, Vaclav, *China's Environmental Crisis: An Enquiry into the Limits of National Development* (Armonk, NY, 1993). The immense challenges facing China in land use, soil erosion, pollution, and population pressures.

Thompson, Roger, *China's Local Councils in the Age of Constitutional Reform* (Cambridge, Mass., 1995). Shows first attempts at democratic structures in rural and urban government.

Tse-Tsung, Chow, *The May Fourth Movement: Intellectual Revolution in Modern China* (Cambridge, Mass., 1960). Encyclopaedic detail and overview of groups, individuals, new journals, and issues.

Wakeman, Frederic, *Policing Shanghai, 1927–1937* (Berkeley and Los Angeles, 1995). The attempt to bring order to the city ravaged by narcotics and corruption, and controlled economically through foreign concessions. Much detail on criminal syndicates and political terror.

19. South-East Asia

Bastin, John, and Benda, Harry J., *A History of Modern South East Asia* (Englewood Cliffs, NJ, 1968). Specific focus on the colonial impact and the regional responses.

Benda, Harry J., *The World of Southeast Asia: Selected Historical Readings* (New York, 1967). A representative selection of authentic South East Asian voices.

Kahin, George McT. (ed.), *Governments and Politics of Southeast Asia* (Ithaca, NJ, 1964). Close attention to historical background.

Leifer, Michael, *ASEAN and the Security of Southeast Asia* (London, 1990). The rise and role of a regional diplomatic community.

—— *Dictionary of the Modern Politics of Southeast Asia* (London, 1995). A summary of politics and international relations since the end of the Pacific War.

Osborne, Milton, *Southeast Asia: An Illustrated Introductory History* (Sydney, 1990). A succinct comprehensive introduction.

Pluvier, J. M., *Southeast Asia from Colonialism to Independence* (Kuala Lumpur, 1974). An account of the rise of nationalism.

Sandhu, K. S., *et al.* (eds.), *The ASEAN Reader* (Singapore, 1992). An extensive selection on all dimensions of the Association of South-East Asian Nations.

Steinberg, David J., *et al.* (eds.), *In Search of Southeast Asia: A Modern History* (Honolulu, 1987). Limited but scholarly attention to the twentieth century.

Tarling, Nicholas (ed.), *The Cambridge History of Southeast Asia*, ii. *The Nineteenth and Twentieth Centuries* (Cambridge, 1993). A good summary account.

20. South Asia

BAXTER, C., *Bangladesh: A New Nation in an Old Setting* (Boulder, Colo., 1984).

BRASS, P. R., *The Politics of India since Independence* (Cambridge, 1990).

BROWN, JUDITH M., *Gandhi: Prisoner of Hope* (London, 1989).

—— *India: The Origins of an Asian Democracy* (2nd edn., Oxford, 1994). Good general survey.

GOPAL, S., *Jawaharlal Nehru: A Biography* (3 vols.; London, 1975–84).

JALAL, A., *The State of Martial Rule. The Origins of Pakistan's Political Economy of Defence* (Cambridge, 1990).

—— *Democracy and Authoritarianism in South Asia. A Comparative Historical Perspective* (Cambridge, 1995). Comparative political survey.

ROBINSON, F. C. R. (ed.), *The Cambridge Encyclopaedia of India, Pakistan, Bangladesh, Sri Lanka . . .* (Cambridge, 1989). Key reference work.

STERN, R. W., *Changing India: Bourgeois Revolution on the Subcontinent* (Cambridge, 1993). Interpretative account of late twentieth-century India.

TAMBIAH, S. J., *Sri Lanka: Ethnic Fratricide and the Dismantling of Democracy* (Chicago, 1986).

TOMLINSON, B. R., *The Economy of Modern India 1860–1970* (Cambridge, 1993).

WOLPERT, S. A., *Jinnah of Pakistan* (New York, 1984).

21. North Africa and the Middle East

AHMAD, FEROZ, *The Making of Modern Turkey* (London, 1993). A complete socio-economic and political history of twentieth-century Turkey.

HOROWITZ, DAN, and LISSAK, MOSHE, *Trouble in Utopia: The Overburdened Polity of Israel* (Albany, NY, 1989). An excellent study of Israeli political history and the strains imposed upon the system in the 1980s.

KERR, MALCOLM, *The Arab Cold War 1958–1967: A Study of Ideology in Politics* (2nd edn., London, 1967). The best account of intra-Arab relations at a time when unity was one of the basic political issues.

KHADRA, SALMA, *Modern Arabic Poetry: An Anthology* (New York, 1987). Contains examples of poems by the best-known Arab poets of the twentieth century.

KHALIL, SAMIR, *The Republic of Fear* (Berkeley and Los Angeles, 1989). A novel attempt to examine the role of violence and fear in the government of Ba'thi Iraq.

LEVEAU, REMY, *Le Sabre et le tourban: L'Avenir du Maghreb* (Paris, 1993). A prescient analysis of the main political forces at work in late-twentieth-century North Africa.

LUCIANI, GIACOMO (ed.), *The Arab State* (London, 1990). Contains a variety of essays seeking to define the significance of oil revenues in the management of the Gulf states.

MOTTAHEDEH, ROY, *The Mantle of the Prophet: Religion and Politics in Iran* (New York, 1985). A classic combination of religious biography and political analysis as Iran moves towards its Islamic revolution.

SEALE, PATRICK, *Assad: The Struggle for the Middle East* (London, 1988). The best biography of a major twentieth-century Arab political leader.

SPRINGBORG, ROBERT, *Mubarak's Egypt: Fragmentation of the Political Order* (Boulder, Colo., 1989). A hard-hitting analysis of the strengths and weaknesses of Egypt's authoritarian political system.

YAPP, MALCOLM, *The Near East since the First World War* (London, 1991). A good general account of Middle Eastern history since the First World War.

ZAHAN, ROSEMARY SAID, *The Making of the Modern Gulf States* (London, 1989). A well-informed study of the history and contemporary government of the Gulf states and Saudi Arabia.

22. Africa

BAYART, FRANÇOIS, *The State in Africa: The Politics of the Belly* (London, 1993). A classic, if controversial, account of post-colonial Africa.

BERMAN, BRUCE, and LOSDALE, JOHN, *Unhappy Valley: Conflict in Kenya and Africa* (2 vols.; London, 1992). Profound analysis of the nature of the colonial state and of African ethnicity.

CHABAL, PATRICK, *Power in Africa: An Essay in Political Interpretation* (London, 1992). A historically conscious analysis of contemporary African politics.

CHANOCK, MARTIN, *Law, Custom and Social Order* (Cambridge, 1985). A brilliant account of the interaction of colonial rule and African custom.

FEIERMAN, STEVEN, *Peasant Intellectuals: Anthropology and History in Tanzania* (Madison, Wisc., 1990). A seminal exploration of 'the unbounded local' in colonial Africa.

HASTINGS, ADRIAN, *The Church in Africa, 1450–1950* (Oxford, 1994). A magisterial account of Africa's recent religious history.

ILIFFE, JOHN, *Africans: The History of a Continent* (Cambridge, 1995). The most recent, and best, single-volume history of Africa.

MAMDANI, MAHMOUD, *Citizen and Subject: Contemporary Africa and the Legacy of Late Colonialism* (London, 1996). A vigorously argued account of colonial structures of rule and development and of the failures of African independent states to modify them.

MOORE, HENRIETTA, and VAUGHAN, MEGAN, *Cutting Down Trees* (London, 1994). A study of gender, nutrition, and changing colonial agrarian policies.

PEEL, JOHN, *Ileshas and Nigerians* (Cambridge, 1983). An illuminating study of colonial social change.

VANSINA, JAN, *Paths in the Rainforests: Towards a History of Political Tradition in Equatorial Africa* (London, 1990). An account of how colonial inventions of tradition undercut indigenous vitality.

WATTS, MICHAEL, *Silent Violence: Food, Famine and Peasantry in Northern Nigeria* (Berkeley, and Los Angeles, 1983). A ground-laying account of famine and African rural society.

WERBNER, RICHARD, *Tears of the Dead* (Edinburgh, 1991). Revelatory account of the effects on an African family of colonial conquest, dispossession, guerrilla war, and post-colonial violence.

—— and RANGER, TERENCE, (eds.), *Postcolonial Identities in Africa* (London, 1996). A debate between the editors on the continuities and discontinuities of colonial and post-colonial Africa accompanied by solid contemporary case studies.

23. Latin America

BEEZLEY, WILLIAM H., and EWELL, JUDITH (eds.), *The Human Tradition in Latin America: The Twentieth Century* (Wilmington, Del., 1987). Twenty-one brief but illuminating biographies—of 'ordinary' Latin Americans.

BETHELL, LESLIE (ed.), *The Cambridge History of Latin America* (Cambridge, 1986–91). Detailed histories of particular countries and themes as well as useful up-to-date biographies.

—— *Mexico since Independence* (Cambridge, 1991).

—— *Central America since Independence* (Cambridge, 1991).

—— *Argentina since Independence* (Cambridge, 1993).

—— *Chile since Independence* (Cambridge, 1993).

—— *Cuba: A Short History* (Cambridge, 1993).

BULMER-THOMAS, VICTOR, *The Economic History of Latin America since Independence* (Cambridge, 1994). A sophisticated economic survey.

DONGHI, TULIO HALPERIN, *The Contemporary History of Latin America* (Basingstoke, 1993). The best general history of modern Latin America.

24. The Old Commonwealth: The First Four Dominions

BAMBRICK, SUSAN (ed.), *The Cambridge Encyclopedia of Australia* (Cambridge, 1994). A wide-ranging set of essays by many experts.

BARBER, JAMES, and BARRATT, JOHN, *South Africa's Policy: The Search for Status and Security 1945–1988* (Capetown, 1990). The best one-volume survey of South Africa's foreign policy until just before the end of apartheid.

BEINART, WILLIAM, *Twentieth-Century South Africa* (Oxford, 1994). A succinct yet wide-ranging survey.

CREIGHTON, DONALD, *Canada's First Century* (Toronto, 1970). A beautifully written survey of the century 1867–1967 by one of Canada's most distinguished controversial and conservative historians.

DAVENPORT, T. R. H., *South Africa. A Modern History* (Cape Town, 1988). A comprehensive, well-nigh encyclopaedic, and rather dense textbook treatment.

HAWKE, G. R., *The Making of New Zealand: An Economic History* (Cambridge, 1985). The best complement to Sinclair on the economic side.

HILLMER, NORMAN, and GRANATSTEIN, J. L., *Empire to Umpire: Canada and the World of the 1990s* (Toronto, 1994). An excellent survey of Canada in world affairs from the twentieth century to joining NAFTA.

LOWER, ARTHUR R. M., *Colony to Nation: A History of Canada* (1946; 5th edn., Toronto, 1977). A classic survey history by a Prairie-based historian.

McKINNON, MALCOLM, *Independence and Foreign Policy: New Zealand in the World since 1935* (Auckland, 1993). The best single-volume survey of New Zealand's foreign policy.

RICE, GEOFFREY W. (ed.), *The Oxford History of New Zealand* (Oxford, 1992). A good overview of recent and some revisionist historiography.

RICKARD, JOHN, *Australia: A Cultural History* (London, 1988). Australia's history written from a cultural perspective and weighted towards the twentieth century.

SHAW, A. G. L., *The Story of Australia* (London, 1960). A lucid survey, good on the economic and social conditioning factors.

SINCLAIR, KEITH, *A History of New Zealand* (London, 1959; rev. ed., 1969). The classic short account.

WOODCOCK, GEORGE, *A Social History of Canada* (Toronto, 1988). A challenging spirited social, and in parts intellectual, history.

25. Towards a World Community? The United Nations and International Law

ARCHER, CLIVE (ed.), *International Organizations* (2nd edn., London: Routledge, 1992). Very useful introduction to the role of the UN and other bodies.

BEST, GEOFFREY, *War and Law since 1945* (Oxford, 1995).

BROWNLIE, IAN (ed.), *Basic Documents in International Law* (4th edn., Oxford, 1995).

CASSESE, ANTONIO, *International Law in a Divided World* (Oxford, 1986).

JAMES, ALAN, *Peacekeeping in International Politics* (London: Macmillan, 1990). Relates peacekeeping activities to the broader political processes which they are intended to ameliorate.

NORTHEDGE, F. S., *The League of Nations: Its Life and Times, 1920–1946* (Leicester, 1986).

PARSONS, ANTHONY, *From Cold War to Hot Peace: UN Interventions 1947–1994* (London, 1995).

ROBERTS, ADAM, and KINGSBURY, BENEDICT (eds.), *United Nations, Divided World: The UN's Roles in International Relations* (2nd edn., Oxford, 1993).

SCOTT, JAMES BROWN (ed.), *The Proceedings of the Hague Peace Conferences: Translation of the Official Texts* (4 vols. plus index vol.; New York, 1920–1).

UNITED NATIONS, *The Blue Helmets: A Review of United Nations Peacekeeping* (3rd edn., New York, 1996). Useful factual survey of each operation.

WALTERS, F. P., *A History of the League of Nations* (Oxford, 1960).

26. The Close of the Twentieth Century

FERNÁNDEZ-ARMESTO, FELIPE, *Millennium* (London, 1995). A stimulating and iconoclastic interpretation of the last 1,000 years, with non-Eurocentric implications for the next 1,000.

HOBSBAWM, ERIC, *The Age of Extremes* (New York, 1994). Written from a Marxist perspective, the end of the book provides a stimulating general assessment of the last part of the century.

KENNEDY, PAUL, *Preparing for the Twenty-First Century* (New York, 1993). By using the same methods as in one of his previous books, *The Rise and Fall of the Great Powers*, Paul Kennedy analyses developments in technology, economic change, and population growth.

LOUDON, IRVINE (ed.), *Western Medicine: An Illustrated History* (Oxford, 1997). Fundamental for an assessment of the advances in medicine at the end of the century.

NEUSTADT, RICHARD E. and MAY, ERNEST R., *Thinking in Time* (New York, 1986). An original contribution to understanding the uses of historical analogy in attempting to resolve problems of the present and future.

ULLMAN, RICHARD H., *The World and Yugoslavia's Wars* (New York, 1996). The introductory chapter is an incisive treatment of the Balkan conflict.

ZELDIN, THEODORE, *An Intimate History of Humanity* (London, 1994). An imaginative and unorthodox approach filled with compassion and insight.

1900 Second year of second South African (Boer) War; relief of Kimberley, Ladysmith, and Mafeking between January and May; destruction of the Boer army and re-annexation of the Transvaal in October, but guerrilla war continues

Spring: Boxer uprising breaks out in China with slogan 'Support the Qing, destroy the foreigner'; foreign legations in Peking besieged in June, relieved by multinational force on 14 August; Dowager Empress Cixi flees to Sian

British occupation of Northern Nigeria begins

Ottoman government grants Germany concession to build railway from Berlin to Baghdad

USA engaged in war in Philippines against nationalist guerrillas in aftermath of Spanish-American War

Currrency Act makes gold the sole monetary standard in USA

1901 22 Jan.: Queen Victoria dies after more than 63 years on the throne

Commonwealth of Australia created, becomes second Dominion (after Canada) in British Empire

Sept. 1901: Boxer Protocol ends Boxer affair as China agrees to Great Powers' demands

6 Sept.: US President McKinley shot by anarchist, dies a week later; Vice-President Theodore Roosevelt becomes President

Socialist Revolutionary Party formed in Russia

Australian financier W. K. D'Arcy obtains concession from Persian government and begins intensive exploration for oil in Persia

Social Democratic Party formed in Japan

1902 30 Jan.: Britain and Japan sign Anglo-Japanese Alliance

Ultra-conservative Dowager Empress Cixi returns to power in Peking

31 May: Treaty of Vereeniging ends Boer War

Filipino guerrilla resistance to US rule ends

1903 USA supports Panama's secession from Colombia to facilitate building Panama Canal

11 June: murder of King Alexander of Serbia initiates era of Balkan crises

CHRONOLOGY

Science, Technology, and Medicine	Culture	
Max Planck's radiation law implies 'quanta' of energy: major step towards development of quantum theory of physics; David Hilbert announces his 'Programme for Mathematics' First Zeppelin, a dirigible airship, launched in Germany	Sigmund Freud, *The Interpretation of Dreams* Joseph Conrad, *Lord Jim*; Theodore Dreiser, *Sister Carrie*; Anton Chekhov, *Uncle Vanya* Giacomo Puccini, *Tosca*; Antonin Dvorak, *Rusalka*; Jean Sibelius, *Finlandia*; Edward Elgar, *The Dream of Gerontius*	**1900**
12 Dec.: Guglielmo Marconi transmits wireless signals across the Atlantic Oil discovered at Spindletop, Texas J. P. Morgan forms US Steel, first billion-dollar corporation; General Electric establishes first research laboratory	Rudyard Kipling, *Kim*; Thomas Mann, *Buddenbrooks*; August Strindberg, *The Dance of Death*; Chekhov, *Three Sisters* Sergei Rachmaninov, *Piano Concerto No 2*	**1901**
First trans-Pacific cable laid First hormone, secretin, discovered by W. M. Bayliss and E. H. Starling A. E. Kennelly and O. Heaviside correctly infer a strongly ionized region in the upper atmosphere (Kennelly–Heaviside layer) which deflects wireless waves	V. I. Lenin, *What Is To Be Done?* Conrad, *Heart of Darkness*; Henry James, *The Wings of the Dove*; Sir Arthur Conan Doyle, *The Hound of the Baskervilles* Claude Debussy, *Pélleas and Mélisande* Frank Lloyd Wright completes Willits House, Illinois Georges Méliès, *A Trip to the Moon*	**1902**
17 Dec.: first successful controlled flights in a power-driven aeroplane by the Wright brothers, Orville and Wilbur, at Kitty Hawk, North Carolina	Bertrand Russell, *Principles of Mathematics* James, *The Ambassadors*; Bernard Shaw, *Man and Superman*	**1903**

Politics and International Relations

1903   At a congress in London of the Russian Social Democratic Labour Party Lenin's faction wins majority; they are thereafter known as the *Bolsheviki* (members of the majority)

1904   8 Feb.: Russo-Japanese War begins

8 Apr.: Britain and France conclude Entente Cordiale

USA acquires Panama Canal Zone on lease

1905   2 Jan.: Port Arthur falls to Japanese; in late January revolution breaks out in Russia, resulting in concession of constitutional government by Tsar in 'October Manifesto'

Beginning of Constitutional Revolution in Persia

First Moroccan Crisis, over Tangier, between Germany and France

Norway achieves peaceful independence from Sweden

British partition of Bengal sparks first large-scale resistance movement organized by Indian National Congress under Gopal Gokhale

5 Sept.: Treaty of Portsmouth, New Hampshire, ends Russo-Japanese War

China enacts reforms, abolishing Confucian examination system for civil service and substituting 'new learning' (Western style education) as basis of political or scholarly career

Outbreak of Maji-Maji revolt against German rule in German East Africa

---

1906   Election in January of first Duma (parliament) in Russia

Captain Alfred Dreyfus, a French Jew falsely accused of treason in 1894, is finally rehabilitated, ending the bitterly divisive Dreyfus Affair in France

In Britain, Liberal Government comes to power; Labour Party formed; under Liberal Government policies, Boers regain self-government in Transvaal and Orange Free State, but within British Empire

17 Apr.: San Francisco earthquake and fire

Muslims in India, alarmed by Hindu nationalism, establish all-India Muslim League

---

1907   Mohandas Gandhi launches first campaign of *satyagraha*, or non-violent resistance, against anti-Indian racial policies in South Africa

Indian National Congress splits between moderates led by Gokhale and revolutionaries advocating violence led by B. G. Tilak

Japanese–American 'Gentleman's' agreement limits Japanese emigration to USA

Japan establishes formal protectorate over Korea

Second Hague Peace Conference

31 Aug.: Anglo-Russian Convention on spheres of influence in Central Asia concluded

Dutch consolidate control of Sumatra

Science, Technology, and Medicine	Culture	
Completion of the trans-Siberian railway	J. M. Synge, *Riders to the Sea*; Chekhov, *The Cherry Orchard* Puccini, *Madame Butterfly*	**1903**
Invention of photo-electric cell, ultra-violet lamp, safety razor blades Frederick Soddy proves that chemically identical atoms may have different masses (isotopes)	Conrad, *Nostromo*; James, *The Golden Bowl* Leoš Janáček, *Jenufa*	**1904**
Albert Einstein formulates special theory of relativity; explains photo-electric effect in terms of light quanta; develops Brownian theory of motion	Freud, *Three Essays on the Theory of Sexuality*; George Santayana, *The Life of Reason* Edith Wharton, *The House of Mirth*; Oscar Wilde (posth.), *De Profundis*; Baroness Orczy, *The Scarlet Pimpernel* Richard Strauss, *Salome*; Debussy, *La Mer*; Franz Lehar, *The Merry Widow* Paul Cezanne, *Les Grandes Baigneuses* Antonio Gaudi y Cornet, Casa Mila, Barcelona First regular movie theatre established, Pittsburgh, Pennsylvania	**1905**
Walther Nernst establishes 'Heat Theorem', now the third law of thermodynamics Roald Amundsen determines position of magnetic North Pole In response to revelations in Sinclair's *The Jungle*, the US passes Pure Food and Drug Act	Upton Sinclair, *The Jungle*, a scathing indictment of US meat-packing industry John Galsworthy, *The Forsyte Saga* (to 1928)	**1906**
Ivan Pavlov investigates conditioned reflexes Leo Baekland develops synthetic resin, Bakelite, which becomes a trademark name applied to a variety of synthetic resins and plastics	Henri Bergson, *L'Évolution créatrice*; William James, *Pragmatism* Pablo Picasso, *Les Demoiselles d'Avignon* George Bernard Shaw, *Major Barbara*; Synge, *The Playboy of the Western World*; Conrad, *The Secret Agent* Frederick Delius, *A Village Romeo and Juliet*	**1907**

Politics and International Relations

1907   New Zealand becomes self-governing Dominion

End of Maji-Maji revolt in German East Africa

1908   Young Turks force Abdul Hamid II to restore Ottoman Constitution of 1876

Oct.: Austria annexes Bosnia–Hercegovina

International outrage over forced-labour policies forces Belgium to take over Congo Free State from Leopold II

Empress Dowager dies; constitutional reform gathers momentum in China

Discovery of oil in south-west Persia under the D'Arcy concession results in formation of Anglo-Persian Oil Company

---

1909   National Association for the Advancement of Colored People (NAACP) established in USA

Forced abdication of Ottoman sultan Abdul Hamid II

Morley–Minto Reforms in India

1910   Egyptian prime minister Butros Ghali assassinated by Egyptian nationalists

Natal, Cape Colony, Transvaal and Orange Free State unite with dominion status in Union of South Africa, under leadership of Louis Botha and Jan Smuts

Japan annexes Korea

Revolution overthrows monarchy in Portugal; which becomes republic

Mexican revolution begins

First provincial assemblies convene in China; China abolishes slavery

---

1911   Second Moroccan crisis, over Agadir, between Germany and France

Portugal adopts liberal constitution

Sept.: Italo-Turkish war results in Italian victory and annexation of Tripoli and Cyrenaica from Ottoman Empire

Oct.: Chinese revolution breaks out; leads to end of Manchu Dynasty

US Supreme Court upholds antitrust legislation in *Standard Oil Company of New Jersey v. United States*, breaks up Standard Oil Trust

First Lord of the British Admiralty, Winston Churchill, switches Royal Navy from coal to oil

Science, Technology, and Medicine	Culture	
	R. Baden-Powell establishes Boy Scout movement	**1907**
	Georges Sorel, *Reflections on Violence*	**1908**
	Gertrude Stein, *Three Lives*; E. M. Forster, *A Room with a View*; Kenneth Grahame, *The Wind in the Willows*	
	Constantin Brancusi, *The Kiss*	
6 Apr.: Commander Peary reaches the North Pole	Nicolai Rimsky-Korsakov, *Le Coq D'Or*; Strauss, *Elektra*	**1909**
25 July: Louis Blériot makes first flight across the English Channel	Picasso and Georges Braque develop Cubism; first use of term 'Futurism' in the arts (Filippo Marietti)	
Henry Ford begins mass production of Model T car	Sergei Diaghilev's Ballets Russes, with Nijinsky as leading dancer, takes Paris by storm	
Marie Curie, *Treatise on Radiography*	Bertrand Russell with A. N. Whitehead, *Principia Mathematica*	**1910**
Paul Ehrlich develops cure for syphilis	Forster, *Howards End*	
International Psychoanalytical Association founded with C. G. Jung as president	Igor Stravinsky, *The Firebird*; Aleksandr Scriabin, *Prometheus*; Ralph Vaughan Williams, *A Sea Symphony*; Puccini's *La Fanciulla del West* [The Girl of the Golden West] opens in New York	
Sir Arthur Evans excavates Knossos on the island of Crete	Amedeo Modigliani, *The Cellist*; Post-Impressionist Exhibition in London of works by Matisse, Cezanne, van Gogh	
Amundsen reaches South Pole	D. H. Lawrence, *The White Peacock*; Rainer Maria Rilke, *The Duino Elegies*; Gaston Leroux, *The Phantom of the Opera*; Rupert Brooke, *Poems*	**1911**
Marie Curie wins Nobel Prize for Chemistry		
Ernest Rutherford proposes nuclear structure of atom		
Heike Kammerlingh Onnes first observes superconductivity	Richard Strauss, *Der Rosenkavalier*; Gustav Mahler completes *Symphony No. 9* and dies shortly thereafter; Arnold Schoenberg, *Manual of Harmony*; Stravinsky, *Petrouchka* ballet; Irving Berlin, *Alexander's Ragtime Band*	
Charles Wilson takes first cloud chamber photos of sub-atomic particles		
Chaim Weizmann develops process critical to acetone production for manufacture of cordite	Marc Chagall, *I and the Village*; Leonardo da Vinci's *Mona Lisa* stolen from Louvre in	

Politics and International Relations

1911

1912 1 Jan.: Dr. Sun Yat-sen installed as provisional President of Chinese Republic; 12 Feb.: last Chinese emperor, P'u-yi, abdicates; Dr Sun resigns in favour of General Yuan Shih-k'ai who is inaugurated president on 10 Mar.: Sun founds Kuomintang

Arizona and New Mexico achieve statehood in USA

17 Oct.: First Balkan War breaks out as Balkan League (Serbia, Greece, Bulgaria, and Montenegro) attack Ottoman Empire

South African Native National Congress, subsequently known as African National Congress (ANC), founded in Bloemfontein by Zulu Methodist minister J. W. Dube

Woodrow Wilson elected president of USA

1913 30 May: Treaty of London ends First Balkan War; June, Bulgaria launches Second Balkan War, which ends 10 Aug. with Treaty of Bucharest and Bulgarian defeat

Yuan Shih-k'ai exiles Sun Yat-sen, purges Chinese Assembly

US Federal Reserve System legally established (not activated until 1914)

1914 Unification of Northern and Southern Nigeria under indirect rule policies of first Governor-General Frederick Lugard forms largest British colony in Africa

British Admiralty obtains controlling interest in Anglo-Persian Oil Company

Tampico incident between USA and Mexico; Apr.–Nov.: American occupation of Vera Cruz; July: resignation of Mexican dictator Victoriano Huerta

28 June: Archduke Franz Ferdinand of Austria and wife assassinated in Sarajevo by Gavrilo Princip, Bosnian Serb nationalist; 28 July: Austria declares war on Serbia; Aug.: outbreak of First World War

31 July: Jean Jaurès, socialist leader, assassinated in Paris

Aug.–Sept.: battles of Tannenberg and the Masurian Lakes on Eastern Front; First Battle of the Marne halts German advance on Paris, resulting in failure of the Schlieffen Plan

Aug.–Sept.: New Zealand forces occupy German Samoa; Australian forces occupy New Guinea, Bismarck Archipelago, and Solomons; Oct.: Japan occupies German Pacific islands in Marianas, Marshalls, Carolines, and Palau

Oct.–Nov.: First Battle of Ypres results in French and British holding the line against German efforts to take the North Sea ports

Science, Technology, and Medicine	Culture	
	Paris (recovered in 1913); Vassily Kandinsky and Franz Marc establish 'Blue Rider' (Blauen Reiter) group of artists in Munich	**1911**
Victor Hess discovers cosmic rays	C. G. Jung, *Psychology of the Unconscious*; Alfred Adler, *The Nervous Character*	**1912**
R. F. Scott reaches South Pole		
Invention of stainless steel; first manufacture of cellophane	Rabindranath Tagore, English translation of *Gitanjali* (awarded Nobel Prize for Literature in 1913)	
Remains of so-called 'Piltdown Man' claimed to be from the early Pleistocene period 'discovered' at Piltdown in England; exposed as a hoax in 1953	Maurice Ravel, *Daphnis et Chloë*; Schoenberg, *Pierrot Lunaire*	
First successful parachute jump	Marcel Duchamp, *Nude Descending a Staircase*	
15 Apr.: 1,500 people die when *Titanic* sinks in the North Atlantic after striking an iceberg	F. W. Woolworth Co. founded	
Henry Ford develops first moving assembly line in Detroit	Freud, *Totem and Taboo*	**1913**
Niels Bohr constructs quantum model of hydrogen atom; Einstein develops quantum theory of radiation	Lawrence, *Sons and Lovers*; Mann, *Death in Venice*; Maxim Gorky, *Childhood*; Marcel Proust, *Du coté de chez Swann*, opening volume of *A la recherche du temps perdu* (to 1927)	
Bela Schick develops diphtheria immunity test	Stravinsky, *The Rite of Spring*; Charles Ives, *Holidays Symphony*	
Sir James Jeans, *Radiation and Quantum Theory*	James Joyce, *Dubliners*; Conrad, *Chance*; Wyndham Lewis, a leader of the Vorticist movement, edits with Ezra Pound the magazine *Blast* (until 1915)	**1914**
Panama Canal opens		
Robert Goddard begins rocketry experiments	W. C. Handy, *St Louis Blues*	
	Oscar Kokoschka, *Bride of the Wind*	

Politics and International Relations

1914	Nov.: Japanese and British troops take German-held Wei-hai-wei; Japan takes control of Shantung
	Dec.: Britain declares protectorate over Egypt
	Gandhi returns to India and supports British war effort
	Blaise Diagne of Senegal elected first black Deputy to French Assembly
1915	Jan.: Japan presents 21 Demands to Yuan Shih-k'ai in effort to establish a virtual protectorate over China
	Germany and Britain impose reciprocal naval blockades
	Feb. (to Jan. 1916): Allies launch unsuccessful naval attack on the Dardanelles followed by landings on Gallipoli peninsula which are eventually repelled by Turkish forces
	Apr.–May: Second Battle of Ypres; first widespread use of poison gas as a weapon
	May: Italy enters war on Allied side
	7 May: German submarine sinks *Lusitania*, raising outcry against submarine warfare in USA
	16 May: secret Sykes–Picot Agreement concluded on Anglo-French division of Middle East after the war
	USA intervenes in Haiti (to 1934)
	Nov.: Turkish victory over British forces at Ctesiphon followed by 5-month siege of Allied forces in Kut; Turks conduct mass deportations and killings of Armenians
	Occupation of German South-West Africa by South African forces under Louis Botha; campaign in German East Africa by British and South Africans under Smuts against von Lettow-Vorbeck; Dec.: British forces take control of Lake Tanganyika
	First German Zeppelin attacks on Britain
1916	Mar.: Pancho Villa raids Columbus, New Mexico, leading to expedition by US General John J. Pershing into northern Mexico
	25 Apr.: Easter Rebellion breaks out in Dublin; suppressed by British
	21 Feb.–Aug.: Battle of Verdun, *c.* 700,000 total casualties; 1 July–Nov.: Battle of the Somme, *c.* 1.2 million total casualties; British use tanks for the first time (September)
	31 May: Battle of Jutland: German High Seas Fleet damages British Grand Fleet but fails to shake its control of North Sea
	June: Russian offensive under Brusilov breaks through Austrian lines but finally exhausts Russian army
	June: Yuan Shih-k'ai dies and China descends into era of warlordism
	June: Sharif Hussein of Mecca revolts against Ottomans and is proclaimed King of the Arabs; T. E. Lawrence appointed British liaison officer to army of Prince Faisal
	Home Rule Leagues formed in India under Annie Besant and B. G. Tilak
	Lucknow Pact establishes united front between Muslim League and Indian National Congress calling for constitutional reform, greater Indian participation in government
	16 Dec.: Grigori Rasputin, adviser of Russian Tsar and Tsarina, assassinated by Russian nobles

Science, Technology, and Medicine	Culture	
		1914
Einstein, *General Theory of Relativity*	Ezra Pound, *Cathay*; Lawrence, *The Rainbow*; Ford Madox Ford, *The Good Soldier*; W. Somerset Maugham, *Of Human Bondage*; Edgar Lee Masters, *Spoon River Anthology*; John Buchan, *The Thirty Nine Steps*	1915
Hugo Junkers develops first fighter plane; Henry Ford produces first motorized farm tractor		
Alexander Graham Bell makes first transcontinental telephone call from New York to San Francisco; wireless service begins between USA and Japan	Duchamp produces the first Dadaist paintings	
British develop the world's first military tank	D. W. Griffith, *Birth of a Nation*	
American chemist Gilbert Newton Lewis propounds valence theory	Joyce, *Portrait of the Artist as a Young Man*	1916
	Claude Monet, *Water Lilies*; anarchist Dadaist art movement flourishes in Zurich	
	Gustav Holst, *The Planets*; jazz becomes widely popular in USA	
	Lloyd Wright designs the Imperial Hotel in Tokyo	
	New Culture Movement under way in China as Western-educated Chinese scholars debate need for modernizing reform	
	Griffith, *Intolerance*	

Politics and International Relations

1917 E. S. Montagu, Secretary of State for India, declares Britain's goal for India to be responsible government within British Empire

Mexico adopts radical constitution

9 Feb.: Germany proclaims unrestricted submarine warfare

February revolution in Russia; Tsar abdicates on 16 Mar.

China enters war against Germany, sending 150,000 labourers to Europe

5 Apr.: US Congress declares war on Germany

Apr.: French offensive under Nivelle fails

May–June: mutinies break out in French army but are suppressed

July: mutinies break out in Russian army and navy; Aug.: factory workers strike in Moscow demanding end to war

Aug.–Nov.: British attacks in Flanders (Passchendaele): 400,000 British casualties

2 Nov.: Balfour Declaration promises British Government's support for establishment in Palestine of a 'national home for the Jews'; Dec.: British forces enter Jerusalem

7 Nov.: 'October Revolution' breaks out in Petrograd (St Petersburg); Bolsheviks under Lenin take control of Russian government

5 Dec.: Bolshevik government signs armistice with Central Powers

---

1918 Worldwide influenza epidemic kills more than ten million

8 Jan.: US President Wilson proposes 'Fourteen Points' as basis for peace and post-war reconstruction

Mar.: Germans launch last major offensive on Western Front, followed in July by successful Allied counter-offensive, including US troops

3 Mar.: Treaty of Brest–Litovsk ends war between Russia and Central Powers

16 July: Russian imperial family murdered at Ekaterinburg by local Bolsheviks

19–21 Sept.: Battle of Megiddo, last battle of Middle East campaigns, ends in British victory near Jaffa and subsequent fall of Damascus, Beirut, Homs, and Aleppo to British forces

Oct.: Austria-Hungary begins to collapse; Czechs and Slovaks declare independence, create Czechoslovakia

30 Oct.: Ottoman Empire agrees to armistice with Allies

Nov.: mutinies and revolution break out in Germany; Kaiser abdicates and flees into exile in Holland; 11 Nov.: armistice signed between Germany and Allied Powers ends First World War; Hungary, Yugoslavia, and Poland declared independent states; Austria and Germany become republics

Throughout 1918 civil war rages in Russia between Reds (Bolsheviks) and Whites; intervention by British, French, US, and Japanese forces in support of Whites

Mexico nationalizes its oil fields

Dec.: Britain's 'Coupon Election' overwhelmingly returns Lloyd George and Coalition Government to power, but fatally splits Liberal Party, allowing Labour Party to become major alternative to Conservative Party

---

Science, Technology, and Medicine	Culture	
	Carl Gustav Jung, *Psychology of the Unconscious*; Freud, *Introduction to Psychoanalysis*	**1917**
	T. S. Eliot, *Prufrock and Other Observations*; W. B. Yeats, *The Wild Swans at Coole*; Paul Valéry, *La Jeune parque*	
	Modigliani, *Crouching Female Nude*; J. S. Sargent, *Portrait of John D. Rockefeller*	
	C. D. Carra and Giorgio de Chirico establish school of 'metaphysical painting' in Italy; first use of the term 'surrealist' by Guillaume Apollinaire	
	Ottorino Respighi, *The Pines of Rome*; Sergei Prokofiev, *Classical Symphony*; Bela Bartok, *The Wooden Prince*; Eric Satie, *Parade*; George M. Cohan, *Over There*; Handy, *Beale Street Blues*	
Sir Arthur Stanley Eddington, *Gravitation and the Principle of Relativity*	Joyce, *The Exiles*; Luigi Pirandello, *Six Characters in Search of an Author*; G. M. Hopkins (posth.), *Poems*; Lytton Strachey, *Eminent Victorians*; Willa Cather, *My Antonia*; Chou Shu-jen (pseudonym Lu Hsun), *Madman's Diary* [short story on Western model]	**1918**
Harlow Shapley discovers true size of the Milky Way; Mount Wilson observatory telescope completed		
Max Planck awarded Nobel Prize for Physics for quantum theory		
Leonard Woolley begins archaeological excavations in Mesopotamia	Bartok, *Bluebeard's Castle*; Elgar, *Cello Concerto*; the 'Original Dixieland Jazz Band' tours Europe	
Regular airmail service begins between Washington and New York City		

Politics and International Relations

1919   Early January, 'Spartacist Revolt', an armed Communist uprising in Berlin led by Rosa Luxemburg and Karl Liebknecht, fails; 15 Jan.: Luxemburg and Liebknecht assassinated

18 Jan.: Paris Peace Conference opens; results in formal treaties ending First World War: treaties of Versailles with Germany, signed 28 June; Saint-Germain, with Austria, 10 Sept.; Neuilly, with Bulgaria, 27 Nov.; Trianon, with Hungary, 4 June 1920; and treaties of Sèvres (10 Aug. 1920) and Lausanne (24 July 1923) with Turkey; also establishes League of Nations, and Mandate system under which German and Turkish colonies in Africa, the Middle East, Asia, and the Pacific are divided among victorious Allies

Government of India Act establishes bicameral legislature for all India and elected provincial assemblies; Rowlatt Act continues harsh wartime emergency powers aimed at preventing sedition

10 Apr.: assassination of Emiliano Zapata at Chinameca hacienda, Mexico

13 Apr.: British-led troops fire on crowd in Amritsar, a city in the Punjab, killing over 300, wounding over 1,000, and causing outcry against British rule in India

May: Third Afghan War breaks out; major hostilities end within the month but guerrilla activity continues into 1920s

Chinese outrage at refusal of Versailles Conference to force Japan to give up Shantung leads to riots and May 4th Movement

Anton Drexler, Munich locksmith, founds Deutsche Arbeiterpartei or German Workers' Party, renamed in 1920 Nationalsozialistiche, or National Socialist, German Workers' Party (NSDAP), Nazi Party for short

In Italy, Benito Mussolini, former editor of Socialist paper Avanti, helps form Fasci d'Italiani di Combattimento, or Fascist party

Nationalist-inspired riots lead to general uprising against British in Egypt which is bloodily suppressed

Lenin establishes Comintern at Congress of Third International in Moscow to facilitate world revolution

---

1920   League of Nations and Permanent Court of International Justice established

US Senate votes against joining League of Nations

18th Amendment introduces Prohibition in USA; 19th Amendment grants women's suffrage

Britain granted mandate for Palestine; Emir Faisal, son of Sharif Hussein of Mecca, briefly becomes King of Syria before being evicted by French, who take Syria as a mandate

Gandhi supports Khilafat Movement in India and launches civil disobedience campaign (to 1922)

10 Aug.: Treaty of Sèvres triggers armed Turkish nationalist resistance led by Mustafa Kemal against Allied plans to dismember Turkey

Russian civil war ends

Italian immigrants Sacco and Vanzetti, both anarchists, are arrested and, in 1921, tried for murder in the USA; the ensuing *cause célèbre* lasts for years, with many believing in the men's innocence

---

Science, Technology, and Medicine	Culture	
Scientists observing total eclipse of the sun confirm Einstein's theory of relativity J. W. Alcock and A. W. Brown fly non-stop across the Atlantic in just over 16 hours First successful flight of a helicopter Radio Corporation of America (RCA) founded	J. M. Keynes, *The Economic Consequences of the Peace*; Karl Barth, *Der Romerbrief* [Epistle to the Romans]; Henri Bergson, *L'Energie spirituelle*; Havelock Ellis, *The Philosophy of Conflict*; Karl Jaspers, *Psychologie der Weltanschauungen*; Johan Huizinga, *The Waning of the Middle Ages*; Hu Shih, *Outline of Chinese Philosophy* Robert Wiene, *The Cabinet of Dr Caligari*; Manuel de Falla, *The Three-Cornered Hat*; Thomas Hardy, *Collected Poems* Vassily Kandinsky, *Dreamy Improvization* and *Arabian Cemetery*; Monet, *Nympheas*; Picasso, *Pierrot et Harlequin*; Georgia O'Keefe, *Blue and Green Music* Walter Gropius founds the Bauhaus (school of architecture and design) in Weimar, Germany	**1919**
Herman Rorschach develops inkblot test for diagnosing mental disorders John T. Thompson, a retired American army officer, patents his 'Tommy' submachine gun	Alfred Adler, *The Practice and Theory of Individual Psychology*; Jung, *Psychological Types*; Alfred North Whitehead, *The Concept of Nature*; H. G. Wells, *Outline of History* F. Scott Fitzgerald, *This Side of Paradise*; Sinclair Lewis, *Main Street*; Edith Wharton, *The Age of Innocence*; Hu Shih, champion of *pai-hua*, or literary use of the vernacular, publishes collection of *pai-hua* poems, *Ch'ang-shih chi*; Eugene O'Neill, *The Emperor Jones* and *Beyond the Horizon* Satie, *Socrate* Pope Benedict XV canonizes Joan of Arc	**1920**

Politics and International Relations

1921   Feb.: head of Cossack Brigade, Reza Khan, carries out *coup d'état* in Iran

Japanese prime minister Takashi Hara assassinated; Crown Prince Hirohito named regent

Evicted by French from Syria, Faisal is made King of Iraq by British

Mar.: Kronstadt rebellion suppressed; Lenin ends War Communism, adopts New Economic Policy (NEP)

Trial and conviction of Sacco and Vanzetti in USA spark worldwide protest

July: Chinese Communist Party founded

Nov.: (to Feb. 1922), Washington Naval Conference results in Four Power Treaty on the Pacific (13 Dec. 1921), which also ends Anglo–Japanese Alliance; Nine Power Treaty on China (6 Feb. 1922), and Five Power Treaty limiting naval strengths among the major powers (6 Feb. 1922)

6 Dec.: Anglo–Irish treaty creates Irish Free State within the British Empire, partitioning Ireland between largely Protestant north and largely Catholic south; civil war breaks out among Irish nationalists

1922   Lenin suffers debilitating stroke; Stalin becomes General Secretary of Communist Party in Russia; Soviet states formally establish Soviet Union

Britain separates Transjordan from rest of Palestine mandate and establishes Emir Abdullah, one of Sharif Hussein's sons, as ruler

Britain unilaterally recognizes Egyptian independence under King Fuad, but reserves right to control defence, Suez Canal, and the Sudan

Sept.–Oct.: Chanak crisis results in Turkish nationalist victory; Nov: Mustafa Kemal abolishes Ottoman sultanate, proclaims Turkey a republic; Greek population expelled from Turkey

Oct.: Benito Mussolini and Fascists threaten to march on Rome, forcing King Victor Emmanuel III to name Mussolini prime minister

1923   10 Jan.: Southern Rhodesia achieves self-government within the British Empire

10 Jan: France occupies Ruhr

24 July: Treaty of Lausanne recognizes new Turkish Republic

8–9 Nov.: Beerhall *putsch* in Munich results in Hitler's imprisonment; he writes *Mein Kampf* (published 1925)

Science, Technology, and Medicine	Culture	
Thomas Hunt Morgan proposes chromosome theory of heredity	Ludwig Wittgenstein, *Tractatus Logico-Philosophicus*	**1921**
Meghmed N. Saha formulates his thermal ionization equation for use in analysing stellar spectra	Lawrence, *Women in Love*; Italo Svevo, *The Confessions of Zeno*; O'Neill, *The Emperor Jones*; Lu Hsun, *The True Story of Ah Q*; J. Hasek, *Good Soldier Schweik*	
	Prokofiev, *The Love of Three Oranges*	
	Charlie Chaplin, *The Kid*; Rudolph Valentino stars in *The Sheik*	
Lord Carnarvon and Howard Carter discover tomb of Tutankhamen in Egypt	Joyce, *Ulysses*; Eliot, *The Waste Land*; Valéry, *Le Cimetière marin;* Forster, *A Passage to India*; Sinclair Lewis, *Babbit*; Herman Hesse, *Siddhartha*; Osip Mandelstam, *Tristia* (poems)	**1922**
	Chagall and Kandinsky are among writers and artists who leave Russia for the West; in Mexico Diego Rivera, David Siqueiros, and Jose Orozco begin painting murals	
	Ludwig Mies van der Rohe designs steel and glass skyscraper; Le Corbusier publishes plan for 'The Contemporary City'	
	Schoenberg establishes 'twelve-tone composition' method	
	F. W. Murnau, *Nosferatu: A Symphony of Horror*; Robert Flaherty, *Nanook of the North*	
Calmette and Guerin develop tuberculosis vaccine	Freud, *The Ego and the Id*; Le Corbusier, *Towards a New Architecture*	**1923**
Juan de la Cierva develops idea of autogiro	Lu Hsun, *Na-han*	
B. F. Goodrich Co. uses Gideon Sundback's Hookless No. 2 slide fastener on line of rubber galoshes, calls device a 'zipper'	Duchamp, *The Bride Stripped Bare by her Bachelors, Even* (begun in 1915, now left 'definitively unfinished')	
	Alexander Rodschenko produces photomontages for Mayakovsky's poem *Pro Eto*	
	Cecil B. de Mille, *The Ten Commandments*	

Politics and International Relations

1924   21 Jan.: Lenin dies; power struggle ensues within Communist leadership

19 Feb.: Reza Khan deposes Shah of Iran and is himself appointed regent; later assumes throne

Mar.: Ataturk abolishes caliphate

Ibn Saud captures Mecca from Sharif Hussein, King of Hijaz

24 Mar.: Greece proclaimed republic

Apr.: Dawes plan proposes a settlement of European debt crisis

10 June: Italian Deputy Giacomo Matteotti murdered by Fascists

---

1925   Stalin emerges as ruler of Soviet Union and proclaims new policy of 'socialism in one country'

17 June: Geneva Protocol prohibiting use of gas and bacteriological weapons signed by 38 countries

Abd el-Krim revolt breaks out in Morocco against French and Spanish

1 Dec.: Locarno Conference treaties guarantee boundaries of Germany, France, and Belgium

---

1926   8 Jan.: Ibn Saud proclaimed King of the Hijaz

25 Apr.: Reza Khan crowns himself Reza Shah, and proclaims new Pahlavi dynasty in Iran

Summer: General Strike called by trades unions in Britain

8 Sept.: Germany admitted to League of Nations

USA intervenes in Nicaragua (to 1933)

Cristero (Catholic) rebellion breaks out in Mexico against revolutionary regime (to 1929)

Imperial Conference agrees that 'group of self-governing communities composed of Great Britain and the Dominions' are 'autonomous Communities within the British Empire'

Chiang Kai-shek reorganizes Kuomintang; leads Northern Expedition to reunify China

Abd el-Krim revolt ends in Morocco

1927   Trotsky expelled from Soviet Communist Party

Chiang Kai-shek attempts to destroy Chinese Communist Party

Italian immigrants Sacco and Vanzetti, tried and convicted for murder in 1921, are executed in USA after an appeal for a re-trial is denied; anti-American riots follow in Europe

---

Science, Technology, and Medicine	Culture	
Henry S. Hele-Shaw and T. E. Beacham develop variable-pitch airplane propeller; self-winding watch is patented; first portable radio marketed by Zenith; first spiral notebook introduced	Mann, *The Magic Mountain*; Shaw, *Saint Joan*	**1924**
	Janáček, *The Cunning Little Vixen*; George Gershwin, *Rhapsody in Blue*	
E. V. Appleton uses radio-ranging (precursor of radar) to determine distance to objects; locates heaviside layer of ionosphere	André Breton, *First Manifesto of Surrealism*	
	Erich von Stroheim, *Greed*; F. W. Murnau, *The Last Laugh*	
Wolfgang Pauli formulates 'Exclusion Principle' in quantum mechanics; Werner Heisenberg formulates first version of his 'uncertainty principle'; Heisenberg, Born and Jordan publish first version of *New Quantum Theory*	Adolf Hitler, *Mein Kampf*	**1925**
	Franz Kafka, *The Trial*; Fitzgerald, *The Great Gatsby*; John Dos Passos, *Manhattan Transfer*; Virginia Woolf, *Mrs Dalloway*; Noel Coward, *Hay Fever*; P. G. Wodehouse, *Carry On, Jeeves*	
Bell System establishes the Bell Telephone Laboratories	Alban Berg, *Wozzek*; Ravel, *L'Enfant et les sortilèges*, Josephine Baker appears in *Revue Nègre* in Paris	
AT&T offers first wirephoto service		
Bronx River Parkway, first public road with entrances and exits rather than intersections, opens in New York City and Westchester County	Sergei Eisenstein, *Battleship Potemkin*; Chaplin, *The Gold Rush*	
	In Japan, potters Kawai Kanjiro, Yanagi Soetsu, and Hamada Shoji establish folk art movement, drawing on traditional Japanese and some English designs to produce ceramic ware for daily use	
Erwin Schrödinger publishes first version of wave mechanics; Paul Dirac shows that the Heisenberg and Schrödinger theories are identical	T. E. Lawrence, *The Seven Pillars of Wisdom*; Kafka, *The Castle*; André Gide, *The Counterfeiters*; Lu Hsun, *P'ang-huang*; A. A. Milne, *Winnie the Pooh*	**1926**
John Logie Baird demonstrates television in London	Puccini, *Turandot* (posth.); Dmitry Shostakovich, *Symphony No 1*	
Robert H. Goddard launches first liquid-fuel rocket	Kandinsky, *Point and Line to Plane*	
	Fritz Lang, *Metropolis*; Vsevolod Pudovkin, *Mother*	
	Rudolph Valentino dies after filming *Son of the Sheik*, millions mourn	
Lindbergh flies solo over the Atlantic	Kafka, *Amerika*; Hesse, *Steppenwolf*	**1927**
Rolex markets first waterproof watch	Bartok, *Piano Concerto No 1*; Zoltan Kodaly, *Hary Janos*; Jerome Kern and Oscar Hammerstein, *Showboat*, Duke Ellington plays at the Cotton Club in Harlem, New York	
Cellophane tape invented		
First iron-lung device invented		
	Abel Gance, *Napoléon*; talking motion pictures begin with Al Jolson in *The Jazz Singer*	

Politics and International Relations

1928	Chiang Kai-shek elected president of China
	Stalin launches first Five Year Plan in Soviet Union
	Mar.: Hasan al-Banna, an Egyptian schoolteacher, establishes Society of Muslim Brothers, subsequently known as the Muslim Brotherhood
	17 July: Mexican president-elect Obregon assassinated
	28 Aug.: Kellogg–Briand Pact (General Treaty for the Renunciation of War as an Instrument of National Policy) signed in Paris
1929	11 Feb.: Lateran Treaties between papacy and Italy establish the Vatican as a state
	28 Oct.: Wall Street crash; beginning of Great Depression
	31 Oct.: Lord Irwin, Viceroy of India, declares that Britain's goal for India is 'Dominion Status'
	Chinese Communists regroup in rural soviets
	Arab–Jewish riots over incidents at Wailing Wall in Jerusalem
	Establishment in Mexico of governing Revolutionary National Party, subsequently known as Institutional Revolutionary Party or PRI
1930	Stalin decrees forced collectivization and 'liquidation of the kulaks as a class' in Soviet Union
	Mar.–Apr.: Gandhi leads Salt March, major civil disobedience campaign against British rule in India; 12 Nov.: Round Table Conference on India opens in London
	Ras Tafari ascends throne as Emperor Haile Selassie of Ethiopia
	Revolution in Argentina brings Jose Uriburu to power as president
	Revolution ends 'Old Republic'; brings Getulio Vargas to power in Brazil
	Passfield White Paper on Palestine proposes limits on Jewish immigration
1931	Feb.–Mar.: Gandhi–Irwin talks result in Congress participation in Round Table Conference in London

Science, Technology, and Medicine	Culture	
Alexander Fleming discovers penicillin; George Papanicolau develops Pap test to discover cancer in the uterus Radio beacons begin to be used as navigational aids Joseph Schick develops the first modern electric razor	Evelyn Waugh, *Decline and Fall*; Lawrence, *Lady Chatterley's Lover*, published privately in Florence, but banned as obscene in many countries; Yeats, *The Tower* Ravel, *Bolero*; Kurt Weill and Bertolt Brecht, *The Threepenny Opera*; Gershwin, *An American in Paris* Le Corbusier designs Villa Savoye Walt Disney introduces Mickey Mouse; G. W. Pabst, *Pandora's Box*; Carl Theodor Dreyer, *The Passion of Joan of Arc*	**1928**
Airship, *Graf Zeppelin*, flies around the world Dirac predicts the existence of a new particle to partner the electron Edwin Powell Hubble proves the universe is expanding	William Faulkner, *The Sound and the Fury*; Ernest Hemingway, *A Farewell to Arms*; Virginia Woolf, *A Room of One's Own*; Alfred Doblin, *Berlin-Alexanderplatz*; Erich Maria Remarque, *All Quiet on the Western Front*; Robert Graves, *Goodbye to All That*; C. Day Lewis, *Transitional Poems*; Jean Cocteau, *Les Enfants terribles*; Tanizaki Jun-Ichiro, *Tade kuu mushi* [Some Prefer Nettles] Henry Moore, *Reclining Figure* King Vidor, *Hallelujah* (all-black film)	**1929**
C. W. Tombaugh discovers the planet Pluto Sir C. Raman wins Nobel Prize for work on light diffusion Dirac publishes *The Principles of Quantum Mechanics* Max Theiler discovers yellow fever vaccine Amy Johnson flies solo to Australia from London	W. H. Auden, *Poems*; Eliot, *Ash Wednesday*; Wyndham Lewis, *The Apes of God* Paul Robeson and Peggy Ashcroft star in stage production of *Othello*; Noel Coward and Gertrude Lawrence in Coward's *Private Lives* Picasso, *Crucifixion*; Grant Wood, *American Gothic* Chrysler Building completed in New York Josef von Sternberg, *The Blue Angel*; Alfred Hitchcock's first sound film, *Blackmail*; René Clair, *Sous les toits de Paris*; Lewis Milestone, *All Quiet on the Western Front*; Luis Bunuel, *L'Age d'or*	**1930**
Positron is discovered First cyclotron is built at Berkeley, California	Pearl Buck, *The Good Earth*; George Seferis, *Strophe* (poems); Edmund Wilson, *Axel's Castle*	**1931**

Politics and International Relations

1931   In England Oswald Mosley leaves Labour Party to form British Union of Fascists

In Spain monarchy overthrown and republic declared

Austrian Credit-Anstalt bank (11 May) and German Danatbank (13 July) collapse, causing bank closures across Central Europe and Germany

15 Sept.: British cuts in pay precipitate mutiny among naval forces at Invergordon

21 Sept.: Britain abandons Gold Standard; economic crisis forces general election (27 Oct.), resulting in 'National Government' composed largely of Conservatives supporting Labour Prime Minister Ramsay Macdonald

Sept.: Japanese troops stage incident on railways at Mukden, using it as pretext for occupying Manchuria

11 Dec.: Statute of Westminster defines Dominion status in British Empire

1932   Worldwide Depression deepens; famine in Soviet Union as a result of Stalin's collectivization programme

Japanese establish puppet state of Manchukuo in Manchuria with last Qing emperor as titular head of state

2 Feb.: League of Nations convenes World Disarmament Conference in effort to reduce offensive weapons (Conference dissolves in failure in 1934)

July–Aug.: Ottawa Conference establishes Imperial Preference system in British Empire and Commonwealth

Gandhi restarts civil disobedience campaign; Indian National Congress declared illegal and Gandhi jailed

Chaco War breaks out between Bolivia and Paraguay (to 1935)

King Ibn Saud consolidates his realms into single kingdom of Saudi Arabia

May and June: veterans' 'Bonus March' on Washington, DC, ends in violence when troops under General Douglas MacArthur disperse marchers

8 Nov.: Franklin Delano Roosevelt elected US President

1933   30 Jan.: Adolf Hitler becomes Chancellor of Germany

27 Feb.: Reichstag fire in Berlin gives Hitler excuse to claim dictatorial powers and to crush all opposition, in Emergency decrees of 28 Feb. and Enabling Law of 23 Mar.; 14 July: all parties outlawed except Nazi Party; first concentration camps established in Germany

Mar.: newly inaugurated US President Roosevelt launches New Deal to combat Depression; Apr.: USA goes off Gold Standard; Roosevelt recognizes, and resumes trade with, Soviet Union

27 Mar.: Japan leaves League of Nations, rejecting condemnations of Japanese policy towards China

Revolution in Cuba ousts dictator Machado

21st Amendment to US Constitution repeals Prohibition

14 Oct.: Germany withdraws from World Disarmament Conference and League of Nations

Science, Technology, and Medicine	Culture	
Du Pont introduces Freon	William Walton, *Belshazzar's Feast*; William Grant Still, *African–American Symphony*; USA officially adopts *Star-Spangled Banner* as national anthem	**1931**
	Chaplin, *City Lights*; William Wellman, *The Public Enemy*, with James Cagney; Fritz Lang, *M*; Boris Karloff, *Frankenstein*	
	Empire State Building completed in New York City	
James Chadwick discovers the neutron	Hemingway, *Death in the Afternoon*; Aldous Huxley, *Brave New World*	**1932**
Kurt Gödel, *Undecidability Theorem*		
Amelia Earhart becomes first woman to fly solo across the Atlantic	Leni Riefenstahl, *The Blue Light*; Gary Cooper appears in *A Farewell to Arms*; Johnny Weissmuller makes first *Tarzan* film; Shirley Temple makes her first film, *Red-Haired Alibi*, aged 4	
Polyethylene produced by British Imperial Chemical Industries	André Malraux, *La Condition humaine*	**1933**
Wiley Post makes first solo around the world flight	Gertrude Stein, *The Autobiography of Alice B. Toklas*; Wells, *The Shape of Things to Come*	
Ernst Ruska invents first electron microscope	Alexander Korda, *The Private Life of Henry VIII*, with Charles Laughton; Busby Berkeley, *42nd Street*; David O. Selznick, *King Kong*; *Flying down to Rio*, first screen pairing of Fred Astaire and Ginger Rogers	
	The game Monopoly is invented	

Politics and International Relations

1934   Roosevelt inaugurates Good Neighbor Policy of non-intervention in Latin America; USA ends quasiprotectorate over Cuba

30 June: Hitler orders liquidation of Ernst Röhm's Brownshirts in 'Night of the Long Knives'; 24 July: Nazis seeking *anschluss* with Austria assassinate Austrian Chancellor Engelbert Dollfuss; 19 Aug.: Hitler proclaims end of republic, beginning of Third Reich, with himself as Führer

Oct.: under attack by Kuomintang, members of Jianxi Soviet begin Long March (to Oct. 1935), during which Mao Zedong emerges as leader of Chinese Communist Party

Japan repudiates Washington treaties limiting armaments

Dec.: Sergey Kirov assassinated, almost certainly, on Stalin's orders; beginning of Great Purge in Soviet Union; millions killed or imprisoned in slave labour camps

1935   Mustafa Kemal continues Westernizing reforms in Turkey and adopts surname Ataturk

7 Mar.: Hitler incorporates Saarland into Germany; 16 Mar.: he repudiates disarmament clauses of Versailles Treaty, reinstitutes compulsory military service; 18 June: Anglo-German Naval Agreement; 15 Sept.: Nuremberg Laws enacted against Jews in Germany

Stalin's purge continues with enormous bloodshed

2 Oct.: Mussolini invades Abyssinia; League of Nations declares Italy an aggressor; imposes sanctions with little effect

Reza Shah officially changes name of Persia to Iran

Government of India Act establishes provincial government and federal system

1936   20 Jan.: Edward VIII accedes to British throne; abdicates 10 Dec.; succeeded by George VI

Indian National Congress wins most elections under new constitution

7 Mar.: German troops re-enter Rhineland in defiance of Versailles Treaty and Locarno Pact

3 May: Popular Front government comes to power in France under Leon Blum

9 May: Italy annexes Abyssinia

18 July: army revolt under General Franco marks beginning of Spanish Civil War; USSR supports Republic; Italy and Germany support Franco

Aug.: first 'show trial' in Moscow, involving ex-Politburo members Zinoviev and Kamenev

25 Nov.: Germany and Japan sign anti-Comintern Pact

Chiang Kai-shek declares war on Japanese invaders; kidnapped by Communists from Xian, he agrees to united front against Japanese

Science, Technology, and Medicine	Culture	
The ocean-liner *Queen Mary* is launched	Hu Shih, *Chinese Renaissance*; Shu She-yu, *Niu T'ien-tz'u chuan*; Mikhail Sholokov, *And Quiet Flows the Don*	**1934**
	Frank Capra, *It Happened One Night*; Berkeley, *Gold Diggers of 1933*	
	Socialist Realism decreed only acceptable artistic form in Soviet Union	
Kodak introduces colour photography; IBM markets electric typewriter; nylon patented	Sydney and Beatrice Webb, *Soviet Communism: A New Civilization?*; Karl	**1935**
First radar developed in Britain	Jaspers, *Suffering and Existence*; Barth, *Credo*	
Kendall discovers cortisone; Gerhard Domagk successfully tests the first sulfa drug, Prontosil	Malraux, *Le Temps du mépris*; Eliot, *Murder in the Cathedral*; Robert E. Sherwood, *The Petrified Forest*; Sinclair Lewis, *It Can't Happen Here*	
	Gershwin, *Porgy and Bess*; Paul Hindemith, *Mathis der Maler*	
	Shimazaki Toson writes *Yoakemae* [Before the Dawn]	
	Marx Brothers, *A Night at the Opera*; Riefenstahl, *Triumph of the Will*; Hitchcock, *The 39 Steps*; John Ford, *The Informer*; Selznick, *David Copperfield*; Clark Gable and Charles Laughton star in *Mutiny on the Bounty*	
Boulder dam completed	Keynes, *The General Theory of Employment, Interest, and Money*; A. J. Ayer, *Language,*	**1936**
Carrel creates artificial heart	*Truth and Logic*; Beatrice Webb, *My Apprenticeship*	
Porsche designs the Volkswagen, or 'people's car'; Focke develops first practical helicopter; first Spitfire airplane test-flown	Auden, *Look, Stranger!*; Shu She-yu, *Lo-t'o Hsiang-tzu*, published in unauthorized English translation in 1945 under title *Rickshaw Boy* (best-seller); Margaret Mitchell, *Gone With the Wind*	
In Germany the Reichspost develops the first picturephone service, connecting Berlin, Leipzig, Hamburg, and Nuremberg	Henry Luce establishes *Life* magazine; Penguin markets the first paperback books	
	Schoenberg, *Violin Concerto*	
	Lloyd Wright designs 'Falling Water' in Pennsylvania	

Politics and International Relations

1936   King Farouk ascends Egyptian throne; 26 Aug.: Anglo-Egyptian Treaty normalizes relations between Britain and Egypt

Arab Higher Committee formed in Palestine to co-ordinate resistance to Jewish immigration; Arab Revolt breaks out; British appoint Peel Commission to investigate and make recommendations for mandate

---

1937   Spanish civil war continues; 27 Apr.: German bombers destroy ancient Basque city of Guernica

28 May: Neville Chamberlain becomes British Prime Minister

1 June: Prince Konoye named Prime Minister in Japan; Japanese militarists pursue more aggressive war policy; 7 July: incident at Marco Polo Bridge, near Peking, leads to full-scale war between Japan and China; Japanese occupy Tientsin and Peking in Aug.; 12 Dec.: Japanese troops capture Chiang Kai-shek's capital, carry out 'Rape of Nanking'

Italy joins Anti-Comintern Pact; leaves League of Nations

Germans in Sudetenland riot

Soviet purges continue

1938   12 Mar.: Hitler engineers *Anschluss*, or union, with Austria; through spring and summer he demands Sudetenland from Czechoslovakia; in Munich Agreement (29 Sept.) British prime minister Chamberlain and French premier Daladier give in to Hitler's demands

9–10 Nov.: *Kristallnacht* [Night of Broken Glass], Nazi pogrom against Jews in Germany

By end of Nov. Japanese troops have taken control of most of China except Szechwan; Chinese resistance continues from Chiang Kai-shek's wartime capital at Chungking

Science, Technology, and Medicine	Culture	
	Chaplin, *Modern Times*; Capra, *Mr Deeds Goes to Town*	**1936**
	US athlete Jesse Owens wins four gold medals at Olympic Games in Berlin; German boxer Max Schmeling defeats American Joe Louis	
	BBC begins television service	
	Bruno Hauptman convicted of kidnap and murder of Lindbergh baby	
Golden Gate Bridge completed in San Francisco	Dos Passos, *U.S.A.*; Hemingway, *To Have and Have Not*; Malraux, *L'Espoir*; George Orwell, *The Road to Wigan Pier*; John Steinbeck, *Of Mice and Men*; Jean-Paul Sartre, *La Nausée*; Auden, *Spain*; Shiga Naoya, *Anya Koro*	**1937**
Wernher von Braun and other German scientists begin first rocket tests at Peenemunde research facility; German dirigible Hindenburg explodes while landing in USA; in England, A. A. Griffith and Frank Whittle build first jet engine; a similar engine is developed independently in Germany by M. Muller and Pabst von Ohain	Picasso paints mural, *Guernica*; Paul Mellon endows National Gallery in Washington, DC	
Grote Reber builds first radiotelescope in his backyard, begins receiving signals from space the following year; British Government builds chain of radar stations along eastern coast	Shostakovich, *Symphony No 5*; Carl Orff, *Carmina Burana*; Berg, *Lulu* (posth., unfinished)	
Insulin used to control diabetes; Bovet develops first antihistamine; Theiler develops vaccine against yellow fever	Walt Disney, *Snow White and the Seven Dwarfs*; Jean Renoir, *La Grande Illusion*	
Biro patents first commercially successful ball-point pen; fluorescent lamps introduced; Nestlé Company develops instant coffee	Whitehead, *Modes of Thought*; Santayana, *The Realm of Truth*; Franz Boas, *General Anthropology*	**1938**
Reber picks up short waves from the Milky Way	Orwell, *Homage to Catalonia*; William Faulkner, *The Unvanquished*; Thornton Wilder, *Our Town*; Emlyn Williams, *The Corn is Green*; Archibald MacLeish, collection of poems, *Land of the Free*; exiled Russian-Jewish poet Osip Mandelstam reported dead in Siberian labour camp	
	Aaron Copland, *Billy the Kid*	
	Joe Louis knocks out Max Schmeling in return match	
	Orson Welles's radio broadcast of Wells's *War of the Worlds* causes panic among radio listeners in USA	

Politics and International Relations

1938

1939   Feb.–Mar.: London Conference on Palestine ends in failure; 17 May: Britain issues White Paper outlining new policy to restrict Jewish immigration to 75,000 over the next 5 years, and establishment within 10 years of independent Palestinian state, with safeguards for minority communities

Mar.: Spanish Civil War ends with surrender of Loyalist government to Franco; thousands of Loyalist refugees flee into France

23 Mar.: Germany invades Czechoslovakia; 23 Aug.: Nazi–Soviet Pact; 1 Sept.: Hitler attacks Poland; 3 Sept.: Britain and France declare war on Germany, and Second World War begins; 17 Sept.: Soviet troops enter Poland; 29 Sept.: Germany and USSR partition Poland; Oct.: Soviets occupy Latvia, Lithuania, and Estonia; 30 Nov.: USSR attacks Finland in campaign that lasts until Mar. 1940

Chinese construct Burma Road to obtain supplies from outside world

1940   Apr.–May: German troops launch blitzkrieg attacks on Denmark, Norway, Holland, Belgium, and France; 10 May: Winston Churchill becomes British Prime Minister; 27 May–4 June: over 300,000 troops evacuated to Britain from Dunkirk; 10 June: Italy declares war on Britain and France; 17 June: Vichy regime in France signs armistice with Germany; General Charles de Gaulle proclaims Free French movement in London; Aug.–Sept.: Battle of Britain as Luftwaffe tries to bomb Britain into submission; 2 Sept.: USA trades 50 over-age destroyers for leases on British bases in Caribbean; 7 Sept.–Apr. 1941: German air raids on British cities; 28 Oct.: Italy attacks Greece; 9 Dec.: successful British offensive against Italian forces in Western Desert, North Africa; subsequently British conquer Italian East Africa; 29 Dec.: Roosevelt declares USA must become 'arsenal for democracy'

1941   11 Mar.: US Congress passes Lend-Lease aid to Allies

Apr.: German forces overrun Yugoslavia and Greece

20–31 May: German airborne landings capture Crete; British forces in North Africa are driven back to Egyptian frontier

22 June: Germany invades USSR, overrunning much of Western Russia and besieging Leningrad (till Jan. 1944)

14 Aug.: Churchill and Roosevelt meet off Newfoundland coast, issue Atlantic Charter, statement of goals for post-war world

Science, Technology, and Medicine	Culture	
	Eisenstein, *Alexander Nevski*; Hitchcock, *The Lady Vanishes*; Riefenstahl, *Olympia*	**1938**
	Lloyd Wright builds Tailesin West; Gropius and Marcel Breuer design Haggerty House in Cohasset, Mass., USA	
Otto Hahn and Fritz Strassman discover nuclear fission	Freud, *Moses and Monotheism*	**1939**
	Joyce, *Finnegans Wake*; Christopher Isherwood, *Goodbye to Berlin*; Mann, *Lotte in Weimar*; Steinbeck, *The Grapes of Wrath*; Eliot, *The Family Reunion*; Gide, *Journal 1885–1939*; Antoine de Saint Exupéry, *Terre des hommes*; Louis MacNeice, *Autumn Journal*	
	Bartok, *Mikrokosmos*	
	Selznick, *Gone With the Wind*; Ford, *Stagecoach*; Sam Wood, *Goodbye Mr Chips*; Capra, *Mr Smith Goes to Washington*; Ernst Lubitsch, *Ninotchka*; Victor Fleming, *The Wizard of Oz*; Berkeley, *Babes in Arms*	
Giant cyclotron built at the University of California	Arthur Koestler, *Darkness at Noon*; Edmund Wilson, *To the Finland Station*; Richard Wright, *Native Son*; Graham Greene, *The Power and the Glory*; Hemingway, *For Whom the Bell Tolls*; O'Neill, *Long Day's Journey Into Night*; Thomas Wolfe (posth.), *You Can't Go Home Again*	**1940**
Penicillin developed		
Tacoma Narrows Bridge in Tacoma, Washington, collapses due to wind stress; leads engineers to rethink future bridge designs	Duke Ellington acclaimed as jazz pianist and composer	
	Disney, *Fantasia*; Ford, *The Grapes of Wrath*; Hitchcock, *Rebecca*; George Cukor, *The Philadelphia Story*; Chaplin, *The Great Dictator*	
	Lascaux Caves with prehistoric wall paintings discovered in southern France	
First aerosol spray containers introduced	Benedetto Croce, *History as the Story of Liberty*; Reinhold Niebuhr, *The Nature and Destiny of Man* (to 1943)	**1941**
First Jeeps produced on designs developed in 1940; adopted for general use by US Army in June	Fitzgerald, *The Last Tycoon*; Coward, *Blithe Spirit*; Franz Werfel, *Das Lied der Bernadette*	
	Shostakovich composes *Symphony No 7* during siege of Leningrad; Benjamin Britten, *Violin Concerto*	

Politics and International Relations

1941 6 Dec.: Soviet forces counter-attack north of Moscow, halting German offensive

7 Dec.: Japanese forces attack US fleet at Pearl Harbor; 8 Dec.: USA and Britain declare war on Japan; Japanese forces attack and overrun Philippines and Hong Kong; 11 Dec.: Germany and Italy declare war on USA

1942 20 Jan.: Wannsee Conference of senior Nazis finalizes plans for 'Final Solution' of 'Jewish Problem' — extermination of Jews in Europe

Jan.–Feb.: Japanese forces overrun the Malay peninsula and Netherlands East Indies. 15 Feb.: British surrender at Singapore; Japanese take 130,000 prisoners of war

Feb.: US Government orders forced removal of Japanese-Americans from coastal areas to inland camps

Cripps Mission on post-war independence for India fails to achieve agreement; in Aug. Gandhi launches 'Quit India' movement, is jailed in Oct. with other Congress leaders

30 May: RAF begins 1,000 bomber raids on Germany

4 June: Battle of Midway turns tide in the Pacific

28 June: Germans launch offensive in Russia towards Caucasus

7 Aug.: US forces land on Guadalcanal

23 Oct.: British Eighth Army in North Africa defeat German–Italian forces at el Alamein, subsequently pursue them to Tripolitania

7 Nov.: Anglo–American forces land in French North Africa

22 Nov.: Soviet forces launch counter-attack at Stalingrad

William Beveridge makes his 'Report on Social Security'

1943 14 Jan.: Casablanca Conference between Roosevelt and Churchill; proclamation of Allied goal of unconditional surrender by Axis powers

31 Jan.: Germans surrender at Stalingrad, 300,000 taken prisoner; 5 July: Soviet victory in largest tank battle in history at Kursk marks turning point on Eastern Front

7 May: last Axis forces in North Africa surrender, 250,000 taken prisoner

24–8 June: Allied air attack on Hamburg initiates Combined Allied Air Offensive against German homeland

9 July: Allies invade Sicily; Sept.: invasion of mainland Italy leads to deposition of Mussolini and Italy's surrender; however, German troops rescue Mussolini and take over defence of Italy; 11 Oct.: new Italian government declares war on Germany

In India famine ravages Bengal as war conditions hamper relief efforts

22 Nov.: Cairo Conference between Churchill, Roosevelt, and Chiang Kai-shek discusses Allied policies of unconditional surrender by Japan and post-war settlement of East Asia

28 Nov.: Tehran Conference between Roosevelt, Churchill, and Stalin discusses post-war settlement in Europe

---

1944 4 June: Rome liberated by Allied forces; 6 June: D-Day, Allied cross-Channel invasion of Europe leads to 25 Aug. liberation of Paris

June: Japanese invasion of India thrown back at Imphal and Kohima

Science, Technology, and Medicine	Culture	
	Orson Welles, *Citizen Kane*; John Huston, *The Maltese Falcon*; Berkeley, *Babes on Broadway*; Ford, *How Green Was My Valley*; anti-British Nazi film, *Ohm Kruger*	**1941**
Enrico Fermi initiates first self-sustaining nuclear reaction; Manhattan Project begun to develop atomic weapon in the USA	Albert Camus, *L'Etranger*; Jean Anouilh, *Antigone*; Sartre, *Les Mouches*; C. S. Lewis, *The Screwtape Letters*	**1942**
In Germany first successful prototype of the V-2 rocket is tested	May: Mao Zedong lays down guidelines for Chinese Communist literature in *Talks at the Yenan Forum on Art and Literature*	
	John Cage, *Imaginary Landscape No 3*	
	Michael Curtiz, *Casablanca*, with Humphrey Bogart and Ingrid Bergman; Welles, *The Magnificent Ambersons*; William Wyler, *Mrs Miniver*; Disney, *Bambi*	
Jacques Yves Cousteau and Emile Gagnan develop first Scuba gear	Sartre, *L'Etre et le néant*	**1943**
Waksman develops streptomycin	Sinclair, *Dragon's Teeth*; Bertolt Brecht, *The Good Woman of Setzuan*; Betty Smith, *A Tree Grows in Brooklyn*; William Saroyan, *The Human Comedy*	
	Rodgers and Hammerstein, *Oklahoma*	
Quinine first synthesized	F. A. von Hayek, *The Road to Serfdom*	**1944**
Uranium pile built in Clinton, Tennessee	Saul Bellow, *Dangling Man*; Tennessee Williams, *The Glass Menagerie*;	

Politics and International Relations

1944   July: leaders of French West and Equatorial Africa meeting with de Gaulle in Brazzaville issue Brazzaville Declaration, reaffirming continuance of French empire, rejecting possibility of independence, but calling for democratic reforms in colonies

20 July: officers' plot to kill Hitler fails, suspected plotters killed

22 July: international finance conference signs agreement at Bretton Woods, New Hampshire, establishing parameters for post-war world economy, including establishment of World Bank and International Monetary Fund

24–5 Sept.: British airborne landings at Arnhem defeated

Dec.: German counter-offensive through the Ardennes repulsed

1945   9 Jan.: US forces land on Philippines, fighting continues to July

4–11 Feb.: Yalta Conference between Churchill, Roosevelt, and Stalin discusses final strategies to end war and fate of post-war Germany

19 Feb.: US forces land on Iwo Jima, fighting lasts until 15 Mar.

9 Mar.: US air forces destroy 20% of Tokyo in fire raids

1 Apr.: US forces land on Okinawa, fighting continues until July

12 Apr.: Roosevelt dies; Harry Truman becomes US president

25 Apr.: Soviet and Allied armies meet at Torgau on the Elbe

28 Apr.: Mussolini and mistress captured and shot by Italian partisans

Hitler marries Eva Braun, both commit suicide on 30 Apr. as Russians take Berlin

7 May: Germany surrenders; 8 May: V.E. Day ends war in Europe; Allied Control Commission divides Germany into British, American, French, and Russian occupation zones; British, Americans, Russians occupy Berlin

Allied troops liberate Auschwitz and other Nazi death camps; it is later estimated that as many as 6,000,000 Jews were put to death by the Nazis in what comes to be known as the Holocaust

Apr.–June: international conference meeting in San Francisco drafts United Nations Charter, signed by 50 nations on 26 June, ratified at first meeting of UN General Assembly, in London, 24 Oct. establishing General Assembly, Security Council, and, subsequently, specialized agencies such as International Court of Justice (1945), Food and Agriculture Organization (1945), International Monetary Fund (1946), and World Health Organization (1948)

3 May: Rangoon captured, completing British reconquest of Burma

16 July: first successful test of atomic bomb near Alamagordo, New Mexico

17 July–2 Aug.: Potsdam Conference deals with questions of post-war Germany and Eastern Europe, offers Japan unconditional surrender of armed forces or total destruction

July: British General Election ousts Churchill and Conservatives and returns Labour Government under Clement Attlee

6 and 9 Aug.: US planes drop atomic bombs on Hiroshima and Nagasaki, Japan; on the 8th USSR declares war on Japan; 10 Aug.: Emperor Hirohito decrees Japan must 'endure the unendurable' and surrender; on 2 Sept.: Japan signs unconditional surrender, ending Second World War

In India Congress leaders released, negotiations begin for Indian independence

Aug.: fighting breaks out between Nationalists and Communists in North China; US General George Marshall unsuccessfully tries to mediate dispute

Science, Technology, and Medicine	Culture	
	Jean Giraudoux, *The Mad Woman of Chaillot*	**1944**
	Copland, *Appalachian Spring*; Michael Tippett, *A Child of Our Time*; Bartok, *Violin Concerto*; Prokofiev, *War and Peace*; Leonard Bernstein, *On the Town*	
	Laurence Olivier, film version of *Henry V*; Marcel Carné, *Les Enfants du paradis*; Hitchcock, *Lifeboat*; Otto Preminger, *Laura*	
Hungarian scientist Lajos Janossy explores properties of cosmic radiation	Karl Popper, *The Open Society and Its Enemies*; Hesse, *The Glass Bead Game*	**1945**
Atomic Energy Research Establishment established at Harwell, England	Orwell, *Animal Farm*; Evelyn Waugh, *Brideshead Revisited*; Leopold Sedar Senghor, *Chants d'Ombre*	
	Bartok, *Concerto for Orchestra*; Benjamin Britten, *Peter Grimes*; Zoltan Kodaly, *Missa Brevis*; Rodgers and Hammerstein, *Carousel*	
	'Bebop' becomes popular	
	Eisenstein, *Ivan the Terrible*, part I; Roberto Rossellini, *Rome, Open City*; David Lean, *Brief Encounter*	

Politics and International Relations

1945 Republic of Yugoslavia established under Marshal Tito

Aug.: President Truman announces end of Lend-Lease, precipitating financial crisis in Britain and eventual extension of American loan of 3.75 billion dollars

Nuremberg tribunals begin trials of Nazi leaders for war crimes

Pan-African Congress held in Manchester, England

1946 International Military Tribunal at Tokyo begins trials of Japanese war criminals

5 Mar.: Churchill denounces Soviet Union in 'Iron Curtain' speech at Fulton, Missouri.

Apr.: civil war resumes in China (to 1949)

Spring: Anglo-American Committee of Inquiry on Palestine recommends allowing 100,000 Jewish refugees into mandate but envisages single, secular, democratic Palestinian state; July: Zionist terrorists bomb King David Hotel in Jerusalem

Juan Peron elected president of Argentina

Transjordan becomes independent (renamed Hashemite Kingdom of Jordan in 1949)

USA recognizes Philippine independence; Ferdinand Marcos becomes president

Italy becomes a republic

New York announced as permanent home of UN

Nov.: war breaks out in French Indochina (to 1954) between Communist nationalist forces led by Ho Chi Minh and French occupying forces

1947 9 Feb.: peace treaties signed with Italy, Hungary, Romania, Bulgaria, and Finland

Feb.: Britain announces plans to return Palestine mandate to UN; in summer UN Special Committee on Palestine (UNSCOP) proposes partition into Jewish state, Arab state, and internationally administered zone

5 June: in speech at Harvard, US Secretary of State George C. Marshall proposes 'Marshall Plan' for European recovery

July: Dutch launch 'police action' against Indonesian Nationalist Party led by Achmad Sukarno; brutality of campaign precipitates debate in UN and truce in Dec.

15 Aug.: last Viceroy Lord Mountbatten presides over partition of India and creation of independent states of India and Pakistan; hundreds of thousands die in communal strife attending partition; Oct.: armed conflict breaks out between India and Pakistan over Kashmir, which is effectively partitioned between the two

Greek civil war breaks out (to 1949), precipitating Truman Doctrine

Cominform established at Warsaw Conference

Belgium, Netherlands, and Luxemburg establish Benelux customs union

Montego Bay Conference on Federation of British West Indies

General Agreement on Tariffs and Trade (GATT) signed in Geneva

Science, Technology, and Medicine	Culture	
		1945
ENIAC, first electronic digital computer, demonstrated at University of Pennsylvania	Robert Penn Warren, *All the King's Men*; O'Neill, *The Iceman Cometh*; John Hersey, *Hiroshima*	**1946**
Baruch Plan for internationalizing nuclear energy turned down at the UN; Dec.: first Soviet nuclear reactor begins operation	William Wyler, *The Best Years of Our Lives*; Howard Hawks, *The Big Sleep*	
US navy conducts atomic test blast at Bikini Atoll		
First supersonic flight	Camus, *The Plague*; Lionel Trilling, *The Middle of the Journey*; Auden, *The Age of Anxiety*; Williams, *A Streetcar Named Desire*; Mann, *Doktor Faustus*; publication of *The Diary of Anne Frank*; Guido Ruggiero, *Existentialism*; Jaspers, *The Question of Guilt*; Kawabata Yasunari completes *Yukiguni* (published in English as *Snow Country*, 1956)	**1947**
Dead Sea Scrolls found at Qumran in Palestine; Francis Steele reconstructs the Code of Hammurabi from texts found in the Nippur excavations in Mesopotamia		
Bell Laboratories produces the first transistors		
	Leopold Senghor of Senegal, Aimé Cesaire of Martinique, and Léon Damas of French Guiana establish *Présence Africaine*, leading African literary journal, as forum for literature of Negritude, Black cultural movement that began in the 1930s and sought to reunite cultural experience of all peoples of African descent	
	Giacometti sculpts *The Pointing Man*	
	The 'New Look' introduced by Christian Dior dominates women's fashion	

Politics and International Relations

1948   Jan.: Gandhi assassinated by Hindu fanatic

Feb.: Soviet bloc condemns Tito regime in Yugoslavia

Feb.–Mar.: Soviet-backed coup establishes Communist government in Czechoslovakia

Marshall Plan for reconstruction of Europe goes into effect

Count Folke Bernadotte, acting as UN mediator in Palestine dispute, is assassinated by Zionist terrorists

May: Britain leaves Palestine; 14 May: State of Israel proclaimed; Arab armies invade, precipitating first Arab–Israeli war

Apr.: ceasefire declared in Kashmir

Sept.: Indonesian Communist Party (PKI) joins revolt in East Java, quickly suppressed by nationalist government under Sukarno

Burma becomes independent republic outside British Commonwealth

Ceylon becomes independent (renamed Sri Lanka 1972)

Malayan Emergency declared as British combat Communist insurgency

June: Berlin blockade and airlift create greater Cold War tensions

Organization of American States established at Pan-American Conference in Bogota

Afrikaner-dominated National Party comes to power in South Africa and begins institution of apartheid laws

Assassination of popular radical Liberal leader Jorge Gaitan in Bogota precipitates violent riots, triggers the Colombian 'Violencia' (to 1957)

1949   Soviet Union successfully tests atomic bomb

Federal German Republic established in West Germany with Konrad Adenauer as Chancellor; German Democratic Republic established in East Germany

Britain devalues sterling

Ireland leaves British Commonwealth as independent republic

India becomes republic but remains within British Commonwealth

International outrage at Dutch military action in Indonesia leads to conference at The Hague between Dutch and PNI; in Dec. Indonesia becomes independent

North Atlantic Treaty, establishing NATO alliance, signed in Washington, DC

Chinese Communists drive Nationalists off mainland to island of Taiwan; 1 Oct.: Mao proclaims People's Republic of China (PRC)

Communist rule established in Hungary

1950   US occupation of Japan ends

Prime Minister Jawaharlal Nehru institutes first Indian Five Year Plan

Britain recognizes Communist China

China and USSR sign 30-year pact

Communist Chinese occupy Tibet, which appeals unsuccessfully to UN

US Senator Joseph McCarthy warns President Truman that State Department is 'riddled with Communists'; Alger Hiss convicted of perjury; Klaus Fuchs found guilty of passing atomic secrets to USSR

Science, Technology, and Medicine	Culture	
Alfred Kinsey, *Sexual Behavior in the Human Male* Lajo Janossy, *Cosmic Rays and Nuclear Physics*	Alan Paton, *Cry, the Beloved Country*; Tanizaki Jun-Ichiro completes *Sasame-yuki* (published in English as *The Makioka Sisters*, 1957); Senghor, *Anthologie de la nouvelle poesie negre et malagache* [Anthology of the New Negro and Madagascan Poetry]; F. R. Leavis, *The Great Tradition* Strauss, *Four Last Songs* Vittorio de Sica, *Bicycle Thieves*; Hitchcock, *Rope*	**1948**
In USA guided test missiles reach height of 250 miles, highest ever to date; USSR explodes its first atomic device Cortisone developed	Simone de Beauvoir, *Le Deuxième Sexe* Orwell, *Nineteen Eighty-Four*; Arthur Miller, *Death of a Salesman* Fernand Braudel, *La Méditerrannée et le monde méditerranéen à l'époque de Philippe II* Rodgers and Hammerstein, *South Pacific*; Kurt Weill, *Lost in the Stars*; Orff, *Antigonae*; Bartok, *Viola Concerto*; Hindemith, *Concerto for Flute, Oboe, Clarinet, Bassoon, Harp, and Orchestra* Gene Kelly and Stanley Donen, *On the Town*; Carol Reed, *The Third Man*	**1949**
Einstein publishes *General Field Theory* in effort to restore a single theoretical base for physics Antihistamines become popular treatment for colds and allergies	Trilling, *The Liberal Imagination* Doris Lessing, *The Grass is Singing*; Ray Bradbury, *The Martian Chronicles*; Hersey, *The Wall*; Thor Heyerdahl, *Kon-Tiki*; Margaret Mead, *Social Anthropology*; Gilbert Ryle, *The Concept of Mind*; Octavio Paz, *El laberinto de la soledad* Giacometti sculpts *Seven Figures and a Head*	**1950**

Politics and International Relations

1950 President Truman orders development of hydrogen bomb

25 June: North Korean invasion of South Korea begins Korean War (to 1953)

USA gives military aid to French in Indochina

28 Nov.: Colombo Plan goes into effect to help economic development of countries in South and South-East Asia

---

1951 Mohammed Mossadegh becomes Prime Minister of Iran and nationalizes oil industry, precipitating a major crisis with Britain

Pakistani Prime Minister Liaquat Ali Khan assassinated by Afghan fanatic; Pakistan enters period of civil disorder

Libya becomes independent

Apr.: General MacArthur relieved of his command in Korea after advocating use of atomic weapons

Apr.: Julius and Ethel Rosenberg sentenced to death as Soviet spies in USA

8 Sept.: peace treaty signed with Japan in San Francisco

1952 Spring: Egyptian revolution overthrows monarchy and establishes republic in Egypt, first under General Muhammad Neguib and eventually under Gamal Abdul Nasser

Apr.: Movimiento Nacionalista Revolucionario under Dr Victor Paz Estenssoro successfully launches Bolivian Revolution; Paz Estenssoro becomes president of Bolivia

Mau Mau rebellion breaks out in Kenya among Kikuyu bitter over British colonial land policies; Oct.: British authorities declare State of Emergency (to 1959)

Elizabeth II succeeds to British throne on death of her father George VI

Greece and Turkey join NATO

Nationalist leader Kwame Nkrumah becomes Prime Minister of Gold Coast

Britain conducts first atomic tests

6 Nov.: USA tests first hydrogen-fuelled thermonuclear fusion device at Eniwetok Atoll in Pacific

Dwight D. Eisenhower elected president of USA

Science, Technology, and Medicine	Culture	
	Jackson Pollock paints *Lavender Mist*, marking the emergence of Abstract Expressionism as leading movement in modern art	**1950**
	Billy Wilder, *Sunset Boulevard*; Jean Cocteau, *Orphée*; Akira Kurosawa, *Rashomon*; Huston, *The Asphalt Jungle*	
First transistors developed for commercial production	J. D. Salinger, *The Catcher in the Rye*; Carl Sandburg, *Complete Poems*; Anthony Powell, *A Dance to the Music of Time: A Question of Upbringing*; Ting Ling, *T'ai-yang chao tsai Sang-kan-ho shang* [The Sun Shines over the Sangkan River]; Chou Li-Po, *Pao-feng tsou-yu* [The Hurricane]; Shu She-yu, *The Yellow Storm*; Ooka Shohei, *Nobi* [Fires on the Plain]	**1951**
Chrysler introduces power steering for automobiles		
American surgeon John Gibbon, Jr, develops first heart-lung machine		
Antabuse developed as treatment to prevent alcoholics from drinking		
Transcontinental television broadcasting begins in the USA	Britten, *Billy Budd*	
	Vincente Minelli, *An American in Paris*; Mervyn Leroy, *Quo Vadis*; Marlon Brando stars in *A Streetcar Named Desire*	
First contraceptive pill developed	Hemingway, *The Old Man and the Sea*; Ralph Ellison, *The Invisible Man*; Lessing, *Martha Quest*; Dylan Thomas, *Collected Poems*; Agatha Christie, *The Mousetrap*; Anouilh, *The Waltz of the Toreadors*; Cesare Pavese, *Il Mestiere de Viviere*; Samuel Beckett, *Waiting for Godot*; Steinbeck, *East of Eden*; Edna Furber, *Giant*; Shaw, *Don Juan in Hell*; Shu She-yu, *The Drum Singers*	**1952**
Jacques-Yves Cousteau and Fernand Benoit first use Scuba gear to investigate ancient shipwreck		
First nuclear power plant accident occurs at Chalk River in Canada without casualties		
First hearing aids using transistors marketed		
Douglas Bevis develops amniocentesis for determining genetic heritage of foetus in the womb	Chagall, *The Green Night*; Pollock, *Number 12*; Georges Rouault, *End of Autumn*	
Robert Wallace Wilkins develops first tranquillizer	Barbara Hepworth, *Statue*	
George Jorgensen undergoes first sex-change operation; subsequently known as Christine	Kurosawa, *Ikiru*; Welles, *Othello*; Fred Zinneman, *High Noon*; Jacques Tati,	
Canadian-built CF-100 is first straight-wing combat plane to break sound barrier		

Politics and International Relations

1952

1953 5 Mar.: Joseph Stalin dies and power struggle ensues in USSR

London Conference of Northern and Southern Rhodesia and Nyasaland held; over protests of African nationalist leaders all three territories are amalgamated for ten-year trial in Central African Federation

Jomo Kenyatta and others sentenced to prison for directing Mau Mau rebellion in Kenya

Anti-French riots in Morocco (to 1955)

27 July: Korean armistice signed

Mossadegh overthrown as prime minister of Iran in coup engineered by USA and Britain; Muhammad Reza Shah restored to full power

Second Conference on Federation of West Indies takes place in London

12 Oct.: Soviet Union tests hydrogen bomb

1954 Mar.–May: siege of Dien Bien Phu results in French capitulation to Communist forces; subsequently two regimes emerge: South Vietnam (the Republic of Vietnam) under Ngo Dinh Diem, with its capital in Saigon; and North Vietnam (the Democratic Republic of Vietnam) under Ho Chi Minh, capital in Hanoi; Cambodia and Laos also become independent

USA and Japan sign defence agreement; USA signs treaty guaranteeing security of Republic of China (Taiwan)

In Egypt Nasser seizes power

In Nigeria a new constitution creates a federal structure uniting Northern, Eastern, and Western Nigeria, along with the UN Trust Territory of the Camerouns and the federal territory of Lagos

USA and Canada agree to build Distant Early Warning (DEW) line of radar stations to protect against air attack over the Arctic

Science, Technology, and Medicine	Culture	
	Monsieur Hulot's Holiday	**1952**

W. Le Gros Clark exposes 'Piltdown Man' as a hoax

29 May: Edmund Hillary and Tenzing Norgay are first to summit of Mt Everest

Kinsey, *Sexual Behavior in the Human Female*

US rocket-powered plane flies at over 1,600 mph

CBS begins first commercial colour television broadcasts in USA

IBM 650 Computer first to be manufactured in large numbers, memory capacity of 1,000 10-byte words; P. L. Spencer of Raytheon Corporation develops first microwave oven; Charles Townes invents Maser (Microwave Amplification by Stimulated Emission of Radiation), precursor of laser

First kidney transplant operation performed in Paris, fails due to tissue rejection; John H. Gibbon uses heart–lung machine successfully; in Britain, Frederick Sanger discovers molecular structure of insulin

Francis Crick and James Watson propose the double helix structure of the DNA molecule, thus explaining how genetic information is carried in living organisms and how genes replicate

B. F. Skinner, *Science and Human Behavior*; Czeslaw Milosz, *The Captive Mind*; Martin Heidegger, *Introduction to Metaphysics*; J. B. Rhine, *The New World of the Mind*; Jaspers, *Tragedy is not Enough*

Saul Bellow, *The Adventures of Augie March*; Jorge Luis Borges, *Labyrinths*; Nadine Gordimer, *The Lying Days*; Miller, *The Crucible*; Camara Laye, *L'Enfant noir*

Georges Braque, *Apples*; Jean Bazin, *Chicago*; Chagall, *Eiffel Tower*

Britten, *Gloriana*; Vaughan Williams, *Sinfonia antarctica*; Hindemith, *A Composer's World*; Gottfried von Einem, *The Trial* (based on Kafka's novel)

1953

USA continues testing hydrogen weapons; concerns about nuclear fall-out mount; critic Robert Oppenheimer, head of Manhattan Project, is fired, loses security clearance; UK Atomic Energy Authority established to develop civilian uses of atomic power

Vaccine for polio developed by Dr Jonas Salk in 1952 is used for first time for mass inoculations; Thorqazine first used to treat mental disorders

US nuclear-powered submarine *Nautilus* commissioned; British develop first vertical-lift airplane

Kingsley Amis, *Lucky Jim*; William Golding, *Lord of the Flies*; J. R. R. Tolkien, *The Lord of the Rings*; Françoise Sagan, *Bonjour Tristesse*; Williams, *Cat on a Hot Tin Roof*; Laye, *Le Regard du Roi*

Lynn Chadwick sculpts *Two Dancing Figures*

Chagall, *The Red Roofs*; Fernand Léger, *Acrobat and Horse*; Roger Bissière, *Composition*

World Council of Churches convenes at Evanston, Illinois

1954

Politics and International Relations

1954 US Senator Joseph McCarthy extends his witch-hunt for Communist infiltrators in the US Government; Army–McCarthy hearings expose his tactics to the public, leading to his censure by the Senate

May: General Alfredo Stroessner seizes power in Paraguay, establishing 35-year dictatorship

May: US Supreme Court rules in *Brown v. Board of Education of Topeka, Kansas* segregation of black and white in public education to be unconstitutional

June: a coup supported by CIA overthrows Guatemalan president Jacobo Arbenz, whose nationalist, reformist policies included expropriation of land belonging to United Fruit Company

Aug.: threatened by a military coup, President Getulio Vargas of Brazil commits suicide

Sept.: Manila Pact, which leads to South East Asia Treaty Organization (SEATO)

Nov.: open insurrection breaks out in Algeria as the FLN (National Liberation Front) under Ben Bella demands independence from France; the Algerian War continues until 1962, contributing to the downfall of the Fourth Republic in France

---

1955 24 Feb.: Baghdad Pact signed (becomes Central Treaty Organization, or Cento, 21 Aug. 1959)

Apr.: Sukarno hosts Conference of some 29 Asian and African post-colonial states at Bandung, Indonesia

In China period of 'New Democracy' ends and collectivization begins

Warsaw Treaty signed establishing the Warsaw Pact

EOKA (National Organization of Cypriot Fighters) led by Colonel Georgios Grivas launches violent attacks on British troops in Cyprus demanding *enosis*, or unity, with Greece (to 1959)

May: State Treaty ends occupation of Austria

West Germany joins NATO

Sept.: Argentinian military overthrows President Peron, forcing him into exile in Spain

Dec.: in Alabama African–American Rosa Parks refuses to give up her bus seat to a white man, sparking successful black boycott of Montgomery bus system

---

1956 1 Jan.: the Sudan unilaterally proclaims its independence from both Britain and Egypt

Feb.: Nikita Khrushchev emerges as Stalin's successor in USSR and in 'secret' speech at 20th Congress of the Soviet Communist Party he denounces Stalin's crimes against the Soviet people

2 Mar.: Morocco becomes independent as French protectorate ends

British deport Archbishop Makarios, Cypriot nationalist leader, to the Seychelles

July–Nov.: Suez Crisis breaks out; 26 July: Nasser nationalizes the Suez Canal; 29 Oct.: Israel invades Egypt, followed by Anglo-French attacks on Egyptian airfields and invasion of the Canal Zone ostensibly to separate Israeli and Egyptian forces; USA forces Britain, France, and Israel to withdraw

Adoption of new constitution makes Pakistan an Islamic republic

Following unrest in Hungary during the spring and summer, in Oct. open revolution breaks out but is suppressed on 4 Nov. by Soviet invasion force

Nov.: Fidel Castro lands on eastern coast of Cuba and launches Cuban revolution

Science, Technology, and Medicine	Culture	
Steerable radiotelescopes commissioned in USA and Britain	Fellini, *La Strada*; Elia Kazan, *On the Waterfront*; Kurosawa, *The Seven Samurai*	**1954**
TV dinners developed and marketed in USA	Bill Haley, *Rock around the Clock*	
Malcolm MacLean begins transporting goods in containers between New York and Houston; container transport soon becomes most popular form of shipping in the world		
Gordon Teal of Texas Instruments develops first silicon transistor; first transistor radio, the Regency, is marketed		
Electricity generated by atomic power first used in Schenectady, New York	Claude Lévi-Strauss, *Tristes Tropiques*	**1955**
Scientists at Massachusetts Institute of Technology produce ultra high frequency waves	Vladimir Nabokov, *Lolita*; Waugh, *Officers and Gentlemen*; Graham Greene, *The Quiet American*; Tchicaya U Tam'si, *Le Mauvais sang*	
Lloyd H. Conover patents tetracycline	Nicholas Ray, *Rebel without a Cause*; Satyajit Ray, *Pather Panchali*; Ingmar Bergman, *Smiles of a Summer Night*; Sidney Poitier stars in *Blackboard Jungle*	
First industrial-use artificial diamonds produced; Velcro patented		
Narinder S. Kapany develops optical fibre		
Antineutron discovered by scientists at Berkeley; neutrino, atomic particle without an electric charge, produced at Los Alamos Laboratory in New Mexico	W. H. Whyte, *The Organization Man*; John F. Kennedy, *Profiles in Courage*; Winston S. Churchill, *History of the English-Speaking Peoples*; Karl Mannheim, *Essays on the Sociology of Culture*	**1956**
Ion microscope invented by F. W. Muller	Giuseppe Tomasi di Lampedusa, *The Leopard*; Mongo Beti (Alexandre Biyidi), *Le Pauvre Christ de Bamba*; Ferdinand Oyo, *Une vie de boy*	
Transatlantic cable telephone service begins		
Construction begins on Brasilia as the new capital of Brazil	Alan Lerner and Frederick Loewe, *My Fair Lady*; Gian Carlo Menotti, *The Unicorn, the Gorgon and the Manticore*	

Politics and International Relations

1956

1957   6 Mar.: the Gold Coast becomes the first of Britain's African colonies to achieve independence as the state of Ghana, with Kwame Nkrumah as Prime Minister

Malaya becomes independent

25 Mar.: Treaty of Rome establishes European Economic Community

Sept.: Federal troops enforce desegregation of public schools in Little Rock, Arkansas

1958   Federation of the West Indies goes into effect (to 1961)

Army opposition and threat of civil war due to the government's Algerian policy leads to the downfall of the Fourth Republic in France and the return of De Gaulle to head the Fifth Republic; De Gaulle gives French African colonies choice of immediate independence with loss of French aid and cultural ties, or membership in on-going French Community; only Guinea under Sékou Touré opts for independence

1 Feb.: United Arab Republic proclaimed as loose federation between Egypt and Syria with Nasser as president, collapses in 1961 when Syria withdraws

Venezuela returns to democratic rule following the fall in 1957 of dictator Marcos Perez Jimenez due to charges of corruption and electoral fraud

Mao launches the Great Leap Forward in China in effort to speed up industrialization

July: revolution breaks out in Iraq, overthrowing monarchy and bringing left-wing regime

Science, Technology, and Medicine	Culture	
	Maria Callas debuts in Bellini's *Norma* at New York's Metropolitan opera; Elvis Presley achieves international popularity	**1956**
	Renais, *Nuits et Brouillard*; Mike Todd, *Around the World in Eighty Days*; Preminger, *The Man with the Golden Arm*; De Mille, *The Ten Commandments* (remake)	
	Jorn Utzon designs Sydney Opera House	
Aug.: USSR successfully launches its first intercontinental ballistic missile, followed by *Sputniks I* and *II*, alarming the West and initiating the space race	Boris Pasternak, *Dr Zhivago*; Beckett, *Endgame*; John Osborne, *The Entertainer*; Jack Kerouac, *On the Road*; O'Neill, *Long Day's Journey into Night*; Lawrence Durrell, *Alexandria Quartet*; Dr Seuss, *The Cat in the Hat*	**1957**
International Atomic Energy Commission established in Vienna		
Discovery of the anti-matter version of the proton at Berkeley	Leonard Bernstein, *West Side Story*; Meredith Willson, *The Music Man*; Britten, *The Turn of the Screw*; John Gardener, *The Moon and Sixpence*; Stravinsky, *Agon*; Hindemith, *Harmonie der Welt*; William Walton, *Concerto for Cello and Orchestra*	
Mackinac Straits Bridge, longest suspension bridge in the world, opens in Michigan		
Albert Sabin develops oral polio vaccine; Alick Isaacs and Jean Lindenmann discover interferons; CAT scan being developed at University of Cape Town, South Africa	Chagall, *Self-Portrait*; Carlo Levi, *Anna Magnani*; H. G. Adam, *Beacon of the Dead*	
	Le Corbusier designs Tokyo Museum of Art	
	Preminger, *Bonjour Tristesse*; Bergman, *Wild Strawberries* and *The Seventh Seal*	
	Wolfenden Report leading to legalization of homosexuality published in Britain	
	The 'Beat Generation' described by Kerouac gives rise to the 'beatnik' movement	
Introduction of commercial stereo recordings	Chinua Achebe, *Things Fall Apart*; Truman Capote, *Breakfast at Tiffany's*; John Kenneth Galbraith, *The Affluent Society*; Cyril N. Parkinson, *Parkinson's Law*	**1958**
Jack Kilby and Robert Nooyce independently invent the integrated circuit		
USA launches first satellite; begins Explorer series of unmanned space probes; discovers Van Allen radiation belt around earth	Mies van der Rohe designs Seagram Building in New York City	
	Andrej Wajda, *Ashes and Diamonds*	

Politics and International Relations

1958 under Brigadier Qasim to power; US troops intervene in Lebanon to prevent civil war at the request of President Chamoun

July: Dr Hastings Banda returns to Nyasaland to lead African nationalist movement against the Central African Federation

Alaska becomes 49th state of the USA

Nov.: Khrushchev precipitates another Berlin Crisis by demanding the removal of all Western forces from Berlin; Eisenhower and NATO stand firm and Khrushchev backs down

1959 1 Jan.: after several years of guerrilla warfare, Castro enters Havana and proclaims Cuban revolution, ousting Batista regime and making himself prime minister

European Free Trade Association is formed

Emergency in Nyasaland

Hawaii becomes 50th state of the USA

Archbishop Makarios returns from exile to Cyprus; Cyprus becomes independent republic in Dec. with Makarios as president

In China the Great Leap Forward is destroying the fragile Chinese economy and contributing to the deaths of millions from starvation

Uprising in Tibet against Chinese rule is brutally repressed and Dalai Lama flees to India

In Sri Lanka, Prime Minister S. W. R. D. Bandaranaike assassinated by disaffected Tamil, is succeeded as prime minister by his wife, SirimavoRatwatte Dias Bandaranaike, who thereby becomes the world's first female prime minister

Sukarno proclaims 'Guided Democracy' in Indonesia

1960 Jan.: Congo Crisis begins when Belgium announces intentions to grant independence to Congo; during May elections inter-tribal fighting breaks out; more fighting develops on independence day 30 June and the entire country descends into civil war and chaos; Congolese police mutiny against European officers; in Katanga province Moise Tshombe proclaims independent republic; in the summer UN Secretary-General Dag Hammarskjöld sends peace-keeping force on request of Congo government under President Kasavubu and Prime Minister Patrice Lumumba

3 Feb.: British Prime Minister Harold Macmillan makes 'wind of change' speech in South Africa acknowledging growth of African nationalism and need to accommodate it

Protests organized in South Africa by the Pan-Africanist Congress against apartheid lead on 21 Mar. to the Sharpeville Massacre, when police open fire on peaceful demonstrators, killing more than 60 and wounding over 100

May: American U-2 spy plane shot down by USSR; President Eisenhower refuses to

Science, Technology, and Medicine	Culture	

Introduction of commercial stereo recordings

Jack Kilby and Robert Nooyce independently invent the integrated circuit

USA launches first satellite; begins Explorer series of unmanned space probes; discovers Van Allen radiation belt around earth

1958

Soviet space probe Luna 3 takes first photos of dark side of moon

St Lawrence Seaway connecting St. Lawrence River and Great Lakes opens for first time to ocean-going vessels

Saul Bellow, *Henderson the Rain King*; Gunter Grass, *Die Blechtrommel* [The Tin Drum]; William Burroughs, *Naked Lunch*; Alan Sillitoe, *The Loneliness of the Long Distance Runner*; Mishima Yukio (Kimitake Hiraoka), *Kinkaku-ji* [Temple of the Golden Pavilion]; Ezekiel Mphahlele, *Down Second Avenue*; Ian Fleming, *Goldfinger*

Wilder, *Some Like It Hot*; François Truffaut, *A Bout de souffle*, and *Les Quatre cent coups*; Resnais, *Hiroshima, Mon Amour*; Michelangelo Antonioni, *L'avventura*

1959

First laser built in Houston, Texas

Ban on D. H. Lawrence's *Lady Chatterley's Lover* finally lifted in Britain after much-publicized obscenity trial

Eugene Ionesco, *Rhinoceros*; Harold Pinter, *The Caretaker*; John Updike, *Rabbit, Run*; Kawabata Yasunari, *Sembazuru* [A Thousand Cranes]; Achebe, *No Longer at Ease*

Fellini, *La dolce vita*; Hitchcock, *Psycho*

1960

Politics and International Relations

1960   apologize for incident and Premier Khrushchev uses it as pretext to break up Paris Summit conference

1 Oct.: Nigeria, Britain's largest African colony, becomes independent

After plebiscite, Ghana becomes a republic with Nkrumah as president; under Nkrumah country moves towards dictatorship

Synghman Rhee overthrown in South Korea

John F. Kennedy elected president of USA

1961   Jan.–Sept.: Congo Crisis continues (to 1963) as President Kasavubu invites military coup led by Colonel Mobutu to overthrow Prime Minister Patrice Lumumba, who is soon murdered with connivance of Moise Tshombe; Sept.: Hammarskjöld is killed in plane crash while on inspection tour in the Congo

Jan.: USA breaks diplomatic relations with Cuba

Sino-Soviet break becomes public

UN condemns *apartheid* in South Africa; South Africa withdraws from British Commonwealth and becomes a republic

Apr.: Bay of Pigs invasion of Cuba by anti-Castro Free Cuban forces supported by the USA fails

30 May: dictatorial ruler of Dominican Republic, president Trujillo, is assassinated, leading to establishment of short-lived democratic regime in 1962

13 Aug.: In Berlin, the East German Government builds the Berlin Wall overnight to halt access to the West

9 Dec.: Tanganyika becomes independent under prime minister Julius Nyerere

---

1962   Algeria becomes independent

Military seizes power in Burma

Early in the year, Uganda achieves full self-government within the British Commonwealth as a federation of five kingdoms but in Sept. Prime Minister Milton Obote overturns the constitution and declares a republic

Oct.: China attacks India across disputed border of Tibet

Second Vatican Council (Vatican II) begins in Rome (to 1965)

Adolf Eichmann is hanged in Israel

Oct.: Cuban Missile Crisis develops when American aircraft spot Soviet nuclear missile bases being built in Cuba; President Kennedy delivers ultimatum and establishes blockade to prevent missiles from being delivered; eventually Khrushchev backs down and crisis is resolved with Soviet missiles being withdrawn from Cuba and obsolescent American missiles being removed from Turkey

Science, Technology, and Medicine	Culture	
		1960
Soviet cosmonaut Yuri Gagarin becomes first man in space; Alan Shepherd becomes first American to orbit the earth	New English Bible published; Michel Foucault, *Histoire de la folie*; Fritz Fischer, *Griff nach der weltmacht*	**1961**
Trans-Siberian Railway electrified	Frantz Fanon, *The Wretched of the Earth*; V. S. Naipaul, *A House for Mr Biswas*; Henry Miller, *Tropic of Cancer* (first legal publication in USA, published in Paris in 1934); Joseph Heller, *Catch-22*; Jean Anouilh, *Becket*; Bernard Malamud, *A New Life*; Steinbeck, *The Winter of Our Discontent*; Robert Heinlein, *Stranger in a Strange Land*; Irving Stone, *The Agony and the Ecstasy*	
Tanganyika Conference convened to protect African wildlife		
	Renzo Rossellini, *Uno sguardo dal ponte*; Luigi Nono, *Intoleranza*; Henri Barraud, *Lavinia*	
	Truffaut, *Jules et Jim*; Robert Rossen, *Judgement at Nuremberg*; Luis Bunuel, *Viridiana*; Robert Wise, *West Side Story*; Resnais, *Last Year in Marienbad*	
F.H.C. Crick, J.D. Watson, and M.H.F. Wilkins share Nobel Prize for Physiology on Medicine	Friedrich Dürrenmatt, *The Physicists*; Milton Friedman, *Capitalism*, Barbara Tuchman, *The Guns of August*	**1962**
Rachel Carson writes *Silent Spring*, contributing to popular concern over environmental problems of industrial society	Alexander Solzhenitsyn, *One Day in the Life of Ivan Denisovich*; Edward Albee, *Who's Afraid of Virginia Woolf?*; Camus, *Notebooks, 1935-1942*; Williams, *The Night of the Iguana*; Edmund Wilson, *Patriotic Gore*; Ken Kesey, *One Flew Over the Cuckoo's Nest*; Carlos Fuentes, *The Death of Artemio Cruz*; Christopher Okigbo, *Heavensgate*; Wole Soyinka, *The Trials of Brother Jethro*; Ousmane Sembene, *God's Bits of Wood*	
NASA continues Mercury manned space programme in USA; Telstar communications satellite launched; Mariner 2 launched to probe Venus		
Thomas S. Kuhn, *The Structure of Scientific Revolutions*	Britten, *War Requiem*; Shostakovich completes 12th Symphony;	
	David Lean, *Lawrence of Arabia*; Stanley Kubrick, *Lolita*	
	The Beatles have first hit, *Love Me Do*	

Politics and International Relations

1962

1963   Congo Crisis is largely resolved when Katanga separatist movement of Moise Tshombe is defeated and Tshombe himself goes into exile, though UN troops remain in the country until mid-1964

Formation of Organization of African Unity

29 Jan.: French president Charles de Gaulle refuses British entry into the European Economic Community

Federation of Malaysia is created

Amid opposition from all leading African groups, Central African Federation dissolves

Aug.: Revd Martin Luther King leads March on Washington for Jobs and Freedom

Oct.: trial of Black African leader Nelson Mandela under the Suppression of Communism Act begins in South Africa (to June 1964)

1 Nov.: President Ngo Dinh Diem of South Vietnam assasinated in US-supported coup

22 Nov.: President Kennedy assassinated in Dallas, Texas; Lyndon Johnson becomes US president

1964   Jan.: revolution overthrows sultanate in Zanzibar; 26 Apr.: Zanzibar and Tanganyika merge to form United Republic of Tanzania, with Julius Nyerere as president

Northern Rhodesia achieves independence as Republic of Zambia under president Kenneth Kaunda; Nyasaland becomes independent state of Malawi with Hastings Banda as Prime Minister

Formation of the Palestine Liberation Organization (PLO)

US Congress passes Civil Rights Act

Indian Prime Minister Nehru dies; succeeded by Lal Bahadur Shastri as Congress Party remains in power

Revolts break out in Congo as UN forces leave the country; President Kasavubu invites Moise Tshombe to return as premier but soon removes him from power; Kasavubu overthrown by Army under General Mobutu, who establishes dictatorial rule as Mobutu Sese Seko

Military coup in Brazil inaugurates period of authoritarian military regimes (to 1985)

Oct.: Nikita Khrushchev removed as Soviet leader. Replaced by Leonid Brezhnev and Aleksei Kosygin

Aug.: North Vietnamese forces involved in incident with US ships in Gulf of Tonkin; US Congress passes Gulf of Tonkin Resolution giving President Johnson wide powers to respond

Science, Technology, and Medicine	Culture	
	Andy Warhol achieves celebrity status and launches 'Pop Art' movement using images from popular culture such as Campbell Soup cans and brillo pads in a variety of media	**1962**
Valentina Tereshkova becomes first woman in space T. A. Matthews and A. R. Sandage discover first quasar (3C273)	Hannah Arendt, *Eichmann in Jerusalem: A Report on the Banality of Evil*; Betty Friedan, *The Feminine Mystique*	**1963**
	Grass, *Dog Years*; Iris Murdoch, *The Unicorn*; James Baldwin, *The Fire Next Time*; John Le Carré, *The Spy Who Came in from the Cold*; George Seferis becomes first Greek author to win Nobel Prize for Literature	
	Richard Lippold, *Orpheus and Apollo*	
	Guggenheim Museum in New York exhibits Pop Art including work of Warhol, Jasper Johns, and Robert Rauschenberg	
	Tippett, *Concerto for Orchestra*; Menotti, *Labyrinth*, *Death of the Bishop of Brindisi*	
	Singers Bob Dylan and Joan Baez gain worldwide popularity	
Fundamental particle, omega-minus, discovered	Martin Luther King, Jr, *Why We Can't Wait*;	**1964**
Fred Hoyle and J. V. Narlikar propose new theory of gravitation	Bellow, *Herzog*; Pinter, *The Homecoming*; Philip Larkin, *The Whitsun Weddings*; Ngugi wa Thiang'o, *Weep Not Child*	
Verrazano Narrows bridge, longest suspension bridge in world, opens in New York	Deryck Cooke completes Gustav Mahler's *Symphony No 10*; Jerry Herman produces musical *Hello Dolly*; Jerry Bock, *Fiddler on the Roof*	
Britain grants licences for oil and gas development in North Sea	Picasso, *The Painter and His Model*	
	Peter Brook, *Lord of the Flies*; The Beatles, *A Hard Day's Night*; Michael Cacoyannis, *Zorba the Greek*; Stevenson, *Mary Poppins*; Ray, *Charulata*	

Politics and International Relations

1965   21 Feb.: Black leader Malcolm X assassinated in New York; in the summer, major riots break out in Watts neighbourhood of Los Angeles, California, illustrating growing racial tensions in USA

Apr.: US forces intervene in Dominican Republic (to 1966)

US Congress passes Voting Rights Act to protect black voters in South

President Ben Bella of Algeria deposed

Angered by British demands for Black African participation in government, Rhodesian Prime Minister Ian Smith issues Unilateral Declaration of Independence (UDI), denounced as illegal by British Government; Britain imposes oil embargo on Rhodesia

US combat troops arrive in South Vietnam; regular US bombing of North Vietnam begins

Oct.: after abortive coup attributed to Indonesian Communist Party (PKI), army massacres hundreds of thousands of suspected plotters and other dissidents; Sukarno becomes little more than figurehead

Singapore becomes independent republic

Apr.–June: Indo–Pakistan war breaks out over Pakistani aid to Muslims in Kashmir, fighting renewed in September (to Jan. 1966)

1966   Jan.: Nigerian army mutiny results in assassination of federal prime minister Alhaji Sir Abubakr Tafawa Balewa and the premiers of East and West Nigeria; July: General Gowon leads counter-coup and tries to establish new constitution; Sept.: Ibos massacred in Northern Nigeria

In China, Mao launches the Great Proletarian Cultural Revolution to break hold of 'bureaucrats' on the revolution

UN orders first mandatory general economic sanctions against Rhodesia

Mar.: General Suharto takes power from Sukarno in Indonesia

In Ghana, military coup overthrows Nkrumah

Indira Gandhi, daughter of Nehru, becomes Prime Minister of India

Sept.: Milton Obote overthrows President Mutesa II and proclaims himself President of Uganda

British Guiana becomes independent state of Guyana

South African Prime Minister Dr Hendrik Verwoerd assassinated

---

1967   May: full-scale civil war breaks out in Nigeria (to 1970) when Colonel Odumegwu Ojukwu declares Iboland independent Republic of Biafra

5–10 June: Six Day War between Israel and an alliance of Arab states — Egypt, Jordan, and Syria — ends in Israeli victory; the Israelis occupy Sinai, the Old City of Jerusalem, the West Bank, and the Golan Heights

European Community (EC) comes into being with merger of European Economic Community, European Atomic Energy Commission, and European Coal and Steel Community

Science, Technology, and Medicine	Culture	
Soviet and American astronauts conduct first space walks; France launches first satellite Ralph Nader, *Unsafe at any Speed*; Nader becomes major consumer advocate in USA	Norman Mailer, *An American Dream*; Soyinka play, *The Road* and novel *The Interpreters*; Ngugi, *The River Between*	**1965**
First lunar soft landing made by Soviet Lunar 9; US Surveyor 1 makes soft landing and sends back photos of the moon's surface	Paul Scott, *The Jewel in the Crown*, first volume of the *Raj Quartet* (completed 1975); Okot p'Bitek, *Song of Lawino*; Capote, *In Cold Blood*; Sagan, *Le Cheval évanoui*; John Barth, *Giles Goat-Boy*; Heinlein, *The Moon is a Harsh Mistress*; Mao Zedong, *Quotations of Chairman Mao* (The 'little red book') Andrei Tarkovsky, *Andrei Rublev*; Truffaut, *Fahrenheit 451*; Sembene Ousmane, *La Noire de...* Soviet writers Andrei Sinyavsky and Yuri Daniel imprisoned	**1966**
Dr Christiaan Barnard performs first heart transplant at Groote Schuur Hospital, Cape Town, South Africa; American Dr Irving Cooper develops cryosurgery	William Styron, *The Confessions of Nat Turner*; Gabriel Garcia Marquez, *One Hundred Years of Solitude*; Tom Stoppard, *Rosencrantz and Guildenstern Are Dead*; Ibuse Masuji, *Kuroi ame* [Black Rain]; Ngugi, *A Grain of Wheat*; Jacques Derrida, *De la Grammatologie* and *L'écriture et la différence*	**1967**

Politics and International Relations

1967   Association of South-East Asian Nations (ASEAN) established

Che Guevara, Marxist guerrilla leader, killed in Bolivia

Thurgood Marshall becomes first black Justice of US Supreme Court

Anti-Vietnam War demonstrations in Washington, DC

Nov.: British withdraw from Aden, last possession in Middle East

---

1968   Jan.: Alexander Dubcek becomes first secretary of Czechoslovakian Communist Party and introduces liberal reforms; Aug.: invading Warsaw Pact forces crush the 'Prague Spring'

29 Jan.–25 Feb.: Tet Offensive in Vietnam discredits US military leaders' assurances that war is almost won; President Johnson announces he will not seek re-election

4 Apr.: Martin Luther King assassinated in Memphis, Tennessee, precipitating racial violence across USA

3 Jun.: Senator Robert F. Kennedy, frontrunner for Democratic presidential nomination, assassinated in Los Angeles

Summer: anti-war demonstrators disrupt Democratic National Convention in Chicago; protest suppressed by Chicago police

Student protests turn violent in Paris and other cities in Europe; in Mexico City student protesters are killed in confrontation with police on eve of the Summer Olympics

In Peru a military coup brings left-wing junta to power

USS *Pueblo* captured by North Koreans

Britain announces complete military withdrawal from east of Suez

Richard Nixon elected president of USA

1969   De Gaulle resigns as French president

Yasser Arafat becomes head of PLO

Outbreak of 'Troubles' in Northern Ireland

Mar.–Sept.: fighting breaks out between Chinese and Soviet forces along border

Nov.: negotiations begin between USA and USSR on limiting strategic arms

---

1970   Jan.: Nigerian Civil War ends with collapse of Biafran resistance; as many as a million Ibos have perished from fighting or starvation

Mar.: Military coup removes Cambodia's head of state, Norodroi Sihanouk: US and South Vietnamese forces invade Cambodia to cut supply lines of North Vietnamese into South Vietnam

Mar.: Willy Brandt, Chancellor of German Federal Republic, opens negotiations with East Germany and Warsaw Pact powers, leading to normalization of relations

Science, Technology, and Medicine	Culture	
	Franco Zeffirelli, *Romeo and Juliet*; Arthur Penn, *Bonnie and Clyde*; Antonioni, *Blow-Up*; Norman Jewison, *In the Heat of the Night*	**1967**
Apollo 8, with 3-man crew, orbits the moon and returns safely to earth Pulsars discovered Intelsat 3, first of new generation of communications satellites is launched	Robert Conquest, *The Great Terror*; Tom Wolfe, *The Electric Cool-Aid Acid Test*; Kawabata Yasunari is first Japanese author to win Nobel Prize for Literature Stanley Kubrick, *2001: A Space Odyssey*; Sergei Paradjanov, *Sulat Nova* [The Colour of Pomegranates] Pope Paul VI issues encyclical *Humanae Vitae* against use of artificial contraceptives	**1968**
20 July: Apollo 11 lands on lunar surface; on the 21st Neil Armstrong becomes the first human to set foot on the surface of the moon; 24 July: Apollo 11 returns with all 3 crew members safely to earth; Mariner space probes send back pictures of Mars to earth	Nadezhda Mandelstam, *Hope against Hope*; Alexander Solzhenitsyn expelled from Soviet Writers' Union; Norman Mailer, *Armies of the Night*; Philip Roth, *Portnoy's Complaint*; Kurt Vonnegut, *Slaughterhouse-Five*; Michael Crichton, *The Andromeda Strain*; Mario Puzo, *The Godfather* *Oh Calcutta!* sex review staged in London and New York causes sensation Music festivals like that at Woodstock, New York, feature pop artists, including Jimi Hendrix and Bob Dylan Robert Altman, *MASH*	**1969**
Boeing 747 jumbo jets first introduced into regular service Soviet probe Venera 7 lands on surface of Venus Scientists at University of Wisconsin announce first complete synthesis of a gene	Mishima Yukio (Kimitake Hiraoka) completes tetrology, *Hojo no umi* [Sea of Fertility], and then commits public seppuku to protest against Japan's military weakness and Westernization; Maya Angelou, *I Know Why the Caged Bird Sings*; Patrick O'Brian, *Master and Commander*	**1970**

Politics and International Relations

1970   4 May: four students protesting against Vietnam War shot by National Guard at Kent State University

In Chile, Marxist leader Salvador Allende wins election as president and speedily institutes radical Marxist programme of wholesale nationalization and sweeping social reform

General upsurge in terrorist attacks around the world; Palestinian terrorists hijack three jumbo jets to Jordan

---

1971   Jan.: General Idi Amin overthrows President Obote and becomes dictator of Uganda, initiating period of extreme violence and terror until his overthrow in 1980

Under President Nixon and National Security Adviser Henry Kissinger, USA pursues 'detente' with Soviet Union; July: Kissinger secretly visits Beijing

People's Republic of China admitted to UN in place of Taiwan

Aug.: USA suspends convertibility of dollar to gold; marks collapse of Bretton Woods system and beginning of floating exchange rates

Sept.: Jordan expels PLO, which shifts headquarters to Lebanon; expulsion leads to formation of extremist 'Black September' Palestinian terrorist group

Civil war in Pakistan between East and West Pakistan; India intervenes in Dec., defeating Pakistan Army; Bangladesh becomes independent

---

1972   30 Jan.: 'Bloody Sunday' in Londonderry when British troops fire on Republican demonstrators, killing 14; Britain reimposes direct rule from London on Northern Ireland

US President Richard Nixon visits China after years of American refusal to acknowledge legitimacy of Communist regime and recognizes Taiwan as part of China

May: Nixon and Brezhnev sign Strategic Arms Limitation Treaty (SALT) limiting construction of ICBMs and development of anti-ballistic missile systems (ABM)

Israeli athletes massacred by 'Black September' Palestinian terrorist group during Summer Olympics in Munich, West Germany

During US election campaign, Nixon White House authorizes break-in at Democratic National Headquarters in Watergate apartment building, Washington, DC

1973   Jan.: Britain joins EEC, followed by Ireland and Denmark

27 Jan.: Paris Agreement ends US involvement in Indochina

July: first stage of Conference on Security and Cooperation in Europe (CSCE) opens in Helsinki

July: Afghan prime minister Muhammad Daoud overthrows monarchy and declares Afghanistan a republic with himself as president

Sept.: Against a background of spiralling inflation and massive political and social unrest, Chilean army led by General Augusto Pinochet (supported by CIA) overthrows Marxist president Salvador Allende, who is killed; ruthless military dictatorship established

Sept.: after years of exile, Juan Peron briefly returns to power in Argentina when he is elected president, but dies one year later

Science, Technology, and Medicine	Culture	
		1970
US astronauts continue manned exploration of moon's surface	Friedman, *A Theoretical Framework for Monetary Analysis*	**1971**
US satellite Mariner 9 orbits Mars; USSR soft-lands a space probe on Mars	Pablo Neruda, Chilean poet and diplomat, wins Nobel Prize for Literature; Sylvia Plath, *The Bell Jar*; Pentagon Papers published by the *New York Times*	
Choh Hao Li synthesizes human growth hormone at University of California	Kubrick, *A Clockwork Orange*	
Pocket calculators first introduced	Solzhenitsyn, *August 1914*	**1972**
Richard Leakey and Glynn Isaac discover 2.5 million year old hominid skull in Kenya	Tom O'Horgan, *Jesus Christ Superstar*; Tom Moore, *Grease*; Francis Ford Coppola, *The Godfather*; Andrei Tarkovsky, *Solaris*	
US successfully launches Skylabs I, II, and III; American space probe Pioneer 10 transmits television pictures from vicinity of Jupiter	Thomas Pynchon, *Gravity's Rainbow* Bernardo Bertolucci, *Last Tango in Paris*	**1973**

Politics and International Relations

1973 1 Oct.: Yom Kippur War breaks out as Egypt invades Israel on Day of Atonement

US aid for Israel precipitates Arab Oil Embargo (Oct. 1973–Mar. 1974) by OPEC, leading to higher petrol and oil prices, and subsequent energy crisis in industrial world

Major famine strikes Ethiopia

1974 Summer: Watergate hearings in Congress lead to potential constitutional crisis in USA; 9 Aug.: Richard Nixon resigns presidency rather than face impeachment; Gerald Ford becomes 38th US president

Military coup in Portugal; Guinea Bissau gains independence from Portuguese rule

July: abortive coup of Greek Cypriot officers briefly forces president, Archishop Makarios, into exile (restored to office in 1975); provides pretext for Turkish invasion and establishment of Turkish Federated State of Cyprus in northern part of the island

Emperor Haile Selassie deposed in Ethiopia; Sept.: radical military officers overthrow short-lived liberal government and establish brutally repressive military dictatorship

India conducts underground nuclear tests

IRA terrorists bomb public buildings in London

1975 Saigon falls to North Vietnamese; Vietnam reunited under Hanoi's rule

Apr.: the Communist Khmer Rouge capture Cambodian capital Phnom Penh and institute regime of terror (to 1979), forcibly depopulating Cambodia's cities and exterminating all intellectuals, government workers, and other potentially dissident groups; estimated 1–2 million dead

Apr.: civil war in Lebanon

1 Aug.: leaders of 35 countries sign Helsinki Accords at Conference on Security and Cooperation in Europe, declaring European frontiers inviolable and agreeing key principles on human rights, security, and cooperation

Indonesian forces occupy East Timor with heavy fighting after left-wing Fretilin movement proclaims region's independence from Portugal

Papua New Guinea becomes independent

Indian prime minister Indira Gandhi accused of electoral violations, declares State of Emergency and rules with dictatorial powers

Nov.: after years of opposition to nationalist armed struggle, Portugal recognizes independence of Angola and Mozambique; in Angola civil war breaks out between Marxist MPLA, supported by Soviet Union and some 40,000 Cuban 'volunteers', and UNITA led by Jonas Savimbi, supported by USA and South Africa; under weak Marxist government of Samori Machel, Mozambique becomes involved in armed struggle against white regimes in South Africa and Rhodesia

General Franco dies, King Juan Carlos is restored to the throne, and democracy returns to Spain

---

1976 East Timor formally incorporated into Indonesia; thousands of Fretilin supporters interned; guerrilla war of resistance continues

Science, Technology, and Medicine	Culture	
		1973
	Alexander Solzhenitsyn forced into exile after publication of *The Gulag Archipelago*	**1974**
	Roman Polanski, *Chinatown*; Sembene, *Xala*; Coppola, *Godfather Part II*	
Video recorders and floppy disks introduced for home use	Bellow, *Humboldt's Gift*; Peter Shaffer, *Equus*; Albee, *Seascape*	**1975**
Apollo–Soyuz joint space mission by USA and USSR	Milos Forman, *One Flew Over the Cuckoo's Nest*; Steven Spielberg, *Jaws*; Huston, *The Man who Would be King*	
Concorde supersonic airliner begins transatlantic flights	Bellow, *To Jerusalem and Back: A Personal Account*; Alex Haley, *Roots*	**1976**

Politics and International Relations

1976 Apr.: Syrian forces intervene directly in Lebanese civil war; cease-fire negotiated in Oct.–Nov. but fighting continues in the south

4 July: Israeli commandos raid Entebbe airport in Uganda, freeing 98 victims of 27 June terrorist hijacking of Air France flight

Sept.: Mao dies in Beijing; power struggle ensues in China between 'moderate' reformers like Deng Xiaoping and hardline radicals led by Mao's widow and other members of the 'Gang of Four'

In Argentina the military installs new regime and conducts terror campaign, killing thousands of suspected leftist dissidents

Parti Quebecois wins provincial elections in Quebec, Canada

South Africa establishes first 'bantustan' in Transkei

1977 Jan.: In Czechoslovakia Charter 77 Declaration published, signed by over 200 citizens, calling on regime to honour its commitments to international human rights accords

Feb.: Colonel Mengistu Haile Mariam seizes power in Ethiopia in violent and bloody coup; guerrilla fighting in Eritrea continues; war breaks out between Ethiopia and Somalia over grazing rights in the Ogaden (to 1978)

Steve Biko, leader of Black Consciousness movement in South Africa is murdered in police custody; UN Security Council orders mandatory arms embargo against South Africa

Indira Gandhi ends State of Emergency in India and loses elections to Janata Party under Morarji Desai

July: Prime Minister Zulfikar Ali Bhutto overthrown in military coup led by General Muhammad Zia al-Haq

President Anwar Sadat of Egypt unexpectedly flies to Israel where he addresses the Israeli Knesset and calls for peace

1978 Deng Xiaoping rises to power in China; begins 'Four Modernizations' programme involving agriculture, industry, national defence, and science and technology, emphasizing individual management in place of former communal approach

US Senate ratifies Panama Canal treaties promising to turn the Canal over to Panama by 2000

Cardinal Karol Wojtyla of Poland elected first non-Italian pope since 1522, assumes papal throne as John Paul II

Mar.: Israeli forces invade Lebanon, supporting Christian forces in effort to halt PLO attacks on Israel, then withdraw in June

Apr.: left-wing military coup overthrows (and kills) Afghan president Muhammad Daoud and proclaims Democratic Republic of Afghanistan under Nur Mohammad Taraki

17 Sept.: Camp David Accords between US President Carter, Israeli Prime Minister Menachem Begin, and Egyptian President Sadat lay groundwork for 'peace process' in Middle East

Dec.: Vietnamese invade Cambodia in effort to crush Khmer Rouge

1979 7 Jan.: Phnom Penh falls to Vietnamese; Khmer Rouge regime overthrown; Feb.–Mar.: brief Sino–Vietnamese war breaks out over Vietnamese invasion of Cambodia; mass graves of huge numbers of victims of Khmer Rouge discovered

Science, Technology, and Medicine	Culture	
Archaeologists begin excavation of Ebla in Syria	Nagisa Oshima, *Empire of the Senses*; Martin Scorsese, *Taxi Driver*	**1976**
First cases of AIDS diagnosed in New York City	Dan Jacobson, *The Confessions of Josef Baisz*	**1977**
US Voyager space probes launched to investigate the solar system	George Lucas, *Star Wars*; Woody Allen, *Annie Hall*; Spielberg, *Close Encounters of the Third Kind*	
Louise Brown becomes the world's first 'test-tube' baby, born in Britain	Edward Said, *Orientalism*	**1978**
Astronomers discover a moon orbiting Pluto	John Irving, *The World According to Garp*; Gillian Armstrong, *My Brilliant Career*;	
Sony introduces the Walkman portable cassette player	Jean-François Lyotard, *The Post-modern Condition*	**1979**
	Naipaul, *A Bend in the River*; Italo Calvino, *If on a Winter's Night a Traveller*;	

Politics and International Relations

1979   Jan.: American ambassador to Afghanistan assassinated, followed in Feb. by assassination of President Taraki by supporters of deputy prime minister Hafijullah Amin, who seizes power and seeks US support; in Dec. Soviet troops invade, Amin is killed, and Communist rule restored under Babrak Karmal; millions of refugees flee into neighbouring Pakistan and 10-year armed resistance by Mujaheddin guerrillas begins

Jan.: China and USA establish diplomatic relations; Democracy Wall appears in Beijing

16 Jan.: Shah flees Iran in face of revolution; Feb.: Ayatollah Ruhollah Khomeini returns from exile in France, seizes control of the government, and eventually establishes a theocratic Islamic state; Nov.: 66 American hostages are seized at US Embassy in Tehran, precipitating the 'Iran hostage crisis' (to Jan. 1981)

26 Mar.: Israel and Egypt sign peace treaty

Saddam Hussein becomes President of Iraq

Tanzanian forces invade Uganda and topple government of dictator Idi Amin

Opposition forces in Nicaragua finally overthrow the Somoza regime; Marxist Sandinistas establish provisional government but are accused by some Opposition members of 'highjacking' the revolution; civil war breaks out (to 1990) when the Contras, supported by USA, oppose the Marxist regime imposed by the Sandinistas and call for free elections

Indira Gandhi re-elected prime minister in India

First direct elections held for European Parliament

Conservative Margaret Thatcher becomes first woman Prime Minister of UK; leads Conservative 'revolution'

Former Prime Minister Bhutto executed in Pakistan

IRA assassinates Earl Mountbatten of Burma and grandson in bomb attack

1980   Green Party established in West Germany devoted primarily to ecological concerns; watershed in political development of the broader Green Movement concerned with global environmental problems

Iraq invades Iran. War continues till 1988

Strikes in the Gdansk shipyards in Poland lead to emergence of independent Solidarity labour movement demanding reforms

Rhodesia becomes independent majority-ruled state of Zimbabwe under Robert Mugabe

Failure of referendum favouring separation of Quebec from the rest of Canada

24 Apr.: airborne commando raid to rescue American Embassy hostages in Iran ends in disaster

Nov.: US voters elect Republican Ronald Reagan in landslide

1981   20 Jan.: Ronald Reagan inaugurated as President of USA; the same day Iran releases Embassy hostages; Reagan Administration soon supports Contra movement fighting Sandinista regime in Nicaragua

Spring: Israeli jets destroy Iraqi nuclear power plant near Baghdad

Science, Technology, and Medicine	Culture	
	Mailer, *The Executioner's Song*; William Styron, *Sophie's Choice*; Milan Kundera, *The Book of Laughter and Forgetting* Coppola, *Apocalypse Now*	**1979**
World Health Organization announces worldwide eradication of smallpox Voyager 1 space probe returns photos of Saturn and six new moons	Golding, *Rites of Passage*; Naipaul, *The Return of Eva Peron*; Mark Medoff, *Children of a Lesser God* Paul Schrader, *American Gigolo*; Akira Kurosawa, *Kagemusha*; Robert Redford, *Ordinary People*; Scorsese, *Raging Bull*	**1980**
IBM introduces first personal computer Scientists identify Acquired Immune Deficiency Syndrome (AIDS)	Paul Theroux, *The Mosquito Coast*; Paton, *Ah! But Your Land is Beautiful*; Salman Rushdie, *Midnight's Children*	**1981**

Politics and International Relations

1981   6 Oct.: Egyptian President Sadat assassinated by Islamic fundamentalists

IRA hunger strikers die in Northern Ireland

Greece joins EEC

Indonesian Army carries out massive campaign of repression against suspected Fretilin separatists in East Timor

Martial law declared in Poland

1982   Apr.–June: Falklands War between Argentina and Britain when Argentina invades the Falkland Islands and British forces recover them

Israel completes withdrawal from Sinai Peninsula begun in 1974

June: Israeli forces invade Lebanon, reaching Beirut; Aug.: negotiations led by USA result in withdrawal of PLO and Syrians from Beirut and the insertion of an international peacekeeping force; Sept.: Christian Phalangist forces massacre inhabitants of Palestinian refugee camps Sabra and Chatilla

Spain joins NATO

Fall in oil prices causes Mexico to default on international debts; beginning of world debt crisis

Oct.: military regime in Bolivia returns power to civilian democratically elected government

China speeds up economic liberalization programme

1983   In Argentina, discredited by loss of Falklands war, military regime allows elections; newly elected President Raul Alfonsin tries to restore democracy

President Reagan denounces USSR as 'evil empire' and announces Strategic Defense Initiative (SDI), also called 'star wars' programme, for space-based missile defence system

1 Sept.: Soviets shoot down civilian Korean airliner KA 003

Oct.: US forces respond to earlier left-wing coup by invading island of Grenada

Oct.: PLO finally withdraws from Lebanon, relocating headquarters in Tunisia

31 Dec.: Brunei becomes fully independent from UK

1984   Famine again becomes critical in Ethiopia, leading to worldwide fundraising effort for famine relief

Mar.: South Africa and Mozambique sign Nkomati Accord, designed to curb ANC attacks into South Africa and South African incursions into Mozambique

Spring: Sikh separatist movement gains ground in Punjab, India; Prime Minister Indira Gandhi orders assault against Sikh militants occupying holiest Sikh shrine, the Golden Temple in Amritsar; Sept.: Gandhi is assassinated in retaliation by her Sikh bodyguards

Britain and China agree on procedures to return Hong Kong to China in 1997

1985   Reformer Mikhail Gorbachev comes to power in USSR; inaugurates *perestroika* or 'restructuring' of the economic and political system, *glasnost* or 'openness', and 'New Thinking'

Science, Technology, and Medicine	Culture	
First US space shuttle Columbia makes successful flight; European rocket Ariane makes successful launch; Voyager 2 flies by Saturn Chinese scientists successfully clone a golden carp fish World's fastest train, the French TGV, goes into operation	Andrew Lloyd-Webber's *Cats*, musical based on poems by T. S. Eliot. Spielberg, *Raiders of the Lost Ark*; Hugh Hudson, *Chariots of Fire*	**1981**
First use of genetic engineering comes on the market in the form of insulin manufactured from bacteria	Thomas Keneally, *Schindler's Ark*; Dominique Fernandez, *Dans la Main de l'Ange*; Stoppard, *The Real Thing*; Carlos Fuentes, *Distant Relations* Spielberg, *ET*; Richard Attenborough, *Gandhi* Vietnam War Memorial dedicated in Washington, DC	**1982**
Compact discs marketed, soon replace tapes and records France tests neutron bomb; Soviet nuclear-powered submarine sinks in North Pacific World's first artificially created chromosome created at Harvard University US space shuttle Challenger successfully makes maiden flight	Garcia Marquez, *Chronicle of a Death Foretold*; Alice Walker, *The Color Purple*; J. M. Coetzee, *Life and Times of Michael K*	**1983**
Apple Macintosh computer with mouse is marketed American and French medical research teams independently discover HIV, virus believed to cause AIDS Genetic research and artificial fertilization of human eggs gives rise to ethical concerns over control of human evolution	Milan Kundera, *The Unbearable Lightness of Being* Chen Kaige, *Yellow Earth*	**1984**
British Antarctic survey team discovers hole in ozone layer over Antarctica	Primo Levi, *Periodic Tables*; Raul Hilberg, *The Destruction of the European Jews*	**1985**

Politics and International Relations

1985 South Africa withdraws troops from Angola

Responding to Greenpeace protests against French nuclear testing in the Pacific, on 10 July French secret agents sink Greenpeace flagship *Rainbow Warrior* in Auckland harbour, New Zealand

---

1986 Uruguay Round of GATT sets up World Trade Organization

26 Apr.: nuclear disaster at Chernobyl

11–12 Oct.: Reykjavík Summit between Reagan and Gorbachev ends inconclusively

State of Emergency declared in South Africa

Former Emperor of Central African Empire, Jean-Bedel Bokassa, is tried for mass murder and cannibalism

Corazon Aquino sworn in as president in the Philippines after disputed elections and the flight of President Marcos

Revolution forces Haitian dictator Jean-Claude Duvalier into exile; Haiti moves towards democracy

Iran-Contra scandal, in which funds from US arms sales to Iran were funnelled to support Contras fighting Sandinistas in Nicaragua, shakes Reagan administration

Portugal and Spain join EEC

1987 Students riot against government repression and corruption in Kwangju, South Korea

Chinese suppress nationalist uprising in Tibet

USA and USSR sign treaty eliminating intermediate-range missiles

Indian Government imposes direct rule in the Punjab to fight Sikh terrorism

Palestinians in the occupied territories begin 'Intifada', an uprising against Israeli rule

---

1988 Cease-fire ends Iran–Iraq War

US court indicts General Manuel Noriega, ruler of Panama, on drug-trafficking charges

PRI candidate Carlos Salina elected president of Mexico with bare majority

Mar.–Sept.: 'Burmese Spring', hundreds of thousands of students and others demonstrate for democratic reform, leading to army crackdown on 18 Sept., killing hundreds of protestors and arresting dissidents; military regime changes country's name to Myanmar

Aug.: a Geneva Accord negotiated between UNITA and the MPLA puts a temporary end to Angolan civil war

Widespread strikes in Poland

After nine years of occupation, Soviet troops begin withdrawal from Afghanistan

Dec.: PLO Chairman Yasser Arafat addresses UN General Assembly rejecting military violence, recognizing the existence of Israel, and calling for a political solution of the Palestinian problem

---

Science, Technology, and Medicine	Culture	
Space shuttle Atlantis makes maiden voyage	Merchant–Ivory, *A Room With a View*	**1985**
Surgeons use lasers to clean out clogged arteries		
USA and UK withdraw from UNESCO		
Space shuttle Challenger explodes on take-off, killing all on board; Voyager 2 discovers 10 more moons around Uranus; European space probe Giotto photographs core of Halley's Comet	Nigerian writer Wole Soyinka awarded Nobel Prize for Literature; Kazuo Ishiguro, *An Artist of the Floating World*; Irina Ratushinskaya, *No, I'm Not Afraid*	**1986**
25,000 cases of AIDS diagnosed in USA	Claude Berri, *Jean de Florette* and *Manon des sources*; Spike Lee, *She's Gotta Have It*	
Bill Gates, founder of Microsoft, becomes first microcomputer 'billionaire'	Chinua Achebe, *Anthills of the Savannah*; Tahar Ben Jelloun, *La Nuit sacré*; Toni Morrison, *Beloved*	**1987**
	Bertolucci, *The Last Emperor*	
Stephen Hawking, *A Brief History of Time*	Garcia Marquez, *Love in the Time of Cholera*; Rushdie, *The Satanic Verses*; Wolfe, *The Bonfire of the Vanities*; Egyptian Naguib Mahfouz wins Nobel Prize for Literature	**1988**
First transatlantic optical fibre telephone cable links USA, Britain, and France		
Internet computer virus created by student affects over 6,000 US military computers	John Adams, *Nixon in China*; Luciano Berio, *Ofarin*; Witold Lutoslawski, *Piano Concerto*; Andrew Lloyd Webber, *Phantom of the Opera*	
US space shuttle Discovery makes first successful shuttle flight since Challenger disaster	Zhang Yimou, *Red Sorghum*	
US B-2 stealth bomber shown publicly for the first time		

Politics and International Relations

1989 Feb.: in Paraguay dictatorship of General Alfredo Stroessner overthrown after 35 years in power; General Andres Rodriguez elected president

Soviet Army completes withdrawal from Afghanistan

China imposes martial law in Lhasa, Tibet

June: pro-democracy demonstrations culminate in Tiananmen Square massacre as government troops forcibly disperse demonstrators in Beijing

In Chile, General Pinochet allows free elections and military dictatorship is peacefully replaced by a return to democratic rule and continuing free market economic policies

Sept.: F. W. de Klerk becomes State President of South Africa and moves towards principle of universal suffrage and ending of apartheid

Aug.–Sept.: Communist rule ends in Poland and later Hungary

9 Nov.: East German Government opens entire border; Berlin Wall comes down amid massive celebrations; Dec.: Communist rule collapses in East Germany and Czechoslovakia; on the 25th, Romanian Communist dictator Nicolae Ceausescu and wife executed

Late Dec.: US forces invade Panama to arrest General Manuel Noriega, indicted by US court on drug-trafficking charges

---

1990 3 Jan.: General Noriega leaves refuge in Vatican Embassy and surrenders to US forces; new Panamanian Government under President Guillermo Endara installed 20 Dec.

Mar.: Lithuania declares its independence from USSR; elections in East Germany and Hungary bring down Communist regimes; Apr.–May: multiparty elections held in Yugoslavia; 1 July: union of currencies between East and West Germany prelude to reunification of Germany on 3 Oct.; Dec.: Lech Walesa becomes President of Poland

2 Aug.: Iraqi forces invade Kuwait proclaiming it a province of Iraq; USA under President George Bush mounts Operation Desert Shield to provide protection against Iraqi attack on Saudi Arabia; Bush also organizes international coalition against Iraq; UN imposes economic sanctions and gives Iraq ultimatum to retreat from Kuwait by 15 Jan. 1990 or suffer consequences

May: after release from prison, black South African leader Nelson Mandela negotiates ending of apartheid with President de Klerk

Namibia becomes independent

Sandinista regime in Nicaragua agrees to free elections and loses to coalition anti-Marxist parties led by Violeta Barrios de Chamorro, who becomes president

Mary Robinson elected as Ireland's first woman president

Challenged for the UK Conservative Party leadership, Margaret Thatcher resigns as Prime Minister; John Major elected in her place

---

1991 Mid-Jan.: Gulf War breaks out as US-led Alliance with sanction of UN invades Kuwait and Iraq, expelling Iraqi forces from Kuwait; Iraq subjected to UN supervision of weapons of mass destruction and restrictions on military activities in northern and southern provinces

1 Apr.: Warsaw Pact annulled

June: Boris Yeltsin becomes president of Russia; 18–21 Aug.: hardline coup against Gorbachev fails in USSR; Chechnya declares its independence; Gorbachev resigns as President and in Dec. USSR is dissolved; some of the republics form the Commonwealth of Independent States

Science, Technology, and Medicine	Culture	
Computer viruses infect computers around the world	Ishiguro, *Remains of the Day*; Islamic regime in Iran pronounces death sentence on Salman Rushdie for his novel *The Satanic Verses*; Umberto Eco, *Foucault's Pendulum*	**1989**
Worldwide efforts to limit use of CFCs thought to be damaging earth's ozone layer		
NASA launches Galileo space probe to Jupiter; Voyager 2 reaches Neptune	I. M. Pei designs controversial glass pyramid to cover new entrance to the Louvre museum in Paris	
DNA 'fingerprinting' allowed as evidence in rape trials in Florida and Virginia		
Electron-positron supercollider begins operation in Switzerland		
Ornidyl, new drug treatment for African sleeping sickness, approved by WHO	Mexican poet Octavio Paz made Nobel Laureate for literature; Hou Xiaoxian, *City of Sorrows*	**1990**
First gene therapy begun on human patients	György Ligeti, *Concerto for Violin and Orchestra*; John Adams, *The Death of Klinghoffer*	
	Scorsese, *Goodfellas*	
	Bret Easton Ellis, *American Psycho*	**1991**
	Quentin Tarantino, *Reservoir Dogs*; Zhang, *Raise the Red Lantern*; Jonathan Demme, *The Silence of the Lambs*	

Politics and International Relations

1991 June: war begins in Yugoslavia as Slovenia and Croatia declare their independence; Sept.: Yugoslavian Army (which is increasingly the Serbian Army) begins assault on Croatia, initiating war that lasts into mid-1990s

In South Africa, government repeals apartheid laws; Nelson Mandela elected president of ANC

21 May: former Indian Prime Minister Rajiv Gandhi assassinated by 'Tamil Tigers'

23 Oct.: Paris Peace Accords on Cambodia signed scheduling elections under UN supervision for 1993

Brazil, Argentina, Uruguay, and Paraguay sign Mercosur trade pact

1992 Bosnia-Hercegovina becomes independent; secession sparks ethnic violence, primarily between Muslims and Serbs; Serbs engage in 'ethnic cleansing'; UN imposes arms embargo on both sides, in fact favouring the better-equipped Serbians, as well as sanctions on Serbia and Montenegro. UN peacekeeping force (UNPROFOR) established

Sept.: USA sends troops to Somalia under UN authority on humanitarian mission

In China, Deng Xiaoping reaffirms free market economic growth

First free general elections are held in Taiwan

In Brazil President Fernando Collor de Mello is impeached and resigns

Peace accords end 12 years of civil war in El Salvador

Crisis occurs in the European Exchange Rate Mechanism, UK forced to leave

1993 1 Jan.: Czechoslovakia splits into Czech Republic and Slovakia

Maastricht Treaty comes into effect. All 12 members of EU agree to introduce a common currency, drop all trade barriers, and accept a common defence and foreign policy.

Israel signs peace agreement with PLO

Cambodia is restored to constitutional monarchy under King Norodom Sihanouk

Apr.: Russian President Yeltsin survives a referendum on his government; he crushes Supreme Soviet rebellion; Dec.: new Constitution adopted and new Duma elected

UN Security Council establishes International Criminal Tribunal for the Former Yugoslavia at The Hague

In Colombia, security forces kill Medellin Cartel drug lord Pablo Escobar

1994 Jan.: the North American Free Trade Association (NAFTA) goes into effect between Canada, USA, and Mexico

Jan.: Zapatista revolt breaks out in Chiapas, southern Mexico

May: Nelson Mandela elected first black President of South Africa after ANC victorious in South African elections; South Africa rejoins the British Commonwealth

Civil war and genocide in Rwanda bring UN intervention and the creation of a UN-sponsored International Criminal Tribunal

Russian forces invade the breakaway republic of Chechnya

Science, Technology, and Medicine	Culture	
		1991
UN-sponsored ecology conference held in Brazil results in 150 nations signing a Convention on Biological Diversity	Howard Brodkey, *The Runaway Soul*; Jung Chang, *Wild Swans*; Michael Ondaatje, *The English Patient* Merchant–Ivory, *Howards End*; Tony Kushner, *Angels in America*	**1992**
	Spielberg, *Schindler's List*; Chen Kaige, *Farewell My Concubine*	**1993**
Channel Tunnel connecting Britain and France under the English Channel is officially opened	Tarantino, *Pulp Fiction*	**1994**

Politics and International Relations

1994   US forces intervene in Haiti to oust military government and restore President Aristide to power

UN troops, including Russians, attempt to maintain 'safe areas' for Muslims and others under UN protection in the Bosnian civil war; Serbs become even more aggressive, taking UN peacekeepers hostage

Israel and Jordan sign peace treaty

Dec.: Mexican financial crisis sends shockwaves throughout Latin America

1995   Serb massacre of Muslims at Srbenica, under eyes of UN peacekeepers, sparks sustained attacks by NATO air forces on Serb targets in Bosnia-Hercegovina; negotiations at Dayton, Ohio, lead to Dayton Accords settling the status of the former Yugoslavia, including a peace agreement for Bosnia-Hercegovina; NATO-led force, including US troops, created to oversee implementation of settlement; UN War Crimes Tribunal indicts Bosnian Serb leaders, including President Radovan Karadzic, for genocide and crimes against humanity

Sept.: Israel and PLO agree to expand Palestinian self-rule on the West Bank; Israeli troops begin gradual withdrawal from West Bank after nearly 30 years of Israeli military rule

Terrorist bombing destroys Federal Building in Oklahoma City, kills 168

On 50th anniversary of bombing of Nagasaki, US President Clinton announces a halt to all nuclear testing; on 50th anniversary of end of Second World War, Japanese prime minister offers 'heartfelt' apology for suffering caused by his country

2 Nov.: Israeli Prime Minister Itzhak Rabin assassinated by anti-peace extremist

1996   Binyamin Netanyahu becomes Israeli prime minister; peace process slows

Prime Minister Benazir Bhutto dismissed in Pakistan amid accusations of massive corruption and bringing the country to the brink of disaster

IRA resumes campaign of violence

Controversy develops over claims to property, confiscated from Jews by Nazis, still being held by Swiss banks 50 years after the end of Second World War

1997   Russia and Chechnya sign peace treaty

Labour Party under Tony Blair wins British elections, ending 18 years of Conservative rule

Deng Xiaoping dies

30 June: Hong Kong is returned to China

July: devaluation of Thai currency sets off regional economic crisis

In Britain death of Diana, Princess of Wales, provokes widespread emotional reaction

In Mexico, PRI loses its hold on local governments

Overthrow of President Mobutu Sese Seko of Zaire by Laurent Kabila

Science, Technology, and Medicine	Culture	
		1994
Microsoft launches Windows 95 computer software system Internet use continues to grow with new companies like Netscape and America Online providing easy access Princeton-based British mathematician Andrew Wiles is first person to publish a general proof of 'Fermat's last theorem'		**1995**
		1996
Fears for environment grow as 'El Niño' effect on climate produces extreme weather conditions and variations, especially in North America; fires sweep equatorial forests in Brazil and Indonesia; and evidence of global warming increases in Antarctica Cloning of a sheep by British scientists causes widespread disquiet over implications of genetic engineering		**1997**

INDEX

Note: **Bold** indicates main references